525
16
541

P. 479 Test to find kids' interests

P. 413

211 spelling

Core Studies

311

How to Increase Reading Ability

THIRD EDITION
REVISED AND ENLARGED

How to Increase Reading Ability

A GUIDE TO DEVELOPMENTAL AND REMEDIAL METHODS

by Albert J. Harris

DIRECTOR OF THE EDUCATIONAL CLINIC
AND PROFESSOR OF EDUCATION
QUEENS COLLEGE
NEW YORK

LONGMANS, GREEN AND CO.

NEW YORK LONDON TORONTO

LONGMANS, GREEN AND CO., INC.
119 WEST 40TH STREET, NEW YORK 18

LONGMANS, GREEN AND CO. LTD.
6 & 7 CLIFFORD STREET, LONDON W 1

LONGMANS, GREEN AND CO.
20 CRANFIELD ROAD, TORONTO 16

HARRIS
HOW TO INCREASE READING ABILITY

PUBLISHED SIMULTANEOUSLY IN THE DOMINION OF CANADA BY
LONGMANS, GREEN AND CO., TORONTO

FIRST EDITION JANUARY 1940
SECOND EDITION JANUARY 1947
THIRD EDITION JUNE 1956
REPRINTED NOVEMBER 1956
REPRINTED AUGUST 1957
REPRINTED AUGUST 1958
JUNE 1959
JUNE, 1960

LIBRARY OF CONGRESS CATALOG CARD NUMBER 56-9217

Printed in the United States of America

To

EDITH

Preface to the Third Edition

In preparing this thoroughly revised and considerably enlarged third edition, I have attempted to retain the essential character which has given the previous editions popularity over nearly two decades. Three points of major concern to me have been scope, balance, and practicality.

Breadth of scope has been a distinctive feature of the two previous editions. This has allowed the book to be used successfully as an introductory textbook on reading instruction for students preparing to teach, as an advanced text for graduate courses in corrective and remedial reading, and as a desk reference for teachers and reading clinicians. Although most of its illustrative material is from the elementary-school level, it has been used considerably in planning secondary and college reading programs. The present edition maintains this broad coverage.

A strong effort to maintain a balanced point of view is a second guiding principle common to this and the preceding editions. On important controversial issues I have attempted to explain opposing points of view, to indicate what I believe to be the strengths and weaknesses of the differing viewpoints, to cite the most significant research findings, and to express my personal beliefs or opinions. In line with this is my conviction that no method provides a panacea, but rather that there are many alternative teaching procedures which incorporate sound psychological and educational principles, and that artistry in teaching involves the judicious selection of methods which are particularly suited to a specific situation.

The third major emphasis has been on keeping the book practical. I have tried to avoid technical terminology as much as possible, to be definite, to give illustrations, to recommend specific materials, and to answer the important questions which teachers ask over and over again. Because I believe in the wise selection of procedures to fit conditions, enough theory has been included to provide a basis for judging when and why a particular technique may be useful.

In organization, the book can be divided into three main parts: the over-all classroom reading program, methods for evaluating and diagnosing group and individual reading needs, and developmental and remedial teaching of specific reading skills. Throughout the entire work runs the theme that reading instruction can be most effective when it is based on an understanding of pupils as individuals, and when organization for instruction, reading materials, and instructional methods are suited to individual and group needs. More fundamental than any details of technique is the importance of a wholesome teacher-pupil relationship.

Although every chapter has been revised and extensively rewritten, four topics have been expanded so much as to require an additional chapter each. The general survey of the reading program now occupies two chapters. The vital question of how to meet individual and group needs has been greatly amplified, and I have attempted to provide a clearer and more detailed description of individualized and group techniques than has hitherto been available. Discussion of the causation of reading difficulties has been greatly enlarged, especially in regard to visual problems, directional confusion, and personality, and a new theory on the significance of hand and eye dominance in relation to reading disability is presented. The centrally important question of how best to develop word recognition skills now occupies three chapters, the first two discussing in detail the developmental program in word recognition and the third covering remedial practices.

One former chapter, "Teaching Reading to Specially Handicapped Children," has been dropped. It did not seem possible to treat the special needs of such groups as the mentally retarded, the hard of hearing, and others, with sufficient adequacy in just a few pages each. With four additional chapters and one deletion, the number of chapters has increased to nineteen.

The listings of helpful materials and references have been enlarged and brought up to date. These include descriptions of tests and equipment, word lists, bibliographies, workbooks, and games and teaching devices included at appropriate points. The appendixes have been thoroughly revised. Appendix A provides an alphabetical descriptive listing of all tests mentioned in the book. Appendix B consists of a graded list of books recommended for poor readers, with special symbols identifying books of exceptional appeal or secondary-school interest.

The research of the past ten years has been carefully sifted for ideas that would enrich the book. Footnotes have been used rather generously to guide the serious student into further reading, especially on controversial issues and on technical matters that could not be treated in detail. I have consulted William S. Gray's annual summaries in the *Elementary School Journal* and *Journal of Educational Research,* the three-year summaries in the *Review of Educational Research,* Traxler and Townsend's *Eight More Years of Research in Reading, The Education Index,* and *Psychological Abstracts,* and hope that I have overlooked no major contributions. With a total possible bibliography of many thousands of items, it is possible to include in a book of this type only the references which seem most relevant or useful.

Much effort has been spent to make this a readable book. The style of writing has aimed at simplicity and clarity. The format has been chosen with careful consideration of the reader's visual comfort.

During the ten years in which this revision gradually was formulated, I had the opportunity to discuss reading with groups of teachers in many parts of the United States and in Canada. Most of my teaching has been by a discussion method with small graduate classes, and the ideas in this book have been influenced greatly by many hours of give and take in which I have learned the necessity of striving to be practical and specific. I wish I could acknowledge individually the numerous excellent suggestions I have received from classroom and remedial teachers, as well as from the many people with whom I have shared platforms at reading conferences and meetings. I want specifically to acknowledge the insights I have gained from my friend and former colleague, Professor Florence G.

Roswell of The City College of New York, and from years of close collaboration with the staffs of the Educational Clinics of Queens College and The City College.

In a rather unique way, this book is a family affair. The section on vision has benefited from the comments and suggestions of my brother-in-law, Bernard Fread, M.D., associate clinical professor of Ophthalmology at the Medical College of New York University. My sister-in-law, Stella F. Rapaport, interrupted her own work on a new children's book to do the drawings for me. But most of all I am indebted to my wife. Not only has she patiently given up evenings, week ends and vacations so that the book could be written, but she has also read every page of the manuscript from the viewpoint of a teacher with many years of experience in both classroom teaching and individualized remedial reading. Her comments have led to greater clarity and specificity in many parts of the book.

Many publishers have graciously consented to the use of quotations or to the reproduction of samples from tests or workbooks. Specific acknowledgments will be found at appropriate places in the text.

Albert J. Harris

March, 1956

Contents

Illustrations

Tables

How to Increase Reading Ability

· I ·

About Reading

I. The Importance of Reading

DESPITE THE CHALLENGES from the movies, radio, the comic book and television, reading is here to stay. Our society is a reading society, in which enormous quantities of reading matter are consumed. We read newspapers, magazines, comic books, trade papers, racing forms; adventure stories, love stories, crime stories, science-fiction stories, "true" stories, literary stories; novels, biography, history, travel, drama, poetry; science, psychology, religion, astrology; how-to-do-it books on a thousand and one topics; dictionaries, almanacs, encyclopedias – the list is endless. From this reading material our people acquire the basis of much of their way of living. They read to acquire knowledge, to achieve recreation, relaxation, or emotional stimulation, to build attitudes, and to solve problems.

More reading of all kinds is done today than ever before. On the one hand, comic books sell at the hard-to-believe rate of about 70 million copies a month. On the other hand, worthwhile reading also circulates in larger quantities than ever before. Book clubs and inexpensive paper-bound editions have brought the sales of many "highbrow" books above the half-million mark, and the circulation of nonfiction books has shown slow but steady increases for many years. "The combined circulation of all magazines in the United States and Canada is now more than 170 million copies per issue – almost the combined population of both countries. . . . Forty-two magazines have sales of a million copies or more per issue." [1]

[1] *Reader's Digest,* November, 1953, p. 180.

As compared to movies, radio, and television, reading has certain unique advantages. Instead of having to choose from a limited variety made available to him by courtesy of the advertising sponsor, or from the currently available pictures, the reader can select from the finest writings of the present or past. He can read in a place and at a time chosen for his own convenience. He can go at his own pace and can slow down or speed up, take an intermission, reread, or pause and think, at his own pleasure. He can read what, when, where, and how he pleases. This flexibility insures the continuing value of reading both for education and for entertainment.

The importance of reading becomes even more obvious if one considers what happens in our culture to those who fail to learn to read well. As he gets older, the poor reader is increasingly handicapped by his difficulty. He is almost sure to repeat grades and, if he gets into high school, he is practically certain to leave without graduation. Many desirable occupations will be closed to him. He learns to cover up and conceal his illiteracy. When asked how he managed to fill out a job application, one boy answered: "Huh, I wasn't gonna let that guy know that I couldn't spell all those hard words! So I said, 'Hey look at my hands; they're dirty! How about letting that girl type this for me. I'll tell her what to write.'" Not always does this succeed.[2]

The nonreader is to a large extent cut off from cultural activities and finds it difficult to mingle with educated people. If his dislike for school becomes sufficiently intense, he may progress by easy stages to truancy, association with undesirable companions, and juvenile delinquency. Juvenile delinquents as a group include many whose reading abilities are far below their mental abilities. Among those tested by the psychiatric unit of the Children's Court in New York City, 76 per cent were found to be two or more years retarded in reading, and more than half of those were disabled five or more years.[3] This does not prove that reading difficulties cause delin-

[2] Mullen, Frances A., "Mentally Retarded Youth Find Jobs," *The Personnel and Guidance Journal*, Vol. 31, 1952, p. 23.

[3] Margolin, J. B., Roman, M., and Harari, C., "Reading Disability in the Delinquent Child: a Microcosm of Psychosocial Pathology," *American Journal of Orthopsychiatry*, Vol. 25, 1955, pp. 25–35.

quency, or that delinquency causes reading difficulty, but it does show a very strong tendency for the two types of problems to occur together. Although many poor readers avoid delinquency, the frustrations caused by years of unsuccessful effort and invidious comparisons with other children are practically certain to create severe feelings of inferiority which interfere with normal personality development.

During World War II, hundreds of thousands of men were unable to meet the Army's minimum literacy standard, which was placed at about fourth-grade reading level. To reduce this tremendous waste of manpower, the armed forces set up special training units in which thousands of illiterate draftees were taught within a period of eight to thirteen weeks to read, write, and do simple arithmetic.[4] An illiterate was as useless to the Army as a man who was blind, deaf, or crippled.

II. Reading in the Schools of Today

THE IMPORTANCE of reading is clearly recognized by the elementary schools. In the primary grades, more time and effort is spent on teaching reading than on any other phase of the school program. More money is spent on reading matter than on any other type of school supplies. Poor reading is recognized as the most important single cause of retardation in the elementary school (although it, in turn, may be due to low intelligence). At the first- and second-grade levels, children are very rarely kept back for any reason other than failure in reading.

In the past, high schools and colleges took for granted the reading ability of their students. Today an increasing number of secondary schools, colleges, and universities recognize that many of their students cannot do the reading expected of them. More and more of these schools have come to the conclusion that they too must provide for the teaching of reading, and in one way or another are

[4] Witty, Paul A., and Goldberg, Samuel, "The Army's Training Program for Illiterate, Non-English-Speaking, and Educationally Retarded Men," *Elementary English Review*, Vol. 20, 1943, pp. 306–311.

attempting to do so. The lead in developing such programs at the college level has come, not from schools with inferior student populations, but from such schools as Dartmouth and Harvard.

Reading and the Changing Curriculum

Reading is unique among school activities in being both a subject of instruction and a tool for the mastery of other phases of the curriculum. Formerly one of the major goals in elementary education was "learning to read"; now the emphasis is placed upon "reading to learn." It is not true that "learning to read" has no place in the modern school, as some extremists have suggested. In the primary grades, skillful teaching of reading is of the highest importance. In the upper grades many pupils fail to continue to develop in reading skill, in schools which discontinue teaching reading skills as such and rely entirely upon incidental learning for further development of reading. It is true, however, that the modern school places less emphasis on reading for its own sake, but makes far greater use of reading as a tool, when compared with the typical school of twenty years ago. The total amount of reading done in school is much greater than it used to be. While formerly pupils usually read one reader a term, today they are reading many books in each grade. Purposeful independent reading has to a large extent supplanted the class reading lessons of the past. Individual pupils and committees read and report on a great variety of topics, finding their information in an equally great variety of sources.

Reading and Other School Subjects

It is only natural that proficiency in reading should be found to be closely related to school success. The fast, accurate reader possesses a valuable tool that lays open to him the vast storehouse of knowledge that lies between the covers of books. The poor reader either reads so slowly that he has not time to read much, or reads so inaccurately that he is little better off when he has finished than when he started. He must depend to a large extent on what he can learn by listening. In consequence he tends to fall behind in subjects that require reading. Arithmetic, spelling, writing, composition, and all of the content subjects that require the use of books are related to reading ability.

Arithmetic problems are usually presented in written or printed form, and so have to be read before they can be solved. It is obvious that a pupil who cannot read well may be completely helpless when given a problem to be read, even when he might be able to solve it easily if it were given to him orally. There is in general a high correspondence between good problem-solving and good reading ability, although some good readers are very poor at solving arithmetic problems.

The mastery of arithmetic fundamentals – addition, subtraction, multiplication, and division – is not nearly so dependent upon reading as problem-solving is. Most of the early work of mastering combinations is done orally. Later, when most of the computation is done from written examples, it is found that many poor readers have no trouble with reading numbers, and make normal or superior progress in arithmetic. Monroe has found the arithmetic computation ability of 415 reading disability cases to average about one and a half grades better than their reading ability.[5] This does not mean that the poor readers as a group were above average in arithmetic, but simply that they were not as bad in arithmetic as they were in reading.

In recent years we have become aware of the close interrelationships among the various forms of oral and written communication, and in consequence much attention has been given to an integrated approach to language arts. People express themselves in speech and writing; they interpret the expressions of others by listening and reading. Basic to all four is a grasp of the structure of the language and the personal development of ideas, concepts, and attitudes. Successful teaching of reading must necessarily be related to the other phases of the language arts.

The ability to recognize and remember words is fundamental to

[5] Monroe, Marion, *Children Who Cannot Read,* p. 14. Chicago: University of Chicago Press, 1932.

both reading and spelling. The child who finds it difficult to recognize a word when he sees it is apt to have even more difficulty trying to reproduce its sequence of letters from memory. Reading and spelling are closely associated because many of the abilities required for one are also required for the other. The correlation between scores on reading tests and scores on spelling tests usually falls in the range of .80 to .85.[6] This is a high relationship and indicates that good spellers who are poor readers or good readers who are poor spellers are comparatively rare. The vast majority of reading disability cases are also extremely poor spellers. Analysis of a pupil's errors in spelling often helps in understanding his reading difficulties, and remedial teaching in reading and spelling can often be carried on together with profit to both.

In contrast to the close relation between reading and spelling, reading and penmanship are not closely allied. Some retarded readers produce illegible scrawls; the same difficulties that prevent them from seeing words clearly when they try to read interfere with their attempts at written reproduction. Some poor readers have poor general control of their muscles, and show the same clumsiness in writing as in other activities. However, it is not at all unusual to find poor readers whose handwriting is neat and legible, or good readers whose penmanship is atrocious.

Reading and composition are each dependent upon the other. Wide and extensive reading broadens the child's range of knowledge, enriches his vocabulary, and provides him with desirable models of style that he can imitate. On the other hand, a lack of ability to understand and use good English will naturally handicap a child in understanding what he reads. Children are sometimes found whose good spoken English stands out in sharp contrast to poor reading ability; these children often make very rapid improvement under appropriate remedial treatment.

As soon as children start to use textbooks, reading disability becomes a general handicap. The large amount of oral work done in the elementary school makes it possible for some poor readers to do

[6] Peake, Nellie L., "Relation Between Spelling Ability and Reading Ability," *Journal of Experimental Education*, Vol. 9, 1940, pp. 192–193.

acceptable work in content subjects. The higher up these children go, however, the more important the study of books becomes. In the upper grades such studies as history and geography are seriously affected by poor skill in reading.

An investigation by Lee[7] demonstrated clearly the importance of reading for general scholarship in elementary school. Six tests of reading ability were given to pupils in the fourth, fifth, and sixth grades, and the results were correlated with an achievement score obtained from the *Modern School Achievement Tests* (In getting this score, the reading sections of the tests were omitted.). Even after the influence of intelligence was eliminated, substantial relationships between reading and general achievement remained. From her results Lee concluded that reading ability of low fourth-grade level is a minimum requirement for satisfactory work in these grades.

Reading ability is important for scholarship in secondary school as well as in elementary school. This has been clearly shown in a careful study by Bond.[8] She gave a number of reading tests and also standardized achievement tests in all subjects to three hundred ninth-grade pupils. A suitable statistical method was used to make sure that the results were not influenced by differences in age or intelligence. General reading comprehension was found to be significantly related to average scholarship and to all separate subjects except mathematics. Evidence was also obtained that the reading abilities essential to achievement differed considerably from one subject to another. For instance, fast readers excelled slow readers in tests of vocabulary and literary acquaintance, but the slow readers had a slight advantage in general science, spelling, and mathematics. Bond concluded that there is a definite need for teachers of the content subjects to instruct their pupils in the particular reading skills that are important in the study of their subjects.

[7] Lee, Dorris M., *The Importance of Reading for Achieving in Grades 4, 5 and 6*, Contributions to Education, No. 566. New York: Bureau of Publications, Teachers College, Columbia University, 1933.

[8] Bond, Eva, *Reading and Ninth-Grade Achievement*, Contributions to Education, No. 756. New York: Bureau of Publications, Teachers College, Columbia University, 1938.

III. The Nature of Reading

LONG BEFORE he starts to read, the young child learns to communicate with others. He becomes increasingly capable of understanding what others say to him, and of making his thoughts and feelings known to them. Reading is an extension of communication and naturally builds upon the listening and speech skills already developed.

In its beginning stages, learning to read means learning that queer-looking marks stand for speech. The child "reads" when he is able to say the words which are represented by the printed marks. The child may say the words out loud, or he may say them to himself; in either case, reading means saying the correct words. If the child says the right words, they fall into a familiar sequence whose meaning is apparent to him because of his previously acquired facility in comprehending speech. If he says the wrong words, if he has to leave out too many words because he does not recognize them, or if his recognition is so slow and halting that the words are not heard as coming in meaningful sequences, the approximation to heard speech will not be good enough to convey the correct meaning. The discovery that printed words "talk" is the first step in learning to read.

That reading is a process involving meaning is self-evident, but it can hardly be overemphasized that meaningful response is the very heart of the reading process. "It can and should embrace all types of thinking, evaluating, judging, imagining, reasoning, and problem-solving."[9] Not only are intellectual meanings involved; feelings of considerable intensity may be aroused and emotional attitudes may be profoundly altered through reading.

Skill in the recognition of words continues to develop as the child's reading ability matures. Recognition of common words becomes faster and more accurate. New words are continually being added to the child's store of sight words. Gradually the child becomes able to recognize short, familiar phrases as perceptual and

[9] *Reading in the Elementary School,* p. 3. 48th Yearbook of the National Society for the Study of Education, Part II. Chicago: University of Chicago Press, 1949.

meaningful units. Skill in attacking new words is also acquired gradually, so that the child no longer has to be told each new word. The necessity for translating the printed symbols into the corresponding speech sounds recedes; reading becomes inaudible, lip and tongue movements cease, and to many an expert reader the meaning seems eventually to leap from the printed page with scarcely any awareness of inner speech.

As the child gets beyond the beginning stages in reading and the task of recognizing words becomes more nearly automatic, he finds his reading material becoming more complicated. Ideas are introduced which are outside the range of his experience and words are employed which he has never heard spoken. Sentences become longer and their structure grows more complex. Finding out what the book means becomes harder because the language is more involved than the conversation to which the child is accustomed. To keep up with his reading the child must increase his vocabulary, enlarge and refine his store of concepts and ideas, and develop his mastery of more complex forms of expression.

The child meets a variety of reading materials and finds that he reads to satisfy many different needs and purposes. Story-type reading becomes differentiated from work-type reading. In pleasure reading, exclusive concern with the plot becomes gradually enriched by the development of appreciation for humor, characterization, accuracy and vividness of description, and the sheer beauty of artistic expression. In work-type reading, study habits must be formed. They differ from subject to subject, and different methods of study must be learned to cope with the different phases of one subject. The efficient student learns how to locate what he needs, to distinguish major from minor points, to follow directions, to interpret, to summarize, to outline.

Finally reading becomes reflective and evaluative. To grasp the meaning and organization of a writer's ideas is important but not sufficient. The mature reader brings his previous knowledge and experience into relation with his present reading, compares the facts and arguments presented by one author with those of another, and is on the alert for errors in logical reasoning. He has learned to distinguish factual reporting from biased propaganda, and objective reasoning from wishful thinking.

To summarize, we may define reading as the act of responding appropriately to printed symbols. For the beginner, reading is mainly concerned with learning to recognize the printed symbols which represent speech, and to respond intellectually and emotionally as he would if the material were spoken rather than printed. The reasoning side of reading becomes increasingly important as recognition is mastered. As proficiency in reading increases, the individual learns to adapt his method of reading in accordance with his purpose for reading and the restrictions imposed by the nature of the material. The nature of the reading task, therefore, changes as the learner progresses from less mature to more mature levels. Reading is not one skill, but a large number of interrelated skills which develop gradually over a period of many years.

IV. Objectives of Reading Instruction

When teachers of reading are asked to state their objectives the answers are frequently very general. Many teachers do not get beyond the statement that their aim is to help their children to become better readers. This praiseworthy desire is much too broad and vague to be helpful in the planning of the specifics of teaching.

Everyone knows that when one plans a trip he has to decide where he wants to go before he can make decisions about how to get there. If a New Yorker has decided that he wants to spend a vacation in Yellowstone National Park, he can choose among many possibilities: plane, train, bus, and private car, with competing lines and alternative roads. But if he decides to go to Europe instead, the possible ways of going are quite different. "Europe" is also vague as a travel goal and a trip to Great Britain and Scandinavia will bear little resemblance to one concentrating on France, Switzerland, and Italy.

It is as important to be definite about educational objectives as about travel objectives. Teachers who set up as a major objective the development of a love for reading as a form of recreation can find many different ways of working toward it and each can achieve substantial success. But if developing a love for independent reading is not one of the teacher's goals it is unlikely that his pupils will develop such an attitude as a result of his efforts. Having the right goals and knowing what they are is the necessary first step in developing a sound reading program.

There are some objectives which should characterize the reading program as a whole. In setting down a list of eight major criteria of a sound reading program, the Yearbook Committee of the National Society for the Study of Education has pointed out the interrelations between the reading program and the school program as a whole, and has emphasized that reading must fit harmoniously into the total plan of a good educational program. According to this committee, a good reading program in an elementary school –

1. Is consciously directed toward specific valid ends which have been agreed upon by the entire school staff;
2. Coordinates reading activities with other aids to child development;
3. Recognizes that the child's development in reading is closely associated with his development in other language arts;
4. At any given level, is part of a well-worked-out larger reading program extending through all the elementary and secondary school grades;
5. Provides varied instruction and flexible requirements as a means of making adequate adjustments to the widely different reading needs of the pupils;
6. Affords, at each level of advancement, adequate guidance of reading in all the various aspects of a broad program of instruction: basic instruction in reading, reading in the content fields, literature, and recreational or free reading;
7. Makes special provisions for supplying the reading needs of cases of extreme reading disability, in other words, the small proportion of pupils whose needs cannot be satisfied through a strong developmental program;
8. Provides for frequent evaluation of the outcomes of a program and for such revisions as will strengthen the weaknesses discovered.[10]

[10] Whipple, Gertrude, "Characteristics of a Sound Reading Program," Ch. III in *Reading in the Elementary School,* 48th Yearbook of the National Society for the Study of Education, Part II. Chicago: University of Chicago Press, 1949, pp. 34–38. In the Yearbook, the specific meaning of each of the eight criteria is developed further in a number of subheadings.

The present writer is entirely in sympathy with these eight criteria and believes that they describe very well the broader aspects of the reading program. Each of them needs to be spelled out in greater detail for its applications to be clear. These applications will be developed in later chapters. At this point it seems desirable to point out in somewhat greater detail the meaning of the sixth criterion, which mentions different aspects of a broad reading program.

The teacher of reading wants his pupils to be able to read, to use reading effectively as a learning tool, and to enjoy and appreciate reading. Using somewhat more technical language, we can talk about developmental reading, functional reading, and recreational reading. *Developmental reading* activities are those in which the main purpose of the teacher is to bring about an improvement in reading skills – activities in which learning to read is the main goal. *Functional reading* includes all types of reading in which the primary aim is to obtain information; in other words, reading to learn. Some writers prefer to call it study-type reading or work-type reading. *Recreational reading* consists of those reading activities which have enjoyment, entertainment, and appreciation as major purposes.

A somewhat more detailed analysis of these three types of reading is as follows:

A. Developmental Reading

1. Skill in the mechanics of reading
   a. Development of a large sight vocabulary
   b. Development of skill in identifying unfamiliar words
   c. Development of good eye-movement habits
   d. Development of proper habits of posture, holding books, and so on
   e. Development of speed and fluency in silent reading
   f. Development of oral reading skills; phrasing, expression, pitch, volume, enunciation

2. Skill in reading comprehension
   a. Acquisition of a rich, extensive, and accurate vocabulary
   b. Ability to grasp the meaning of units of increasing size; phrase, sentence, paragraph, whole selection
   c. Ability to find answers to specific questions

d. Ability to select and understand main ideas
e. Ability to understand a sequence of events
f. Ability to note and recall details
g. Ability to grasp the organization of the author's plan
h. Ability to follow directions accurately
i. Ability to evaluate what one reads
j. Ability to remember what one has read

B. Functional Reading

1. Ability to locate needed reading material
   a. Use of index
   b. Use of table of contents
   c. Use of dictionary
   d. Use of encyclopedia
   e. Use of library card files
   f. Use of other bibliographic aids
   g. Use of skimming in search for information
2. Ability to comprehend informational material
   a. Application of general comprehension skills listed under A, 2, above
   b. Development of specific skills needed by special subject matter, e.g.,
      (1) Reading of arithmetic problems
      (2) Reading of maps, charts, and graphs
3. Ability to select the material needed
4. Ability to organize what is read
   a. Ability to summarize
   b. Ability to outline

C. Recreational Reading

1. Development of liking for reading as a voluntary leisure-time activity
2. Development of ability to locate interesting and enjoyable reading matter
3. Satisfaction of present recreational interests and tastes through reading
4. Development of more varied, more mature, and more refined reading tastes
5. Development of liking for oral reading as a means of entertaining others

6. Development of discriminative taste with regard to literary merits of reading matter

These three major types of reading purposes cannot and should not be kept entirely separate. In a developmental lesson children must read material which is either recreational or functional in character. An enjoyable story may be used for the development of particular reading skills, and developmental lessons can be planned to help the pupils in their reading of science material.

A sound reading program must have balance among these major types of reading. If the desire to read for fun is killed by overemphasis on drills and exercises, one of the major aims of reading instruction is defeated and the result is the pathetic graduate who never opens a book after commencement. What that balance should be changes grade by grade. For the beginner, nearly all reading activities are primarily developmental; by the upper elementary grades, functional reading is most important and developmental lessons take the least amount of time.

V. Stages in Reading Instruction

In a historic report which had a tremendous influence upon the development of reading instruction, the National Committee on Reading described five main stages of reading instruction.[11] A generation later, this division into broad stages or periods remains quite satisfactory. These stages will be briefly summarized here, and will be discussed in greater detail in the chapters immediately following.

Stage 1. Development of Reading Readiness. From birth on, the necessary background for success in learning to read is built up through a combination of inner maturation and learning. The meaning of reading readiness, ways of evaluating it, and procedures for helping children to become ready are considered in Chapter II.

Stage 2. Initial Stage in Learning to Read. A proper start in read-

[11] *Report of the National Committee on Reading,* 24th Yearbook of the National Society for the Study of Education, Part I. Bloomington, Ill.: Public School Publishing Co., 1925.

ing is crucially important. When to start to teach reading, whether to begin with published materials or with informal material developed by teacher and pupils, and how to insure the building of a sight vocabulary, are some of the main problems. Much of the reading is oral, but silent reading is introduced very early and stress is placed on getting meanings rather than just calling words. Experience stories, preprimers, primers, and first readers are the main materials.

Stage 3. Rapid Development of Reading Skills. This stage includes the normal instructional program of the second and third grades. In these grades a thorough grounding in basic reading habits and skills should be provided. Comprehension is emphasized. Training in the techniques of word recognition and word analysis receives much attention. By the end of this period a child should be able to attack unfamiliar words by a variety of methods, including use of context, phonics, and structural analysis. Fostering interest in reading and encouraging children to read widely in varied sources are other important aims. In the latter part of this stage, the development of new concepts and ideas begins to present problems.

Stage 4. Stage of Wide Reading. During this stage, which includes the reading program of the fourth, fifth, and sixth grades, the normal reading program should emphasize wide reading that extends and enriches the child's experience. Although the basic skills of comprehension and word recognition should be acquired in the primary grades, it is necessary to work for the improvement of these skills in the middle grades. Silent reading should become more rapid than oral reading and should occupy most of the reading time. Training in the use of books and in location of information should be definitely provided. Special attention should be devoted to the development of skills involved in reading factual material. Fostering the habit of reading for pleasure should be a major goal, and increasing amounts of independent reading should be accomplished, both in and out of school.

Stage 5. Refinement of Reading. During secondary schools and college there is a definite need for continued guidance in reading, although this need is not recognized in many schools. The development of varied, flexible study skills is achieved by some students without help, but others, including many very bright students, need assistance in learning to study efficiently. As the student reaches higher levels of instruction the reading he is required to do increases both in amount and in difficulty. Voluntary reading seems to reach a peak in the early teens; the decline in voluntary reading after the age of thirteen is a source of concern.

Implications of Individual Differences

In the above discussion of stages in reading instruction a false impression may have been created that uniformity in progress is expected or can be achieved. In a typical first grade in April the majority may be in Stage 2, but some children are probably still in Stage 1. In a modern second grade the teacher should be able to provide not only for those who are ready for Stage 3, but also for the fairly large number who are still in Stage 2, and in many schools will have a small number who are still at the readiness level at the beginning of the year. In a typical fifth grade the range of reading proficiency will probably vary from second- or third-grade level to secondary school level. Similar problems of wide differences in reading attainment exist at every age and grade level.

Efficient teaching of reading requires, therefore, that the teacher be able to plan and carry out a program in which children with widely varying abilities can be effectively guided to achieve the goals of reading instruction, in accordance with their individual learning capacities. The need for such a program is generally recognized, and teachers are more worried about how to accomplish this than they are about any other aspect of the reading program.

VI. Remedial and Corrective Reading

Reading Retardation and Reading Disability

Children differ in their potentialities for learning, and the achievement of a child should be judged in relation to the child's learning capacity. Of major importance in determining learning capacity is the child's general intelligence. Other factors which must be taken into account are the child's experiential background, his attainment in the other language arts, his freedom from interfering physical handicaps, and his motivation or lack of motivation to read.

The terms *retarded* and *retardation* have unfortunately come to be used in education in ways that create ambiguity of meaning. When a child's general mental development is slow, he is called a retarded child. If a child's school achievement lags behind that of most children of his age he is said to be educationally retarded. This term does not distinguish between those children whose retardation is primarily one of limited mentality and those whose retardation is due to other causes.

In the past few years, some people have used the term *retarded reader* to refer to those whose reading is poor and who have the capacity to do better in reading. This is an unfortunate use of the term, since it is so easily confused with other meanings. It is desirable to use the term *retarded reader* in its original sense as referring to any individual whose development of reading skills is below the normal performance for his age or grade. Retarded readers, according to this recommended usage, include all whose reading is poor. They include those whose limited reading skill is just one aspect of generally slow mental development, and those who have the potential capacity to do better. For the latter group we have special terms that are unambiguous: we say they have a special reading difficulty or a *reading disability*.

Children with reading disabilities possess mental ability that should enable them to read considerably better than they do. Sometimes all of the child's school work is below average, but on intelligence tests he shows that he has the mental capacity to do much better work in school than he has achieved thus far. Sometimes the child's scholastic difficulties are confined to reading and the closely related skills of spelling and composition, or are most extreme in those areas; in arithmetic or other subjects he may be doing normal or superior work. The retarded reader whose achievement in reading is significantly below the normal expectancy for his mental ability is said to be a case of reading disability.

An example may make this distinction clearer. Suppose that two children, John and James, are both ten years old, both in the fourth grade, and both have third-grade reading ability. Since normally a ten-year-old should be able to do fifth-grade work,[12] both are two years retarded in reading. Let us suppose that John has an IQ of 80 and a mental age of eight years. A child with a mental age of eight who can do third-grade work is up to normal performance for his mental ability, so John is not a case of reading disability. Let us suppose that James has an IQ of 100 and a mental age of ten years. His reading ability should be up to fifth-grade level, and since his reading is two years below expectancy for his mental ability, he is properly called a case of reading disability.

In addition to the children with reading disability whose ineffective reading is easy to recognize, there is a small group which is usually overlooked. These are children who have superior mental ability but are merely average in reading. If we define reading disability as reading skill which is significantly below expectancy for the child's mental ability, these bright children should be counted as cases of reading disability, even though they are able to do the reading expected in their grades.

The Frequency of Reading Disabilities

Surveys indicate that in typical elementary schools, about one third of the children read at their grade level, about one third read one or more years above their grade level, and about one third are retarded in reading one or more years. Of the retarded readers, the majority are dull children whose reading is on a par with their other abilities. A substantial minority, comprising about 10 to 15 per cent of all the children, are cases of mild or severe reading disability. For example, in one survey,[13] 6000 pupils in grades two to six inclusive

[12] The typical school child enters the first grade very close to his sixth birthday and is promoted regularly. He is seven years old when entering the second grade, eight years old when entering the third grade, and so on. To find the normal grade placement for an average child, subtract five years from his chronological age. To determine approximately the expected grade level of achievement for a child whose intelligence is above or below average, subtract five years from the child's mental age.

[13] Durrell, D. D., *Improvement of Basic Reading Abilities,* p. 45. Yonkers, New York: World Book Co., 1940.

were given tests of reading capacity and reading achievement. Of the whole group, 18 per cent of the boys and 9 per cent of the girls scored one or more years lower on the achievement test than on the capacity test.

For some unknown reason, boys are much more subject to difficulty in all phases of language development than girls are. The superiority of girls over boys in speech is marked even in the preschool years.[14] Stuttering is more than twice as common in boys as in girls.[15] Boys constitute about two-thirds of the milder reading disability cases, and make up 75 to 90 per cent of the severe cases which are seen in reading clinics.[16] It seems safe to conclude that between 10 and 15 per cent of elementary school children have at least mild reading disabilities, and that boys outnumber girls in frequency of reading disabilities about three to one.

The Causes of Poor Reading

There is no one cause of reading disability. The general result of the large number of investigations that have attempted to find the causes of reading difficulties is that there are many handicaps which are found more frequently in poor readers than in good readers. None of these handicaps will of itself necessarily prevent a child from becoming a normal reader, but any of them may, in an individual case, interfere seriously with the child's learning. When we investigate a case thoroughly we usually find evidence of a number of factors, each of which may have been important in the creation of his disability. The most important of these factors will be briefly described now; more complete treatments will be found in Chapters IX and X.

[14] Stoddard, G. D., and Wellman, B. L., *Child Psychology,* p. 156. New York: The Macmillan Co., 1934.

[15] Louttit, C. M., *Clinical Psychology,* p. 426. New York: Harper & Bros., 1935.

[16] Note the percentages in the Durrell survey cited above. Witty and Kopel found that the 100 poorest readers in a large group of elementary school pupils contained 66 boys and 34 girls. See: Witty, P. A., and Kopel, D., "Heterophoria and Reading Disabilities," *Journal of Educational Psychology,* Vol. 27, 1936, pp. 222–230. Monroe found that boys constituted 84, 86, and 94 per cent of three groups of reading disability cases whom she studied; see *Children Who Cannot Read,* p. 98.

1. *Lack of Reading Readiness.* When forced to compete with children who are making normal progress, immature children not only fail to learn, but also develop feelings of frustration and avoidance reactions which interfere with later efforts to learn to read.

2. *Mental Retardation.* The majority of children who are retarded in reading are children whose general mental growth is slower than average. Their attainment in reading, although below average, is frequently up to or even slightly ahead of their general mental development. Such children have no disability in reading and should not be given remedial instruction. When a dull child is reading well below his own limited mental level, he may properly be considered to have a reading disability.

3. *Physical Handicaps.* Any physical condition which lowers a child's vitality, impairs his vision or hearing, or causes significant absences from school may interfere with the learning process.

4. *Directional Confusion.* Although there is still disagreement about the importance of deviations from the usual right-sided preferences as causes of difficulty in reading, spelling, and speech, many believe that directional confusions are important factors in some language disabilities.

5. *Special Brain Defects.* There are some children with neurological peculiarities that make it very difficult for them to learn to read, but such conditions account for only a small proportion of poor readers.

6. *Emotional Handicaps.* The fact that failure in school learning is intimately connected with the child's emotional state has become increasingly apparent. Poor motivation or emotional blocking is found in most children with reading disabilities who are studied clinically. In many it may be a reaction to prolonged failure, but in others it is an important causative factor.

7. *Accidental Interference with Learning.* A child's progress in school may be disrupted by frequent or prolonged absence, or by changes from one school to another. The degree to which this handicaps a child depends mainly on how much effort the school makes to help the child bridge the gaps.

8. *Poor Teaching.* All too often, much of the blame can be attrib-

uted directly to previous teachers. Things that teachers do which create difficulty include assigning work which is beyond the child's capacity, using disparagement and sarcasm as forms of motivation, and giving the child the impression that he is disliked and inferior. Of the errors of omission, perhaps the most important is failure to notice and correct difficulties while they are new and minor, allowing them to grow into severe and persistent defects.

Adapted, Corrective, and Remedial Reading Programs

Children whose retardation in reading is due to below-average mental ability need a reading program which is geared to their abilities, which accepts their limitations and is designed to meet their needs and interests. Such a reading program, different from the typical reading program in its slower pace and use of different materials and interests, can be called an *adapted* program. About 25 per cent of American children have IQ's below 90 and would benefit from reading programs which are at least in some respects adapted to their needs.

The 10 to 15 per cent who are definitely reading below their potential capacity should have reading programs which are planned to teach them the specific reading skills they have failed to master, using the best methodology, materials, and motivation possible. Efforts to help these children are broadly described as *remedial reading*. Within this broad heading a useful distinction can be made between *corrective* reading programs and *remedial* reading programs. When the remedial activities are carried on by a regular classroom teacher within the framework of regular class instruction, the term *corrective* reading applies. When the help takes place outside of the framework of class instruction, it is called *remedial* reading. Remedial reading may be conducted by the regular class teacher with an individual or small group during a special period when the rest of the class is not present; or by a special teacher, meeting with an individual child or small group in school, in a clinic or on a private tutoring basis. When a special reading teacher works with a class of a size which is typical for the school, this should be called corrective rather than remedial reading.

Developmental Reading and Remedial Reading

It is tempting to speculate on the results that would be achieved if all teachers could come close to perfection in the teaching of reading. Under these conditions, those reading problems which are presently the result of faulty educational practices would not arise. Would the need for remedial reading disappear?

It seems probable that even in an educational Utopia there will be some children with neurological handicaps, visual handicaps that resist correction, emotional problems arising out of early family experiences, and so on. These children would need diagnostic study of a depth beyond most classroom teachers' capabilities, and many of them would need, as they do now, an amount and kind of individual help which it is very difficult to provide in a classroom situation. Utopian teaching would lessen the number of reading disabilities but would not eliminate them, and some need for special remedial facilities would remain.

At present, and at least for the next decade or two, most reading programs will continue to fall short of Utopia. With the best of teacher efforts to meet individual needs there will be thousands of children who will get lost in the early stages of reading instruction. If the supply of well-trained teachers increases at a slower rate than the number of children, as seems quite likely to occur, the proportion of retarded readers may increase rather than decrease. We can be sure that most of these children do not just outgrow their reading problems; the large number of severe disability cases of secondary school age prove this conclusively. The need for corrective and remedial programs is not likely to diminish soon.

Light is cast upon this issue if we compare it with the situation in the field of physical health. There is no argument over the principle that great emphasis should be placed upon hygienic living, and that with proper attention to the teaching of principles of nutrition, safety education, and so on, much poor health and many accidents can be avoided. This does not mean that first aid becomes unnecessary. Accidents will continue to happen and germs will continue to circulate. Knowledge of what to do for common, minor physical ailments and mishaps is just as important as ever. Finally, when a serious illness or accident occurs, nobody denies the need for the diagnostic skill of a capable physician or the expert care of trained nurses. There is a need for all three: general practice of hygienic living, widespread knowledge and use of approved first-aid practices, and expert medical care.

The situation with regard to the teaching of reading is similar. There can be no quarrel with the proposition that major efforts should be devoted to improving the general efficiency of classroom teaching. As this takes place, the frequency of reading disabilities will diminish. However, under the best of teachers, children will continue to be handicapped by physical defects, to miss school because of illness, and for other reasons to fall behind. Detecting weak points in the child's achievement and helping the child to overcome these weaknesses are integral parts of the effective classroom teacher's method. This corrective instruction is a sort of educational first aid. It is, of course, remedial teaching, but remedial teaching conceived of without capital letters, as a normal part of good methodology. As corrective teaching in its simpler forms becomes taken for granted because it is part of every good teacher's procedure, the need for calling it by a special name diminishes. In this sense, remedial reading is losing its distinctive character by becoming normal rather than unusual procedure. Finally, there will continue to be a few stubborn cases of children whose special handicaps in reading will require the application of refined diagnostic procedures by experts, and individual teaching by skilled remedial teachers. There is, then, no conflict among the three phases of a good reading program: superior first teaching which is adapted to the needs and individual abilities of the children, frequent classroom use of simple corrective procedures as they are needed, and careful diagnosis and special remedial help for the severe reading casualty.

Suggested Additional Reading

ADAMS, FAY, LILLIAN GRAY, and DORA REESE. *Teaching Children to Read,* Chs. 1, 2. New York: The Ronald Press Co., 1949.

Association for Supervision and Curriculum Development, N.E.A. *The Three R's in the Elementary School.* Washington, D.C.: The Association, 1952.

Betts, Emmett A. *Foundations of Reading Instruction,* Chs. 1, 6, 7. New York: American Book Co., 1946.

Bond, Guy L., and Eva Bond Wagner. *Teaching the Child to Read,* Revised Edition, Chs. 1, 2. New York: The Macmillan Co., 1950.

Russell, David H. *Children Learn to Read,* Chs. 1–4. Boston: Ginn & Co., 1949.

Whipple, Gertrude. "Characteristics of a Sound Reading Program," *Reading in the Elementary School,* pp. 33–53. 48th Yearbook of the National Society for the Study of Education, Part II. Chicago: University of Chicago Press, 1949.

Yoakam, Gerald A. *Basal Reading Instruction,* Chs. 1, 2. New York: McGraw-Hill Book Co., 1955.

· II ·

Developing Readiness for Reading

SCHOOLS OF TODAY realize that individual differences are as significant when children enter school as they are at any later time. Some first-grade entrants are not as mature as a typical kindergarten child, while others are far ahead of their age group in many respects. These tremendous differences in maturity have great implications for curriculum planning and teaching technique. To confront an immature child with tasks that are far beyond his abilities is practically certain to make him fail. A successful program for young children, in reading as in other curricular areas, should be based on a realistic appraisal of what they can do now and what they are ready for next.

I. The Nature of Reading Readiness

BEFORE A BABY can walk he must develop strength in his back and legs and must be able to balance himself. He has already become able to sit without support, to stand holding on to something, and to stand for a few moments without support. In this process the maturing of the nervous system is even more important than the strengthening of muscles, but both learning and growing are involved. After the baby has developed these necessary abilities he is usually ready to begin to walk; before then, no amount of teaching and helping by his parents will produce results. At this point learning comes more strongly into play. A painful fall on a slippery floor may retard progress for several weeks, while successful beginning efforts tend to result in quick accomplishment.

Reading, like walking, can be mastered only after a long process of growing and learning has taken place. It is a much more complex activity than walking and requires both a much higher level of general growth and brain development, and a host of specific learnings. Some of the traits involved depend primarily on the growth potentialities of the child as determined largely by constitutional make-up. Other traits, equally important, develop through learning from every day living. The intimate interplay of inner growth and environmental stimulation is present in all aspects of child development, and readiness for reading is no exception.

Reading readiness may be defined as a state of general maturity which, when reached, allows a child to learn to read without excess difficulty. It is a composite of many interconnected traits. A child may be more advanced in some aspects of reading readiness than in others. The major characteristics which are important in reading readiness are age, sex, general intelligence, visual and auditory perception, physical health and maturity, freedom from directional confusion, background of experience, comprehension and use of oral English, emotional and social adjustment, and interest in reading. These will be discussed below in the order in which they have just been listed.

The Age Factor

In most school systems children are accepted into the first grade once a year and there is a minimum age limit. The entering class is likely to vary almost a full year in age, from the child just barely old enough to the child who was almost old enough the year before. If the minimum entering age is 5 years 9 months, the age difference of almost a year between youngest and oldest amounts to about 17 per cent; if the minimum is 5 years 4 months, the difference is about 19 per cent. Such a difference in chronological age is highly significant because general development takes place rapidly during this period, and a difference of 10 per cent or more in age between two children is likely to be accompanied by important differences in the levels of physical, intellectual, linguistic, and emotional maturity attained.

In making a transition from semiannual to annual promotion (a prevalent but not always wise move) some schools have lowered their entering age. In doing this they have automatically changed the first-grade population so that a much larger proportion than formerly are not ready for reading when they enter. When the entering age is lowered by half a year, it takes a half year longer for the average child to become ready for reading. Maturity in children cannot be created by regulations.

The Sex Factor

It is well known that girls tend to mature earlier than boys in many aspects of growth. While the individual differences within each sex are much greater than the average differences between the sexes, the average differences are still significant.

Girls tend to reach puberty about one and a half years earlier than boys, and from birth on there are detectable differences in physiological maturity, particularly as shown by the date of appearance of teeth and by the hardening or ossification of the skeleton. Girls begin to talk somewhat earlier than boys and through childhood tend to have larger vocabularies and to do a larger volume of talking than boys. Boys tend, even in preschool years, to spend more time on large-muscle activities, while girls spend more of their time in sedentary activities. Feminine practice in weaving, sewing, or doll play may be advantageous in developing good close vision and fine manual skills. The sex differences in language development may also have a cultural basis, as McCarthy has pointed out.[1] Probably these differences are partly constitutional and partly due to differences in upbringing; in either case, they are important. When we note that boys constitute about two-thirds of the milder reading disability cases and make up 75 to 90 per cent of the severe cases,

[1] McCarthy, Dorothea, "Some Possible Explanations of Sex Differences in Language Development and Disorders," *Journal of Psychology,* Vol. 35, 1953, pp. 155–160.

it is easy to infer that more boys than girls are not ready for reading instruction when they enter school.

Intellectual Factors

General Intelligence. The most important single factor in reading readiness is general intelligence, which, being an average of many phases of mental growth, is significantly related to most of the other factors. The results of tests of general intelligence for children are expressed in terms of Mental Age (MA) and Intelligence Quotient (IQ). Saying that a child has an MA of 6 years 0 months means that his score on a particular intelligence test is equal to the average score of children who are exactly six years old. The MA is a measure of degree or level of mental maturity and tends to increase at a quite steady rate as the child gets older. The IQ is a measure of brightness or rate of mental growth and tends to remain fairly stable as children get older. About 50 per cent of children have IQ's between 90 and 110, which is considered the average range. Of the two measures, the MA tends to give a better short-range prediction of performance during the next few months, while the IQ give the better long-range prediction.

In 1931 an experimental report was published by Morphett and Washburne which has had a profound effect upon school practice.[2] In this report, the progress of first-grade children in Winnetka, Illinois, was studied in relation to their mental ages. Two critical points were reported. Children whose mental ages were below six when they entered usually failed. The proportion of failure dropped as mental age increased up to six and one half years; above that point, nearly all succeeded. Many writers have since that time stated dogmatically that there is a minimum mental age necessary for success in first-grade reading. Some have placed the lower limit at an MA of six years, and some at six and a half years. Nearly all have based their conclusions on the Morphett-Washburne study. Most of them have ignored the facts that the reading materials used in that study were difficult by today's standards, and that the pass-

[2] Morphett, M. V., and Washburne, C., "When Should Children Begin to Read?" *Elementary School Journal,* Vol. 29, 1931, pp. 496–503.

ing standard set in that study would be considered high in many school systems today.

While there is unquestionably a substantial relationship between mental age and learning to read, present evidence does not justify the establishment of an absolute dividing line at any one mental age, such as six years or six and one half years. Davidson succeeded, with much effort, in teaching some dull five-year-olds to recognize words.[3] Winch has reported from England a beginning reading program which was generally successful with five-year-old children from lower-class homes.[4] Roslow has described the results of a first-grade program in which differentiated instruction was given to children with mental ages below six years; the majority of them reached second-grade level in reading by the end of the year.[5] As Gates[6] has sensibly pointed out, the progress of a child is not dependent entirely upon his ability; such things as the difficulty of the material used, the speed with which the pupils are required to move along, the specific methods used, and the amount of individualized help, all influence the progress of the child.

However, the fact that reading *can* be taught to children with five-year-old minds does not prove that it *should* be taught to such children. Conclusive evidence concerning the ideal age or stage of maturity at which to begin reading would require careful comparative studies in which large groups of children, carefully equated, were started on reading at different ages and their progress followed for several years. How much the children learn during the first year of instruction is not a satisfactory basis for judgment. For example, Keister[7] has reported on the progress of three first-grade classes in

[3] Davidson, Helen P., "An Experimental Study of Bright, Average, and Dull Children at the Four-Year Mental Level," *Genetic Psychology Monographs*, Vol. 9, Nos. 3, 4, 1931.

[4] Winch, W. H., *Teaching Beginners to Read in England*, Educational Research Monographs, No. 8. Bloomington, Ill.: Public School Publishing Co., 1925.

[5] Roslow, S., "Reading Readiness and Reading Achievement in the First Grade," *Journal of Experimental Education*, Vol. 9, 1940, pp. 154–159.

[6] Gates, A. I., "The Necessary Mental Age for Beginning Reading," *Elementary School Journal*, Vol. 37, 1937, pp. 497–508.

[7] Keister, B. V., "Reading Skills Acquired by Five-Year-Old Children," *Elementary School Journal*, Vol. 41, 1941, pp. 587–596.

which most of the children were five years old. Reading ability at the end of the year was practically up to the norm, on standardized tests. However, when the children entered the second grade the following September, they had forgotten so much that the teachers practically had to start all over again; by the end of the second grade they were still well below the norm. It seems decidedly questionable whether all the effort expended by the teachers and pupils in the first grade was worth while.

Reports of programs in which the teaching of reading was delayed one or more terms are generally favorable. Such cities as Chicago and Los Angeles have experimented with setting up special nonreading first-grade classes for immature first-grade entrants, with favorable results.[8] Some private schools, whose pupils are for the most part bright and from superior homes, give no instruction in reading in the first grade. The assertion is that the children achieve normal standing in reading by the end of the third grade with much less effort on the part of teachers and pupils than is customary.

One research study has traced the effects of a delayed start for several years.[9] In Winnetka, one first-grade class was not started on reading until the middle of the second grade. Each child in the class was carefully matched for intelligence and other characteristics with three children in other classes which started reading at the beginning of the first grade. The delayed class caught up with the others in reading ability by the end of the third grade, was a half year ahead by the end of the fourth grade, and was one and a half years ahead, on the average, by the end of the eighth grade. While this study does not prove the desirability of postponing reading for all children, it certainly casts some doubt upon the advisability of rushing children into reading as soon as they reach the first grade.

[8] Johnson, W. H., "Development of the Chicago Program to Aid Pupils Lacking in Reading Readiness," *Elementary School Journal*, Vol. 42, 1942, pp. 337–344.

Woods, E. L., and staff, "A Study of the Entering B1 Children in the Los Angeles Public Schools," *Journal of Educational Research*, Vol. 31, 1937, pp. 9–19.

[9] Washburne, Carleton, "Individualized Plan of Instruction in Winnetka," in *Adjusting Reading Programs to Individuals*, Supplementary Education Monographs, No. 52, pp. 90–95. Chicago: University of Chicago Press, 1941.

Two cases may be cited to show the bad effects of starting children on reading before they are mentally mature enough.

Bronson entered school at the age of five, and, as the school had no kindergarten, was placed in the first grade. He came from a good home, was of average intelligence, and had no physical or sensory defects. Throughout the year he was at a complete loss, and at the end of the year he made zero scores on reading tests. He repeated the year and made fairly satisfactory progress. All the effort expended on him during the first year was wasted. When he entered school, Bronson was too young and immature to tackle reading. His mental age was growing at a normal rate, however, and in another year became high enough for successful reading.

More frequent in the schools are children like Lawrence, who was of average age but below average in intelligence when he entered the first grade. Lawrence entered school at the age of six, with an IQ of 80 and a MA of less than five years. He was, of course, confronted with work beyond his mental capacity and, in addition, the type of instruction he received was not adapted to children whose rate of mental growth is slow. His initial handicap was reinforced by inappropriate instruction, and he became a real case of reading disability. At the age of ten, he was still struggling with second-grade work.

The way in which mental age is related to both chronological age and IQ is shown in Table I. From the table one can readily see that the lower a child's IQ, the older he must be to reach an MA adequate for success in learning to read. If we take an MA of six years as a desirable minimum, then the child with an IQ of 120 has reached it by the age of 5 years 3 months; with an IQ of 110 it is attained by 5 years 9 months; with an IQ of 100, by 6 years; with an IQ of 90, not until 6 years 9 months; with an IQ of 80, not until 7 years 9 months; and with an IQ of 70, not until the child is about nine years old.

About 50 per cent of all children have IQ's below 100 and are probably not intellectually ready for reading until after the age of 6 years. Approximately 25 per cent have IQ's below 90 and are not expected to be ready until some time after 6 years 9 months. Obviously many of them spend a year in the first grade before they are able to undertake reading instruction with profit.

Table I. Reading Readiness: Relation of Mental Age to Chronological Age and Intelligence Quotient

	Intelligence Quotient						
	70	80	90	100	110	120	130
Chronological Age	*Corresponding Mental Age*						
5 yrs. 3 mos.	3–8	4–2	4–9	5–3	5–9	6–4	6–10
5 yrs. 9 mos.	4–0	4–7	5–3	5–9	6–4	6–11	7–6
6 yrs. 3 mos.	4–5	5–0	5–8	6–3	6–9	7–6	8–2
6 yrs. 9 mos.	4–9	5–5	6–1	6–9	7–5	8–1	8–9
7 yrs. 3 mos.	5–1	5–10	6–6	7–3	8–0	8–8	9–5
7 yrs. 9 mos.	5–5	6–2	7–0	7–9	8–6	9–4	10–1

NOTE: Mental ages for other chronological ages and IQ's may be computed with the formula: Mental Age = Chronological Age times IQ. In using the formula it is desirable to change Chronological Age into months and then divide the resulting MA by 12 to express it in years and months. One must remember, also, that the IQ is really a decimal fraction. For example: To find the MA of a child who is 6 years 6 months old and has an IQ of 85, 78 mos. (.85) equals 66.3 mos. which equals 5 years 6 months.

In the absence of decisive evidence, the following conclusions concerning the relationship of mental ability to beginning reading seem justified: (1) There is a substantial relationship between mental age and ease of learning to read; most children who fail in reading in the first grade have mental ages below six years. The more mature children not only learn more easily but also retain what they learn better than the less mature children. (2) Most children who have normal IQ's, have MA's above six years, and are free from special handicaps, can be successfully taught to read in the first grade. However, a delayed start does these children no harm. (3) It is not possible to set a definite minimum mental age for learning to read because too many other factors are involved.

Children with mental ages as low as five years can be taught to read first-grade materials. There seems to be no lasting advantage in such an early start, however, and many of these children fail to make any headway when the pace of instruction is geared to the progress of older or brighter children. (4) Schools which provide a first-grade program which is rich in experiences and social activities, with no formal reading instruction, avoid many problems of reading failure and achieve as good or better reading in the higher grades as the schools which teach reading from the beginning of the first grade.

Specific Mental Abilities. It is natural to suppose that when children whose general intelligence seems to be adequate for the requirements of learning to read fail to do so, they may have some special kind of mental defect that prevents them from making progress. Intelligence tests contain many different kinds of items, and it seems possible that the child's total score might be good while he might do very poorly on some one type of question. The best available evidence seems to indicate that in young children such traits as memory and attention are not separate, but are closely interrelated and are not clearly distinguishable from general intelligence.[10] This is true, at any rate, for most children. It does not rule out the possibility of finding an occasional child who shows very poor memory, inability to concentrate and pay attention, or difficulty in following directions, which is in marked contrast to otherwise satisfactory mental ability. The question of the occurrence of special mental difficulties as handicaps to progress in reading is dealt with in greater detail in Chapter IX. While a teacher may suspect the presence of such a defect, the diagnosis of such conditions requires the services of a trained psychologist.

Visual Perception. Even if the eyes are normal, the child may have immature visual perception. Seeing a thing does not always mean noticing its details. Many young children pay attention only to the main characteristics of visual stimuli — the size, shape, and

[10] McNemar, Quinn, *The Revision of the Stanford-Binet Scale.* Boston: Houghton Mifflin Co., 1942.

color — and ignore the details. When asked to match letters or words they make many errors, not because of faulty vision, but because they do not notice differences which are obvious to older children.

Prominent among the perceptual tendencies of immature children is the tendency to make *reversal* errors. To such children, *b, d, p,* and *q* are the same; the differences are ignored. The letters *m* and *w* may be confused; this is an example of a vertical reversal. Pairs of words such as *on* and *no, saw* and *was, tap* and *pat,* also tend to be confused, since the children have not yet learned to look at a word always from left to right. Studies by Teegarden [11] and Davidson [12] have shown that reversal errors are very common among young children and tend to decrease as children get older, and Teegarden's results indicate that children with marked reversal tendencies make less than normal progress in the first grade.

Because the ability to perceive visual similarities and differences is so important for progress in reading, items designed to measure this ability are found in all reading readiness tests.

Auditory Perception. Inability to distinguish between words which sound somewhat alike may prove a severe handicap in learning to read. In some children it is due to faulty hearing. In others hearing acuity may be normal, but the child has not learned to perceive the differences in the sounds of the words. Deficiency in auditory sensation or perception often results in the persistence of infantile pronunciation. If a six-year-old still pronounces his *r*'s like *w*'s or mixes up his *th* and *v* sounds (*muvver* for *mother*), or slurs and mispronounces words of more than one syllable, the chances are good that he does not notice the difference between his pronunciation and the correct pronunciation. If a child does not hear the difference between two words, he will have difficulty distinguishing between their printed symbols. Such children also have difficulty learning the sound of the letters.

[11] Teegarden, L., "Clinical Identification of Non-Readers," *Child Development,* Vol. 3, 1932, pp. 346–358.

[12] Davidson, H. P., "A Study of the Confusing Letters B, D, P, and Q," *Journal of Genetic Psychology,* Vol. 47, 1935, pp. 458–468.

Physical Fitness

In some school systems, every child entering the first grade is given a comprehensive examination by a physician. This is a desirable practice which should be more widely followed. A school is negligent which allows children to flounder along handicapped by physical defects which are correctible. The physical defects which most frequently interfere with beginning reading are poor vision and poor hearing.

Any marked departure from normal vision may give a child hazy or incorrect images when he looks at words. Few first-grade children are nearsighted, but the majority of them are farsighted and tend to outgrow the condition as they get older.[13] Astigmatism and poor coordination of the eyes are also common in six-year-olds.

Judy was a total loss in the first grade. She not only failed to make any progress in reading, but also was quite a nuisance in the classroom. That summer her mother took her to a reading clinic. There it was found that Judy had normal intelligence (IQ 104), but had poor visual acuity. She had probably been unable to see charts or the blackboard clearly from her seat, and so had missed much of the instruction. Provided with suitable glasses and given some individual help, Judy began to make good progress in reading. Judy's poor vision should have been discovered at the beginning of her year in the first grade, not at the end.

When a medical examination is not possible, an alert teacher can still notice many signs which suggest physical problems, and which are unfortunately overlooked very often. A child whose eyes turn pink and begin to water in the classroom may need glasses. The child who looks stupid may have a hearing defect. No child is intentionally clumsy; when motor incoordination is very marked, it may be caused by something wrong in the child's nervous system, making a neurological examination desirable. Listlessness, laziness, and lack of effort may be related to anemia, malnutrition, and endocrine disorder, or a focal infection, such as diseased tonsils.

[13] Betts, Emmett A., *The Prevention and Correction of Reading Difficulties*, pp. 153–156. Evanston: Row, Peterson and Co., 1936.

The good first-grade teacher looks for signs of health problems in the daily behavior of her children.

Physical Maturity. Children differ in their rates of growing up. The most obvious aspects of physical growth are height and weight. Any teacher who has lined up a kindergarten or first-grade class in order of size is aware of the marked differences that exist. By comparing the average heights and weights obtained by measuring thousands of children at each age, it is possible to express a child's status in these characteristics in terms of a height age and a weight age.

Another significant index of physical maturity is the development of the child's skeleton. A baby's bones are comparatively soft and many of the bones are still only masses of flexible cartilage. X-ray pictures of a child's bones, when compared with a series selected to show typical development at different ages, allow an expert to judge the skeletal age of a child. X-rays of the wrist and hand are usually employed, since this region contains many small bones whose sequence of development has been carefully studied. Wide differences in skeletal maturity exist among children of the same size and age. Girls are on the average a year more advanced in skeletal maturity than boys of the same age.

Research studies conducted by Olson and Hughes[14] suggest that the physical maturity of a child, as indicated by his height, weight, and skeletal development, may be an important correlate of reading readiness. At the present time, however, it seems unwise for teachers to place much reliance on the aspects of physical maturity that they can easily observe, as indicators of reading readiness.

Lateral Dominance. One of the issues concerning reading about which there is still much disagreement is the importance of hand and eye dominance in relation to reading progress. This issue is a complex one, and is discussed in greater detail in Chapter X. There

[14] Olson, Willard H., and Hughes, B. O., "The Concept of Organismic Age," *Journal of Educational Research,* Vol. 35, 1942, pp. 525–527. An as yet unpublished doctoral study by Robert Karlin at New York University indicates a significant relationship between skeletal maturity of first-grade children and their progress in reading.

seems to be some truth in the idea that children who are not consistently right-sided sometimes have difficulty in learning to follow a left-to-right direction in reading and are troubled by marked reversal tendencies. Castner stated that he could usually pick out a future reading disability child when the child is still in kindergarten, largely on the basis of the child's hand and eye preferences.[15] While much research has been done on the relation of lateral dominance to reading ability at higher-grade levels, the significance of variations in hand and eye dominance for reading readiness work is still in doubt. It is desirable, however, for first-grade teachers to let a child use whichever hand he prefers for writing and drawing.

Experience

The general cultural level of a child's home is the most important determiner of the adequacy of his background of knowledge and experience. The young child whose parents are educated and cultured grows up in a home which provides many opportunities for favorable development. He is surrounded by adults who speak good English with a rich vocabulary, and naturally tends to develop the same kind of speech. Through trips and excursions he is provided with broadening experiences. Books and magazines in the home attract him with their bright pictures, and the stories which are read or told to him tend to develop an early interest in books and reading. Such a home is valuable in providing the child with a background of knowledge that will aid him in reading.[16]

Many children who are normal in intelligence come to school from homes that are quite lacking in intellectual stimulation. Chil-

[15] Castner, B. M., "Prediction of Reading Disability Prior to First Grade Entrance," *American Journal of Orthopsychiatry,* Vol. 5, 1935, pp. 375–387.

[16] Hilliard, G. H., and Troxell, E., "Informational Background as a Factor in Reading Readiness," *Elementary School Journal,* Vol. 38, 1937, pp. 255–263.

Almy, Millie, *Children's Experiences Prior to First Grade and Success in Beginning Reading,* Contributions to Education, No. 954. New York: Bureau of Publications, Teachers College, Columbia University, 1949.

Milner, Esther, "A Study of the Relationship between Reading Readiness in Grade One School Children and Patterns of Parent-Child Interaction," *Child Development,* Vol. 22, 1951, pp. 95–112.

dren who grow up in city slums or on isolated farms sometimes know astonishingly little about the world in general, although they may know a great deal about certain phases of it. They are often completely ignorant of many things that are commonplace to the average first-grade child. One child known to the writer lived only half a mile from one of the world's most famous zoos but had never been taken there; he did not know a cow from a horse, and had never seen a chicken outside of a butcher shop. It is no wonder that he found his primer (which dealt with farm life) hard to understand.

It sometimes happens that children who live in homes of very superior economic status are so sheltered as to be quite retarded in experience when they enter school. The parents may be too busy or too uninterested to give their children much personal attention, servants may take practically complete charge, or the children may be given few or no opportunities to play with other children. What counts for child development is not the wealth of the home but the intellectual and social environment with which the child is surrounded.

Language Factors

Adequate mastery of spoken language is important for progress in reading. The major aspects of language that seem most significant in reading readiness are: (1) the child's vocabulary, which is basic both to his understanding of what is said to him and to his ability to communicate; (2) mastery of sentence structure, shown most clearly in the child's spontaneous conversation; and (3) clarity of pronunciation. Since typical first-grade reading employs only a few hundred words and the typical six-year-old understands the meaning of thousands of words, sentence structure and clarity of speech are more likely to be deficient at the beginning level than vocabulary.

Mastery of language is dependent on many factors. The most important of these are intelligence, hearing, and home environment. The dull child is slow at learning to talk because language is a highly intellectual acquisition. There is in general a close relationship between a child's intelligence and his mastery of speech. When children of normal intelligence are retarded in speech it is usually because of a special handicap, such as defective hearing or a very restricted home background.

Children who come from homes of low cultural level do not have normal opportunities to develop an adequate language background. If a foreign language is spoken in the home the handicap is more intense, as the child tends to develop a small English vocabulary, incorrect pronunciation, and faulty sentence construction. Foreign-born parents who do not try to learn English are usually poorly educated and their homes are often deficient in many other respects besides language.

Pedro is an example of the hampering effect of a foreign-language background. Although born and brought up in New York City, he heard little English until he entered school. His parents had immigrated from Latin America and lived in a compact little community of other Spanish-speaking people. Pedro picked up what little English he knew on the streets, but even there Spanish was the major language. His reading reflected this poor background. He mastered the mechanics of reading fairly well (although he ignored endings and spoke with a marked accent), but showed extremely poor comprehension. A great many commonplace words meant nothing to him.

Children like Pedro form a large part of the school population in the larger cities and in many smaller communities. They often find it hard to progress in reading even when they have normal intelligence. If they are also dull — and many of them are — they are doubly handicapped in their schoolwork.

Emotional and Social Maturity

The social and emotional development of first-grade children is just as varied as their mental development. Some newcomers to school are cheerful, stable, self-reliant children who fit into the new routine without difficulty. Others are very babyish. They may show immaturity in a great variety of ways: they cannot take off or put on their outer clothing; they need help in the toilet; they cannot play independently; they do not know how to get along with other children; they are extremely timid; they are too shy to open their mouths in class; they do not know what it means to take orders or obey; they are crybabies; they talk baby talk; or they try to monopolize the teacher's attention. These and many other forms of immature behavior may be found in varying degrees of severity and in many combinations. It is not uncommon to find a bright child who is quite immature in nonintellectual traits, and who consequently makes less progress than one would expect from his mental test scores.

Three aspects of emotional and social maturity are significant in reading readiness. The first of these is emotional stability. The unstable six-year-old has not outgrown the emotional volatility which characterizes the child of nursery-school age. Among the ways in which he may show his instability are rapid changes of mood, crying at the least provocation, and fits of temper or tantrums. Difficulties in the home situation are usually responsible for marked instability in young children.

The ability and desire to help oneself, or self-reliance, is another aspect of social maturity that is significant in school adjustment. Some children have parents who wisely encourage their first fumbling efforts at feeding, dressing, and washing themselves, choosing their playthings, and solving their own problems. Some neglected children develop self-reliance to a high degree through necessity Other children are still very helpless when they enter school, often because their mothers baby them and do everything for them.

The ability to participate actively and cooperatively in group activities is a third extremely important aspect of social development. So much of the learning in the primary grades is done in groups that a child who is too shy, too restless, or too antagonistic to take a normal part in group activities is bound to miss a great deal.

In order to understand the reasons for immaturity in social behavior or for peculiar emotional reactions, it is necessary to inquire into the family situation in which the child has spent most of his time and has learned most of his emotional and social habits. A tactful interview with the child's mother frequently discloses highly significant information.

The teacher can expect to find, in the home life of a socially retarded or emotionally disturbed child, one or more of the following conditions:

1. A broken home, with one or both parents missing because of separation, military service, death, or other causes. The effect is greatest if the cause of the disruption is one about which the family is ashamed, such as illegitimacy or imprisonment.
2. Dissention or quarreling between the parents. Emotional tension in the home is felt by the child and makes him insecure and nervous.
3. Poor disciplinary procedures. Home discipline may be harsh and arbitrary, excessively lenient, or inconsistent and unpredictable.
4. Rejection. The child may be made to feel that he is unwanted, a burden, a nuisance, that his parents do not love him. Threats to give a child away or send him away are often taken seriously by young children, even if the parents do not mean them. The continued feeling of being rejected or disliked by his parents is one of the most damaging experiences that a child can have.
5. Unsuccessful competition with brothers or sisters. In some families the parents openly show favoritism. The child may be exhorted to emulate the favored one until real jealousy and hatred develop. If the favorite is a good student, the other child may become hostile to the school activities because he associates them with the disliked brother or sister.
6. Overprotection. Some mothers gain such satisfaction from taking care of their babies that they are reluctant to see the children grow up. In many little ways they try to keep the child dependent upon them and try to delay each step toward maturity. They usually find fairly plausible excuses behind which to hide their real motives from others, and sometimes even from themselves.

Interest in Books

One of the most important aspects of readiness is the desire to learn to read. Children who have spent many pleasurable hours listening to stories and looking through picture books usually look forward to reading with eager anticipation.

Children's expectations about reading are strongly influenced by what they hear at home. In one study, 700 kindergarten children were interviewed shortly before promotion to the first grade.[17] More children expected reading to be hard than expected it to be easy. Often their expectations were based on what they were told by older brothers and sisters. Some were discouraged before they even started: "You make mistakes and the teacher hollers at you." For a few children who are trying to maintain a babyish dependence in their home relationships, learning to read means growing up and is therefore put off as long as possible.

The attitudes which the child brings to the first grade are quickly modified by his experiences in school. A good first-grade program satisfies those who expect to like reading and want to read, and changes the attitudes of those whose attitudes are negative or indifferent.

II. Methods for Evaluating Reading Readiness

In the preceding section, it was pointed out that reading readiness is a combination of many different characteristics. Some of these can be measured by standardized tests, some can be judged from information obtained from the child's family, and some can be noted only by observing the child in his daily behavior.

Use of Intelligence Tests

Since general intelligence is the most important single factor in readiness for reading, it is obvious that intelligence tests are useful for appraising certain phases of readiness to read.

Most schools rely upon group intelligence tests. These tests are comparatively simple and economical. They can be given and scored by a classroom teacher, and so are practical for routine use. Group intelligence tests for first-grade children are all somewhat alike. Directions are given orally, and the children indicate their answers by making marks on pictures. No reading ability is involved. Items which are commonly included are intended to measure such abili-

[17] Brumbaugh, F., "Reading Expectancy," *Elementary English Review,* Vol. 17, 1940, pp. 153–155.

ties as range of information, understanding of single words and sentences, memory, ability to follow directions, recognition of similarities and differences, and logical reasoning. The following group tests are recommended for use near the end of kindergarten or beginning of the first grade: the *Pintner-Cunningham Primary Test*,[18] the *Detroit Beginning First Grade Intelligence Test*, the *California Test of Mental Maturity, Pre-Primary Battery* (long or short form), and the *Kuhlmann-Anderson Intelligence Test*, grade 1A.

In comparative studies, group tests have sometimes shown higher correlations with achievement in the first grade than individual intelligence tests do. This is probably because the child's ability to conform to the group situation influences both his classroom learning and his score on a group test.

To obtain a measure of mental ability which is as nearly as possible a measure of the child's mental capacity, uninfluenced by emotional and social factors, it is necessary to use an individual intelligence test. In such a test the examiner can watch what the child is doing all the time, and has a better chance to keep the child doing his best throughout the test. He can also observe the child's attentiveness, effort, or carefulness. The individual intelligence test most widely used in the United States for children is the *Revised Stanford-Binet Intelligence Scale*. This test should be given only by a person with special training. Each child must be tested separately. Average time for testing, at the age of six, is about thirty minutes. The *Wechsler Intelligence Scale for Children* is a newer individual test whose value as a measure of readiness for reading has not yet been determined.

For most schools the practical procedure, if intelligence tests are to be given to entering children, is to give a group test. The few children whose scores are quite low, or who are thought to be brighter than the test results indicate, should then be retested individually or in a small group with another group test. If there is still doubt about the accuracy of a child's results, or if his score is

[18] A descriptive list of all of the tests mentioned in this book, with information about cost, publishers, and so on, will be found in Appendix A.

so low that special class placement must be considered, the child should be referred to a psychological examiner for individual examination.

Reading Readiness Tests

A number of tests are available which are designed specifically to measure readiness for reading. These are similar to the intelligence tests in many respects, but there are also important differences. While the intelligence tests attempt to measure general mental ability, the readiness tests attempt to measure the particular phases of mental functioning that are most closely related to success in reading. Some of the subtests in readiness tests are measures of acquired information, such as knowledge of the names of the letters of the alphabet.

In selecting a readiness test, attention should be paid to the following questions: (1) How good is the test's validity in terms of predicting reading achievement? This is by far the most important question. (2) Does the test have adequate reliability? For satisfactory measurement of individual children the reliability coefficient should be at least .90. (3) Are the norms satisfactory? Are they based on a sufficiently large and representative number of children? Are there norms for the separate parts as well as for the total score? (4) Are the directions for administering and scoring the test clear and complete? (5) How time-consuming is the test to give and score? Tests which have parts that must be given individually to each child are generally quite time-consuming. (6) Does the test provide helpful diagnostic information? Does it show specific weaknesses of individual children? A very large number of brief subtests is not necessarily an advantage since the parts may be so short and unreliable as to be quite undependable measures when considered separately. (7) What is the cost per pupil? In general costs of test blanks are sufficiently similar so that this factor should not be given much weight.

When readiness test results are going to be combined with carefully recorded teacher judgments, intelligence test results, or both, it may not be practicable to give one of the longest and most valid

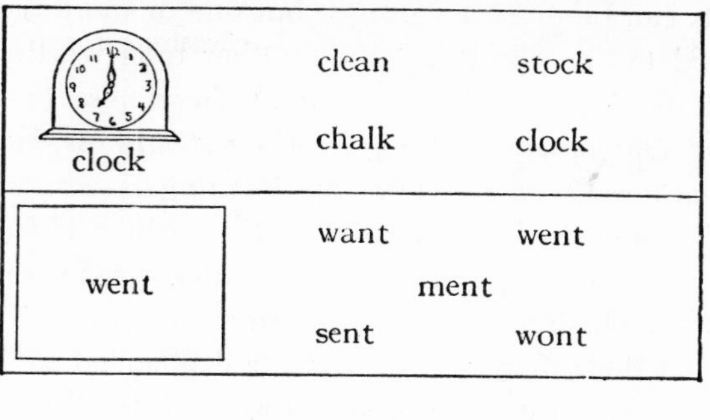

a red apple

a red ball
the red apple
a yellow apple
a red apple

Fig. 1. Samples of exercises in the perception of similarities and differences. Top, reproduced from the *Stone-Grover Classification Test for Beginners in Reading,* by permission of Webster Publishing Co.; middle, from the *Metropolitan Readiness Test,* 1933, by permission of World Book Co.; bottom, from the *Stevens Reading Readiness Test,* by permission of the American Education Press, Inc. All are reduced in size.

readiness tests, and one of the shorter tests such as the *Lee-Clark* may serve quite well. The *Metropolitan Readiness Test* is a long and reliable test for group administration which has shown up well in many comparative studies. The *Gates Reading Readiness Tests* and *Monroe Reading Aptitude Tests* are well-constructed tests in which parts can be given to groups, but one or more parts must be administered to one child at a time. Other tests worthy of consideration are the *Harrison-Stroud Reading Readiness Test,* the *Murphy-Durrell Diagnostic Tests of Reading Readiness,* the *American School Readiness Test,* the *Webster Reading Readiness Test,* and the *Van Wagenen Reading Readiness Test,* which is for individual administration. Some publishers of primary-grade readers issue readiness tests which are correlated with their readers. These should be judged on their merits, since the small financial saving possible hardly justifies the use of an inferior test; some of these are reasonably satisfactory, others are mediocre or worse.

Teacher Judgment

Teachers have always tended to form judgments about the rate of progress different pupils would achieve. With the development of standardized intelligence and reading readiness tests, some first-grade teachers have become hesitant to trust their own opinions about pupils. The judgment of a reasonably competent teacher who has had a few weeks in which to observe the daily behavior of her pupils is by no means to be disregarded. In one research study [19] each of fourteen first-grade teachers ranked her pupils in order of learning ability after six or eight weeks of school, and at the end of the year all of the children were given standardized reading tests. The average correlation between teacher ratings and reading test scores was .79, which compares favorably with the predictive value of the best tests.

This should not be taken to mean that all teachers are perfect judges, or that tests are useless. The tests provide the teacher with a quick, convenient, standardized basis for judging the status of the children in certain highly important intellectual abilities. They help the teacher to locate quickly the pupils who require further careful study. When test results and teacher observations agree, the teacher naturally feels more confident in her opinion; when they disagree, the need for further consideration is shown. Moreover, there are

[19] Carr, J. W., Jr., and Michaels, M. O., "Reading Readiness Tests and the Grouping of First Grade Entrants," *Elementary English Review,* Vol. 18, 1941 pp. 133–138.

some aspects of reading readiness which tests do not measure, for which teacher judgment, based upon observation and interviews, is needed.

It is comparatively easy to form a general over-all impression of a child. It is somewhat more difficult, but also more rewarding, to try to analyze the child's strong and weak points. The teacher who does that can determine what specific handicaps may interfere with the child's progress and in many instances can take measures to strengthen the weak abilities.

In some schools, anecdotal records are kept. The teacher has a large folder or envelope for each child's records. Whenever the child does something worth remembering, the teacher writes a brief description of the incident on a slip of paper and inserts it in the child's folder. From time to time the slips are reviewed and summarized. Teachers who use this procedure for the first time are often amazed at the number of important things they have forgotten, which the little anecdotal records bring back to mind. If a class is large, however, keeping up a set of anecdotal records may become very time-consuming.

A form which provides a quick and convenient way to record teacher judgments about reading readiness is shown in Figure 2. The teacher can use the symbols S and U for satisfactory and unsatisfactory, G, F, and P for good, fair, and poor, or any other scheme she prefers. Traits which she finds difficult to rate can be omitted. Additional comments can be written in. If the teacher has spent a few weeks in observing her pupils, the rating should not take much time. A minimum of writing is required, and it is possible for the teacher or supervisor to see on one sheet of paper a comprehensive picture of the class. By looking down a vertical column, the children who are deficient in that trait and need special attention for it can be quickly selected. By looking across one line, a comprehensive picture of one pupil is obtained. Since the headings in the rating scale correspond to the organization of the first part of this chapter, the meaning and significance of each trait can be quickly located and reviewed.

Whether the teacher records her opinions on a form like this or

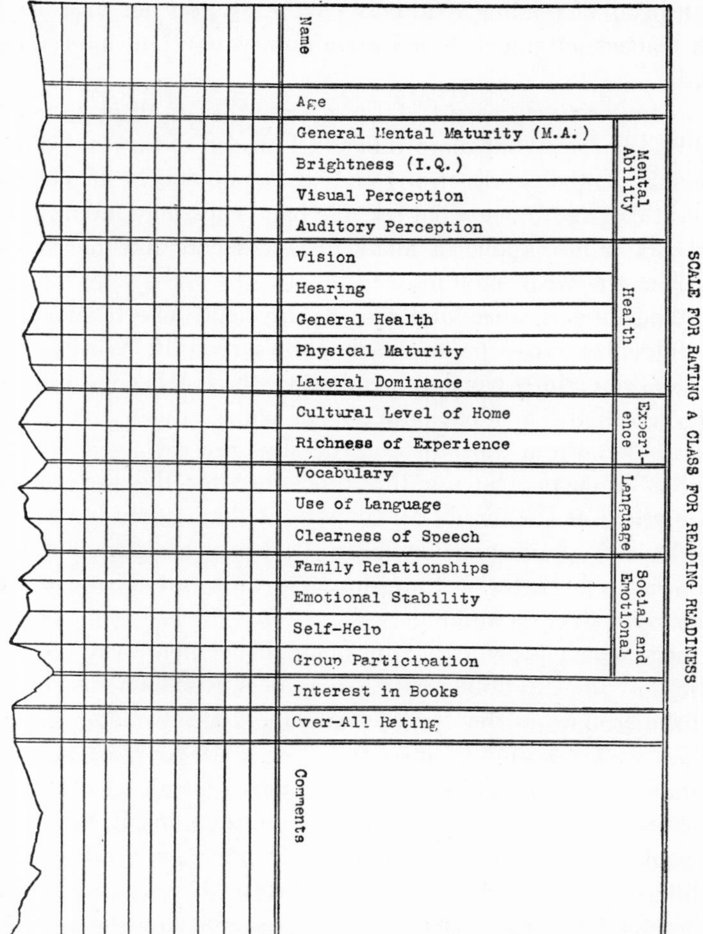

SCALE FOR RATING A CLASS FOR READING READINESS

Name

Age

Mental Ability: General Mental Maturity (M.A.); Brightness (I.Q.); Visual Perception; Auditory Perception

Health: Vision; Hearing; General Health; Physical Maturity; Lateral Dominance

Experience: Cultural Level of Home; Richness of Experience

Language: Vocabulary; Use of Language; Clearness of Speech

Social and Emotional: Family Relationships; Emotional Stability; Self-Help; Group Participation

Interest in Books

Over-All Rating

Comments

Fig. 2. A scale for rating a class in the important aspects of reading readiness.

keeps them in her head, it is advisable for her to reconsider them and revise the ratings that are no longer correct. Many changes will result from growth or improvement in the pupils. Some changes may involve the revision of an opinion that proved to be incorrect. By changing her ratings as the children overcome or outgrow their difficulties, the teacher can keep track of the progress of her pupils and at any time can get a bird's-eyes view of her readiness problems.

Planning the Evaluation of Reading Readiness

Many schools routinely test all children for readiness. Although it is possible to give the tests near the end of the kindergarten year and might be advantageous to do so in some schools, it is ordinarily better to wait until the children are in first grade. The best time is usually two or three weeks after the beginning of the school year. This allows time for the children to get accustomed to classroom activities and teacher directions, and at the same time is early enough to make the results useful in decisions about such matters as how to group the children and when to start reading.

In some school systems administrative policy requires that children reach their sixth birthday before they are tested for reading readiness, and no reading instruction may be given until after the children have been tested. This kind of rigid policy ignores the fact that young, bright children are often farther advanced in readiness than their older classmates, and prevents the teacher from working out the best possible adaptations to individual abilities.

For this testing either a group intelligence test or a group readiness test can be used. Not more than ten or twelve first-grade children should be tested as a group, so arrangements need to be made to take care of part of the class while the rest are being tested. The test should be administered by the teacher or a person known to the children, and the directions in the manual should be followed as exactly as possible. After the test papers have been scored, at least a sampling of them should be rescored by another person, since scoring errors are made with deplorable frequency even by experienced scorers.

Using the test results in combination with the teacher's observations, an estimate of each child's readiness can be made which will prove accurate in most cases. If the test and teacher judgment disagree, further study of the child is needed and further testing may be arranged. Individual testing by a school psychologist is desirable for children whose scores on two or more group tests are very low.

The combination of a group intelligence test with a readiness test lessens the chance of making erroneous judgments about the readiness of individual children. This was shown clearly by a study in which the *Metropolitan Readiness Test* and the *Detroit First Grade Intelligence Test* were given to sixty-six first-grade pupils at the beginning of the year. The results were compared with the success or failure of the children in learning to read. Of the 47 for whom success was predicted on both tests, 43 passed and only 4 failed. Eight of the ten whose scores indicated success according to one test and failure according to the other test also passed. However only two of the nine who scored poorly on both tests managed to pass.[20] If teacher ratings had been combined with the scores of these tests, it is probable that still fewer errors of prediction would have resulted.

For those children who are found to be not yet ready, reading readiness activities and an informal reading program should be carried on until the teacher thinks that perhaps they are now ready. At that point, retesting with an equivalent form of the same test or with a similar test provides evidence which can be helpful in deciding whether to start reading or to continue the readiness program.

III. Development of Reading Readiness

Since reading readiness is not a single trait but a state of all-round development or maturity, it is best developed in a class atmosphere which provides optimum conditions for physical, intellectual, and social development. There should be a rich variety of stimulating and informative experiences which encourage children to look and listen attentively, and to express their thoughts and feelings in many different forms of creative and expressive activity. In order to create such an atmosphere, the teacher must be in harmony with

[20] Fendrick, P., and McGlade, C. A., "A Validation of Two Prognostic Tests of Reading Aptitude," *Elementary School Journal*, Vol. 39, 1938, pp. 187–194.

the modern trend which conceives of the major task of education as fostering child development. Learning to read, or learning any other specific fact or skill, is subordinate to the encouragement of healthy physical, intellectual, and social growth.

In a first-grade class there usually are some children who are ready to read before the year begins, others who are nearly ready and benefit from spending part of the year in readiness activities, and still others who will not become fully ready until a year or two later. A good modern reading program takes account of these differences in ways which will be discussed in the next two chapters. Here we are concerned with the question of what can be done with those children whose readiness is not yet sufficient.

Practically every aspect of a well-rounded kindergarten program has some value in building readiness for reading. In such a program the child engages in both group and individual activities. Eyes and hands are trained through work with blocks, clay, crayons, paint, scissors, weaving, and so on. Language growth is stimulated in many ways, including listening to stories, discussing experiences, conversation, "show and tell," rhymes and poetry, and dramatization. New ideas and concepts are introduced through many kinds of experiences, including trips and visits. Among the very important social learnings are learning to live in a group, to take one's turn, to curb one's temper, to listen attentively, to follow directions. This list could go on almost indefinitely. When first-grade children are not ready for reading, their program should be very much like that of a rich kindergarten program.

Within this framework it is possible to incorporate activities planned to develop specific aspects of readiness in which growth may be needed. Table II takes up the various aspects of reading readiness which were discussed earlier in this chapter, lists for each aspect the kinds of evidence that point to a need for improvement, and provides a few practical suggestions concerning what can be done to foster improvement. More detailed descriptions of readiness activities can be found in the references listed at the end of this chapter.

Table II. Reading Readiness Handicaps and Their Correction

Handicap	*Evidence of Handicap*	*Helpful Procedures*
Low in general intelligence	MA is below 6-0 on a test.	Mental age will increase steadily as child gets older.
	IQ is below 90 on a test.	If child has been handicapped by poor environment, sometimes shows increase in IQ with good schooling
	Seems lacking in curiosity Ideas seem vague and confused. Comprehension is poor. Range of information is poor. Unable to give explanations Language development is retarded	If MA below 5-0 or IQ below 80, may take a year or more to become ready for reading instruction General readiness work with litle emphasis on reading until child reach MA of at least 6-0 is recommended.
Poor memory	Forgets instructions	Give motive for wanting to remember; send on errands with oral messages.
	Unable to recall events of story	Tell a simple story; ask child to retell the story after other children have done the same.
	Memory span below 4 digits or words	Play memory games: One child says something, second tries to repeat it; if correct, he takes lead. Several objects on table. Child who is "it" turns back, tries to tell which one was removed.
	Poor memory for visual details Memory is tested in various ways in the Gates, California, Betts, Monroe, Stevens, Van Wegenen tests.	Have children inspect picture. Remove picture, ask for list of things in the picture.

Inability to follow directions	Needs repetition of directions Becomes confused if given more than one direction at a time Look for evidence of low intelligence language handicap, or poor hearing. Difficulty in following directions on any readiness or intelligence test	Give directions slowly and clearly. Gain the child's attention before starting. Play "following directions" games. At first, give one direction at a time, then two, then three. Allow children to take turns in giving directions for games and other classroom activities. Check for possible hearing difficulty.
Poor attention	Does not listen when directions are given Tires of an activity quickly Is very distractible Seems dreamy, absorbed in own thoughts	Check for possible hearing difficulty. This is normal in young children. Watch for signs of restlessness and change to another activity. For individual activities, give a seat away from other children. Give opportunity to tell his stories and ideas. In general, provide interesting activities. Children are attentive when their interest is aroused.
Poor visual perception	Insensitive to similarities and differences in pictures, words, letters Draws and copies drawings poorly All readiness tests contain subtests to measure visual perception.	Practice in clay modeling, drawing, cutting around outlines Assembling picture puzzles Finding missing parts in pictures Describing pictures in detail Exercises for noting visual similarities and differences, such as those in reading readiness workbooks If very poor, delay reading. Check for possible visual difficulty.

Handicap	*Evidence of Handicap*	*Helpful Procedures*
Poor auditory perception	Seems to have poor hearing but does well on hearing test	Provide a good model of speech
	Speech is indistinct or defective.	Encourage accurate pronunciation. See suggestions under "Defective speech" below.
	Does not recognize rhymes	Much use of rhymes, jingles, poems, and songs
	Is insensitive to similarities and differences in word beginnings or word endings	Call child's attention to the difference between two words which he confuses.
	Cannot recognize (or blend) a word if it is sounded out	Play "word family" games. One child says a word; the next child has to say a word which begins (or ends) the same way.
	Tests of auditory perception are included in the Gates and Monroe tests.	Say a list of words. Have child listen for the one that does not sound like the others. Many teachers do much of their training in auditory or phonic readiness after the children have begun to read.
Poor general health	One or more of these: overweight; underweight; pale, looks anemic; listless; tires easily; frequent colds; mouth breather; poor posture; other signs of poor health	Recommend a thorough medical examination. Take special precautions to avoid strain and fatigue for frail or sickly children. Give rest period. Discuss with mother the child's eating and sleeping habits.
	Report from physician or nurse	Check up to see that defects are corrected.

Physical immaturity	Child is very short for age.	In some cases where evidence of endocrine deficiency is present, medical treatment speeds up growth.
	Child looks much younger than his age.	Child should not be teased or made to feel conspicuous.
		If child is generally immature, retention in kindergarten may be advisable.
Poor vision	Does poorly on vision tests	Refer for eye examination. If glasses are needed, see that they are obtained and used.
	Teacher observes that: eyes tear or become bloodshot; child squints or closes one eye to see better; gets close to board or chart to see; complains of headaches	Place in a favorable seat.
		If difficulty is severe, sight-saving activities and materials may be necessary.
Poor hearing	Does poorly on whisper or watch test	Refer to an ear specialist or hospital clinic.
		Give child a favorable seat.
	Teacher notes that child: has a chronic ear infection seems inattentive misunderstands directions asks to have statements repeated comprehends better in conversion than at usual classroom distances	Speak slowly and distinctly to the child.
		Emphasize visual approach in reading.
		Poor hearing is no reason for delay in starting reading, unless other handicaps are present.

Handicap	*Evidence of Handicap*	*Helpful Procedures*
Poor muscular coordination	Clumsy: poor at walking, running, skipping, hopping, dancing, climbing stairs, throwing, catching Often drops and spills things Poor hand-eye control in using scissors, crayon, pencil	Be patient; clumsiness and slowness are not intentional. In severe forms, lack of coordination may be a sign of a neurological difficulty. Refer for medical examination. Rhythmical games to music: dancing, skipping, etc. Rhythm band Show careful ways of holding objects. Simple types of handwork: cutting, pasting, coloring, clay or plasticine, weaving, construction Use of manipulative toys: peg-boards, form-boards, etc.
Poor cultural background	Parents are uneducated, ignorant. Foreign language is spoken at home. Home is lacking in common cultural assets: telephone, radio, magazines, books, etc.	If possible, encourage taking adult education courses. Provide a good model. Give rich oral language activities (see below). Explain to parents the desirability of child's hearing and speaking English at home. Provide rich, varied experiences (see below).
Meager background of experience	Child's experience is confined to his own neighborhood. Unacquainted with traditional rhymes and stories Range of information very limited	Plan a sequence of visits; the school itself, stores, fire station and other points of interest in the neighborhood, more distant parts of the community, the zoo, a farm, etc. Develop new concepts and vocabulary during the trip and in subsequent discussion. Make use of pictures and lantern slides. Provide rich experiences in the classroom. Encourage children to bring pets and possessions to school, sharing experiences. Have appropriate, simple units of activity. Read stories and poems to children. Children retell and dramatize stories.

Limited vocabulary	Limited comprehension Has difficulty finding words to express his ideas; uses circumlocutions Nearly all readiness and intelligence tests contain vocabulary tests.	Vocabulary develops normally out of rich, varied experiences (see above). Acting games. Teacher says a sentence, children (taking turns) act it out. Different games can be played in which children act out nouns (animals, etc.), verbs (walk, run, hop), adverbs (quickly, quietly), prepositions (under, behind, in). Pictures are used for introducing new concepts. Children list all the words they know of one type (toys, pets, flowers, etc.). Those not generally known are described and illustrated.
Poor use of language	Speaks in one or two words, or in fragmentary sentences	Put child's idea into a complete sentence, have him repeat it. All statements should be in complete sentences.
	Uses immature speech forms ("I runned" etc.) Uses awkward or confused word order	Correct gently grammatical errors, awkward constructions, slang, etc., by stating child's idea in more appropriate language; praise him when he repeats teacher's statement.
	Uses undesirable speech forms which are characteristic of his cultural background	Provide opportunities for natural growth in language ability through free conversation, group discussions, "telephone conversations," "radio broadcasts," composing group stories. telling experiences, dramatization of stories.

Handicap	*Evidence of Handicap*	*Helpful Procedures*
Defective speech	Speaks too fast, runs words together	Speak slowly and distinctly to children. Encourage child to take his time. Promote relaxation.
	Lisping	Is normal in children who have lost front baby teeth
	Baby talk; defective pronunciation of consonant sounds	If marked, requires special training in production of speech sounds. Mild cases usually clear up without special attention.
	Marked hesitation, stammer or stutter	This is a problem for a speech correctionist or psychologist. Classroom teacher should encourage relaxation, rhythmical activity, freedom from strain.
Emotional instability	May be shown in: shyness, timidity, excessive self-consciousness	Do not rush timid child into group activities; give him time to become used to school.
	quick temper, tantrums stubbornness, negativism extreme restlessness	Remove overexcited, rebellious, stubborn, or angry child from group temporarily; provide a quiet individual activity.
	extreme sensitivity; crybaby	Teacher should show warmth, liking for the child, appreciation.
	specific nervous habits	Underlying cause of nervousness needs to be removed.
	poor concentration	Severe cases of emotional instability should be referred to a psychologist or mental hygiene clinic.
Lack of self-reliance	Child makes excessive requests for help.	Encourage child to try to do things. Provide help and support when needed.

	Child gives up quickly when he meets difficulties.	Build self-confidence through experience of success in a graded series of activities, starting with very easy ones.
Poor group participation	Child is bossy; picks fights and quarrels.	Remove from group temporarily. Look for cause in the home situation.
	Submissive, shy, afraid to speak up.	Ask the child easy questions. Praise generously. If too shy to talk in front of group, allow to recite to teacher privately.
Bad family situation	Interview with mother or older children in family. Look for evidence of: Poor discipline—too harsh, too lax, or inconsistent Quarreling and dissention Child is unloved Child is overprotected.	When family situation is very bad, parents should be encouraged to seek help of a social service agency or mental hygiene clinic. Some mothers are receptive to tactfully given suggestions concerning discipline and child management.
Lack of interest in reading	Child seems restless, uninterested, when teacher reads or tells stories.	Language may be too difficult or ideas too strange for child's comprehension. Vary the type and difficulty of stories.
	Child shows no interest in books or in learning to read.	Provide library table with interesting picture and story-books. Read stories from books in class library. Have a bulletin. Post simple notices, etc. Build simple reading stories from children's own experiences. Praise generously the first signs of interest or attempts to read.

Reading Readiness Workbooks

In a readiness program the teacher's task can be lightened somewhat by making use of readiness workbooks. Every modern set of primary readers now has at least one readiness workbook, with an accompanying teacher's manual containing suggested lesson plans. These workbooks provide colorful, interesting pictures which can serve as a basis for description, discussion, storytelling, and learning new concepts and vocabulary. They also contain graded series of exercises for making comparisons, noting similarities and differences, and learning to observe in a left-to-right direction. In addition to the readiness books which are parts of reader series, there are some which are published independently.

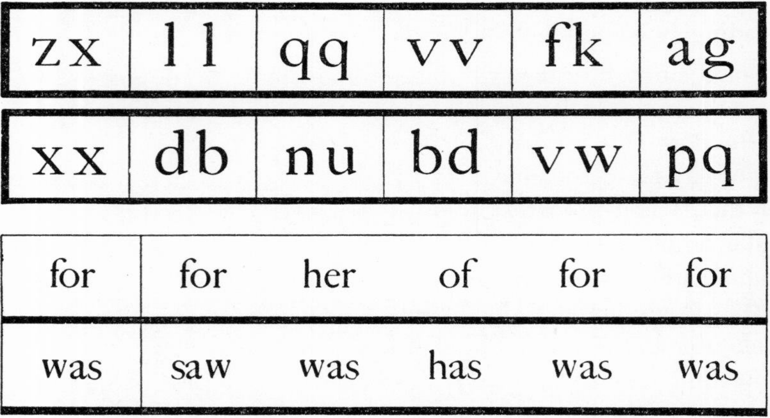

Fig. 3. Exercises to develop visual discrimination for letter and word forms. From: *Getting Ready,* by Paul McKee and M. Lucile Harrison. Boston: Houghton Mifflin Co., 1949. Top two lines are from page 20 and require deciding whether or not the two letters in each box are alike; bottom two lines, from page 60, involve marking each word on the right which is like the one in the box at the left. Reproduced by permission of the publisher and reduced in size.

One of the complaints made about readiness workbooks has been that they are too difficult for some immature children. In consequence, some publishers are now providing workbooks of an even simpler nature which can be used to prepare children for the use of the regular readiness books. How far this trend will go it is hard to tell. One can even envisage a readiness series starting with a rattle.

The fact is that no teaching materials can be expected to produce miracles in slow-maturing children, even though specific, well-planned learning experiences can help somewhat. Furthermore, a readiness program can fulfill only a few of its many aims by relying on a workbook. These materials are useful, but only as a subordinate part of a rich and varied program. Teachers must avoid the temptation to let the workbook carry the full instructional load.

Reading Readiness and Beginning Reading

Some authorities believe that reading should be entirely omitted from the programs of children who are not ready for formal reading instruction. This is taking a too pessimistic attitude about the learning ability of such children. It was pointed out earlier in this chapter that, when properly taught, the majority of five-year-olds can make progress in reading. If it is decided to postpone systematic reading instruction, it is not necessary to eliminate all reading activities. A gradual introduction of reading activities is in many ways preferable to the attempt to eliminate reading entirely.

Reading may be introduced to these children by labeling the objects in the classroom such as the desks, chairs, blackboard, and so on. Each child's name can be printed on cards and the cards used to identify his desk and his locker or clothes hanger. Colorful pictures can be displayed with a brief title below each. A bulletin board can be kept up with weather reports, special events, or messages to children. The children can compose little stories based on their experiences and the teacher can print the stories on the blackboard or on a chart. Gradually the children begin to recognize some common phrases or words. Meanwhile, they do not have the feeling of being excluded from reading.

When systematic instruction is started, a preprimer that presents a small and simple vocabulary with a great deal of repetition should be selected. The words of the preprimer should be introduced gradually in blackboard and chart reading. Seatwork can be utilized which involves matching words with pictures, arranging sentences and words in the correct order, or printed directions for coloring and cutting out pictures. Workbooks which accompany the preprimer can be used, or the teacher can make up similar materials and mimeograph or hectograph them. The rate at which the group advances should be determined by the progress of the group rather than by an arbitrary standard. If the work is taken up gradually enough and each new achievement is noted and praised by the teacher, nearly all of the children will make some progress.

Suggested Additional Reading

Anderson, Irving H., and Walter F. Dearborn. *The Psychology of Teaching Reading*, Ch. 2. New York: Ronald Press, 1952.

Betts, Emmett A. *Foundations of Reading Instruction*, Chs. 8–19.

Bond, Guy L., and Eva Bond Wagner. *Teaching the Child to Read*, Revised Edition, Chs. 5–7.

Harrison, M. Lucille. *Reading Readiness*, Revised Edition. Boston: Houghton Mifflin Co., 1939.

Hildreth, Gertrude. *Readiness for School Beginners*. Yonkers-on-Hudson: World Book Co., 1950.

McKee, Paul. *The Teaching of Reading in the Elementary School*, Ch. 7. Boston: Houghton Mifflin Co., 1948.

Monroe, Marion. *Growing Into Reading*. Chicago: Scott, Foresman & Co., 1951.

Russell, David H. *Children Learn to Read*, Ch. 6.

Tinker, Miles A. *Teaching Elementary Reading*, Chs. 2–4. New York: Appleton-Century-Crofts, 1952.

· III ·

How Children Start to Read

THE OBJECTIVES OF READING INSTRUCTION which were summarized in Chapter I call for a flexible but coordinated and planned reading program designed to develop effective reading skills, to adapt these skills to many functional purposes of learning and study, and to foster reading as a recreational activity. In that chapter, also, five major stages of reading instruction were briefly described. The first of these, the reading readiness stage, has been discussed in Chapter II. The present chapter gives more detailed consideration to the second stage, the stage of getting started in reading. The other stages are described in Chapter IV.

I. Reading in the Total School Setting

THE WAY in which reading is taught in a school is inescapably influenced by the aims, philosophy, and organization of the entire school program. There is no such thing as *the* ideal reading program. A superior reading program which is a harmonious part of the curriculum in one school day may be entirely out of step if transplanted to another school.

Some of the most conspicuous differences come right in the first grade. These may be pointed out by comparing two schools which we may call School A and School B.

In School A it is generally taken for granted by the principal, teachers, parents, and children that the one really important job of the first grade is learning how to read. A set standard must be met for promotion to the second grade and those who cannot read passably in a first reader by the end of the year must repeat the grade. The pace of the program is determined by the goals that must be reached and the first-grade teachers are judged in terms of the number of children who fail of promotion. In consequence, only lip service is paid to the idea of readiness. Reading is started early in the fall; every child must read to the teacher every day; a major part of each day is spent in systematic reading lessons; when children have trouble keeping up they are given extra drill after school and their parents are asked to read with them at home. Because covering a specified amount in a series of basal readers is required, reading is centered around the covering of these books.

In School B, the first grade is considered to be primarily a period during which the child learns gradually to adjust to a new kind of social environment. Reading is thought of as part of the language arts rather than as a separate curricular entity, and opportunities are created for linking it to listening, speaking, and writing. The teachers are expected to provide a program with rich, varied experiences, many forms of creative self-expression, and multiple opportunities for learning social skills. The teacher normally stays with the class through the second grade and so has a two-year period to get to know the children intimately and to get them well started. Children begin to read in small groups as they show readiness and each group progresses at its own rate. No child is required to repeat the first grade, and nonpromotion at the end of the second grade requires agreement between parents and school that it is for the child's benefit. The reading program includes experience stories and many library books as well as basal and supplementary readers.

These two examples, brief as they are, highlight some of the striking differences one finds in the beginnings of reading between the "traditional" schools and the "child-development" centered schools. A successful teacher in School A would probably have some difficulty adapting to the ways of School B, and vice versa.

The fact that the writer is in sympathy with the general point of view of School B is probably quite evident in the above descriptions. Yet this does not blind him to the fact that some schools of the A type do a much better job than some schools of type B. Without skill in execution the best of plans may fail of accomplishment, and it is unfortunately true that some schools that attempt to be flexible and child-centered succeed only in being confused and disorganized.

Teachers who are trying to adapt to newer ways sometimes wonder what happens to reading. This question has been well answered as follows: "As the variety of activities included in the curriculum increases, the greater the need is for reading ability, because children must read in so many different types of situations. On every hand children must read in order to accomplish the ends for which they are striving. The contrast, then, between reading in the modern school and in the early school is that the early school tended to see reading as an end in itself, whereas the modern school sees reading as an essential whereby children may realize their varied purposes. In brief, the modern school is characterized by reading for a purpose." [1]

There has been considerable disagreement among proponents of the newer curriculum concerning the retention of special periods for teaching reading. Some have said that reading ability does not have to be specifically taught, but will develop naturally out of situations which create a need and a desire for reading. "Let children read to learn, incidentally they will learn to read." [2] Schools which follow this line of reasoning sometimes discontinue reading instruction as soon as the pupils are able to do easy independent

[1] Goodykoontz, Bess, "The Place of Reading in the Curriculum," *The Teaching of Reading: A Second Report,* 36th Yearbook of the National Society for the Study of Education, Part I, p. 44. Bloomington, Ill.: Public School Publishing Co., 1937.

[2] Meriam, J. L., "Avoiding Difficulties in Learning to Read," *Educational Method,* Vol. 9, 1930, pp. 413–419.

reading, relying upon abundant, varied reading to produce improvement. In these schools, surveys of reading achievement are made periodically and remedial work is given to those pupils who have fallen behind.

Since reading is a complex skill, a comparison with other complex skills should prove helpful. Provided with appropriate facilities, a child who wants to learn to play tennis, to swim, or to typewrite can learn to do so. Expert instruction is not absolutely necessary for any of these activities. But those who teach themselves usually develop faulty habits of performance that prevent them from ever becoming really expert. No one who has had the chance to compare the self-taught tennis player, swimmer, or typist with those who started from the beginning under competent instruction, can doubt the value of specific training in those skills.

Experimental comparisons of systematic, direct teaching of reading as compared with incidental growth in reading are not entirely conclusive, but seem in general to favor systematic instruction. "Available evidence from both experiments and progressive practice tends to favor specific provision for guidance in reading at times reserved for the purpose." [3]

Developmental reading lessons should have a definite place in the curriculum of the modern school, as well as in schools adhering to a more conservative program. But while some of the more conservative schools still consider learning to read as an end in itself, the modern school clearly recognizes that developmental reading has value in proportion as it prepares the children for more effective recreational and functional reading.

The organization and general plan of an activity- or project-type of elementary school curriculum requires the use of a much larger and more varied collection of reading material than was needed in the conventional school of the past. In addition to basic reading materials, the teacher must be able to provide reading matter covering many different aspects of each activity or project. The children learn at an early age to hunt for appropriate reference material, to assemble and correlate ideas and facts from several dif-

[3] Goodykoontz, Bess, *op. cit.*, p. 52.

ferent sources, to compare one reference with another. They learn to read inquiringly and critically at an age at which most of their present teachers assumed that anything found in a book (unless labeled fiction) had to be true. The teacher in an activity school must learn how to discover and procure adequate reading materials in quantity and variety, and teach his pupils how to make effective use of them.

An activity-centered curriculum makes it somewhat easier to adapt reading instruction to individual differences. It is difficult to teach social studies to a fifth-grade class which varies in reading ability from third to seventh grade, if all of the pupils have to study a rather difficult geography or history book which assumes at least fifth-grade reading ability. If, however, the project for the term is to become acquainted with "Our American Friends" (formerly, the study of the geography and history of Central and South America), the children will get their information from a large number of sources: encyclopedias, formal histories and geographies, books of fiction set in the regions being studied, pamphlets written in simple and entertaining style with the needs of slower and poorer readers in mind, circulars distributed by travel companies, and so on. At the same time, a rich experience background will be developed through nonreading activities, such as listening to South American music, learning South American dances, tasting regional foods, making costumes and staging plays, or seeing lantern slides and moving pictures. In such a setting, the poorer as well as the better readers have an opportunity to learn effectively.

The school's policies on promotion and pupil classification have a great effect upon the reading program. The older type of promotion policy is to require pupils to repeat if they do not achieve the required level of competence for the next grade. Theoretically, one might expect that this would reduce the range of individual differences in reading ability in a grade by eliminating the low end of the distribution. Sometimes it works that way, but Cook [4] has shown

[4] Cook, Walter W., *Grouping and Promotion in the Elementary School,* Series on Individualization of Instruction, No. 2. Minneapolis: University of Minnesota Press, 1941.

that often the range of differences remains practically as great in the schools which retard children, and the average reading achievement is no higher grade by grade. Two reasons for this have been advanced: (1) The child who repeats because of poor reading often does no better the second time; and (2) after repeating the grade once the child is usually promoted regardless of improvement. The elimination of poor reading in the upper grades by a policy of non-promotion is therefore often an illusion which, when used to justify requiring every pupil to read at official grade level, blinds the teacher to the real reading needs of many of the pupils.

On the other hand, the results of a policy of automatic promotion regardless of achievement sometimes are far from ideal. Such a policy can work very well so long as each teacher accepts the necessity of molding the reading program to fit a wide range of reading skill, and is able to carry out a successfully differentiated program. In some schools this is carried out well in the primary grades, but is far less successful above the third grade. Promoting a child with third-grade reading ability into a sixth grade in which no curricular adaptations are made for the poor readers confronts the child with problems which are different from, but no less serious than, those of being left back. Continuous promotion works well only if combined with adaptation to individual needs all the way up the grades.

There are many other phases of the school's total program that influence the reading program — the provisions or lack of special provisions for exceptional children, the funds available for purchase of books and supplies, and so on — but these cannot be considered at this point.

In the rest of this chapter references will be made frequently to reading levels. In stating that a particular kind of activity is appropriate at a second-grade level what is meant is that children are usually ready for this activity when they can appropriately use material of second-grade level; this may occur for some children in the first grade, and for others in the third, fourth, or fifth grade.

II. How Children Start to Read

Discarded Methods

Before considering how reading is introduced to children today it is instructive to take a look at some of the older methods which have passed into disuse. During the past century almost every decade has witnessed the birth of a new method of teaching reading, whose author was sure it would solve all reading problems. For interesting descriptions of many of these obsolete methods one can turn to Huey,[5] whose book is still a mine of useful information, or to Smith's [6] systematic history.

The earliest method was the alphabet-spelling method, in which the letters of the word are named in sequence and then the word is pronounced: e.g., *c-a-t, cat.* In most languages this is an effective procedure because the letter names are essentially the same as their sounds; in English, however, we get something like *seeaytee* from the letter names instead of *cat.* As the inadequacy of this procedure became recognized, phonic and phonetic systems developed which also started with the letters but used their sounds rather than their names, and built words by pronouncing the sounds and then blending them to get the word. The alphabet-spelling and phonic methods are similar in that they go from the parts to the whole, and therefore are sometimes called the *synthetic* methods.

Critics of the synthetic alphabet and phonic methods have emphasized several shortcomings: (1) The English language has so many irregularities and exceptions that an adequate phonic system has to be quite complicated and difficult to learn. (2) The synthetic methods tend to produce slow, labored reading. (3) They encourage attention to the words and do not place enough stress on the thought-getting side of reading.

In contrast to the synthetic methods, which go from the parts to the whole, several "analytical" methods were developed in which

[5] Huey, Edmund B., *The Psychology and Pedagogy of Reading.* New York: The Macmillan Co., 1908.

[6] Smith, Nila B., *American Reading Instruction.* New York: Silver, Burdett, 1934.

the general program was to start with a whole as a unit and then proceed to the study and use of the parts.[7] Three types of analytical methods could be distinguished – the word method, sentence method, and story method. The first of these was the word method. In this the usual procedure was for the teacher to put a word on the board, pronounce it, have several children pronounce it, and then combine it with other words to form various sentences. Flash cards were commonly employed to develop speed and accuracy. Word-picture associations were also employed. The study of word parts followed sight recognition and sometimes was given very little attention. Depending on the association of the name and meaning of the word with its total appearance, this method is often referred to as the "look and say" method.

Proponents of the sentence method argued that the sentence was the real unit of meaning; the child should first be taught a whole sentence at a time, and then the sentence could be divided into words. The same words could be presented in many different sentence arrangements. The need for continuity of meaning from one sentence to the next was ignored in many of these systems.

The story method attempted to put main stress on meaning. The teacher would read a cumulative folk tale (such as *Chicken Little* or *The Gingerbread Boy*) to the children over and over until most of them had memorized it. She would then present the first few sentences in print, read it to them, and have them recite the memorized lines as they looked at the print; in this way recognition of words was developed. This method assumed that the child would look at the words in proper sequence and in time with the story; failure to do this produced many cases of pseudoreading in which the children would know the story perfectly and be able to recite it, without having made any associations to the printed symbols.

Proponents of the synthetic methods stressed the child's need to be able to attack unfamiliar words and be able to work out their pronunciation. Proponents of the analytical methods emphasized

[7] William S. Gray has recently used the term "global method" to describe approaches of the sort called "analytical" here.

the need for meaningful reading and for immediate sight recognition of words and phrases. All of these methods dogmatically tended to assume that there was one correct way of learning that was the same for everyone. They all had some good points and each one succeeded with the majority of children. Current methodology tries to utilize the good features of all these older methods and combine them into a comprehensive, flexible program that is adaptable to individual differences.

Most elementary schools today start children on reading with a basal reader approach, with an experience approach, or with a combination of the two.

The Basal Reader Approach

In most American elementary schools the current practice is to choose a set of basal readers for the primary grades and to follow fairly closely the teaching methods recommended by the authors, as explained in the manuals for teachers which accompany the readers. It is necessary to have a clear idea of what these materials are like in order to develop a real understanding of the methodology. It is strongly recommended, therefore, that each reader of this book choose a series of basal readers popular in his community and take the time to study it, starting with the first-grade materials. Such study should involve using the reader, the manual, the correlated workbook, and sometimes correlated material such as filmstrips and large word or phrase cards. It is desirable to go through the steps of several typical lessons as outlined in the manual, at each of several grade levels. As one becomes familiar with the methodology of one series, it is helpful to make a similar study of other series.

The Materials. A generation ago, a typical series of basal readers had two books for the first grade, the primer (first book) and a first reader. From the second grade on there was one reader for each grade. Manuals for teachers, if provided, were brief. Aside from word or phrase cards for the first grade, there usually were no correlated teaching aids.

Today's series tends to be far more elaborate. It starts with one or more reading readiness books or workbooks. The first book involving actual reading is a thin, paper-covered preprimer, and there are usually three of these. Next comes the first hard-covered book, the primer; there may be two primers, or a regular primer and an optional "junior primer" to follow the preprimers. After the primer comes the first reader (sometimes two of them). At the second- and third-grade levels there are usually two readers for the grade. From the fourth grade on there is usually one reader for the grade, but these are thick books with many pages. A series usually stops at sixth- or eighth-grade level.

Many accessory materials are provided. These include large word and phrase cards (mainly for first grade), a workbook to go with each reader in the series, and manuals. Some series provide a giant reproduction of the first preprimer for group reading, and correlated sets of filmstrips are rapidly being developed. Additional supplementary material with vocabulary related to that of the basal readers may include supplementary readers, single paper-bound stories, and correlated series of textbooks on health, social studies, science, or arithmetic.

Almost without exception, today's readers deserve excellent ratings for their paper, print, and colorful illustrations. Great care is taken to introduce new words slowly and to provide abundant repetition. This has brought about a corresponding reduction of the total number of words introduced, so that some series have a total primary vocabulary of only about 1100 words, while others use as many as 2000 in their primary readers. Analysis of seven currently popular series shows the following approximate averages: preprimers, 60 words; primers, 115 new words; first readers, 170 new words; second readers, 430 new words; third readers, 790 new words; total for three grades, 1575 words. From fourth-grade on vocabulary is not so carefully controlled and there is great variation in practices. The trend toward smaller vocabularies has probably already gone too far, since a sight vocabulary of about 3000 words is desirable for effective reading in fourth-grade materials and the typical primary series of today teaches only half that number.

The content of the books used in the first grade is in most series based on the idea of keeping to familiar experience, so as to complicate the task of learning the beginnings of reading as little as possible with unfamiliar settings and ideas. Commonly the preprimers, primer, and first reader center around a single family. The cast of characters usually consists of a boy and a girl (Dick and Jane, Alice and Jerry), father, mother, a younger child, a dog, and a cat. Other characters, such as grandmother, child friends, the postman, a storekeeper and so on, are variable. Nearly always the family seems to be middle class in status, lives in an attractive one-family house, is well dressed, and has a new-looking car. It has been pointed out by many people that this idealized family does not come very close to the lives of the millions of children who live in slums, in apartment houses, or on farms. However, as compared to the fairy stories and folk tales of a past generation of readers, the current first-grade materials do seem to come closer to many first-grade children's experiences.

Preprimers are paper-bound booklets of thirty to fifty pages which tell their stories mainly through pictures, with a small amount of reading matter in the form of conversation. In spite of the restrictions of a very limited vocabulary which is introduced gradually, well-written preprimers succeed in telling stories which have plot and suspense. The language, however, tends to be artificial, stilted, and repetitious because of the vocabulary limitations. The primer continues with the same cast, achieving somewhat more natural language structure and telling more of the story in print as the vocabulary expands. With the addition of new people the cast continues usually through the first reader, in which the vocabulary taught in preprimers and primers is repeated and new words are added in a carefully controlled fashion.

The manuals for teachers are actually textbooks on how to teach reading with the particular reader. Typically, the manual has more pages than the reader it accompanies. The manuals present first a general plan, and then give detailed lesson plans story by story, sometimes page by page, or even, at preprimer level, line by line. One set of manuals presents three different sets of plans for fast, average, and slow groups.

All series now provide workbooks correlated with the basal

readers. Most are organized so that doing one or more pages of the workbook is an optional supplementary activity following the reading of the corresponding pages in the reader. The alternative plan, of using the workbook in advance of the reader as a preparatory experience, has failed to achieve wide popularity but is used in two currently popular series. Workbooks vary greatly in the suitability of their practice material and adaptability for independent use by the child. Some provide a basis for rich and varied learning experiences while others call for relatively useless busy work.

Methodology. Although no two series agree perfectly on the details of method, the similarities far outweigh the differences and there is a large amount of agreement concerning the basic structure of good reading lessons. In general five main steps are discernible in typical basal reader lessons. These are: (1) preparations; (2) guided reading; (3) rereading for specific purposes; (4) related activities; and (5) enrichment activities.

Preparation involves developing readiness for the specific reading to be done. It usually includes three different phases. The first is motivation and arousal of interest. The second is the introduction and explanation of new concepts, ideas, and meanings. Third, and closely related to the second, is the oral and visual presentation of new words to be met in the selection.

The first reading of the selection is usually stimulated by questions which give the children purposes for reading. The amount read before the teacher provides more guidance varies from one line at a time in early preprimer lessons to an entire story or selection in upper grades. This first reading is usually done silently, and is followed by discussion or the answering of questions, either orally or in writing.

Rereading usually follows, and is generally done orally. Care is taken to provide purposes for rereading and to vary these purposes. Sometimes rereading may be silent. The amount of rereading suggested varies quite a bit from one series to another.

Related activities most commonly include reviews of words previously studied, teaching word analysis and phonics, and doing related workbook exercises.

Enrichment activities may include drawing or painting something in the story, dramatization of the story, listening to the teacher read related stories or poems, listening to records, or individual supplementary reading.

A representative lesson for the early stages of preprimer reading is shown in the following excerpt: [8]

PREPARING FOR READING

Establishing background. Scrambling up and down steps, over fences, and up trees seems a never-ending source of fun to youngsters. After a preliminary conversation about climbing, encourage girls and boys to tell about special climbing games they play. "Do your little brothers and sisters like to climb up, down, and over things too? Do they like to play on the stairs inside or outside the house? Tell us about some of the climbing games they play."

Presenting vocabulary. (NOTE: The new words are *go, down.*) "Sally likes to play on the stairway. Sometimes she pretends that Tim can walk up and down the stairs just as she can. She holds him by the paw and makes him look as if he were really walking up and down the stairs When she wants Tim to go upstairs, Sally says *Go up.*" Present this line and have it read silently and orally: place *Tim* after *up* and have this sentence read. Changes the line to *Go up, up, up,* and have it read silently and orally. Clear the chart.

"What do you think Sally says to Tim when she wants him to go down the stairs?" Elicit *Go down* and present the sentence. Add *Tim* and have the new sentence read. Clear the chart and present these lines one at a time for silent and oral reading: *Go, go, go. Go down, down, down.*

Checking the presentation: Place the line *Go up* in the chart and ask, "Does Sally want Tim to go up or down the stairs when she says this? Find the word that tells where Tim is to go." Add the word *Tim* and have that sentence read. "Find the word that tells us to whom Sally is speaking." Change the sentence to *Go up, up, up* and have it read. Ask someone to point to all the words in the line that say the same thing. In a similar manner, check comprehension of *Go down. Go down, Tim. Go down, down, down. Go, go, go.*

[8] Gray, W. S., Monroe, M., Artley, A. S., and Arbuthnot, M. H., GUIDEBOOK to Accompany THE THREE PRE-PRIMERS, pp. 102–104. Copyright © 1956 by Scott, Foresman and Company.

INTERPRETING THE STORY

Guided reading: "Here's another story about Tim. The last time we saw the toy bear, he gave Dick a surprise shower. Maybe something unexpected happens in this story, too."

Page 31: Obviously the toy and the pet are the center of attraction. Children's comments about picture details may include reactions to these remarks: "Who do you suppose left Tim at the foot of the stairs? Do you think Sally should have left Tim there? Why not? What is Spot doing? Can you guess what our story is going to be about? Read the name of the story to find out (Tim and Spot)."

Page 32: During the picture interpretation, point out that Sally has now come back to play with Tim. "What do you think Sally is pretending?" Add to the discussion by encouraging the use of such words as *stairway, stairs,* and *banister.* "Sally often talks to Tim as she plays. Do you think she is talking to Tim in this picture? What do you suppose Sally is saying to Tim as she helps him 'walk' up the stairs? Read the first line to yourselves. What is she telling Tim to do?" Have the line read and go on with the silent reading of the second line. Continue guiding the silent and oral reading of the remaining two lines. Finally, have the page read aloud as a unit.

Return to the picture with: "Do you think Tim can do what Sally wants him to? How is he 'going up' the stairs? Is Spot paying any attention to Sally and Tim? What do you think Sally will do when she and Tim are at the top of the stairs?"

Following similar suggestions for pages 33 and 34, it is suggested that in rereading the selection one child should give the picture action while another child reads the verbal text. In the manual, the next section is "Extending Skills and Abilities" with directions for "contrasting word meanings," "making judgments," "scrutiny of word forms," "meeting individual needs," and use of the workbook. The final section is called "Extending Interests" with suggestions for "sharing experiences," "enjoying literature," and "art activities."

As the children progress in the first-grade material the general pattern continues to be preparation, guided silent reading, oral rereading, related word study and workbook activities, and enrichment activities. Motivating and guiding questions may center on a single line or may introduce the reading of a whole page. The change from line by line guidance proceeds gradually through the higher preprimers, primer, and first reader.

For the inexperienced teacher, the detailed directions in the manual are usually of great value and should be followed quite closely. With increasing experience the teacher will discover many ways of improving on the manual's plans. A fast-learning group may need very little of the careful preparation and extensive supplementation and review provided; a slow group may require a much slower pace. If the teacher is to follow all of the suggestions in some manuals, so much time will be spent on preparation, discussion, rereading, and follow-up that the amount of forward progress in the reader will be disappointingly small. In some manuals a sound plan is used over and over with unrelieved monotony. Teachers should, therefore, regard the manuals as resources from which ideas may be selected rather than as bibles to be followed with literal exactness.

A question often asked is whether it is better to follow a series of basal readers straight along, or to read supplementary books on the same level before moving on to the next level. The vocabulary continuity is usually better between adjacent books of the same series than between books of the same level in different series. However, some books of the same level have a great deal of vocabulary in common and make excellent supplements for each other, while others have relatively small overlapping of vocabulary and therefore present many difficulties as supplementary books for each other. In general it is probably best to follow a series in sequence through the first-grade materials. Preprimers and easy primers of other series can be used as supplementary reading by a child who is well along in a primer, and primers and easy first readers of other series can be used as supplementary reading by the child who is progressing in a first reader. In individualized first-grade programs (see p. 116) it is usually desirable for a child to read several books at one level before progressing to the next level.

The Experience Method

Many teachers and supervisors who have been trying to develop their programs around the needs and interests of children believe that the child's earliest reading activities should grow out of his own experiences. Instead of reading about children who may be quite different from him, living in an unfamiliar type of environment, and doing things that he has never done, they believe that his early reading should be about himself and his classmates, telling about his own experiences in his own language. In this way, they say, the reading matter is sure to be phrased in language that is natural to him and to be vitally interesting because he has helped to write it.[9]

During the readiness period some incidental reading activities may be started through labeling objects around the room and identifying coat hooks and desks with their users' names. After the children complete an interesting experience, the teacher may suggest that they make up a story about it. Through group discussion a series of sentences is worked out which the group regards as its own account. This is an experience story. Almost any interesting event can be made the basis of a little story: a birthday, a holiday, the sprouting of some seeds, plans for a trip, what was done on the trip, what was learned on the trip. The teacher helps the group to select a title, and to decide upon the exact wording of the story.

As Betts [10] has pointed out, not all experience stories are useful as material for teaching reading. Many experience records are fine for summarizing an event or experience and for language development, but require too varied a vocabulary and sentences that are too complicated to serve well as beginning reading material.

When a story is to be made the basis of definite reading practice the teacher develops the story on the board and later prepares two copies, one on newsprint or other chart paper and one on a fairly stiff paper such as oak tag, which can be cut into line strips, phrases, and separate words.[11] In preliminary reading the teacher reads the story to the group as a whole and line by line, using a pointer to show the left-to-right direction and to indicate where she is. Then

[9] Zirbes, Laura, "The Experience Approach in Reading," *The Reading Teacher,* Vol. 5, November, 1951, pp. 1–2, 15–16.

[10] Betts, Emmett A., *Foundations of Reading Instruction,* p. 394. New York: American Book, 1946.

[11] The description of the experience method given here is based on the explanation of the method given in: Lamoreaux, Lillian A., and Lee, Dorris M., *Learning to Read Through Experience.* New York: D. Appleton-Century Co., 1943.

children who volunteer are called on. Leading questions may be asked, such as: "Who can read the sentence that tells what kind of a pet we have?" Sentences, phrases, and single words can be "framed" with the hands. Commonly the procedure is from whole story to single sentences to phrases to single words. The second copy is cut into lines, which can be arranged in proper order in a chart holder with pockets, and can be cut into phrase cards and word cards for further practice. This procedure is continued with different charts until the children are judged to have built up sufficient reading vocabulary to be able to start reading preprimers with little or no difficulty. The use of experience charts can be continued as a form of supplementary reading throughout the primary grades.

The use of experience charts as a basis for beginning reading has been severely criticized by Stone, who has attacked it on the following grounds: (1) the method encourages memory reading; (2) too many words are introduced, many of which will not appear in the readers of the first and second grades; (3) there is not enough repetition of the words that are introduced; (4) the content is often too difficult; and (5) the method is not adaptable to individual differences.[12]

There seems to be real justification for the complaints concerning too many different words, insufficient repetition, and lack of correlation with the vocabulary of the books to be used. In one study, the words employed in the diary of stories about daily experiences, used by a first-grade class as reading material, were tabulated and studied. The number of words was far greater and the amount of repetition was far less than in any recent set of first-grade readers.[13] At the close of an extended description of the use of the experience method in a first-grade class, Lamoreaux and Lee present a tabulation of all the words used in the twenty-six charts that had been studied, and in each of the six preprimers that were

[12] Stone, Clarence R., *Progress in Primary Reading,* Ch. I. St. Louis: Webster, 1950; also, "The Current-Experience Method in Beginning Reading," *Elementary School Journal,* Vol. 36, 1935, pp. 105–109.

[13] Sister Richardine and Wilson, Frank T., "A Reading Activity in Grade One," *Elementary English Review,* Vol. 15, 1938, pp. 170–178.

considered for selection as the first book for the class.[14] Some counting (by the present writer) discloses that a total of 180 words were introduced in the 26 charts, an average of seven new words per chart. The average number of new words introduced in modern preprimers, in contrast, is less than one per page. Of these 180 words, 101 occurred in none of the preprimers, 19 were found in only one preprimer, and only 60 were common to the charts and two or more of the preprimers. On the other hand, the charts did contain the majority of the words in each of the preprimers. Since this illustration is presumably a superior example of the use of the experience method, it is probable that in the hands of many teachers even less vocabulary control would be evident.

The need for careful control of vocabulary is minimized by some advocates of the experience method. "In real life situations, where interests are natural and motivate learning, the need for repetition is largely supplanted by intensity of experience, and by the much more extensive associations and integrations resulting from deeply satisfying experience." [15] While this statement cannot be entirely dismissed as wishful thinking, its acceptance can easily be carried too far. Teachers using experience charts should try to keep the vocabulary load down and to introduce and repeat many times those words which are known to be important in preprimer reading.

Whether "memory reading" will be encouraged or not depends upon the skill of the teacher in getting the children to notice and learn to identify progressively smaller units in the story: the line, the phrase, the word. If practice in word recognition is provided, "memory reading" can be avoided. As to individual differences, various amounts of repetition and review can be provided according to the needs of the children.

The experience method fits into the modern primary-grade program in a natural way. It provides a kind of prebook reading experience that can be continued along with reading readiness activities of various kinds until the children seem clearly ready to start book reading. It has an important place in modern practice, although, as

[14] Lamoreaux, Lillian A., and Lee, Dorris M., *op. cit.*, pp. 156–168.
[15] Sister Richardine and Wilson, F. T., *loc. cit.*

pointed out already, it can easily be misused. In most schools it will probably continue as an introduction to preprimer reading and as a form of supplementary reading rather than as a substitute for preprimers and primers.

Some Dissenting Opinions

In the early 1940's considerable attention was given to the Non-Oral Method. McDade, its originator, was impressed by the fact that the persistence of lip movements and subvocal speech seemed a major factor in the slow reading of many adults. He reasoned that if children could learn to read without ever involving speech associations, reading could be made more efficient. His method attempted to develop a direct meaningful response to the printed symbol without accompanying speech. The two cardinal rules were: "(1) The positive rule is: There must *always* be an association of the printed word with its meaning. . . . (2) There must *never* be an association of the printed word with the oral word." [16] Pantomime and pictures were used to teach meanings. Many kinds of individualized seatwork were developed to provide for word study and silent meaningful reading. Books were read silently and discussed orally.

A large-scale experimental comparison of the Non-Oral with a conventional method was carried out by Buswell.[17] Children taught by these methods in the first and second grades were tested at the end of the third and sixth grades. No statistically significant advantage for either method was found. A crucial finding was that almost as many of the Non-Oral group showed observable lip movements in the sixth grade as of the "oral" group, indicating that speech associations had developed with both methods.

The trouble with the Non-Oral Method is that it ignores the psychological processes of normal child development. Oral communication precedes written communication and provides the foundation on which reading and writing are erected. To the beginner,

[16] McDade, James F., *Essentials of Non-Oral Reading*, 30 pp. Chicago: The Plymouth Press, 1941.

[17] Buswell, Guy T., *Non-Oral Reading: a Study of Its Use in the Chicago Schools*, Supplementary Educational Monographs, No. 60. Chicago: University of Chicago Press, September, 1945.

the process of reading is one of realizing that print represents meaningful speech and then learning to associate the printed symbols with the meaningful speech units they represent. Children, if told that they must not say words out loud while reading, will naturally say the words under their breath. To understand, the beginner must get the cues of inflection and emphasis as well as the pronunciation of the words. This writer agrees with McKee when he says ". . . there is good reason to believe, therefore, that in order to understand the meaning of a given sentence, the young child must reconstruct in his mind the intonations that he would hear if someone spoke or read the sentence to him meaningfully or if he himself spoke the sentence." [18] In trying to eliminate these cues to meaning, the Non-Oral Method tries to eliminate the natural advantages that the normal child has over the deaf and dumb. The Non-Oral Method probably achieved its results because of enthusiastic teaching and clever individualized practice materials rather than because of any merit of the nonoral idea. Lip movements and subvocal reading can be overcome in other ways (see Chapter XVIII).

In Chapter II it was pointed out that most experts favor the postponement of systematic reading instruction until the child shows signs of real readiness, meanwhile working to develop those aspects in which the child is insufficiently ready. There is a minority view that favors incorporating readiness in actual reading lessons, starting all children on reading from the beginning of the first grade. Dice,[19] who compared a "direct" approach with a "preparatory" approach, found that the "direct" approach seemed to give slightly better results with the slower pupils, while the average and above-average pupils learned about equally well with both methods. However, her experiment is inconclusive because there were differences in methodology as well as in time of starting, and there was no follow-up beyond the first grade.

[18] McKee, Paul, *et al., Teachers' Manual for* WITH JACK AND JANET, p. 6. Boston: Houghton Mifflin, 1949.

[19] Dice, Leah K., *An Experimental Study of Two Methods of Teaching Beginning Reading: The Direct versus the Preparatory Approach.* Baltimore: Johns Hopkins Press, 1942.

Deserving of very serious consideration is the project carried on in New Castle, Pennsylvania,[20] using filmstrips intensively as an important part of the first-grade reading program. All first graders were started together and apparently there was neither teaching by small groups nor individualized instruction. At the end of the year all of the children had learned to read, including those whose IQ's suggested a lack of readiness. Follow-up of the children through the third grade indicated that the early rapid progress was not being maintained, individual differences in achievement were increasing, and a close approximation of average achievement to capacity was taking place. Nevertheless, this is a project that deserves to be repeated with carefully controlled conditions elsewhere. If the New Castle results are verified, a thorough modification of our present first-grade programs may be required.

A major issue on which current practice is being challenged is the ever-controversial issue of phonics. The basal reader systems of the 1950's provide for more systematic instruction in word analysis techniques, including phonics, than did the systems of the 1930's and 1940's. But this does not satisfy some, who want intensive phonics instruction to be a very important part of first-grade reading. Several new "phonic systems" have been developed. These are generally planned to be used in parallel with basal readers, not to supplant them. As yet no convincing experimental evidence has been produced to show that these intensive phonic systems produce lasting benefits.

Every popular set of readers in use in America today uses a primarily analytical or global approach in the teaching of word recognition, supplemented by instruction in word analysis techniques after the sight vocabulary has been started. This seems to be a psychologically sound and experimentally justified procedure. The phonics question is discussed in detail in Chapter XIII.

[20] McCracken, Glenn, "We Must Modernize Reading Instruction," *The Reading Teacher,* Vol. 8, December, 1954, pp. 100–106; "Have We Overemphasized the Readiness Factor?" *Elementary English,* Vol. 29, 1952, pp. 271–276; "The New Castle Reading Experiment: a Terminal Report," *Elementary English,* Vol. 30, 1953, pp. 13–21.

This chapter has surveyed the crucial question of how to get children off to a good start in reading. After a brief consideration of the shortcomings of both the synthetic alphabet and phonic methods and the word method, the type of methodology followed in modern basal readers was described. Some minority opinions have been included, for in some of them may lie the promise of better methods for the future.

Suggested Additional Reading

See references at the end of Chapter IV.

· IV ·

Continuing Growth in Reading

THIS IS THE THIRD of three chapters which provide an overview of the total program of reading instruction. Reading readiness was the topic of Chapter II, and beginning reading was taken up in Chapter III. In the present chapter the later stages in reading instruction are described, and some special problems in the teaching of reading are considered.

I. Later Stages in Reading Instruction

STAGE 1, readiness for reading, and Stage 2, the initial stage in learning to read, have already been discussed in some detail. The other three stages in reading instruction will now be described. It must be kept in mind that these stages are not sharply separate but merge one into another, and that the range of individual differences at each grade level is such that the teacher is likely to have children whose reading ability spans two of these stages, and sometimes three, or more.

Stage 3. Rapid Development of Reading Skills

The reading program of the second and third grades is of crucial importance, since in these grades the foundation for later reading should become firmly established and rapid progress is normally achieved in all important phases of reading. By the end of this period the child should be able to recognize at sight a large number of words, should be able to work out successfully the pronunciation of many unfamiliar words, should read orally with fluency and expression, should read silently with good comprehension and at a rate faster than oral reading, should be able to do factual reading at a simple level in textbooks and references, and should be well started on reading for pleasure.

In this stage developmental reading lessons still form the major part of the reading program, although functional reading and recreational reading gradually increase in importance. For developmental reading the class is usually divided into groups reading at different levels of difficulty. Problems of group instruction are considered in detail in Chapter VI. Reading instruction tends to occupy a larger part of the school day than any other part of the curriculum, averaging around ninety minutes a day.

Basal readers for these grades generally are collections of short stories, arranged in groups with similar themes. Some readers put major emphasis on enjoyable fiction while others stress the social studies value of their content. One finds stories about the farm and city, about trips to various places by airplane, train, and boat, animal stories of both the "talking animal" and realistic types, folk tales and fairy tales. At third grade there tends to be a shift toward stories about children in foreign lands. Vocabulary, as in first-grade books, is carefully controlled. Illustrations are colorful and plentiful, but no longer tell a major part of the story. Correlated workbooks are supplied and can be quite helpful in providing useful supplementary silent reading activities. Supplementary readers, phonics workbooks, a class library for individualized reading, textbooks in other curriculum areas, and informational books related to units or special projects are desirable in addition to the basal readers.

The general structure of lesson planning remains basically the same as at first-grade level: preparation, silent reading, oral rereading, related activities, and enrichment activities. In preparatory work, teaching the meanings of unfamiliar ideas increases in importance, although providing motivation and presenting new sight words continue to be essential. Silent reading is usually a few pages at a time, followed by answering questions (these may be provided in the workbook), oral discussion, and oral rereading. Systematic teaching of word analysis techniques is a very important related activity, since most basal reader systems place the major part of instruction in word attack skills in the second and third grades. Enrichment activities are expanded in scope by the growing ability of the children to read independently.

Functional reading increases in importance in these grades. In some schools this mainly takes the form of the reading of textbooks in spelling, arithmetic, and other subjects. In other schools it consists mainly of reading in varied sources to obtain the information needed in the carrying on of units or projects. Weekly newspapers provide a basis for current events and other phases of the social studies in many schools.

As children become better able to read, the range of possible recreational material increases markedly. At first-grade level the classroom library consists mainly of picture books, supplementary preprimers and primers, and books for the teacher to read to the class. At second-grade level many children can read simple story books for pleasure, and at third-grade level there is a wide range of books and stories suitable for individual reading.

Stage 4. Stage of Wide Reading

The reading program at fourth-, fifth-, and sixth-grade levels is characterized mainly by a broadening scope of reading, with diminishing emphasis on developmental reading and growth in importance of both functional reading and recreational reading.

Developmental reading activities are concerned mainly with the further refinement and improvement of skills already well started. Time devoted to developmental reading lessons decreases to about five hours a week in fourth grade, four hours in fifth grade, and three hours in sixth grade. While the basic outline of a complete reading activity persists as a desirable general plan, considerable flexibility is desirable. Preparation and oral reading usually take proportionally less time than in the primary grades. Word study is concerned more with meanings than with pronunciation. Word analysis skills involve review of the primary-grade word attack program, the teaching of syllabication, and systematic teaching of the use of the dictionary for both pronunciation and meanings. Silent reading is done in larger units, often a complete story or selection, and comprehension questions may be given either before or after the first reading. Comprehension may be checked by written answers to questions as well as in oral discussion, and an attempt is made to develop skill in answering different kinds of questions and in reading for different purposes. Rate of reading deserves some attention and some practice to speed up silent reading may be appropriate.

In these grades the basal reader is again the primary focus of developmental reading, after a decade or so during which many schools considered basal readers to be unnecessary above third-grade level. The readers are typically collections of stories which have been shortened and adapted from the originals or written expressly for the reader. Most of the stories are fiction but some factual material may be included. A representative fifth reader presents stories in the following general categories: animal stories, stories about young Americans, inventions, funny stories, children in other countries, old tales, sea stories, and stories about hunting for gold. Workbooks to accompany the readers are available and are useful in the management of group reading. Manuals are somewhat less detailed than those for the primary grades.

Functional reading of many kinds occupies much of the time devoted to other curricular areas, since children in these grades get much of their information and instruction through reading. Materials for functional reading include textbooks in various subjects, pamphlets, informational books, magazines, newspapers, encyclopedias, and so on. Frequently it is found that a textbook in a content field requires more advanced reading skill than many of the pupils possess, requiring use of the textbook in ways different from those intended by its author. Most children in these grades need guidance in learning how to adapt their general reading skills to the specific requirements of these special kinds of reading matter. This guidance may be incorporated in the content work such as social studies or science, using the regular text material. Techniques of locating information, and of summarizing and organizing it in various ways should also be taught in these grades.

As children become more competent in reading, their capacity for independent reading grows. Much can be done in these grades to strengthen children's interest in reading for pleasure. A rich variety of good books should be made available and time for pleasure reading should be provided in school, in addition to stimulating the use of leisure hours at home for reading. Through this independent, individualized reading a major part of the child's reading improvement and general educational growth can take place.

Stage 5. Refinement of Reading

As a student progresses through junior high school, senior high school, and college, the reading he is expected to do increases both in amount and in difficulty. There is definite need for continued guidance in reading, although this need is not recognized in many schools. The adaptation of reading to the study requirements of different kinds of courses is achieved by many students without special help, but others, including many bright students, need assistance in learning how to study effectively.

Since at these levels reading is usually no longer a separate subject in the curriculum, definite planning for the provision of reading guidance is needed; otherwise it is everyone's responsibility in general and no one's responsibility in particular. At junior high school level, developmental reading and recreational reading are usually the responsibility of the English teacher, or core teacher. Increasingly it is recognized that guidance in functional reading is the responsibility of every subject-matter teacher, since efficient learning requires different reading patterns in science, mathematics, history, and other subjects. Developmental reading may center around the use of basal readers, of which there are several appropriate for junior high school use. The poorer readers at junior high school level are still reading at various elementary school grade levels and therefore the junior high school teacher of reading needs to understand the reading methodology of the first six grades, and should be prepared to analyze the reading problems of the pupils and provide special help when needed. Recreational reading usually is a combination of the rather intensive reading and discussion of selected "classics," and individualized outside reading on which book reports are required.

At the high school and college level, conscious attention to reading mainly takes the form of special provisions for poor readers. Remedial reading classes and groups may be organized in a variety of ways. The study of literature to a large extent replaces the earlier emphasis on wide independent reading for pleasure. The tendency for recreational reading to reach a peak in junior high school and then decline in amount is due in part to the pressure of increased homework and in part to greater absorption in social activities, but remains a real problem for curriculum planners.

II. Some Special Problems

IN DISCUSSING stages in reading instruction, it is possible to develop the misconception that these stages are discreet and quite distinct from one another, like the steps in a staircase. On the contrary, development of reading skill is continuous from week to week, month to month, and year to year, and the stages have no sharp dividing points. Certain problems and issues are present at all levels and stages. A few of these will now be discussed.

Word Analysis and Phonics

While phonic methods are no longer recommended for use as systematic procedures for starting children on reading, it is desirable that children should learn how to figure out unknown words without help from the teacher. The greater the emphasis that is placed upon wide independent reading, the more necessary it is for children to be able to attack new words when they meet them. Formerly, reliance was placed exclusively on the teaching of phonic sounding and blending as the major aid in unlocking new words.

Today it is recognized that there are many ways of attacking words, and that a good reader is not dependent upon any one of these procedures, but has several techniques and makes use of the one that best fits the situation. The term "word analysis" is used to include all methods by which a word can be analyzed and its pronunciation worked out.

Modern teaching of word analysis makes use of four main approaches, which are used in conjunction in solving an unknown word, not as alternatives. First, children are helped to make intelligent use of the context or meaningful setting in which the new word appears. Second, children are taught to apply structural analysis techniques of several kinds – recognition of root words and endings (play-ing), prefixes, roots and suffixes, separation of a word into known parts, and syllabication. Third, phonics is definitely taught, since knowledge of the sound equivalents of letters and letter combinations is essential. And last, the use of the dictionary is taught as a dependable aid in determining the pronunciation, meaning, and correct spelling of words.

Despite some recent efforts to turn the clock back and persuade us to return to a slow, plodding, meaningless, uninteresting, and difficult type of phonics instruction,[1] there is almost unanimous agreement among those regarded as authorities on the teaching of reading that for most children it is easier to proceed from the whole to the part, to start with whole words and to be introduced to structural and phonic learnings later, and to develop understandings from comparison and analysis of meaningful material rather than from rote learning of meaningless sound combinations. Words are to be analyzed when they cannot be recognized as wholes, and the analysis need be carried only so far as necessary to solve the word. Thus, it would be foolish to attack the word "schoolmaster" one phonic element at a time if a child already has "school" and "master" in his sight vocabulary. Structural and phonic clues should be used in combination with the context, and therefore instruction

[1] Flesch, Rudolph, *Why Johnny Can't Read.* New York: Harper & Brothers, 1955.

should not be concerned primarily with words in lists, but rather should emphasize meaningful material.[2]

The teaching of independence in word recognition is dealt with in greater detail in Chapters XII and XIII.

Oral Reading

Many years ago instruction in reading was predominately oral. When research began to show that children taught in this way tended to be slow, laborious readers, silent reading became the vogue. In many schools the pendulum swung so far that oral reading was almost completely neglected above the first-grade level. This tendency in turn had its bad effects, among which were inaccurate word recognition, poor spelling, and lack of opportunity to give desirable training in speech and diction.

The traditional oral reading lesson was one in which all the pupils had the book open at the same place and were expected to follow along as each one arose in turn, stumbled or mumbled through two or three sentences, and sat down as quickly as possible. Such a procedure has only a limited utility, as a rapid method of testing. Each oral reading lesson should have a specific goal and should be planned to contribute a definite value to the reading program as a whole.

It is now recognized that oral reading contributes to the total development of the child in many ways. Among them, the following are noteworthy: (1) oral reading gives the teacher a quick and valid way to evaluate progress in important reading skills, particularly those of word recognition and phrasing, and to discover specific instructional needs; (2) oral reading provides practice in oral communication for the reader, and in listening skills for the audience; (3) oral reading aids in the development of effective speech patterns; (4) oral reading provides a vehicle for dramatization and effective portrayal of stories in situations where memorization would not be practical; and (5) oral reading provides a medium in which

[2] Witty, Paul A., "Phonics Study and Word Analysis," *Elementary English*, Vol. 30, 1953, pp. 296–305, 373–379, 383; Witty, Paul A., and Sizemore, Robert, "Phonics in the Reading Program: a Review and an Evaluation," *Elementary English*, Vol. 32, 1955, pp. 355–371.

the teacher, by wise guidance, can work to improve the social adjustment of children, particularly those who are shy and retiring.[3]

Some reading authorities have stated that oral reading should always follow a silent reading of the selection. Like other dogmatic assertions, this is one which teachers should feel free to challenge. Although in the usual pattern of developmental reading lessons it is desirable for silent reading to precede oral reading, there are some situations in which oral reading at sight is preferable. One of these is for diagnosis, when the teacher wants to get a clear picture of the child's word-recognition skills; preliminary silent reading would eliminate many of the mispronunciations and hesitations. In remedial or corrective reading, difficulties in word recognition can be corrected more quickly when the first reading is oral, since an error made in silent reading goes unnoticed by the teacher until later. In group reading, children may enjoy from time to time getting away from the usual pattern and reading the story aloud at sight; this is particularly true of the better readers. What may be undesirable as routine procedure has real value as an occasional variation.

A partial list of types of oral reading lessons that seem to have real worth follows.

1. *Taking Turns in a Small Group.* The bad effects of taking turns, as described above, are minimized if the child is a member of a small group who are similar in reading ability. Expecting a turn soon, each child is more likely to pay attention. He has a turn oftener and gets more practice in oral reading than in a whole-class lesson. Self-consciousness on the part of the poorer readers is less likely because the rest of the group are not markedly better than he is. This type of oral reading activity is especially important with retarded readers.

2. *Individual Reading to the Teacher.* Oral reading gives the teacher an opportunity to observe and note pupils' errors and reading habits that need correction. Having the child read a fairly long, representative selection out loud is an important phase of checking up on the pupil's reading abilities. This can be done as a class or

[3] Robinson, Helen M., ed., *Oral Aspects of Reading*, Supplementary Education Monographs No. 82. Chicago: University of Chicago Press, 1955.

group exercise in which each pupil takes his turn. It is more effective, however, to call one pupil at a time to the teacher's desk and have him read to the teacher while the rest of the class is engaged in some activity that does not require the constant attention of the teacher.

3. *Finding and Reading Answers to Questions.* After the silent reading of a selection, some kind of checkup on comprehension has become a nearly universal practice. One procedure which brings in oral reading in a natural and significant way is to ask the children to locate in the selection the answers to specific questions. The answers are then read aloud. This provides purposeful review in silent reading as well as desirable practice in oral reading, and may serve as a stimulus for interesting discussions about the correctness of the answers.

4. *Audience Reading.* Each pupil is given a chance to select and prepare a selection to read to the class, preferably from material that is *not* familiar to the other pupils. After considerable practice at home, and, if possible, a preliminary rehearsal with the teacher, the child reads his carefully prepared selection to his classmates. Since the material is new to them and well presented, the interest of the class is usually well sustained and the pupil experiences satisfaction from a job well done. Many good teachers of reading make a period of audience reading a weekly event. Sometimes an imitation microphone is employed, a member of the class serves as announcer, and the pupils broadcast their selections in typical radio fashion. Another variation is to present a short play, with each of several pupils reading a different part.

5. *Choral Reading.* Certain definite values can be derived from occasional periods in which the class reads aloud in unison. The better readers carry along the poorer ones, who may gain a better appreciation of pronunciation, phrasing, rhythm, and interpretation. This kind of oral reading is especially suitable for poetry and other strongly rhythmical material.

6. *Reading Parts in Radio Scripts or Plays.* There is no type of oral reading that is more interesting to children or that helps them more to read with natural expression than reading a part in a play.

The influence of the radio is helping to break down the tradition that plays must be given from memory. When children are allowed to read their parts from the script, plays can be prepared and presented in a fraction of the time formerly required, and a great many more informal dramatizations can be introduced into the classroom than were formerly possible.

Silent Reading

Changes have also taken place in the teaching of silent reading. One of them is the tendency to think in terms of specific kinds of reading and to plan lessons designed to improve a particular reading skill. One lesson is designed to give practice in finding the central idea of a selection, another to improve ability at locating answers to specific questions, a third to develop ability to remember the sequence of events, and so on. Each lesson should have a definite aim. Reading for appreciation and pleasure is clearly distinguished from work-type reading or study. Minute dissection of plot and characters is avoided in pleasure-type reading because of its tendency to spoil enjoyment, while habits of careful and accurate reading are built up with carefully planned exercises in the reading of informational material.

Another trend in silent reading has been toward increasing the amount and broadening the scope of the reading done in the schools. The use of basic readers is supplemented by wide reading in a variety of sources. Magazines, pamphlets, and newspapers are brought into the classroom and used as instructional materials. The "classics," while not ignored, have had to make room for a large amount of reading that is intimately related to contemporary life. Functional reading of many varied types absorbs a major part of the total time spent in school.

Recognition of Individual Differences

Even more significant than the specific changes in teaching procedures has been the increasing awareness of the importance of individual differences as a factor in reading. Some teachers still seem to believe that if their teaching is good it should bring all or nearly all of their pupils up to a fairly uniform level of achievement. The schools are realizing more and more the falsity of this belief. Children when they enter school differ widely in their abilities and in their potentialities for future development. With efficient instruction, these differences should increase rather than decrease as they progress through school. Even when the dull child is brought by highly efficient instruction up to the highest level that his capacity allows, he will still be far behind his bright classmates. Uniformity of achievement in a class is more apt to indicate neglect of the abler pupils than generally effective teaching.

With this recognition of the significance of individual differences have come all sorts of attempts to adjust the school program to the varying abilities of the pupils. These have included plans for classifying pupils into instructional groups on the basis of reading ability, and plans which attempt to provide complete individualization of the reading program. Realization of the importance of meeting the needs of each pupil has brought remedial instruction into the foreground. This should not be conceived too narrowly. The aim of the teacher should be not merely to help those who are poor in reading, but rather to help every pupil, the good as well as the poor, to develop the maximum power in reading of which he is capable.

III. Some General Considerations

There is no one plan for teaching reading that is ideally suited to meet the needs of all teachers. Classes of pupils differ in mental ability, in background, in previously acquired skill in reading, and in the amount of variation within the class. Materials also differ; some teachers have nothing to use except one set of readers, while others are provided with extensive and varied instructional material. Finally, teachers themselves are unlike in many significant ways — in amount and kind of training, in resourcefulness, in energy, in temperamental characteristics. A method which works well with one teacher may be very difficult for another to apply effectively. The best program for a particular teacher to follow is one which is adapted to his pupils, makes efficient use of his materials, and is suited to his abilities as a teacher.

There are, however, certain general principles which should be incorporated into any method of teaching reading. While specific applications may and should differ according to circumstances, these principles are fundamentally important and provide a basis for evaluating the probable effectiveness of any plan.

1. *Reading must be made an enjoyable activity.* Methods which conceive reading narrowly as a collection of word recognition and comprehension skills, to be taught by drill methods, often fail to achieve this important goal. If pupils are to develop a genuine liking for reading, provision must be made to encourage large amounts of silent reading in materials which are interesting and of suitable difficulty. Every reading plan should try to build up the habit of reading for fun.

2. *Systematic training must be given in the mastery of specific reading skills.* In the primary grades much emphasis has to be placed on the acquisition of a fundamental reading vocabulary, on the development of accuracy and independence in word recognition, and on reading for meaning. Above the primary level, attention should be given to the continued expansion of vocabulary and to the mastery of the many varied skills that are required in work-type reading and study.

3. *A good reading program is balanced and contains varied activities.* The relative emphasis to be placed on silent and oral reading, on specific drills and unsupervised reading, on recreational and informational reading, naturally differs according to local conditions. A program which emphasizes any one phase of reading to the virtual exclusion of all others, however, is practically certain to produce a corresponding lack of balance in the reading abilities of the pupils.

4. *Provision must be made for individual differences.* Pupils differ widely in every significant trait that can be observed. An effective plan of teaching reading must take account of variations in intelligence, in maturity, in interest, and in the presence or absence of handicaps to learning. If a teaching method is to succeed with all

pupils, it must be flexible enough to give different pupils the kinds of instruction that they need.

5. *Special attention must be given to pupils whose reading is below normal.* Every teacher should be alert to notice the difficulties of individual children, and should arrange his teaching so as to leave time for giving these pupils the assistance they need. It does not matter very much whether this assistance is given in regular class periods or before or after school, individually or in small groups, by the regular teacher or by a special remedial teacher, so long as it is based on an intelligent diagnosis of his needs and helps to overcome his difficulties.

Suggested Additional Reading

ADAMS, FAY, LILLIAN GRAY, and DORA REESE. *Teaching Children to Read,* Chs. 7–10.

BETTS, EMMETT A. *Foundations of Reading Instruction,* Chs. 20, 22.

BOND, GUY L., and EVA BOND WAGNER. *Teaching the Child to Read,* Revised Edition, Chs. 8, 12.

MCKEE, PAUL. *The Teaching of Reading in the Elementary School,* Chs. 8–11.

MCKIM, MARGARET G. *Guiding Growth in Reading in the Modern Elementary School,* Chs. 5–7, 10, 11. New York: The Macmillan Co., 1955.

Reading in the Elementary School. 48th Yearbook of the National Society for the Study of Education, Part II. Chicago: University of Chicago Press, 1949.

RUSSELL, DAVID H. *Children Learn to Read.* Chs. 5, 7, 8.

SIMPSON, ELIZABETH A. *Helping High-School Students Read Better,* Chs. 4, 5. Chicago: Science Research Associates, 1954.

STONE, CLARENCE R. *Progress in Primary Reading,* Chs. 1, 2, 6. St. Louis: Webster Publishing Co., 1950.

STRANG, RUTH, CONSTANCE M. MCCULLOUGH, and ARTHUR E. TRAXLER. *Problems in the Improvement of Reading,* Second Edition, Chs. 3–6. New York: McGraw-Hill Book Co., 1955.

TINKER, MILES A. *Teaching Elementary Reading,* Chs. 5–7, 13–15.

YOAKAM, GERALD A. *Basal Reading Instruction,* Chs. 3, 5, 6.

· V ·

Meeting Individual Needs in Reading

THE ONE REQUEST which teachers have made to this writer most often is: Please tell us how we can teach reading so as to meet the needs of all the children. Some are more concerned with the poorer readers, some with how to stimulate the good readers. Some want only to know how to manage three groups, as if that were the final solution. Some have heard about individualized reading and want to know how it can be done. The specific questions vary, but interest in this general question is universal among teachers who are awake to their classroom problems.

I. The Significance of Individual Differences in Reading

ALTHOUGH ALL TEACHERS know that there are important differences in reading ability among children, few are aware of how great these differences really are. A look at the magnitude of the problem will show vividly why it is essential that continuing efforts be made to improve our methods of adapting to individual abilities.

Some results of a recent nationwide study to establish norms for Form J of the *Stanford Reading Test* are shown in Table III. The Intermediate level of the Paragraph Meaning subtest was used in grades five and six, and the Advanced level was used in grade seven. Results for the Word Meaning subtest and the Average Reading

Table III. Distribution of Paragraph Meaning Grade Equivalents of the Stanford Achievement Test, Form J, for Grades 5, 6, and 7

Grade Equivalents	*Grade 5 Per Cent*	*Grade 6 Per Cent*	*Grade 7 Per Cent*
12.0–12.9			1.6
11.0–11.9	0.4	1.3	5.4
10.0–10.9	2.5	6.1	9.7
9.0– 9.9	3.0	6.1	8.9
8.0– 8.9	6.7	11.4	15.6
7.0– 7.9	10.0	13.4	15.6
6.0– 6.9	19.5	22.5	13.4
5.0– 5.9	20.9	17.6	16.6
4.0– 4.9	21.8	13.6	9.0
3.0– 3.9	12.4	6.4	3.8
2.0– 2.9	2.6	1.4	0.5
Below 2.0	0.3	0.1	0.01
Number	14,227	13,679	10,327
75th Percentile	6.8	7.9	9.0
Median	5.6	6.4	7.4
25th Percentile	4.4	5.1	5.7

These are the results of the National Standardization Groups tested in Spring, 1952. The grade equivalents are the so-called "modal-age" grade equivalents (based on children of normal age for grade), which run 3 to 5 months lower than grade equivalents based on all pupils in given grades. This table is adapted from data supplied by World Book Company, and used by permission.

scores were quite similar. Since the "average group" is often defined as the pupils in the middle 50 per cent, it is instructive to note how these 50 per cent vary among themselves. The range from 25th percentile to 75th percentile is 2.4 grades in grade five, 2.7 grades in grade six, and 3.3 grades in grade seven. This hardly is encouragement for those who think of "average" pupils as being very much alike.

Teachers tend to think of the pupils in a given grade as reading at that grade level. According to the results in Table III, only 21 per cent of the fifth graders were reading at fifth-grade level, only 22.5 per cent of sixth graders were reading at sixth-grade level, and only 16 per cent of seventh graders were reading at seventh-grade level. It is no wonder that there is often a lack of fit between the materials supplied for children to read and their capacity to use the materials.

Those who were found to read two or more years below grade placement were uncomfortably numerous: 15 per cent in grade five, 21.5 per cent in grade six, and 21 per cent in grade seven. A significant number were found to be reading three or more years below grade placement: 3 per cent in grade five, 8 per cent in grade six, and 13 per cent in grade seven. An approximately equal number were found to be reading two or more years above grade placement.

The spread in grade equivalents is not as large as this in the primary grades, since it tends to increase year by year. It also may be considerably less than this in a particular school, because of a relatively homogeneous population or an untypical promotion policy. Taking these factors into account, it is still conservative to say that it is unusual to find a class in which as many as one-third score within six months of this actual grade placement. A difference of five or more years in reading grade between the best and poorest readers in a classroom is normally to be expected.

The overlapping of reading ability in different grades is also tremendous. Some additional statistical work on the data in Table III reveals that 32 per cent of the sixth graders and 23 per cent of the seventh graders scored below the fifth-grade median. On the other hand, 16 per cent of the fifth graders and 30 per cent of the sixth graders did better than the median child in grade seven. Obviously there is not only a great range at each grade level, but also a large amount of overlapping of reading ability from grade to grade.

The implications of such findings as these – and they are not very much different from those of similar surveys in the 1930's and 1940's [1] – call for determined efforts to provide school situations that can

[1] Gray, William S., "The Nature and Extent of the Reading Problem in American Education," *Educational Record,* Supplement No. 11, Vol. 19, 1938, pp. 87–104.

Bond, Guy L., and Handlan, Bertha, *Adapting Instruction in Reading to Individual Differences,* Series on Individualization of Instruction, No. 5, pp. 16–24. Minneapolis: University of Minnesota Press, 1948.

deal with the realities of individual differences. Efforts to do this have been of two major kinds. One kind includes many types of administrative efforts to reduce the range of differences in a class to teachable levels. The other kind includes the various ways of adapting instruction within the classroom to individual differences.

Goals for Differentiated Reading Instruction

Before taking up the details of plans that aim at meeting the problem of wide individual differences in reading ability, it is desirable to consider what the specific objectives should be for any plan of differentiated reading instruction. Such objectives fall naturally into four categories.

There is, first of all, the objective of providing opportunities for the maximum growth of each child in the important phases of reading. A plan that is concerned only with developmental reading is too limited in scope; recreational reading and functional reading must be given careful consideration also.

Second, a sound plan for reading instruction must necessarily be one that favors the social and personal adjustment of all of the children and helps to foster the development of truly democratic attitudes and practices. Many complaints against specific classification or grouping procedures have arisen from experiences in which snobbishness, social ostracism, defeatism, and bitter resentment seemed to result from the procedure. A sound plan should be acceptable to administrators, teachers, pupils, and parents. It should be one in which children are helped to become happier and more secure, as well as better in reading skills.

In the third place, the plan should be one which can be carried out by teachers of average training and ability. Some of the plans which have been praised in the professional literature portray an exceptionally expert and creative teacher carrying out a program which requires a great deal of planning and preparation. Exhorting average teachers to adopt such a plan sometimes discourages them from trying anything new, because they feel quite unable to meet the requirements. Realistic plans must be usable by most teachers, while at the same time providing scope for creative work by superior teachers.

Finally, a good plan should fit the school and its pupils. Some good plans are workable only in large schools with hundreds of pupils. Others require an abundance and variety of materials far beyond the resources of the typical school. The little red schoolhouse, with eight grades in one room, enforced a kind of differentiated instruction rarely seen in graded schools. Each school has to appraise its own situation and work out solutions that fit its own needs.

II. Administrative Provisions for Reading Instruction

Retardation and Acceleration

In the typical school of a generation ago, individual differences among pupils did not form a basis for planning. The work was laid out in neat weekly and daily segments so that the primer would be finished by January and the first reader by June. The rate of progress was determined by the average pupils. The children who did well were commended; those who did poorly were exhorted to pay closer attention and were kept after school for extra drill. When the end of the year came, a very few exceptionally able pupils "skipped" into a higher grade; the majority were promoted; and a substantial minority were required to repeat the term or the year.

The supposed benefits of repeating grades are more illusory than real. According to the *Encyclopaedia of Educational Research,* retention does not significantly increase a slow rate of learning, make for better student morale, assure mastery of subject matter, reduce variability in achievement, increase grade-achievement averages, or improve the personal adjustment of the retained pupil. "The present trend is away from the practice of failing pupils in order to adjust them to the curriculum. Rather the curriculum is being adjusted to the pupil." [2]

Some school systems, however, have attempted to abolish retarda-

[2] Monroe, Walter S., ed., *Encyclopaedia of Educational Research,* Revised Edition, p. 1124. New York: The Macmillan Co., 1950.

tion without setting up adequate plans for individualizing work. So-called "one hundred per cent promotion" plans which do not provide work at each grade which fits the varying abilities of the children are probably worse in some respects than the older plan which required the slow pupil to repeat grades. In such schools, pupils can be promoted regularly and finish the elementary school grades without ever having the experience of being able to do the work assigned to them. Abolishing nonpromotion is useless unless at the same time provisions are made for teaching pupils in each grade in accordance with their abilities.

Ideally, promotion policy should allow each child to be with the group in which he can make the best total adjustment, socially and educationally. This is usually — but not always — his own age group. Children of exceptional all-round maturity usually benefit from some acceleration, and children who are quite immature in general are sometimes better off in a younger group. Allowing for a few exceptional cases, reliance on retardation and acceleration is no longer acceptable as a general way of adjusting instruction to individual needs.

Postponing Reading for All Children

In the first flush of enthusiasm for reading readiness, it was seriously proposed by some [3] that the way to eliminate difficulties in reading instruction was to postpone instruction in reading until the age of eight or nine, when practically all children would have become ready for reading. A little later the proposal was to eliminate reading entirely from the first grade.[4] Evidence was cited in Chapter II which seems to show that reading can be postponed a year or more with good results. However, it does not seem likely that making all children wait a year or more before starting to read is the best solution. We do not make all of the people at a picnic delay their lunches because two or three are not yet hungry; and there

[3] Witty, Paul A., and Kopel, David, "Preventing Reading Disability: The Reading Readiness Factor," *Educational Administration and Supervision*, Vol. 12, 1936, pp. 401–418.

[4] Kopel, David, "The Prevention of Poor Reading," *Elementary English Review*, Vol. 20, 1943, pp. 321–326.

seems to be no more reason to make children who are ready for reading wait because some other children are not ready. Furthermore, postponing reading does not make all children equal in learning ability when they finally do start; it simply postpones the time at which adjustment to varying learning rates will have to be made.

Reading Readiness Classes

In a large school there are sometimes enough first-grade children lacking in reading readiness to justify the formation of a special class. Such classes are called by various names, such as "junior primary," "kindergarten extension," "transition," and so on. In such a class the teacher starts with a program similar to that of a good kindergarten. The major goal is the development of all phases of reading readiness. The whole term may be spent on readiness work, or the teacher may watch for indications that some of the children are ready to start reading and may start formal reading work with that group while continuing readiness work with the rest of the class.

This procedure is practicable in cities, where schools are large and there may be enough immature first-grade pupils to warrant the formation of such classes. The results in general have been favorable in reducing the rate of failure in the first grade in cities like Los Angeles and Chicago.[5]

Homogeneous Grouping

The inadequacies of the old plan of skipping some pupils and making others repeat grades as the only concession to individual differences has long been recognized. Once its shortcomings were known, many plans of "homogeneous grouping" were tried out. All of these plans have as their main idea the organization of classes in each grade on the basis of abilities. Grouping is usually done on the basis of intelligence tests, the recommendations of teachers, or a combination of the two. Typical plans divide the children in each

[5] Johnson, W. H., "Development of the Chicago Program to Aid Pupils Lacking in Reading Readiness," *Elementary School Journal,* Vol. 42, 1942, pp. 337–346.

grade into three classes (bright, average, and dull) or in large schools sometimes into five or more classes. In some schools the only instructional differences are that the bright groups go faster and the dull groups slower than the average; all study the same curriculum. It is generally thought, however, that homogeneous grouping should be accompanied by differentiated courses of study. The bright children should be given an enriched curriculum, with less drill work and more emphasis on the development of initiative in working under relatively little supervision. By enriching the course of study rather than acceleration, the dangers of social maladjustment that often occur when bright children are placed with children two or three years older than they are can be avoided. The dull child also needs something other than merely a slowing down of the conventional program of study.[6]

It was originally hoped that when classes were set up in this way, the children in each class would be sufficiently alike so that they could be taught as a unit. However, regardless of the method of assigning pupils – whether on the basis of mental age, IQ, teacher judgment, achievement test scores, or some combination of these – it has been found that in each class there remain differences sufficiently great as to constitute a real instructional problem. Even if the grouping is done solely on the basis of reading ability, it is found that children reading at the same level have different patterns of abilities and need different emphasis in their instruction.

Research has for the most part compared undifferentiated classroom instruction in heterogeneous classes with undifferentiated instruction in homogeneous classes, and has not shown a clear advantage for either; the majority of teachers and pupils have expressed attitudes favorable to homogeneous grouping.[7] The results obtainable from differentiated instruction within homogeneous classes have not been adequately studied. As subgrouping within classes

[6] Detailed consideration of this problem is to be found in *The Grouping of Pupils,* 35th Yearbook of the National Society for Study of Education. Bloomington, Ill.: Public School Publishing Co., 1936.

[7] *Encyclopaedia of Educational Research,* Revised Edition. New York: The Macmillan Co., 1950.

became popular many schools discontinued homogeneous grouping. There has not been a real experimental tryout of combining the best features of both.

One of the main criticisms against homogeneous grouping is that it fosters the development of unfavorable attitudes in both teachers and pupils toward classes known to be limited in scholastic performance. It seems to this writer that prejudice against slow pupils can be fostered or discouraged in any kind of school organization and is not inherent in homogeneous grouping; however, it may be harder to prevent the development of such attitudes when slow children stay together for all activities.

The Special Class for Poor Readers

Some large elementary schools have tried the idea of gathering together into one room all of the poorest readers at a particular grade level, while the rest of the school has heterogeneous classes. Such a special class is kept small (preferably under twenty), the teacher is selected on the basis of ability to work with poor learners, extra materials are supplied, and the teacher is free to deviate from the usual curriculum of the grade. Such classes are often called "opportunity classes," although it is probably better not to give them a special designation. If such a class is set up and works well, it may be desirable to keep the teacher and children together for a two-year period.

One of the major advantages of this plan is that it relieves the other teachers of the children who require a disproportionate share of the teacher's time and energy in a regular class, and reduces individual differences in the regular classes to the point where the teachers feel competent to deal with them.

The special class, of course, requires a teacher whose skills include a practical working knowledge both of mental hygiene principles, and of corrective and remedial techniques. Even with such a teacher, the special reading class may become very difficult to manage if it is overloaded with children who are severely maladjusted.

Homogeneous Grouping for Reading Only

Another plan which has produced favorable results in graded elementary schools involves assigning children to reading classes that are relatively homogeneous, while keeping classes heterogeneous for other activities. Such plans involve the giving of reading tests to all the children in the grades in which the plan is to be used. On the basis of test results and teacher judgment the pupils are divided into reading classes, all of which are scheduled for reading at the same time. When the bell rings, each child goes to his reading teacher. In the reading class he will find some children from his own grade and some from higher or lower grades. When the reading period is over he returns to his regular class.

Such plans are not new, since many of them were developed in the 1930's. Several good ones were described in the Seventeenth Yearbook of the Department of Elementary School Principals, of the National Education Association.[8] In one of them, O'Bannon told of an experiment in which the children in grades three to six of an elementary school were classified into nine instructional groups for reading. In the two lowest groups the teachers found it necessary to devote a great amount of time to word recognition. In the upper groups quite informal reading programs were devised, with large amounts of time spent in library reading. At the end of the term, it was found by means of a questionnaire that 85 per cent of the children preferred the plan, including 53 of the 67 who were placed in reading classes below their regular grades. Retesting at the end of the term showed quite large gains for the lowest groups.

Bigelow [9] described a program in which the fourth-, fifth-, and sixth-grade pupils in a school were reclassified for reading instruction. The majority of the pupils came from foreign-language homes, and average attainment in reading was low. Three classes were set

[8] *Newer Practices in Reading in the Elementary School,* Seventeenth Yearbook of the National Elementary School Principal, Vol. 17, No. 7. Washington, D.C.: National Education Association, July, 1938.

[9] Bigelow, E. B., "Improvement in Reading as Shown by Standard Tests," *Educational Method,* Vol. 13, 1934, pp. 258–263.

up, with median reading grade scores of 4.9, 3.7, and 2.2. Each class was in turn subdivided for small group instruction. The best group was given a large amount of library work. The poorest class was given training in the mechanics of reading and in vocabulary development, easy reading material, and individual help as far as possible. In this group two days a week were devoted to remedial work, two days to reading for appreciation, and one day to reading of materials chosen by the pupils.

All of these published accounts report good results in raising the reading abilities of the children on whom the plans have been tried. There is no doubt but that grouping children into reading classes on the basis of reading ability produces classes which are more homogeneous for the teaching of reading than when grouping is based on general intelligence.

There is not, however, any unanimous agreement that homogeneous grouping for reading gives a complete solution to the problem of organizing a school for reading. The necessity for a set and limited period of reading instruction interferes with the elasticity of programming which is favored in many modern schools. When reading is taught a child by one teacher and the other subjects by another teacher, there is apt to be serious interference with the integration or correlation of the work of the pupils. There is little opportunity to combine training in word recognition with spelling, to utilize historical or geographical material for training in work-type reading, and so on. The fact that reading is a tool more than a subject tends to be obscured. These objections are raised most strongly in schools which emphasize a unit or activity program. They are least significant in schools where the different subjects of the curriculum are kept rigidly separated or where a departmental organization is already in operation.

When homogeneous grouping for reading is tried, it is probably desirable to restrict it to a two-grade range if the school is large enough. For example, the third and fourth grades, fifth and sixth grades, and seventh and eighth grades, can be reclassified for reading. This lessens the variations in age, size, and social maturity.

Classification for Reading in Secondary School

Grouping plans similar to those employed in elementary schools have been employed successfully in some secondary schools as an aid to more effective work in teaching reading. In secondary schools reading is not usually considered a separate subject, but is included in the curriculum in English. A representative grouping program of a kind suitable for junior and senior high school English classes has been reported by Miller.[10] Nine classes of seventh-grade pupils were given standardized reading tests and reclassified on that basis. A three-track program was worked out, with different materials and teaching procedures for the superior, average, and inferior classes. The poorer pupils were provided with specially selected books and library lists, and made use of reading workbooks. Somewhat similar plans, involving ability grouping in English on the basis of reading tests, intelligence tests, or a combination of the two, have been employed in many secondary schools.

A different approach to the improvement of reading ability in secondary school has been described by Strang.[11] Conferences of the teachers in a high school were held in which the need for attention to reading thoroughout the school and methods of improving reading ability were discussed. An all-school program was worked out in which the teachers of all subjects stressed the improvement of one reading skill (such as selecting the main idea of a passage) for a period of two weeks, and then another skill was stressed during the next two weeks. By the end of the term a well-rounded program had been covered. In addition to the all-school program, the twenty poorest readers, selected on the basis of intelligence and reading test results, were gathered together in a remedial reading class. Such an all-school program has the important advantage of providing instruction in the adaptation of reading skills to the requirements of the different secondary school subjects, and, used in combination

[10] Miller, G. E., "Adapting Reading Materials to Varying Ability Levels," *English Journal,* Vol. 27, 1938, pp. 751–759.

[11] Strang, R., "Improvement of Reading in High School," *Teachers College Record,* Vol. 39, 1937, pp. 197–206.

with special provisions for the poorer readers, has many things in its favor.

In many secondary schools the only administrative procedure aimed directly at the improvement of reading is the segregation of the poorest readers into special remedial classes, usually scheduled as English classes. Such a procedure is beneficial to the remedial pupils, but neglects the large potentialities for improvement which the majority of the pupils possess. There is no good reason why systematic effort to develop the reading ability of normal and superior readers should be restricted to the elementary school.

The Primary Division or School

An increasing number of schools are finding the solution to many problems in the elimination of hard and fast grade boundaries. Each teacher is expected to consider herself a teacher of children rather than a teacher of a fixed curriculum, set by an official syllabus. If this is the second year the children have been in school and some of them are still reading at primer level, the teacher must work with them at that level. If others in the class are capable of using third-grade materials, their needs also must be met. Children stay with the group in which they are likely to make the most adequate total adjustment.

In order to provide continuity of instruction, teachers stay with their classes for longer periods of time. They frequently move up with the children. The undesirability of changing teachers every few months is recognized. When the teacher stays with a class for two years or more, she has time to study their needs and to carry out individual adjustments. She also is relieved of pressure to get quick results, and therefore does not have to rush the pupils along faster than they can go. Individual differences are expected and accepted. Accordingly, some schools have experimented successfully with plans in which the primary teacher stays with the class for two or even three years.

Some schools have abolished primary-grade divisions. The kindergarten and subsequent two or three years are conceived as an ungraded primary division or school. Children usually stay with the group with which they enter. The different classes are known by their teacher's names rather than by grade numbers. Teachers move along with their pupils in a continuous integrated program in which grade boundaries become obscure.[12]

In one such plan, reported by Boney,[13] the first-grade teacher stayed with the same class for three years; all the children were promoted regardless of what they had learned. The method used stressed individual and small-group instruction for the most part, and each child was allowed to proceed at his own rate. Careful measures of achievement were made at fairly frequent intervals and after each checkup those children who were found not to have progressed much since the preceding tests were given special help. The significant result was that nearly all of the children were able to meet fourth-grade standards after three years in the experimental class. Furthermore, several children who made such slow progress in the first year that they would ordinarily have repeated the grade made rapid strides in the second and third years and were up to the average by the end of the experiment.

An account of the use of such a plan with a group of children from foreign-language backgrounds has been given by Wahlert.[14] After a year in kindergarten, they were placed in the first grade and stayed with the same teacher for two years. At the beginning, major emphasis was placed on developing readiness for reading. Reading instruction was introduced gradually and was taught on a highly individualized basis. At the end of the two-year period all of the children had developed a liking for reading, and most of them were ready for third-grade work. Wahlert said that the emotional effects of the plan were very beneficial, since there was no sense of failure,

[12] "Schools Can Change Grouping Practices," *Grouping . . . Problems and Satisfactions,* pp. 14–18. Washington, D.C.: Association for Childhood Education International, 1954.

[13] Boney, C. DeWitt, "The Disposition of a Group of Slow First-Grade Readers," *Elementary School Journal,* Vol. 37, 1936, p. 203–208.

[14] *Newer Practices in Reading in the Elementary School,* Seventeenth Yearbook of the National Elementary School Principal, Vol. 17, No. 7, pp. 552–556. Washington, D.C.: National Education Association, July, 1938.

no comparison of one child's achievements with those of other children, and no fear of low grades or of nonpromotion during this critical period.

If similar individualized procedures are carried on in the subsequent grades, there is no promotion problem at the end of the primary school. If the upper grades in the elementary school are less capable of coping with varying levels of achievement than the primary grades, nonpromotion may be desirable at the end of the primary sequence for those who need more time in which to be able to meet fourth-grade work successfully.

As one reads about the various administrative plans that have been tried, the striking fact is that all of these plans seem to have produced quite favorable results in the local situations in which they were developed. Probably the enthusiasm and ability of the people operating the plan and the appeal of novelty will give any sensible innovation an advantage over what was done before. In this, as in many other important questions about reading instruction, research has produced no final answers.[15]

III. Differentiated Learning within the Classroom

If a reading program is to be richly varied in its objectives and learnings, it is reasonable to expect that no one way of organizing the class will serve all of these purposes equally well. A few years ago there were arguments about whether or not to use reading groups; whether reading should be taught by group methods or by individualized methods, and so on. Today, a well-rounded reading program includes several different kinds of class organization, each used for the reading activities for which it is best suited. The question is no longer one of choosing between individualization and grouping, but rather of how to combine several kinds of organization, including whole-class activities, individualized reading, and group reading, into a harmonious whole.

[15] Figurel, J. A., "What Recent Research Tells Us about Differentiated Instruction in Reading," *The Reading Teacher,* Vol. 6, No. 1, September, 1952, pp. 27–33.

Whole-Class Reading Activities

There are several kinds of reading activities which can profitably be carried on with the entire class. They include audience situations, common new learnings, current events reading, open-book textbook sessions, and choral reading. Each of these has a legitimate place in the total reading program.

Audience Situations. One type of oral reading approved for modern schools involves the presentation to the class of an oral reading selection which has been prepared and rehearsed. Materials can include poems, jokes, selections from stories and books, radio scripts, or short plays. The presentation may be by an individual or small groups. Sessions in which children give oral book reports or present reports based on individual or committee reading also can provide whole-class audience situations. The two important features are: (1) advance preparation, so that the performance is reasonably good; and (2) the class does not read along silently, but is a real audience.

Common New Learnings. There are many occasions when a new reading skill can be introduced to the whole class, even though not all will learn it with equal rapidity. Alphabetizing, the use of such aids as the table of contents, index, dictionary and encyclopedia, and new phonic principles and word meanings are among the reading skills that can be introduced in this way.

Current Events. School newspapers provide opportunities for current events periods in which all can participate. Weekly graded editions make it possible for all to do the same kind of reading together, while some may be reading an advanced edition and others an edition intended for lower grades. In the primary grades, experience stories can be used for the same purpose.

Textbook Reading. When a textbook is the focus of a particular curriculum area, it may be necessary to have "open book" sessions in which the textbook is used like a basal reader. Often the unavailability of simpler textbooks makes it necessary to use the one book with the entire class. The poorer readers get the content mainly by listening and are called on only for comparatively easy passages or questions.

Choral Reading. The occasional use of choral reading is not only helpful for the appreciation of poetry and rhythm, but also assists in developing the spirit of belongingness and group cohesion in he class.

Individualized Reading Activities

A completely individualized reading situation is one in which no two children in the class are reading the same thing at the same time. Individualized reading makes it possible to provide maximum flexibility in adjusting reading to individual abilities, interests, and needs. It naturally requires an abundance of varied materials. An entire class may be engaged in individualized reading at one time, or part of the class may be reading individually while other children work in groups. Individualized procedures have been developed for four different kinds of reading activity: recreational reading, research reading, practice on reading skills, and developmental reading.

Individualized Recreational Reading. Periods for recreational reading in which each child is free to read what he pleases (from the materials available) have been called *free-reading* periods. During such a period the teacher can circulate among the class, spending a minute with one child and five minutes with another. These individual contacts can be spent in discussing a book already finished, considering with the child what he might like to read next, finding out more about the child's interests or problems, listening to some oral reading, providing help on a specific difficulty, and so on.

Since in a free-reading program the pupils read only what they like, there are great possibilities for developing and broadening interest in reading. Extensive reading will in itself bring about some enrichment of vocabulary and improvement of speed and comprehension. It is necessary, of course, to have books available covering a wide variety of subject matter and of suitable difficulty. Arrangements can often be made to borrow an appropriate collection of books from the school library or from a public library; librarians are ordinarily glad to cooperate with teachers. In many schools, periods can be provided during which the pupils are allowed to browse through the library shelves. It is usually advisable to provide some guidance in the choice of books, as without it some of the pupils will make inappropriate selections and lose interest. Reports on books should not be lengthy and detailed; a one-paragraph writ ten report or an oral report usually suffices. The teacher employing free reading must always keep in mind that the success of the method depends on the extent to which it builds more favorable attitudes toward reading and gets the pupils to read more.

Individualized Research Reading. Modern teaching procedures create many occasions for a child to read by himself to find out needed information. For good readers this highly functional reading provides multiple opportunities for intellectual enrichment and personal development. For the poor reader, the absence of relevant material simple enough for him to comprehend is often a cause of frustration and the decline of intellectual curiosity.

Individualized Skills Practice. In the middle and upper grades there is room for a period, once or twice a week, in which each child can work on particular reading skills in which he needs to improve. For this to be effective one must have ways of determining individual needs, making individual assignments, and providing practice materials which have been set up with clear, self-administering directions and scoring keys.

Individualized Developmental Reading

Although several plans for teaching developmental reading by individualized methods were described in the 1930's, there are relatively few school systems in which such procedures have been generally adopted.

Individualized Reading in the First Grade. An individualized developmental reading program should be most difficult to operate in the first grade, because the children are less mature, less independent, less capable of self-direction, and less able to sustain attention than in succeeding grades. The writer has therefore been very much intrigued by the success of some of his graduate students in substituting individualized reading for group developmental reading lessons in the first grade. The following brief account is a composite based on detailed reports from several teachers.

At the beginning of the year a readiness program is continued from the kindergarten and experience stories are gradually introduced with the whole class. When a child displays readiness in such ways as scoring well on a test, recognizing story words used in previous stories, and showing interest in library books and in the stories read by the teacher, he is allowed to start a first preprimer. The teacher sits next to him for a few minutes a day, discussing the pictures, telling the words as needed, and listening to oral reading. One child at a time is started in this way. The rest continue meanwhile with readiness activities.

After several children have started to read, more organization is needed. Several centers of interest (painting, crayons, clay, store, doll house) are set up and children choose their activity for a particular period. During this activity period, in which most of the children do not need teacher help or supervision, the teacher calls four children to her and seats them around her. While one child reads with her orally for about five minutes, the other three read silently in their separate stories. If a child needs help with a word he points to it, and the teacher tells him the word without interrupting the child who is reading orally. Each group of four is with the teacher for about twenty minutes; three or four such groups can be worked with during a morning. In this way, each child gets to read with the teacher two or three times a week. Those doing readinesss work have their regular turns, as well as those already reading.

Instead of having a regular afternoon session for the whole class, the teacher may invite a few children to return for an extra period after lunch. This period can be used for training in word attack skills, concept development, extra individual help for some children, and so on. Different children can be invited on different days. Other reading activities, such as experience stories, may be continued on a whole-class basis.

A number of factors seem to be helpful in making such a program work effectively. (1) The plan is much easier to operate in a small class (twenty-five or fewer) than in a large one. (2) Before the plan can go into operation the children must be helped to become independent in a variety of nonreading activities. (3) Preprimers, primers, and first readers should be arranged in a sequence which provides for gradual introduction of new words and extensive repetition, so that the children's reading can be easy and pleasurable and requires a minimum of preparatory teaching. Children should read several books at one level of difficulty before going on to the next level. The first-grade materials of several basal series should be on hand. (4) A rich classroom library should be well stocked with picture books and storybooks. (5) The teacher should work out a simple record system for keeping track of the reading progress of each child. (6) Ample opportunities should be provided in other parts of the school day for oral discussion, storytelling, dramatization, rhythms, music, and the other activities that make for a rich first-grade program.

Individualized Developmental Reading in Other Grades. The plan just described for the first grade provides nonreading activities for all children except those called to read with the teacher. As children become able to carry on silent reading independently, it becomes possible to have many children reading quietly at their seats, while the teacher moves from one to another or calls one at a time to her desk. Children who are unable to read independently may need to be assigned to nonreading activities during such a period, or competent readers may be asked to act as helpers, to whom a child can turn when he needs assistance with a word.[16]

[16]Evans, N. D., "An Individualized Reading Program for the Elementary School," *Elementary School Journal,* Vol. 54, 1953, pp. 157–162.

Kaar, H., "An Experiment with an Individualized Method of Teaching Reading," *The Reading Teacher,* Vol. 7, No. 3, February, 1954, pp. 174–177.

Hugerth, C., "It's Different—for Each One," *The Reading Teacher,* Vol. 7, No. 1, October, 1953, pp. 5–9.

McLeod, J., "'When I First Started Teaching'—the Tape-Recorded Comments of One Teacher," *The Reading Teacher,* Vol. 7, No. 4, April, 1954, pp. 226–228.

Lee, J. Murray, "Individualized Instruction," *Education,* Vol. 74, 1954, pp. 279–283.

Olson, W. C., "Seeking, Self-Selection, and Pacing in the Use of Books by

In such a program, it is probably desirable to continue with a carefully arranged sequence of basal readers through the third-grade level. Beyond that, free recreational reading may emphasize library books rather than readers, or readers may be utilized as collections of short stories. Supplementary reading can, of course, be introduced as soon as children are able to engage in it.

The Sacramento program described by Dean [17] emphasized individualized reading. A typical fifth-grade class, with pupils varying widely in intelligence and reading ability, was provided with a class library of forty-five books ranging in difficulty from third to seventh grade and covering a wide variety of topics. No general reader was used. The reading periods were devoted to silent reading, with each pupil reading a different book. When a pupil finished a book the teacher tested him on it and helped him to select another. During the reading periods the pupils were called to the desk one at a time for oral reading, practice on new words in their vocabulary notebooks, and corrective help when needed. The last five minutes were usually devoted to carefully prepared audience reading. Dean commented: "While the individual plan does not lessen the work of the teacher, it does take away much of the drudgery because pupils are more interested and progress is more apparent."

The Chicago Individualized Program. In Chicago, the individualization of developmental reading in grades four to six has been fostered by providing teachers with specially adapted materials. Directions have been prepared for separating a number of readers into individual stories and mounting each selection in an oak-tag folder. Each story is provided with mimeographed directions, comprehension questions, and an answer key. The selections are numbered and arranged in sequence in a file box. By using just a few

---

Children," *The Packet*, Vol. 7. Boston: D. C. Heath & Co., Spring, 1952, pp. 3–10.

Schmidt, Ethel, "I Used Individualized Instruction," *The Reading Teacher*, Vol. 5, September, 1951, pp. 7–9.

Jacobs, Leland, "Reading on Their Own Means Reading at Their Growing Edges," *The Reading Teacher*, Vol. 6, March, 1953, pp. 27–32.

[17] Dean, R. B. in *Newer Practices in Reading in the Elementary School*, Seventeenth Yearbook of the National Elementary School Principal, Vol. 17, No. 7, July, 1938, Ch. IX.

graded readers, each teacher can assemble stories ranging in difficulty over a number of grades. Each pupil can start at a level appropriate for him and progress at his own rate. For the teachers using these materials, individualized reading has largely supplanted reading by groups.[18]

It is unlikely that completely individualized reading can provide all the learnings needed to achieve a well-rounded reading program. When appropriately combined with whole-class activities and some group activities, a well-managed program of individualized reading should provide more effectively for differentiated learning than the much more popular grouping plans can.

Individualized Reading within a Group

A teacher who generally likes to organize reading instruction on a group basis in preference to an individualized program may find it appropriate to consider the use of individualized reading with one group rather than with the entire class. For example, a third-grade teacher was satisfied with the way her high and middle groups were working. The low group, however, included eight children ranging from preprimer to first-reader level, and it was impossible to make group lessons profitable for all. With a primer, two children were at a frustration level, and three were unchallenged; only the three children actually at primer level seemed to be profiting. She therefore tried an individualized approach with these eight children. In a twenty-minute period with this group she was able to spend about two minutes with each child, and the others read ahead silently, asking for help when they met new words. Each child progressed at his own rate, and no two were at the same point. Four or five minutes were used for group discussion, motivation, words difficult for several children, and the like. She reported a tremendous improvement in interest and a doubled rate of reading growth for this group. Whenever the range of individual abilities in a group is so large that it is impossible to choose a basal reader for the group that is reasonably satisfactory for all members of the group, the possible advan-

[18] Information supplied by Miss Mary DeKoker, supervisor of the program, as of July, 1953.

tages of using an individualized approach with that group should be given serious consideration.

This chapter has been concerned with the omnipresent problem of great individual differences in rate of learning and their implications for reading instruction. Different kinds of administrative provisions designed to cut down the range of differences were reviewed, with the conclusion that skillful administrative procedures in pupil classification can help but cannot completely solve the problem. The importance of the social aspects of learnings arrangements was stressed. The need of a balanced program involving some whole-class reading activities, some individualized reading, and some reading in groups was pointed out, and different kinds of whole-class and individualized reading activities were described. Group reading procedures will be discussed in the next chapter.

Suggested Additional Reading

See references at the end of Chapter VI.

· VI ·

Group Instruction in Reading

A WELL-ROUNDED READING PROGRAM, as we have seen in Chapter V, involves some whole-class reading activities, some individualized reading, and some group reading activities. This chapter attempts to provide answers to the questions that teachers ask about group reading instruction.

I. Problems of Group Instruction

THE MAIN PROBLEMS of group instruction are those concerned with group organization, scheduling, assignments, use of helpers, group names, and equipment needed.

Organization of Groups

Because classes differ so widely, there is no one plan for grouping that fits every need. A method of grouping that may be appropriate for one class may not adequately meet the needs of another class. The range of ability within the class, the age of the pupils, the previous experience of the pupils in working in groups, the materials available, and the teacher's competence, all have to be considered. Grouping children for reading is not an end in itself, but a means for achieving desirable objectives of learning and adjustment.

A clearer understanding of the instructional problem requires a consideration of the range of differences in reading ability to be found in normal classrooms. Let us assume that we are studying a school in which the children are representative of the general population in intelligence, there is one class at each grade, all children are promoted regularly regardless of achievement, and reading instruction is of average quality. In such a school, the distribution of reading ability would correspond closely to the figures given in Table IV. This tables includes the second, fourth, and sixth grades; results in other grades would be similar.

Table IV. Probable Distribution of Reading Abilities in the Second, Fourth, and Sixth Grades of an Elementary School

		Beginning of Year Reading Grade Levels		
IQ	*Approx. No. of Pupils in a class of 36*	*Grade 2*	*Grade 4*	*Grade 6*
120 and up	3	3.4 and up	5.8 and up	8.2 and up
110–119	6	2.7 to 3.3	4.9 to 5.7	7.1 to 8.1
100–109	9	2.0 to 2.6	4.0 to 4.8	6.0 to 7.0
90–99	9	1.4 to 1.9	3.1 to 3.9	4.9 to 5.9
80–89	6	1.0 to 1.3	2.2 to 3.0	3.8 to 4.8
Below 80	3	Readiness	Below 2.2	Below 3.8

At the beginning of each grade, half of the children in such a school are reading at or above the grade norm and half are reading below the grade norm. In the second grade, the range is likely to be from children still in the readiness stage to high third-grade level. At the beginning of the fourth grade, the range is likely to be from high first- or low second-grade level to sixth-grade level. At the beginning of the sixth grade, the range is likely to be from third- to ninth-grade level. If the school is one in which the child who does poorly is not promoted, there will be fewer pupils with low reading scores in each grade, but a corresponding number of overage pupils If the school as a whole is above or below average, the distribution of reading ability will show about the same range, but will be shifted up or down.

Grouping by Reading Level

When the range of ability in each class is wide, as in the example just cited, it is usually advisable to set up reading groups primarily on the basis of reading grade levels. When the range of ability is comparatively small, because of homogeneous grouping or excessive nonpromotion, grouping can be done on the basis of other characteristics.

The simplest form of grouping divides the class into two groups: those who can do the normal reading for the grade, and those who cannot. The groups will vary in size according to the ability of the class. In an average class it is usually desirable to place about two thirds of the class in the upper group and about one third in the lower group. The upper group can use reading material normal for the grade, and the lower group preferably should use a reader of a difficulty level appropriate for the average child in the group.

This kind of grouping, into two groups, is probably the most effective kind for the teacher who is just learning the technique of group instruction. As the teacher becomes more skilled, he can either increase the number of groups, or supplement the two-group plan with a greater amount of individualized work.

There is nothing magical about the number three. Two groups will often suffice, especially if combined with some individualized reading. On the other hand, sometimes three groups are not enough. For example, a second-grade class like the one in Table IV would seem to need at least four groups: the nonreaders, a preprimer group, a first-grade group (primer or first reader), and the rest of the class as a large group able to use second-grade books. Within this upper group, a substantial amount of individualized reading could provide for the wide range of skill.

Durrell recommended the use of several small groups rather than two or three larger groups.[1] Teachers who follow his system make use of pupil "assistant teachers" to lead the group activities, while

[1] Durrell, Donald D., *Improvement of Basic Reading Abilities,* Ch. 9. Yonkers, N.Y.: World Book Co., 1940.

the teacher plans, supervises, and spends as much time as possible with the slower groups. A good description of the Durrell plan as used in a retarded fourth-grade class, using five groups, has been given by Donnelly.[2] Such a program can produce excellent results when the teacher is capable of managing it. It seems to require a teacher who is well above the present average in resourcefulness and organizing ability, and who does not mind spending a great deal of time in preparing lesson plans and rehearsing the pupil teachers. At the present time, most teachers are doing well if they can handle three groups effectively. A well-managed two-group plan is superior to an ambitious multigroup plan that gets out of hand.[3]

Grouping according to Specific Needs

Grade level in comprehension is not the only basis on which reading groups have been set up. When the range of reading ability is comparatively narrow, it may be preferable to set up groups on the basis of special needs, such as deficiency in phonics, speed, accuracy, and so on. Shields used a classification of sixth-grade pupils into four groups: the best readers, those who were slow but thorough, the skimmers who were poor in comprehension, and those who were generally poor.[4] Youngman reported a division of a seventh-grade class into five groups: rapid-accurate (superior in both rate and comprehension); median-balanced (average in both rate and accuracy); rapid-inaccurate (weak in comprehension); slow-accurate (weak in rate); and slow-inaccurate (weak in both rate and comprehension).[5] Davis, working with pupils in grades four to six, has given as an example the division of a class of forty pupils into three groups.[6] Group one consisted of twenty-two pupils who were up to

[2] Donnelly, Helen E., "The Remedial Reading Classroom," *Education,* Vol. 59, 1938, pp. 31–36.

[3] Harris, Albert J., "Grouping in the Teaching of Reading," *The Reading Teacher,* Vol. 5, No. 1, September, 1952, pp. 1–3.

[4] Shields, J. M., "Teaching Reading Through Ability Grouping," *Educational Method,* Vol. 9, 1927, pp. 7–10.

[5] *Seventeenth Yearbook of the National Elementary Principal,* Vol. 17, No. 7, July, 1938, Ch. 9.

[6] Davis, G., "Procedures Effective in Improving Pupils of Poor Ability in Regular Reading Classes," *Elementary School Journal,* Vol. 31, 1931, pp. 336–348.

the norms and did not need corrective teaching; group two contained ten pupils who needed training in thought-getting; and group three included eight pupils who needed training in word recognition, vocabulary building, and phrasing. McLatchy and Beavers grouped sixth-grade pupils into fast, average, and slow groups with regard to rate of reading.[7] These examples indicate the wide range of grouping plans that have been tried.

It may often be desirable to set up a special group consisting of children who need help in a particular skill. In a fourth-grade class, this might include those whose phonic knowledge needs improvement, and could include one or two of the better readers as well as some of the poorest. In a sixth grade, a special group might be formed to improve speed and accuracy in alphabetizing. Such groups should usually be temporary and disband as soon as their purpose has been accomplished, whereupon the teacher can start another special group with a different specific need.

Grouping according to Interests

A teacher may find that a few children in the class have a hobby or interest in common, such as raising tropical fish, collecting stamps, having dogs or cats as pets, and so on. Such a group can be encouraged to meet, discover common problems, find reading material related to their special interest, read it, exchange information, and report to the class. Several interest groups may be set up in a class, with membership entirely voluntary. Such groups would not have to meet often; once a week or even once in two weeks might be sufficient.

Reading in Heterogeneous Groups or Committees

Many projects, units, or activities are organized on a committee basis in modern schools. Each committee usually takes responsibility for one part of the total project. Within the committee the questions to be answered are decided upon and each member has his allotted

[7] McLatchy, J. H., and Beavers, E. B., "A Sixth Grade Teacher Studies Reading," *Educational Research Bulletin,* Ohio State University, Vol. 13, 1934, pp. 141–147.

responsibilities. Committees are usually set up by the teacher so that each contains a cross section of the class in abilities.

When reading is to be done to find the answers to questions, a project committee consults as wide a variety of sources as it can. The better readers tackle the hard references; the less capable readers pore over the simpler books. Each finds what he can to contribute. Ideally this can be an excellent way of individualizing functional reading. In practice it is often hard to find any relevant material that is easy enough for the poorest readers to use.

Size of Groups

Since the distribution of reading ability within a class varies so much from one class to another, the size of the groups should also vary. It would be undesirable to set arbitrary rules concerning group size. Some guiding principles, however, can be set down.

A group in which the children require a good deal of individual attention should preferably be kept small; one capable of much individual or self-regulated activity can be larger. When in doubt about the best group placement for a child, it is usually better to place him in the lower of the two groups being considered; this more nearly insures successful participation, and allows him to be moved up later if he seems ready. If a class has two groups, it is generally desirable for the lower group to be the smaller; similarly, the lowest of three groups should usually be smaller than the middle group. Groups set up on the basis of special needs or special interests can be of any size. Groups of two children can be effectively used for such activities as testing one another on word or phrase cards and for some kinds of reading games.

Flexibility in Grouping

Although there is general agreement that flexibility in grouping is highly desirable, some striking examples of inflexibility can be found. In one school, achievement tests were given in May and on the basis of the reading scores, the principal divided each class into groups which the teachers were not allowed to modify until the next reading tests were given the following May. This is about as bad a misuse of the idea of grouping as one can find. Flexibility in grouping can be of two main kinds.

1. *Changing Group Placements.* Children should be moved from one group to another whenever it becomes evident that their reading needs can be better met in the new group. Children differ in their rates of progress; some outgrow a slow group, others are unable to keep up with a faster group. Sometimes a child who has been floundering as the poorest reader in a group takes on a new lease of life when he finds that he is one of the best readers in his new group. Similarly, a child who glides through his group assignments with a minimum of effort may respond with redoubled energy to the challenge of working at a higher level of difficulty. In making such decisions, it is often desirable to consult the child and respect the child's desires concerning his group placement.

2. *Using Different Groupings Simultaneously.* At least two different forms of grouping should be in operation. In classes with a wide range of ability grouping for developmental reading should be according to reading level, with some use of specific needs grouping as special needs become apparent. Grouping for functional reading can often be in heterogeneous groups, especially if a project or activity unit plan is followed. Recreational and functional reading both provide opportunities for setting up interest groupings. When children belong now to one group and now to another, the possibility of developing a rigid caste system in which the poorest readers become "untouchables" is held to a minimum.

One must avoid the danger of assuming that flexibility is an end in itself, since that leads to the changing of groupings just for the sake of change. Under such a system it is hard to see how either the teacher or the children would be able to settle down and get much work done. Flexibility has value when it improves learning conditions and social interrelationships, and too much change can be as undesirable as too little.

Equipment and Materials

A suitable classroom for instruction by groups should be large enough so that the groups can be separated physically, and classroom furniture should be movable so that it can be rearranged in many patterns. For any group activity involving intercommunication the group should be seated so that all can see one another; a rectangular arrangement with desks pushed together as if to make a large table is often most practical. A large area of chalkboard and bulletin board is desirable. There should be convenient shelving for books and supplies. A library corner should have in it not only space for books, but also a table and chairs to encourage browsing, and a colorful display of books or book jackets. These are desirable features, but none of them is absolutely essential.

Materials for a rich, well-rounded reading program should include:

1. Several sets of basal readers, in numbers appropriate for the groups using them, ranging in difficulty from readers appropriate for the lowest group to difficult readers intended for the grade.
2. Workbooks which accompany the readers. Without these, the teacher has a heavy additional burden of creating suitable comprehension questions and other kinds of written questions or duplicated seatwork.
3. Reading games and puzzles. These can be used when an assignment is finished early, or in a free reading period instead of a book; some simple group games are also desirable.
4. A classroom library of at least fifty books, covering a wide range in difficulty and interest appeal, and changed several times during the year.
5. Reference works. In primary-grade rooms, picture dictionaries should be available. Above the primary grades there should be an encyclopedia, dictionaries, atlases, an almanac, and the like.
6. Special teacher-devised materials, to fill gaps in the commercial materials that are available.
7. Children's magazines and picture magazines. These have a place on the library table.
8. Workbooks not correlated with specific readers. These can be helpful in providing additional practice material for particular reading skills.
9. Related pictures, filmstrips, slides, recordings, and movies to help provide ideational background.

The teacher in a school where supplies are meager should not feel utterly discouraged about being able to provide some differentiated instruction in reading, but it is unquestionably more difficult with insufficient materials.

One of the major sources of difficulty in group management arises from giving a group a basal reader that is too difficult for them. This encourages restlessness, inattention, excessive requests for help, and whispering. The writer has often found, when consulted about a classroom in which group reading was not working well, that excessively hard material was the main source of trouble.

Reading Materials for Group Instruction

In most group plans at least two different readers are required, one of below-grade difficulty and one of normal difficulty for the grade. If there are middle and high groups, they may proceed through the reader at different rates of speed and the high group may be given more supplementary reading or individualized reading.

Materials especially written to ease the problems of group instruction are still few in number. Noteworthy is the *Developmental Reading Series,* edited by Guy L. Bond for Lyons & Carnahan, in which the same stories are provided in two levels of difficulty. There are readers of normal difficulty for the grade, and there are "Classmate" editions which present the same stories with the same paging, and the same illustrations, but with simpler and shorter sentences and easier vocabulary, so as to be about one grade lower in difficulty. The teachers' manuals for this series recommend keeping the whole class together for preparatory activities and discussion, while conducting oral reading and some other activities in two groups. Such a plan certainly simplifies planning and provides a synthesis of whole-class and group-reading activities. It may work very well in classes in which the range of individual differences is not too great to allow an effective two-group plan.

Assignments

In group instruction, while the teacher is working directly with one group, the other group or groups must have definite assignments which they can carry on without help from the teacher.

At the earliest levels, it is often true that one or more groups are unable to carry on any kind of reading activity without the active participation of the teacher. When this is the case, it is desirable to alternate reading with other kinds of activity that the children are able to carry on independently. At first-grade level, independent activities include play in a doll-house corner, painting at easels, clay, weaving, crayons, cutting and pasting pictures, and so on. These can be combined with reading in a rotating plan so that the group reads only when the teacher is with them, and engages in quiet self-directed activities when the teacher is with another group. This procedure is essential in the first grade, and is often needed in grades above the first for one or more groups.

Before starting the group activities of the day it is helpful to take a few minutes to go over the specific assignments for all groups. A group should always have supplementary activities to which they can turn if they finish an assignment before the end of a period. It is helpful to have, for each group, a poster which they can consult if they forget what to do next. The following list was drawn up by one group in a fifth-grade class:

1. Read the pages in your book.
2. Write the new words in your notebook.
3. Look them up in the dictionary.
4. Write answers to the questions.
5. Read a library book, *or*
6. Draw a picture about the story.

With such a plan, it was easy for the group to keep busy for a thirty- or forty-minute period. The faster readers had more time than the others for reading their library books.

Interference between groups should be kept at a minimum. Movable classroom furniture makes it possible to rearrange the classroom for group activities, and is far better for group instruction than furniture which is fastened to the floor. Many teachers keep a semicircle of small chairs near the chalkboard or teacher's desk. When working with a group, the teacher should keep his voice low; the children soon learn to speak quietly also. Routines for distributing

and collecting books, workbooks, paper, and other supplies quietly and efficiently need to be developed and practiced.

Time Schedule. It is necessary to consider with care the total amount of time to be devoted to the reading program per day and per week, the duration of reading periods, and appropriate spacing of reading periods in the school day. In the primary grades the reading program should take on the average an hour or more in the first grade, and about an hour and a half a day in the second and third grades. From the fourth grade on the amount of time specifically scheduled for developmental and recreational reading decreases grade by grade (see p. 87), but the amount of time spent in functional reading in a variety of curricular fields more than makes up the difference.

Each teacher has to experiment to determine the length of period that seems to work best in the particular class. When periods are too short, so much time is spent in getting materials out, warming up to the task, and putting things away again that inefficiency results. When periods are too long, children get fatigued or bored and their increasing restlessness and noise signals to an alert teacher the fact that effective learning has stopped. Young children, with their short attention spans, need somewhat shorter periods than older children; in consequence, the teacher may find it desirable to have two or three short periods a day with a group, rather than one long one. Periods devoted to easy, pleasurable activities can be relatively prolonged; periods requiring intense concentration on difficult tasks should be comparatively brief. Suggested durations for different kinds of reading activities at different grade levels are shown in the specimen group plans in Figures 4–7.

Many teachers plan their reading as a solid block of an hour or more, during which they work with each group in turn. The known facts about the psychology of learning indicate that it is efficient to separate periods of similar activity by periods in which quite different activities are carried on, so as to avoid the effects of retroactive inhibition. "If one period of study is to be followed immediately by another, we should arrange our schedule so that we may switch to the lesson that is least similar to the one on which we have been working."[8] In the planning of a reading program it would seem desirable to interpolate nonreading activities between reading periods, or to follow one reading activity by another quite different kind of reading activity.

Group Names. Some teachers are quite concerned about what to call their groups. They think of them as "the high group" or "the low group," but they realize it would be bad for morale to use such terms with the children. Numbering the groups is not very desirable for the same reason. The assignment of names that imply relative size, speed, or competence is to be avoided, as in Eagles, Robins, and Sparrows, or Airplanes, Trains, and Autos. Teachers should be sensitive to the feelings of the children about the traits implied by group names: Roses, Pansies, and Lilies may be quite acceptable to girls, but certainly would arouse strong objections in boys. Children are quite aware of the comparative proficiencies of groups. "The teacher calls us the red, white, and blue groups, but she might as well call us the fruits, vegetables, and nuts." Choosing names wisely does not eliminate this awareness; it merely avoids rubbing it in.

One way of selecting group names that is quite popular is by discussion and voting, allowing each group to choose its own name. During a unit on Indians, for examples, the groups may wish to choose the names of Indian tribes. This procedure avoids the dangers cited above. It sometimes gives the groups an implication of permanence and stability that one may prefer to avoid. It has, however, worked very well for many teachers.

Perhaps the best way of treating this problem is to make it as casual as possible. Thus, groups with chairmen can be referred to as Billy's group or Annette's group, or the group can be named according to the color of the cover of the book they are currently using. The less fuss made about group names, the better.

Chairmen and Helpers. There are many group activities in which pupils can act as group leaders, making it unnecessary for the teacher to be with the group for that activity. Often a few of the best readers are assigned by the teacher to be the leaders of the less capa-

[8] Kingsley, Howard L., *The Nature and Conditions of Learning,* p. 485. New York: Prentice-Hall, Inc., 1946.

ble groups. Sometimes this privilege is rotated among several children, so that no one child gets conceited or misses too much of his own group's reading activities. An alternative is to let each group select its own chairman, or to have the chairmanship rotate among the members of the group, with each child having a turn. The chairman who is a member of a group is often accepted with better grace than the leader who comes from another group. When a group is not yet able to function without help, it may be possible to have a chairman from within the group who assigns turns to read and keeps order, and a helper from a higher group who can supply unknown words and correct errors.

Helpers can be used during silent reading or workbook practice, as well as during oral reading. One child can be the helper for a group, or each child who needs help may be allowed to select another child as his personal helper. In the latter case, the helper and the child helped may be assigned neighboring seats.

Children do not naturally know how to be effective chairmen or helpers. Sometimes they will give too much help, or too little, or they may become officious or sarcastic. It is desirable to train helpers or chairmen for their jobs, and it is certainly necessary to keep an eye on how they carry out their functions. Since many children consciously imitate their teacher when placed in a teaching role, evaluation of child leadership performance sometimes leads to modification of teacher behavior.[9]

II. Illustrative Group Plans

FOR SEVERAL YEARS the writer has discussed grouping problems with classroom teachers in graduate courses, has presented specimen plans to them for criticism, and has encouraged them to develop program plans that fit their own classes. From this he has become convinced that classes at the same grade level vary tremendously, so that it is impossible to present a plan for a given grade that will

[9] For additional discussions of good practices in grouping, see: McCullough, Constance, "Groping or Grouping?" *Elementary English,* Vol. 31, 1954, pp. 136–138, and Whipple, Gertrude, "Good Practices in Grouping," *The Reading Teacher,* Vol. 7, 1953, pp. 69–73.

fit all classes. The plans described below are intended to be used as sources of ideas, not as specifications to be followed exactly.

In these specimen plans an attempt has been made to adhere to five basic principles. (1) Each plan combines reading by groups with some whole-class and some individualized reading. (2) The teacher is with the group for those activities for which he is most needed. (3) Expectancy concerning what a group may be able to do without the teacher (but with a chairman or helper) is realistic. (4) Length of periods has some relationship to the maturity and attention span of the children. (5) All groups get a reasonable share of the teacher's attention.

Figure 4 shows a week's plan for an average first-grade class in February. The low group is still using a preprimer; the middle group has started a primer; and the high group is near the end of a primer and able to do supplementary reading in preprimers and primers of other series. Reading periods are generally short (fifteen minutes). The teacher guides all reading of the low group, including their use of workbooks. The middle group is expected to be able to cut and mount pictures for a picture-dictionary scrapbook, to play simple word games, and to do some easy workbook or teacher-made seatwork without the teacher. The high group can carry on several kinds of reading activities independently, including individualized supplementary reading, but gets personal attention from the teacher every day. Whole-class activities are included every day and include word analysis, experience stories, dramatizations, and listening to stories and poems read by the teacher.

In Figure 5 a two-group plan is shown, which could be used late in the first grade or early in the second, at a time when the low group is working in a primer and the high group is doing well in a first reader or easy second-grade reader. The low group has the teacher for preparatory activities, guided silent and oral reading, and checking workbooks; they are expected to be able to play simple word games, cut and mount illustrations for picture-dictionary notebooks, and do simple workbook exercises with a helper. Teacher time is evenly divided between the two groups, although some teachers would prefer to spend more time with the low than

Low Group (preprimer)	Middle Group (early primer)	High Group (late primer)
	MONDAY	
T Preparation, Guided reading (15 min.)	Picture Dictionary scrapbooks (15 min.)	Individualized reading in supplementary preprimers and primers, Draw picture about the story (30 min.)
Non-reading activities (20 min.)	**T** Preparation, Guided reading (15 min.)	
	Workbook, word games (15 min.)	**T** Preparation for reader (5 min.) Silent reading in reader
T Guided use of workbook (10 min.)		Workbook page (10 min.)
Whole class: Initial consonant study, ear training games, listing words with similar beginnings (15 min.) Teacher reads a story. (15 min.)		
	TUESDAY	
Non-reading activities (20 min.)	Non-reading activities (35 min.)	**T** Discussion of story, Oral reading, Check workbook, Preparation (20 min.)
T Preparation, Guided reading (15 min.)	**T** Check workbooks Preparation, Guided reading (15 min.)	Silent reading in reader Oral re-reading, group chairman (15 min.)
Duplicated seatwork (15 min.)		Free reading (15 min.)
Whole class: Teacher reads a poem. Children recite poems and rhymes that they know. Children listen for words that rhyme. (15 min.)		

Group 1	Group 2	Group 3
WEDNESDAY		
T Preparation, Guided reading (15 min.)	Picture dictionary scrapbooks (15 min.)	Silent reading in reader, Workbook, Individualized supplementary reading (30 min.)
Non-reading activities (30 min.)	**T** Preparation, Guided reading (15 min.)	
	Workbook, word games (15 min.)	**T** Discussion, Check workbook, Oral reading (15 min.)
Whole class: Initial consonants as on Monday (15 min.) One group dramatizes a story (10 min.), or choral reading (10 min.)		
THURSDAY		
T Preparation, Guided reading (15 min.)	Non-reading seatwork (15 min.)	Individualized reading as on Monday (35 min.)
Non-reading activities (25 min.)	**T** Preparation, Guided reading Word study (20 min.)	**T** Preparation (5 min.)
T Guided use of workbook (10 min.)	Workbook, word games (15 min.)	Silent reading in reader (10 min.)
Whole class: Develop experience story about some new experience, practice reading it. (20 min.) Teacher reads a story. (15 min.)		
FRIDAY		
Non-reading activities (15 min.)	Non-reading activities (30 min.)	**T** Discussion, Oral reading (15 min.)
T Preparation, Guided reading (15 min.) Non-reading activities (15 min.)	**T** Check workbooks, Review new words (15 min.)	Non-reading activities (30 min.)
Whole class: Re-read experience charts or review word analysis of week. (15 min.) Teacher reads story or group dramatizes story. (15 min.)		

Fig. 4. A three-group plan for the first grade. **T** indicates the group with which the teacher is working.

Lower Group (primer)	Upper Group (1^2 or 2^1 reader)
MONDAY	
Whole class: Word recognition skills. Assignments and directions (10 min.)	
T Preparation; guided silent and oral reading (15 min.)	Writing stories (15 min.)
Workbook (15 min.)	**T** Preparation; guided silent and oral reading (15 min.)
Whole class: Teacher reads story (15 min.)	
Whole class: Individualized silent reading, science, social studies and health readers, storybooks, supplementary primers and preprimers. Teacher gives individual help as needed. (30 min.)	
TUESDAY	
Whole class: Develop an experience story and read it together. Assignments and directions (10–15 min.)	
T Check and discuss workbooks Continue in reader (15 min.)	Workbooks (15 min.)
Drawing (15 min.)	**T** Check and discuss workbooks Continue in reader (15 min.)
Whole class: Reading and carrying out directions for number work (15 min.)	
Whole class: Children report on books or stories read individually; audience reading. (15 min.)	

WEDNESDAY

Whole class: Word recognition skills. Assignments and directions (10 min.)

Group 1	Group 2
T Preparation; guided silent and oral reading (15 min.)	Silent reading in reader (15 min.)
Word games (15 min.)	T Discussion of story; oral re-reading (15 min.)

Whole class: Teacher reads story. (15 min.) Individualized silent reading, as on Monday. (30 min.)

THURSDAY

Whole class: Re-read experience charts. Assignments and directions (10 min.)

Group 1	Group 2
T Preparation; guided silent and oral reading (15 min.)	Workbook (15 min.)
Workbook (15 min.)	T Check and discuss workbooks Preparation for next story (15 min.)

Whole class: Dramatization by each group of a story recently completed. (30 min.)

FRIDAY

Whole class: Word recognition skills. Assignments and directions (10 min.)

Group 1	Group 2
T Check workbooks and read orally (15 min.)	Silent reading in reader (15 min.)
Word games, construct picture dictionaries (15 min.)	T Discussion and oral re-reading (15 min.)

Whole class: Reading and carrying out directions for number work. (15 min.) Teacher reads story. (15 min.)

Fig. 5. A two-group plan for upper first grade or second grade.

with the high group. About half of the total reading time is spent in whole-class or individualized activities. If the low group should prove unable to carry out these simple activities without the teacher, they would be given nonreading activities while the teacher works with the high group, and the high group could do nonreading activities while the teacher spends a second period a day with the low group.

The three-group second-grade plan shown in Figure 6 introduces some activities, not shown in the other plans, which can be used in several grades. These include a library visit, a catch-up period, groups organized according to special needs meeting once a week, use of a supplementary reader, and use of a filmstrip. A succession of activities is provided, especially when a group has a long period without the teacher. The program averages about ninety minutes a day, of which one hour is planned for group activities on three of the five days. Whole-class activities of several kinds are introduced, with alternatives provided. Free recreational reading is provided for all groups, with the alternative of nonreading activities for those not yet ready to read independently. When library visits are not made on Tuesdays, a fourth day of group reading would be substituted. The special-needs groups on Thursdays could also be replaced by additional periods for the regular groups. The intention of this plan is to suggest the rich variety of reading activities that can be used to keep the program fresh and interesting. This program, although labeled a second-grade plan, would fit many third grades very well with minor modifications.

The fourth-grade plan outlined in Figure 7 is one that can be used in the fifth and sixth grades also with little change. The low and middle groups follow a fairly conventional program using readers and correlated workbooks. The high group spends most of its group time on free reading, independent workbook and teacher-made practice material, and research reading, with a reader used once or twice a week. The high and middle groups can carry on with chairmen some kinds of activities for which the low group still needs the teacher. In consequence the teacher works with the low group every day, but is scheduled for only three short periods a week with the high group. Two whole-class periods of free reading a week provide an opportunity for attention to individual members of all three groups. The time has been cut to an hour a day, and does not include most of the functional reading that would be carried on in the middle grades.

III. Special Provisions for Remedial Reading

THE PROGRAMS for differentiating and individualizing reading instruction discussed above are based on the assumption that a good developmental reading program must provide for marked differences in rate of learning. Children are expected to progress at individual rates of speed, and a child is not considered in need of remedial help just because he is not up to the majority of his classmates. These plans also include provisions for giving specific corrective help as needed, which can take place during a whole-class activity, during a group session, or during a period of individualized reading. In this way much of what formerly was considered to be remedial activity is now provided for within the framework of the regular classroom program.

Even in schools where well-differentiated reading programs are in operation, the need for special remedial help for a few pupils is not eliminated. The program of the lowest reading group in the class may still be at a frustration level for the most retarded child or two in the class, and the teacher may find it impossible to give those children enough individual attention to meet their needs. It is very difficult for the typical teacher in the fourth, fifth, or sixth grade to provide adequate individual help to a child whose reading ability is three or more years below grade placement. In the seventh and eighth grades the problem of meeting the needs of the very poor reader within the structure of the regular program is even harder. A second difficulty is the necessity for detailed diagnosis when dealing with severe cases of reading disability. A classroom teacher, even when able to carry through such a diagnosis, may not be able to spare the time required when several such cases are present in one class. A third, and probably crucial, difficulty is the fact that some

Low Group (First reader)	Middle Group (2^1 reader)	High Group (2^2 reader)
Whole class: Directions and assignments, each day (5–10 min.)		
	MONDAY	
Silent reading, story introduced Friday Workbook (20 min.)	T Preparation Guided silent and oral reading (20 min.)	Silent reading Workbook Illustrate story (20 min.)
T Preparation Guided silent and oral reading (20 min.)	Silent reading Write and study new words Workbooks	Silent reading in supplementary reader (20 min.)
Art or weaving or free reading (20 min.)	Free reading or art (40 min.)	T Preparation Guided silent and oral reading (20 min.)
Whole class: Phonics (10 min.); weekly reader or free reading (20 min.)		
	TUESDAY	
Whole class: Visit to school library Preparation: Discussion of behavior, book selection, etc. (10 min.) Visit: Librarian tells or reads story. Children select books to take back to class, librarian and teacher helping (45 min.) Catch-up period for absentees and those behind in assignments. Others read library books. (30 min.)		

WEDNESDAY

Group 1	Group 2	Group 3
T Vocabulary review Check workbooks Preparation (20 min.)	Silent reading Workbooks (20 min.)	Silent reading Workbooks Free reading (40 min.)
Silent reading Workbooks Free reading or non-reading activity (40 min.)	T Oral reading Review new words Preparation (20 min.) Silent reading in reader (20 min.)	T Discussion of story Oral reading, selected parts Preparation (20 min.)

Whole class: Phonics (10 min.). Listening to a poem, or oral reports on free reading (10–20 min.)

THURSDAY

Groups organized according to special needs (phonics, expression in oral reading, punctuation, etc.) Teacher spends 5–15 min. with each group. Groups do free reading or non-reading activities for rest of period. (45 min.)

Whole class:

Showing of film strip related to reading program, discussion (15 min.)
Audience reading of favorite parts of library books (15 min.)
Plan a dramatization of a favorite story (15 min.)

FRIDAY

Group 1	Group 2	Group 3
T Guided silent and oral reading (20 min.)	Workbooks (20 min.)	Silent reading in reader (20 min.) Workbooks, free reading (20 min.)
Sound-picture scrapbook (20 min.) Workbooks Word games (20 min.)	T Check workbooks Discussion, oral reading (20 min.) Sound-picture scrapbook or phonics workbook (20 min.)	T Check workbooks Discussion and oral reading (20 min.)

Whole class: Free reading or audience reading or dramatizations (30 min.)

Fig. 6. A three-group plan for second grade.

Low Group	Middle Group	High Group
Whole class: Directions and assignments given to each group every day (10 min.)		
MONDAY		
T Preparation, new words, silent and oral reading in reader (20 min.) Correlated workbook (20 min.)	Free reading (20 min.) T Preparation, new concepts, silent and oral reading in reader (20 min.)	Free reading (40 min.)
Whole class: Reading and discussion of weekly newspapers (20 min.)		
TUESDAY		
T Discuss story Check workbooks Oral re-reading (20 min.) Practice exercises in word analysis, word games (20 min.)	Correlated workbook Compare and discuss answers under group chairman (20 min.) T Discuss story Oral re-reading Preparation for next story (20 min.)	Workbook not correlated with reader. Compare and discuss answers under group chairman (20 min.) Oral reading at sight in reader, group chairman (20 min.)
Whole class: Free reading period, teacher circulates and gives help as needed (20 min.)		

WEDNESDAY

Group 1	Group 2	Group 3
T Preparation (10 min.) Silent reading Correlated workbook (20 min.)	Silent reading in reader Correlated workbook (20 min.)	Practice sheet on alphabetizing (10 min.)
T Check workbooks (10 min.)	T Discussion of story (10 min.) Check workbooks, group chairman (10 min.)	T Check practice sheet, brief speed test (10 min.) Free reading (20 min.)

Whole class: Word analysis, syllabication, using words from reading and spelling; synonyms and antonyms (20 min.)

THURSDAY

Group 1	Group 2	Group 3
T Oral re-reading Preparation (20 min.)	Oral re-reading, group chairman (20 min.)	Research reading for individual or group report topics (25 min.)
Silent reading in reader (20 min.)	T Preparation (5 min.) Silent reading in reader (15 min.)	T Discussion of progress of research (15 min.)

Whole class: Free reading period as on Tuesday (20 min.)

FRIDAY

Group 1	Group 2	Group 3
T Discussion of story Oral reading (20 min.)	Silent reading in reader Correlated workbook (20 min.)	Individualized practice on skills or free reading (20 min.)
Workbook, free reading (20 min.)	Rehearse dramatization (20 min.)	T Oral reading, supplementary reading (20 min.)

Whole class: Book club meeting; audience reading; dramatization; oral reports (20 min.)

Fig. 7. A three-group plan for the fourth grade.

children just are unable to concentrate in the face of the many kinds of stimulation and distraction present in a typical classroom. Strauss and Lehtinen [10] found that the most essential factor in helping brain-injured children to get started on reading was removal to a quiet location where distracting influences were cut to a minimum. Once they had acquired basic reading skills they could return to a classroom and adjust to it. This inability to resist distracting stimulation is found also in restless, hyperactive, nervous children who show no signs of neurological difficulty. For some disabled readers the embarrassment of being watched or overheard by the other children is a severely inhibiting factor.

It is the firm conviction of this writer, therefore, that a good total reading program needs to provide special facilities for children with reading disabilities. Special provisions for diagnosis should be made. At a first level, a reading consultant or remedial teacher can make an intensive analysis of the child's reading performance and can outline a specific program of corrective instruction for the classroom teacher to carry out. At a second level, the child may be referred to a school psychologist for testing of intellectual and personality characteristics, and to an eye specialist or other medical services for study of possible health problems. At a third level, it should be possible to refer the child to a child guidance or mental hygiene clinic where an intensive social, psychological, and psychiatric study can be made.

Special provisions for remedial help should also be available. At the elementary school level two main forms of organization for remedial reading instruction have been evolved. The first is the provision of a remedial teacher to meet the children with reading disabilities in small groups. A special room is set aside and the teacher works with one group at a time. The group (often called a "reading club") is usually no larger than five or six children and has two to five sessions a week with the remedial teacher. As pupils become able to function in their regular classrooms they are discharged and replaced by other children. This plan requires, of course, an extra

[10] Strauss, Alfred A., and Lehtinen, Laura E., *Psychopathology and Education of the Brain-Injured Child*, Ch. 11. New York: Grune & Stratton, 1947.

teacher who has no classroom assignment. Such a plan has been in operation in New York City for about twenty years. In Chicago, the "adjustment teachers" are responsible both for remedial teaching and for some guidance assignments such as conducting the school's testing program. The practical problems involved in such a remedial program are discussed in greater detail in Chapter XI.

The number of school systems employing special teachers for remedial work has been gradually increasing. Some school systems have tried and discontinued such programs, either because of financial reasons or because of the unfortunate accident of having hired teachers poorly qualified for remedial work, whose disappointing results caused the program to be abolished. Nationwide, however, the demand for well-qualified remedial teachers increases faster than the supply. The successful remedial teacher often finds his position expanding to include consultations with classroom teachers and leadership in curriculum reconstruction and in-service training.[11]

Another plan often used in the elementary school involves the creation of a corrective reading home room. The most severe disability cases from a range of two or three grades (four and five or four through six) are gathered together under a specially qualified teacher and stay in that class throughout the day; reading is given a very prominent part in the class program but other subjects are not neglected. In a school large enough to have several classes at each grade, one home room with retarded readers may be set up at each grade level, with the rest of the classes heterogeneous. The class should be small, preferably not more than fifteen children. Necessarily the teacher of such a class must be well versed in methods of individualized instruction, not only in reading but in other curriculum areas as well. By juggling class enrollments it is sometimes possible to set up a corrective reading home room without enlarging the size of the teaching staff. However, when such a class is given to the newest teacher or substitute because the other teachers don't want it, the results are likely to be unfortunate.

[11] Robinson, Helen M., "Qualifications for Teachers of Remedial Reading," *School Review*, Vol. 63, 1955, pp. 334–337.

Many schools have found ways of providing special remedial teaching for their poor readers without expanding their staffs. In some schools the first-grade children are dismissed earlier than the rest of the school, and the first-grade teachers devote the remainder of the school day to remedial work with their own poorest pupils and with disability cases from upper grades. A teacher is detached for remedial work a few times a week in other schools by doubling up classes for lessons in painting, nature study, music, handwork, and so on. One school known to the writer was so crowded that it was necessary to double up, with one set of teachers and pupils in the morning and another set in the afternoon. The morning classes met from eight o'clock to noon, and the afternoon classes from noon to four o'clock. The school was in a poor neighborhood and had a high percentage of poor readers and disciplinary cases. By having the morning teachers stay until one o'clock and the afternoon teachers come at eleven, a full set of teachers was available for remedial work and other special duties for two hours a day. In this way a handicap was turned into an asset. When there is a genuine desire to provide remedial instruction a way can usually be found.

The pioneering efforts of people like Donald D. Durrell at Boston University, Emmett A. Betts at Temple University, Helen M. Robinson at the University of Chicago, and Arthur I. Gates and Ruth Strang at Teachers College, Columbia University, in establishing reading clinics with accompanying training programs in remedial reading, have borne fruit in the rapid increase in the number of reading clinics and reading laboratories in operation. Most of these are connected with colleges or universities; a few, like the one established in St. Louis by William Kottmeyer, have become integral parts of local school systems.[12]

In practically every remedial program a few children (usually 5 to 10 per cent) are found who do not improve under good remedial teaching. While these failures are sometimes the result of injudicious remedial methods, they are probably more often cases in which causal factors such as unsuspected neurological injuries or

[12] *Reading Clinics Directory*, compiled by Walter B. Barbe. Chattanooga, Tenn.: Junior League Reading Center, University of Chattanooga, 1955.

deep-lying emotional difficulties are present. To care for such cases there should be available in the community a child guidance clinic, whose staff of psychiatrists, psychologists, and social workers can make a more intensive and thorough diagnosis than can be expected of a remedial teacher. Child guidance clinics would be swamped if they tried to care for the majority of reading disability cases, and most poor readers do not need psychiatric treatment. It is desirable, however, to have a clinic available to which the small proportion of baffling cases can be sent.

Treatment of these cases may require psychotherapy, or completely individual remedial teaching, or a combination of the two. A growing number of well-trained private remedial teachers, whose background should include supervised practice in a good reading clinic, can be called upon for help with many of these cases.

Provisions in Secondary Schools

At the secondary-school level, with relatively few exceptions (such as specially organized classes for mentally retarded children and serious behavior problem cases) the program of study is departmentalized, so that the corrective home room plan is not employed. The majority of secondary schools that have provided for remedial work in reading have relied on the organization of remedial reading classes, for which the poorest readers are selected on the basis of silent reading tests. These classes take the place of English in the pupil's regular program. Often no distinction has been made between genuine disability cases and retarded readers who are intellectually dull and need an adapted program suited to their abilities rather than a definitely remedial program. Remedial instruction has often proceeded what might be called a "shot-gun" method; that is, instead of basing the instruction of each child on difficulties disclosed by an individual diagnosis, the whole class is given doses of everything that might help some of them, in expectation that each one will get out of the program what he needs. For pupils who have a fairly sound mastery of the mechanics of reading but have little interest in reading, engage in little or no voluntary reading, have restricted vocabularies, or have failed to develop systematic study habits, such programs are usually beneficial, and often result in highly satisfactory improvement. For the more extreme disability cases, individual diagnosis and individual or small-group instruction should be available.

The opinions of eighty-eight junior high school principals in New York City concerning practices with retarded readers in junior high school were summarized by Lazar.[13] The retarded reader was considered a severe problem by 60 per cent and a mild problem by 39 per cent of the principals. Ninety-seven per cent thought that English teachers in junior high school should be able to teach elementary basic reading skills, but only 10 per cent thought that they are equipped to do so. About three out of four thought that the English teacher can meet the needs of pupils reading at fifth- and sixth-grade levels in regular English classes, but only 9 per cent thought this possible for those reading below fifth-grade level. Almost all (96 per cent) of the principals favored the provision of additional special teachers for remedial reading.

Nine recommendations resulted from this questionnaire study. (1) Severely retarded readers should be given special instruction in an out-of-class program. (2) The out-of-class reading program now in existence in selected junior high schools merits expansion. (3) A program designed to train junior high school teachers in methods of teaching reading should be instituted. (4) A consistent effort should be made to develop and supply appropriate reading materials. (5) A developmental reading program should be specifically provided in the regular classroom. (6) The departmentalized program of instruction in the junior high school needs to be re-evaluted. (7) Child guidance services should be expanded so that they are more available for retarded readers. (8) Supervisory services must be extended. (9) The possibility of formulating a new position for Teacher of Reading should be explored.[14]

These recommendations, although developed specifically for New York City, merit serious consideration in other school systems. Aside

[13] Lazar, May, ed., *The Retarded Reader in the Junior High School,* A Guide for Supervisors and Teachers, pp. 43–46. Bureau of Educational Research, Publication No. 31. City of New York: Board of Education, September, 1952.

[14] *Ibid.*, pp. 45–46.

from the sixth recommendation, they would seem to apply with equal cogency to the senior high school also.

Individual differences in reading performance are, as was pointed out at the beginning of Chapter V, uncomfortably great and increase as one goes up the grades. The old-fashioned teacher was protected from some of this range by severe promotion policies and resolutely ignored much of the rest. In some schools a reconsideration of administrative procedures in pupil classification can lighten the burden considerably. The modern teacher has gone beyond the rigid three-group instructional system of a few years ago to develop flexible combinations of whole-class reading, individualized reading, and group-reading activities of several kinds into harmonious patterns that fit their particular classes. Even with the best of classroom procedures there are some children who do not respond to corrective instruction in the classroom, and a well-rounded total reading program should include provisions for intensive diagnostic study and special remedial instruction for these children.

Suggested Additional Reading

BETTS, EMMETT A. *Foundations of Reading Instruction,* Ch. 25.

DURRELL, DONALD D. *Improvement of Basic Reading Abilities,* Ch. 4. Yonkers, N. Y.: World Book Co., 1940.

Grouping . . . Problems and Satisfactions, Reprint Service Bulletin No. 26. Washington, D.C.: Association for Childhood Education International, 1954, 39 pp.

MCKIM, MARGARET G. *Guiding Growth in Reading in the Modern Elementary School,* pp. 134–144, 161–167, 189–215, 324–327, 331–335, 351–361.

RUSSELL, DAVID H. *Children Learn to Read,* Ch. 15.

SIMPSON, ELIZABETH A. *Helping High-School Students Read Better,* Ch. 5.

STRANG, RUTH, CONSTANCE M. MCCULLOUGH, and ARTHUR E. TRAXLER. *Problems in the Improvement of Reading, Second Edition,* Ch. 11.

· VII ·

Evaluating Performance in Reading, I

THE IMPORTANCE of adjusting reading instruction to group and individual needs, which has been the theme of the two preceding chapters, leads directly to the necessity of being able to determine what those needs are. If instruction is pitched at too difficult a level for a child, or attempts to develop skills for which he is not yet ready, small-group or individualized instruction is not likely to be much more helpful than mass instruction.

Determining instructional needs involves setting up objectives, measuring attainment, evaluating the results of measurement, and diagnosing difficulties that come to light. The objectives of reading instruction have been discussed in Chapters I and III. Measurement and evaluation of reading skills are discussed in this and the following chapter. The diagnostic analysis of reading skills is considered in these two chapers, and exploring the causal background is taken up in Chapters IX and X.

I. The Meaning of Evaluation and Diagnosis

THE EVALUATION of reading involves considerably more than the collection of scores on reading tests. Evaluation means arriving at judgments about the degree to which the objectives of the reading program are being achieved. Evaluation can make use of data from many sources: standardized test scores, observation of pupil performance during reading lessons, workbook exercises, evidence of reading interests derived from discussion periods or written compositions, reports on independent reading, success in using subject-matter textbooks, and so on. The data used in evaluation do not have to be quantitatively exact. The important thing is to have some usable evidence concerning the degree to which each important objective is being reached.

The term *diagnosis* is used when a difficulty is discovered and explored. Diagnosis means a careful study of the condition to determine its nature and find out about its causation, with the aim of correcting or remedying the difficulty. The first part of diagnosis, studying the nature of the reading difficulty, is taken up in these two chapters; the causes of reading difficulties are discussed in Chapters IX and X.

II. Determining General Level of Reading Ability

THE MOST IMPORTANT single question to answer about a child's reading is: *how difficult a book can this child read?* On the answer to this question depends not only the classification of pupils into instructional groups, but also the selection of basal readers and supplementary reading materials.

The answer to this question varies somewhat according to the kind of reading and the degree of perfection in reading that is expected. In general, material which is to be read under the guidance of the teacher can be somewhat more difficult than material in which the child is to read independently.

More Than One Level of Reading Ability

Betts has suggested that several levels of reading competence should be distinguished.[1] The *independent* reading level is the highest level at which a child can read easily and fluently, without assistance, with few word recognition errors and very good compre-

[1] Betts, Emmett A., *Foundations of Reading Instruction,* Ch. 21. New York: American Book Co., 1946.

hension and recall. The *instructional* level is the highest level at which the child can do satisfactory reading provided that he receives preparation and supervision from a teacher; word recognition errors are not frequent, and comprehension and recall are satisfactory. The *frustration* level is the lowest level at which the child's reading skills break down; fluency disappears, word recognition errors are numerous, comprehension is faulty, recall is sketchy, and signs of emotional tension and discomfort become evident.

This is a very useful set of concepts and has helped to clarify thinking about the meaning of "reading level." For example, a child may be able to read fifth-grade material with considerable strain, difficulty, and inaccuracy (frustration level); fourth-grade material with acceptable accuracy and comprehension after the teacher explains new words and concepts and provides guiding questions (instructional level); and third-grade material with ease, fluency, and almost complete accuracy (independent level). If the teacher assigns him to a group using a fifth-grade reader and expects him to do supplementary reading in fourth-grade material, his effort and accomplishment are likely to be disappointing. If he is placed in a group using a fourth-grade reader and encouraged to read independently in material of third-grade level the results are apt to be gratifying. If all of his reading is at fourth-grade level he will probably do reasonably well in group lessons but engage in a minimum of other reading. If all of his reading material is third grade in difficulty he may complain about a lack of challenge and maturity in his reader, while enjoying story books at that level.

Making a Quick Class Survey

Dolch has suggested a quick way to use a basal reader to locate the poor readers in a class.

> It is astounding how, in middle and upper grades, children can go on for weeks or months as poor readers without the teacher's realizing the fact. If, however, the teacher takes the precaution at the beginning of the term of having every child read something orally, these mistakes could not happen. She can best make this oral test by telling the class that they are going to become acquainted with a new book, and she wants to know

> how hard the book is. To find out how hard the book is, they will all take part in reading it aloud.
>
> As fast as they can, each will read a sentence in turn. Then several things may happen. First, some child may refuse to read. The teacher will cheerfully say, "All right. Next one read on." Or a child will read with great hesitation and difficulty. To him, the teacher will instantly supply any word that stops him, say "Good," and go on. Since each reads but one sentence, there will be little embarrassment.
>
> But the teacher will have her poor readers picked out for her at once. . . .[2]

One sentence is a very brief and unreliable sample from which to attempt to evaluate a child's reading, even in such a rough, preliminary way, and this writer would prefer to have each child read two or three sentences. Otherwise this procedure recommended by Dolch seems practical and effective as a quick screening test. Since it is intended to get at mastery of the mechanics of reading and does not include any check on comprehension, it can disclose only one side of the reading picture.

A quick test on comprehension can also be given for preliminary screening of the pupils unable to get adequate meaning from a particular book. One can choose a short selection (four or five pages) from near the beginning of the book and ask the children to read it silently. As each pupil finishes, he closes the book and looks up; in this way the slowest readers can easily be spotted. When all have finished, the teacher can read a list of questions and the pupils write their answers. For this kind of brief test, short answer questions are generally preferable to objective-type questions. The children who are unable to score at or above 70 per cent are likely to have difficulty in understanding the book.

A combination of a quick oral reading survey and a silent comprehension test provides a good way to locate the children for whom a particular book is too difficult. It not only discloses the children who are not ready for the book, but also indicates if the book is suitable for the majority of the class. If teachers will take the trouble

[2] Dolch, E. W., "How to Diagnose Children's Reading Difficulties by Informal Classroom Techniques," *The Reading Teacher,* Vol. 6, Jan. 1953, pp. 10–14.

to "try the book on for size," [3] not only with basal readers but also with textbooks in such content areas as social studies and science, many frustrating learning experiences can be prevented.

Using Book Samples to Measure Reading Levels

The simplest and most straightforward way in which to find out if a child can read successfully in a book is to try him out on a small portion of the book. When trying to find out a child's independent and instructional levels (the frustration level is less necessary), a representative series of graded readers can be used.

Preparing Materials. The teacher should start with a well-graded series of readers, of average difficulty, preferably one that is unfamiliar to his pupils. The objection to using a familiar series is the danger that some children may have practically memorized the content of the books they have been exposed to, through listening to others read. The selections chosen should be near the beginning of the book and should be representative of reader material of that level in language and vocabulary. It is usually advisable to start at the beginning of a story. The teacher should mark the starting place in the margin in pencil, and then count off twenty-five, fifty, one hundred and two hundred words, marking each place with a vertical pencil line and the number of words. Usually fifty-word selections are sufficient at preprimer level, one hundred-word selections at primer- and first-reader levels, and two hundred-word selections at and above second-reader level. Sometimes a short sample is enough to show that the material is very easy or too hard, but usually samples of the lengths suggested are little enough on which to base a judgment. If quite a few children are to be tested, it is advisable to prepare two or three equivalent selections in each book and to use them in rotation.

Administration. It is desirable to start with a book expected to be very easy for the child, and to go up through the series one book at a time until a frustration level is reached. Starting with a very easy book helps the child to overcome initial nervousness and to settle

[3] Chall, Jeanne, "Ask Him to Try on the Book for Fit," *The Reading Teacher*, Vol. 7, December, 1953, pp. 83–88.

down in performance before reaching the difficulty levels at which he meets a real challenge.

The teacher should try to put the child at ease and to keep the procedure as relaxed and informal as possible. Before reading each selection, a look at the pictures and a bit of discussion helps to maintain similarity to a guided reading lesson. At first- and second-grade levels, proper names of characters should be told and pointed out. The child is asked to read the selection out loud as well as he can, with no preceding silent reading. If he pauses for about five seconds, or asks for help, he is told the word. When the child finishes the selection he is asked to tell the story that he read. If his account is sketchy or incomplete, supplementary questions are asked. Some people prepare in advance a list of five or ten short-answer or objective questions on each selection. Since it is often impossible to frame that many good questions on such short selections, and variations in the difficulty of questions make the exactness of per cent scores on them highly questionable, this writer prefers the free response kind of comprehension check.

The teacher should select a time when about fifteen minutes will be available without interruption, either during a quiet seatwork period for the entire class, or when the class is out of the room. Teacher and child should sit side by side if there is only one copy of the book. Voices are kept low so as not to disturb the other children.

When pupils are able to read above third-grade level it may be desirable to test both oral and silent reading. The oral test is given as just described, with the addition that the number of seconds needed to finish the selection is timed with a watch. An equivalent selection is then read silently and timed. Comprehension is checked with similar questions on both selections. From the comparison of the two results one can draw conclusions about the child's relative rate and comprehension in silent and oral reading, and this may cast light on the causation of slow silent reading.

Recording. Although clinics in which a great deal of testing is done often mimeograph the selections used so that an examiner can use the mimeographed copy as a record form, for most classroom teach-

First Reader **100 word sample**

Said	for	Words aided
fix	far	far
so	soon	
you	your	
Repetitions //		
Omissions / little		

Total errors: 7
Total words missed: 4 96% accuracy Comprehension: good
Level: instructional

2[1] Reader **50 word sample**

Said	for	Words aided
big		Singing
ast	fast	
Summer	Singing	
riden	river	
garden /	yard	
we	I	
Later	Late	
everything	overnight	
covered	come	
our	the	
was	had	
in	a	
friends	family	
the	of	
Insertions //	big, our	

Comprehension: fair
Total errors: 18 64% accuracy Level: frustration

Fig. 8. Record of oral reading in book samples taken with Harry, a boy of 10 with a severe reading disability.

ers it is not worth while to do this. A useful, accurate record can be kept without it.

It is helpful to use a blank sheet of paper for each book tried. At the top enter the child's name, date, name of book, selection used, and number of words read. An example of this kind of record is shown in Figure 8.

Mispronounced words are recorded in two columns, the word said by the child on the left and the correct word to its right. Words pronounced by the examiner are listed in a third column, labeled "Words aided." Repetitions (R), omissions (O), other types of errors, and qualitative comments are recorded below. When a mistake is made a second time, a check mark is made to the right of the first entry. Comprehension is briefly rated as good, fair, or poor; if a series of prepared questions is used, the per cent score can be entered. At the bottom one can enter the number of errors in word recognition, the accuracy per cent, and one's conclusion as to whether the book is at the independent, instructional, or frustration level for this child. If a parallel silent reading sample is taken, all one needs to record is the rate, comprehension rating, and qualitative observations such as the presence of lip movements.

Interpretation. Essentially the teacher has to decide, for each selection tried, which of the three possibilities is correct: (1) The child can read this book independently with good fluency, accuracy, and comprehension; (2) the child can read the book with instructional guidance; or (3) the child is not ready for the book and shows a frustration pattern when trying to read it. In arriving at conclusions, the following criteria can be applied.

For independent reading, oral reading at sight is fairly fluent. Word-recognition difficulties are not common; nonrecognitions, substitutions, and mispronunciations should total not more than two or three errors per hundred words. In counting errors, mistakes that are spontaneously self-corrected are not included, and minor slips such as omitting a final *s* or substituting *a* for *the* may be disregarded. The child is able to continue reading after an error without feeling blocked. The major parts of the story are recalled spontaneously and correctly, and additional details can be supplied in answer to supplementary questions. The child feels that the selection is easy.

For the instructional level, word recognition errors usually total between 2 and 5 per cent. Comprehension is mostly correct, but free recall is incomplete and some details are forgotten or recalled incorrectly. Reading is mostly fairly fluent, but slows down or becomes hesitant when word recognition or comprehension difficulties are encountered, and some repetitions and omissions may appear. The child's feeling is that the selection is not easy, but that he can handle it.

The frustration level is most clearly evident in the qualitative pattern of the reading. Fluency tends to break down and hesitations, repetitions, and word-by-word reading are common. Signs of emotional tension or distress can be found in the child's color, breathing, facial expression, voice, and so on. He makes mistakes not only on unknown words but also on some words that he usually recognizes without difficulty. If not helped he becomes blocked and has trouble continuing; when allowed to stop he shows relief. Comprehension generally ranges from fair to poor, although bright children sometimes can understand quite well selections through which they stumble with great difficulty. Most children begin to show signs of frustration when word recognition errors rise above 5 per cent. When the child is highly motivated or the selection is very interesting, some children can cope with material of 5 to 10 per cent difficulty without getting upset. Material of higher than 10 per cent difficulty is nearly always frustrating.

The specific errors recorded during these book samples provide material for a qualitative analysis of the child's oral reading problems. Specific suggestions on how to make such an analysis will be found in the next chapter.

No short sample of reading matter used as a test can give perfectly accurate results. Even if the child is not nervous and reads as he usually does, marked variations are found among books that are all supposedly at the same grade level, and even among different stories or chapters in the same book. Estimates of a child's reading level, based on a series of short samples, should therefore be recognized as crude approximations. The child's subsequent degree of success in reading the assigned books should be watched, and easier or harder material substituted if it seems necessary.

Sometimes there is a marked difference between a child's oral reading and silent reading performance. When in doubt, it is probably safest to assign reading material of the difficulty suggested by whichever of the two is the lower.

III. What to Evaluate in Silent Reading

The most important silent reading characteristic to evaluate is the *level of difficulty* at which the child can comprehend. This can be determined by means of book samples, as discussed in the preceding section, or by means of standardized tests. The tests designed to measure this aspect of reading consist of a series of graded selections, varying in difficulty from easy to hard, and usually covering a difficulty range of several grades. One or more questions is asked about each paragraph. There is either no time limit or enough time is allowed so that most pupils have done as much as they can before time is called.

Because *vocabulary* is so important in reading comprehension, most standardized silent reading tests include a separate section for measuring it. In primary-grade tests the child is usually asked to mark the one word out of several that corresponds to a picture. In vocabulary tests above the primary level, each test word is usually presented in a short sentence, with several possible synonyms from which the correct one is to be selected.

Rate of silent reading should be measured on material which is of the same level of difficulty throughout. There are two plans commonly used in measuring rate. One is to use a test containing a large number of short paragraphs of equivalent difficulty, with a question to be answered on each paragraph. Such tests employ a time limit, and the rate is determined from the amount read in the time allowed. Sometimes the score is called "rate of comprehension" and is based on the number of correct answers, rather than on total number of answers; this is neither a pure rate score nor a very good comprehension measure. The other plan presents a fairly long selection of several hundred words and the time required to finish is recorded, or time is called and the child marks the last word read. Informal teacher-constructed rate tests as well as standardized tests can be built on this basis.

Accuracy in silent reading is measured in terms of the proportion of correct answers to the total number of answers. Although few standardized tests provide norms for accuracy, the person scoring tests should make note of a test paper in which unusually high or low accuracy is shown, as this characteristic often has diagnostic significance.

Very few people are equally good at comprehending all kinds of reading material, and tests designed to measure *specific kinds of comprehension* are of considerable value above the primary grades. In tests for the upper grades and secondary school one can find sections for measuring ability to get the central thought of a selection, to note specific details, to follow directions, to find supporting arguments, to locate the answer to a question, to arrange a sequence of events in proper order, and so on. Some tests include sections for measuring abilities that are more properly classified as study skills, such as the ability to locate information in a table of contents or index, or to interpret maps and charts. Tests of specific comprehension skills are helpful in locating kinds of reading in which pupils need more practice.

IV. Informal Appraisal of Silent Reading Abilities

Testing Reading Comprehension

The most important use of comprehension testing is in connection with daily work in silent reading. Much of this is done by means of oral questions and answers. In the early grades, it is often desirable to ask questions which will disclose whether each line or sentence as been understood.

In first-grade reading, the teacher should attempt to insure an active interest in the story by proper preparation. There is an introduction for each story, and for each page in the story. In modern sets of primary readers, the teachers' manuals often contain excellent detailed suggestions on how to proceed, step by step, through the introduction, preteaching of new words and ideas, motivated silent reading, checking on comprehension by means of thought questions, rereading to select parts for oral reading, and the like. The following extract from the manual which accompanies a popular first reader is a sample of how silent reading for comprehension can be guided and checked.

Page 51: Pupils' interpretation of the picture will be extended by reading of the first three lines. After silent reading, suggest, "Look at the car. Now close your eyes and tell us what people you can see in the car. What do you suppose the children are talking about? Let's read the next two lines to find out what Jane said first." After someone has told what Jane said, encourage pupils to make use of the visual imagery suggested during "Presenting vocabulary": "What kinds of buildings would you tell Jim and Patty to look for? Let's read the next three lines to see whether Jane said what we would have said." After silent and oral reading of the rest of the page, encourage pupils to tell how they think Sally felt.[4]

As children improve in reading, they become able to read and comprehend longer units. In contrast to the almost sentence by sentence questioning suggested for first-reader material above, a corresponding page in the third-grade manual of the same series reads as follows:

Page 50: "On this page you will find out what trading has to do with a party." After pupils have read silently, ask, "What kind of party did Susan want to have for Betty Jane? Had Mrs. Hall ever heard of a trading party? What kind of a party do you think it would be? The first two paragraphs on page 51 will tell you what Susan meant by a trading party." [5]

Comprehension of the central idea of a paragraph, understanding the feelings of the characters, and being able to anticipate what is likely to happen next in a story are some of the aspects of comprehension that can be checked by oral questions and answers. When the reading matter is factual in nature, many varied kinds of questions can be asked. Oral questioning has several advantages: (1)

[4] Gray, W. S., Monroe, M., Artley, A. S., and Arbuthnot, M. H., GUIDEBOOK *to Accompany The New* OUR NEW FRIENDS, p. 110. Copyright © 1956 by Scott, Foresman and Company.

[5] Gray, W. S., Monroe, M., Artley A. S., and Arbuthnot, M. H., GUIDEBOOK *to Accompany the New* STREETS AND ROADS, p. 83. Copyright © 1956 by Scott, Foresman and Company.

The question can allow freedom in response, while questions requiring written answers of equal length would usually be too time-consuming; (2) errors in understanding can be immediately detected and corrected; and (3) socialized discussions and exchanges of opinion are possible. The major disadvantage, of course, is the fact that usually only one child has a chance to answer a particular question. For testing purposes, oral questioning is inferior to written questions because the oral questions asked of different children vary in difficulty; but for use during a reading lesson, oral questioning is very useful.

There are many occasions on which a written comprehension test is desirable. This is particularly true when the teacher assigns a selection for silent reading by one group while the teacher works with another group. Usually the teacher provides the group that is working independently with a set of questions to answer. In general, short-answer or objective questions are more efficient for this purpose than questions that call for answers in sentence or paragraph form because they take up much less time. Completion and multiple-choice items allow less opportunity for guesswork than yes-no or true-false items and are therefore somewhat more satisfactory. On the other hand, free-response questions should be employed part of the time, to develop ability to explain and defend answers. Suggestions about different kinds of informal comprehension tests will be found in Chapter XVI. Workbook exercises and standard test items may be used by the teacher as models for framing questions. The questions at the end of stories in some readers, or in their correlated workbooks, may also be used to good advantage.

Measuring Rate of Reading

Informal tests of reading rate are easy to give and should be administered from time to time as a routine procedure in reading instruction above the primary grades. The selection used should be easy for the group, and should be of approximately uniform difficulty throughout. The proper length varies with the grade level of the pupils; in general, one should use a selection long enough to take the average child in the class five to seven minutes, if one wants a fairly accurate measure.[6]

Perhaps the simplest way to measure rate is to start the pupils off together and measure the time necessary for each child to finish the selection. The pupils should be instructed to read at their normal rate, and should be informed that they will be questioned about the selection after they finish. They should be told to look up as soon as they finish and copy on their papers the number that is written on the board or displayed on a card. The teacher should expose a new number at regular intervals; every ten seconds or fifteen seconds will give sufficient accuracy. Knowing the number of words in the selection, the teacher can prepare in advance a little table which gives in words per minute the rate corresponding to each number.[7] If the selection is a long one, some time can be saved by finding the average number of words in a sampling of ten lines from different parts of the selection and multiplying by the total number of lines to get the approximate number of words.

Another technique that can be used is to say "Mark" at the end of each minute and have the pupils mark the last word they read before the signal. The number of words read in each minute can then be counted and averaged. Another variation is to give only one signal to mark, and divide the number of words read by the number of minutes allowed. This procedure is especially suitable for use with selections found in some readers and workbooks in which the cumulative total of words is given at the end of each line. After the rate test is over, the slower pupils should be allowed to finish the selection so as to have a fair chance in the comprehension test.

When a pupil is being tested individually, it is a simple matter to get the total time for reading the selection, using a stop watch or a watch with a second hand, and to divide the number of words by

[6] Traxler, A. E., "The Relationship Between the Length and the Reliability of a Test of Rate of Reading," *Journal of Educational Research,* Vol. 32, 1938, pp. 1–2.

[7] If the number is changed four times a minute, the rate in words per minute for any number is obtained by multiplying the number of words read by four and dividing by the number. If the number is changed six times a minute, multiply by six and divide by the number.

the time to get the rate in words per minute. Norms for rate of reading are given in Table X on page 508.[8]

General Observations

The teacher should be alert to notice the presence of habits which interfere with efficiency in reading. One of the most common interfering habits is the tendency to make lip movements during silent reading. When children begin to read they pronounce each word as they read it. Early silent reading is usually quiet oral reading. With further practice this becomes reduced to inner speech; the person "hears" the words as he reads, but does not say anything. There is a gradual reduction from complete pronunciation through successive stages until completely silent reading is attained. Many children, even in the upper grades and high school, mumble or move their lips when they are supposed to be reading silently. These movements prevent them from reading silently at a faster rate than they can read orally. Lip movements definitely retard speed when they occur above the third-grade level. They can be easily detected simply by watching the child in silent reading. Other habits which interfere with rate of reading and can easily be observed are keeping the place with a finger or pencil, and turning the head instead of moving the eyes as one reads.

The reading difficulties of some children are aggravated by their inability to concentrate on the reading matter. They are restless and fidgety in their seats, and often interrupt their reading to look around the room or out of the window, or to whisper or get into mischief. In many cases such behavior is not a cause of their difficulties but is a natural result of giving them reading matter which is uninteresting or too difficult, and disappears when more appropriate materials are used. In other cases close checking on their accomplishments by frequent comprehension questions is needed. Restlessness and inattention are significant and should not be ignored.

It is not necessary for the classroom teacher to observe the eye movements of most of his pupils, as the information to be gained is

[8] Since speed of reading varies greatly according to the material read, any norms for rate must be considered rough approximations.

not ordinarily of sufficient importance to justify the large amount of time required to observe each child separately. The teacher of reading should, however, know how to observe eye movements, and should for his own information try the procedure with a few pupils so as to get a clearer understanding of the way the eyes work in reading. Observing eye movements should be a routine part of the examination of reading disability cases. Methods for observing eye movements are described on pages 514–516.

V. Characteristics of Standardized Tests

THE CONSTRUCTION of a good standardized test in reading is a long and laborious job that should be undertaken only by specialists in test construction. The general characteristics of standardized tests and methods of constructing them have been admirably described in some of the recent books on testing. Here it is important to note only those characteristics which must be understood for intelligent use of such a test.

The material in a test is selected after careful analysis of the kind of reading a child in the grades for which the test is intended may be called upon to do. Since the test is designed for use in a wide variety of school systems, it must not parallel too closely the content, style, or vocabulary of any one set of books. It must also include a wide enough range of difficulty so that the poorest reader in the lowest grade for which the test is intended can get something right, and so that the best reader in the highest grade for which the test is intended cannot get a perfect score. Nearly always two or more forms are provided which are equivalent in type of question and in difficulty. This makes it possible to retest a child without using exactly the same material.

Every standardized test is accompanied by a manual of directions which tells in detail exactly how the test should be given and scored. It is essential to follow these directions closely. If this is not done, the norms will not be applicable, since they are based on performances under standard conditions.

There are certain points which are involved in the administration of all group tests. In the lower grades tests should not be given in the first few days of a new term, as the children often need some time to become accustomed to a new class and teacher, and cannot do their best until they have settled down. Each child should be provided with two pencils, to avoid loss of time if a point breaks. The directions should be explained clearly in accordance with the printed instructions. Since the test is one of reading rather than of ability to understand directions, it should not be started until all the children know what they are expected to do. If during the test a child asks a question which shows that he has not understood the directions, the teacher may show him what he is supposed to do but must not help him to find the correct answer. During the test the teacher should move around the room and encourage any child whose effort is lagging. If the teacher believes that for any reason a child has not been able to show on the test what he can really do, he should be given another test under more favorable circumstances.

After a test has been constructed it is given to several thousand pupils in schools selected so as to be representative of all the schools in the country. A table of norms is simply a statement of results obtained in this preliminary testing, and may be used as a basis for interpreting results on the test when given to other pupils. The three kinds of norms commonly used in reading tests are reading grade, reading age, and percentiles.

In computing the table of *reading grades* that is found in any reading test manual, the test author first classifies his results according to the grade position of the children. He then finds the median score for each grade.[9] If the median score of all children in the first month of the fifth grade was 46, then any child obtaining a score of 46 is said to have a reading grade of five years and one month, or 5.1. Reading grade scores are usually given in terms of years and tenths, since there are ten months in the school year.

[9] The median is the point above which are half of the scores and below which are half of the scores.

Some tests have two kinds of grade scores, the usual kind based on the scores of all the children in the norm group, and the "modal age" type, based only on the scores of the children who have not been retarded or accelerated. The same number of right answers usually results in a slightly lower grade score when the "modal age" tables are used.

The *reading age* is similar to the reading grade except that the norms are based on the age of the child rather than on his grade position. Thus a reading age of 9–7 (nine years and seven months) means that the child's score is equal to the median score of children who are nine years and seven months old. Reading ages are expressed in years and twelfths.

Percentiles are ways of stating how a child compares with other children of his own age or grade. Saying that a child has a percentile score of 89 means that he has done better than 89 per cent of the children with whom he is being compared, and is surpassed by only 11 per cent. A percentile score of 42 means that the child has done better than 42 per cent of the comparison group, and has been surpassed by 58 per cent. Important percentile scores are the twenty-fifth, the fiftieth (which is the same as the median), and the seventy-fifth. Tables of percentile scores often use steps of five or ten percentile points, from which intermediate values may be estimated.

The *reliability* of a test means the degree to which the test gives consistent results. It is usually found by giving two forms of the same test to a large group of pupils. If each pupil makes practically the same score on one form that he does on the other form, the test is highly consistent and reliable. If many pupils make scores on one form much higher or lower than their scores on the other form, the test has a low reliability. The reliability of a test is usually stated in one of two ways: the coefficient of self-correlation, or the probable error. If a test is being used merely to compare the average scores of different classes, it is not necessary to use a test of high reliability. For the purpose of measuring the ability of an individual pupil, however, only a test of high reliability should be used. Such a test should have a self-correlation of at least .90 for a single grade, or a standard error of not more than five months.[10]

The *validity* of a test is the degree of accuracy with which it meas-

[10] The standard error is a measure of the amount of change that may be expected on repetition of a measurement, through the operation of chance factors producing variations in scores. If the standard error of a test score is 5 months, the chances are 68 in 100 that on retesting the new score will vary from the present one by between 0 months and 5 months, and 32 chances in 100 that the new score will differ from the present one by 5 or more points.

ures what it is intended to measure. If a test has low reliability it cannot be very valid, but a high reliability does not insure high validity. Let us suppose we have a test consisting of thirty paragraphs of equal difficulty, with one easy question on each. The test is given with a fairly short time limit, and has a high reliability. Such a test is intended to measure speed of reading, and may have high validity as a measure of speed. If someone mistakenly attempted to use this test as a measure of level of comprehension the results would be highly misleading, and thus of low validity. Evidence about the validity of a test is nearly always given in the manual of directions. This evidence need not be accepted at its face value, and should be checked by looking up impartial opinions about the test [11] and by a careful inspection of the test to see if the items seem to be designed to measure the phases of reading ability that one wants to measure.

VI. Standardized Silent Reading Tests

STANDARDIZED silent reading tests can be classified according to the grade levels for which they are intended and according to the reading functions they are designed to measure. Under the second method of classification, the major divisions include survey tests, analytical tests, and tests of a single function such as vocabulary or rate. Since the primary purpose of this section is to acquaint the reader with the characteristics of reading tests rather than serve as a test catalogue, no attempt has been made to include descriptions of all available tests.

Survey Tests

The major purpose of a survey test reading is to give a fairly accurate measure of the level of difficulty at which a pupil can read. These tests generally have long time limits, so that the pupil is stopped primarily by the increasing difficulty of the items rather than

[11] For this the reader may consult the *Mental Measurement Yearbooks*, edited by Oscar K. Buros, published by Rutgers University Press, New Brunswick, N.J.

19. Every morning the cows leave the big barn. They go to the fields to eat grass. Look for the barn in the picture. Draw a line under it.

"Mother buys bread at the

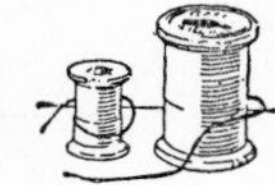

Henry and his brother Peter go to the country every summer. They go wading and fishing in the brook. One day Henry caught three fish and Peter caught five.

28. This story tells about two
boys fish farms brooks

29. Who caught the more fish?
Father Henry Peter Helen

Fig. 9. Samples of paragraph reading tests at the primary level. *Top:* From the *Gates Primary Reading Test.* Type 3, Form 2. Reproduced by permission of the Bureau of Publications, Teachers College, Columbia University. *Bottom:* Items of different levels of difficulty. From the Reading test of the *Metropolitan Achievement Tests,* Primary II Battery, Form R. Reproduced by permission of World Book Co.

by the calling of time. Most survey tests have two parts, one designed to measure reading vocabulary and the other a test of paragraph comprehension. Measures of ability to read sentences and of rate of reading are included in some of them.

At the primary level, the *Gates Primary Reading Tests* [12] are good examples of tests for survey purposes. These include three types of

Stanf. Inter. Partial: Form D TEST 1. READING: PARAGRAPH MEANING 3

DIRECTIONS. In the paragraphs below, each number shows where a word has been left out. Read each paragraph carefully, and wherever there is a number decide what word has been left out. Then write the missing word in the answer column at the right, as shown in the sample. Write JUST ONE WORD on each line. *Be sure to write each answer on the line that has the same number as the number of the missing word in the paragraph.*

SAMPLE. Answer

A-B Dick and Tom were playing ball in the field. Dick was throwing the —A— and —B— was trying to catch it. A ball B

1-2 A mother bird was picking worms out of the ground. Instead of eating them herself, she carried them to her —1— to feed to her —2—. 1 2

25-26 In speaking of gold, the term "carat" is used to indicate the proportion of gold in a given mass. A carat is one twenty-fourth of the whole mass. Thus, a fourteen-carat ring is one with fourteen parts of pure gold and ten parts of some other metal, usually copper. A twenty-four-carat watch chain is pure —25—. A bracelet that is half gold and half copper would be called a —26—carat gold bracelet. 25 26

44-45 Dryden tells us that "Solitude is as needful to the imagination as society is wholesome for the character." By this he means that the art of thinking and contemplation is developed by —44—, but that good character requires that one live in the —45— of his fellow men. 44 45

End of Test 1. Look over your work.

Fig. 10. Sample of a paragraph reading test. From the *Stanford Reading Test, Intermediate,* Form D, 1940. Reproduced by permission of World Book Co., reduced to size.

tests, printed in separate booklets, and designed to measure word recognition, sentence reading, and paragraph reading. The items are arranged in order of increasing difficulty and the time limits are fairly long. In the opinion of this writer, these are not good tests to use with poor readers, who often make artificially high scores on the basis of successful guessing despite a penalty for wrong answers. Other widely used survey tests for the primary grades are the

[12] A list of tests, with data about forms, publishers, etc., will be found in Appendix A.

primary levels of the reading tests that form part of achievement test batteries such as the *Stanford Achievement Tests,* the *Metropolitan Achievement Tests,* and the *California Achievement Tests.*

A representative example of survey tests in reading above the primary level is the *Stanford Reading Test,* which has been very widely used. This test has two parts, one to measure reading vocab-

IX 9→

Sugar beets must be raised where cheap labor can be secured because the plants require a great deal of cultivation, most of which must be done by hand. First the plants are thinned and then blocked to get the correct number in the rows. The roots from which the sugar is extracted are not like the red beets which are eaten as vegetables, but are more like the common turnips. These roots are washed, sliced, and soaked in water. The water is later drawn off and boiled into beet syrup. Then the syrup is changed to a brown sugar called raw sugar. The last step is to send the raw sugar through the refinery, where it is cleaned and whitened. Then the white sugar is ready to be boxed and sold for use in our homes.

41. Sugar beets must be raised where labor is not expensive because they require — 1 much care 2 much washing 3 many plants in a row 4 soaking in water 5 much boiling . . . 1 2 3 4 5

42. What kind of labor is most used in the raising of sugar beets? 1 machine 2 manual 3 difficult 4 easy 5 unusual . . . 1 2 3 4 5

43. The raw sugar is — 1 made into syrup 2 refined and whitened 3 boxed and sold 4 left as it is 5 changed to brown sugar. . . . 1 2 3 4 5

44. The best title for this story is — 1 Blocking and Thinning Beets 2 Colorado Sugar Beets 3 How Beet Sugar Is Obtained 4 Cleaning Raw Sugar 5 How Beet Sugar Is Whitened . . . 1 2 3 4 5

45. Raising sugar beets requires — 1 inexpensive labor 2 syrup changed to sugar 3 sugar to be cleaned 4 many common turnips 5 raw sugar. . . . 1 2 3 4 5

Fig. 11. Sample of a paragraph comprehension test. The answer to each question is indicated by filling in with a pencil between the appropriate pair of dotted lines. A perforated stencil is used in scoring, with correct answers showing through holes in the stencil and needing only to be counted. This test is also adaptable for use with a separate answer sheet that can be scored on the International Test Scoring Machine. Many recent tests are arranged in this way. From the *Durrell-Sullivan Reading Achievement Test, Intermediate,* Form A, 1937. Reproduced by permission of World Book Co., reduced in size.

ulary and the other a test of paragraph comprehension. Each word in the vocabulary test is followed by several others from which an appropriate synonym is to be selected. The paragraph test consists of a series of short paragraphs, in each of which one or more words have been left out. Comprehension is shown by selecting the correct word for the blank space. This test is available in several levels of difficulty, and has several equivalent forms.

Most other survey tests for the intermediate and upper grades follow a similar pattern, although there are minor differences in the kind of questions used to measure paragraph comprehension. They include the *Metropolitan Elementary, Intermediate,* and *Advanced Reading Tests,* the *Durrell-Sullivan Reading Achievement Test,* and the *Nelson Silent Reading Test.* Tests of the same general nature for higher levels include the *Nelson-Denny Reading Test for Colleges and Senior High Schools* and the *Minnesota Reading Examination for College Students.*

Tests which, while intended primarily for survey purposes include measures of rate and accuracy as well as vocabulary and paragraph comprehension, are the *Gates Reading Survey,* usable in grades three to ten, the *Traxler Silent Reading Test for Grades 7 to 10,* the *Traxler High School Reading Test,* the *Diagnostic Reading Tests, Survey Section,* lower and upper levels, and the *Cooperative Reading Tests* C1 and C2, for secondary school and college.

Analytical Tests

In contrast to the survey tests, which are designed mainly to indicate general level of comprehension, are a number of tests intended to give a more detailed analysis of silent reading.

At the primary level, *The Chicago Reading Test B* (grades two to four), and the primary levels of the *California* and *Ingraham-Clark* tests are examples of analytical tests. The *Chicago* test measures comprehension of words, sentences, paragraphs, and rate of reading. The *California Primary* test contains three subtests on vocabulary (word form, word recognition, and meaning of opposites) and three subtests on comprehension (following directions, directly stated facts, and interpretations).

Among the analytical tests available for the intermediate and upper grades, the *Sangren-Woody Reading Test,* the *Iowa Silent Reading Tests,* and the *Gates Silent Reading Tests* have been widely employed. The *Sangren-Woody* is a test for grades four to eight designed to measure seven different phases of silent reading: word meaning, rate, fact material, total meaning, central thought, following directions, and organization. Norms are provided for each part as well as for the total score. The *Iowa* tests, which include an Elementary test for grades four to eight and an Advanced test for high school and college, resemble the *Sangren-Woody* in general organization. They include measures of comprehension for scientific and social science material, general and technical vocabulary, selection of a central idea, sentence meaning, location of information in index and alphabetizing, and rate of reading.

The *Gates Basic Reading Tests* for grades three to eight are intended to measure rate and accuracy in four types of reading: to appreciate general significance, to predict the outcome of events, to understand precise directions, and to note details. They do not measure level of comprehension, as all the paragraphs in each test are on the same level of difficulty. This fact has been overlooked by some people who have used the tests. The time limits are short, making speed an important factor in the scores. They are best used in combination with a level of comprehension test.

The *California* series has an Elementary test for grades four to six, an Intermediate test for grades seven to nine, and an Advanced test for high school and college. Each has four vocabulary subtests and three comprehension subtests. The *Chicago Reading Tests* C and D (grades four to six and seven to nine) include measures of word, sentence, and paragraph comprehension, rate, and interpretation of graphs and maps.

The *Diagnostic Reading Tests* published by the Committee on Diagnostic Reading Tests, Inc., include in addition to a Survey Test, separate tests of vocabulary, silent comprehension, auditory comprehension, general rate of reading, rate in social studies material, rate in science material, and word attack oral and silent. These are intended for secondary school and first year of college. The lower level, for grades four to six, includes tests of comprehension, vocabulary, rate, and word attack. *The SRA Reading Record,* although it has numerous subtests, has such short time limits that it is in all probability mainly a test of rate of comprehension.

Two highly analytical silent reading tests are the reading and study skills sections of the *Iowa Every-Pupil Tests of Basic Skills* and the *Diagnostic Examination of Silent Reading Abilities* devised by Van Wagenen and Dvorak.* The *Iowa Every-Pupil* tests contain subtests on reading comprehension, vocabulary, map reading, use of references, use of index, use of dictionary, alphabetization, and reading of graphs. The *Iowa* tests are available in two levels of difficulty, Elementary for grades three, four, and five, and Advanced for grades five to nine. The *Diagnostic Examination* contains sections entitled rate of comprehension, perception of relationships, vocabulary in context, vocabulary-isolated words, general information, central thought, clearly stated details, interpretation, integration of dispersed ideas, and drawing inferences. Both of these tests make use of separate answer sheets for quicker scoring. They both take about two hours to administer. The *Diagnostic Examination* has three levels of difficulty, covering the range from grade four to college.

The SRA Reading Analysis attempts to provide a wealth of diagnostic information by means of group test techniques. The Aptitude booklet contains tests of visual discrimination and memory, auditory discrimination and memory, motor abilities (cancellation and handwriting), and hearing vocabulary. The Achievement booklet contains tests of paragraph understanding, word discrimination, word recognition, spelling, and arithmetic computation.

The *Silent Reading Diagnostic Tests* devised by Bond, Clymer, and Hoyt attempt to provide a detailed analysis of both comprehension and word recognition skills. Grade scores are provided for vocabulary and four comprehension and appreciation scores, and a profile chart provides a way to show strengths and weaknesses in word recognition pattern, types of errors, visual analysis, and phonic knowledge. This new test seems practical and will probably be widely used.

Analytical tests have the potential advantage over general survey tests of providing the teacher with a profile of the silent reading skills of the pupil in which his relatively strong and weak points may be discovered. In judging one of these tests several points should be kept in mind. If the number of subtests is very large, the separate parts may be too short to be accurate measures, even though the total score may be highly reliable. The time limits for

* This test is now out of print.

the subtests may be so brief as to place an unwarranted premium on rate of reading. The test may require a very long time to score. Finally, in the attempt to provide easy scoring, types of items may be used that do not resemble closely the kinds of reading that pupils ordinarily do. These criticisms do not apply to all analytical tests, but should be kept in mind when making a selection.

Vocabulary Tests

Vocabulary tests for the primary grades are mainly tests of word recognition; above the primary grades the major function tested is comprehension of meaning. The vocabulary sections of any of the good reading survey tests will usually provide satisfactory measures of general vocabulary. Some of the tests for upper grades and secondary school provide separate vocabulary tests in different curriculum areas.

Tests of Rate of Reading

Reasonably satisfactory tests of rate of silent reading are incorporated in the *Iowa Silent Reading, Sangren-Woody, Chicago, Traxler,* and *Diagnostic Reading Tests* which have already been briefly described. A more artificial kind of rate test is exemplified in the *Gates Reading Survey* (see Fig. 12); there are several others like it, including the pioneer *Chapman-Cook,* which has been used extensively in experiments on the relation of type size and illumination to rate of reading.

The results of rate tests are somewhat hard to interpret, since they are strongly influenced by the mind-set of the reader and the nature and difficulty of the material employed.

The Selection of Silent Reading Tests

As there are many satisfactory tests available, the selection of tests naturally depends to some extent upon the amount of time available for testing and scoring, the money available for purchasing tests, and other practical considerations. If the school can provide for the use of only one silent reading test, the test selected should be of high reliability and should include as a minimum good measures of

SPEED TEST

Directions: Read these paragraphs. Draw a line under the word which best answers the question. Draw a line under *one* word only. Do the exercises as rapidly as you can without making errors.

Sample: The sun is warm in summer. Boys and girls like to swim and,play games on the grass. When do we get very hot days?

winter **spring** **<u>summer</u>** **fall**

1. Mary was walking in the snow. She pulled her coat closer but the wind blew the icy snow against her face. What kind of day was it?

pleasant **warm** **tiresome** **cold**

8. At night when all is still, a cat can hear tiny creatures moving. She can also see quite well on a dark night. What can see quite well on a dark night?

boy **girl** **cat** **man**

2. They were pretty, red woolen mittens. They were sure to keep out the snow. How do you think they would feel in the winter time?

cold **heavy** **warm** **wet**

9. The blue roadster was in the ditch. The wrecking car got it out again with just one pull. What do you think the wrecking car had to be?

beautiful **strong** **old** **light**

Fig. 12. Sample of a standardized test of rate of silent reading. From the *Gates Reading Survey for Grades 3 to 10*. Reproduced by permission of the Bureau of Publications, Teachers College, Columbia University.

vocabulary and level of paragraph comprehension. The use of several relatively short and inexpensive tests measuring different functions is sometimes preferable to a single test that is highly analytical. When it is intended to use a single test to select poor readers for more intensive study, a test emphasizing comprehension may be used.

Before ordering any test in quantities, it is desirable to make a tentative selection of a few tests that might be suitable and to order a specimen set of each of those tests. Careful inspection of the test blanks and manuals of directions will usually show one of the tests to be the most desirable one in that situation.

VII. How to Interpret Silent Reading

All the educational testing in the world would be of no practical value if it did not lead to a better understanding of pupils and their instructional needs. Too often in the past tests have been given, scored, tabulated, and then filed away and forgotten.

In the hands of the school administrator silent reading tests are useful instruments for measuring the effectiveness of instruction, and as a basis for the classification of pupils according to their abilities.

The Teacher's Use of Silent Reading Tests

The classroom teacher may use reading tests to determine the average and range of reading ability in the class, to divide the class into smaller groups for instructional purposes, to determine the specific phases of silent reading in which the class as a whole and individual pupils need more instruction, to aid in the selection of reading materials of appropriate difficulty, and to measure progress. When used as part of the diagnostic procedure in studying individual cases of reading disability, silent reading tests furnish valuable clues about the nature of the child's difficulties, help determine the level at which remedial teaching should start, and serve as a means of checking up periodically to determine whether the remedial work is properly directed.

One of the important steps in planning remedial teaching is to determine what materials the pupil is capable of reading. This may be done by using a set of graded readers, as described earlier in the chapter, or by finding the grade score on one or more standardized silent reading tests. Children should not be expected to read materials above the level of their reading grade. In remedial work it is sometimes desirable to start with materials that are one or two grades below the indicated level, so as to insure a feeling of success from the start. It is much better to start below the child's level and work up than to start above it and have to work down.

A real problem in the teacher's interpretation of test results stems from the fact that as yet no standardized tests attempt to distinguish between independent, instructional, and frustration levels. For the most part, their scores tend to indicate instructional rather than independent reading level. Sometimes the difficulty of a test for a particular child makes the experience a frustrating one. When the score on a test contains a large component of lucky guessing, the score is most probably indicative of a frustration level.

Interpretation of Silent Reading Patterns

From a comparison of a pupil's scores on different types of silent reading, valuable clues about the nature of his difficulties can be obtained. Almost any combination of good and poor scores can be found occasionally, but there are a few patterns of reading performance that are found rather frequently. Some of these will now be described.

Suppose that in your reading you came across the following sentence: "The _______ led _______ _______ of _______ _______, which _______ in the _______ _______." It is very doubtful that you could make much sense out of it. If, however, the sentence read as follows: "The road led _______ fields of rippling wheat, which _______ in the bright sunlight," you would get the general idea, even if the words you filled in were not the exact ones intended. There are many children who depend almost entirely on this kind of guessing process when they come across a word that is unfamiliar to them. They are called *context readers,* because they depend on the context or general setting of a word when they cannot recognize it.

Using the context as a clue to the meaning of words is in general a desirable practice. Most good readers make use of it frequently and to good effect. If the reader has no other method of attack on unknown words, however, he will be helpless when the number of unknown words in a selection is large.

There are several characteristics which serve to distinguish the context readers as a group from other types of reading cases. Their performance is usually better on tests of paragraph reading than on tests of vocabulary or word recognition, as there are usually more clues in a long selection than in a short one. They generally score higher on a test which involves finding the central idea of a selection than on one which calls for painstaking attention to details. Their scores on rate tests are usually higher than on tests of level of comprehension. Their reading tends to be rapid and somewhat inaccurate. They are apt to do markedly better on tests of silent reading than on oral reading tests. They are usually of average or above average intelligence, since considerable mental ability is necessary to be able to make correct guesses.

In general, context readers need training in word recognition techniques and in careful, accurate reading. Suggestions for remedial treatment of such cases will be found in later chapters.

For some children the reading of paragraphs is a very difficult task. They can do fairly well on short units such as brief sentences, but get lost as soon as the material gets long or complex. In many such cases it is found that the child is reading each word separately. Word-by-word readers (sometimes called "word callers") usually do better on vocabulary or sentence reading tests than on tests of paragraph meaning. Their speed is usually low, and below their level of comprehension. They can read orally with fair accuracy material which they cannot comprehend. Many of them move their lips while reading silently, and point with a finger to each word in succession. It is often necessary for them to reread material before it conveys any meaning to them.

These children need training designed to increase their recognition span, teach them to recognize phrases and thought units, improve their rate of reading, and give training in reading for meaning.

Some children's reading is slow but otherwise fairly satisfactory. They may be detected by comparing their scores on level of comprehension tests with scores on rate tests. Such children are not very much handicapped on tests like the *Stanford* or *Metropolitan,* because of the generous time limits. They score considerably lower on tests in which speed plays a large part in determining the total score. On such tests they often get right most of the questions that they answer, but are able to complete only a small part of the test within the time limit. Observation of their eye movements usually discloses a short recognition span, many fixations, and frequent regressions. They often make movements of the lips and head and point to each word with a finger as they read.

Figure 13 shows the scores of Pedro, a twelve-year-old boy of Latin-American ancestry, on the *Sangren-Woody* Test. Pedro was in the sixth grade. He seemed slightly inferior in intelligence on verbal tests (IQ 86) but showed normal ability on nonverbal mental tests (IQ 99). The general reading level shown on the silent reading test is low fourth grade. Marked difficulty is shown on the rate test and on the test of finding the total meaning of a paragraph, while his vocabulary score is comparatively good. The test indicates very slow reading, with greater ability to understand sentences than to comprehend the meaning of paragraphs or larger units.

Many reading disability cases show equally poor work on all types of silent reading. These cases show more extensive disability than the groups already described, and need training designed to improve all aspects of reading. In addition to the meager vocabulary, slow speed, and poor comprehension which silent reading tests can disclose, the word recognition techniques used by these children are usually discovered to be sadly deficient when their oral reading is examined.

As an illustration of the diagnostic use of silent reading measures the following case is of interest.

Konstantine was promoted from a bright fourth-grade class to an average fifth-grade class, marked "good" in everything but reading. The class was given the *Stanford Reading Test,* on which she made a grade score of 3.0, and a group intelligence test on which her IQ was 91. Her oral

Sangren-Woody: Form A

READING PROFILE CHART

SHOWING THE READING STATUS OF THE PUPIL IN SILENT READING

Grade Equivalent	Part I Word Meaning	Part II Rate	Part III Fact Material	Part IV Total Meaning	Part V Central Thought	Part VI Following Directions	Part VII Organization	Total	Grade Equivalent
10^{10}, 10^5, 9^{10}, 9^5, 8^{10}, 8^5, 7^{10}, 7^5, 6^{10}, 6^5, 5^{10}, 5^5, 4^{10}, 4^5, 3^{10}, 3^5, 2^{10}, 2^5	33, 32, 31, 30, 29, 28, 27, 26, 25, 24, 23, 22, 21, 20, 19, 18, 17, 16, 15, 14, 13, 12, 11, 10, 9, 8, 7, 6, 5	27, 26, 25, 24, 23, 22, 21, 20, 19, 18, 17, 16, 15, 14, 13, 12, 11	15, 14, 13, 12, 11, 10, 9, 8, 7, 6, 5, 4, 3, 2, 1	11, 10, 9, 8, 7, 6, 5, 4, 3, 2	9, 8, 7, 6, 5, 4, 3, 2, 1	10, 9, 8, 7, 6, 5, 4, 3, 2, 1	12, 11, 10, 9, 8, 7, 6, 5, 4, 3, 2, 1	115, 110, 105, 100, 95, 90, 85, 80, 75, 70, 65, 60, 55, 50, 45, 40, 35, 30, 25, 20, 15	10^{10}, 10^5, 9^{10}, 9^5, 8^{10}, 8^5, 7^{10}, 7^5, 6^{10}, 6^5, 5^{10}, 5^5, 4^{10}, 4^5, 3^{10}, 3^5, 2^{10}, 2^5

DIRECTIONS. Draw a small circle around the number in each column representing the score of the pupil in that part; then join the circles with lines to form the profile. The abilities in which the pupil is strong or weak then stand out clearly.

[2]

Fig. 13. Silent reading profile of Pedro on the *Sangren-Woody Reading Test,* Form A. Scores on the separate subtests range from below the norms on the Rate test and below 2.5 on Total Meaning to 5.3 in Word Meaning. The grade equivalent for the total score is 4.2. Reproduced by permission of World Book Co., and reduced in size.

reading was worse than her silent reading, with much guessing and many mispronunciations of all sorts. As her work was excellent in everything but reading, the teacher doubted the accuracy of the IQ and decided to give her special help in reading. Questioning disclosed the fact that Konstantine attended a private school every afternoon where she received lessons in reading and writing Greek, and after eliminating other possibilities the teacher decided that confusion between the Greek and English alphabets was the main cause of the girl's difficulties. For six months Konstantine was given intensive training in phonics and word recognition, in addition to the regular class reading lessons, and then was tested again. On another form of the *Stanford* her reading grade was 5.5, a highly satisfactory gain of two and one-half years in six months. She was also given two of the *Gates Silent Reading Tests*. On Type C (Reading to Understand Precise Directions), her grade score was 7.0, but on Type A (Reading to Appreciate the General Significance of a Paragraph), her score was only 4.3. Since rate of reading is a more important factor in Type A than in either Type C or the *Stanford*, Konstantine was given a rate test and the judgment of accurate but very slow reading was confirmed. This disclosed the need to change completely the direction of the remedial efforts, dropping entirely the stress on word recognition (since that had been brought up to a highly satisfactory level), and concentrating upon the improvement of rate and ability to grasp main ideas.

Skill in the interpretation of reading test results is not attained all at once. Patterns of high and low scores, and comparisons of silent with oral reading become meaningful gradually as one studies the results of child after child. Like any other instrument, a silent reading test is useful only in the hands of one who has learned how to employ it. Ability to understand test results is, however, well within the ability of a capable teacher who is willing to go through a period of learning.

Suggested Additional Reading

See references at the end of Chapter VIII.

· VIII ·

Evaluating Performance in Reading, II

WHILE IT IS POSSIBLE to develop meaningful interpretations on the basis of patterns of high and low scores in silent reading, as was shown in the last part of Chapter VII, the reason for a particular wrong answer to a comprehension question based on silent reading is not easily located through a study of silent reading only. Faulty comprehension may be due to errors in word recognition, to lack of understanding of word meanings, to incorrect phrasing or misinterpretation of punctuation, to the difficulty or strangeness of the thought being presented, and so on. Some of these possibilities, such as word recognition and phrasing difficulties, are most easily studied through oral reading. In oral reading one can follow a child's reading word by word and phrase by phrase, and the errors are clearly in evidence. Even when one's intention is primarily to find out the reasons for comprehension difficulties in silent reading, an analysis of oral reading performance is likely to be helpful.

I. What to Look for in Oral Reading

Comparison with Silent Reading

One of the first things to find out about a child's oral reading is how it compares with his silent reading. This can be done by determining his grade level with informal silent and oral tests, as described in the first part of Chapter VII, or by comparing grade scores on standardized silent reading tests with grade scores on standardized oral reading tests. Children whose oral reading is superior to their silent reading abilities are usually comparatively good in word recognition. Their oral reading difficulties are likely to be deficiencies in fluency, phrasing, and expression rather than in pronouncing the words. Because of this fact, a detailed analysis of the word recognition skills of these children is often unnecessary. The oral reading of most retarded readers is at least as poor as their silent reading, and in a great many cases it is much worse. Since word recognition errors make up the majority of the errors of these children, a careful analysis of word recognition difficulties is usually profitable when one is working with retarded readers.

Fluency, Phrasing, and Expression

Deficiencies in fluency, phrasing, and expression are readily noted in oral reading. Good oral reading proceeds smoothly and rhythmically. The words are grouped in phrases, and meaningful thought units are indicated by appropriate pauses and inflections of the voice.

One of the common defects in fluency is *word-by-word reading*. The word-caller plods along slowly, tending to make a noticeable pause after each word. When he does attempt to phrase his reading, he may group the wrong words together and may disregard or misinterpret punctuation marks. The voice is usually monotonous. Keeping the place with a finger is fairly common. Recognition may be slow even for familiar words. Some word-by-word readers have marked deficiencies in their word recognition techniques, while others have learned fairly good methods of word analysis but have not outgrown the habit of reading one word at a time. Understanding and memory for what is read are usually poor in word-by-word readers.

In contrast to the word-caller, the *context reader* may be fairly fluent although quite inaccurate. He goes merrily along, skipping words, adding words, substituting one word for another, and when there are too many unknown words he may invent a new story as he goes along. His reading is marked by carelessness and inattention to details. He can often read a sentence correctly after being told that he made a mistake in it. Many a context reader is unable to attack a word that is not in his sight vocabulary by any method except guessing from the context.

Jerkiness, hesitations, and repetitions are other defects in fluency that are easily detected. In some children these are simply indications of nervousness or self-consciousness. In many cases, however, hesitations and repetitions are accompaniments of slowness in word recognition and are employed to gain more time to decipher the next word.

Word Recognition and Analysis

There are several methods that may be used by a child in attempting to solve a word that is not immediately recognized. The word may be guessed from the context in which it is found. If it has been taught in spelling lessons, spelling it may stimulate recall. The words may be sounded out and then blended to get the pronunciation. The size and shape of the word may serve as clues, or the resemblance of the word to another word which is already known may be noticed. A good reader is resourceful. If one method of attack does not succeed he tries another. He knows how to utilize the context, how to blend, and how to employ visual resemblances. Poor readers often restrict themselves to one method of attack and employ even that method poorly. It is important to find out what method or methods a child tries to use as well as how successful he is.

Some children have apparently never learned any technique of word analysis thoroughly enough to use it successfully. They know the sounds of only a few letters, and cannot blend a word when they succeed in sounding it. They have not learned to look for common recognizable parts or phonograms in a word, or to look for resemblances to words they know. They have laboriously acquired a small stock of sight words which is quite inadequate for their needs. They may or may not try to make use of the context. In these cases remedial teaching must necessarily start at the beginning and should consist of a thorough, intense, and systematic teaching of primary-grade reading skills.

Reversal errors are prominent in the oral reading of about one out of ten disability cases. The child who frequently reverses letters or whole words has not learned to follow a consistent left-to-right direction in reading. This tendency may result from any of several causes, among which are immaturity, difficulties with dominance, poor eye coordination, or simply failure to receive appropriate instruction. Methods which are successful in overcoming reversal tendencies all stress the development of a steady left-to-right direction in reading.

The technique of observing the first one or two letters of a word and guessing the rest is quite common. The intelligent context reader is often surprisingly successful with his guesses. Duller children also often attempt to use this technique, but their guesses are apt to be quite inappropriate. Among the commonest errors made by children who rely on this procedure are confusions of words which begin with *wh* or *th* (*who, when, where, which*; or *then, the, there, these*).

Errors on the beginnings of words are less common than errors on the middles of words and on word endings. Many children ignore endings such as *es, ed, ly,* and *ing*. The middles of words are especially apt to be misread. Confusions of letter sounds are common. Among the most common confusions are: *b, d, p,* and *q: u* and *n; l* and *i; h* and *n; m* and *w*; and vowel errors.

Speech

Many teachers of speech and speech correction ask their pupils to read orally for them so that they can make a careful analysis of the child's speech patterns. The classroom teacher cannot help noticing salient facts about the child's clarity of speech and use of his voice while listening to him read. Major speech faults such as stuttering, stammering, lisping, or lalling are, of course, very easily detected. Unclear enunciation and faulty pronunciation should also be noted. Certain types of speech habits are characteristic of regional or cultural groups. For example, it is common in the South to pronounce a long *i* as *ah*; children who speak Spanish or Italian at home often ignore word endings, particularly *d* and *s*; the substitution of *d* for *th* (*dat* for *that*) is frequent among children whose cultural background is poor. The quality, pitch, and intensity of the child's voice also deserve attention. A weak, tense, strained, or high-pitched voice may be a highly significant indication that the child is nervous in the reading situation. Excessively loud, nasal, and singsong voices may also be encountered.

Posture

Few teachers need to be reminded to observe the posture of their children as they read. It is important for general hygiene, and particularly to avoid eyestrain, that the child should sit or stand while reading in a natural, easy posture, with his back reasonably straight, and the book held firmly or supported about twelve to eighteen inches from his eyes, on a proper level, and with adequate light that is devoid of glare. Excessive movement, particularly of the head, should be noted. The persistence of such habits as pointing with the finger beyond the time when they are useful should also be observed.

The Relative Importance of Different Oral Reading Faults

The frequency of different kinds of faults in oral reading varies with the abilities of the children, the grades studied, and the methods of teaching that have been employed. Some idea of the relative frequency of different kinds of faults can be gained from an inspection of Table V, in which the third-grade data come from a study of children in Cambridge, Massachusetts, and the data for the fourth and fifth grades are from the schools of Shorewood, Wisconsin. The five types of faults that were most common in all three grades are inadequate word mastery skill, poor enunciation, inadequate phrasing, errors on small words, and lack of expression. These five difficulties were about as frequent in the fifth grade as in the third, while the other faults common in the third grade were much less frequent by the fifth grade.

A detailed study of the frequency of different kinds of errors in

Table V. The Frequency of Different Kinds of Oral Reading Faults among Pupils in the Third, Fourth, and Fifth Grades

Difficulty	*Number of Children Showing Fault* Grade 3*	Grade 4**	Grade 5
1. Inadequate word mastery skill	28	41	38
2. Poor enunciation	33	39	40
3. Inadequate phrasing	30	37	29
4. Errors on small words	33	26	33
5. Lack of expression	28	24	28
6. Volume too loud or too soft	21	23	8
7. Habitual repetition	22	20	12
8. Bad head movements	30	20	12
9. Word-by-word reading	22	19	4
10. Insertion and omission	39	14	5
11. Ignoring punctuation	43	12	13
12. Inaccurate guessing	36	7	6
13. Strained voice	21	6	1
14. Extreme tenseness while reading	9	6	1
15. Poor posture	8	2	2
16. Improper position of book	8	2	2
17. Uses finger as pointer	10	1	1
18. Loses place	4	0	0
Number of pupils	87	100	100

* Data for the third grade are taken from: Duffy, G. B., and Durrell, D. D., "Third Grade Difficulties in Oral Reading," *Education,* Vol. 56, 1935, pp. 37–40.

** Data for fourth and fifth grades are taken from: Daw, S. E., "The Persistence of Errors in Oral Reading in Grades Four and Five," *Journal of Educational Research,* Vol. 32, 1938, pp. 81–90.

word recognition was made by Madden and Pratt.[1] They tested the oral reading of 1154 pupils in grades three through nine, on both social study material and science material. By far the most

[1] Madden, M., and Pratt, M., "An Oral Reading Survey as a Teaching Aid," *Elementary English Review,* Vol. 18, 1941, pp. 112–126, 159.

common errors were mispronunciations, constituting 50 to 60 per cent of errors in all grades. Repetitions came second, making up 9 to 21 per cent of the errors in different grades. Omissions came next, ranging from 5 to 17 per cent. Additions were found to make up 5 to 12 per cent of errors in different grades. Refusals to attempt words made up 21 per cent of errors in the third grade, but did not make up as much as 10 per cent in any grade from the fourth up. Reversals were least common, amounting to 1 per cent or less in all grades. The additions and omissions were mainly of articles (*a, an, the*), with prepositions next in frequency and verbs third.

In analyzing 37,274 errors made by retarded readers in the third and fourth grades, Bennett [2] found that errors in which the middle of the word was wrong were most frequent, followed by errors in which only the beginning of the word was correct, errors in which only the ending of the word was correct, and reversals, in that order. Failures to observe the middles and ends of words were the most important causes of mispronunciations. Reversals made up 12 per cent of all errors; while this was a minor category, it should be noted that this is more than ten times the proportion of reversals made by the third- and fourth-grade pupils in the Madden and Pratt study, in which the majority of the pupils were normal in reading ability.

An Oral Reading Check List

The check list below is of practical value in analyzing oral reading performance. It does not attempt to provide a complete and exhaustive list of all the kinds of errors or faults that can be found in oral reading, but rather to direct attention to significant patterns of response that are frequently found in oral reading.

1. *Comparison with silent reading*
. . . a. Oral reading poorer than silent
. . . b. Oral reading faster than silent
. . . c. Comprehension poorer after oral

[2] Bennett, A., "An Analysis of Errors in Word Recognition Made by Retarded Readers," *Journal of Educational Psychology,* Vol. 33, 1942, pp. 25–28.

2. *Fluency*
. . . a. Word by word reading
. . . b. Monotone: lack of meaningful inflection
. . . c. Ignores punctuation
. . . d. Phrases poorly
. . . e. Hesitations
. . . f. Repetitions
. . . g. Very slow
. . . h. Rapid and jerky
. . . i. Loses place

3. *Word recognition, general*
. . . a. Small sight vocabulary
. . . b. Errors on very common words
. . . c. Unsuccessful in solving unknown words
. . . d. Inserts words that are not there
. . . e. Omits words
. . . f. Skips lines

4. *Use of context*
. . . a. Excessive guessing from context
. . . b. Fails to use context as word recognition aid
. . . c. Substitutes words of similar meaning
. . . d. Substitutes words of similar appearance, different meaning
. . . e. Omits or skips unknown words
. . . f. Makes errors which spoil or change meaning
. . . g. Makes errors which produce nonsense
. . . h. Reads words correctly in context which he misreads in isolation

5. *Attack on unknown words*
. . . a. Spells
. . . b. Attempts to sound out: . . . single letters . . . phonograms . . . syllables
. . . c. Uses configuration, size, and shape
. . . d. Attends mainly to one part of word: . . . beginning . . . middle . . . end
. . . e. Uses structural analysis: . . . . prefixes . . . roots . . . endings
. . . f. Lacks flexibility in word attack
. . . g. No method of word attack

6. *Specific difficulties in word attack*
. . . a. Lacks auditory discrimination
. . . b. Unable to blend
. . . c. Unclear visual perception
. . . d. Reversal tendency
. . . e. Letter confusions

. . . f. Gaps in phonic knowledge
. . . consonants . . . consonant blends . . . short vowels . . . long vowels . . . diphthongs . . . word families . . . syllabication . . . prefixes . . . suffixes

7. *Use of voice*
. . . a. Enunciation generally poor
. . . b. Leaves off or slights word endings
. . . c. Slurs and runs words together
. . . d. Sound substitutions
. . . e. Stuttering or cluttered speech
. . . f. Voice sounds nervous or strained
. . . g. Volume: . . . too loud . . . too soft
. . . h. Pitch: . . . too high . . . too low
. . . i. Peculiar cadence

8. *Postural habits*
. . . a. Holds book too close
. . . b. Posture poor while reading
. . . c. Moves head while reading
. . . d. Book held unsteadily
. . . e. Points with finger

II. How to Measure Oral Reading

Informal Appraisal of Oral Reading

The practice of calling upon children to read orally, one after the other, has lost its former place as the major activity in reading lessons and has been largely supplanted by more dynamic types of learning activities. Preparation is usually followed by guided silent reading, and oral reading is usually a form of rereading for a definite purpose (see pp. 92–95). The teacher may, for example, ask a child to read the sentence that contains the answer to a specific question. Under these conditions, the teacher and the pupil are both likely to focus their attention on the appropriateness of the choice more than on the qualities of the oral reading. When one wishes to evaluate oral reading as such, the oral reading activity should be planned to provide optimum conditions for a careful appraisal.

The use of book samples to determine the child's independent and instructional levels has been described on pages 156–161 and need not be repeated here. By using a somewhat similar technique, a teacher can make a satisfactory detailed analysis of the oral reading difficulties of each child in a class without using special material.

Each child can be called to the teacher's desk in turn to read ahead at sight. Since preliminary silent reading would give the child an opportunity to puzzle over some of the words, or reread when it doesn't make sense, this kind of oral reading should be done at sight; preparatory silent reading would only conceal some of the child's problems from the teacher. The child should read for a long enough time to give the teacher a good picture of his oral reading; one to three minutes will usually suffice. A written record of mispronunciations, nonrecognitions, and so on, can be taken in the same way as in determining reading level (see Fig. 8). While one child is reading to the teacher, the rest of the class can be busy with seatwork or free reading.

The teacher's first problem is to get a survey of the major kinds of faults the child shows in his oral reading. For this purpose, a check list like the one given on pages 189–193 can be conveniently used. Copies of the check list can be mimeographed, and as the child reads, or immediately after he has finished, the teacher writes the child's name and the date on a copy of the check list and runs down the list, marking those items that are characteristic of the child's reading with a check mark, or a double check if the tendency is very marked.

Some teachers prefer to use a briefer check list, so that the results from the whole class can be summarized on one sheet of paper. A form convenient for this purpose is shown in Figure 14. Teachers are welcome to copy this form. After each child finishes reading, the teacher marks the particular faults that he shows, by making checks or double checks in the appropriate columns. From a record sheet like this it is easy to select the names of a group of children who have a particular fault in common and therefore should be brought together in a special group for remedial work to correct that fault.

Many teachers are skeptical of the value of systematically recording observations about oral reading habits, as suggested in the

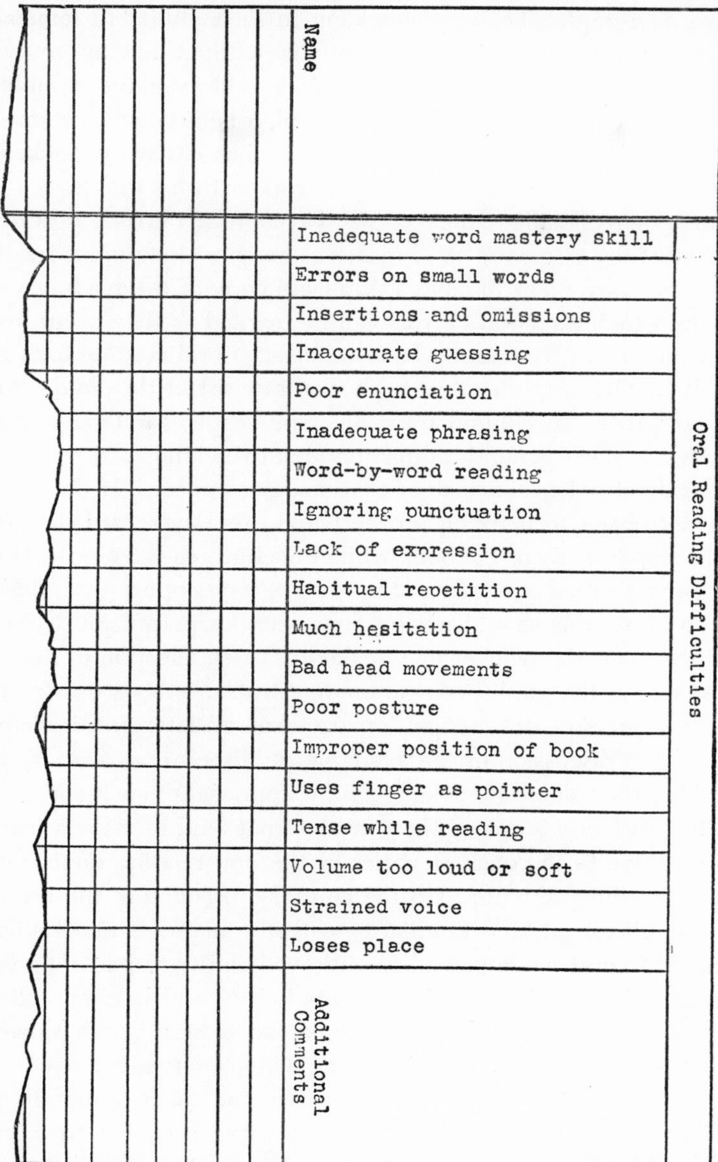

Name										
Oral Reading Difficulties										
Inadequate word mastery skill										
Errors on small words										
Insertions and omissions										
Inaccurate guessing										
Poor enunciation										
Inadequate phrasing										
Word-by-word reading										
Ignoring punctuation										
Lack of expression										
Habitual repetition										
Much hesitation										
Bad head movements										
Poor posture										
Improper position of book										
Uses finger as pointer										
Tense while reading										
Volume too loud or soft										
Strained voice										
Loses place										
Additional Comments										

Fig. 14. A check list for recording the oral reading difficulties of a class.

above paragraphs. They are confident in their ability to remember the important facts about their pupils without having to write them down. If such a skeptical teacher will take the trouble to employ the check-list system once, he will, if he is honest, be amazed at the number of specific faults which he has either overlooked or forgotten during weeks or months of work with his pupils.

For a more detailed study of word recognition errors, it is desirable to list the errors the child makes as he goes along in his reading. It is most convenient to have a duplicate copy of the reading selection, on which the child's errors can be marked as they occur, using a scheme like the one set up for standardized oral reading tests (see Fig. 16). With experience, a fairly accurate list of the child's errors can be written in column form on blank paper for later analysis. Trusting to one's general impression about the kinds of errors made is considerably less satisfactory than making a record. If the teacher does not object to marking up the books, he may record the errors on the pupil's copy of the book while the child reads from the teacher's copy. Another procedure is to mimeograph copies of a selection from a book; this should not be done without permission from the publishers. Or the teacher may make up a test selection of his own, or use one of the published oral reading tests. Methods of analyzing specific errors in word recognition are taken up later in this chapter, following a discussion of the available published oral reading tests.

Taking the trouble to make a careful appraisal of each child's oral reading at intervals during the year does not tend to make a teacher less sensitive to the characteristics of the oral reading done during regular reading activities. On the contrary, practice in the use of a detailed check list, and familiarity with the main characteristics to be noted in oral reading, lead to improved clarity of perception and greater skill in noting significant facts in any oral reading activity. The kind of informal appraisal recommended here is a supplement to, not a replacement of, the teacher's daily observation.

The time that should elapse between one fairly thorough oral reading appraisal and the next should vary according to circumstances. Children whose progress is poor need to be checked more frequently and more carefully than those making good progress.

Once a child has reached a high level of fluency and accuracy in oral reading, thorough periodic rechecks on his oral reading may be a waste of time. If a child does extremely well or very poorly in an oral reading appraisal the teacher should try him out on a harder or easier book. Two-month intervals will prove sufficient in many situations.

Informal Appraisal of Word Recognition Skills

The cleverness that some children show in using the context makes it possible for them to conceal many of the uncertainties that plague them in reading, even in oral reading at sight. Billy may have much trouble distinguishing between *then* and *than,* but if he comes to a sentence that says "John can run faster than Dick," he is unlikely to misread *than.* To get a true picture of sheer word recognition ability, one has to test for ability to recognize words when they are out of any meaningful context. For this purpose, one asks the child to read a list of unrelated words.

A good sample of the total vocabulary of a book can be easily selected. In a book of 145 pages, a twenty-word sample can be taken by taking one word from every seventh page. In order to make it a random, unbiased sample it is desirable to decide in advance to choose each word from a particular position on the page. For example, one twenty-word sample can be taken by choosing the third word on the second line of pages 1, 8, 15, and so on. Equivalent samples can be chosen by starting on page 2, or by taking the word from a different line. No word that appears in the predetermined position should be left out because it seems unsuitable, except proper names, for then the sample would no longer be a random sample. A twenty-word sample is long enough for most teacher purposes.

Sometimes it is preferable to check on the degree to which the new words in the book are known, rather than the total vocabulary. In primary-grade readers the new words are listed by page in the back of the book, and a random sample is easily taken. The glossaries of many books for the middle grades can be similarly used as a basis for a vocabulary test on the new words in the book.

Still another way to construct vocabulary tests for specific reading

QUEENS COLLEGE
EDUCATIONAL CLINIC

Sample Graded Word Lists

Preprimer	Primer	1st Reader	Grade 2
am	all	another	clang
big	cake	cry	fruit
run	how	hopped	quick
dog	from	gate	teach
up	into	snow	sound
look	story	next	music
to	that	bunny	often
me	wanted	thought	straight
it	playing	well	dark
good	milk	running	cannot

Grade 3	Grade 4	Grade 5
cheek	addition	accomplish
reason	blizzard	commotion
plain	compound	decorate
freeze	embrace	essential
knife	groove	marvelous
inch	introduce	grateful
moment	magic	population
president	nonsense	remarkable
shovel	permanent	suggestion
whale	scratch	territory

Fig. 15. Ten-word lists sampling the new words in preprimers, primers, first readers, second-, third-, fourth-, and fifth-grade readers. The difficulty levels are not indicated on copies used with children.

levels is to use the results of word counts. For example, the word lists in Figure 15 were taken from two lists. The words for the pre-primer, primer, first-, second-, and third-grade lists were taken from Stone; [3] the fourth- and fifth-grade lists were taken from Durrell.[4] These short lists of ten words each, prepared on a giant primer typewriter, have proven quite useful in clinical practice. If a child has difficulty with more than three words in any list, he is likely to find many unknown words in typical books of that vocabulary level. If he misses two or three words, the rating for that level is "doubtful."

In using a word list one usually has three purposes. First, one wants to know if the child can recognize the word at sight, with little or no hesitation. If the child does not recognize the word at sight, the next question is whether he can work out the pronunciation. In this, an understanding of the child's method of approach to an unknown word, and of the factors, contributing to success or failure, is more important than getting a score. If the child does not recognize a word immediately, one should encourage him to do his thinking out loud as he tries to figure it out. A child staring blankly at a page does not reveal very much, but if he will verbalize his thoughts, one can find out what he is trying to do and why he succeeds or fails.

Standardized Oral Reading Tests

The *Gilmore Oral Reading Test* [5] is a quite satisfactory standardized oral reading test. There are two forms, each consisting of ten paragraphs ranging in difficulty from first grade to high school. Even in the very easy paragraphs the language is not babyish, and the paragraphs form a continuing story. The pupil reads from a spiral-bound heavy cardboard booklet, with one paragraph on each page. The examiner records errors, time in seconds, and answers to comprehension questions in a separate record booklet (see Fig. 16).

[3] Stone, Clarence R., *Progress in Primary Reading*, pp. 109–130. St. Louis: Webster Publishing Co., 1950.

[4] Durrell, Donald D., *Improvement of Basic Reading Abilities*, pp. 355–376. Yonkers: World Book Co., 1940.

[5] Details about forms, publishers, etc., of tests mentioned in this book are given in Appendix A.

5. On Saturday the two boys do things they enjoy. For them this is the nicest day of the week. Sometimes they help with different household duties. In warm weather Tom and Father mow the lawn. If Mother is especially busy cooking for Sunday, Ned is glad to run errands for her before lunch. The family does not always spend the day working. In summer they often visit a lake near the city, where they spend happy hours swimming and boating. In winter the boys sometimes attend a movie; or, in freezing weather, they skate with their parents. The family takes real pleasure in Saturday activities.

TIME______Seconds

__1. What is the most pleasant day of the week for the boys?
__2. What do Tom and Father do on Saturdays in warm weather?
__3. What does Ned do for Mother?
__4. Where does the family go in summer?
__5. What do the boys do with their parents in the winter?

NUMBER RIGHT ______

ERROR RECORD	Number
Substitutions	
Mispronunciations	
Words pronounced by examiner	
Disregard of punctuation	
Insertions	
Hesitations	
Repetitions	
Omissions	
Total Errors	

Fig. 16. Excerpts from the Record Blank of the *Gilmore Oral Reading Test,* Form B. As the child reads the paragraph, printed in larger type in a separate booklet, the examiner records errors and time, and then asks the comprehension questions. Reproduced by permission of World Book Co.

Norms are provided for accuracy, comprehension, and rate, and directions are provided in a twenty-six-page manual. Although the norms at first-grade level are too severe, this test will probably remain popular for quite a while.

The *Leavell Analytical Oral Reading Test* also consists of a continuous story told in paragraphs of increasing difficulty and has two booklets, one for the pupil and a record booklet for the examiner. There is one form.

The *Gray Standardized Oral Reading Paragraphs* have been widely used since their publication in 1916. A four-page booklet contains twelve paragraphs ranging from first grade to high school in difficulty. A second copy is used by the examiner for recording errors and time; there is no comprehension check. Time and errors are combined to give a single score. This test has been valuable for a long time and is still in wide use, even though so many years have passed, but it is now in need of revision of both content and norms. There is one form.

Section IV of the *Diagnostic Reading Tests* includes a graded series of paragraphs for oral reading. There are two levels of difficulty, Lower and Upper. The other tests of this battery are for group administration.

The only series of oral reading tests providing five equivalent forms at several levels of difficulty is the *Gray Standardized Oral Reading Check Tests.* Although almost as old as the *Oral Paragraphs,* and provided with norms that are very crude, these tests can still be used for repeated measurement of progress at fairly short time intervals.

Other tests of connected oral reading are included in the Gates and Durrell diagnostic batteries, which are described below.

Recording Performance on Oral Reading Tests

All of the standardized tests of reading connected material orally require that each paragraph be timed. For this it is desirable to use a stop watch, although a watch with a second hand can be employed. The examiner follows along in a second copy of the test material, either a copy of the test or a record form which contains a reproduction of the test material. The manual for each test contains directions as to how to record errors and what to count as an error. There are differences on what constitutes an error — for example, hesitations, ignored pronunciation marks, and self-corrected mispronun-

The sun pierced into my large windows. It was the opening of October, and the sky was of a dazzling blue. I looked out of my window and down the street. The white houses of the long, straight street were almost painful to the eyes. The clear atmosphere allowed full play to the sun's brightness.

If a word is wholly mispronounced, underline it as in the case of "atmosphere." If a portion of a word is mispronounced, mark appropriately as indicated above, for example, "pierced" pronounced in two syllables; sounding long a in "dazzling;" omitting the s in "houses," the al in "almost," or the r in "straight." Omitted words are marked as in the case of "of" and "and;" substitutions as in the case of "many" for "my;" insertions as in the case of "clear;" and repetitions as in the case of "to the sun's." Two or more words should be repeated to count as a repetition.

Record the exact nature of each error as nearly as you can. When you are unable to define clearly the specific character of an error, underline the word or portion of the word mispronounced. Be sure you put down a mark for each error. In case you are not sure that an error was made, give the pupil the benefit of the doubt. If the pupil has a slight foreign accent, distinguish carefully between this difficulty and real errors.

Fig. 17. Directions for recording errors on the *Gray Standardized Oral Reading Check Test.* Reproduced by permission of the Public School Publishing Co.

ciations are not counted as errors in the Gray tests, but are counted in the Gilmore — so that it is necessary to follow carefully the directions in the manual of the test being used. This writer uses a wavy line under repetitions, a check mark to indicate a hesitation, a P when the word has to be pronounced by the examiner, encircles omissions, puts parenthesis marks around self-corrected mistakes, and writes in mispronunciations, substitutions, and insertions. As yet no test has attempted to refine its scoring by distinguishing between minor errors, such as omitting a final *s* or substituting *a* for *the,* the major errors. If a large proportion of the errors are minor in character, the resulting grade score probably underestimates the level at which the child can cope with a book.

Classifying and Scoring Errors in Word Recognition

There is no general agreement about the way errors in word recognition should be classified. Monroe uses a classification with ten divisions: vowel errors, consonant errors, addition of sounds, omission of sounds, substitutions, repetitions, addition of words, omission of words, refusals, and words aided. Gates uses four main divisions: omissions, additions, repetitions, and mispronunciations. The mispronunciations include whole reversals, part reversals, wrong beginning, wrong middle, wrong ending, and wrong several parts. Gray makes use of an elaborate classification with sixteen major divisions and fourteen subheads (see Fig. 18). Durrell also uses a highly elaborate set of divisions and subheadings.

The writer has found it most helpful to analyze word recognition difficulties along the lines suggested under headings 3, 4, 5, and 6 of the check list on page 192. The important questions to answer are: (1) To what extent, and how successfully, does the child make use of the context? (2) how does he attempt to attack new words, and with what degree of success can he employ various methods of attack? and (3) what specific kinds of errors does he make, that may require specific remedial attention? Finding the answers to these questions is not an automatic result of counting different kinds of errors, but involves an attempt to understand what the child is trying to do as he reads, as well as noting what he does. It is a qualitative rather than a quantitative method of analysis that is most helpful.

Diagnostic Oral Reading Test Batteries

The *Monroe Diagnostic Reading Tests* employ the *Gray Standardized Oral Reading Paragraphs* (described above) for measuring oral reading of connected material, and two word lists called the *Iota Word Test* and the *Word Discrimination Test* for detecting difficulties in word recognition. The three oral reading tests are used to get a profile of errors. Supplementary tests include a mirror-reading test, a mirror-writing test, an auditory word-discrimination test, a

No. of Set Used_______________

INDIVIDUAL RECORD SHEET
Progressive Analysis of Errors in Oral Reading

Pupil's Name______________________________Age________Grade________

Types of Errors	No. 1	Daily	No. 2	Daily	No. 3	Daily	No. 4	Daily	No. 5	Daily
I INDIVIDUAL WORDS										
1. Non-recognition										
2. Gross mispronunciation										
3. Partial mispronunciation										
a. Monosyllabic Words										
1. Consonant										
2. Vowel										
3. Consonant blends										
4. Vowel digraph										
5. Pronounce silent letters										
6. Insert letters										
7. Pronounce backwards										
8. Rearrange letters										
b. Polysyllabic Words										
1. Accent										
2. Syllabication										
3. Omit syllable										
4. Insert syllable										
5. Rearrange letters of syllables										
6. Incorrect pronunciation of a syllable										
4. Enunciation										
5. Substitutions										
6. Insertions										
7. Omissions										
8. Other types of error										
II. GROUPS OF WORDS										
1. Change order										
2. Add words to complete meaning according to fancy										
3. Omit one or more lines										
4. Insert two or more words										
5. Omit two or more words										
6. Substitute two or more words										
7. Repeat two or more words										
8. Other types of error										
Pupil's test record — Rate										
Pupil's test record — Errors										
Standard Scores for the Grade — Rate										
Standard Scores for the Grade — Errors										
Date of Each Test										

Fig. 18. Record blank for classifying errors on the *Gray Standardized Oral Reading Check Tests.* Reproduced by permission of the Public School Publishing Co., and reduced in size.

visual-auditory learning test, a sound-blending test, and tests of handedness. The material is put up in the form of an individual record blank and a set of test cards. A manual of directions is provided.

The original *Gates Reading Diagnosis Tests* have been replaced by a revised edition, published in 1945. The 1945 edition has two equivalent forms. For each form, the material which is to be read by the child is printed in a spiral-bound booklet. A record booklet of sixteen pages provides space for recording all responses and scores. Included in the battery are the *Gates Oral Reading Test,* a *Phrase Perception Test,* four word lists of twenty words each which provide the material for a *Word-Perception — Flash Presentation Test,* an *Untimed Word Pronunciation Test,* and a test of oral spelling, a reversible words test, an oral vocabulary test, and several short tests for measuring knowledge of phonics and ability to blend. A manual of directions provides the information needed for giving and scoring the tests.

The *Durrell Analysis of Reading Difficulty,* which came out in a new edition in 1955, includes tests of oral and silent reading, listening comprehension, word recognition and word analysis, spelling and handwriting, with supplementary tests for those below second-grade reading. The reading selections, four sets of paragraphs ranging from first to sixth grade in difficulty, are printed on heavy paper in a spiral-bound booklet. There is a record booklet of twelve pages which provides for recording and analyzing results, and a thirty-two-page manual which gives directions for administration and interpretation. Both silent and oral reading are timed and are provided with comprehension checks. Unfortunately, the norms for the oral reading test are based on rate rather than on accuracy. The listening test is read to the child and checked for comprehension, and may be used as a measure of reading capacity. The word recognition and word analysis tests use tachistoscopic exposure, the word first being shown in a hand tachistoscope for quick recognition; if the child misses it, the shutter is opened and he is encouraged to try to analyze it. The supplementary tests include naming and matching of letters, identifying sounds, visual memory for words, hearing sounds in words, knowledge of single and double consonant sounds, and learning rate. This battery has many commendable features and is certain to have wide use.

Oral Reading Word Lists

The *Monroe Iota Word Test* consists of 53 words printed on three cards. The child is asked to read the words out loud one by one, and his exact responses are recorded. All but six of the words are of one syllable, and are chosen to give opportunity for a variety of errors. The norms cover grades one to five.

In his 1945 edition, Gates has four lists of 20 words each. Two of the lists are used for testing quick recognition, using a card with a narrow opening to uncover each word for a brief time interval. The other two lists are for use as a test in which the child has time to inspect each word carefully.

Another useful word list is the one which forms the reading part of the *Wide Range Achievement Test*. This list of 128 words contains a larger number of difficult words than any of the others, and provides grade norms from kindergarten to college graduate level. It is therefore usable in upper grade, secondary school, and college levels for which the other word lists are too easy.

The *Durrell Flashed Word-Word Analysis Test* consists of several lists of words, ranging in difficulty from grade one to grade six. The lists are designed to be used in a quick-exposure device called a *tachistoscope*.[6] This instrument makes it possible to expose a word for about one quarter of a second – long enough to recognize a well-known word but not long enough for more than one quick look. If the child makes an error on a word the shutter is opened and the child is allowed to inspect the word carefully and try again. Norms are given separately for the number of flashed words correct and the number of analyzed words correct. The use of the tachistoscope makes it possible to distinguish between a child's sight vocabulary

[6] Durrell's tachistoscope is a simple cardboard container into which the word list is placed. The movement of a shutter by hand exposes the word through an opening. A simple handmade tachistoscope is shown in Figure 19. Much more elaborate tachistoscopes with mechanically operated shutters are also available; see pages 525–526.

and the words which he can decipher if given enough time. The errors made provide a basis for analyzing the child's method of attack.

Some clinics test poor readers on all 220 words of the *Dolch Basic Sight Vocabulary* list, using a printed list rather than individual word cards. This writer prefers to try only a small sample of the Dolch list to determine if work on it will or will not be needed, leaving to the remedial lessons the identification of the specific words that need to be learned. Tryout on the entire list is unnecessarily tedious and frustrating for most children with severe reading disabilities.

The idea of testing a child for both quick recognition and careful analysis of words is a good one. Flash cards, with a word or phrase printed on each card, have long been used to give practice in speedy word and phrase recognition. For testing purposes, the usual procedure with these cards — covering the card with a blank card, lifting the covering card for a moment and then replacing it — may be used, but is somewhat crude, and makes it difficult to keep the time of exposure approximately constant. A simple tachistoscope can be easily made, and then can be used either for testing or for drill.

An illustration of a homemade tachistoscope is given in Figure 19. It consists of a sheet of stiff cardboard with an opening cut in it, and another piece of cardboard fastened to the first by a brass paper fastener so that it serves as a shutter. The material to be exposed is printed on index cards. Any flash card material can be used in a device like this.

Multiple-Choice Word Recognition Tests

The tests just described present a printed word to the child and note the errors he may make in pronouncing it. Another approach to analyzing methods of word recognition is to pronounce a word and then ask the child to select the correct printed word from a list designed to allow him to make several kinds of errors. A test of this nature is the *Monroe Word Discrimination Test.* It contains forty-seven items. Each item contains, in addition to the word pronounced, six wrong words designed to allow vowel errors, consonant errors, reversals, additions of sounds, omissions of sounds, and complete substitutions.

A discrimination test may be employed when the examiner doubts the accuracy of his diagnosis of errors and desires additional information. In most cases a satisfactory diagnosis can be made without it.

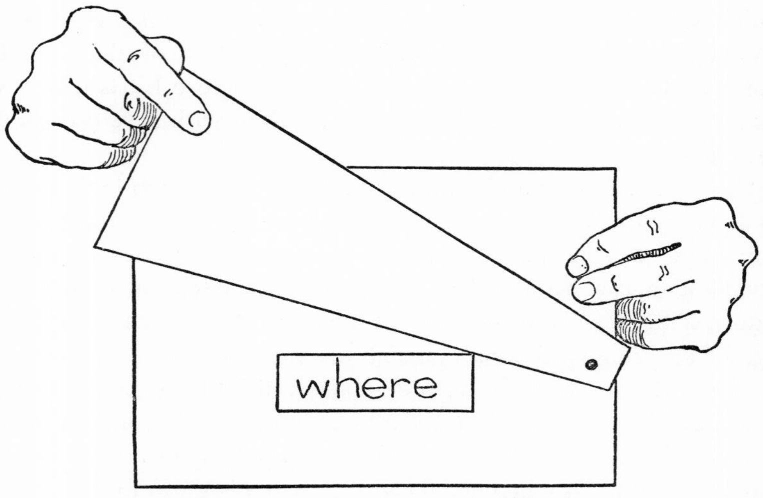

Fig. 19. A simple hand tachistoscope. This can be made in sizes to fit the use of 4 x 6 or 3 x 5 in. index cards. The shield and shutter can be cut out of stiff cardboard or the sides of the grocery carton with a sharp razor blade. To use, hold the shield upright on table top with the left hand. Pick up a card with the right hand and place it against the shield, with the bottom of the card resting on the table, so that the material to be exposed is in the opening. Place the left thumb against the card, holding it in place. With the right hand lift the shutter quickly until its lower corner is level with the top of the shield and let go; this gives a fairly rapid exposure. Very rapid exposures can be obtained by placing the left index finger across the top of the shield and bouncing the shutter against it.

Tests of Phonic Elements and Blending

Because of the importance of phonetic analysis for the attainment of independence in reading, it is advisable whenever a child's oral reading is very poor to find out whether he knows the sounds of the letters of the alphabet and of common combinations of letters. Gates includes in his battery several tests by which the child may be tested for ability to pronounce the small and capital letters, and common two-, three-, and four-letter phonograms and syllables. These tests of word elements are valuable and they, or similar tests, should be employed whenever a child shows weakness in phonetics. Durrell also includes a *Phonetic Inventory* in his battery. It is less complete than the one presented by Gates, as it includes only the alphabet and a few two-letter combinations. Informal tests of a similar nature can easily be devised. It is important to present the letters in a mixed order when testing knowledge of letter sounds.

There are many children who know the individual letter sounds but seem to be unable to blend the sounds into words. Short tests designed to measure blending ability are included in the Gates and Monroe batteries. Informal tests of ability to blend sounds are easy to devise. Take a list of words, such as man, hit, top, spin, mother, penny, and so on, and pronounce each word one sound at a time, as *m-a-n*. In pronouncing consonants one should be careful to avoid adding an *uh* sound. If a child cannot pronounce simple words after hearing them sounded, he is not ready to use blending as a procedure in word recognition.

The *Roswell-Chall Diagnostic Reading Test* is a quick, convenient test for analyzing a child's word attack skills. It contains parts dealing with knowledge of letter and phonogram sounds, solving one-syllable words, short and long vowels, and syllabication. The *Silent Reading Diagnostic Tests* (see page 176) provide a group testing approach to the analysis of word recognition techniques. The *Diagnostic Reading Tests* (see page 175) contain both oral and silent word-recognition tests.

Selection of Oral Reading Tests

For the classroom teacher who wants to use a published oral reading test, the basic requirement is that it contain connected reading material. Such a test in many cases gives sufficient information by itself, although the teacher may want to make a more thorough diagnosis of a few of the poorest readers in the class. In that case he may use in addition an oral reading word list, in which the child gets no help from a story in his attempts to recognize single words. Tests of knowledge of phonetic elements are also useful in the extreme cases, and consume little time.

A clinic or an examiner who expects to handle many reading disability cases should have on hand a variety of tests from which the ones that seem most useful for each individual case can be selected. Most of the oral reading tests now available are included in three batteries (by Gates, Monroe, and Durrell), each of which attempts to include all the tests necessary for a thorough diagnosis and each of which must be purchased as a whole. As these batteries are not very expensive, there is no reason why a clinic or remedial teacher should not have all three of them ready for use.

Even if one wants to make a very thorough diagnosis of a reading disability case, it is not necessary to use all of the tests in a battery. The two basic elements of an oral testing program are a test of connected reading material and a test of reading isolated words. From these one can judge the adequacy of a child's oral reading and determine the kinds of errors commonly made. In many cases this is quite sufficient. If serious difficulties in word recognition are discovered, tests of phonetic elements and ability to blend should be added. Supplementary tests that are not concerned specifically with oral reading will be discussed in the next chapter.

Analysis of Errors in Spelling

There is a close relationship between errors in word analysis in reading and errors in spelling. Not only are poor readers usually poor spellers, but they also tend to make the same kind of errors in spelling that they make in recognizing words. It is therefore advisable to include a spelling test as part of the procedure for diagnosing word analysis techniques. Spelling errors should be examined for the same tendencies that are looked for in oral reading.

III. How to Interpret Oral Reading

In interpreting oral reading one must keep in mind that understanding the pupil's difficulties is the important goal. The errors made should be carefully inspected for the information that they may give about fluency, about the utilization of meaning or context, about the pupil's method of attack on words, and about the particular errors in word recognition that he is most prone to make. These findings must be considered in relation to his silent reading and the other information available about the pupil.

A few cases will be presented at this point to illustrate different kinds of errors in oral reading and the procedure followed in interpreting them.

A record of Harry's reading in book samples of high first grade and easy second-grade material is shown in Figure 8, page 158. Although he made seven errors in the first-grade sample, only four different words were involved, since *far* was missed twice and two errors were repetitions. This material can be judged to be near the upper limit of his instructional level. In the second-grade sample the excessive number of errors in the first fifty words made it painful and unnecessary to proceed any further; the frustration level had obviously been reached.

Inspection of the errors shows that Harry made some use of initial consonants, and occasionally (*ast* for *fast, garden* for *yard*) recognized a word family phonogram. Most of his errors were substitutions involving guesses from context. In the first-grade material some of the words he read correctly were probably good guesses from context. In material as full of unknown words as the second-grade sample he made many errors in his anticipation of meaning so that many of his substitutions ruined the sense; other substitutions, however, like *friends* for *family* and *garden* for *yard,* combined partial cues in combination with context to keep the meaning essentially correct. It was evident that Harry had no consistent methods for attacking unknown words, had a very small sight vocabulary, and depended mainly on guessing from context.

Floyd was a boy eight years and nine months old, with an IQ of 105, in the high third grade. His average silent reading score on the *Gates Primary* tests was 3.0 and on the *Gray Oral Check,* Set II, Test 1, he made 11 errors and took 140 seconds, both scores being below the norms for the middle of the second grade. His reading was slow and inaccurate in both silent and oral reading. Nearly all of his errors in oral reading were mispronunciations; there were no omissions or additions of words, and he tried to pronounce every word. A collection of his mistakes from this test and other samples of his oral reading includes the following:

almost	*for*	among	first	*for*	front
party	*for*	pretty	grass	*for*	glass
rigs	*for*	rags	window	*for*	windows
were	*for*	will	her	*for*	hear
hiding	*for*	hidden	pin	*for*	pine
stood	*for*	stone	feets	*for*	feet
every	*for*	very	spot	*for*	spots
well	*for*	wall	five	*for*	four
want	*for*	wants	like	*for*	likes
cold	*for*	cool	those	*for*	these
that	*for*	there	had	*for*	has
for	*for*	from	slow	*for*	slowly
these	*for*	lies	back	*for*	black
clamb	*for*	climb	neck	*for*	kick

A classification of the errors shows one substitution (*these* for *lies*), two wrong beginnings (*every* for *very* and *neck* for *kick*), eleven wrong middles (such as *well* for *wall*), ten wrong endings (such as *feets* for *feet, slow* for *slowly*), four wrong several parts (such as *almost* for *among*), and one partial reversal (*for* for *from*). From a somewhat different point of view in classification one would note that fourteen vowels were mispronounced, mainly in the middle of words, and relatively few errors were made on consonant sounds. Several of the errors consist of the addition or omission of a final *s* or *ly*. It should be noted that people may differ on how to classify particular errors; *that* for *there* might be classified variously as wrong ending, wrong several parts, vowel error, consonant error, or as two or more of these. No uniform rules for tabulating errors have been established.

The tabulation given above did not supply an immediately meaningful interpretation of Floyd's difficulties in word recognition. For this a different approach was needed. It was noted that in all but two of these words Floyd got the beginning of the word right. He evidently looked mainly at the first letter or two, got a vague impression of the rest of the word, and said a word he already knew which looked like the one before him and started with the same letter. In order to determine whether the vowel and consonant errors were due to lack of knowledge of letter sounds or carelessness, it was necessary to test his ability to give the sounds of the letters when presented one by one. These showed confusion about vowel sounds but no consonant errors. It was also noted that he made poor use of the context, as half of his errors spoiled the sense of what he was reading. The conclusion was drawn that major emphasis should be placed on exercises to develop the habit of paying attention to the whole word rather than just the beginning, on teaching vowel sounds and providing exercises for overcoming vowel confusions, and on getting him to use the context more effectively when faced with an unknown word.[7]

Theresa, a girl of above average intelligence in the high sixth grade, obtained a grade score of 5.8 on the *Metropolitan Intermediate Reading Test.* In oral reading her performance was at the fourth-grade level for rate and third-grade for errors. Her errors showed considerable variety, including omissions, additions, and substitutions of words, reversals of word order, and mispronunciations of polysyllabic words. In reading isolated words her performance was far more accurate than in reading connected material. She had a good phonetic background and could work out the pronunciation of long and difficult words. When she came to an unknown word in connected reading, however, her usual tendency was to guess from the context rather than observe the word carefully and work it out. In addition to this habit of depending too much on the context she read slowly and in a monotonous voice, phrased incorrectly, and sometimes skipped lines. She needed training to improve phrasing and expression and directed practice in utilizing her phonetic knowledge.

Philip's errors in oral reading included many reversals of letters (*bid* for *did, baby* for *body*), reversals of words (*top* for *pot, on* for *no*), reversals of word order (*there was* for *was there*), and errors on the beginnings of words (*hand* for *land, father* for *mother*). He had difficulty keeping the place, and would sometimes jump from the middle of one line to the middle of the next line. These errors were judged to indicate a failure to establish consistent left-to-right eye movements, and training was instituted to encourage proper direction in reading and placing emphasis on the beginnings of words.

IV. Diagnostic Use of Sample Lessons

In some of the early approaches in diagnosing reading disabilities, tests of associative learning were used to try to give a clear picture of why the child had trouble learning to recognize words. Tests were used that involved the associating of nonsense syllables with geometric forms, meaningful words with geometric forms, real words with squiggles that looked something like printed words, and so on. These tests fell into disuse when most users found that the results

[7] Remedial procedures for improving word recognition are discussed in detail in Chapter XIV.

were of little help in planning a remedial approach. However, the idea that it is desirable to test the child's ability to learn by trying him in genuine learning tasks has real merit.

The idea of using miniature sample remedial lessons as a diagnostic procedure for reading was developed by the writer and his colleague Florence Roswell several years ago, and has been used in their diagnostic procedures ever since. A similar approach was used by Gates and Russell in their *Spelling Diagnosis Tests.* The directions currently being used are as follows: [8]

The entire session is informal and permissive. There is a considerable amount of give and take and flexibility in approach.

The examiner should note qualitative observations about the child's ability to profit from reading instruction. Such factors as quick or slow grasp, tempo of work, need for repetition of instructions, degree of motivation required, resistance to specific materials, ability to exert effort, to give sustained attention, and to recall what is taught, are of significance in interpreting the results of sample lessons.

Several procedures should be tried until success with at least one method is clearly apparent. If time allows, a variety of materials should be presented so as to obtain some impression of the child's reactions to readers, workbooks, and game-type devices. Any success should be liberally praised and failure minimized. In such a brief period we have been able to demonstrate to many children that they have the ability to learn to read. We have found that, in most cases, this experience has proven to be a powerful motivating force for future reading instruction.

The procedures that are described below are to be used at the discretion of the examiner, following careful analysis of the diagnostic reading test results. Thus, which methods to use and what level at which to begin the sample lessons will be based on an appraisal of the child's basic reading skills as indicated on the tests.

1. *Visual Method.* For the child who is a non-reader or almost a non-reader it is advisable to begin with a simple visual approach to word recognition which is essentially one of learning words by means of picture clues.

For materials, one needs several cards, each with one picture illustrating a well-known object such as a cake, a window, a table, a book, etc.

[8] Harris, A. J., and Roswell, Florence G., "Clinical Diagnosis of Reading Disability," *Journal of Psychology,* Vol. 36, 1953, pp. 323–340.

The word is printed or typed under the picture. On another set of cards the words are printed without pictures. Test the child to make sure he does not already know the words, and select about five for teaching.

Present the first picture card, point to the word, and tell the child the word. Ask him to say the word several times while looking at it. Then ask him to find the non-illustrated card with the same word on it. When the child thinks he has learned the word, proceed to the next illustrated word. After five words have been studied, shuffle the five non-illustrated cards and test him on them. If he is successful, re-test about 30 minutes later.

It may be desirable to follow up by teaching a few words in a preprimer workbook, followed by reading the corresponding preprimer. If the child objects to this material, it may be necessary to avoid using readers in the early stages of remedial instruction.

If the child cannot succeed with a visual approach of this sort, it will probably be necessary to use either a visual motor or kinaesthetic procedure in the early phases of remediation. If none of these three is successful, one is probably dealing either with a severe emotional blocking requiring psychotherapy, or with an organic neurological condition similar to an aphasia. In the latter case, progress is likely to be very slow, and work on a reading readiness level may be needed for a long time before the child is capable of learning and remembering word forms.

2. *Word Family Approach.* If the child can grasp a visual procedure readily and shows some knowledge of letter sounds a Word Family method may be tried. This technique of word analysis is especially useful for those children who possess only rudimentary blending ability and who are not yet able to cope with a letter by letter sound-blending procedure described under Phonic Method. It affords a limited degree of independence in word analysis. For example a known word such as "man" may be transformed into "fan, can, ran," by changing the initial consonant. The words learned in the visual lesson may be developed in the same way: "cake, lake, bake, rake, take; book, look, cook, took, hook," etc.

3. *Phonic Method.* If a child shows ability to blend together three sounds that are presented orally such as *b-a-t,* it is safe to try a phonic approach. Teach or review the sounds of about four consonants and the short vowel *a.* The sounds of the letters are presented singly as follows: Show him the letter *m* (use lower case letters). "This is *m* and the sound is mmm as in man. Now I am going to give you some other words that begin with *m.* Listen and try to hear the *m* at the beginning of each word: meat, must, make, milk, etc. Can you hear the *m*? Now give me some words that begin with *m.*" Help him with suggestions if necessary. Proceed the same way with *f, s, t, d.*

Teach short vowel sound of "a." "This is *a,* and the sound is ă as in apple."

"Now I am going to say a word quickly, then slowly. Listen. The word is 'cat.' Now I am going to say it slowly 'c-a-t.' This is how it looks in writing." Use anagrams to form the word "c-a-t," "cat." "See if you can put them together to make 'cat.'" Ask him to sound the word out as he does it. Help him, if necessary. Then show him how you can change it to mat, fat, sat, etc.

Write a sentence containing the words, such as "The fat cat sat on the mat."

Change the final sounds: sat to sad, mat to mad, mad to man, fat to fan. Dictate the words to ascertain whether he can write them and sound them as he writes them.

Present words in mixed order: sat, fan, mad, bat, etc. If he is able to read them, there is evidence that he is likely to succeed with a phonic approach.

If a child shows lack of blending ability or is unable to name words that begin with letter sounds it would be advisable to postpone the use of a phonic procedure until after he has had training in auditory discrimination and sound-blending.

4. *Visual-Motor Method.* Choose about three words with which the child is unfamiliar (about 5 to 8 letters in length) such as *friend, airplane, pilot.* Present each word separately. Print the word clearly on a card. Say, "This word is 'friend.' Take a good look at it. What is the word? Now close your eyes. Can you see it with your eyes closed? Look again. What is the word?" Remove the word and ask him to write it. Have him compare his word with that on the card. If incorrect, repeat the above procedure, present the word, pronounce it, have him try to visualize it and then write it again. Sometimes it is necessary to show the card several times before he is able to write it. If he has much difficulty with a word, try another. If he reproduces the word correctly, have him write it again, covering up his previous writing so as to be sure he is recalling the word from memory rather than merely copying it. Check each time to see that it is done correctly. After a period of time has elapsed, review the words.

5. *Kinaesthetic Method.* The brief summmary given below is based on the method fully described by Fernald. Only the initial stages used in teaching by a Kinaesthetic procedure are presented here.

A short period of orientation is suggested. Tell the child that you are going to teach him to read by means of an entirely new method. Assure him as to its value by telling him that other people who have had difficulty with their reading learned in this way. Describe the procedure to him.

Write the word with a crayon on paper in large size script, or in print (letters approximately 2 inches high). The child traces the word with his index finger (or index finger and thumb, if he wishes) saying each part of the word as he traces it. He repeats this as many times as necessary in order to write the word without looking at the original one. When he appears to know it, he writes it on another sheet of paper. In cases of error or if the child hesitates and seems unable to complete the word, he retraces the word as a whole. He is not permitted to erase in order tc correct errors. If he has difficulty recalling the word he should be encouraged to trace it over and over and then to write it without consulting the original writing.

It is evident that any approach may be used as a starting point so as to insure success in learning to read from the very outset of remedial instruction. However, before long, such procedure must be supplemented by others because a successful reader must have a variety of techniques at his command. It is not necessary to try all five methods listed above. It will be found that most children can learn by at least one of the first three methods. In such cases it is usually unnecessary to try Procedures 4 and 5. However, in cases of severe disability where children cannot learn by a simple visual approach and cannot synthesize sounds together as required in a phonic procedure, the Visual-Motor and Kinaesthetic methods should be tried. Trial lessons may be used similarly at all levels and should be varied according to the needs of the case.

The principle of sample word-study lessons has been developed into a standardized technique by Mills.[9] Four methods are used: visual, phonic, kinesthetic, and combined. The examiner spends fifteen minutes with each method, teaching ten words. While his adaptation seems to this writer to be quite time-consuming and very fatiguing to the child, reading clinics and remedial teachers may find it a real addition to available diagnostic procedures. The picture-word cards at primer, first-, second-, and third-grade levels which form part of the Mills test material are in themselves well worth having.

The Learning Rate test which is part of the 1955 edition of the *Durrell Analysis of Reading Difficulty* utilizes only a purely visual method of word study and presents too much material to be learned for one lesson. A good result on this test is probably a safe indicator

[9] Mills, Robert E., *Manual for the Learning Methods Test.* Gainesville, Florida: Reading Laboratory and Clinic, University of Florida, 1954.

that the child can build a sight vocabulary by visual study, but a poor result may be ambiguous.

To this writer the essence of the sample lesson is a situation in which the child's behavior as a learner can be carefully observed and evaluated. Qualitative observation and interpretation are more important than numerical scores or ratings. Such characteristics as interest, attentiveness, distractability, perseverance, effort, reaction to success, reaction to failure, anxiety, discouragement, and efforts to evade the task are some of the characteristics which may be observed and judged. A standardized procedure and scoring may not draw one's attention away from these qualitative factors, but the temptation to rely on scores is strong. For these reasons the writer prefers to use sample lessons in a flexible, unstandardized way.

In these two chapters the analysis of reading performance has been treated in some detail. Consideration has been given both to informal teacher-constructed procedures and to standardized tests. Methods were considered for determining reading level, comprehension, and rate, fluency and accuracy in oral reading, word recognition skills, and learning potentialities in word recognition. These techniques form an important part of reading diagnosis. Equally important is the study of the types of handicaps which may create or intensify a reading problem. This important question will be taken up in the next two chapters.

Suggested Additional Reading

Broom, M. E., Mary A. E. Duncan, Dorothy Emig, and Josephine Steuber. *Effective Reading Instruction,* Second Edition, Ch. 11. New York: McGraw-Hill Book Co., 1951.

Brueckner, Leo J., and Guy L. Bond. *The Diagnosis and Treatment of Learning Difficulties,* Chs. 4 and 6. New York: Appleton-Century-Crofts, 1955.

Durrell, Donald D. *Improvement of Basic Reading Abilities,* Chs. 2 and 13.

Gates, Arthur I. *Improvement of Reading,* Third Edition, Chs. 3, 6, and Appendix 2. New York: The Macmillan Co., 1947.

GREENE, HARRY A., A. N. JORGENSEN, and J. R. GERBERICH. *Measurement and Evaluation in the Elementary School,* Second Edition, Ch. XV. New York: Longmans, Green & Co., 1953.

MCKIM, MARGARET G. *Guiding Growth in Reading in the Modern Elementary School,* Ch. 13.

STRANG, RUTH, CONSTANCE M. MCCULLOUGH, and ARTHUR E. TRAXLER. *Problems in the Improvement of Reading,* Second Edition, Chs. 12 and 13.

TORGERSON, THEODORE L., and GEORGIA SACHS ADAMS. *Measurement and Evaluation for Elementary School Teachers,* Chs. 9 and 11. New York: Dryden Press, 1954.

· IX ·

Exploring the Causes of Reading Difficulties, I

LEARNING TO UNDERSTAND a child who is having trouble in reading is, like any other form of exploration, a challenging and exciting task. This learning process, which we call *diagnosis,* can be carried out to different degrees of completeness, by teachers, by remedial specialists, and by special clinical centers. It is not expected that a classroom teacher should make a thorough diagnosis of every pupil; such an undertaking would leave little time or energy for teaching. Fortunately many of the simpler difficulties in reading can be corrected by direct teaching of the missing skills, without an intensive search for reasons why the skills were not learned before. Teachers should, nevertheless, know what the possible causes of reading difficulties are, and should be able to carry out the simpler parts of a diagnostic study. When a diagnostic study is being made by a remedial specialist, there is no good excuse for careless work or for failure to consider the full range of possible contributing factors.[1]

I. The Nature of Diagnosis

MAKING A READING DIAGNOSIS means studying the nature of the individual's reading performance and of the factors, both in the present

[1] Harris, A. J., and Roswell, Florence G., "Clinical Diagnosis of Reading Disability." *Journal of Psychology,* Vol. 36, 1953, pp. 323–340.

and in the past, which have contributed to the development of the difficulties he is showing. In the process of making a diagnosis it is necessary to collect facts, and tests can contribute many of the facts needed. But the heart of diagnosis is not testing. It is, rather, the intelligent interpretation of the facts by a person who has both the theoretical knowledge and the practical experience to know what questions to ask; to select procedures, including tests, which can supply the needed facts; to interpret the meaning of the findings correctly; and to comprehend the interrelationships of these facts and meanings. The natural outcome of a diagnostic study is a plan for treatment which involves two parts: a plan for correcting or minimizing those handicapping conditions which are still interfering with learning; and a plan for remedial instruction that is most likely to be successful in the light of what has been found.[2]

Methods of studying the individual's reading skills have been discussed in Chapters VII and VIII. Analyzing the nature of the person's present reading skills and faults is a very important part of the total diagnosis, and contributes most of the information on which the instructional part of the treatment plan is based. This chapter and Chapter X are concerned with the other side of diagnosis, the exploration of the causal setting.

Most reading disabilities are not caused by special types of mental defect, but arise from causes such as mental or social immaturity, physical handicaps, poor motivation, interrupted schooling, emotional disturbance, and exposure to ineffectual teaching. Many of these can be fairly readily discovered by an alert classroom teacher. For example, one published study lists the causes contributing to the reading difficulties of eighty-three children (all but four reading below third-grade level) as classified by three experienced teachers.[3] The frequencies of the main types of causes were as follows: use of inappropriate reading material, 76; too early introduction of the

[2] For a more extended explanation of this point of view, see Harris, A. J., "Diagnosis of Reading Disabilities," *Corrective Reading in Classroom and Clinic*, pp. 80–87, compiled and edited by Helen M. Robinson, Supplementary Educational Monographs, No. 79. Chicago: University of Chicago Press, 1953.

[3] Whipple, Gertrude, "Remedial Programs in Relation to Basic Program of Reading," *Elementary School Journal*, Vol. 44, 1944, pp. 525–535.

child to reading, 59; uncorrected physical defects, 44; insufficient rest, 42; physical deficiencies, 42; poor diet or wrong eating habits, 37; emotional difficulties, 33; poor home environment, 32; gaps in the child's schooling, 29; inferior language equipment, 23; extreme nervousness, 13; undue amount of work outside of school, 12; extremely limited experience outside of school, 8; limited powers of concentration, 5; confusion of direction because of left-handedness or change in handedness, 4; lack of effort, 2. More than half of the children had five or more of these handicaps each.

The teachers in the study just summarized probably missed some of the subtle physical, social, or psychological factors that might have been found if these children had been given thorough clinical study, but they certainly learned a great deal about the children and discovered many handicaps about which something could be done.

The task of the teacher is to find out as well as he can what difficulties are present in each case, and then to apply common sense and a knowledge of remedial procedures to the problem of overcoming the child's handicaps and teaching what he has not learned. When the teacher finds, after a good trial, that he is not getting satisfactory results with a child, he should then refer the child for a more intensive diagnostic study by specialists.

II. Intelligence and Reading Ability

When intelligence and reading tests are given to all the pupils in a school, a fairly marked tendency for reading scores to agree with intelligence scores is usually found. The exact size of the relationship varies with the grade level and with the tests used. In general, the better the teaching of reading, the closer the relationship. However, there are always some children whose achievement in reading is much below the level that one would expect from their intelligence scores. Among the children who have been referred to the writer as complete nonreaders there have been several with IQ's of 115 to 130. Most children with severe reading disabilities have average or low average general intelligence.

The opposite finding — of reading ability substantially higher than intelligence level — is less common. Dull children do sometimes score a year higher on reading tests than on intelligence tests, and a difference of two years is rare but not impossible. Such findings are to some extent the result of errors of measurement in the tests, and are also to some extent due to unevenness in the child's development.

The Selection of Intelligence Tests

Accurate measurement of the intelligence of children who are retarded in reading is difficult because some of the handicaps that interfere with reading may also hinder the child from showing his true ability on intelligence tests. The better individual intelligence tests such as the *Revised Stanford-Binet* give the most trustworthy results, and whenever possible an individual test given by a trained psychologist should be employed. Even on the *Stanford-Binet,* however, the IQ of a retarded reader may be too low because of the weight given to vocabulary and the inclusion of a few items requiring reading.

Although the individual intelligence tests devised by Wechsler (the *Wechsler Intelligence Scale for Children,* the *Wechsler-Bellevue,* and the *Wechsler Adult Intelligence Scale*) have become deservedly popular, the present writer believes that the sampling of the verbal intellectual abilities related to reading is more thorough in the *Stanford-Binet* than in the Wechsler tests and so generally prefers the former for use with reading problem cases, supplemented by the performance part of the appropriate Wechsler test.

In general school practice, group intelligence tests must be used because of the expense in time and personnel of using individual tests. Most intelligence tests that are intended for use in the primary grades are reasonably satisfactory for use with retarded readers because of the use of pictures with no reading matter. Such tests include the *Pintner-Cunningham;*[4] *Detroit Primary; Otis Quick-Scoring Alpha; Otis Primary; Kuhlmann-Anderson; California Tests of Mental Maturity; Pintner-Durost Elementary: Picture Content,* and *SRA Primary Mental Abilities Tests.*

[4] See Appendix A for data about the tests mentioned in this chapter.

From the fourth grade up, most group intelligence tests present all or most of their questions in printed form. On those tests, a very poor reader has difficulty in reading the questions and so often makes a low score even if he has average or superior intelligence. The writer has seen many cases whose group test IQ's were below 80 and whose *Stanford-Binet* IQ's were 100 or over. Many of the tests which are commonly used in elementary schools and secondary schools are subject to this criticism. They include the *National Intelligence Test, Henmon-Nelson, Otis Self-Administering, Otis Quick-Scoring Beta, Pintner General Ability Verbal Series, Terman Group Test,* and *Terman-McNemar.* If the child's retardation in reading is not extreme, however, his mental test results from one of these tests may be fairly correct. At the college level, for instance, results on the *Otis* tests do not seem to be influenced by marked improvement in reading ability.

With increasing recognition of the dangers of judging a child's intelligence entirely on the basis of printed questions, a number of recent tests have been constructed so as to include both a part which requires reading and a part which does not require reading, so that one can get separate verbal (reading) and nonverbal (no reading required) mental ages and IQ's. Tests which have this type of organization are the *California Tests of Mental Maturity, Elementary* (grades four to eight), *Intermediate* (grades seven to ten), and *Advanced* (grade nine to adult), the *Pintner-Durost Elementary Test, Reading Content* and *Picture Content* (grades two to four), the *Pintner Intermediate Test, Verbal Series* and *Non-Language Series* (grades five to eight), and the *American Council on Education Psychological Examination,* high-school and college levels. The child who is a generally retarded, mentally slow child will usually do equally poorly on both parts of such tests as those just mentioned. The child with a marked reading disability will usually do much better on the nonverbal part.

As an example of the discriminative value of testing with both reading and nonreading content, we may consider the results of two boys who were in a high school remedial reading class. Both were reading at fourth-grade level at the beginning of the year.

On the *California Tests of Mental Maturity,* Nat made a language IQ of 63 and a nonlanguage IQ of 64. He was a sickly child, with markedly defective vision, underweight, potentially tubercular, and with a severe spinal deformity; he had been grossly neglected through much of his childhood, and at the age of seventeen seemed a generally retarded boy, whose retardation could be explained largely in terms of chronic physical and social handicaps. Remedial reading did not seem to offer a solution to his difficulties. Mario, the other boy, obtained a language IQ of 77 and a nonlanguage IQ of 102. This seemed to show a special difficulty in the language area, preventing him from showing his otherwise normal ability. Investigation showed that he had come from Italy only three years previously and was still handicapped by imperfect ability to comprehend and express himself in English; and an intensive reading and English program seemed to have much value for him.[5]

The *Davis-Eells Games* and other so-called culture-free tests of mental ability are designed to emphasize those phases of intelligence in which children from lower-class homes and deprived backgrounds can do as well as middle-class and upper-class children. The verbal skills which are closely related to reading are definitely influenced by culture and education, and it would seem reasonable that a test which leaves out everything that is correlated with education and culture would have very low correlations with success in reading, and therefore cannot serve as a measure of potential reading capacity.

Determining Reading Capacity

The procedure by which one starts with the MA or IQ of a child and comes out with an estimate of the grade level at which he should be able to understand reading material is considered in Chapter XI, pages 299–302. At that point, also, the reader will find a discussion of techniques other than intelligence tests for judging the reading capacity of children.

Reading Expectancy for the Mentally Slow Child

The importance of mental maturity for reading readiness was stressed in Chapter II. The use of group readiness tests and group

[5] Harris, A. J., and Sternberg, W., "An Analysis of the Characteristics of Pupils in Three Remedial Reading Classes at the High School Level," *High Points,* Vol. 26, No. 7, September, 1944, pp. 43–59.

IQ tests early in the first grade makes it possible to locate the child whose rate of mental growth is below average. The reading program can be adapted to his limited capacities by prolonging the period of reading readiness activities and by gearing the pace of reading instruction to his rate of learning.

It is generally agreed that it is futile to start such children on systematic reading instruction before they reach a mental age of six years. The ages at which mentally slow children reach the mental age of six, at various IQ levels, are shown in Table VI. By this

Table VI. Attainment of Mental Readiness for Reading in Children of Limited Intellectual Ability

IQ	*Age at Which Child Reaches Mental Age of 6–0*	*Mental Maturity at Various Ages*					
		Age 9–0		*Age 12–0*		*Age 15–0*	
		Mental Age	*Mental Grade*	*Mental Age*	*Mental Grade*	*Mental Age*	*Mental Grade*
90	6–8 *	8–1 *	3.1	10–9 *	5.8	12–11 *	7.9
85	7–1	7–8	2.7	10–3	5.3	12–3	7.2
80	7–6	7–2	2.2	9–7	4.6	11–6	6.5
75	8–0	6–9	1.8	9–0	4.0	10–9	5.8
70	8–7	6–4	1.3	8–5	3.4	10–1	5.1
65	9–2	5–10	Kgn.	7–10	2.8	9–4	4.4
60	10–1	5–5	Kgn.	7–3	2.3	8–8	3.7

* Figures in these columns were taken from: Terman, L. M., and Merrill, M. A., *Measuring Intelligence*. Boston: Houghton Mifflin, 1937, IQ tables in Appendix.

criterion children with IQ's between 80 and 90 become ready between the ages of six and one-half and seven and one-half; those with IQ's in the 70's become ready between the ages of seven and one-half and eight and one-half; and those with IQ's below 70 are usually nine or older before they are ready for reading instruction. For many of these children an extra year in kindergarten or first grade is much kinder than promotion with their chronological age group. For those with IQ's below 70 or 76 (depending on local regulations) special classes are desirable.

Since roughly 25 per cent of our school population have IQ's below 90, it is important to consider what happens to them as they ascend the grades. Their IQ's usually do not improve substantially, and the gap between what they can learn and what the average child can learn tends to widen as they get older. The right-hand side of Table VI shows the level of mental maturity they can attain by their ninth, twelfth, and fifteenth birthdays. For each mental age the corresponding mental grade is given, which can be used as an indicator of potential reading capacity.

When he reaches his ninth birthday, the child with an IQ between 80 and 90 is mentally capable of reading at second-grade level; the child with an IQ below 80 is doing reasonably well if he has started to read at all. At the age of twelve, when most children are in seventh grade, the child with an IQ in the 80's has the mental capacity to understand reading material of fourth- to fifth-grade level; those with IQ's below 80 range downward in reading capacity from mid-fourth grade level. At the age of fifteen (ninth or tenth grade) those with IQ's in the 80's can comprehend at sixth- to seventh-grade level, those with IQ's in the 70's can understand at fifth- or sixth-grade level, and even those with IQ's in the 60's can grasp the meaning of material of third- or fourth-grade level.

Certain conclusions come inevitably from consideration of these data. First, children of limited mental ability cannot be brought up to age and grade norms in reading, and schools have to accept this as a fact and set realistic goals for them. Second, although they are behind their normal grade placement in reading skills, they often learn up to the limits of their mental ability and are therefore not suitable candidates for remedial instruction. Failure to realize this has clogged up many remedial programs with the wrong children. Third, from the age of nine to the age of fifteen even the very slow are capable of substantial growth in reading skills; unfortunately, both the school and the children have often given up hope by the time the children are ready to respond to reading instruction.

The Effect of Remedial Reading on Intelligence

Many teachers who plan to select a small number of pupils for special attention in reading find it hard to resist the temptation to select the poorest readers, regardless of their intelligence. Some of them find it difficult to distinguish between retarded readers (meaning simply those whose reading is below expectancy for their age and grade) and reading disability cases (whose reading is also well below their mental level). Others recognize this distinction but argue that the dull child will become brighter as a result of the remedial teaching.

Cases do occur in which a marked change in IQ is found after remedial teaching (see Case III in Chapter XIX). But in most of these cases the true reason for the change is the use of a group test which gave an untrue impression of mental retardation, or the presence of unrecognized handicaps which prevented the child from showing his ability at the time of the first testing. Unfortunately there is no factual basis for a belief in the efficacy of remedial reading as a cure for dullness. Moreover, if the dull child's reading ability is up to his mental age, relatively little return may be gained from remedial instruction.

While no radical changes in brightness should be expected, the effective functioning of a child may improve as his vocabulary enlarges, his range of knowledge expands, and his interest in schoolwork increases. These results, which may not show very much in intelligence test scores, are worth while in themselves.

Teachers should not make the mistake of labeling a child dull because his reading and other schoolwork are poor.

An excellent illustration of how erroneous such a conclusion may be is furnished by Richard, who entered junior high school at the age of fourteen with second-grade reading ability. When Richard was in the fourth grade his teacher suspected him of being feeble-minded and referred him to a clinic for a psychological examination, the result of which showed average intelligence (IQ 98). The junior high school was unwilling to accept this evidence of normal mentality because of his extremely poor work, and had him examined again at another clinic. This time his IQ was found to be above 100. The pity of it is that the boy spent eight years in school before any real attempt was made to understand his difficulties and to do something to improve his reading.

Special Mental Defects and Reading

Early investigators of reading disabilities usually assumed that, if the child showed no observable deficiencies of general mental development or health, the reading difficulties were the result of brain defects which made it difficult or impossible for a child to remember and identify printed words.[6] Several imposing technical terms were proposed—*word-blindness, alexia, dyslexia, strephosymbolia*—by those medical men who looked for a fundamental defect or deficiency in the child's nervous system as the reason for his failure to learn to read. As the prevalence of other, more remediable handicaps became known, educators and psychologists tended to use the diagnosis of "congenital word-blindness" less and less. It seems probable at the present time that only a small proportion of the reading disabilities to be found in the schools are of this type. This question will be discussed in greater detail later, in the sections on neurological difficulties and lateral dominance.

Poor memory for sequences of letters, numbers, or words may be found in children of otherwise normal mental ability. Usually it is a sign that the child is anxious or emotionally very tense while taking the test, and suggests that anxiety interferes similarly with his efforts to read. More rarely it indicates a special type of intellectual deficiency which would tend to slow up the child's rate of learning even in a good remedial program. When this seems to be the case, one should look for other signs of a possible neurological deviation. Memory tests should usually not be attempted by teachers, but judgments can be formed on the basis of daily work.

A child's inability to remember what a word looks like may be the result of failure to perceive it clearly in the first place. Deficiencies in visual perception are common, if not universal, among children who have serious difficulty in building up a sight vocabulary. In most of these children, the poor visual perception cannot be explained in terms of defective visual acuity; the child can see

[6] Hinshelwood, James, *Congenital Word-Blindness*. London: H. K. Lewis, Ltd., 1917.

well enough by vision tests, but he does not notice the finer points in the appearance of words or single letters. Sherlock Holmes' ability to notice and obtain meaning from clues that totally escaped Dr. Watson was not a matter of better eyes, but of a keener mind. Many of the children who have great difficulty in perceiving the details of words have no similar difficulty with tests involving perception of visual forms or numbers; other children show general vagueness in their perception of visual details. In clinical testing, many clues about the child's visual perceptive abilities can be gained from performance tests and such tests as the *Rorschach,* the *Bender Visual-Motor Gestalt Test,* and the *Mosaic Test.* Tests of visual memory are included in the *Monroe-Sherman Group Diagnostic Reading Test,* the *SRA Reading Record, Aptitude,* and the *Detroit Tests of Learning Aptitude.* Very poor ability in analyzing visual objects, in perceiving their parts accurately, and in grasping how the parts fit together may be suggestive of a neurological defect.

Poor auditory perception is also very prevalent among deficient readers. While showing normal hearing on the usual hearing tests, such children do not distinguish small differences in the sounds of words (*man* and *men* sound alike) and have difficulty in hearing the sound of separate letters or phonograms within words. This writer agrees with the stress that Durrell and Murphy have placed on auditory discrimination as basic to the learning of word analysis skills.[7]

Vagueness in perception may also extend to the sense of movement, or kinesthetic sense. French found that poor readers did not do as well as normal readers in tracing designs with their fingers while blindfolded.[8]

Difficulties in visual and auditory perception may at times be the result of neurological difficulties. Sometimes they are accompanied by moderate or severe visual or hearing defects. A foreign-language background may make it difficult for the child to perceive the sounds

[7] Durrell, D. D., and Murphy, H., "The Auditory Discrimination Factor in Reading Readiness and Reading Disability," *Education,* Vol. 73, 1953, pp. 556–560.

[8] French, E. L., "Kinesthetic Recognition in Retarded Readers," *Educational and Psychological Measurement,* Vol. 13, 1953, pp. 636–654.

of spoken English correctly. Very often, however, the most probable explanation seems to be that the child has not learned to pay attention to these details, and still retains the uncritical and unanalytical attitude common in preschool children; in other words, he has not developed reading readiness in these important traits. Often such children make rapid progress in both visual and auditory perception when given specific perceptual training.

III. Vision

Types of Visual Defects

There are many different kinds of visual defects, some of which seem to be more important in the causation of difficulties in reading than others.

The three defects which are best known to the layman are nearsightedness (myopia), farsightedness (hypermetropia), and astigmatism. These are all due usually to structural deviations from the normal shape of the eye. The myopic eye is too long from front to back, so that light focuses before the retina and tends to produce a blurred impression. The farsighted eye is too short from front to back, so that light, especially when coming from a source near the eye, focuses behind the retina. With moderate amounts of farsightedness, normal or better than normal vision for distant objects is often found; it is possible for the farsighted person to get near objects also into clear focus, but long-continued attention to near objects, as in reading, tends to produce eyestrain with accompanying fatigue and headaches. Astigmatism is usually the result of uneven curvature of the front part of the eye, so that light rays coming into the eye are not evenly distributed over the retina; the results are blurred or distorted images and eyestrain. All three of these conditions can be corrected with properly fitted glasses.

The eyes have to make four major types of adjustments for clear vision. There is an automatic reflex adjustment of the size of the pupillary opening to the amount of illumination (pupillary reflex); this permits a larger amount of light to enter in dim lighting, and protects the eye against the dazzling effect of bright illumination.

Second, there is an automatic reflex adjustment of the shape of the lens to the distance of the object being looked at; this is called the accommodation reflex, and acts like the adjustment for distance in a camera. Third, there is an automatic reflex control of the degree to which the eyes turn in so both focus on the same spot (the convergence reflex); the eyes are almost parallel when viewing an object more than ten feet away, but turn in quite noticeably when aimed at a target a foot away. Fourth, the eyes must be aimed so that the objects we wish to see most clearly are in the center of the visual field, where acuity is greatest. This requires smooth, continuous movement when following a moving object, and quick, jerky movements (*saccadic movements*) with intervening pauses (*fixations*) when observing stationary objects. These movements are not easily seen on casual observation, but are easily noted in eye-movement photography or when making special observations of eye movements (see pp. 510–517).

There are some defects which cannot be detected when each eye is tested separately, but which appear when the eyes are used together. For normal two-eyed vision both eyes must be focused accurately on the same target. This allows a fusion in the brain of the slightly different images from the two eyes. Fusion difficulty is often the result of paralysis of an eye muscle. When there is no fusion the person sometimes sees double (as when under the influence of alcohol), but more commonly the image from one eye is ignored or suppressed in the same way that a person looking into a microscope or sighting a rifle ignores the other eye. Continued suppression of the vision of one eye for a period of years may eventually produce blindness in that eye, and the person will have to depend completely on the preferred eye. It is therefore very important to detect cases of visual suppression early. A one-eyed person is not bothered by his lack of fusion and may have clearer vision in the good eye than other people have with two eyes.

Partial or imperfect fusion is more apt to interfere with clear vision than a complete absence of fusion. When fusion is incomplete, a blurred image instead of a clear one is likely, even though the person may see clearly with either eye separately. Some people can fuse the images, but do it slowly. This may not be a handicap in the ordinary use of the eyes, but may interfere with clear vision when rapid, precise focusing is needed, as in reading.

Poor fusion is often associated with a lack of proper balance among the six pairs of muscles which turn the eyeballs. When the lack of balance is extreme, the condition is called *strabismus* ("cross-eyed" or "walleyed"). The person with strabismus usually ignores one eye completely, and so has no interference with the vision of the other eye. Milder cases of poor muscle balance (*heterophoria*) occur in which the eyes turn in too much (*esophoria*), turn out (*exophoria*), or in which one eye focuses a little higher than the other (*hyperphoria*). Most people with these defects are able to obtain proper fusion when the eyes are not tired, but get blurred vision after extended reading or other close and exacting visual work. When the eyes are tired, they may get blurred images, may see a combination of the things each eye is looking at, or may see the two objects in reverse order. There also may be a complete suppression of one eye.

Color blindness of the usual type, which involves difficulty or inability in distinguishing reds from greens, is found in 4 to 8 per cent of boys and is quite rare in girls. There is no evidence to indicate that it has any effect on reading ability. Weakness in ability to perceive depth (called *astereopis*) has been mentioned as possibly being involved in reading disability cases; it is related to poor fusion. A condition in which one eye forms a larger image of the object than the other eye (called *aniseikonia*) has been found to cause visual disturbances in some individuals; it would seem to be a reasonable cause for poor fusion in some cases.

As yet little is known about the possible importance for reading of the speed and precision with which the pupillary, accommodation, and convergence reflexes adapt the eyes to new targets or to a changing target. Vision tests currently in use do not attempt to measure these factors.

In addition to the conditions described above, there are very many ocular conditions, caused by injuries, disease, and so on, that may produce poor vision. The above list contains, however, about all of the visual defects with which the school teacher or clinical psychologist needs to be acquainted.

The Significance of Visual Defects for Reading

Although many studies on the relation of visual defects to reading ability have been made, an exact statement of the degree to which poor reading is caused by poor vision cannot yet be made. One of the reasons for the discrepancies between different research studies is the fact that the subjects used and the vision tests employed are frequently not directly comparable. But there are more fundamental reasons why one cannot state exactly how much poor reading is caused by defective sight. A relatively slight visual defect may give one person acute discomfort, while another person with a more severe defect may not be bothered by it. People vary in their ability to adapt themselves to handicaps. For instance, a moderate degree of exophoria may cause one person no trouble because his ability to compensate for the tendency (that is, his duction power), is good, while a similar amount of exophoria may cause another person considerable difficulty in reading. And then, too, one must remember that poor vision is only one of many handicaps that may interfere with reading. If poor vision is a child's only handicap he may be able to become a good reader in spite of it, while if he has several other handicaps as well the combination may be too much for him.

The research on this topic is already much too extensive to review here; those interested will find good summaries by Robinson,[9] Cleland,[10] and Traxler.[11]

An uncritical reading of the research reveals a lack of agreement.

[9] Robinson, Helen M., *Why Pupils Fail in Reading*. Chicago: University of Chicago Press, 1946.

[10] Cleland, Donald L., "Seeing and Reading," *American Journal of Optometry*, Vol. 30, 1953, pp. 467–481.

[11] Traxler, Arthur, *Ten Years of Research in Reading*. New York: Educational Records Bureau, 1941.

Traxler, Arthur, *Another Five Years of Research in Reading*. New York: Educational Records Bureau, 1946.

Traxler, Arthur, and Townsend, Agatha, *Eight More Years of Research in Reading*. New York: Educational Records Bureau, 1955.

The recent study by Edson, Bond, and Cook[12] adds one more to a fairly long list of researches in which little or no relation was found between vision test results and reading achievement. The present writer believes that positive findings outweigh negative findings, and is inclined to trust the accumulated evidence of such investigators as Park and Burri,[13] Eames,[14] and Robinson and Huelsman,[15] all of whom found evidence of a relationship between certain types of visual defects and reading failures. It is very significant that these research studies place most emphasis on such visual difficulties as poor near-point acuity and poor eye-muscle balance with accompanying deficiencies in fusion and depth perception — significant because these problems are usually not detected by the eye tests commonly used in schools. The Robinson and Huelsman study, probably the most intensive yet undertaken, studied the interrelationships among fifty-nine tests of vision and thirteen tests of reading. with first-grade, fourth-grade, and seventh-grade pupils. Reading success was correlated most highly with depth perception and near acuity; in addition, none of the sets of vision tests used in their study was found to be fully satisfactory.

The Detection of Visual Defects

In view of the great importance of conserving vision, it would be ideally desirable for every child to have a periodic examination by an eye specialist. Since the expense of such a practice is prohibitive

[12] Edson, W. H., Bond, G. L., and Cook, W. W., "Relationships between Visual Characteristics and Specific Silent Reading Abilities," *Journal of Educational Research,* Vol. 46, 1953, pp. 451–457.

[13] Park, G. E., and Burri, C., "The Relationship of Various Eye Conditions and Reading Achievement," *Journal of Educational Psychology,* Vol. 34, 1943, pp. 290–299; "The Effect of Eye Abnormalities on Reading Difficulty," *Journal of Educational Psychology,* Vol. 34, 1943, pp. 420–30; "Eye Maturation and Reading Difficulties," *Journal of Educational Psychology,* Vol. 34, 1943, pp. 535–546.

[14] Eames, T. H., "Comparison of Eye Conditions among 1000 Reading Failures, 500 Ophthalmic Patients, and 150 Unselected Children," *American Journal of Ophthalmology,* Vol. 31, 1948, pp. 713–717.

[15] Robinson, Helen M., and Huelsman, C. B., Jr., "Visual Efficiency and Progress in Learning to Read," in *Clinical Studies in Reading, II,* pp. 31–63. Supplementary Educational Monographs, No. 77. Chicago: University of Chicago Press, 1953.

for most schools, the common school practice is to give simple eye tests to select or screen out those whose eyes require careful examination. Even this limited program, however, is carried out inadequately.

The usual method of measuring vision in school makes use of the Snellen chart or a similar test. The child stands twenty feet away from a wall chart and tries to read letters of different sizes. Each eye is tested separately, the other eye being covered up. A score of 20/20 is considered normal; 20/30, 20/40, and so on, mean defective acuity to the extent that the child can see at twenty feet letters large enough for the normal eye to see at thirty feet, forty feet, and the like. The assumption is sometimes made that the Snellen ratio represents a per cent of normal vision. That this is wrong can be clearly seen by inspecting Table VII; 20/30 acuity, which is usually considered to be borderline, represents an acuity only 8.5 per cent less than 20/20.

The Snellen-type vision test, if it is the only kind of vision test used, has many drawbacks. In addition to the fact that it is often administered in schools in such a way as to allow a child to cheat and simulate good vision by memorizing the chart, it fails to detect moderate degrees of farsightedness or astigmatism and fails completely to detect even severe cases of poor fusion and eye-muscle imbalance. The one defect that it readily discloses is nearsightedness. Eames has reported that in the examination of one hundred children who had visual defects when given a thorough ophthalmological examination, Snellen chart tests disclosed the presence of a defect in only forty-eight children.[16]

In recent years several sets of vision tests have been devised which are less inadequate than the Snellen chart for school eye testing. Three rather expensive instruments using stereoscopic slides for testing several visual functions are available: the *Orthorater*, the *Sight-Screener*, and the *Keystone Visual Survey*. These test acuity, eye-muscle balance and fusion in both distance vision and near

[16] Eames, T. H., "The Effect of Correction of Refractive Errors on the Distant and Near Vision of School Children," *Journal of Educational Research*, Vol. 36, 1942, pp. 272–279.

Table VII. Percentage of Visual Loss for Various Acuity Fractions *

	Per Cent	
	Efficiency	*Loss*
20/20	100.0	0.0
20/30	91.5	8.5
20/40	83.6	16.4
20/50	76.5	23.5
20/70	64.0	36.0
20/100	48.9	51.1
20/200	20.0	80.0

* This table is reproduced from Louttit, C. M., *Clinical Psychology,* p. 572. New York: Harper & Brothers, 1936. By permission of the publishers.

vision, with additional tests of depth perception and color vision. They can be administered by a teacher, nurse, or psychologist after a short period of training. The *Orthorater* (which has professional and industrial models) has rated slightly better in comparative evaluations, while the *Keystone* tests, using an instrument called the *Telebinocular,* has the advantage of somewhat easier portability. The *Massachusetts Vision Tests* [17] add measures of eye-muscle balance to far-point acuity, but are limited in that they do not test near vision. The *Eames Eye Tests* are quite inexpensive; although not as accurate or comprehensive as the *Orthorater, Sight-Screener* or *Keystone* tests, they do detect some of the conditions overlooked by the Snellen test, are within the budget of any school, and are not difficult to administer. The *Orthorater* and *Keystone* tests now have briefer versions for very fast testing to pick out those needing more careful screening.

With any of these tests one does not attempt to specify the kind of visual defect present, but simply to select or screen out those who should be referred to an eye specialist for examination. Unfortunately some ophthalmologists and optometrists stop when they have examined each eye separately and do not pay much attention

[17] Sloane, A. E., "Massachusetts Vision Test," *Archives of Ophthalmology,* Vol. 24, 1940, pp. 924–939.

in their examinations to those aspects of coordinated close binocular vision that are most likely to have a significant effect on reading. It sometimes is not the fault of the visual screening test if a child who has done poorly on it is reported by the eye specialist to have normal vision.

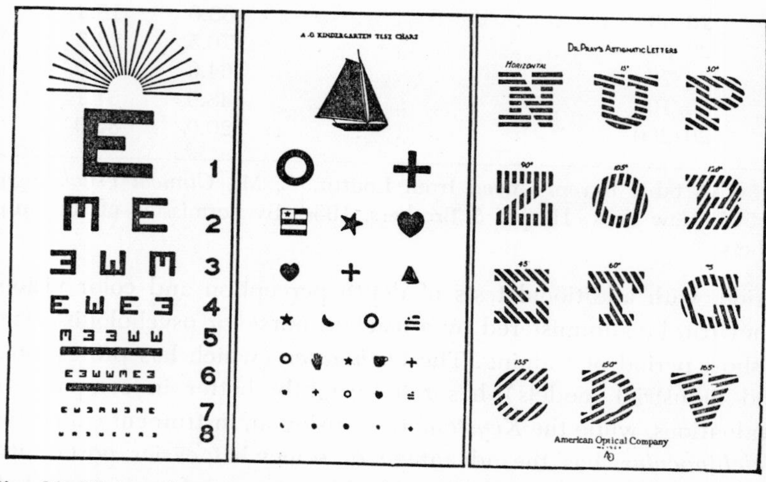

Fig. 20. Vision charts suitable for use with reading disability cases. Left, an E chart; the child points to show the direction to which the E is pointing. Center, a kindergarten chart; the child names the objects. Right, a chart for detecting astigmatism. Courtesy of the American Optical Co.

For schools that want to improve their vision testing procedures but do not wish to purchase any of the above screening tests, a number of suggestions can be made. First of all, the typical Snellen chart should be replaced, when testing poor readers, by an E chart, in which only the letter E is used, facing in different directions. Second, in order to detect the presence of significant amounts of farsightedness a plus 1.00 diopter spherical lens [18] should be obtained. After testing the eyes in the usual way, each eye should be retested looking through the lens; a farsighted child will see as well or better with the lens as without it, but those who have normal

[18] Lenses and vision charts can be purchased through local opticians or optometrists, or directly from the American Optical Co., Southbridge, Mass.

vision or are nearsighted will see less well with the lens. Third, acuity in near-point vision can be tested with a Guibor near-vision E chart, which is quite inexpensive.[19] Fourth, such binocular factors as near-point fusion and suppression can be quickly detected with the *Worth 4-Dot Test* for near vision.[20] In this test the child looks through a pair of spectacles with one red and one green lens, at a flashlight with a special cap that shows one spot of white light, one of red, and two of green. Any response other than seeing four spots indicates an eye-muscle difficulty.

The teacher should always be alert to detect signs of visual discomfort in the appearance or behavior of a child. Among the things to look for are bloodshot, swollen, teary, or discharging eyes; inflamed eyelids; complaints of sleepiness, fatigue, headache, nausea, dizziness, blurred, double, or distorted vision, and pain, or feelings of dryness, itching, burning, or grittiness in the eyes; strained and tense facial expression; rapid blinking or twitchings of the face; and such habits as holding a book very close or far away, or holding the head on one side while reading.

No matter how complete the vision tests in a school may be, no teacher, nurse, or psychologist should attempt to prescribe treatment for eye defects. The school's function is to find those who are in need of expert attention; children who are found or suspected to have defective vision should be sent to an eye specialist.

Before leaving the subject of vision testing, mention should be made of two tests that have had some use in reading clinics. One of these is an adaptation of the *Gray Standardized Oral Reading Check Tests* on stereoscopic slides, by which the relative efficiency of the two eyes in reading can be compared.[21] The other is the *Spache Binocular Reading Test,*[22] which uses stereoscopic slides in which some words are omitted from the left-eye selection and other

[19] Obtainable from the House of Vision, Chicago, Ill.; cost is about $2.

[20] Obtainable from E. B. Meyrowitz, Inc., 520 Fifth Ave., New York, N.Y. For a description of this test and explanation of how to use it, see: Kramer, Mary E., *Clinical Orthoptics: Diagnosis and Treatment,* p. 221. St. Louis: C. V. Mosby Co., 1949.

[21] The *Keystone Tests of Binocular Skill,* obtainable from the Keystone View Co., Meadville, Pa.

[22] Obtainable from Keystone View Co., Meadville, Pa.

words from the right-eye selection, to indicate whether either eye is failing to contribute its share.

IV. Hearing

THE DEGREE to which poor hearing is a handicap in learning to read depends on the amount of emphasis given to oral instruction in reading. In a careful study Bond[23] found significant differences in hearing between good and poor readers in the second and third grades, and reported that partly deaf children were seriously handicapped in classes where oral-phonetic methods were stressed, but made normal progress in classes which stressed visual teaching materials and silent reading. This is another impressive bit of evidence to demonstrate that teaching methods must be adapted to the learning abilities and disabilities of the individual child.

As with defective vision, the handicapping effect of a partial hearing loss is much greater for some people than for others. Some make up for their sensory weaknesses by concentrating intently and getting the greatest possible meaning out of what they do hear; others, combining inattention or disregard for small differences with their sensory loss, seem greatly handicapped.

While the majority of children with somewhat impaired hearing show lessened acuity across the full range of pitch represented by the piano keyboard, there are others whose deficiency is concentrated in the higher frequencies. An example of high-frequency hearing loss is shown in Figure 21.

Raymond was a ten-year-old boy, barely able to read a primer. His *Stanford-Binet* IQ was 85, but his IQ on the *Pintner-Paterson Performance Scale* was 120, showing inferior verbal ability but superior ability in nonverbal situations. His speech was marked by a lisp and general indistinctness in the pronunciation of *s, sh, z, th, f,* and *v* sounds; he also spoke very jerkily. His father, a mechanic, had exactly the same speech pattern. It seems probable that Raymond's inability to hear high-frequency sounds clearly was responsible for his inability to pronounce

[23] Bond, Guy L., *Auditory and Speech Characteristics of Poor Readers,* Contributions to Education, No. 657. New York: Bureau of Publications, Teachers College, Columbia University, 1935.

them well, and resulted in confusing him in reading because words that sounded alike to him had different letters in them and different meanings.

Testing Hearing

By far the most satisfactory way to measure hearing in the schools is to use an audiometer. For the purpose of singling out pupils who need careful medical examination of their hearing, audiometers are

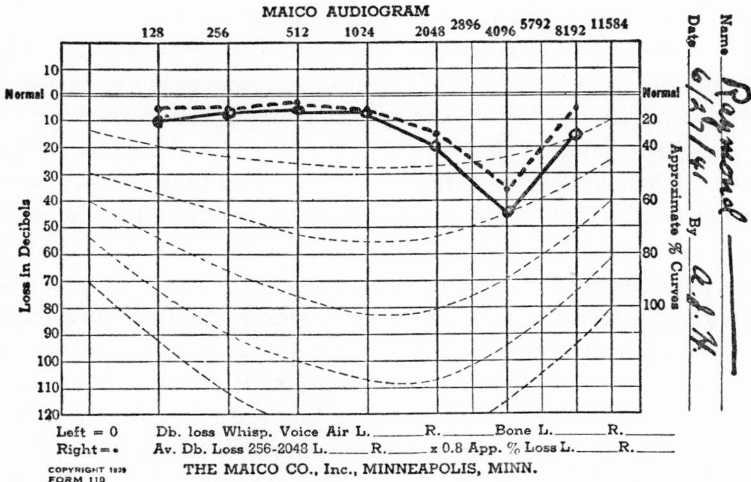

Fig. 21. Chart of audiometer test results for a ten-year-old boy with a severe reading disability. The chart shows an impairment of acuity in the higher frequencies, in both ears, with the left ear slightly poorer than the right. Reproduced by permission of the Maico Co., Inc.

available that can be used to test as many as forty children at one time. In such a test each child listens through an earphone and writes down the numbers that he hears. The numbers, spoken with different degrees of loudness, are played on a special phonograph and from the child's written answers the degree of hearing loss can be readily calculated. For individual testing an audiometer [24] that measures amount of hearing loss for pure tones of low, medium, and high pitches should be used. The record blank for one make of individual audiometer is shown in Figure 21. A hearing loss of up

[24] Among the makers of good audiometers are the Maico Co., Inc., and the Audio Development Co., both in Minneapolis.

to 10 decibels is normal; a loss of 10 to 20 decibels is probably a handicap; a loss of over 20 decibels is almost certain to handicap a child in hearing in classroom situations, and is usually accompanied by some indistinctness in speech.

When audiometer tests are not available, cruder and less satisfactory tests must be used. The best of these is the whisper test. When properly given, the child stands at least twenty feet away from the examiner, in a quiet room, facing sideways so that he cannot see the examiner's mouth. The exact distance should be determined for each room by finding the distance at which the majority of the children can hear, since acoustic properties of rooms differ greatly. The examiner should whisper with residual breath; that is, he should breathe out so as to empty lungs, and then whisper softly with clear enunciation. The child attempts to repeat each word as he hears it. If he does poorly, at the average distance, he moves closer. The per cent of hearing efficiency is obtained by dividing the distance at which the child can hear by the normal distance. Each ear is tested separately.

The other common test is the watch-tick test. A loud-ticking watch should be used. One ear is covered while the other is tested. The child stands with eyes closed while the watch is moved toward and away from him, saying "Yes" and "No" to indicate when he can hear it. Distance is measured with a yardstick, or a scale can be chalked on the floor. The normal hearing distance has to be discovered for each watch and for each room in which it is used.

Some conditions that lead to progressively increasing deafness can be cured if treated early enough, and careful periodic tests of hearing should be part of the routine health procedure in every school. Teachers should watch for signs of poor hearing in a child's general behavior. Children with inflamed or running ears should of course be referred for medical treatment. Poor hearing should be suspected if a child asks to have statements repeated, cups a hand behind his ear, scowls, or otherwise shows intense effort in listening, confuses words of somewhat similar sounds, or has indistinct speech. Teachers sometimes mistakenly decide that a child is stupid because his face has a blank expression due to his inability to hear.

V. Other Physical Conditions

Illness

There is no evidence that surgical operations or the common infectious diseases of childhood are related to reading disability. Prolonged illness of any kind may influence reading ability if the child is out of school for a long period of time and misses important work. A history of a series of long absences in the first and second grades is found fairly often among children with severe reading handicaps. Many children show no lasting scholastic effects of such absences because they were ahead of the class, or because their mothers and teachers give them special help to make up the lost ground. When neither of these conditions is present, the child may never catch up.

There are certain chronic conditions which lower a child's general vitality, so that he tires quickly and cannot put forth a normal amount of effort. Rheumatic fever is the major offender in this group, according to the writer's experience. Asthma, heart trouble, tuberculosis, sinus trouble, other chronic infections, and malnutrition are other conditions which cause intermittent absence and lower the child's energy output. Insufficient sleep is also common among poor readers.

Muscular Coordination

A considerable number of poor readers are generally clumsy. They are below average in athletic skill, awkward in walking and running, and make poorly formed letters and numbers in writing. While there does not seem to be any direct causal connection between awkwardness and poor reading, in some cases they may both result from the same condition. Gesell [25] suggests that mild injuries to the brain at birth may be responsible for both poor muscular coordination and for speech and reading disabilities.

[25] Gesell, Arnold, and Amatruda, Catherine S., *Developmental Diagnosis: Normal and Abnormal Child Development.* New York: Paul B. Hoeber, Inc., 1941.

Speech

There are many kinds of speech defects, among which stuttering, lisping, slurring, and generally indistinct speech are common. The two kinds of speech defects which the writer has noted most frequently in poor readers are indistinctness, with blurred consonant sounds and a generally "thick" quality, and a rapid, jerky, stumbling kind of speech which is sometimes called cluttering. Any kind of speech defect may produce embarrassment in oral reading and a consequent dislike for reading if oral reading is stressed. Phonic analysis may also be very difficult for children with defective speech. They should usually be taught reading by methods which do not stress oral reading and phonics, and at the same time remedial speech work should be carried on.

Glandular Disturbances

The endocrine or ductless glands are small organs which have tremendous influence on human growth and efficiency. Marked thyroid deficiency is usually accompanied by obesity and mental sluggishness; an overactive thyroid gland may cause loss of weight, fatiguability, and nervous irritability. Abnormalities of the pituitary gland may cause dwarfism and giganticism, obesity, and sexual immaturity. Each of the endocrine glands has important regulative functions, and medical authorities are still far from a complete understanding of them. Among the poor readers seen by the writer, the frequency of endocrine deviations has been greater than in normal child population. Most of these children have been overweight, with signs of either a thyroid deficiency, or of a general endocrine disturbance involving the thyroid, pituitary, and sex glands.[26] Many of these children have shown marked improvement

[26] From studies of the relation of physical to mental growth, Olson concludes: "It is also interesting to note that we get certain instances of split growth involving delayed progress in reading in cases which are marked by hypothyroidism, delay in descent of the testicles, and similar growth retardations." Olson, W. C., "Reading as a Function of Total Growth," *Reading and Pupil Development,* pp. 233–237. Supplementary Education Monographs, No. 5. Chicago: University of Chicago Press, October, 1940.

in mental alertness, effort, and learning ability after appropriate endocrine treatment.

Neurological Difficulties

In recent years neurologists have emphasized that the difficulties of many children are explainable in terms of injuries to the brain suffered at the time of birth. Many birth-injured babies die in infancy. Others grow up with severe paralyses, or with very retarded general mental development. These cases are comparatively easy to classify. According to Ford, the number of children who suffer brain injuries at birth without showing signs of it may outnumber those who do show clinical signs. "The absence of clinical symptoms of birth injury does not disprove the possibility that injury may have occurred, for numerous cases are described in which serious lesions of the brain have been found at post-mortem examination which were not suspected during life." [27] Gesell says: "In many instances the symptoms of minimal injury are so benign that they escape attention. . . . The type which expresses itself in speech difficulties, poorly defined unilateral dominance, and in delayed integration may later result in serious difficulty in the acquisition of reading. . . . The surprising prevalence of reading disabilities, so-called, and their frequent association with minimal birth injuries tends to support our thesis that these injuries are more common than is ordinarily supposed." [28] That comparatively mild birth injuries are important in the causation of reading difficulties is also suggested by Jensen, who points to the frequency of a history of difficult birth, awkward gait, minor speech defects, faulty eye coordination, and deficient auditory discrimination among his cases, as indicating the presence of some neurological injury.[29]

Schilder, an eminent neuropsychiatrist, also favored the idea that severe reading disability results from a basic deficiency in certain

[27] Ford, Frank R., *Diseases of the Nervous System in Infancy, Childhood, and Adolescence*, Second Edition, pp. 877–886. Springfield, Ill.: Charles C. Thomas, 1944.

[28] Gesell, Arnold, and Amatruda, Catherine S., *Developmental Diagnosis*, pp. 238–239.

[29] Jensen, M. B., "Reading Deficiency as Related to Cerebral Injury and to Neurotic Behavior," *Journal of Applied Psychology*, Vol. 27, 1943, pp. 535–545.

parts of the brain.[30] His view seems similar in the main to the older theory of Hinshelwood,[31] who explained word-blindness as caused by a constitutional localized deficiency in the brain, probably in the part called the angular gyrus. The difference is that Hinshelwood stressed a lack of visual memory for word forms, while to Schilder an inability to analyze and synthesize visual-auditory associations was the main defect.

It seems probable that only a small proportion of the reading disability problems found in the schools have difficulties of neurological origin. Such cases are, however, more common among the severe cases that are referred to diagnostic specialists and clinics after their school teachers and parents have been unable to help them.

Diagnosis of cerebral birth injury or of other neurological problems naturally requires a competent medical specialist. Symptoms which may lead a psychologist or teacher to recommend a neurological examination include the following: a history of difficult birth, with prolonged labor, instrumental delivery, marked deformity of the head, difficulty in getting breathing started, syanosis, difficulty in sucking and swallowing, and so on; poor equilibrium and general awkwardness; delayed speech development with otherwise normal mental abilities; a history of convulsive seizures or lapses of consciousness; and responses characteristic of the brain-injured on such tests as the *Rorschach,* the *Bender Visual-Motor Gestalt,* the *Mosaic,* and the *Kohs Block-Design,* all of which should be interpreted only by well-trained clinical psychologists.

During the past few years this writer has referred many reading cases suspected of neurological defect for neurological study, including the EEG (*electro-encephalograph,* a recording of the electric impulses of the brain). Up to now the results have been inconclusive. On many of these children the report is that there is some peculiarity in the brain-wave pattern; on others the reports state that the child falls within the normal range. The interpretation of the EEG's of children is a relatively new medical problem and one in which there

[30] Schilder, P., "Congenital Alexia and Its Relation to Optic Perception," *Journal of Genetic Psychology,* Vol. 65, 1944, pp. 67–88.

[31] Hinshelwood, James, *op. cit.*

is still considerable uncertainty. At present it is doubtful that the kinds of neurological defect most likely to produce some delay in readiness to learn to read in children of normal intelligence and motor skills can be accurately detected by either psychological or neurological techniques, and this writer believes that the psychological tests are more sensitive to the particular difficulties in brain functioning in such cases than the types of neurological study usually employed.

Very often the parents of a child who cannot read ask if the difficulty could be the result of a head injury. Nearly always they can recall some occasion when the child fell out of a crib or otherwise bumped his head. The writer came across a child nonreader who had had a severe head injury with concussion. The mother had convinced herself that his mind was no good because of this injury, and her constant repetition caused the boy to believe it also. The most thorough neurological and psychological examinations failed to find any evidence of brain impairment when he was examined three years after the accident, and the boy made satisfactory progress with remedial help. While a medical examination is always desirable in any reading disability case, usually the worry about a possible aftereffect of a fall or blow turns out to be unfounded.

Relatively few reports have come out which relate reading problems to specific neurological defects. For this reason, Lyle's report describing five cases of reading difficulty based on brain lesions is of special interest.[32] Heinz Werner's pioneering research on brain-injured mental defective children, which is conveniently summarized in the book by Strauss and Lehtinen,[33] should also be carefully studied by anyone venturing into this special field.

This chapter has considered the nature and meaning of diagnosis, and the significance of mental ability, vision, hearing, and other types of physical handicaps including neurological conditions, in

[32] Lyle, Donald J., "Reading Disability (Paralexia) from Impairment of Visuo-oculogyric Adjustment," *American Journal of Ophthalmology,* Vol. 36, 1953, pp. 1234–1237.

[33] Strauss, A. A., and Lehtinen, Laura, *Psychopathology and Education of the Brain-Injured Child.* New York: Grune & Stratton, Inc., 1947.

their bearing on the causation of reading disabilities. The exploration of the causes of poor reading is continued in the next chapter.

Suggested Additional Reading

See references at the end of Chapter X.

· X ·

Exploring the Causes of Reading Difficulties, II

THIS CHAPTER continues the discussion of the handicaps that interfere with progress in learning to read. After a new look at the controversial issue of lateral dominance, the contributions to be gained by study of the school history and achievement in other basic skills are considered, and the final section discusses the relation of personality maladjustment to reading difficulty.

I. Lateral Dominance

ONE OF THE MOST PUZZLING and most controversial issues in the whole field of reading is the significance of lateral dominance. By lateral dominance is meant the preferred use and superior functioning of one side of the body over the other. A person who uses his right hand in preference to the left and is more skillful with the right hand shows right-hand dominance. Similarly, the person who relies predominantly on his left hand shows left-hand dominance. Hand dominance has interested people for hundreds of years. The left-handed, because they are a minority, have often been regarded with suspicion. The word "sinister," which originally meant left-handed, now means evil or ominous, and the word "dextrous," meaning skillful, comes from the Latin word meaning right-handed.

Many people are unaware of the fact that they also show a definite eye dominance, or preference for one eye in tasks such as aiming, looking into a microscope, and so on, which can be done with only one eye at a time. The dominant (preferred) eye is usually but not always the eye with stronger acuity. In about one out of three people, it is on the opposite side of the body from the dominant hand. Foot dominance and ear dominance have been but little studied.

Dominance is said to be *crossed* when the dominant hand and eye are on opposite sides. It is said to be *incomplete* when the individual shows nearly equal use of both sides, in either hand or eye dominance. The term *mixed dominance* has been used to include both crossed and incomplete dominance. *Converted* dominance means that the person formerly preferred the other hand; usually it refers to the preferred use of the right hand by formerly left-handed individuals.

The causes for the preference for one side or the other are still unknown, although many theories have been advanced, ranging from hereditary predisposition to social conditioning. Most babies use both hands equally. A definite preference for one hand usually appears between the ages of eighteen months and five years. During the period in which the child shows no definite hand dominance, gentle encouragement of the use of the right hand, by placing toys nearer that hand, and so on, is probably harmless. After a definite dominance has been established, it is probably unwise to attempt to change it.

Theories of Lateral Dominance in Relation to Reading

Hundreds of investigations have been made on the relationships between different types of lateral dominance and the presence of many different kinds of defects, including not only reading, writing, and spelling difficulties, but also speech defects, delinquency, and nervous disorders. Many investigators have concluded that reading disability is less common among children who show consistent right-sided dominance than among the consistently left-sided and those showing mixed or converted dominance. Many other studies have come out with negative results. There is a tendency for reports based on intensive clinical studies to find a relationship, while surveys of large numbers of school children tend to give negative findings. This difference may have two reasons: the use of more complete tests in the clinical studies, and the inclusion of a higher proportion of very severe cases of reading disability in the clinical studies than in the school surveys. The writer has become convinced, from his own experience, that there is more than a chance relationship between lateral dominance and reading disability.[1]

The most widely discussed theory of dominance is that of Dr. Samuel T. Orton, a neurologist. Orton started with the generally accepted fact that the right hemisphere (side) of the brain controls the left side of the body, and the left hemisphere controls the right side of the body. He assumed that the right-sided person develops memory traces for printed words in a part of the left hemisphere, and also develops memory traces in the right hemisphere which are mirror images of those on the dominant side. When the clearly right-sided person reads, only the memory traces on the dominant side are aroused. In the consistently left-sided person, the right hemisphere is similarly dominant. If, however, the individual fails to develop a consistent dominance of one side over the other, difficulties arise. In that case, according to Orton, there will be confusion and conflict between the two sides of the brain. The child will have great difficulty in learning to read and spell and reversal errors will be prevalent. Orton suggested the term *strephosymbolia* (meaning twisted symbols) to describe what he calls "the reading disability" and seemed to assume that poor reading which can be explained on other grounds is of little importance.[2]

The present status of the Orton theory is still that of an unproved hypothesis. While it has met with fairly wide acceptance among neurologists, its basic neurological assumptions have been chal-

[1] The experimental literature is much too extensive to review here. Those who want to read it themselves will find convenient starting points in Traxler's summaries (see footnote 11, p. 234) and in Harris, A. J., "Reading and Other Subject Disabilities," *Progress in Clinical Psychology,* Vol. 2, edited by D. Brower and L. E. Abt. New York: Grune and Stratton, 1956.

[2] Orton, Samuel T., *Reading, Writing, and Speech Problems in Children.* New York: W. W. Norton Co., 1937.

lenged by studies of the effects of brain operations upon lateral dominance.[3]

Another major theory is that of Dearborn.[4] Dearborn said that it is easier for the left-handed person to move his left hand from right to left than from left to right, and easier for the left-eyed person to look from right to left than from left to right. Deviations from right-sidedness, then, would be expected to be accompanied by greater than average tendencies to move the eyes in the wrong direction in reading. With mixed dominance or a lack of consistent preference for either side, confusion in the direction of eye movements in reading, and reversals and other types of word-recognition difficulties, would be expected.

Orton and Dearborn agreed that consistent left-sidedness is less of a problem than mixed dominance, and that left-eye dominance is more important, so far as reading is concerned, than left-hand dominance. Orton's theory stresses confusion in mental imagery, while Dearborn places the major responsibility on confusion in motor activity.

Results with the Harris Tests of Lateral Dominance

Hitherto unpublished data which cast new light on the problem of lateral dominance are shown in Table VIII. The unselected children were obtained by testing children chosen at random from second- and fourth-grade classes in several Manhattan and Bronx public schools. The two groups include some Negro children, contain approximately equal numbers of boys and girls, and since no effort was made to check on achievement, probably contain about 15 per cent of children with some reading disability. The reading disability cases include 98 cases from the City College Educational Clinic (1941–1947) and 210 cases from the Queens College Educational Clinic (1949–1954), with IQ's of 80 or over, mental ages over

[3] Smith, K. U., "The Role of the Commissural Systems of the Cerebral Cortex in the Determination of Handedness, Eyedness, and Footedness in Man," *Journal of General Psychology,* Vol. 32, 1945, pp. 39–79.

[4] Dearborn, Walter F., "Structural Factors Which Condition Special Disability in Reading," *Proceedings of the American Association for Mental Deficiency,* Vol. 38, 1933, pp. 266–283.

Table VIII. Hand and Eye Dominance in Reading Disability Cases and Unselected Children on the Harris Tests of Lateral Dominance

	Unselected Children		*Reading Disability Cases*				
	Boys and Girls		*Boys and Girls*				
	7 yrs.	*9 yrs.*	*7 and 8 yrs.*	*9 yrs.*	*10 and 11 yrs.*	*12 yrs. and up*	*All Cases*
Hand							
Strong Right	52.5%	53.2%	32.3%	48.6%	47.5%	57.3%	47.4%
Moderate Right	14.7	29.3	22.0	13.3	17.5	19.0	17.9
Mixed	18.0	8.2	32.2	25.0	20.6	10.5	21.1
Moderate Left	6.6	7.7	10.2	4.4	3.1	7.2	5.8
Strong Left	8.2	2.2	3.4	8.9	11.4	6.0	7.8
Eye							
Strong Right	27.9	47.3	42.5	45.7	42.3	47.7	44.5
Moderate Right	14.8	9.2	10.2	10.6	6.2	10.7	9.1
Mixed	6.6	7.1	10.2	7.4	7.2	9.4	8.4
Moderate Left	21.3	15.8	6.8	11.7	12.4	6.0	9.4
Strong Left	29.6	20.3	30.6	25.0	32.0	26.2	28.2
Hand and Eye							
Right, Right	37.0	50.0	28.9	42.7	38.1	51.3	40.9
Right, Left	29.5	26.0	22.0	14.7	23.7	15.5	19.2
Right, Mixed	3.3	6.0	3.4	4.4	3.1	9.5	5.2
Left, Right	4.4	2.7	6.8	2.9	5.2	3.6	4.5
Left, Left	8.2	6.5	6.8	10.3	9.3	9.5	9.1
Left, Mixed	1.6	0.5	0	0	0	0	0
Mixed, Right	3.3	3.8	17.0	10.3	5.2	3.6	8.1
Mixed, Left	13.1	4.3	8.5	11.8	11.4	7.1	9.8
Mixed, Mixed	1.6	0	6.8	2.9	4.1	0	3.2
Number	61	184	59	68	97	84	308

At the seven-year level, the reading disabilities are significantly different from the unselected children in all three parts of the table. At the nine-year level there are significant differences (at the 1 per cent level) in hand dominance and in hand-eye combinations, but not in eye dominance. The total reading disability is significantly different from both unselected groups in all three divisions. There are no significant differences between the unselected seven-year-old boys and girls; the unselected nine-year-olds are not significantly different in hand dominance and hand-eye combinations, but the girls have more mixed eye dominance and less moderate right-eye dominance.

7–0, and definite reading disabilities. The median age was ten years and the median reading achievement was about at second-grade level, with many nonreaders. Roughly 90 per cent were boys.

The most striking fact is the high proportion of mixed hand dominance. One-fifth of the unselected seven-year-olds and one-third of the corresponding reading disability group (seven-year-olds and eight-year-olds were put together to get a larger group) showed mixed hand dominance. These are far higher percentages than have been reported with the use of other tests, and indicate that these tests are sensitive to something which most other tests of hand dominance do not pick up. The nine-year-old groups both show less mixed hand dominance than the younger groups, but the rate of decrease is far smaller in the disability group, so that the proportion of mixed hand dominance is more than three times as great in the nine-year disability than in the nine-year unselected group. This is true for both the boys and the girls. Even among the disability cases of twelve and over, the proportion of mixed hand dominance is higher than in the unselected nine-year-olds, despite a trend toward increasing frequency of right-handedness with increasing age. Strong left-handedness was also significantly more frequent in the older disability groups.

The eye dominance results show less change with increasing age, and less difference between the unselected and disability groups. The hand-eye combinations are influenced by the smaller per cent of right handedness and larger per cent of mixed handedness in the disability groups. In addition, the per cent of left-handed, left-eyed children is higher in the older disability groups.

A more detailed analysis of these and other results with the *Harris Tests of Lateral Dominance* will be published elsewhere. The present data show quite dramatically that a very high proportion of young reading disability cases show mixed dominance on these tests, and that the development of a fairly consistent preference for one hand takes place later than the age of nine in a far higher proportion of reading disability cases. Since mixed hand dominance in these tests is usually a sign of directional confusion, shown mainly by untypical results in the simultaneous writing test, a reappraisal of the relation of dominance to the causation of reading disability is in order.

Directional Confusion

After fifteen years of pondering the conflicting and confusing results of the research on lateral dominance, the writer has come to the conclusion that the significant question is whether or not a person shows directional confusion, rather than what pattern of lateral dominance he has. Directional confusion is typically shown by the presence of reversals in reading. It may also show up in spelling and the writing of numbers, in typing, or in speech in the form of stuttering. In some cases there seems to be a related difficulty in distinguishing east from west or downtown from uptown.

Such directional confusion can be present with any pattern of lateral dominance including complete right-sidedness, but it is most likely to occur in those with mixed dominance as measured by the Harris tests.

It seems probable that there is a physiological basis for the directional confusion in many cases. Many of the children showing severe reading disability with directional confusion are cases of delayed and irregular neurological maturation. In these cases there is usually a history of some delay in beginning to talk, approximately equal use of both hands until the age of five or later, mixed or incomplete dominance, and a lack of really good coordination with either hand. Some of these children have birth histories that suggest minimal brain damage of the sort referred to on page 245. In other cases inquiry into the development of the child's siblings and parents reveals that the pattern of delay in establishing dominance of one hand, a strong reversal tendency, some speech difficulty, and early difficulty in learning to read characterizes several members of the family, suggesting a familial growth pattern.

Conversion of a left-handed child to the use of the right hand can create a picture of incomplete dominance accompanied by directional confusion, similar to that found in the cases of delayed maturation. After a year or two of practice, the right hand tends to establish definite superiority. If the transition period takes place before the child begins to read it is not likely to produce directional confusion in reading. If the changeover takes place while the child is in the beginning stages of reading, or just before, a serious directional confusion may result. Once off to a poor start in reading, the child's reading difficulties may continue long after the directional confusion has cleared up. In some cases the right hand never establishes a consistent superiority, and directional confusion continues for many years to interfere with reading and other language activities.

In cases where there is a physiological basis for directional confusion, whether caused by neurological injury or defect, by a family growth pattern which includes slow and somewhat irregular neurological maturation, or by conversion from left to right, it is possible that both the Orton and the Dearborn theories are correct in part. There may be an Orton type of rivalry between the two hemispheres of the brain, and at the same time a conflict between left-to-right and right-to-left motor tendencies such as Dearborn emphasized.

Some directional confusion accompanied by reversal tendencies is so common among preschool children that it has to be considered a normal characteristic up to the age of six. The data in Table VIII suggest that it is present in nearly one-fifth of unselected seven-year-olds. It is only when such a confusion persists after considerable instruction in the left-to-right direction in reading and writing that it requires careful consideration.

Barger has recently reported some spectacular results in remedial reading with children showing strong reversal tendencies, by having them read material by looking into a mirror which reverses the material both vertically and horizontally.[5] He believes that this corrects a functional neurological peculiarity which causes these children to see normal print the way it looks to most people in the mirror, so that the use of the mirror allows them to see the print normally. After a few weeks of practice the mirror can be discarded. If Barger's results are substantiated by others, he will have made a

[5] Barger, William C., "An Experimental Approach to Aphasic and to Non-Reading Children," *American Journal of Orthopsychiatry,* Vol. 23, 1953, pp. 158–170.

substantial contribution to the understanding and treatment of directional confusions.

Leavell has recently brought out a method of overcoming directional confusions in cases of crossed dominance by training the nondominant eye to coordinate with the dominant hand.[6] This is done by requiring practice in the tracing and drawing of designs presented in a stereoscope. This procedure, like the Barger mirror technique, is at this writing too new to be evaluated. Both of these procedures deserve to be tried out carefully in independent experimental research studies.

There remains the probability that some cases of directional confusion are emotional in origin. The use of force, compulsion, or ridicule to make a left-handed child use his right hand quite often has harmful effects which may include the beginning of stuttering, assorted nervous habits, and emotional upset in addition to the directional confusion which otherwise might be quickly outgrown. Blau attempted to show that left-sidedness in general is a form of neurotic negativism or defiance; while as a general explanation of left-sidedness his theory seems farfetched, it may very well apply to a few cases.[7] Park has reported two cases in which a strong directional confusion in reading seemed to be a disguised form of negativism.[8] In cases of this sort — and there are probably more of them — directional confusion can be found in a completely right-sided individual.

The point of view that directional confusion interferes with learning to read, and that directional confusion can in turn be the result of either physiological or psychological factors, makes it possible to explain why the results of the many research studies on lateral dominance and reading success are conflicting. One starts by assuming that the consistently right-sided child has an advantage over the

[6] Leavell, Ullin W., *Manual of Instructions for the Leavell Language-Development Service.* Meadville, Pa.: Keystone View Co., 1955.

[7] Blau, Abram, *The Master Hand.* Monograph Series, No. 5. New York: American Orthopsychiatric Association, 1945.

[8] Park, George E., "Mirror and Reversed Reading," *Journal of Pediatrics,* Vol. 42, 1953, pp. 120–128.

left-sided child or the child with crossed, mixed, or incomplete dominance, in learning to follow a consistent left-to-right direction. With appropriate instruction, however, most of these children who are not consistently right-sided do learn the left-to-right sequence and make progress in reading consistent with their abilities. But when an inconsistent lateral dominance pattern is complicated by neurological or emotional difficulties, a disabling directional confusion is likely to be established, and the usual classroom help is not sufficient to overcome it. Since these cases are a minority of all reading disability cases, and from this number those whose directional confusion is emotionally based would have to be subtracted, the remainder is really a small group. These would be the cases where directional confusion is related to untypical lateral dominance as a sign of neurological immaturity or defect. Whether or not a particular investigator would find enough of them in his reading disability group to show some statistical relationship between reading disability and lateral dominance patterns would depend on the severity of disability in the group studied, and the degree to which his tests were sensitive to directional confusion.

Measurement of Lateral Dominance and Directional Confusion

Since perfect consistency in the choice of hand, eye, or foot is the exception rather than the rule, it is necessary to use a variety of tests rather than rely upon one or two. Until the writer published the *Harris Tests of Lateral Dominance* in 1947 (Second Edition, 1955), there was no set of hand, eye, and foot dominance tests available with a manual of directions and printed record form. In this series the hand dominance tests include tests of hand preferences, several tests in which the relative speed and skill of the two hands are compared, and one test for directional confusion. The eye-dominance tests include both tests of sighting with one eye and tests of eye dominance in binocular vision. There are two tests of foot dominance. The series is reasonably comprehensive, it takes little time to administer, and most of the equipment can be inexpensively purchased at a local toy store.

Van Riper's *Critical Angle Board Test* was the first which revealed

2nd Edition

THE HARRIS TESTS OF LATERAL DOMINANCE

Record Blank

Name..Age.......... Date.......................... Examiner..........................

1. Knowledge of Left and Right
R hand.......... L ear.......... R eye..........

HAND DOMINANCE

2. Hand Preferences R..........%
.1 Throw a ball ....
.2 Wind a watch ....
.3 Hammer a nail ....
.4 Brush teeth ....
.5 Comb hair ....
.6 Turn door knob ....
.7 Hold eraser ....
.8 Use scissors ....
.9 Cut with knife ....
.10 Write ....

3. Simultaneous Writing
No. of Reversals:
R.......... L.......... ....
Co-ordination better: ....

4. Handwriting
Time: R.......... L..........
Co-ordination better: ....

5. Tapping
Number: R.......... L..........
Co-ordination better: ....

6. Dealing Cards
Time: R.......... L..........
Co-ordination better: ....

7. Strength of Grip (optional)
R.......... L.......... R.......... L..........

EYE DOMINANCE

8. Monocular Tests
.1 Kaleidoscope ....
.2 Telescope ....
.3 Sight rifle
Eye ....
Shoulder ....

9. Binocular Tests
.1 Cone: ....
.2 Hole: ....

10. Stereoscopic Tests (optional)
.1 Teleb: R..........% L..........% Supp?..........

FOOT DOMINANCE

11.1. Kick
Pref.......... Other.......... Better..........

11.2. Stamp
Foot used..........

RATINGS

Test					
	KNOWLEDGE OF LEFT AND RIGHT				
1	:	:			
	Confused	Hesitant	Normal		
	HAND DOMINANCE				
	:	:	:	:	
	L	L	M	R	R
2	:	:	:	:	
	L	L	M	R	R
3	:	:	:	:	
	L	L	M	R	R
4	:	:	:	:	
	L	L	M	R	R
5	:	:	:	:	
	L	L	M	R	R
6	:	:	:	:	
	L	L	M	R	R
7	:	:	:	:	
	L	L	M	R	R
	EYE DOMINANCE				
	:	:	:	:	
	L	L	M	R	R
8	:	:	:	:	
	L	L	M	R	R
9	:	:	:	:	
	L	L	M	R	R
10	:	:	:	:	
	L	L	M	R	R
	FOOT DOMINANCE				
11	:	:	:	:	
	L	L	M	R	R
11.1	:	:	:	:	
	L	L	M	R	R
11.2	:	:	:	:	

Family Background:

Conversion:

Qualitative Comments:

Fig. 22. First page of the Record Blank for the *Harris Tests of Lateral Dominance*, Second Edition. New York: Psychological Corp., 1955. Each of the hand, eye, and foot dominance tests is rated on a five-point scale: strongly left, moderately left, mixed, moderately right, and strongly right. Reduced in size.

latent tendencies for directional confusion.[9] It involves blindfolded drawings on two vertical surfaces at the same time with both hands, and the angle of the two surfaces is changed until mirroring occurs. Used for many years in speech clinics, it seems to reveal a basic tendency for directional confusion. Several other tests incorporating the same idea have since been developed, including the Simultaneous Writing Test which is part of the *Harris Tests of Lateral Dominance*. In these tests it is normal to draw or write mirrorwise with the nondominant hand, but any mirror-drawing or mirror-writing with the dominant hand points to the presence of a directional confusion. A series of hand dominance tests which does not include a test of directional confusion cannot be considered adequate.[10]

Eye-dominance tests of many kinds have been developed. In addition to those in the *Harris Tests of Lateral Dominance*, the reader may wish to look up Crider's battery of eye dominance tests,[11] to try out the recent test by Berens,[12] and to explore the possibilities of Spache's *Binocular Reading Test* (see p. 239).

The foot dominance tests in the current revision of the writer's tests have survived many years of tryout, and include kicking and stamping out a fire. The testing of ear dominance has been omitted, as being of little known theoretical significance.

II. The School Record

THE RECORD of a child's school career should always be examined carefully, as it often contains information of considerable value. The

[9] Van Riper, C., "The Quantitative Measurement of Laterality," *Journal of Experimental Psychology*, Vol. 18, 1935, pp. 372–382.

[10] Significant support of the point of view expressed here that directional confusion rather than untypical dominance is the important factor comes from Smith's research; cf. Smith, Linda, "A Study of the Laterality Characteristics of Retarded Readers and Reading Achievers," *Journal of Experimental Education*, Vol. 18, 1950, pp. 321–329. She found no relationship between reading success and patterns of lateral dominance, but a significant relationship between reading difficulty and mirroring on the Critical Angle-Board Test.

[11] Crider, Blake, "A Battery of Tests for the Dominant Eye," *Journal of General Psychology*, Vol. 31, 1944, pp. 179–190.

[12] Berens, Conrad, and Zerbe, Jean, "A New Pinhole Test and Eye-Dominance Tester," *American Journal of Ophthalmology*, Vol. 36, 1953, pp. 980–981.

child's age at entering school should be noted, as poor progress may be partly a result of starting at too young an age. His report-card marks indicate when his poor progress in reading was first noticed by his teachers, and the evidence about repeating terms or grades shows how serious his retardation was estimated to be.

His attendance record should be looked over for long absences that may have handicapped him, and for frequent short absences that may indicate poor physical condition or possible truancy. If he has changed schools or classes frequently the reasons for the changes should be investigated. Failure to acquire good reading habits is sometimes the direct result of frequent changes of teachers in the primary grades, with consequent confusion of teaching methods. Ratings on conduct, effort, and personality traits may be highly significant. If scores on standardized tests of intelligence and achievement are on the record, they should of course be noted.

The health record may give valuable information about sensory or physical defects. Defects of vision and hearing are often not detected by the routine tests used in schools and may escape the notice of teachers, so a clear physical record should not be accepted at its face value. When possible it is desirable to have a thorough physical examination given to the child. Similarly it is desirable to test the child's intelligence even if an IQ or MA appears on the record.

Teachers who have had a child in their classes in previous terms should be consulted for information that is not placed on record cards. It is important to find out what methods of teaching reading have been used with the child, especially in the first grade. Such information can be obtained only from his former teachers. They also can often contribute valuable facts about the child's behavior and conduct in class, his attitude toward reading, and his home conditions.

Such an inquiry will sometimes bring surprising results. A fourth-grade teacher looked up the record of her poorest reader and noticed that he received a B for work in the first term of the first grade, but failed the second term, and was marked deficient in reading from then on. She asked the child for the name of his 1B teacher and then went to that teacher for some information about the boy. The teacher indignantly denied that he had ever been in her class, stalked into the fourth-grade room, singled out the boy (whom she was not supposed to know), and asked him before the other pupils why he lied in saying he had ever been in her room. It does not take a great stretch of the imagination to infer that dislike and fear of that teacher had played an important part in creating the boy's difficulties in reading.

III. Arithmetic, Spelling, and Handwriting

Usually the child's school record card indicates whether or not his work in arithmetic has been satisfactory. If one wants to use a standardized arithmetic test to get a more accurate picture of the child's ability in that subject, any of the widely used achievement tests, such as the *Stanford,* or the *Metropolitan,* have appropriate parts. For research purposes it is highly desirable to have an accurate measure of ability in arithmetic, but in practical remedial work such refinement is usually not necessary. Reading disability cases often do considerably better in arithmetic computation than in problem-solving, in which their poor reading is more of a handicap. The child who is poor in problem-solving should be asked to explain his attempts at solution step by step. It is then possible to determine if his errors are due to lack of understanding of the vocabulary, careless errors in reading, choice of the wrong operation, skipping of a necessary step, errors of computation, and so on.

It has already been pointed out in Chapter VIII that poor reading is usually accompanied by poor spelling, and that children are apt to make similar errors in word recognition and spelling. From the standpoint of diagnosing reading difficulties it is more important to get a clear idea of the kinds of errors a child makes in spelling than it is to get an exact grade score. Convenient short lists of spelling words are included in the Monroe, Durrell, and Gates diagnostic batteries. Standardized spelling tests such as those found in general achievement tests may be used but are not necessary. A teacher can make up a satisfactory list by selecting words from the lists given in spellers or from printed spelling lists.[13] The words should include a variety of sounds, should contain nonphonetic as well as phonetic words, and should cover a difficulty range of about three grades.

In analyzing spelling errors, part of the check list of oral reading errors given on page 192 may be used as a guide. Reversals, omissions, additions, substitutions, and ignorance of the alphabet are common mistakes of poor spellers. Other common sources of error in spelling are attempts to spell nonphonetic words phonetically (*nees,* for *niece*), spelling which reflects mispronunciation (*liberry* for *library*), forgetting the end of a word while writing the first part, and lack of familiarity with the word or its meaning.[14]

Poor penmanship occurs frequently in poor readers. Much of their difficulty is the result of failure to learn letter forms and inability to spell correctly. In order to test writing independently of spelling it is advisable to dictate words for a penmanship test letter by letter, or to provide a printed selection that may be copied. Since writing words is employed as one method of teaching them in both reading and spelling, it is highly desirable to improve legibility of penmanship as part of a remedial program.[15] One should not overlook the possibility that poor penmanship in a reading disability case may be nothing more than a reflection of the child's dislike for reading and everything that goes with it. A history of previously better writing is significant in this regard.

IV. Emotional and Social Problems

CHILDREN who fail in reading are usually studied a few years after their troubles started, and because of the time that has passed and

[13] Such as the *Morrison-McCall Spelling Scale,* the *Iowa Spelling Scales,* or the *Buckingham Extension of the Ayres Spelling Scale.*

[14] A good reference on remedial teaching of spelling is: Gates, Arthur I., and Russell, D. H., *Diagnostic and Remedial Spelling Manual.* New York: Bureau of Publications, Teachers College, Columbia University, 1937.

[15] Some excellent suggestions about remedial work in penmanship may be found in Cole, L., "Heresy in Handwriting," *Elementary School Journal,* Vol. 38, 1938, pp. 606–618. See also Hildreth, Gertrude, *Learning the Three R's,* Revised Edition. Minneapolis: Educational Test Bureau, 1947; Brueckner, Leo J., and Bond, Guy L., *The Diagnosis and Treatment of Learning Difficulties,* Ch. 12. New York: Appleton-Century-Crofts, 1955.

the difficulty of getting accurate information about the past, it is always difficult to determine what part emotional problems may have played in causing the reading difficulty. Usually there are evidences of other types of handicaps also, and the relative importance of the different handicaps is frequently impossible to determine. Estimates of the significance of emotional factors in the causation of reading disabilities vary widely. Most children with reading difficulties show signs of emotional maladjustment which may be mild or severe. The percentage of maladjustment reported by a particular investigator varies with the standards he uses, as well as with the kind of child population he has studied.

Some time ago Gates estimated that among cases of severe reading disabilities, about 75 per cent show personality maladjustment, and in about 25 per cent the emotional difficulty is a contributing cause of the reading failure.[16] The writer believes that Gates' estimates are too low. Among reading disability cases seen in the Queens College Educational Clinic, close to 100 per cent show maladjustment of some kind, and the per cent in which the emotional difficulties are thought by the staff to have had a causal relationship to the reading problem runs over 50 per cent.

Emotional Problems as Causes of Reading Difficulties

Attempts to find a type of personality or type of maladjustment characteristic of children with reading disabilities have failed completely. Among children with reading problems one finds a few emotionally healthy children, some very inhibited "good" children, some children with definitely neurotic symptoms, some children whose misbehavior is conspicuous, some predelinquents, and some prepsychotic and psychotic children. Reading disability is not a unique entity, but rather is found in combination with practically all other forms of child maladjustment. While case studies of children often reveal intimate connections between the child's emotional difficulties and his reading difficulties, research studies comparing the personalities of poor readers with good readers have failed to reveal any

[16] Gates, Arthur I., "The Role of Personality Maladjustment in Reading Disability," *Journal of Genetic Psychology,* Vol. 59, 1941, pp. 77–83.

consistent group differences. This is probably due to the mistaken attempt to find a common personality type or problem in the reading disability cases.[17]

Teachers have come in recent years to blame reading problems on "emotional blocking." Unfortunately the term "emotional block" is a very vague one which is only the beginning of the description of what is wrong. There are different kinds of emotional blocking, and corrective procedures should differ according to the kind of blocking that has taken place. Even when an emotional problem has been identified and seems to have a causal relationship to the reading difficulty, one must remember that there are other children with similar emotional problems who read well. Often it is the combination of an emotional problem with an eye defect, a directional confusion, absence at crucial times for learning, or a particularly disliked or ineffectual teacher that centers the focus of the problem on reading.

Because reading is the first of the three R's to be systematically taught to children and is the one with which parents and teachers are most deeply concerned, it becomes quite naturally the first major educational issue around which problems of reluctance to grow up, resistance to going to school, or defiance of adult authority may be worked out. And because successful reading requires application and sustained concentration, emotional problems which prevent a child from concentrating and paying attention during reading lessons also prevent him from learning to read.

The attempt to describe carefully and accurately the different kinds of emotional problems that are contributary causes in reading disabilities is just in its early stages. Nevertheless several different types can already be distinguished.

1. Conscious Refusal to Learn. The child feels real hostility to parents or teachers or both, hostility which is consciously realized and readily expressed, and rejects reading because it is identified with the adult or adults against whom these feelings are directed.

[17] This argument has been presented by the writer in greater detail in two symposia. See Harris, A. J., "Egoistic Learning," *American Journal of Orthopsychiatry*, Vol. 24, 1954, pp. 781–784, and Harris, A. J., in "Unsolved Problems in Reading, II," *Elementary English*, Vol. 31, 1954, pp. 416–418.

This frequently occurs when there is a conflict between the cultural values of teacher and pupil; the child from a low socio-economic background may not be willing to accept the goals which teachers approve. To do so might jeopardize his social standing in the gang and place him in danger of being considered a sissy. Or the child may be imitating an admired parent who frequently voices contempt for "book-learning."

2. *Overt Hostility.* In some children, self-control is hard to maintain because the child has built up intense feelings of resentment, and his angry feelings are apt to break out with relatively little provocation. Such children are generally regarded as "bad" and school tends to become for them a continuing series of skirmishes and battles, interrupted by punishments. For the children of this kind, the teacher-pupil relationship rarely is of a type conducive to good conditions for learning.

3. *Negative Conditioning to Reading.* The child has built up a negative emotional response to reading (fear, anger, dislike) through the normal working of the principles of learning by association. Reading, having been present with someone or something already feared or disliked, becomes capable by itself of producing negative emotional reactions. As an example, a child had a first-grade teacher who walked around the room rapping knuckles with a ruler, and this teacher placed great stress on reading. The child's paniclike reaction to the teacher continued in response to reading lessons from other teachers in later years.

4. *Displacement of Hostility.* The child may be quite jealous of a favored brother or sister who is very good in reading, and his hostility becomes transferred to the act of reading which is the sibling's strong point. Another pattern is that of the child whose parent is an avid reader and who is unable to express hostility toward the parent in any open and direct fashion. The hostility may be expressed indirectly by failure in reading which is so important to the parent. Displaced hostility is rarely recognized as such by either parent or child.

5. *Resistance to Pressure.* It has been known for many years that

mothers who are overanxious about a child's eating and so try during early childhood to cram as much food as possible into the child, often find their children becoming feeding problems. Similarly the overambitious parent who wants Jimmy to be a Quiz Kid can develop a resistance to pressure for intellectual attainment that may take the form of disinterest in reading. Reading in such cases can become the main battleground on which the child fights for his rights.

6. *Clinging to Dependency.* The child who is overprotected and babied may, consciously or unconsciously, prefer to remain infantile and get attention through helplessness. Learning to read may mean growing up and becoming self-reliant, which the child is not yet ready to attempt. This is a common pattern among children who were only children for four or five years, the first brother or sister arriving while they were in kindergarten or first grade. Such children tend to interpret being sent to school as an attempt to get them out of the house so mother can give her full attention to the baby.

7. *Quick Discouragement.* Some children start off with a desire to learn to read, but meet with some initial difficulty and quickly give up and stop trying. These children, as a rule, are boys and girls who come to school with marked feelings of inferiority and insecurity already well established. Their home life fails to provide them with security and affection. Often they come from broken homes or homes in which much quarreling goes on. Many of them have the feeling (justified or unjustified) that their parents do not care for them. In various ways their lives have failed to give them wholesome feelings of self-confidence and self-respect. Because of this, they are easily convinced that they are stupid, and accept their inferior status in reading as natural when other, more self-confident children would exert extra effort.

8. *Success Is Dangerous.* In some children with deep-lying emotional problems almost any successful form of self-expression may stir up feelings of intense anxiety and distress, related to unconscious fears of destruction or damage. For such a child success in reading may symbolize entering into an adult activity and therefore

attempting to compete as a rival with a parent; such competition, in turn, implies the possibility of dreadful forms or retaliation. On an unconscious level such a child feels that safety lies in self-restriction and passivity. This type of reaction, based on deep-lying unconscious conflicts, tends to be quite resistive to remedial help unless psychotherapy is also provided.

9. *Extreme Distractability or Restlessness.* A high degree of tension in a child may build up an uncontrollable need for relief in the form of physical activity. The child who is unable to sit still is likely to fall behind in learning, and once he is aware of being behind, quick discouragement is likely to set in. Distractability is often closely related to restlessness and complicates the picture, since the child's attention is pulled away from the reading task by almost any stimulus. In cases of neurological deviation, distractability is one of the main problems to be overcome and often requires that the remedial work be completely individual, be conducted in a bare, distraction-free place, and be done calmly since high motivation may bring about disorganization.

10. *Absorption in a Private World.* Some children are absorbed in thoughts of their own to such an extent that they can give only intermittent attention to their environments, and cannot devote to reading the sustained attention needed for good learning. Many of their daydreams and reveries are of a wish-fulfilling type, in which they hit home runs, score touchdowns, and fulfill other romantic ambitions. Sometimes their ruminations are of a morbid character. In either case, their inner preoccupation interferes with the attentive concentration that good reading requires. When retreat into fantasy is so severe as to interfere with progress in a good remedial situation, referral for study by a clinical psychologist or psychiatrist is desirable. Some of these children, who seem merely to be inattentive so far as the teacher is concerned, are found to have severe mental disturbances (obsessive-ruminative psychoneuroses or schizoid states) for which intensive psychotherapy is urgently needed.

In describing these ten types of emotional reactions found in reading problems, an attempt has been made to make them understandable to teachers. More technical descriptions have been given by Pearson.[18] One must not be surprised to find cases which do not fit neatly into any of these categories; Blanchard's published cases are excellent correctives for any misconception that reading cases fall into neatly separated types.[19] For the psychologist using projective tests the Rohrschach patterns described by Vorhaus, although not specific to children with reading problems, are worth careful study.[20]

Effect of Reading Failure on Personality

Any child who finds himself outdistanced by the other children is apt to be disturbed by his lack of progress. At first he is likely to try harder. If his efforts are misdirected and fail to bring improvement, he eventually develops a strong feeling of frustration. He becomes convinced that he is "dumb" or stupid. When he is called upon to read, he is apt to become tense and emotionally upset, which makes his performance even worse. He generally builds up a strong dislike for reading and takes every opportunity to avoid reading. In school, as he falls farther and farther behind, he loses interest in much of the classwork and becomes inattentive, at least during reading lessons. His parents are likely to show strong disappointment because of his poor report cards and may nag, threaten, or punish him. This in turn tends to intensify his emotional difficulties and increase his dislike for school.

Different children react to feelings of failure in different ways. Some attempt to make themselves as inconspicuous as possible, and

[18] Pearson, Gerald H. J., "A Survey of Learning Difficulties in Children," *Psychoanalytic Study of the Child,* Vol. 7, 1952, pp. 372–386.

[19] Blanchard, Phyllis, "Psychogenic Factors in Some Cases of Reading Disability," *American Journal of Orthopsychiatry,* Vol. 5, 1935, pp. 361–374; "Reading Disabilities in Relation to Difficulties of Personality and Emotional Development," *Mental Hygiene,* Vol. 20, 1936, pp. 384–413; "Psychoanalytic Contributions to the Problem of Reading Disabilities," *The Psychoanalytic Study of the Child,* Vol. 2, 1946, pp. 163–188.

[20] Vorhaus, Pauline G., "Rorschach Configurations Associated with Reading Disability," *Journal of Projective Techniques,* Vol. 16, 1952, pp. 3–19; see also Pugh, Derek S., "A Note on the Vorhaus Configurations of Reading Disability," *Journal of Projective Techniques,* Vol. 18, 1954, pp. 478–480.

develop a meek, timid attitude that seems to say that they hope nobody will notice them. These children often develop the habit of daydreaming to excess. Nervous habits, such as twitching, nailbiting, stuttering, and general fidgetiness develop in reading disability cases who showed no signs of nervousness when they entered school. Some complain of headaches and dizziness or resort to vomiting spells in order to be sent home frequently. One youngster played hooky whenever he had a little money and would ride up and back on the subway until he was caught or hunger got the best of him. Fairly satisfactory compensations are achieved by some through becoming highly proficient in such school subjects as arithmetic and drawing, or by becoming outstanding in mechanical work or athletics. A few attempt to compensate for their shortcomings by boasting, bluffing, and exaggerating. One remedial case was described by his teacher as "a suitable prospect for the Tall Story Club." Still others adopt a truculent, defiant pose, as if to dare anyone — teacher included — to make fun of their weakness. The meaning of their behavior can be understood only by one who is willing to look for the reasons behind their behavior before taking disciplinary measures.

The child with a reading difficulty is very sensitive to the opinions of others and usually feels very keenly the criticism which teachers, classmates, and parents may express, even when the critical attitude is not stated plainly in words but only implied in actions and facial expressions. If the teacher is lacking in sympathetic understanding of the child's problem, the child is likely to become bitterly resentful.[21] The child with a severe reading handicap, although in the class, is often not an accepted member of it; more often than not he is right at the bottom of the class in general social acceptance.[22]

Even if a child is emotionally well adjusted when he enters school, continued failure in the most important part of schoolwork is practically certain to have unfavorable effects on his personality.

[21] Greenblat, Helen J., "I Hate Reading," *Understanding the Child,* Vol. 21, 1952, pp. 78–84.

[22] Buswell, Margaret M., "The Relationship Between the Social Structure of the Classroom and the Academic Success of the Pupils," *Journal of Experimental Education,* Vol. 22, 1953, pp. 37–52.

Investigating Emotional and Social Conditions

Understanding of the child's emotional make-up comes best from learning his past history and from day-to-day contact with him. The first and perhaps the most important phase of remedial procedure is to get on terms of friendship with the child. After the teacher is accepted as a friend he can usually get the child to talk with some freedom about himself, his likes and dislikes, his fears and hopes, his hobbies and interests, his friends and enemies, his family—in fact, about nearly anything. Since many of these children regard themselves as friendless, the remedial teacher is in an ideal position to establish himself as a sympathetic listener.

Personality tests of the paper-pencil questionnaire are often not too helpful with reading disability cases. Frequently it is necessary to read the questions to the child — a procedure that is time-consuming and probably less revealing than the information one could obtain by using the same time for informal talks. However, if the child can read well enough, tests like the *California Test of Personality* and the *Rogers Test of Personal Adjustment* may give helpful information. There are some children who find it very difficult to talk about their feelings, but have less difficulty answering the more impersonal printed questions.

The psychologist working in a clinic, who has only a limited time in which to try to understand the child, relies on interview and observation of the child's behavior during testing, supplemented by case history material and by the use of projective tests of personality. In the writer's clinical practice the *Rorschach* is always used, supplemented by a picture interpretation test (the new *Michigan Picture Test* seems more productive of material related to reading problems than the *Thematic Apperception Test* or the *Children's Apperception Test*), and interpretation of drawings and play activities.[23]

The parents are important sources of information, and the opin-

[23] Explanation of the newer trends in personality study lies outside the scope of this book. A good treatment of personality study for teachers will be found in Torgerson, T. L., and Adams, G. S., *Measurement and Evaluation for Elementary School Teachers,* Chs. 7–9. New York: Dryden Press, 1954.

ions and information they can supply should be sought. With both children and parents it is important to seem understanding, sympathetic, and noncritical, if true feelings are to be expressed. Even when a cordial relationship has been established one must remember that self-protection and self-deception are both very prevalent trends, so that what one is told must be interpreted with discriminating judgment.

Among the questions one should try to answer are the following:

1. Who are the other people in the home? What are their ages? How much education have they had? Which ones work? What are their outstanding traits?
2. What is the social and economic status of the family? How large is the family income? What sort of house and what sort of neighborhood do they live in? Are they living at a poverty, marginal, adequate, comfortable, or luxurious level? Has the status of the family changed markedly since the child's birth?
3. How adequate is the physical care given the child? Is he provided with suitable food and clothing? Does he get proper attention when sick? Have his physical defects been corrected?
4. What intellectual stimulation is provided in the home? What language is spoken? How cultured are the parents and other members of the family? What newspapers, magazines, and books are available in the home? How much has the child been encouraged to read?
5. How is the child treated by his parents? Do they love him, or are there indications of rejection or of marked preference for other children? What disciplinary procedures do they use? Do they compare him unfavorably with other children or regard him as stupid? Are they greatly disappointed in him?
6. How is the child treated by his brothers and sisters? What do they think about him? Do they boss him or tease him about his poor ability?
7. How does the child feel about his family? Does he feel neglected or mistreated? Has he feelings of hatred or resentment against members of his family? Does he resort to undesirable behavior in order to get attention?
8. What efforts have been made to help him at home with his schoolwork? Who has worked with him? What methods have been used? How has the child responded to this help? What have the results been?

9. How does the child spend his spare time? What interests does he show? Does he have any hobbies? Does he show any special talent? What are his goals for the future?
10. Who are his friends, what are they like, and how does he get along with them? Does he play by himself? Does he prefer younger children? Is he a leader or a follower?
11. What signs of emotional maladjustment does he show? Has he any specific nervous habits? Is he a poor eater or poor sleeper? What variations from normal emotional behavior does he show?
12. How does he feel about himself? Has he resigned himself to being stupid? Does he give evidence of open feelings of inferiority and discouragement? If not, what substitute forms of behavior has he adopted?

When there seems to be evidence of a marked emotional disturbance the teacher should not try to analyze this himself but should take the initiative to call the child to the attention of the person responsible for working with such problems in the school system; this may be the school guidance counselor, school psychologist, principal, visiting teacher, or school social worker. Intensive study in a child guidance clinic or examination by a clinical psychologist or psychiatrist is probably needed. Decisions as to what kind of treatment should be started first, and whether or not to proceed with remedial teaching, should preferably be made by the specialist or clinic.

V. Interrelationships of Causal Factors

THE DIAGNOSTIC PROBLEM would be comparatively easy if one could expect to find only one important handicap in each reading disability problem. That would be, unfortunately, a mistaken expectation. Most children who develop severe disabilities labor under the burden of several different handicaps, any one of which could be an important drawback to progress in reading.

Mitchell was seven and a half years old and had just completed the second grade in a private school. His teacher did not think that his reading was very poor, but his mother was very much worried about it. During a morning of testing and interviewing, the following significant facts were discovered: (1) Mitchell had average or slightly above average general intelligence, but showed definite inferiority in visual perception. (2) His speech was also somewhat indistinct, and a slight hearing loss was suspected. (3) He had entered the first grade in public school when only five and a half years old. His teacher rated him as immature and inattentive, and in addition he missed several weeks because of scarlet fever. He was transferred to a private school and entered the high first grade with zero reading ability. Lack of reading readiness because of too early a start was obvious. (4) Tests with the *Keystone Visual Survey* showed marked difficulty in binocular vision, with both vertical and horizontal eye-muscle imbalance. He had been taken to an eye specialist who prescribed stereoscopic exercises to correct the condition, but Mitchell's mother had had difficulty in getting him to do the exercises and had discontinued them. (5) Mitchell showed marked right-hand dominance and equally definite left-eye dominance; he could not remember which was his right hand and which his left, and could be considered a typical case of mixed lateral dominance with directional confusion. (6) He had been exposed to teaching that was undoubtedly ineffective and unsuited to his needs. Although the class was small, there was no individualization of work. The teacher used the now-outmoded story-memory method; one day the teacher would read a selection to the class, and the next day the pupils would take turns in oral reading of the same selection. Mitchell had good auditory memory, and by listening carefully he had been able to "read" well without paying much attention to the printed words. Actually he was unable to read primer material satisfactorily, but he had been trying to read first and second readers. No training in phonics or word analysis had been given. (7) There were several sources of emotional difficulty. Mitchell had been a nervous, overactive child since babyhood. His mother had taken him to a child guidance clinic when he was four years old, because she had had such trouble trying to get him to mind. He had one older sister whose good behavior and excellent schoolwork were frequently held up to him as examples. His father had been in the Army for three years, stationed away from home. Since Mitchell was much more attached to his father than to his mother, this separation was undoubtedly a source of anxiety. (8) Mitchell had never shown evidence of a really strong desire to learn to read.

In this case, as in so many others, it was impossible to determine the relative contribution of each handicap to the total picture of failure. The number of different handicaps he showed is by no means unusual in severe reading disabilities. From a practical standpoint, the aim of a thorough diagnosis is not to fix the blame for the child's difficulties, but to discover each of the many conditions that may require correction. A person who develops an enthusiasm for any one theory of causation can frequently find evidence of the handicap he looks for, but is likely to overlook many other significant complications while doing so. An unbiased search for every possible handicap is needed for a really comprehensive and satisfactory diagnosis.

Suggested Additional Reading

BRUECKNER, LEO J., and GUY L. BOND. *The Diagnosis and Treatment of Learning Difficulties,* Chs. 3, 4.

GATES, ARTHUR I. *The Improvement of Reading,* Third Edition, Ch. 4.

ROBINSON, HELEN M. *Why Children Fail in Reading.* Chicago: University of Chicago Press, 1946.

· XI ·

Basic Principles of Remedial Reading

IT HAS BEEN SAID that remedial teaching is nothing but good, effective teaching; that the only difference between remedial teaching and ordinary teaching is that remedial teaching is done more thoroughly, more systematically, and more efficiently. There is a good deal of truth in such a statement. There is nothing magical about remedial work. On the other hand, there is more to remedial teaching than thoroughness and system. Some teachers who have tried to do remedial work have assumed that what the pupils needed was drill and more drill. They have used the same general methods, have employed the same materials, and have aimed at the same goals as in their regular class teaching. The results in such cases are usually disappointing.

The distinction between remedial teaching and classroom teaching has become less sharp because superior teachers have incorporated into their daily procedures the principles which are fundamental in good remedial work. In their classes, the level and type of instruction is based on an understanding of what the pupils need; drill is not an end in itself but is employed when teacher and pupils recognize the need for it; work is related to vital pupil interests; and happy, busy children move on from one successful learning experience to another.

The problems involved in helping children with reading difficulties are much the same, whether the help is given in a regular classroom or in a special small group or individual teaching situation. For this reason, the term "remedial" is used in the rest of this chapter as applying both to corrective reading in classrooms and to remedial reading in an out-of-class situation.

I. General Characteristics of Remedial Teaching

Basing Remedial Instruction on Diagnosis

When a car is towed into a garage out of commission a good mechanic tries to find out exactly what has gone wrong with it — to locate the particular part that is defective or to discover what adjustment needs to be made. Effective remedial teaching is similarly based first of all on an attempt to find out what is wrong, and in a similar way involves concentrated effort to improve the phases of performance which are deficient.

The slogan, "Teach, test, reteach," has gained considerable popularity. It sums up very briefly a good deal of educational wisdom. It points out the need for accurate measurement of the success of pupils in mastering the subject-matter to which they have been exposed, and the desirability of emphasizing in review the particular phases of the work that escaped them the first time. The teacher who has acquired this point of view is applying the basic principle of remedial teaching in his everyday work.

When children are scheduled for remedial work, the slogan needs a little modification. It now should read, "Test, teach, retest." The pupils have failed to master the material when it was first taught to them, so the teacher starts with testing to determine what needs to be retaught. On the basis of his results he decides upon an appropriate plan of teaching to overcome the difficulties which are apparent. After proceeding with this type of instruction for a while it is necessary to test again to see whether the instruction has been effective. Sometimes the retest shows that the difficulties which were present at the beginning have been overcome but that new difficulties have now arisen. It then becomes necessary to plan another teaching program in the light of the new information and to continue in this way until achievement is generally satisfactory.

Starting from What the Pupil Knows

Laying a foundation before putting up a superstructure is as important in educational work as it is in building construction. In arithmetic it is accepted that a knowledge of number combinations is essential for progress in computation, that addition should be taught before multiplication, and so on. The sequence of instruction in reading is not as clearly established and stages of progress are not as clearly defined as in arithmetic, but the same principle of laying the necessary foundations before proceeding to a higher level holds good. If a twelve-year-old has second-grade reading ability, his instruction should start at the second-grade level. If he has marked weaknesses in word recognition, those must be overcome before one can expect to get satisfactory results from instruction designed to increase rate.

Selecting Appropriate Material

The first important problem in the selection of materials is to find reading of the appropriate level of difficulty. The necessity of providing pupils with material which they can read without too much difficulty can hardly be overemphasized. The interest value of the reading is another very important problem, since pupils try hardest on material that they like, and older boys and girls often express disdain for books written for younger children. An abundance of varied types of books and exercises should be available if a well-rounded program of reading is to be followed.

Securing Motivation

Perhaps the most important problems in remedial work are those which are concerned with arousing interest and maintaining effort. Without good motivation a remedial program is sure to be ineffective. Like a car with a dead battery, it cannot move along because it lacks the needed spark. Because motivation is so important, a separate section is devoted to it.

II. Principles of Effective Motivation[1]

THE CHILD whose initial efforts to read have been unsuccessful gets caught in a vicious cycle. Because his experiences in reading have been unpleasant he has learned to dislike reading. Because he dislikes reading he avoids it when he can. By doing a minimum of practice he achieves a minimum of improvement. Meanwhile those who enjoy reading keep on improving and the poor reader's handicap keeps on increasing.

Without the will to learn, the child in need of help in reading rarely accomplishes very much. The term "remedial teaching" has tended to concentrate attention mainly on what the teacher does. It is time that we talk more about "remedial learning" since the heart of the problem is not what the teacher does but what the learner does. The teacher's main task is to arouse within the learner the motivation to do the necessary but not always easy or interesting jobs that must be accomplished in becoming a competent reader, and to guide the learning situation in such a way that the motivation is sustained.

The poor reader feels his inadequacy not only in reading lessons but also in all other phases of school work in which reading is done. One can accept a limited type of failure, such as being unable to sing in tune or being unable to write very legibly, without being hurt too deeply or having one's self-estimate too badly impaired. The stress which is placed on reading as a criterion of general competence in school, by teachers, by parents, and by fellow pupils, often causes the child who regards himself as a poor reader to feel that he is an intellectual pauper. Being a poor reader is far worse than being an inaccurate speller or a clumsy gymnast or an incompetent artist because the poor reader so often concludes that he must be generally stupid.

From this standpoint, the central task in remedial reading is to help the learner to change his feelings about reading. A thorough program aimed at this goal has four main aspects. First, the poor

[1] Much of the material in this section is taken from Harris, Albert J., "Motivating the Poor Reader," *Education*, Vol. 73, 1953, pp. 566–574.

reader should be helped to feel that he is liked, appreciated, and understood. Second, success experiences are needed to supply the basis for overcoming the negative aftereffects of frustration and failure. Third, active effort must be stimulated and sustained by use of both intrinsically interesting reading matter and extrinsic or somewhat artificial incentives. Finally, the learner should become involved as fully as possible in the analysis of his reading problem, the planning of his own reading activities, and the evaluation of his results.

The Remedial Teacher as a Person

The most important single characteristic of a good remedial teacher is a real liking for children. The liking must be genuine—children quickly detect the difference between a warm, friendly person and one who puts on a show of friendliness without really feeling that way. Appearance, dress, age, speech, theoretical knowledge, experience — all these are less important than a genuine fondness for children as they are, complete with their faults and annoying habits.

A good remedial teacher has a manner which conveys a note of optimism and good cheer to the children. He may be full of contagious enthusiasm, or he may be a quiet person who creates a calm, relaxed atmosphere. In his contacts with children he tries to avoid any display of vexation or irritation. He looks for opportunities to praise, and tries to make all of his criticism kindly and constructive.

A good remedial teacher is also sensitive to the emotional needs of the children. He tries to provide a setting in which children can feel that they are appreciated and that their ideas and feelings are respected. He seeks to build up their self-confidence and to restore their shaken feelings of personal worth. He encourages children to confide in him by accepting their confidences with friendly interest. He never forces a child to do anything, but instead tries to arrange the situation so that the child will do what he wants willingly.

A few people seem to be naturally endowed with warmth, tact, and sympathetic understanding. Such people usually get good results in remedial work even if the methods they employ are far from the best. A few others seem to be completely insensitive to children as people; these, in the writer's opinion, should avoid all branches of the teaching profession. The rest, comprising the majority, can improve their relationships with children greatly by studying the principles of mental hygiene and trying to incorporate them into their everyday relations with children.

The teacher who succeeds with poor readers must be able to convey to them the feeling that they are liked, appreciated, and understood. Each teacher must do this in ways harmonious with his own personality. A quiet teacher who creates a calm, relaxed atmosphere, a vivacious teacher who stirs children up, and a strong teacher whose self-confidence conveys a feeling of security to children, may each get fine results although their ways are different. Children know when they are liked, and also have a keen sense for hypocrisy. The teacher who does not like a child usually cannot help him.

Acceptance, Approval, and Understanding

There are some children who are so deeply discouraged that they have given up trying and have resigned themselves to chronic failure. This attitude may pervade not only their response to school but also their general social relationships. Daydreaming may take the place of any attempt at real accomplishment. For such children it may be wise to delay a new start on reading until the child has found at least one other activity in which he feels successful and for which he has received merited approval and recognition.

Peter, a nonreader, was so withdrawn that a total break with reality was feared. Instead of starting immediately with reading, it was decided to work first on improving his social adjustment. With excellent cooperation from his classroom teacher, Peter was gradually drawn into activity with puppets. His first step was manipulating a puppet, out of sight behind the little stage. Performing at first just for the teacher, then for a couple of classmates, he gradually worked up to larger audiences. This was the entering wedge. Gradually he became more communicative and began to enter more actively into social participation with his classmates. Remedial reading was successfully begun several months later.

Osborne [2] has strongly recommended starting the child with some easy-to-learn skill that is respected by other children, and has found magic tricks to be ideal for this purpose. It makes sense to attack total discouragement first by building success in an area in which good results can be obtained far more quickly than in reading.

The poor reader's needs go beyond being liked; he desperately wants to be understood. He often feels hurt, or discouraged, or angry. The teacher who is sensitive to these feelings and can get across to the child the conviction that the teacher's kindly interest is not shaken by his awareness of these feelings actually can help the child greatly to get his emotions under control.

One of the feelings prevalent among poor readers is the notion that they are not like other children, that their troubles are strange and unusual. The teacher should, therefore, try to convey the ideas that one can be bright in many ways and still have trouble with reading, that many children have trouble learning to read, and that it is a difficulty which is neither unusual nor impossible to overcome.

During the course of a remedial program there are inevitably downs as well as ups. These are times when discouragement returns and effort slackens. These periods are sometimes induced by events outside of the remedial program. A quarrel at home, a cold, insufficient sleep, or a sarcastic remark by another teacher may be the starting point of a slump. At these times the remedial teacher can provide invaluable support, by slowing the pace and maintaining a steady faith in the child. Being a sympathetic listener for the child who wants to pour out his troubles also serves a useful purpose, provided the teacher remains a friendly teacher and does not trespass into psychotherapy.

Nothing Succeeds Like Success

Being understanding, sympathetic, and encouraging will not do much good if the child continues to experience frustration in his efforts at reading. It is essential at the beginning of a remedial program to start at a level easy enough so that a successful learning

[2] Osborne, Worth J., "Emotional Blocks in Reading," *Elementary School Journal,* Vol. 52, 1951, pp. 23–30.

experience is virtually certain. The inexperienced remedial teacher often fails to recognize fully the extent of the child's deficiency and tends to overestimate the level at which he is able to experience success. Because of this, the invaluable lift that comes when hope is reinforced by real achievement may be forfeited.

One of the pitfalls for the unwary is relying too much on the grade scores obtained from standardized reading tests. These scores tend to show the level at which comprehension can be achieved with difficulty, rather than the level at which fluency and reasonable accuracy can be expected. Sometimes it is wise to begin one or two years below the level indicated by test scores. Informal tryouts of sample pages from books of different difficulty levels may provide a better indication of where to start than can be gained from test scores.

After a child has tasted the delightful flavor of an auspicious beginning, good judgment is needed in estimating how much to try to cover, how fast to go, and how soon to move to a higher level of difficulty. If the learner has developed real interest in his progress and is ready to go faster he will often suggest a more rapid pace. The teacher who is patient and willing to proceed very slowly at first is often rewarded by accelerated progress later.

Dramatizing Progress

The principle of celebrating a child's success is very important in remedial teaching. Every sign of improvement in the child's work should be noted and praised. Since most poor readers are insecure and lack self-confidence, visible, concrete evidence of their improvement is more necessary than it is with normal children.

Records of progress do not need to be elaborate in order to be effective. One remedial teacher devised a very simple scheme that worked extremely well. When she was ready to listen to a child read orally, she drew a little box on a sheet of paper. She would select some one fault that she was trying to get that child to eliminate, and tell him that every time he made that kind of error she would make a little cross in the box. When he finished, she would give him a star to paste on his record if he had made fewer errors of that type than at the previous practice reading. This worked especially well for eliminating such faults as careless errors in word recognition, repetitions, or overlooking punctuation marks.

Progress charts can be devised to record progress in any phase of reading. Different kinds of progress charts can be constructed for

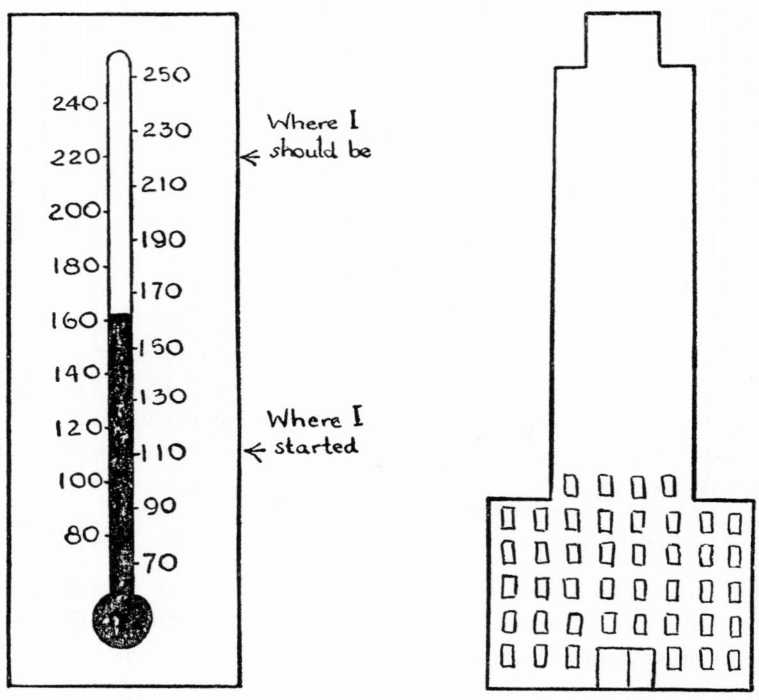

Fig. 23. Individual progress charts. Left, thermometer chart for recording improvement in rate of reading. Right, skyscraper chart for recording the completion of units of work; as a unit is finished the pupil draws in the windows of another floor.

number of pages, stories, or books read; number of new words learned; decrease in number of errors in oral reading; number of word families or phonic principles learned; accuracy of comprehension; rate of reading; and so on. It is desirable to have a separate record for each goal that is being emphasized in the remedial program. At any one time, a remedial pupil should be keeping track of his improvement toward three or four different goals. After these goals have been achieved, new ones should be set up.

There are many different kinds of progress charts. With very young children, colored stars, paper bunnies, or pine trees that can be pasted onto a piece of stiff paper work very well. With older children, more sophisticated forms are usually desirable.

Some of the types of charts that have been used successfully are as follows:

1. The thermometer chart. This is useful for recording a cumulative result, such as the number of pages read or number of words learned. See Figure 23.
2. The skyscraper chart. As the child finishes a unit, he fills in a window. See Figure 23.
3. The race-track chart. Progress is recorded by moving a tiny auto or horse around the track.
4. The map chart. A trip by airplane across the country or to the North Pole represents successive good lessons.
5. The bar graph. This can be used for the whole group. Each child has a line, and fills in another block as he completes each unit.
6. The bookcase chart. The child draws an empty bookcase, and as he finishes each story or book, draws another book in the bookcase. The books can be of various colors. See Figure 59 on page 489.
7. The basket or ship chart. Each child cuts a basket or ship out of colored paper, prints his name on it, and pastes it to a large piece of stiff cardboard in such a way as to leave a little pocket. As he finishes a story or book, he prints the name of it on a small slip of paper and places it in his basket or ship. See Figure 60 on page 490.
8. The line graph. This is best adapted for recording progress in speed and accuracy of comprehension. See Figure 66, on page 531.

Frequently it is advisable to let the child decide on the kind of progress record he wants to make. Many children devise charts that mean more to them than any record that the teacher can devise. For instance, one boy's main enthusiasm was swimming; he devised a chart which represented reading progress in the form of a race back and forth across the swimming pool. A crudely drawn chart made and used by the child usually has greater motivating power than a very pretty one made by the teacher.

The units of improvement should be small enough so that progress can be recorded at frequent intervals. With remedial cases it is usually more desirable to have a child compete with his own record than to compete with other children. If a group is fairly ho-

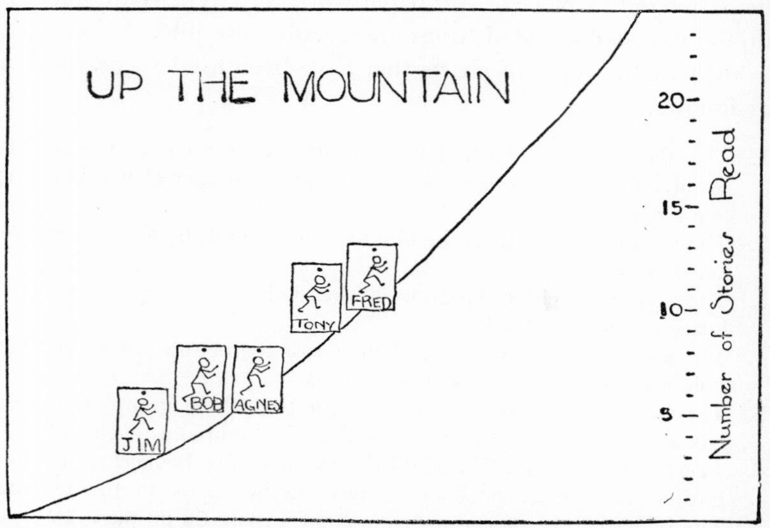

Fig. 24. Progress chart suitable for use with a small remedial group of young pupils; provides recognition for small amounts of progress.

mogeneous, however, a chart which compares the progress of the children in the group may have a desirable motivating effect (see Fig. 24).

Social Recognition

Social recognition is very important. Opportunities can be created for the poor reader to demonstrate his growing competence befoıe his classmates, and their generosity in commending him for his improvement can usually be counted on to serve as a further incentive. The school principal and other teachers may provide appreciative audiences. It is especially valuable to keep the parents well informed about the child's improvement. For many children the anxiety of the parents, shown in nagging, threats, punishment, and ineffectual attempts at tutoring, is one of the major deterrents to progress. When the parents begin to relax and discontinue these pressures at home, the child is able to function better.

The Interest Factor

The desirability of making reading interesting is not a controversial issue in theory. In practice it is often ignored, with teachers relying too much on drill and repetition.

To make reading interesting there are two main alternatives. One is to employ reading material which is intrinsically capable of attracting and holding the reader's interest. The other is to use the material that is available in ways that foster interest. The first places major reliance on finding or creating material, while the second emphasizes procedure. These are not alternatives in the sense that one has to choose one or the other, but rather two aspects which, when successfully combined, produce ideal results.

The teacher who has seen the magical effects obtainable when just the right book is placed in a child's hands cannot ever again disregard the importance of trying to match the book to the child. Some books have earned the honored place of being "starters"—books which over and over again have been a child's first captivating reader.

Two types of stories are particularly successful in this role. One type includes those which, like *Lentil* and *Mike Mulligan and His Steam Shovel,* employ the time-honored plot of the underdog who triumphs in the end. The other includes humorous stories, like *Mr. Popper's Penguins, Mary Poppins,* and the various absurd stories by Dr. Seuss, such as *Bartholomew and the Oobleck.* But no book has magic for all children. For one, animal stories; for another, cowboys and Indians; for a third, old-fashioned fairy tales; for a fourth, nothing will suit but solid scientific information. Mystery, adventure, sports, and hobbies provide spheres of interest for many. To find the right book, one must know both the child and the books. This problem is treated in detail in Chapter XVII.

When unable to find material to fit the child's interests, the resourceful teacher is sometimes able to stimulate interest in material which is available. It is a mistake to assume that one must keep to the interests which a child already manifests. In attempting to sell a new interest it is well to use stories and books known to have wide appeal for many children.

There are some children who cannot read well enough for any book that can appeal to their interests, and will not accept "baby stuff." These children are usually trying to give the impression that they are grown up. Their inner insecurity makes it very difficult for them to acknowledge and accept the low level at which they actually can function in reading.

Creative writing can be both a way of building self-respect and an avenue to reading for these children. The emphasis placed by the late Grace Fernald on the use of stories created by the child was perhaps as great a contribution to remedial reading procedure as the kinesthetic procedures which she advocated.[3]

This approach starts with conversation. The child is encouraged to talk about his recreational outlets — sports, pets, hobbies, or favorite radio and television programs. Careful note is made of anything about which he displays enthusiasm. Selecting one such topic, the teacher suggests that maybe he would like to make up a little story about it which the teacher will write down. With very inarticulate or inhibited children it is helpful to have pictures which can serve as the basis of brief descriptive statements. It is advisable to use the child's exact words, even if somewhat ungrammatical. No effort should be made to simplify the vocabulary, since the child is using language that he understands and perhaps is quite proud of the long or unusual words he is able to employ. The early selections should be kept quite short.

Once dictated, the story is typed or printed in manuscript by the teacher, and then the child reads it. He is helped with the words when necessary. Several repetitions may bring the story to the point where it can be taken home and read to parents. The long and unusual words are likely to be identified quickly, while errors on

[3] Fernald, Grace M., *Remedial Techniques in Basic School Subjects.* New York: McGraw-Hill, 1943.

common little words are apt to persist. Since the arousal of motivation is the most important goal of the early lessons, it is not wise to spend a large amount of time on word study. However, many children enjoy listing the new words they become able to recognize and are quite fussy about keeping the score accurately.

Essentially this procedure is very much the same as the "experience story" method which is widely used with beginning readers and familiarity with that method is necessary if one is to get the most out of this approach. It is important to avoid rote repetition without sufficient attention to the copy. Transfer of responsibility for writing the story to the child may be made as soon as he has enough of a writing vocabulary to feel like trying it; help with many words will continue to be needed. After a while the child will usually express a wish to start reading in a book, and a gradual transition to book reading can then be started.

The priceless ingredient of this approach is its ability to motivate many children who are resistive or antagonistic to easy printed materials. Its drawbacks are fairly obvious. It makes heavy demands on the teacher, who must prepare the reading matter and provide close supervision during the child's reading. It also is deficient in amount of reading and cannot provide the extensive reading practice necessary to develop fluency.

Fortunately, many poor readers are not so resistant to the use of easy and not too exciting books. For many, the experience of being able to read anything with ease and fluency more than makes up for the immature content; success itself generates and maintains interest. Some of these children are emotionally immature enough really to enjoy stories written for children several years their junior. Others can be given the incentive of preparing simple little stories to read to younger brothers and sisters, or to a first-grade or kindergarten class.

The Begin-Over Approach. With older children the teacher may find it desirable to explain the reasons for going back to very easy books. The importance of learning the bothersome little first- and second-grade words can be pointed out. Then the fact that the child is much older and smarter than when he tried these books before can be emphasized. If the child is willing to start over again, things will come much more easily and quickly, and a foundation can be built for progressing to reading matter more appropriate for his age.

The "begin-over" approach just described is not successful with all poor readers. It seems to be most suitable to those who are willing to do almost anything if it will help them, and for those who find the content of primary-grade readers acceptable. For these children, the carefully controlled vocabularies and well-spaced repetition of good modern readers help greatly in building up fundamental reading skills.

Avoiding Monotony

Variety adds spice to the remedial program. Children, even if highly motivated to improve their reading, often get tired of doing the same thing again and again. Each lesson should be subdivided into at least three different kinds of reading activities; some tutors like to break an hour lesson into at least five or six different kinds of activity. When there are daily reading lessons, it is desirable to vary the plan from day to day. From time to time a surprise should be introduced.

Transforming Drills into Games

There are many kinds of remedial activities, such as practice in word and phrase recognition, learning phonic skills, and workbook exercises to sharpen comprehension, that are not particularly enjoyable. The desire to improve will carry the learner through them, but is usually not enough to produce the intense concentration characteristic of highly effective learning. Such activities can often be made exciting by the appropriate use of incentives.

Many kinds of drill can be disguised as games, becoming play rather than distasteful work. Adaptations of *Bingo* are easily constructed, or can be purchased ready made. Card games such as rummy and poker are easily adapted to the use of word or phrase cards. A magnet on a string catches fish (word cards decorated with paper clips) from a pond (desk top). The rules of baseball, football, and basketball provide scoring systems for competitive scoring between two teams, which can be groups of learners, pupil against pupil, or pupil against teacher. A number of devices of this type are described on pages 380–383.

Most effective, if properly used, is the learner's competitive urge to improve his own previous record. This is what gives such motivating power to remedial activities in which the learner can keep his score in comparable units, lesson after lesson. The magic of the *G-score* keeps the McCall-Crabbs exercises popular after thirty years of use.[4] The graphing of rate and comprehension scores on successive practices can be a most effective device for speeding up slow readers. The immediate goal of trying to beat last times' score is a major part of the fascination of such popular forms of recreation as golf, bowling, and fishing. The same type of motivation can be successfully utilized in remedial learning. Failure to try to use it means neglecting one of the most effective types of incentives.

A related issue is the avoidance of fatigue. In general, activities which are easy and pleasurable can be carried on for long periods of time, while those which require self-discipline and concentrated effort soon tire the learner. Even when well motivated in game form, reading activities which demand a high level of effort should be brief and interspersed with less taxing activities.

Cooperation between Teacher and Learner

One of the vital ingredients of a well-motivated remedial approach is the learner's feeling that the program is his program, not something imposed upon him by somebody else. This can be achieved if the reading problem is approached as something on which teacher and pupil can work together. For this to work, there must be a teacher-learner relationship in which the learner trusts the teacher's good intentions and wants to help himself. Under these conditions the learner can take an active part in discussing his problems in reading, in trying to select the particular weaknesses that are most urgently in need of attention, in the selection of materials to be used, and in evaluating progress.

[4] McCall, W. A., and Crabbs, Leila M., *Standard Test Lesson in Reading*, Revised. Books A, B, C, D, E. New York: Bureau of Publications, Teachers College, Columbia University, 1950.

The degree of insight some children possess into their own difficulties is amazing. Sometimes they not only can pick out the major weak points in their reading skills, but also have intelligent ideas about how they came to be poor readers. Such children can often be given wide latitude in selecting their own materials. They delight in devising ways of checking their work and in constructing charts to record their progress.

This does not mean that the teacher adopts a passive role. On the contrary, the teacher is responsible for the entire process. The teacher encourages the learner to make suggestions, but is obligated to point out important issues the learner may have overlooked, to correct erroneous interpretations and proposals, and to provide helpful guidance at every stage. Encouraging the learner to help in planning does not mean abdication of responsibility, but rather creating an atmosphere of truly cooperative work.

Occasionally one finds a pupil who resents the implication that anything is wrong with his reading. "Why pick on me, I can read all right," is a familiar complaint, particularly to junior high school teachers. In a way, many of these boys and girls are right. They can read enough to plow through a passable portion of the assigned reading. But their reading is likely to be laborious, halting, slow, full of minor inaccuracies and misunderstood words, and only partially understood. On standardized tests these pupils usually rate two or more years below grade placement. They are aware that they are not particularly good readers, but usually do not realize how faulty their reading actually is.

Bob was resentful about having been singled out of his class for special help in reading. "Maybe you are right," said the teacher. "You can take a reading test if you want to, and we can score it together. After that you can decide whether or not you want to work on your reading." Bob took the *Iowa Silent Reading Test, Elementary,* on which his subtest grade scores ranged from 3.3 in Rate to 7.6 in Use of Index. A bright boy of thirteen, he was quite shocked at his poor showing. But he had checked the scoring himself, and soon he and the teacher were discussing possible reasons why his reading was so slow and listing some of the things he could do to increase his rate.

Learning exactly where one stands is not a good stimulus for all poor readers. To a sensitive, easily discouraged child it may be disheartening. It is also inadvisable for those whose reading is on a par with their general intellectual development and who are already reading about up to capacity. For them, emphasizing their retardation may be a form of needless cruelty. For pupils like Bob, however, the opportunity to learn just where they stand on objective standardized tests may be exactly what is needed to break through the crust of real or assumed indifference. One of the potential values of standardized tests often overlooked in schools is the function of helping the pupil, as well as the teacher, to appraise progress and become aware of needs.

Children sometimes develop the notion that the main reason for learning to read is to please the teacher. The teacher shows pleasure when one reads well and shows or implies displeasure when one reads poorly. If the child wants to retaliate against the teacher, it may seem logical to get even by not reading, or by reading poorly.

Such an attitude is usually a transfer to the classroom of attitudes learned at home. Many children eat, not because they are hungry, but to please mother. Such children can often beat their mothers in a contest of wills by refusing to eat. If a child who has learned this technique has a mother who is quite concerned over his reading, he is likely to experiment to find out if rejecting reading can be used in the same way as rejecting food. Often the experiment is successful. Not progressing in reading can become a way of keeping mother's attention centered on the child, and this may be more important to the child than the satisfactions of successful learning. Since for young children teachers are to a large extent substitute parents, by not trying to read the child may be attempting to capture a larger share of the teacher's attention.

If the child is refusing to read because he thinks that he can control his mother and teacher that way, obviously the first step is to demonstrate to him that it will not work. Mother and teacher must both switch over to the attitude that they are not concerned whether Johnny reads or not, and must maintain this attitude steadily for a period long enough to convince him. This is a plan that requires perseverance and should not be attempted unless there is good reason to believe that it will be carried through without faltering. In class, the teacher must be able to put across the idea that Johnny doesn't have to read if he doesn't want to, and that while she likes him and would like to see him succeed, Johnny himself is the only one who loses out if he doesn't learn to read.

Underlying such a problem is the fact that the child has learned an undesirable way of getting attention, probably because he wasn't getting enough attention to satisfy him before. Since the underlying need for attention will persist, a really satisfactory solution must involve providing the child with better ways of getting the attention and affection that he craves. Approval must be given for many things he does which deserve commendation if he is to give up less praiseworthy means of attracting notice. When resistance to reading arises out of the fundamental emotional needs of the child, more than a change in teaching technique is required.

Remedial Reading and Psychotherapy

Good remedial teaching has some of the characteristics of good psychotherapy. It is based on the development of a friendly, warm, comfortable relationship between teacher and pupil, for which the term rapport is used. It employs suggestion and reassurance, sometimes used in psychotherapy, to encourage the child and express the faith of the teacher in his ability to learn and improve. It provides the child with the security of feeling that the adult knows what he is doing and can be relied on, while at the same time the child is offered some choice in the selection of activities. It requires that the teacher be clear about what kinds and degrees of freedom the child may be allowed, and that he be pleasantly firm in maintaining the particular limits he feels it necessary to employ. It requires sufficient objectivity on the teacher's part to see the child clearly and to avoid becoming involved as a partisan in the child's struggles with his parents or complaints about his teachers. It is intended to strengthen the child's self-respect and to build his confidence so that he becomes able to attack his problems with courage, energy, and persistence.

There are, however, some important differences. A remedial situation must have a definite structure of planned activities, and the freedom allowed is to choose among approved learning activities whereas in psychotherapy a much wider freedom of action is usually allowed. The major difference, though, is in regard to interpretation. One of the major goals of psychotherapy is the development of insight and self-understanding through the therapist's interpretations of remarks and actions. The remedial teacher should in general avoid interpreting to the child what he thinks the true significance of his remarks or conduct may be.

If a child in remediation wants to spend some of his time talking about problems or pleasant experiences, it is usually advisable to allow this. "If the child chooses to do so, the tutor should listen respectfully and make natural comments, expressing sympathy, understanding, happiness for the child's triumphs, or whatever would be appropriate between any two people who respect one another and have something in common."[5] When in doubt, the safest procedure is to say "You think that . . ." or "You feel that . . ." and to complete the sentence by restating the gist of the child's statement to you. This is one way of using the technique called "reflection of feeling" by Carl Rogers, whose nondirective methods of handling interview material can be very useful to remedial teachers.[6]

Many remedial pupils do not accept their remedial teachers at face value, but test them again and again to try to find out what they are really like. As a guarded, conforming, polite child begins to be less suspicious of the teacher he may let a bit of hostility show, and later may become critical or argumentative. It is important for the teacher to recognize this for what it is — a venture in the direction of self-assertion and the overcoming of shackling inhibitions.

[5] Dahlberg, Charles C., Roswell, Florence G., and Chall, Jeanne, "Psychotherapeutic Principles as Applied to Remedial Reading," *Elementary School Journal*, Vol. 53, 1952, pp. 211–217. The entire article is excellent.

[6] Rogers, Carl R., *Counseling and Psychotherapy*. Boston: Houghton Mifflin Co., 1942.

It is important for the child to feel that he can be liked even when he wants to do objectionable things, and this helps to set the teacher's objectives, which should be to accept and show liking for the child, while drawing the line firmly against unacceptable behavior. Expressions of jealousy of other pupils point to a need for reassurance about the teacher's interest in the jealous one. Attempts to prolong lessons beyond their time limits should be understood as efforts to get a larger share of the teacher's attention. In various ways, children also try to discover whether the teacher is really stable and dependable, or is unpredictable or capable of being manipulated. The setting of reasonable limits in a kindly but firm and consistent manner is in itself a therapeutic process, which provides for some children a basic feeling of security and safety they have lacked in their relationships with other adults.[7]

Some psychologists have explored the possibilities of a therapeutically oriented remedial setting, in which the teacher is quite permissive and the child may choose freely among reading and play activities, and is encouraged to explore and express his feelings about reading, school work, or his family. A skillful psychotherapist may be able to get very good results with such a combined approach. The writer's limited observation of such efforts leads him to believe that results in both reading improvement and better adjustment come faster when remediation and psychotherapy are carried on concurrently by different people.

Enlisting the Cooperation of the Family

The importance of home conditions as causes of unfavorable emotional reactions to reading has been discussed in the preceding chapter. Naturally, the remedial teacher should keep track of how the child is treated at home during the remedial work. With the best of intentions, parents can sometimes defeat the work of the teacher.

William (IQ 105) was a difficult problem when he entered grade 3B after repeating the preceding grade. He was totally uninterested and

[7] Bixler, Ray H., "Limits are Therapy," *Journal of Consulting Psychology*, Vol. 13, 1949, pp. 1–11. Although this article discusses limits in play therapy, the principle is equally applicable to remedial teaching.

created disorder by bothering the children around him. His teacher devoted a great deal of attention to him and succeeded in getting him to work hard at his reading and other studies. After a few weeks she noticed that his work was getting worse again and that he was getting increasingly nervous and restless. The mother was invited to come to school. She told the teacher that she and her husband were trying their best to help. She kept William in the house studying every afternoon, and his father quizzed him every night and beat him when he did not know his lessons.

William's parents were not unusual, but reacted in the way that many parents do when they try to help in remedial work. They are so anxious for success that they lack the patience to allow the child to learn at his own rate of speed. In consequence, they become easily discouraged and emotionally tense, and sometimes resort to severe punishment in an attempt to spur the child on to better work.

In talking with the parents of a child who has a reading disability, it is advisable first to inquire about their ideas concerning the causes of his difficulty. Sometimes they bring out many complaints about the child — he is lazy, he won't work, he must be stupid. Very often their attitude is defensive and they attempt to prove that his poor work is not their fault. After the parents have made their suggestions, one can try to correct their misconceptions. In general, an attempt should be made to restore the parents' confidence in the child and to convey the impression that neither the parents nor the child should be blamed for his failure.

The parents or brothers or sisters of children with reading disabilities usually do more harm than good when they try to tutor the child. Their methods are usually poor, and often at variance with what the school is trying to do. They expect too much and lose patience quickly. In one way or another their efforts fail. This does not mean that children in general should be denied help at home; but those whose families are able to do a good job of tutoring rarely come to our attention as reading disability cases. For this reason, it is often advisable to ask the parents to stop all home tutoring. They should also be asked to stop discussing the child's schoolwork and to discontinue nagging, scolding, punishment, and exhortation to be more like a scholastically brighter brother or sister. Naturally they should freely express pleasure when the child begins to bring home better reports.

On the other hand, parents should be given encouragement to believe that there are important things they can do to help the remedial program. Particularly with younger children, the importance of continuing (or resuming) the reading and telling of stories to the child can be stressed. Many parents do not realize the value of conversation, visits to places of interest, and trips in helping the child to enrich his ideas, expand his vocabulary, and provide a base for improved comprehension. Sharing these and other activities with the child may improve the parent-child relationship.

Many overanxious parents are unable to stop their attempts to teach the child to read, even when they have agreed to do so. When this seems likely, it is often better to give them a very limited job to do than to ask them to step out of the reading instruction entirely. When this is tried the job should be one which can be completed in five to ten minutes, and which consists more of review than of new learning. The exact procedure the parent is expected to use should not only be explained in detail, but should also be demonstrated in a sample lesson.

As the child progresses in his remedial work, it is desirable to send notes home at frequent intervals (once a week is not too often) praising his effort and mentioning some of his new achievements. Cooperative parents welcome opportunities to discuss the child's other adjustment problems, and often very desirable changes in the total home situation can be brought about. The best results are obtained when teacher and parents work together in coordinated effort.

III. Management Problems in Remedial Reading

Selection of Pupils for Remedial Reading

Although more and more school systems are instituting remedial reading programs, the new remedial reading teacher usually finds that the number of pupils who seem to need help is far greater than the number that can be cared for in a well-conceived remedial program. Attempting to serve all usually means giving the right kind of help to none. Lavishing time and energy on the wrong pupils also leads to disappointing results.

Nearly all children will show improvement when special attention is devoted to improving their reading. When the number of pupils that can be given special attention is limited, one should try to give preference to those whose ability in reading is farthest below their potentialities. This is usually done by comparing the child's reading age with his mental age; the greater the discrepancy, the greater the room for improvement.

No test, whether of achievement or intelligence, furnishes results that are completely accurate. Most good intelligence and reading tests have probable errors of measurement ranging between two and six months. Unless the difference between two scores is fairly large, it may be due to errors of measurement. A child's reading ability should be at least six months below his intelligence level before one can be reasonably confident that his reading is definitely below expectation. A safe rule to follow is to select cases for remedial teaching in which the difference between reading age and mental age is at least six months for children in the first three grades, nine months for children in grades four and five, or a year for children above the fifth grade.

Determining Reading Expectancy. When one uses an IQ obtained some time ago, it is necessary to estimate the child's present mental age before comparing with present reading status. To do this, take the child's present chronological age and multiply by his IQ, remembering that this is really a decimal with hundredths. For example, Wallace, who is 9 years 3 months old and obtained an IQ of 86 last year, has an estimated present mental age of 7 years 11 months ($9.25 \times .86 = 7.945$).

The norms for standardized reading tests usually include both reading age and reading grade norms. In planning remedial treatment, the reading grade equivalent is more useful than the reading age. Intelligence tests are scored for mental age but usually do not have mental grade scores.

To convert an age score into a grade score, subtract five years from it; to convert a grade score into an age score, add five years to it. This simple procedure assumes that the normal child enters the first grade at the age of six and is promoted regularly. It agrees completely with the modal age-grade norms for the most recent editions of the *Stanford Achievement Tests.*

It is well established that in elementary school there is a tendency for bright children to do work which is above average but not up to the level indicated by their mental ages, and for dull children (who repeat grades and whose teachers keep after them) to do slightly better work than their mental ages would lead one to expect. Taking this into consideration, it has been suggested that to get a measure of reading expectancy one should average the child's mental age with his chronological age. The desirability of this practice is not clearly evident, as the fact that bright children in general do not live up to their scholastic potentialities is no reason for ignoring those potentialities, and the advisability of forcing the dull child to a level of achievement above reasonable expectation is questionable.

Monroe [8] has employed for the purpose of selecting reading disability cases a Reading Index based on the average of mental age, chronological age, and achievement age in arithmetic computation. This average, minus 5 years, gives an expectancy grade; the Reading Index is the child's reading grade divided by his expectancy grade. Such an involved procedure has only a questionable advantage over the simple process of comparing mental age with reading age, and is too complicated for general school use.

Torgerson and Adams, using formulas devised in Los Angeles by Horn, recommend comparison of reading age with an expectancy age derived by combining mental age with chronological age.[9] For

[8] Monroe, Marion, *Children Who Cannot Read,* Ch. I. Chicago: University of Chicago Press, 1932.

[9] Torgerson, T. L., and Adams, Georgia S., *Measurement and Evaluation for Elementary School Teachers,* Ch. 9. New York: Dryden Press, 1954. The Los Angeles Formulas use an average of MA and CA in the following proportions: ages 6–0 to 8–5, $\frac{MA + CA}{2}$; ages 8–6 to 9–11, $\frac{3MA + 2CA}{5}$; ages 10–0 to 11–11, $\frac{2MA + CA}{3}$; age 12 up, $\frac{3MA + CA}{4}$. This gives an Expectancy Age with which the child's Reading Age is compared.

primary-grade children they average the two ages, and as children get older the weight given to mental age increases. This, like the Monroe Index, requires time-consuming arithmetic and rests on the fallacious assumption that dull children should read above their mental maturity levels and bright children, below their mental ages.

In getting a measure of reading ability to compare with intelligence, it is advisable to include oral reading as well as silent reading. A desirable procedure is to give oral reading equal weight with silent reading in getting a total reading score.

When it is impossible to use a reasonably accurate intelligence test,[10] another method of detecting reading disability cases may be used. The first step is to select a reading test that measures level of comprehension and has at least two equivalent forms. One form is given to the child in the usual way. In giving the other form the test is read to the child as slowly as is necessary, and his spoken answers are recorded. The test used should be one in which speed is of little importance. A normal reader will do as well or better when he reads the test himself as when it is read to him. A reading disability case will usually do much better when the test is read to him. A convenient pair of tests for this purpose has been devised by Durrell and Sullivan. They have published a *Reading Achievement Test* and a *Reading Capacity Test* which are parallel in content and difficulty. The questions in the *Reading Capacity Test*, which can be used as a group test, are read to the children and they record their answers by marking pictures. In using such a procedure care must be taken not to overlook children who score poorly on the capacity test because of poor hearing or a language handicap. In general, however, the scheme is a practical and useful one.

The 1955 edition of the *Durrell Analysis of Reading Difficulty* contains a Listening Comprehension test, with paragraphs that are read to the child, followed by oral questioning. This test is intended as a measure of reading capacity. Somewhat similar techniques for measuring understanding of spoken language as a basis for estimating potential improvement in reading are used in the Auditory

[10] Intelligence tests suitable for use with poor readers have been listed on p. 223.

Comprehension Test which is one of the *Diagnostic Reading Tests* (see p. 175), and in the *Brown-Carlsen Listening Comprehension Test*; both of these are suitable in difficulty for senior high school and college.

Estimates of the mental ability of children who have sensory defects, foreign-language handicaps, or reading difficulties must be made with caution. There is always the possibility in these cases that unsuspected ability may be found after the deficiencies have been corrected.

Criteria for Selection

Some remedial programs have set a minimum IQ below which children are not eligible. This has two disadvantages. The first is that many of the group IQ tests used in school are not fair to the very poor reader. Second, no matter how dull a child may be, he should be able to profit from remedial help if his mental level is substantially higher than his reading level.

Age and grade placement should be considered, as well as the discrepancy between reading and intelligence. There is little sense in starting remedial instruction with children who are immature and not ready to make progress in reading; on the other hand, the sooner a special disability can be overcome the less damage it does to the child's total development and adjustment. For many children who need remedial help the third grade is an appropriate starting place, giving the child two years in which to take hold with the best help the classroom teachers can give. For bright children who are concerned about their poor progress, the sooner remediation can start, the better. In elementary school the major effort should be devoted to third- and fourth-grade pupils, with a few places left open for the most urgent fifth- and sixth-grade cases. In junior high, the seventh grade is the place to concentrate most remedial time; in senior high, the ninth grade; in college, the freshman year.

In a program that can serve a limited number of children, it is necessary to set up a priority system, giving preference to those in the preferred grades, and then to those showing the greatest discrepancy between reading and intelligence or capacity level. Teacher recommendations should be considered, but not substituted for objective measurement.

Remedial Groups

A special remedial teacher in a school generally gets best results working with small groups, ranging from two to six children. The saving as compared to teaching one child at a time is obvious. The small group is not only economical but also has definite psychological advantages. The group is small enough for each child to receive individual attention, yet retains many of the desirable features of a classroom situation. It is usually good for a child to know that he is not the only one who has a handicap, and he may take courage and inspiration from the progress of other members of his group. In many exercises and drills the children can work in pairs or can take turns at testing each other, thus relieving the teacher of some routine work and giving more time for planning, testing, and other necessary work. Games can be introduced in which all of the children in a group can take part.

Not all children need the same intensity of treatment. Some groups can make good progress meeting twice a week; some do much better with three periods; and some children seem to need to see the remedial teacher every school day, or their forgetting almost keeps pace with their learning. One or two children may not be able to adjust to even a small group and need the teacher's exclusive attention; if possible, they should be started with individual help and worked into a group as soon as they are ready.[11]

Arranging a Remedial Schedule

The time of day has relatively little effect on the learning ability of children, so special remedial reading periods may be scheduled for any time that is convenient. The teacher giving special coaching to one or two pupils may meet them before or after school, during assembly periods, or at any other time when the necessary minutes

[11] Traxler, Arthur E., "Current Organization and Procedures in Remedial Teaching," *Journal of Experimental Education,* Vol. 20, 1952, pp. 305–312. This is the report of a research committee of the National Association for Remedial Teaching.

can be found. A regularly assigned remedial teacher usually meets several different groups of children during the day and must schedule them for regular periods. It is desirable to arrange the groups so that the children in one group are at about the same level of reading ability, although it is not necessary. It is also desirable to avoid as far as possible any encroachment on the time required for other necessary activities. The best time to give a child a remedial lesson is the period when the rest of his class is having reading or literature. One should try to avoid interference with lessons in other basic subjects such as arithmetic. It is also inadvisable to schedule remedial reading at the expense of shopwork or physical training, as those may be the only parts of the school day that the disabled readers really enjoy. It is often possible to reduce conflicts to a minimum by conferring with the classroom teachers. When conflicts cannot be avoided, one should remember that the remedial work is for the time being the child's most important school activity and should take precedence over other subjects.

Like any other form of systematic teaching, remedial reading should be scheduled at regular, frequent intervals. One cannot usually expect to get good results if one sees a child only once a week. The length of the period, in most cases, should be about forty-five minutes. Periods shorter than that are not as effective because too large a proportion of the time is spent in getting started and in clearing up. Children whose attention is flighty or who tire easily may be kept occupied through the period by having a variety of things to do and changing their activity every few minutes.

An Illustrative Remedial Set-Up

In February, 1944, New York City began to assign special remedial teachers to schools in which there were many retarded readers. Many of the teachers, who were chosen on the basis of recommendations from their principals, had had previous training and experience in remedial work. The first group of about ten teachers was given a period of intensive training, including lectures, discussions, study of remedial materials, and demonstrations of small-group remedial work. After assignment to a school, the teacher was given two weeks to prepare her room, organize her materials, and select her pupils. After that group was started another group of teachers was trained. In this way, over one hundred remedial teachers were introduced in one year.

In selecting pupils, each classroom teacher in the grades above the second was asked to recommend all pupils who seemed to need remedial help. These pupils were given silent reading tests and a suitable group intelligence test by the remedial teacher. Minimum standards for selection for the remedial program were an IQ above 75 and a mental age at least one year higher than the child's reading age.

Each remedial teacher set up four remedial groups, of about six children each. Each group met with the remedial teacher for a period of fifty minutes, at the same hour every school day. This arrangement left the remedial teacher one free hour, which was used for scoring tests, bringing records up to date, or preparing special materials. After the remedial teachers had a few weeks in which to get settled, they were expected to use many of these free hours for conferences with the classroom teachers and for demonstrations of remedial procedures.

This program has now been in operation over ten years and has been extended upward to include junior high schools and vocational schools. The major complaint about it is that there are not enough remedial teachers to cover all the schools.

Individual Remedial Teaching

There are many children who need more help and attention than they can be given under most classroom conditions. Many schools are so organized that the teachers are not encouraged to individualize their teaching or provided with the materials which individualized methods require. Even when small-group instruction or individualized attention is given in the classrooom, there are usually some children who are so far behind or whose difficulties are so different from those of the other children that they do not seem to profit from teaching which is highly beneficial to the others in the low reading groups.

Most of these children respond well to special remedial group instruction of the type described above. However, there are always a few (usually less than 10 per cent) who do not make progress even under that kind of arrangement. For these few, thorough diagnostic examinations should be provided and completely individual tutoring arranged if necessary. Such examinations, including careful analysis of the child's intellectual, physical, and emotional make-up, require the services of a specially trained psychologist, who is able to make use of medical, psychiatric, and social work facilities for additional help. An increasing number of school systems have psychologists on their staffs who are competent in reading diagnosis. In many localities children can be referred for diagnostic study to special clinics run by universities or teachers' colleges, or to community child guidance clinics.[12] After the child's needs have been determined and his handicaps corrected as far as is possible, the psychologist's recommendations about the kind of reading instruction the child requires can usually be carried out by a competent teacher who has an understanding of the fundamentals of remedial reading, and who has the necessary time to spend.

Very few schools at present have on their staffs special remedial teachers who devote part of their time to completely individual tutoring. Some schools expect their regular teachers to give individual coaching to pupils who need it, and set aside special periods for that purpose. If the kindergarten and first-grade children attend school for only part of the school day, their teachers are sometimes assigned to give individual help to upper-grade pupils during the remaining time. Sometimes assembly and gymnasium periods are arranged so as to free one or two teachers for coaching. In entirely too many schools no provisions at all are made, and help is available to the child who needs it only because a devoted teacher finds time to work with him in private, before or after school.

Outside of the schools, some individual teaching of reading is done by the personnel of clinics, and by private tutors who specialize

[12] *Reading Clinics Directory,* compiled by Walter B. Barbe. Chattanooga: Junior League Reading Center, University of Chattanooga, 1955. *Psychiatric Clinics and Other Resources in the United States.* New York: The National Association for Mental Health, 1955.

in remedial work. The number of people who are qualified and available for this work is small, and the cost of their services is high. When, however, such highly skilled help salvages children who would otherwise remain total failures, the monetary cost is small if balanced against the alternative of ruined lives.

Homework

In learning to read, as in the learning of any other complex skill, the more practice the better. Children who are good readers often read more outside of school than in school, and this voluntary reading is a very important factor in their continued improvement. If the poor reader can be induced to read extensively between lessons, his progress will be that much greater.

One should not, however, impose reading homework on poor readers. At the start of a remedial program it is advisable not to suggest any home reading. One should wait until the child shows that he is gaining confidence in his reading and finds that he can get some pleasure from it. Then one can suggest that perhaps he would like to do some reading between lessons. The importance of doing as much reading as possible can be discussed, and a progress chart for voluntary reading can be started. Books or stories for home reading should be short at first, and should be at the child's independent reading level. Reports on this outside reading should at first be oral, and a page or so of the material read can be used for an oral reading check. If this procedure is handled successfully, the child may soon be reading as much as a book a week in his free time.

Exercises of the workbook type are less interesting than story material, and should usually not be assigned for home reading unless the child shows that he enjoys them. The same principle, that the child should want extra practice, should govern decisions about homework with other types of drill material.

Keeping Records

The remedial teacher should have a separate manila folder or envelope for the records of each child. In this should be kept the

REMEDIAL READING DIAGNOSTIC SUMMARY

Name____________________ Date of Birth__________ Age____

Class_____ Teacher ______________Home Address____________

Test Results

Test	Date	Result	Test	Date	Result
Reading			Intelligence		
			Other		

Physical: General Condition____________________

Defects____________________

Lateral Dominance: Eye____ Hand____ Converted? ____

School History

Grade Progress____________________

Attendance____________________

Marks in Reading____________________

Other Subjects____________________

Remarks____________________

Difficulties in Reading

Word Recognition____________________

Oral Reading____________________

Silent Reading____________________

Attitude Toward Reading____________________

Remarks____________________

Fig. 25. A two-page record form for summarizing the essential points in a reading disability case study.

<u>Family</u>

Cultural____

Parents____

Siblings____

Treatment of Child__________________________________

____

<u>Personality</u>

Relations with Adults__________________________________

Relations with Children________________________________

Temperament, Mood____________________________________

Remarks____

____

<u>Hobbies, Interests, Skills</u>: ______________________________

____

<u>Recommendations</u>:

Reading____

____

____

____

____

____

____

School Adjustment___________________________________

____

Advice to Parents___________________________________

____

____

Other____

____

Date of Summary ___________ Made by _________________

results of all tests and other diagnostic studies, a preliminary analysis of the child's instructional and other needs, an outline of the teaching plan to be followed, and records of the progress of the work. Since record-keeping can become a very time-consuming burden, thought should be given to setting up a record system that will be reasonably comprehensive and, at the same time, require comparatively little writing.

The process of bringing together all of the information about a child in a comprehensive case study is discussed in the next section. Unless a formal report is to be prepared, much of the content of the case study is not written down on paper. However, it is highly advisable to have a concise summary of the most important information. A two-page diagnostic summary form is shown in Figure 25. If many copies are needed, this form, or something like it, can be mimeographed.

If a teacher is working individually with only one or two children, it is frequently worth while to keep a day-by-day diary which contains notations about the child's emotional behavior as well as his reading. This is especially true if the teacher is new to remedial work and wishes to discuss his procedures with a supervisor or instructor. For an experienced and busy remedial teacher such a detailed record is impractical. However, it is desirable to keep a memorandum pad handy and to jot down a brief note, dated, about any unusual behavior or any significant change in the child. These notes are placed in the child's folder. From time to time the brief anecdotal records can be reread, giving the teacher a better perspective on the child's progress.

One should keep a record of the assignments given to each child, notations about when they were finished, and comments about how well they were accomplished. A convenient form for such an assignment record is shown in Figure 26. This form can be left with the child, so that when he finishes one job he knows what to do next. Each child should have a notebook in which he can do his written work, and a large manila envelope in which he can keep his notebook, assignment sheet, progress charts, and other reading materials.

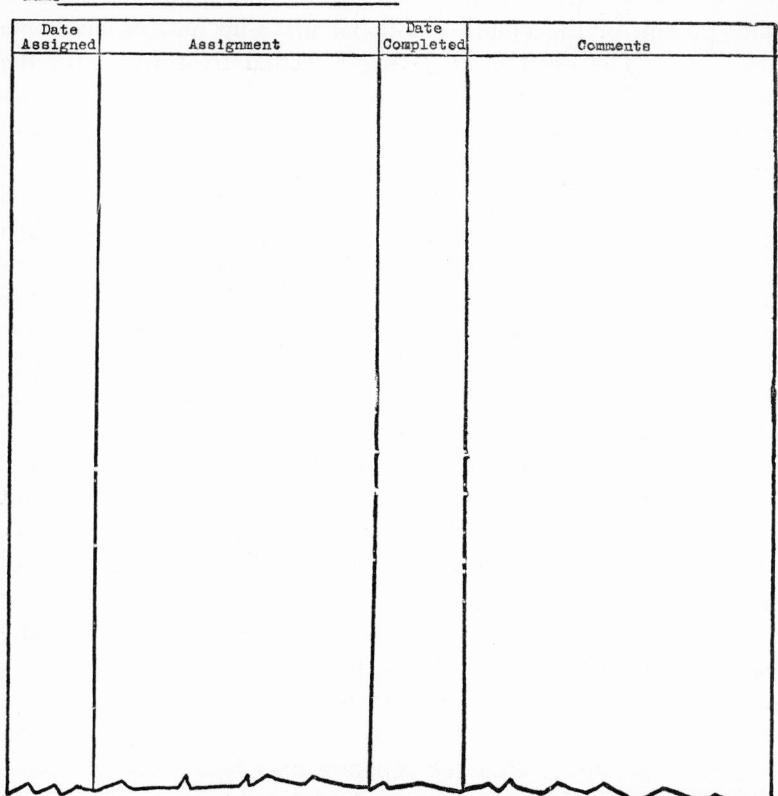
READING ASSIGNMENT SHEET

Name______________________________

Date Assigned	Assignment	Date Completed	Comments

Fig. 26. A form that can be used for individual reading assignments.

IV. How to Make a Case Study

After a child has been selected for intensive study, the teacher should spend the first remedial period or two getting acquainted with him and getting him into the proper frame of mind for the diagnostic and remedial work. The school records should naturally be consulted as soon as possible. Testing may be started as soon as the child seems ready to cooperate. One should be careful not to give too many tests at once; the testing program can be spread over several periods, and some of the tests can be given after remedial work has been started. It may take weeks before one has an adequate picture of the child's emotional make-up and of his home background. The need for delaying remedial treatment until the diagnosis has been fairly well completed can be explained to older pupils in the upper grades or in secondary school. With young and immature pupils it is advisable to begin the remedial work as soon as possible, even though the remedial procedures may have to be changed as soon as a more complete diagnosis has been made. When the diagnostic evidence has been collected, it is necessary to consider the complete picture and arrive at conclusions about what the child's major difficulties in reading are, what seem to be the most reasonable explanations of how these difficulties have come about, and what remedial procedures should be employed to overcome them. After the remedial work is under way one should check up periodically with informal and standardized tests to determine the effectiveness of the procedures that are being used and to find out if a shift in methods should be instituted. Before finishing work with a case one should of course retest to find out how much progress the pupil has made.

All of the factors that need to be considered in the diagnostic phase of a case study have been discussed in the four chapters preceding this one. The selection of appropriate remedial methods will be considered in the chapters that follow. The task of the person making a case study, after the separate data have been obtained, is to get an overall picture of the child and his needs. This task, never too easy, is simplified somewhat if all of the relevant information is briefly summarized in such a way that the interrelations can be seen. Such a summary form is shown in Figure 25.

If a formal case report is to be submitted, it is desirable to follow a definite outline. This is fairly good insurance against omitting important information, as well as an aid to a person reading the report. The writer has found that the following outline is useful to teachers as a guide in writing up remedial reading cases:

A. Objective Data
   1. Child's name

2. Date of birth and age at beginning of study
3. School grade at beginning of study
4. Intelligence test data, including name of test and form, date of administration, MA, and IQ.
5. Silent reading test scores, including name of test and form, date of administration, reading age, and reading grade.

   When separate norms are available for parts of the test, the scores on the parts should be listed as well as the total score.
6. Oral reading test scores, including name of test and form, date, and reading grade
7. Results of standardized tests in other school subjects if such tests have been given

B. Health Data
   1. Results of vision tests and other evidence about vision
   2. Results of hearing tests and other evidence about hearing
   3. Summary of child's present health status
   4. Summary of child's health history

C. Home Background

   The questions listed on p. 272 may be used as a guide in summarizing information about home background

D. Child's Personality
   1. Statement of outstanding personality traits, with illustrations
   2. Child's interests in reading, school, and play
   3. Child's attitudes toward teachers, playmates, and family

E. School History
   1. Record of progress through the grades
   2. Marks in reading and other subjects
   3. Attendance record
   4. Notations about conduct and general behavior
   5. Methods of teaching reading used by former teachers

F. Interpretation of Reading Test Results
   1. Interpretation of silent reading performance
   2. Interpretation of oral reading performance

G. Summary of Diagnosis
   1. Summary of outstanding difficulties in reading
   2. Summary of factors causally related to the child's difficulties

H. Recommendations for Remedial Treatment
   1. Recommendations concerning reading instruction
   2. Other recommendations for school adjustment
   3. Recommendations to the parents
   4. Recommendations for medical examination or treatment
   5. Other recommendations

I. Description of Remedial Treatment

The description of treatment should be given in detail. Preferably a chronological order should be followed, describing procedures used at the beginning and explaining changes made in procedure as the remedial work progressed. Methods should be described in sufficient detail to allow others to reproduce them.

J. Evaluation of Results
1. Tabular summary of initial test scores and retest scores
2. Evaluation of progress shown by the tests
3. Evidence of change shown in the child's general schoolwork
4. Evidence of change shown in the child's personality and behavior

Rigid adherence to an outline such as that given above is not absolutely necessary, but a systematic procedure should be followed. Some cases are more complex than others and need to be described in greater detail. Some illustrative case studies are given in Chapter XIX; others can be found in the references at the end of that chapter.

Suggested Additional Reading

Durrell, Donald D. *Improvement of Basic Reading Abilities,* Ch. 14.
Gates, Arthur I. *Improvement of Reading,* Third Edition, Ch. 5.

· XII ·

Developing Word Recognition Skills, I

THE ABILITY to recognize words quickly and accurately is fundamental to success in reading. This is so obvious that for many centuries teachers of reading were preoccupied mainly with the teaching of word recognition. Whether they used synthetic alphabet or phonic methods or employed an analytical approach, their main concern was with words. Early in this century, when it became evident that many pupils taught in this way were deficient in comprehension and speed, a reaction against this kind of overemphasis set in and methods which stressed comprehension and minimized word recognition skills became popular. These in turn resulted in failure on the part of many pupils to develop independence in attacking new words, and encouraged guessing and inaccuracy. At the present time it is recognized that comprehension is the major goal in reading instruction, but that good comprehension cannot be achieved by one who has failed to develop skill in word recognition.

It is, of course, essential that the meaning of words being taught should be known to the reader. In the first and second grades, in which the major word-recognition skills are developed, most of the words which occur in reading matter have meanings well known to most kindergarten children. While some word meanings need to be taught in those grades, major emphasis in the teaching of words can be placed on recognition skills. As the child progresses in school, the emphasis shifts to the teaching of word meanings. The teaching of meaningful vocabulary will be discussed in Chapter XV.

I. Development of a Sight-Recognition Vocabulary

All of the currently popular methods start with wholes, and proceed later to the consideration of the parts of words, in contrast to the older alphabet and phonic methods which started with single letters and built words out of them. The principle of starting with larger units or wholes is in accord with sound psychological principles. Young children are not very analytical in their perceptions. They respond to the most obvious characteristics of the perceived object. To a baby learning to talk, any animal with four legs may be "doggy" and any person wearing trousers may be "daddy." Differences between one person and another are responded to without any clear awareness of what the distinguishing features are. Only gradually do children become aware of details as such. The earlier, primitive form of response is to the unanalyzed whole; perception of details and of the relationship of the whole to the parts comes later.

Furthermore, effective reading in its later stages requires that words should be recognized immediately, not pieced together bit by bit. The good adult reader has gone beyond reading words as units; he perceives words in phrase groups and takes in an average of nearly two words at each glance. Starting to read in larger units from the beginning prepares the way for rapid, efficient reading later.

Methods of Teaching Sight Words

Children are helped to learn sight words in various ways. Usually the word is introduced by the teacher in a spoken sentence, or story and if the meaning is unfamiliar that is developed first. The sentence can be presented on the chalkboard and the word can be underlined, framed with the hands, or set off by pointers. The children are encouraged to look carefully at it while saying it; this is a "look and say" technique. Phrases consisting of the new word with one or two familiar words may then be presented and read. The word may then be presented by itself on a card, and various types of practice employed, such as selecting from several cards the one which teacher says, matching the word card with the word in the sentence or phrase, or rearranging word cards to form new sentences. Reading of connected material which contains the new words should follow immediately, providing additional repetition and opportunity to recognize the word in a meaningful context. This may be followed by workbook exercises in which the word is to be matched with a picture, written into an incomplete sentence, or used in comprehension questions.

A second commonly used procedure is to present the new word in connection with a picture, which lends vividness of meaning. The child looks at the picture and is told the word or guesses what the word must be. If he forgets the word, he looks back at the picture again. Some workbooks present new words by means of pictures. Published sets of picture-word cards are available and can be used to good advantage. Picture-dictionaries can be placed on the library table and the children can be taught how to look up a new word in the dictionary. Children can also construct their own picture-dictionaries, drawing the illustrations or cutting them out from magazines, and refer back to them when they forget a word.

Children are also encouraged to guess from the context. They study the illustration on the page to find out what new character, object, or action is portrayed. They read the rest of the sentence and try to decide what the missing word must be. As with other techniques, the use of context is valuable, but can become a handicap if the child learns to rely on it too heavily.

When a child forgets a word that has recently been introduced, many teachers encourage him to look back and find the word in a previous sentence. By reading that sentence again, he often can remember what the word says.

Although practice with flash cards has been a widely used method of providing drill on new words, such cards sometimes encourage dependence on the wrong kinds of cues. " 'The one with the dirty thumb mark on it is 'baby.' I always know it by that, else I'd swear it was 'lady.' . . . 'Saw' and 'was' are easy too. 'Saw' is the one with the corner torn off. . . .' "[1]

Flash cards can be used to build sentences, to test new words after they have been taught, and to develop speed of recognition after the words are known. When used for first teaching they not only may encourage dependence on accidental cues, but also may develop disappointingly little carry-over to the recognition of the word in connected meaningful context.

Configuration Clues. Children can be helped to observe salient characteristics of words as an aid to recalling them. Most children have no difficulty with the word *grandmother,* even at the preprimer level, because it is a long word and looks distinctively different from all the other words. Another word that is learned almost at once is *elephant,* which not only is long but also has a distinctive shape, with a unique pattern of ascending and descending letters. The tail at the end of the word *monkey* makes that a very easy word for the beginning reader. In contrast, words which are similar in size and general appearance are easily confused with one another. Words like *went* and *want, and* and *said, no* and *on,* are troublesome to many children long after they should have been well learned. Noticing and calling attention to the distinctive characteristics of words is very helpful to children. However, when the child has to distinguish between *grandfather* and *grandmother,* or between *donkey* and *monkey,* such cues as size, general shape, and a tall letter in the middle or a "tail" at the end no longer suffice, and must be supplemented by more systematic methods of word analysis.

Repetition in the Learning of Sight Words

Many teachers are amazed that children can misread words which they have seen hundreds of times. They remember the "law of exercise" as one of the most important principles of learning; they believe that "practice makes perfect"; and they have relied on repetition and drill as the cure of imperfect learning. Mere repetition, however, was never considered a sufficient basis for learning, and

[1] McCullough, Constance M., "Flash Cards — Opiate?" *Elementary English,* Vol. 32, 1955, pp. 379–381.

the weakness of relying upon it is more clearly recognized today than it used to be. "The 'law of exercise' does not guarantee that mere countless repetitions of any given reaction will serve to fix it, although the erroneous belief that it does has led in some schools to the institution of drill methods diametrically opposed to the principles of effective learning."[2] In the modern psychology of learning, less emphasis than formerly is placed on repetition, and much more attention is given to readiness, motivation, and the attainment of insight. As it relates to the learning of word recognition, insight means attaining a clear and accurate perception of the printed word. If a child has never really seen the word clearly, endless repetition of a faulty perception may only increase the tendency to perceive the word in the same faulty way.

While repetition is now considered to play a subordinate role in the learning process, it is still important. Children differ greatly in their quickness in learning to recognize a word as they do in all other abilities. Some fortunate children can remember a word easily when they have only seen it once or twice before. Mentally slow children may need several times as much repetition as children of average mental ability. To be effective, this repetition should not be monotonous drill, but should be presented in such a way as to maintain the child's interest at a high level and encourage accuracy of perception. Modern sets of primary-grade readers attempt to make the child's task easier by carefully controlling the rate at which new words are introduced and by providing systematic repetition of each new word a large number of times. The use of correlated workbooks provides additional repetition.

Supplementary Word-Recognition Procedures

Much difficulty and discouragement in learning to recognize words can be avoided if systematic reading instruction is delayed until the children have developed a sufficient degree of reading readiness. One of the most important aspects of reading readiness is the ability to perceive similarities and differences in word forms.

[2] Skinner, Charles E., *Elementary Educational Psychology*, p. 165. New York: Prentice-Hall, 1945.

If the teacher finds, after she has started a group of children on book reading, that several of them are still backward in this ability, she can introduce special supplementary practice exercises in visual discrimination of the sort to be found in reading readiness workbooks.

There are some children whose ability to remember the appearance of words after purely visual study remains very poor. These children may be very inferior in visual imagery. They often make surprisingly good progress if the teacher helps them to acquire methods of word study which are easier for them than the "look and say" procedure. Many of them can be helped by the use of a visual-motor method of word study; others are benefited greatly by early, intensive training in phonics; a few may require a systematic kinesthetic procedure.

Tracing Procedures

For some children "look and say" does not work very well because when they look their visual perception of the word is vague and insufficiently clear to provide a basis for effective discrimination from other somewhat similar words, or for recall after an interval of time. For such children additional sensory cues are often quite helpful. Tracing a large copy of the word letter by letter while pronouncing the word is the heart of the kinesthetic method developed by Fernald (see pp. 384–387), and has aided many children who had trouble building a sight vocabulary. Some workbooks now provide large copies of the words with directions for tracing, as part of their regular learning procedure.

Visual-Motor Word Study

Many children do not need extensive practice in tracing, but are helped a great deal by a method which combines visual observation while saying the word with writing the word from memory. As used with a slow group, the procedure can be about as follows:

1. The teacher selects for teaching a small number of new words that are to be met in the next connected reading.
2. Each word is introduced in meaningful context and meanings are checked or taught, as with a purely visual method.

3. The new word is presented on the board in a sentence, and framed or otherwise emphasized, as in the visual method.
4. The teacher holds up a card with the word printed on it, and pronounces it. The children look at it and pronounce it softly, and then a few times to themselves. They should be cautioned *not* to spell letter by letter.
5. Each child shuts his eyes and tries to "make a picture" (visual image) of the word; he then opens them and compares his mental image with the original.
6. The card is covered, and each child attempts to print (or write) the word *from memory.*
7. The word is exposed again and each child compares his reproduction with the original, paying particular attention to any parts not reproduced accurately.
8. The process of looking at the word, saying it, and attempting to reproduce it from memory is repeated until each child can reproduce the word correctly.
9. The other words are taught the same way.
10. The word cards are shuffled and reviewed for speedier sight recognition.
11. The children proceed to read a selection in which the new words are met in meaningful context.

After using the visual-motor method for a month or two, children usually discover that they no longer need to write the word in order to be able to remember it. They then shift to the visual method. Gradually, also, they begin to utilize their developing phonic knowledge in combination with study of the word as a whole.

According to Fernald, who originated the visual-motor procedure (although Durrell gave it that name), the method is a modified kinesthetic procedure, in which the motor imagery of the movements involved in writing the word reinforces the auditory-visual association between the sound of the word and its printed form. It seems probable to this writer that the kinesthetic elements are of minor importance. Instead, it seems likely that writing helps the child to remember the word because he must perceive the word correctly in all of its details in order to reproduce it accurately. The method seems to work just as well whether the child prints the word, writes it, or reproduces it on a typewriter. Whatever the true explanation may turn out to be, it is a fact that many children whose visual memory is very inexact and who show no aptitude for phonics find that they can learn and remember words when they use the visual-motor procedure.

What Sight Words Should Be Taught?

Not all words that occur for the first time are worth teaching. Particularly when using experience stories or charts, teachers need to have some way of knowing whether a word is likely to be met in printed material often enough to justify effort in teaching it, or is better left to later years. The following word lists can be used for this purpose:

Kearney, Nolan C., "An Analysis of the Vocabulary of First Grade Reading Material," *Journal of Educational Research,* Vol. 43, 1950, pp. 481–493. Analyzes 42 preprimers, 38 primers, and 41 first readers, listing the 200 words most common in all three combined and the most common 200 words at each level; also commonest 34 preprimer, 67 primer, and 340 first-reader words.

Gentry, Lillian, "A Study of the Vocabulary Load of Sixty-six Preprimers," *Journal of Educational Research,* Vol. 43, 1950, pp. 525–532. Lists 125 words found in at least 9 of the 66 preprimers, and 125 other words occurring in at least 3 preprimers.

Stone, Clarence R., "Word Lists by Reading Levels," in *Progress in Primary Reading,* pp. 107–132. St. Louis: Webster Publishing Co., 1950. Lists 50 most important preprimer words, 50 other words important in preprimer and easy primer reading, 225 important primer words, 455 first-reader words, 1101 second-reader words, and 1916 third-reader words; each list includes the previous lists; based on a careful analysis of previous word counts. A revision of *1941 Stone's Graded Vocabulary for Primary Reading.* St. Louis: Webster Publishing Co., 1941.

Knipp, Helen B., *Basic Vocabulary Phrases and Sentences for Early Reading Instruction.* Meadville, Pa.: Keystone View Co., 1952. Lists 2646 words derived from previous word lists and from counts of primary readers published between 1944 and 1950, arranged in five levels of difficulty. Also contains phrases and sentences for tachistoscope work.

Dolch, E. W., "A Basic Sight Vocabulary," *Elementary School Journal,* Vol. 36, 1936, pp. 456–460; Vol. 37, 1936, pp. 268–272. A list of 220 words said to make up more than 50 per cent of the running words in any elementary school reading materials. Printed cards for teaching these words can be purchased from Garrard Press, Champaign, Ill.

Dolch, E. W., "95 Nouns Common to the Three Word Lists," in *Teach-*

ing Primary Reading, p. 269. Champaign, Ill.: Garrard Press, 1950. Nouns common to three first-grade vocabulary lists. Printed picture-word cards for teaching these can be purchased from Garrard Press.

Gates, Arthur I., *A Reading Vocabulary for the Primary Grades*, Revised. New York: Bureau of Publications, Teachers College, Columbia University, 1935. A list of 1811 words, arranged in three levels of 500 words each and a supplementary list of 311 words; still used in research studies although based on material now obsolete.

Krantz, L. L., *The Author's Word List for the Primary Grades*. Minneapolis: Curriculum Research Co., 1945. Based on an analysis of 84 preprimers, 69 primers, 84 first readers, 85 second readers, and 47 third readers. It contains 1957 words arranged in levels: 57 preprimer, 156 primer, 334 first-reader, 509 second-reader, and 901 third-reader words.*

Above the primary grades the problem of teaching words becomes more a problem of meaning than one of sight recognition. Word lists which are usable above the primary-grade levels are discussed on page 405.

II. A Modern Program of Word Analysis

ALTHOUGH MOST BEGINNERS respond to the "look and say" method quite well at the start, they tend to become confused and to resort to guessing when they meet with words that are quite similar in length, shape, and conspicuous letters — words such as *look* and *like*, or *this* and *them*. At that point the teacher can help them by pointing out the specific features by which the two words can be distinguished. But that is not enough to produce good readers, since it leaves the child dependent upon someone to tell him what each new word is. A child must become able to attack new words and to work out their pronunciations and meanings, in order to be self-reliant and independent in reading. How best to accomplish this aim has been the subject of violent arguments for many years, and is still a problem to which many different answers are given.

Most of the arguments have revolved around the subject of *phonics*: when, how, and how much phonics to teach.[3] The reading

* This list is now out of print.

[3] *Phonetics* and *phonics* are two words that are often confused or used interchangeably. Phonetics is the scientific study of speech sounds, including their pronunciation, the action of larynx, tongue, and lips in sound production, and

series popular around 1920, such as the *Beacon Readers* (still popular in England), had elaborate phonic systems and devoted much time to the teaching of phonics from the beginning of first-grade reading. Several research studies in the 1920's [4] cast doubt on the value of intensive phonics in that silent reading comprehension scores of groups given intensive phonics training tended to be lower than in comparable groups taught with less stress on phonics. The anti-phonics arguments were well stated by Spache, who pointed out that English is a relatively nonphonetic language; that comparatively few phonic elements in English are sufficiently common and uniform in pronunciation to be worth teaching; that phonic teaching can develop undesirable habits such as paying attention to sound and not to meaning; and that when overemphasized, phonics instruction tends to produce slow, unenthusiastic readers.[5]

Spache, like the earlier researchers, did not advocate doing away with phonics, but rather wanted to limit the amount and to subordinate it to a major emphasis on reading for meaning. Many school people did not read these reports carefully, but only caught the idea that phonics was out of style, and discontinued giving any training at all in word analysis and phonics.

Meanwhile evidence accumulated that phonics instruction does have value. Agnew [6] found that phonics instruction in the first grade increased independence in word recognition, aided the child in learning new words, encouraged correct pronunciation, and improved oral reading; it did not, according to his results, affect com-

---

symbolization of sounds. Phonics is the study of the speech equivalents of printed symbols, and their use in pronouncing printed words; it is therefore a part of phonetics.

[4] Gates, Arthur I., "Studies of Phonetic Training in Beginning Reading," *Journal of Educational Psychology,* Vol. 18, 1927, pp. 217–226.

Sexton, E. K., and Herron J. S., "The Newark Phonics Experiment," *Elementary School Journal,* Vol. 28, 1928, pp. 690–701.

Garrison S. C., and Heard, M. T., "An Experimental Study of the Value of Phonetics," *Peabody Journal of Education,* Vol. 9, 1931, pp. 9–14.

[5] Spache, George, "A Phonics Manual for Primary and Remedial Teachers," *Elementary English Review,* Vol. 16, 1939, pp. 147–150, 156, 191–198.

[6] Agnew, Donald C., *The Effect of Varied Amounts of Phonetic Training on Primary Reading,* Duke University Research Studies in Education, No. 5. Durham, North Carolina: Duke University Press, 1939.

prehension in silent reading. Tiffin and McKinnis, testing pupils in grades five through eight with silent reading tests and a test of ability to pronounce nonsense words, found a significant relationship between the test of applied phonics and the silent reading scores.[7] Even at the college level phonic ability has been found related to general proficiency in reading.[8]

The comprehensive review of the research on phonics by Witty and Sizemore concludes that the nature and amount of phonic instruction needed is still a debatable question; that a readiness program for phonics can safely be recommended; that phonic systems may develop a tendency in children to recognize words piecemeal; that phonics instruction may neglect other techniques which lead to quick, accurate word recognition; that many children do need help in the mastery of phonic skills; and that many basal reading programs give enough attention to phonics to meet the needs of most children, but some children may need some supplementary practice.[9] In line with these conclusions is Russell's report that most teachers believe in teaching phonics as part of a well-balanced total reading program, that they use a combination of sight recognition, context clues, phonics, and structural analysis rather than any one of these exclusively, and that most of them rely on the teacher's manual of the basal reader for guidance in teaching word recognition skills rather than on some independent material.[10]

During the past few years every popular set of basal readers has had a systematic, sequentially developed program for developing independence in word recognition as an integral part of the method of teaching described in its manuals for teachers. These programs vary considerably in the order in which particular items are introduced, exact study and presentation methods suggested, amount of

[7] Tiffin J., and McKinnis, M., "Phonetic Ability: Its Measurement and Relation to Reading Ability," *School and Society,* Vol. 51, 1940, pp. 190–192.

[8] Rogers, M. V., "Phonic Ability as Related to Certain Aspects of Reading at the College Level," *Journal of Experimental Education,* Vol. 6, 1938, pp. 381–395.

[9] Witty, Paul A., and Sizemore, Robert A., "Phonics in the Reading Program: A Review and an Evaluation," *Elementary English,* Vol. 32, 1955, pp. 355–371.

[10] Russell, David H., "Teachers' Views on Phonics," *Elementary English,* Vol. 32, 1955, pp. 371–375.

drill recommended, and so on. They have, however, certain fundamental principles in common. None of them relies mainly on phonic sounding and blending, as the older phonic systems did. Instead they attempt to provide comprehensive, varied word attack skills which include attention to meaning, configuration clues, structural analysis, and phonics. A detailed description of this kind of approach has been given by Gray.[11] Such an approach assumes that a word needs to be attacked analytically only when it cannot be recognized as a whole, and that a good reader is not dependent upon any one way of attacking words, but has several techniques and makes use of the one that best fits the situation.

The term *word analysis* is used to include all methods by which a word can be analyzed and its pronunciation worked out. *Phonic* methods, which include a variety of ways of identifying the sounds of letters or groups of letters and using these in solving the word, are included among the word analysis techniques. So are the various types of *structural analysis,* in which a word is analyzed into major parts, such as root, prefix, and ending or suffix.

Word Analysis Skills

Some of the ways in which a good reader can attack an unknown word are the following:

1. He guesses from context, the rest of the sentence showing what the missing word must be. *Example:* Jerry went into the store to ________ some candy. The missing three-letter word is probably "buy."
2. In addition to the context, he makes use of the first letter or two and the general shape or configuration of the word. *Example:* After getting out of the car, Mr. Smith went into the g______. The *g* shows that the missing word is probably "garage" or "grocery" rather than "house" or "store."
3. Consonant substitution. He notes that the word is similar to a word he knows except for one or two letters, the sounds of which he knows. *Examples:* "mast": Knowing "fast" and *m,* he mentally substitutes the sound of *m* for the *f* to get "mast." "track": Knowing "back" and *tr,* he substitutes the sound of *tr* for *b* to get "track."

[11] Gray, William S., *On Their Own in Reading*. Chicago: Scott, Foresman & Co., 1948.

4. He divides the word into large parts which he already knows as units. *Examples:* "Postmaster" divides into *post* and *master*; "rainfall" divides into *rain* and *fall*; "superimposition," *super im position.*
5. He notes that the word consists of a familiar root and an ending. *Examples:* "playing" *play* and *ing*
   "started" *start* and *ed*
6. He looks for familiar little words within longer words. *Example:* "candidate" *can did ate*
7. He analyzes words structurally into known prefixes, roots, and endings. *Examples:* "reporter" *re port er*
   "independence" *in depend ence*
8. He applies phonic rules, such as the effect of final *e* on preceding vowel. *Examples:* "cane": Knowing *can* and the rule, he gives the *a* its long sound. "decent": Knowing that *c* is soft before *e, i,* or *y,* he uses the sound of *s* instead of the sound of *k*.

9. He uses syllabication, dividing into syllables structurally and sounding the syllables phonically.
   Examples: "unfortunate" *un for tu nate*
   "permitting" *per mit ting*
10. He thinks of a "word family" to which the word belongs. *Example:* "fright": He recognizes it as belonging to the *ight* family along with "night," "right," "fight."
11. He sounds the word out by groups of letters and blends the sounds together.
   Examples: "treaty" *tr eat y* or *tr ea ty* or *trea ty*
   "back" *ba ck* or *b ack*
12. He sounds the word letter by letter and then blends the sounds together.
   Examples: "pant" *p-a-n-t*
   "triangle" *t-r-i-a-n-g-l*
13. He looks the word up in the dictionary and uses the dictionary's syllable divisions, accent marks, and diacritical marks or phonetic respelling to get the correct pronunciation.

Some of the techniques described above (2, 3, 8, 10, 11, 12) are phonic techniques; others (4, 5, 6, 7) are structural analysis techniques; still others (9, 13) involve both phonic and structural analysis principles. With all of them, the good reader is constantly aware of the meaning of the sentence in which the word is found. Thus, he can only decide whether to give the *i* in "live" a long or short sound, or whether to place the accent in "desert" on the first or second syllable, when he grasps the significance of the word in the total sentence. The old-fashioned phonic methods, with their emphasis on sounding words in lists, failed to emphasize this need for meaning.

Flexibility in word attack is also important. A child coming to the new word "everyone" will have no trouble if he sees it immediately as consisting of two known words, "every" and "one." But if he picks out "very" and "on" as his known parts, and adds the *e* at both ends, the result will be a nonsense word that should stimulate him to try to solve the word in a different way. Application of the rule of the final silent *e* making the preceding vowel long will cause the word to rhyme with "bōne." Application of the syllabication rule that a vowel followed by a single consonant generally has the long sound certainly will not help in this case. English is a sufficiently irregular language from the phonic standpoint to make it unwise to follow the rules blindly. Teachers must lead children to expect exceptions and to use intelligent trial and error when the first attempt to solve the word does not make sense.

III. Methods of Teaching Phonics

Readiness for Phonics

A research study by Dolch and Bloomster has had a great effect on phonics instruction.[12] They gave to first-grade and second-grade pupils a test of recognition of uncommon one-syllable words, requiring the application of phonic principles without the aid of meaningful context. They found a substantial correlation between phonic ability as measured by that test, and mental age. The children whose mental ages were below seven years were able to do little or nothing on the phonics test. They concluded that the ability to learn and apply phonic principles requires a higher type of mental maturity than is needed for learning sight words, and recommended that the major part of phonics instruction should be placed in the second and third grades because the majority of first-grade pupils are not ready to profit from such instruction.

[12] Dolch, E. W., and Bloomster, M., "Phonic Readiness," *Elementary School Journal,* Vol. 38, 1937, pp. 201–205.

Most of the currently popular basal readers follow these recommendations and introduce relatively few phonic principles in the first grade (usually the single initial consonants and a few consonant digraphs such as *ch, sh,* and *th*), leaving the vowels and most consonant combinations for later levels. This writer believes that the Dolch-Bloomster phonics test presented the children with a more difficult task than they face in connected, meaningful reading, and that their findings consequently tend to underestimate slightly the phonic readiness of first graders. McKee's general principle that a phonic element can be taught as soon as three or four words in which it occurs have been learned as sight words makes a great deal of sense.[13] This does not imply a return to an old-fashioned phonic system; it does suggest a somewhat richer program of phonics in the first grade than has recently been fashionable.

Auditory Perception

If a child listens to the words *mud* and *sand* and answers "Yes" when asked if they rhyme, or if he listens to *send, sit, soap, mat,* and *sun* and cannot pick out the one that starts differently from the others, he is obviously lacking in auditory perception skills, and therefore in readiness for phonic instruction. Many teachers who have struggled unsuccessfully to impart phonic knowledge to certain children are not aware that the child's ability to perceive similarities and differences in the sounds of words must be developed if phonic teaching is to be effective.

Auditory perception for word sounds can be weak and faulty in children whose hearing, as measured by acuity tests, is excellent. It is not a matter of sensory acuity, but rather one of hearing selectivity the beginning, or end, or middle of the word and comparing it with the sound of the corresponding parts of other words, thus having the basis for comparisons and the recognition of both similarities and differences.

Poor auditory perception is often accompanied by inaccurate or indistinct pronunciation. The child who says *wiv* for *with* is likely

[13] McKee, Paul, *The Teaching of Reading in the Elementary School,* p. 200. Boston: Houghton Mifflin Co., 1948.

not to notice any difference between a *v* sound and a *th* sound within a word, and children who confuse *m* with *n* in reading often mumble the sound in their own speech so as to produce something between *mm* and *nn* for either. A child who says *mudder, fadder,* and *brudder* cannot easily learn the *th* sound for reading. It is particularly hard for many children to discriminate the short vowels: *pin* and *pen, men* and *man,* sound just alike to them.

Since phonics is essentially learning to associate the appearance of a letter or letter combination with a particular sound, a child who is vague in his perception of sounds and unable to recognize similarities and differences in sounds does not have the basis for forming strong visual-auditory associations. Auditory perception skill is an important element in reading readiness and in some studies has outranked all other factors in its contributions to success in reading.[14]

Developing Readiness for Phonics

A series of researches at Boston University has established the importance of providing specific training in auditory discrimination. According to the results of Murphy and others, training in auditory discrimination speeded up the rate of learning new words, and resulted in significantly higher reading scores than those obtained in control groups. When combined with training in visual perception the results were still better. The order of increasing difficulty for children was found to be initial consonant sounds, final consonant sounds, long vowel sounds, and short vowel sounds, but the relative difficulty of specific letter sounds could not be established. Ear training of this type was enhanced by the use of visual aids such as lantern slides. Ear training was especially valuable to those whose initial auditory discrimination scores were low, and of little help to those whose initial scores were high. Ear training also tended to eliminate sex differences in learning rate in the first grade.[15]

The important aspects of phonic readiness are as follows: (1)

[14] Nila, Sister Mary, "Foundations of a Successful Reading Program," *Education,* Vol. 73, 1953, pp. 543–555.

[15] Durrell, Donald D., and Murphy, Helen A., "The Auditory Discrimination Factor in Reading Readiness and Reading Disability," *Education,* Vol. 73, 1953, pp. 556–560.

The child should be able to hear that there is a difference between words that sound somewhat alike, such as *man* and *men,* or *had* and *hat.* (2) He should be able to detect whether two words begin with the same sound or not. To test this ability, one can ask the child to pick out the one word that begins differently in a spoken list such

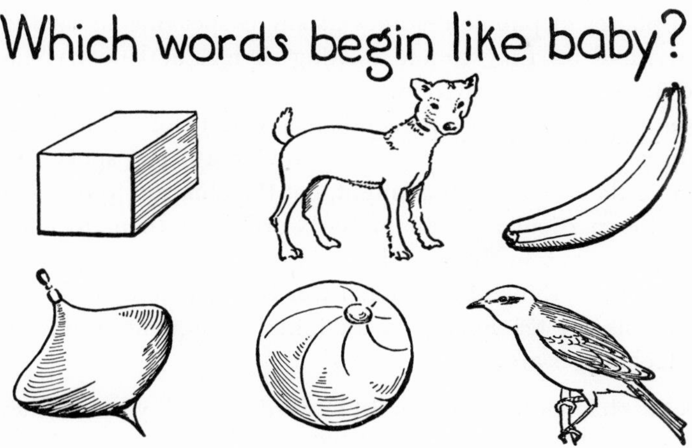
Which words begin like baby?

Fig. 27. Example of one kind of exercise that can be used to develop auditory perception of beginning consonant sounds.

as: *moon, many, soon, make, mother.* He should also be able to listen to a word and supply two or three other words that begin with the same sound. (3) He should be sensitive to rhymes, should be able to pick out words that rhyme, and should be able to supply words to rhyme with a given word. This ability is fundamental to the construction of "word families." (4) He should be able to hear similarities and differences in word endings. (5) He should be able to hear similarities and differences in middle vowels; e.g., he should be able to tell whether *rub* and *rob,* or *hill* and *pit,* have the same middle sound. (6) He should be able to listen to the pronunciation of a word sound by sound and fuse or blend the sounds mentally so as to be able to recognize the word intended.

These six aspects of phonic readiness have been listed roughly in order of increasing difficulty. Stage six is the hardest. While some children find it easy to blend sounds when they enter the first grade, other children go through school without ever becoming skillful at phonic blending. All of these auditory abilities, however, can be improved considerably by special practice. The most effective time to teach any phase of phonic readiness is just before the corresponding discrimination is to be made in printed words. However, certain general phases of phonic readiness, such as speaking distinctly and correctly, and listening to and reciting rhymes and poetry, can be started in the preschool period.

In developing auditory perception, a variety of devices can be used. In general, the technique is to provide a list of spoken words containing the element to be taught, get the children to focus attention on the particular sound in the words, get them to compare words which contain the sound with words which do not, and encourage them to think of additional words which contain the sound. For example, in teaching *f* as an initial consonant, some of the usable techniques are:

1. Ask the children to listen to a list of words and tell you how they are alike. Pronounce such words as: fun, fox, field, fairy, fat, Fred. Ask how they are alike. Then pronounce each word again while printing it on the chalkboard. Explain that all the words begin with the letter *f*, which has the sound *fff*.[16] Underline the *f* in each word as you pronounce it again. Let one child at a time point to the *f* as you pronounce the word a third time.
2. Play a listening game in which the children signal, by raising a hand, clapping, or standing, whenever you pronounce a word which begins with *f*. Use lists such as: fit, fan, make, frog; fence, toy, fireplace, Friday; and so on. Then reverse by having them signal when they do not hear a word beginning with *f*, using lists in which about half of the words do not begin with *f*.
3. Ask the children to suggest other words which begin with *f*. To make this more challenging, it may be done by categories: names, animals, things, or games to play. If desired, the words can be put on the board and the *f*'s underlined.
4. Give incomplete sentences or riddles which the children are to finish by adding a word which begins with *f*. For example:

[16] There has been much argument about the use of letter names only, without ever mentioning the sound as a separate unit, *versus* using the sounds only, without mentioning the letter names. To this writer it is simple common sense to introduce children to both names and sounds at the same time.

Playing ball is lots of (fun).
My cat has nice soft (fur).
What game do boys like to play in the fall? (football)
What do birds do in the air? (fly)

5. After two or more sounds have been taught, practice should be given in discriminating among them. One way of doing this is to pronounce a mixed list of words and have the children either say or write the specific sound and letter they were to listen for.[17]

Types of Phonic Analysis

Many different phonic methods have been evolved. In general they can be divided into two broad types: those which involve sounding the separate parts of a word and then blending them together, and those which avoid the separate sounding of word parts.

Sounding and Blending. Procedures involving sounding and blending have been of three major types. Each of these has certain advantages, and also definite limitations.

1. Probably the oldest of these is letter-by-letter sounding, as *c-a-t, p-i-c-k.* This method teaches a systematic left-to-right sequence in attacking the word and requires the teaching of a relatively small number of phonic elements. It has two main disadvantages: (1) Extraneous sounds may distort the sounding, particularly the addition of an *uh* sound to consonants, as *cuh-a-tuh, puh-i-kuh*; and (2) blending is comparatively difficult, even when extra sounds are avoided.[18]

[17] Additional suggestions can be found in:
Durrell, Donald D., and Sullivan, Helen B., *Building Word Power,* Revised. Yonkers: World Book Co., 1945.
Zedler, Empress Y., *Listening for Speech Sounds.* Garden City, N.Y.: Doubleday & Co., 1955.
Armstrong, Leila, *Come and Hear,* A First Ear-Training Book, including *Teacher's Guide.* Chicago: Follett Publishing Co., 1953.
Cordts, Anna D., *Readiness for Power in Reading.* Chicago: Beckley-Cardy Co., 1953.
Thompson, Lola M., *Teachers' Handbook* for *Happy Times With Sounds.* Boston: Allyn & Bacon, 1951 (The rhymes and poems in this manual are not recommended, but many of the activities suggested are useful.)

[18] For an eloquent defense of letter phonics, see: Dolch, Edward W., *The Psychology and Teaching of Reading,* Revised, Ch. 8. Champaign, Ill.: Garrard Press, 1951.

2. The initial consonant is sounded and the rest of the word is sounded as a phonogram unit of two or more letters, as *c-at, p-ick.* Words with the same final phonogram are taught as families, such as at, bat, cat, fat, hat. Because there are many one-syllable words that belong to such word families, this has been a popular procedure. Since there are only two parts to be blended together, blending is easier than with letter-by-letter sounding. The following sources of difficulty can be anticipated: (1) The child is encouraged to develop the habit of looking at the word ending before the beginning, developing improper eye movements; (2) there is a widely prevalent tendency, among teachers as well as children, to add an extra *uh* sound to the initial consonant, as *cuh-at,* which makes correct blending difficult; (3) practice on word families in list form may have little carry-over to the recognition of the words in printed context; and (4) the phonograms which are taught in this way, like *-ap, -end, -ist, -ong,* and *-uck,* are infrequent in words of more than one syllable.

3. The initial consonant and following vowel are sounded as a unit, and the final consonant is added, as *ca-t, pi-ck.* The advantages claimed for this method are that it avoids extraneous sounds, makes blending comparatively easy, and prepares the way for syllabication of longer words. Critics have pointed out that: (1) The number of consonant-vowel combinations that have to be taught is very large; (2) it is difficult, when sounding in this way, to know whether to give the vowel its long or short sound because that depends on what follows the vowel; and (3) if followed exclusively, the method prevents the teaching of such phonograms as *ight* and *ound,* which are best learned as units.[19] Since a good reader needs flexibility in his attack on words, exclusive devotion to any of these three procedures is probably less desirable than a varied approach.

There are a few important matters of technique which have a great influence over the success or failure of instruction in sounding and blending. (1) In order to achieve good progress, consider-

[19] This method is strongly advocated by Cordts. See: Cordts, Anna D., *Readiness for Power in Reading,* Chicago: Beckley-Cardy Co., 1953; also, Cordts, Anna D., "And It's All Called Phonics," *Elementary English,* Vol. 32, 1955, pp. 376–378.

Your Cues

Work out these words.

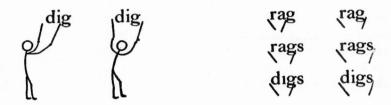

Find the line without a picture.

dipping the milk

lapping the milk

rapping to get in

a bag of rags

digging in the sand

Fig. 28. A page illustrating the use of picture and word cues in developing skill in the use of initial consonant-vowel combinations and consonant endings. From Cordts, Anna D. *I Can Read,* p. 52. Chicago: Beckley-Cardy Co., 1953, reproduced by permission of the publisher, and reduced in size.

able attention should be given to the development of phonic readiness and auditory perception for word sounds. (2) In helping a child to sound out words, the teacher must be very careful to avoid extraneous sounds. (3) Words should be sounded continuously, with the sound of one letter running into the sound of the next letter. If it is necessary to pronounce the sound separately, the time interval between sounds should be as small as possible. (4) When a child is having difficulty in blending a word, the teacher should pronounce the whole word, then pronounce it successively more slowly until the individual sounds are given separately. Then the process is reversed, starting with separate sounds and speeding up gradually, so that the relation between the separate sounds and the usual pronunciation of the word as a whole can be more clearly appreciated. (5) Phonic analysis is very fatiguing to children who are learning the process, and therefore lessons of this type should be short, preferably not more than ten minutes. (6) If the skills developed in phonics lessons are to function in connected reading, abundant practice should be provided in which the child reads interesting material, recognizing most of the words at sight and falling back on phonic analysis only when he meets a new word or has forgotten one learned before.

Whole-Word Phonics

Because so many children taught to sound and blend words either became slow, laborious word-by-word readers, or remained unsuccessful in their attempts at blending, phonic techniques were worked out which attempt to avoid the separate sounding of word parts. The basic principle is to help the child become aware of the contribution of letters and phonogram units to the sound of the word by comparing and contrasting whole words, rather than by separate sounding of the parts.

The basic technique is that of letter substitution (or phonogram substitution). The child, when he comes to an unknown word, is encouraged to think of words which begin and end like the unknown word. For example, if the child comes to a new word, "mast," he may think: "It begins like *man,* and ends like *last,* so it must be *mast.*" He must be able mentally to drop off the ending of *man,* and carry over the beginning while he thinks of the ending of *last,* so this is really a kind of quick mental blending.

Another variant of the method teaches initial consonants by means of cue words; if the child has difficulty remembering the sound of *m* he thinks of the cue word, which might be *milk.* The child is taught four steps: (1) think of a known word that resembles this new word; (2) drop off the part that is different; (3) think the sound of the new part, or think of a cue word that gives the sound of the new part; (4) without sounding the two parts separately, say the new word. Using the same example above, in which "mast" is unknown and "last" is known, the child would think: *last, ast, milk* (cue word for *m*), *mast.* As the consonant sounds become securely learned and skill in the method grows, the second and third steps drop out, and the new part is immediately substituted, so that the child thinks: *last, mast.* The same technique of thinking of a familiar word and making the necessary substitutions can be used also for final consonants (*mea*t, mea*l*), and for vowels (sp*i*n, sp*u*n).

Although some proponents of whole-word phonics are vehemently opposed to ever mentioning the sound of a letter or phonogram as a separate entity, the wisdom of such a prohibition is decidedly questionable. If you point out to children that *baby, book, boat,* and *bunny* all sound alike at the beginning and all start with the letter *b,* the children are going to think "*bee* says *buh*" if you do not tell them that "*bee* says *b,*" being careful to pronounce the consonant without an added vowel. As in the so-called Non-Oral Method, the teacher has no control over what the child is saying to himself, and the children are better off if given a good model to imitate. Thinking the sound of a letter or phonogram is quicker and more direct than thinking of a cue word, and phonic units are easier to apply if they have been learned as separable units than when one has to refer back to a cue word each time.

Obviously the substitution technique requires that a sight vocabulary be learned before phonics can be started, since the cue words must be securely known. For a child who has poor visual abilities but shows an aptitude for learning by primarily auditory techniques, a sounding-blending technique is likely to work better than a substitution technique. For the majority of children, substitution seems to work satisfactorily. Although experimental comparisons of the different kinds of phonic methods are not available, substitution techniques are at present preferred by the majority of authors of basal readers and therefore are the methods by which most of today's children are trained in word attack.

This chapter, the first of three on word recognition skills, has treated methods of developing sight vocabulary, the nature of a modern, comprehensive program of word analysis, and methods of teaching phonics, including the development of phonic readiness. The general topic continues in the next chapter with consideration of structural analysis, phonic elements, the rate and sequence for teaching word analysis skills, and materials useful in the development of proficiency in word analysis.

Suggested Additional Reading

See the references listed at the end of Chapter XIII.

· XIII ·

Developing Word Recognition Skills, II

IN THIS CHAPTER the discussion of word analysis is continued. The different kinds of structural analysis are described, and the need for combining context, structural analysis, and phonics is emphasized. Then the questions involved in determining what phonic elements to teach, and when to introduce them, are considered and a level-by-level word recognition program for the primary grades is suggested. Spelling and its relation to the word recognition program is considered, and the chapter concludes with a descriptive listing of materials available for use in teaching word recognition skills.

I. Structural Analysis

WHEN A CHILD compares *runs* with *run* and observes that the former is *run* with an *s* added, he is using the simplest form of structural analysis. During the first grade children generally are helped to recognize words with variant endings such as *s, es, ed, er,* and *ing.* A second form of structural analysis that is started early is the discovery that some words are compounds made up of smaller familiar words, like *into* and *something.* This technique should be limited to words which naturally separate into known words; children should not be encouraged to look for little words in the interior of bigger words, because that fosters confused eye movements, and often the little word is not a natural unit of the larger word. For instance, the *in* in *final* both provides the wrong vowel sound, and prevents the proper division of the word into two syllables; the *at* and *on* in *nation* similarly do more harm than good.

A third form of structural analysis that become important when polysyllabic words are met with some frequency is the technique of looking for familiar prefixes, root words, and suffixes. This is an effective method with words like *in depend ence* and *en courage ment,* provided the parts can be recognized or sounded. Training in the recognition and meaning of common prefixes and suffixes is useful in the middle grades and secondary school.

Syllabication

The most generally useful form of structural analysis is syllabication. By the third grade, the majority of the new words that a child meets are words of more than one syllable. Many words of two and three syllables have, of course, already been learned as sight words. At the third-grade level one can begin to make children aware of the fact that words are made up of syllables, and can begin to develop skill in noting the number of syllables in a word and whether the vowel sounds are long or short. An exercise of a type that is useful at this level is shown in Figure 29.

Children can learn a word which has been divided into syllables for them, by pronouncing it syllable by syllable, long before they can make independent use of rules of syllabication. It is not necessary, therefore, to wait until rules are taught before using syllabication as an aid in the teaching of word recognition.

Most spelling systems teach the pronunciation of words by syllables as one phase of a multisense approach in learning to spell. It is probably advisable to include the major part of instruction in syllabication in spelling lessons, applying the principles to new words that occur in reading.

Practices vary greatly concerning the teaching of rules of syllabication. Bright children learn such rules easily and can apply them

Directions: Study the words in Section A below. See how they are divided into syllables. Sound each syllable. Find the marked (accented) syllable. Pronounce the whole word. Pronounce the marked syllable more clearly than the others. Notice how these long words are made up of several parts.

A. in hab′ i tant	rec re a′ tion
in for ma′ tion	div′ i dend
for ti fi ca′ tion	sub′ tra hend
ro ta′ tion	im mor′ tal
oc cu pa′ tion	ir ri ga′ tion

B. While your teacher pronounces the words below, slowly and clearly, separate the syllables by drawing vertical lines between them as in mul|ti|pli|ca|tion, and mark the syllables that are pronounced most distinctly. Divide into syllables first.

1. v a c a t i o n	9. r e l a t i v e	17. s y l l a b l e
2. d i v i s o r	10. u n f a v o r a b l e	18. d i s c o v e r

Fig. 29. Part of an exercise on syllabication. From Bedwell, Robert L., and Hutchinson, Mary, *My Own Reading Exercises,* Book Four, p. 36. Auburn, Alabama: Prather Publishing Co., 1944. Reproduced by permission of the publisher, and reduced in size.

satisfactorily, at about the fourth and fifth grades. In general, however, it is probably unwise to spend much time on rules of syllabication below the sixth grade. Among the many rules of syllabication, the following seem most worth teaching to elementary school children:

1. Each syllable has one vowel sound; it may or may not have consonants before and after the vowel.
2. A single consonant is usually joined to the vowel which follows it.
3. When a syllable ends in a vowel, the vowel is usually long; when it ends in a consonant, the vowel is usually short.
4. When two consonants occur together, they are usually divided, one going with the preceding and the other with the following vowel.

Additional rules and many exceptions to the rules can be found in any good handbook of English usage, or in the introduction to a good unabridged dictionary.

Combining Structural Analysis, Phonics, and Context Clues

If the goal is recognizing the word as quickly and economically as possible, the less the child has to do, the better. Thus instantaneous recognition of the word as a whole is quickest and most satisfactory. When the first quick look does not disclose the identity of the word, the combination of an intelligent anticipation based on context with whatever familiar part or parts are immediately discernible is often enough.

Usually the earliest aid to independence in word recognition that is taught is the use of context. The child is asked to look at the illustration (if it is helpful), to think of what the whole sentence is saying, and to guess what the missing word might be.

As soon as children have begun to make use of initial consonants, they can be helped to combine this with use of the context. For instance, a sentence in a first reader might be: "Jim went into the house." The child sees the letter *h* and thinks that the word might be either *house* or *horse*. But a boy could not go into a *horse,* so the word must be *house*. This procedure of combining the anticipation of a certain meaning with the cue supplied by the first letter or so of the word is one which is usually learned in the first grade, and continues to be serviceable to expert adult readers. In the sentence, "We like to watch our television set," either the *tel* at the beginning or the *vision* at the end would be sufficient cue for many children, in combination with context, to determine that the unknown word is *television*. Usually the beginning of the word is more helpful than the ending in this kind of solution.

When context and one familiar part do not suffice, a more systematic attack is necessary. Structural analysis may be sufficient when all, or most, of the parts of the word are already known at sight. For the most part, however, structural analysis is used in combination with phonics and context. The unknown word is divided into reasonable parts, the parts are sounded and blended together, and the result is tried to see if it makes sense in the sentence. At this point the child's listening and speaking vocabularies become impor-

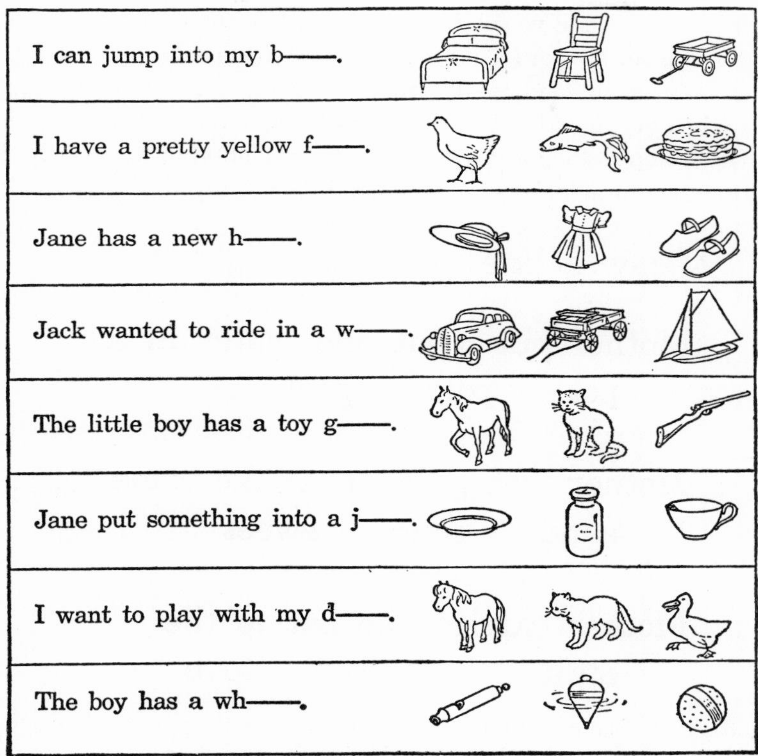

I can jump into my b——.
I have a pretty yellow f——.
Jane has a new h——.
Jack wanted to ride in a w——.
The little boy has a toy g——.
Jane put something into a j——.
I want to play with my d——.
The boy has a wh——.

Fig. 30. An exercise designed to provide practice in combining use of initial consonant sounds with use of the context. From Gray, W. S., and Monroe, M., *Think-and-Do Book* to accompany *Our New Friends,* The Basic Readers, 1². Chicago: Scott, Foresman and Co., 1940. Reproduced by permission of the publisher, and reduced in size.

tant. If the word is one which the child understands, uses, and can pronounce correctly, an approximate or partial sounding is often sufficient for recognition. If the word is completely new to the child he has to guess at both the pronunciation and the meaning, and neither can help him with the other. Thus a fourth-grade child, attacking a word like *incognito,* may divide it neatly into syllables and sound each in a reasonable way, but may accent the wrong syllable or give long vowel sounds where they should be short and so on, because the word is entirely unfamiliar to him.

Skill in the combined use of context, phonics, and structural analysis can be developed by the use of practice material which demands both attention to the meaning and careful attention to the details of words. One form of practice material useful for this purpose is

Draw a line under the right word.

Mother put meat and water in a
pot pole pool

Mother was going to make some
sand soup sweet

Mother carried the pot to the
stairs stones stove

Fig. 31. Part of an exercise to enforce care and accuracy in word recognition. From Gates, Arthur I., Huber, Miriam B., and Peardon, Celeste C., the *Preparatory Book* to accompany *We Grow Up,* The New Work-Play Books. New York: The Macmillan Co., 1939. Reproduced by permission of the publisher.

shown in Figure 31. This kind of exercise, in its many variations, is very useful for enforcing accuracy in word recognition and noting the details of words while reading for meaning. The child has to understand the sentence as a whole in order to know what word to expect; then he has to choose correctly among words that look very much alike in order to complete the sentence correctly.

II. Phonic Elements

There has been much argument about the phonic elements that should be taught, and the proper sequence in which to introduce them. At present there is still much disagreement on the issue.

English spelling is somewhat irregular, and there are many combinations of letters which have sound values which are quite different from those of the separate letters. Furthermore, it is faster and more efficient to break a word into groups of letters than to have to consider each letter separately. For both reasons, it is desirable to teach children to recognize common phonograms as units.

According to Spache,[1] phonograms that deserve to be taught should satisfy the following criteria: (1) They should consist of three or four letters; (2) they should occur frequently in basic vocabularies; (3) they should not be pronounceable in many different ways; (4) they should ordinarily be found in initial and final positions in words, thus forming good units of perception; (5) they should form a syllabic or pronunciation unit; and (6) they should be frequently found at the beginning of words. He presented the following list of phonograms as the only ones that satisfy four or more of these criteria: *ail, ain, al, all, and, ate, ay, con, di, ed, eep, ell, en, ent, er, est, ick, ight, ill, in, ing, ock, se, ter, tion.* Phonograms that meet three of the criteria are: *ai, ake, be, de, ide, ile, ine, it, ite, le, on, ow (low), re, ri,* and *wi.* Initial two-letter consonant combinations worth teaching include: *cl, tr, br, ch, gr, sh, sp, st.* The teaching of these combinations in addition to the long and short vowel sounds and the simple consonant sounds gives, according to Spache, an adequate basis for phonetic analysis.

A sequence for teaching phonic units, including both the single letter sounds and phonograms, was worked out by Hegge, Kirk and Kirk [2] as follows:

Part I. Introductory Sounds

All consonants; the short vowels *a, o, i, u; ee; sh; oo; ch* and *tch; ar;*

[1] Spache, G., "A Phonics Manual for Primary and Remedial Teachers," *Elementary English Review,* Vol. 16, 1939, pp. 147–150, 191–198.

[2] *Remedial Reading Drills;* see description on page 360.

ay and *ai; or; old;* short *e; ea; oa; ck; ow* and *ou;* long vowels with final *e; ing; all; ight; th, wh,* and *que; er, ir,* and *ur.*

Part II. Combinations of Sounds

An, in, and *un; en* and *on; ink, ank,* and *unk: ing, ang, ong,* and *ung; and, ound,* and *est; all, ill,* and *ell; pl, cl, fl, bl, gl,* and *sl; pr, cr, fr, br, gr, tr,* and *dr; sp, st, sc, sm,* and *sw; spl, spr, str,* and *scr.*

Part III. Advanced Sounds

Aw, au, and *ew; ook, ind, oy,* and *oi;* final *y, ly, le,* and *ed; ge, ce, ci,* and *cy; aught, ought, pro,* and *other; re-, be-, de-,* and *pre-; -sion, -tion, -ation,* and *-ution.*

Part IV. Supplementary Exercises

Exceptions: *ea, ow, th, ive.*

Configurations not previously taught: *kn, gn, wr; ph; ould; alk; alm; ex-, con-,* and *dis-; -ous* and *-ful; wor; war; air* and *are; eigh; ie;* monosyllables ending in *y* or *ie; oll; oe; o* and *e* as endings.

Word-building exercises and compound words: *ever, under, sea, post, school, house, some, come, where,* and *there* as parts of compound words; final *e* in compound words; plural of words ending in *y;* plurals.

Exercises for letter confusions: *b, d, p; m* and *n.*

Another usable sequence is the one recommended by Stanger and Donohue. They teach phonic elements in groups. Where vowels are introduced for the first time only the short sound is taught.[3]

Set 1. *a, b, m, s, l, t, i*	Set 7. *g, u*
Set 2. *h, e, th*	Set 8. *n, oo*
Set 3. *r, ee, br, bl, st, sl, sm, tr, thr, sh, th, ble*	Set 9. *j, v.*
	Set 10. *x, z*
Set 4. *o, er*	Set 11. *d*
Set 5. *c, k, f, ch*	Set 12. *ing, ang, ong, ung, ink, ank, onk, unk*
Set 6. *p, y, w, wh*	

Additional sounds: long vowels with final *e, qu, ow, ou, gu, ge, ir, oy, oi, ar, or, ay, ai, eigh, ea, ie, igh, oe, oa, ue, ey.*

Dolch made a careful analysis of the phonograms and syllables that actually occur in children's reading.[4] He analyzed the 19,000

[3] Stanger, Margaret A., and Donohue, Ellen K., *Prediction and Prevention of Reading Difficulties.* New York: Oxford University Press, 1937.

[4] Dolch, E. W., "Phonics and Polysyllables," *Elementary English Review,* Vol. 15, 1938, pp. 120–124.

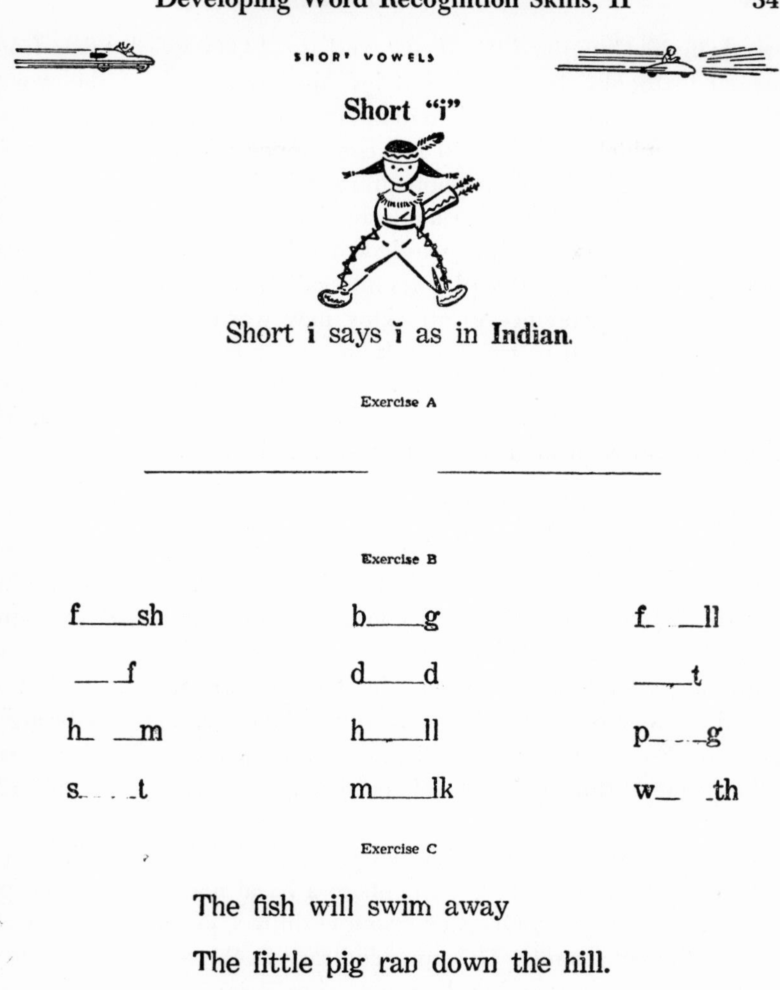

SHORT VOWELS

Short "i"

Short **i** says ĭ as in **Indian**.

Exercise A

________________ ________________

Exercise B

f___sh	b___g	f___ll
___f	d___d	___t
h___m	h___ll	p___g
s___t	m___lk	w___th

Exercise C

The fish will swim away

The little pig ran down the hill.

Is it a very big fish?

Did Bill go with him?

Fig. 32. An exercise to develop the short *i* sound. From Armstrong, Leila, and Hargrave, Rowena, *Building Reading Skills: Jato Car Book,* p. 31. Wichita, Kansas: McCormick-Mathers Publishing Co., 1951. Reproduced by permission of the publisher, and reduced in size.

words in the *Combined Word List,* and also 14,000 words taken from school textbooks. He found that less than one sixth of the words were monosyllables. More than one thousand different syllables were found, of which less than 10 per cent appeared in as many as six words each. The common phonograms which are usually taught in the first and second grades made up less than 12 per cent of the different syllables. Dolch concluded that his findings showed a need for training in both letter phonics and syllabication, if a satisfactory degree of independence in attacking new words is to be attained. Naturally the kind of word attack an author favors determines the kinds of elements to be taught. Thus Cordts, who favors the use of consonant-vowel combinations, teaches such initial units as *ra, ba,* and *chi,* and such final units as *-g, -ck,* and so on.

Sequence in Phonic Instruction

Many different sequences for introducing phonic and structural learnings have been devised. Most authors of basal readers provide for the introduction of initial consonants first, followed by some word families and simple endings, in the first-grade manuals. Two-consonant blends and short and long vowels are usually taught at second-reader level, and less common phonic elements are brought in at third-reader level. Syllabication, prefixes, and suffixes are usually started at third-reader level and developed further in the middle grades.

Some of the special phonics materials which have been designed for independent use as supplements to a basal reading program follow other sequences. One, for example, introduces all short vowels before the consonants. This runs contrary to the available research on phonic readiness and to the practical experience of most teachers, which indicates that vowels are more difficult than consonants for most children, but it is not an impossible sequence.

In attempting to determine a sensible sequence for phonic units, the major guiding principles are to introduce early those elements which are frequently met in primary-grade words, and those which are most readily learned. If one adheres to these common-sense ideas reasonably well, many different sequences can be used with satisfactory results.

It is probably true that the ideal time to introduce a new phonic principle or unit is when the children have need for it and are ready for it. This is what the basal reader systems attempt to do, since

Letter Teams

oi oy aw au

Two horses pulling together make a team of horses. Sometimes two letters work together to make a sound which neither one could make alone. In the words below, *oy*, *oi*, *aw*, and *au* are teams.

Practice pronouncing the words and then select and write the correct word in each blank space.

The teams *oi* and *oy* make the same sound.

boy	toy	joy	Roy	enjoy	joyful	enjoying
boil	toil	join	rejoice	oil	spoil	noise

1. These stories are .... reading.
2. Rain will .... a hat.
3. An automobile must have ....
4. Fire will make water ....
5. A story is something to ....

Fig. 33. Part of an exercise for teaching the sounds of vowel combinations. From Stone, C. R., *Eye and Ear Fun,* Book III. St. Louis, Mo.: Webster Publishing Co. Reproduced by permission of the publisher, and reduced in size.

usually a new phonic idea is introduced at a point where several words exemplifying it have been learned as sight words, and the new idea can be developed from these known words. A good teacher should not hesitate to teach a word attack skill or a new sound when there seems to be a suitable occasion, even if that means deviating from a previously planned sequence.

The contents of Table IX indicate what, in this writer's best judgment, should usually have been covered in word attack skills by the time reading at a given level of difficulty has been completed. At a particular difficulty level no attempt has been made to indicate a sequence in which the items should be taught. As compared to the corresponding table in the preceding edition of this book there have been a few changes in the direction of earlier introduction, such as placing the short vowels at first-reader level rather than at second-reader level. It is the writer's intention that this table may provide a list of objectives and a check list to see what needs to be reviewed or first taught, rather than an instructional sequence. It can be taken for granted that many children will not master a particular phonic skill the first time it is introduced, and therefore review at higher levels of instruction is a necessity. Although an attempt has been made to indicate specific readiness activities at the different levels, the general principle should be that listening for sounds within words and looking for the corresponding visual symbols is part of all phonic instruction.

III. Spelling and Word Recognition

The close relationship between success in reading and success in spelling has already been mentioned in this book several times. Good readers are sometimes poor spellers, but readers who are poor in word recognition are rarely if ever good spellers.

Effective spelling instruction utilizes much the same type of procedure that has been described in this chapter. A typical classroom method of teaching spelling proceeds about as follows: The word is first spoken by the teacher in a sentence, then by itself, and written or printed on the board. The meaning is brought out through use in sentences. The word is then analyzed into component parts, with syllables separated by vertical lines, underlining, or some other device. Attention is called to difficult parts by underlining or using colored chalk. Many types of sensory reinforcement are employed, such as pronouncing the word, spelling it in concert, visualizing the word followed by recall of the visual image with the eyes closed, writing the word in the air while spelling it aloud, and finally, writing the word from memory and checking against the correct form. It is evident that good spelling is based first of all on correct percep-

Table IX. A Planned Sequence of Word Recognition Goals

Reader Level	*Sight Recognition*	*Visual and Auditory Readiness*	*Phonics and Structural Analysis*
Preprimer	40–75 words	Matches objects, pictures, letters, words, phrases, sentences. Notes similarity in the sounds of rhyming words. Notes similarities and differences in initial consonant sounds.	Relies mainly on general configuration, picture cues, and context cues. Recognizes same word beginning with capital or lower-case letter. Recognizes plurals made with *s*. Learns names of most alphabet letters. Begins to use initial consonants in combination with context.
Primer	80–150 new words.	Compares words for similarities and differences in beginning sounds. Compares rhyming words, completes and composes simple rhymes. Compares final consonants in words; notes similarities and differences. Blends and recognizes words spoken by teacher in two or three parts.	Continues use of configuration, context, and picture cues. Uses common initial consonants in combination with context cues. Structural analysis: recognizes familiar words with endings *s, es, d, ed, ing*. Recognizes known whole words in compound words (into). Some common word families with initial consonant substitution. Use of some common final consonants.

Table IX. (Continued)

Reader Level	*Sight Recognition*	*Visual and Auditory Readiness*	*Phonics and Structural Analysis*
First Reader	115–200 new words	Review of previous ear training. Listens to and identifies all initial consonants and common consonant digraphs. Continued use of rhymes. Listens and compares additional final consonants. Notes similarities and differencies in middle vowels: man-men, bill-bell, hat-hot, etc.	Review of previously learned phonic and structural skills. Use of all initial consonants and common consonant digraphs *ch, sh, th, wh.* Additional word families with initial consonant substitution. Learns endings *-er, -est, -ly.* Changes known words by substituting final consonants. Introduction of short vowel sounds.
Second Reader	300–650 new words	Review of previous ear training. Listens to and compares words with single and double initial consonants: *fight-fright, seal-steal,* etc. Listens to and compares words with long and short vowels: *can-cane, bit-bite, hop-hope, cut-cute,* etc.	Review of previously learned word attack skills. Learns common initial two-consonant blends: *br, cr, dr, fr, gr, tr, cl, fl, pl, sl, sp, st,* and final consonant blends, *-ng, -nk, -nt, -st.* Reviews short vowels and learns long vowel sounds, *a, e, i, o, u, y,* and rule of final silent *e.* Learns common vowel digraphs, *ai, ay, ea, ee, ie, oa, oo.* Learns effect of following *r* on vowels: *-ar, -er, -ir, -or, -ur.*

Table IX. (Continued)

Reader Level	*Sight Recognition*	*Visual and Auditory Readiness*	*Phonics and Structural Analysis*
Third Reader	500–1000 new words	Review of previous ear training. Listens to and compares words containing new phonic elements. Listens to divide spoken words into syllable units.	Learns less common two-consonant blends, *gl, sc, sm, sn, pr, sw, tw,* etc. and three-consonant blends, *scr, str, spl, spr, squ.* Learns silent consonants *wr, kn, gn, qu.* Learns vowel diphthongs, *au, aw, ou, ow, ew, ue, oi, oy.* Learns hard and soft *c* and *g.* Prefixes: *re-, be-, de-, pre-.* Endings: *-le, -ble, -tle, -ful, -tion, -sion, -ation, -al.* Recognizes root word in words with these endings. Learns to divide easy two and three syllable words into syllables.

tion of the word, followed by repetition and sensory reinforcement to bring about permanent retention in memory.

Many of the devices used in spelling instruction, such as dividing the word into syllables, pointing out and emphasizing the difficult parts, and using a varied sense appeal are also effective aids in word recognition. When a word is learned so that it can be spelled from memory, it is usually recognized without difficulty in reading. An efficient classroom teacher can use the spelling period for practice on many of the abilities that are necessary for good word recognition.

Dangers of Rote Spelling

Many children whose spelling is poor are victims of an inefficient method of word study. They memorize a word by reciting the sequence of the letters over and over, without paying attention to syllable divisions, without trying to visualize the word, and without trying to note the specific features of the word that may be confusing. Since this type of practice is comparatively uninteresting and devoid of meaning, it is less effective for most children than the kind of procedure described in the preceding paragraphs.

Many children who have difficulty in acquiring a sight reading vocabulary try to learn and recall their reading words by spelling them. This is a very inefficient method of word recognition, and in order to make real progress the child has to give it up in favor of more effective procedures. Rote spelling as an avenue to reading has the following defects: (1) It is a slow procedure and results in halting, word-by-word reading; (2) it usually fails on words of more than five or six letters; (3) the children who resort to spelling as an aid in word recognition are usually poor spellers also; (4) the spelling procedure interferes with the use of more adequate methods of word study; and (5) it prevents the perception of the word as a whole, since the child's attention is not on a word form containing distinctive parts, but on a string of letters possessing no form quality that can be remembered.

In getting a child to discontinue letter-by-letter spelling in his reading, the first step should be an explanation of the weaknesses of the procedure and encouragement to try a different method. As he studies a word, he should be encouraged to pronounce it as a whole, by syllables, or by phonic elements, but not to recite the names of the individual letters.

IV. Materials for Teaching Word Recognition and Phonics

IF A TEACHER is to work effectively with two or more groups in a class, and provide special attention for one or two pupils who cannot keep up with the slowest group, appropriate seatwork which provides useful learning experiences is essential. The teacher whose pupils need extra practice in word recognition and word analysis can choose among many different kinds of published materials. Most of these are workbooks which are to be marked up by the pupil. Some of them are intended for oral work, or for written answers on separate paper. The materials described below are usable in remedial reading programs. None is clearly superior to the others in all respects.

The teacher who wants to know more about these materials can write to the various publishers for descriptive matter and sample copies. Careful inspection of single copies, and perhaps a tryout with one child, can help the teacher to decide which to order in quantity.

It is a pity that so many schools lack funds for the purchase of workbooks and other individualized teaching materials. The cost per pupil is so little when compared to the cost of failure, that the penny-wise, pound-foolish policy followed in so many places cannot readily be justified. Nevertheless, even if prevented by lack of funds from making regular use of perishable workbooks, the resourceful teacher is still not entirely prevented from making some use of them. From single copies, which are generally quite inexpensive, the teacher can get ideas which can be incorporated into blackboard work or developed in duplicated work sheets of his own construction.

Many successful remedial teachers have developed files of useful practice exercises. They order two copies of each of a number of workbooks and cut them up (since pages are printed on both sides,

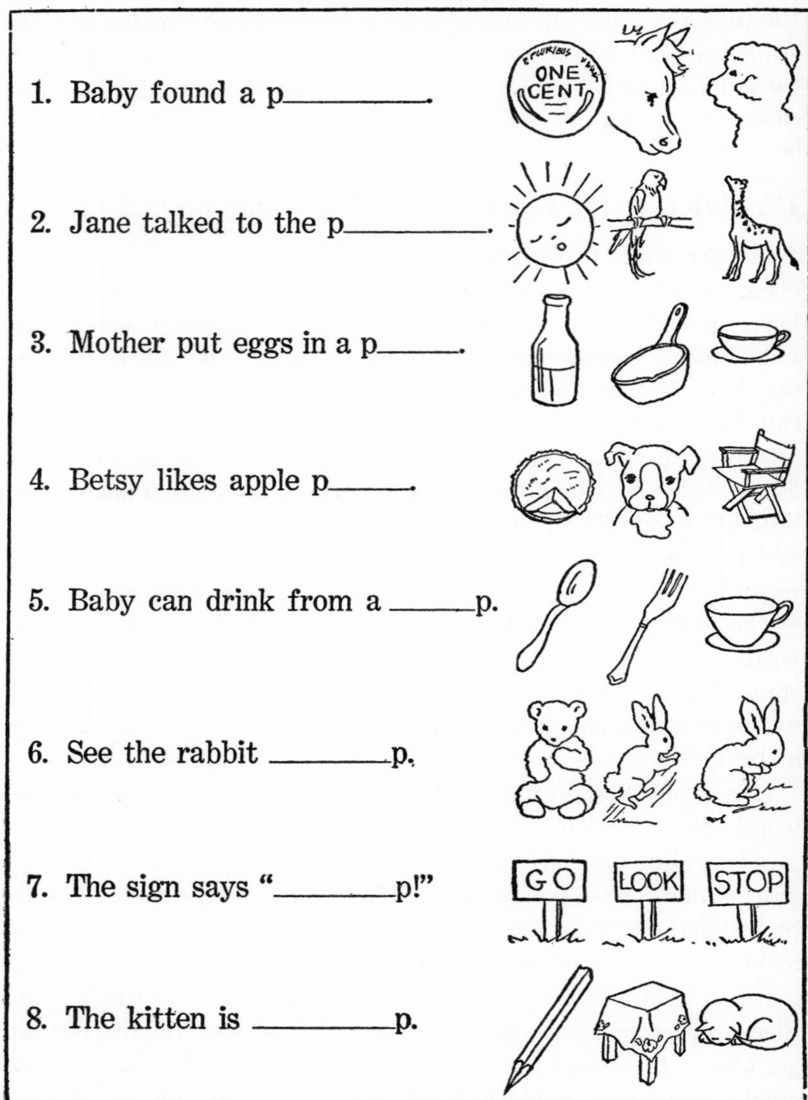

1. Baby found a p______.
ONE CENT
2. Jane talked to the p______.
3. Mother put eggs in a p_____.
4. Betsy likes apple p_____.
5. Baby can drink from a _____p.
6. See the rabbit _______p.
7. The sign says "_______p!"
GO
LOOK
STOP
8. The kitten is _______p.

Fig. 34. An exercise to teach the consonant *p* as both an initial and a final sound. The directions are to put an X on the picture that completes each sentence. From Meighen, M., and others, *Phonics We Use,* Book B, p. 28. Chicago: Lyons and Carnahan, 1946. Reproduced by permission of the publisher, and reduced in size.

two copies are needed). Each page is mounted on heavy paper or oak tag, and can be shellacked or covered with cellophane for permanency. By assembling pages from several workbooks, a comprehensive series of exercises can be built up. Exercises constructed by the teacher can be inserted into the series at any time. A grocery carton can be used as a file drawer. The exercises should be classified by type, and numbered within each type. Care in classifying and numbering the exercises will make it possible for a bright pupil, acting as librarian, to keep the collection in order and to select for each pupil the exercises assigned by the teacher. A separate file of answer keys, corresponding to the exercises, makes it possible for the teacher to correct written work very quickly, or for the pupils to correct their own work.

Practice Materials for Sight Recognition

The most popular materials for supplementary practice to develop sight vocabulary have been the *Basic Sight Vocabulary Cards* and the *Picture-Word Cards* by E. W. Dolch.[5] Other materials which can be used for this purpose include the following:

Mother Hubbard's Seatwork Cupboard, Reading Shelf, Nos. 1 and 2, Kibbe, D. E., ed. Eau Clair, Wis.: E. M. Hale & Co. No. 1, of primer level, introduces a total of ninety-three easy first-grade words in ninety-three pages of exercises which emphasize word-picture matching, coloring, cutting, and pasting; very useful for slow first-grade children, mentally retarded pupils, and nonreaders. No. 2, of first-grade level, puts more emphasis on sentence and paragraph reading.

Puzzle Pages, Books I and II, by F. Shelton and L. L. Tate. Wichita, Kan.: McCormick-Mathers Publishing Co. These workbooks, of primer and first-reader level, provide easy first-grade seatwork with emphasis on cutting and pasting words and sentences in relation to pictures.

Primary Seatwork, by James McDade and others. Chicago: Plymouth Press. Devised for the Non-Oral Method, there are many sets of seatwork involving matching of words with pictures and so on, each set containing material for six children and providing for self-checking.

New Comparison Seatwork, by Clara M. Guibor. Chicago: Primary Educational Service, 8217 So. Halstead St. This and other materials prepared for the Non-Oral Method can be used in other settings.

[5] See description on page 382.

Picture dictionaries can be helpful in building sight vocabulary. In addition to those which are published as parts of basal reader series, there are some good independent picture dictionaries (see page 410).

Practice Materials for Word Attack Skills

The workbooks which accompany basal readers have many pages of practice material on word attack skills, and for many children supplementary material of this type is not necessary. Independent material can be quite helpful in remedial and corrective work, and in teaching children who seem to need a more systematic phonic procedure than the reader method provides. There are many sets of materials on the market, some of which follow sound methodology in the opinion of the writer, and some of which do not. Those for which this writer has the highest regard are the following:

Building Reading Skills, by Leila Armstrong and Rowena Hargrave. Wichita: McCormick-Mathers Publishing Co. A series of six workbooks (Speedboat Book, Jato Car Book, Jet Plane Book, Rocket Book, Atomic Gyro Book, Space Ship Book), developing word attack skills sequentially with emphasis on meaningful content and considerable practice in writing. Each workbook is accompanied by a packet of skill builders (key cards and manipulative devices); there is a separate *Teachers' Guidebook* and a box of large *Phonics Key Cards.*

Eye and Ear Fun, by Clarence R. Stone. St. Louis: Webster Publishing Co. A series of four workbooks (Books 1, 2, 3, 4) with emphasis on exercises which combine meaning, picture, phonic, and structural cues. Book 4 reviews primary-grade phonics and develops elementary syllabication.

Phonics We Use, by Mary Meighan, Marjorie Pratt, and Mabel Halvorsen. Chicago: Lyons and Carnahan. A series of five workbooks (Books A, B, C, D, E) very much like *Eye and Ear Fun* in method; somewhat more gradual in pace.

Happy Times with Sounds, by Lola M. Thompson. Boston: Allyn & Bacon. A series of three workbooks (Books 1, 2, 3) and a separate Teachers' Handbook, with much attention to ear training as a preparation to the practice material, most of which is easy and meaningful. Not all of the ear training material is well chosen.

In addition to the above materials there are many others which have achieved some popularity. A teacher who wishes to have a

Putting in the Right Word: Words with Short u

For each sentence, underline the word that belongs in the blank space.

1. Mary found a big black bug under the ....
   dug hug rung rug
2. The bee .... Bob behind the ear
   stung sung snuff study
3. A .... of wind carried the boy's hat away.
   snuff puff pump punish
4. Watch your step and do not ....
   mumble stuff stumble struck
5. Hear the wind .... through the leaves.
   rusty rubbed husband rushing

Fig. 35. Part of a word discrimination exercise. From Stone, C. R., *Eye and Ear Fun,* Book III. St. Louis, Mo.: Webster Publishing Co. Reproduced by permission of the publisher, and reduced in size.

well-rounded collection of available phonic materials should secure copies of the following:

Phonic Skilltexts, by Mae McCrory and Pearl Watts. Columbus, Ohio: Charles E. Merrill Co. A series of four workbooks (Books A, B, C, D) stressing the use of nursery rhymes and avoiding isolated drill.

Phonovisual Method, by Lucile D. Schoolfield and Josephine B. Timberlake. Washington, D.C.: Phonovisual Products Co., Box 3504. Consists of a large Consonant Chart, a large Vowel Chart, smaller reproduction of the two charts for individual pupil use, a workbook, and an accompanying manual.

Wordland, by Eichler and Snyder. Elgin, Ill.: The Continental Press. A series of six workbooks (Books A, B, C, D, E, F).

Functional Phonetics, by Anna D. Cordts. Chicago: Beckley-Cardy Co. A manual for ear and eye training, *Readiness for Power in Reading,* followed by three hard-cover phonic practice books called *I Can Read, Hear Me Read,* and *Reading's Easy.* Emphasizes initial consonant-vowel combinations. Provides considerable ear training and some practice in meaningful context.

Reading with Phonics, by Julie Hay and Charles E. Wingo. Philadelphia: J. B. Lippincott Co. A hard-cover book for the pupil accompanied by a 128-page teacher's manual and three workbooks. Nearly all of the practice, both in ear training and in sounding, is on isolated words.

Initial consonant-vowel combinations are stressed, and red and black inks are used to make phonic units stand out.

Phonetic Keys to Reading, by Sloop, Garrison, and Creekmore. Oklahoma City: The Economy Co., 24 West Park. Four booklets (*Tag, Dot and Jim, All Around with Dot and Jim,* and *As Days Go By*) and a teacher's manual, using a format like that of preprimers and primers. The first three books are at preprimer, primer, and first-reader level and are intended to be used as basal readers using a phonic method rather than as a supplement to basal readers.

Steps to Mastery of Words, by Nadine Fillmore. Aurora, Ill.: Educational Service, Inc., P.O. Box 10. Includes four guide books for teachers, five phonograph records giving recorded lessons for teachers to imitate, four pupil word-study books, and a Read-More, Spell-More Sound Chart with a black sound stick giving initial consonants, and a red sound stick giving common word endings, with which words are built. This system carries isolated drill in sounding to its logical extreme.

Remedial Reading Drills, by Thorlief G. Hegge, Samuel A. Kirk, and Winifred A. Kirk. Ann Arbor, Mich.: George Wahr, Publisher. A single spiral-bound booklet presenting words in lists arranged for teaching by a combination of letter-by-letter sounding and kinesthetic reinforcement; no meaningful content. Devised originally for use with mentally retarded adolescents.

The materials listed above, with one exception, are intended for use as a supplement to basal readers and as material useful in corrective and remedial programs. There is also a considerable amount of game-type material designed for individualized practice and remedial work, which is described in the next chapter. Additional practice material, for those compiling individual collections for personal use, is to be found in many of the workbooks which accompany basal readers, and in some of the workbooks listed on pages 454–457.

Suggested Additional Reading

ADAMS, FAY, LILLIAN GRAY, and DORA REESE, *Teaching Children to Read,* Ch. 11.

BETTS, EMMETT A. *Foundations of Reading Instruction,* pp. 581–667.

DURRELL, DONALD D. *Improvement of Basic Reading Abilities,* pp. 171–230.

GATES, ARTHUR I. *Improvement of Reading,* Third Edition, Chs. 7, 9.

GRAY, WILLIAM S. *On Their Own in Reading.* Chicago: Scott, Foresman & Co., 1948.

McKee, Paul. *The Teaching of Reading in the Elementary School,* pp. 237–264, 292–303, 363–367.

McKim, Margaret G. *Guiding Growth in Reading in the Modern Elementary School,* Ch. 9.

Stone, Clarence R. *Progress in Primary Reading,* Ch. 11.

Yoakam, Gerald A. *Basal Reading Instruction,* Chs. 8, 9.

· XIV ·

Overcoming Difficulties in Word Recognition

Words are the bricks with which thoughts are built, and when a child cannot recognize many of the words which an author has used he is at a great disadvantage in trying to extract meaning from the printed page. Severe cases of reading disability nearly all need basic retraining in learning to recognize, figure out, and recall printed words. Even in the milder cases where reading comprehension is at the upper elementary or secondary school level, carelessness and inaccuracy in word recognition and the lack of an adequate independent method of attack upon new words may be significant parts of the whole reading picture.

Misunderstanding of the research on phonics caused many schools to swing during the 1930's from somewhat of an overemphasis on oral reading and phonics, to an even more undesirable total elimination of phonic instruction, or to reliance upon incidental or accidental learning of word analysis skills. A sound program of instruction in word analysis, such as has been described in Chapters XII and XIII, would have prevented some of the present cases of reading disability from developing, since many of them have not been taught systematically the techniques necessary for independence in reading. Integral parts of good practice are the teacher's alertness to notice signs of difficulties in their early stages, and the application of comparatively simple corrective procedures in everyday teaching.

Most children who need remedial help in word recognition show a small number of specific weaknesses. One such child may need daily training to overcome a reversal tendency; a second may make mistakes only on vowel sounds; a third may concentrate on neglecting or mispronouncing word endings. These children have made some progress in word recognition, but have developed faulty habits or have failed to learn some important elements of word recognition. Their remedial work should be aimed directly at the specific faults that are evident in their reading. Methods for use with this group are described in Section I. There is a much smaller number of very seriously disabled readers who have never learned an adequate method of studying and learning words, so that they lack a sight vocabulary and need to be taught a basic method for studying words. The needs of this group will be discussed in Section II.

I. Correcting Specific Faults in Word Recognition

Teaching Phonic Units

A great many children who need corrective or remedial help in reading have only a partial knowledge of the sound equivalents of phonic units. They may know the majority of single consonants, but have trouble with consonant blends. Ignorance of short vowel sounds is very prevalent. Many children confuse letter names with letter sounds. Knowledge of phonograms of two, three, or four letters is likely to be uneven, and syllabication is often completely unknown territory. Some of these gaps represent deficiencies in previous instruction, but many of them are aftereffects of teaching for which the child was not yet ready. It is desirable to find out by preliminary testing and observation which sounds are known and which need to be taught, and those that seem to be most urgently needed should be given priority in the teaching sequence.

Ear and Eye Training. Teaching a sound in corrective or remedial work need not be essentially different from the methods advised for developmental instruction. One should start with practice in listening for the sound within known words (see page 332). Then several known words containing the phonic elements are printed in column form and the common element is underlined or circled as the words are pronounced. Additional words containing the sound are suggested by pupil or teacher, pronounced, printed, and marked. Com-

Fig. 36. Part of a page intended to be used in introducing the sound of short *u*. From *King-Size Alphabet Book*, hectograph edition, p. 24. Darien, Conn.: Educational Publishing Co., 1948. Reproduced by permission of the publisher, and reduced in size.

parisons are made with words that sound somewhat similar but do not contain the element, and with words that look somewhat similar but do not contain it.

Vivid Cues. For children who have difficulty in remembering sounds it is important to provide vivid associations which the child can use to recall the sound. Picture cards representing cue words are often helpful. If a child comes to the word "bunny" and has difficulty remembering the short *u* sound, he can look at the umbrella in Figure 36 and, saying "umbrella" to himself, can remind himself of the sound. Cue cards like this can be mounted above the chalkboard for reference, or each child can have a personal set. Sometimes cue cards which the children make themselves are more effective than those which are commercially available.

It is sometimes quite effective to dramatize sounds. Each sound can be associated with a situation in which the sound is made, as: *s* — the hissing of a steam radiator; *t* — the tick of a clock; long *o* — what we say when we are surprised; and so on. Tracing and writing the letter may be used for reinforcement. Clara Schmitt,[1] in an early article that should be read by all who are interested in the history of the development of remedial methods, advocated teaching letter sounds in this way. She employed a continued story, in which bells rang (*l*), dogs barked (*r*), and cows mooed (*m*), one new sound being added each day. This was followed by practice in which the teacher pronounced words sound by sound (r-un to me; f-old your hands), as a preliminary to training in blending.

Monroe pointed out that many children who confuse letters do not hear the differences between letters clearly. She therefore advocated preliminary training in auditory discrimination.[2] To teach an initial consonant sound she started by presenting pictures of several objects, some of whose names begin with the letter. The child was taught to discriminate sounds in the following way: As the child looks at the pictures he says, "S-soap, yes, 'soap' sounds like *s; s* — spoon, yes, spoon sounds like *s; s* — man, no, man doesn't sound like s," and so on. If the child had difficulty in pronunciation with such letters as *d, t,* and *th, s* and *sh, r, l,* and *w,* or *f* and *v,* he was taught the differences in the lip, tongue, and throat movements involved in

[1] Schmitt, Clara, "Developmental Alexia: Congenital Word Blindness or Inability to Learn to Read," *Elementary School Journal,* Vol. 18, 1918, pp. 680–700 and 757–769.

[2] Monroe, Marion, "Remedial Treatment in Reading," *Elementary English Review,* Vol. 10, 1933, pp. 95–97, 112. Also *Children Who Cannot Read,* pp. 116–120.

making the sounds. After the sounds could be correctly distinguished and pronounced, they were then associated with the printed letter form.

A persistent tendency to confuse two letters can be treated by following a sequence of steps: (1) Teach each of the letters in the way suggested above. (2) Present a printed list of words all of which have the first letter to be taught in a prominent place. For

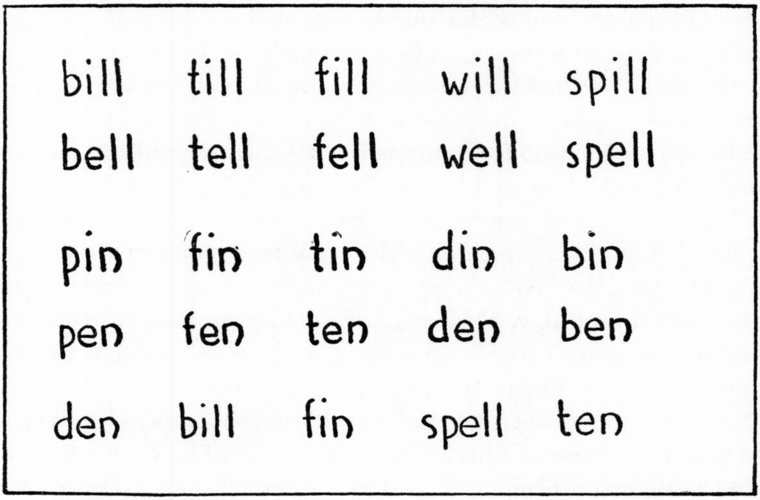

bill till fill will spill
bell tell fell well spell

pin fin tin din bin
pen fen ten den ben

den bill fin spell ten

Fig. 37. Card for practice on short *i* and *e* as middle vowels.

consonants, use words beginning with the letter; for vowels, use one-syllable words with the vowel in the middle. Present a similar list for the other letter. Have the child read each list; help him when necessary. (3) Present pairs of words which are alike except that one contains the first letter while the other contains the second letter, as *hill, till*; *can, pan*; *hat, hit.* (4) Give the child silent reading exercises of a multiple-choice or completion type, as, The cat ran after the (*house, mouse*); The cat ran after the *-ouse.* (5) Give the child sentences to read orally which contain many words in which the two letters are used. This same procedure can be used when there is a tendency to confuse two- or three-letter combinations, such as *th* and *wh, scr* and *str.*

As an example of this procedure, assume that a child confuses *m* and *n*. The letter *m* is presented, and the fact that it has two humps like a camel is pointed out. Then *n* is presented, and the fact that it has only one hump is noted. The two letters are sounded and written. Next a list of words such as *mat, milk, make,* and *melt* is presented and read, followed by a list such as *neat, not, nip,* and *nut*. Then pairs of words are introduced such as *map* and *nap, mail* and *nail*. Sentences are then employed such as: A boy grows into a (man, nan); We get light from the (moon, noon) and the (sum, sun); A -ouse ran across the roo-. Finally, oral reading of such sentences as: Many men went miles to see the sun and moon both shining at noon; or, Men and women need good manners.

Errors on Beginnings, Middles, and Endings of Words

There are many poor readers who observe carefully only the beginning of a word they canot recognize at sight, and guess at the rest. This kind of error is common in context readers, and is also found in children who get little or no help from the context. In either case, such errors tend to destroy the meaning of a passage when there are several unknown words. Some of these children are so poor that they need a thorough, basic training in word recognition of the kind described in Section II below. Others can profit greatly from training directed specifically at this particular kind of error.

The kind of training which is most directly beneficial in these cases is based on the teaching of common phonograms which combine with initial consonants to form many different words. The procedure in teaching phonograms is similar to that described for teaching letters except that the phonogram is taught as a unit, rather than as a group of individual letters.

Let us assume that a child has said *bent* for *band, make* for *main,* and *shine* for *shore*. There are six phonograms to be taught. One may start by teaching each of these phonograms separately, and combining each with different initial consonants. Starting with *and,* the phonogram is presented in printed form, pronounced by the teacher and then by the pupil, and written a few times. Then such words as *hand, sand, land,* and *band* are presented and their similarity pointed out. The same procedure is followed with the other five phonograms, *ent, ake, ain, ine,* and *ore.* Pairs of words starting with the same letter but ending in different phonograms may next

Sharp Eyes and Ears

tap tip top hop	hot hat hut hit	bug big bag beg
but bat bit bet	pit pet pot pat	ham him hem hum

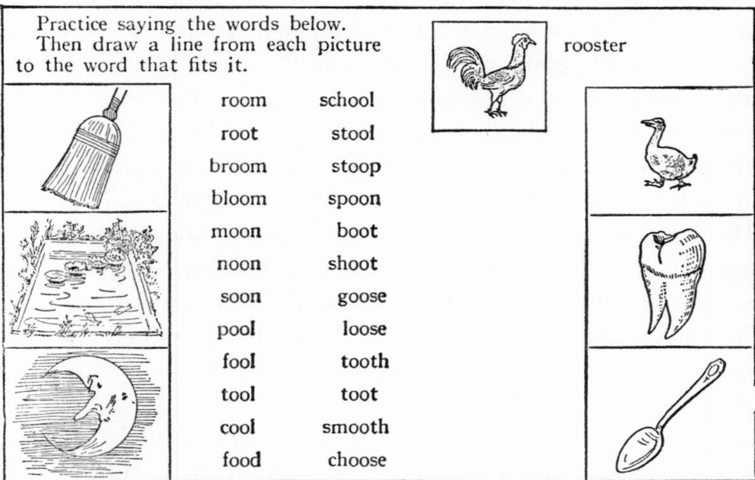

Fig. 38. Samples of word discrimination exercise. From Stone, C. R., *Eye and Ear Fun,* Book II. St. Louis, Mo.: Webster Publishing Co. Reproduced by permission of the publisher, and reduced in size.

be presented, such as *sent* and *sand, rake* and *rain, mine* and *more.*

After practice has been given on reading separate words involving the phonograms, the words should then be presented in context in such a way as to compel the child to pay careful attention to the total word. For this purpose multiple-choice sentences are again useful, as: The man put his money in the (benk, bank, band). Unless practice on isolated words is followed by the reading of the same words in context, the amount of carry-over of the training to connected reading may be disappointingly small.

Some of the errors on word endings consist of failure to note or discriminate endings as *-s, -es, -ed, -ly, -est, -er, -ness.* Usually a little practice is sufficient to overcome these errors. After pointing out how the ending changes the meaning of a word, sentences can be used for practice such as: There are many (horse, horses) in the barn; I can run (fast, faster, fastest) than you.

Confusions on the middles of words usually involve vowel confusions, and therefore call for practice on discriminating vowels. The general procedure is similar to the methods already described. One should give practice on lists of words which are alike except for the median vowel, such as *hit, hat, hot,* and *hut,* and also practice on words which are different except for the same median vowel, such as *man, rat, pack,* and *glad.* A form of error on word middles that is found in individuals of fairly advanced reading level is the confusion of words of several syllables which have similar beginnings and endings, such as *commission* and *communion,* or *precision* and *procession.* In these cases the person must be trained to make use of the context and to attack such words systematically, syllable by syllable.

Errors on the beginnings of words are usually found associated with reversal tendencies or as one phase of serious general weakness in word recognition. When that is the case, the correction of the other errors will tend to eliminate the errors on word beginnings. In cases where the beginnings of words seem to present special difficulty, procedures similar to those used for errors on endings should be employed, except that emphasis is placed on noticing the beginning of the word rather than the ending. Exercises in alphabetizing and the use of dictionaries are also helpful, as they call attention to the beginning of the word.

Word Analysis

These words have only one vowel. If you add a vowel you will have a new word. This will change the sound of the first vowel from the short sound to the long sound. Remember that the second vowel is silent. It is sometimes at the end of the word. Sometimes it is in the middle of the word.

hid	cot	mad	ran
________	________	________	________
set	stem	rod	bet
________	________	________	________
red	bit	fed	pan
________	________	________	________
net	us	pin	hop
________	________	________	________

Fig. 39. Part of an exercise on vowel sounds. From O'Donnell, M., and others, *Companion Book* for *If I Were Going*, The Alice and Jerry Books. Evanston, Ill.: Row, Peterson and Co. Reproduced by permission of the publisher, and reduced in size.

Reversal Errors

The term "reversal" is used to describe a variety of different kinds of errors, including: (1) confusion of single letters such as *b, d, p,* and *q*; (2) complete reversals of words such as *on* and *no, saw* and *was,* and *tap* and *pat*; (3) partial reversals of words such as *ram* for *arm, ate* for *tea,* and *never* for *even*; and (4) reversals of the order of words in a sentence, as "The dog saw a boy" for "The boy saw a dog." Reversals are not the commonest types of errors in word recognition, as they are prominent among the errors of about one reading disability case out of ten. When they are present, however, they are very significant and deserve careful analysis and treatment.

Reversals are very prevalent in young children beginning to read.

Apparently young children tend to think that the difference in position of letters such as *b* and *p*, or of the order of letters in words like *rat* and *tar*, is not important. They take the same attitude as they do toward a picture of a man, which they can recognize about as well when it is sideways or upside down as when it is right side up.

There are other factors besides immaturity which may cause reversal errors. Failure to develop consistent left-to-right eye movements in reading is in many cases the reason for frequent reversals. Due to regressive movements the parts of a word may be inspected in the wrong order, or words may be seen in the wrong order, and reversal errors are the result. Other major causes of reversals are the presence of difficulty with fusion and eye coordination, and incomplete or mixed dominance.

Of all letter confusions, the one involving *b, d, p,* and *q* is probably the most common. These four letters are different orientations of the same form. Other letter confusions that are vertical reversals are *m* and *w,* and *u* and *n.* The general principles described in this chapter for overcoming letter confusions will usually suffice to remove these tendencies to reverse letters. The need for tracing and writing is greater for children who reverse letters than it is for those who make other types of letter errors, and more intensive drill is usually necessary before the confusion is eliminated.

Reversals of words, parts of words, and the order of words in sentences usually indicate that the child needs training to develop a consistent left-to-right sequence in reading. The need for such a consistent direction should first be explained to him, with illustrations of how the words and meanings are changed when the correct order is not maintained. Then various methods may be employed to build up proper directional habits. Among the devices which have been found to work well in overcoming reversal tendencies are the following:

1. Tracing, writing, and sounding words which are frequently confused. These procedures automatically enforce using the correct sequence of letters.
2. Covering a word with a card and removing the card slowly to the right so that the letters are exposed in proper sequence.

3. Underlining the first letter in the word. Sometimes underlining the first letter in green and the last letter in red – "traffic lights" – is effective. The child is told to start on green and stop on red.
4. Encouraging the child to use a finger or pencil as a guide in reading along a line. While this practice is to be discouraged in good readers, it is very helpful as a means of teaching the proper direction for eye movements.
5. Exposing a line of print a little at a time by means of a card, or by means of an opening cut in a card, or by opening a zipper.
6. Drawing an arrow pointing to the right under words which are frequently reversed.
7. Allowing the child to use a typewriter. This has favorable effects on spelling and composition as well as on word recognition.

Fernald stated that reversals quickly disappeared when children were taught by the kinesthetic method, making sure that they started to write at the left edge of the paper.[3] Monroe found that systematic letter-by-letter phonic training, combined with tracing, had a similarly beneficial effect upon the reversal tendency.[4] The mirror method devised by Barger (see p. 256) and Leavell's procedure for training the nondominant eye (see p. 257) are promising new techniques aimed specifically at overcoming directional confusions.

Omissions, Additions, and Substitutions

Omissions and additions of letters or syllables are rarely found unaccompanied by other types of errors. They are commonly associated with errors on word endings and middles. As systematic training in overcoming the other errors is given, the omissions and additions usually disappear. About the only kind of special attention that these errors require is to have the child reread the word on which he made the mistake and to point out the difference between what he said and what the word really is. Such errors are often noticed by the child and corrected immediately. They represent mainly a form of carelessness, and call for somewhat slower and more careful reading until the tendency is overcome. This last statement is true also of most additions and omissions of whole words.

[3] Fernald, Grace M., *Remedial Techniques in Basic School Subjects*, p. 89. New York: McGraw-Hill Book Co., Inc., 1943.

[4] Monroe, Marion, *Children Who Cannot Read*, p. 127.

When a child substitutes a completely different word for the word in print, he is almost always guessing or trying to make use of the context. If the substitutions he makes are reasonable ones which do not alter the meaning, such as *castle* for *palace,* or *boy* for *lad,* and are not very frequent, one can usually ignore them without doing any great harm. If, however, a large number of his substitutions are such as to spoil the meaning of the passage, the fault needs to be remedied. Such meaningless substitutions, as "The boy called a house" for "The man caught a horse," indicate that the child needs thorough basic training in word recognition skills. As he learns how to recognize words the substitutions will disappear. When meaningless substitutions occur in the reading of poor readers at the secondary school or college level, they may indicate reading which is too rapid and careless, or material which is beyond the reader's level of comprehension.

Difficulties with Long Words

Above the fourth-grade level, difficulties in word recognition are more apt to involve long words than short words. The word recognition habits which have been successful in learning such words as *went, their, across* do not seem to work when employed on such words as *migration, provocative, theoretical,* and *constitutionally.* In fact, difficulties in word recognition may arise during the upper grades in children who have previously had little difficulty with reading.

Many of these children have little or no background in phonics. They were either not taught phonics, or were exposed to phonics teaching when they were not yet ready for it and so did not profit from it. They developed satisfactory sight vocabularies so long as the new words were taught to them, and their sight vocabularies, aided by guessing from the context, keep them going fairly well. Their lack of knowledge of letter sounds, however, makes it impossible for them to work out the correct pronunciation of the separate syllables in a long, unfamiliar word. They soon form the habit of guessing from the context, aided by the general appearance of the word with perhaps a more careful inspection of the word beginning. Sometimes they form the habit of skipping the long words altogether, filling in during oral reading with a vague mumble. These children, whose difficulties with the longer words is largely the result of an omission in their previous instruction, are often helped greatly in their attack upon unknown words by teaching of the phonic skills usually covered in the second and third grades.

The main requirement in teaching an adequate method of attack on long words is emphasis on a systematic procedure of dividing a long word into recognizable groups of letters, and combining them in left-to-right order to get the whole word. The teaching of grammatical rules of syllable division is not really necessary. If the pupil shows difficulty in learning these more or less arbitrary rules, he should be encouraged to look for letter groups that seem to him to form natural units. Skill in dividing words into prefixes, word roots, and endings should be developed, and in general the combination of structural analysis skills with phonic sounding in combination with the meaningful context should be the aim. Remedial help along these lines need not differ essentially from good first teaching.

Inability to Make Use of the Context

Because it has been emphasized that pupils who rely greatly on the context may develop habits of carelessness in word recognition or may fail to develop other important techniques, there may be a temptation to assume that pupils who need training in word recognition should be discouraged from attempting to utilize the context at all. Nothing is farther from the truth. Pupils who have failed to acquire other methods of attack in recognizing words need to be taught the other methods, but should not be discouraged from utilizing the context. All good readers make use of context clues, so there is no reason to discourage poor readers from doing the same, except as a temporary measure while other techniques are being learned.

There are also many children — word-by-word readers — who have not learned how to employ the context as a way of figuring out a new word. They should be taught first of all how to guess at a word from the meaning of the rest of the sentence. In the sentence: "The man has a ________ with two doors," the child should be asked what the missing word could be. If he says car, he should be shown that there are other possibilities, such as house and garage. He should then be given the same sentence with the first letter of the missing word supplied, and be shown that if the letter is *h,* the missing word is probably house; if *c,* car; if *g,* garage; or if *s,* store. Sentences such as Cows give m____; dogs like to eat b____; and boys like to play b____, can be used for practice. Exercises like the one in Figure 30 can be used. After the pupil has grasped the idea, he will enjoy reading paragraphs in which a few words have been blotted out.

Slowness in Word Recognition

Children who have been given intensive phonetic training often develop the habit of reading painstakingly and very slowly. They try to sound out most words, and this keeps their speed far below what it would be if they could recognize the words at a glance. Readers of fairly advanced levels are sometimes slow because they have to sound out all long words, although they have no difficulty with short ones. When it is evident that because of a letter-by-letter or syllable-by-syllable attack a reader's rate is being kept unnecessarily low, practice should be given to increase speed of word recognition.

The most helpful procedure for increasing speed of word recognition is to use flash cards or tachistoscopic exposure. One should start with one-syllable words, printed one on a card. The card can be exposed in a simple tachistoscope (see p. 208) or by covering the card with a blank one which is withdrawn and quickly replaced with a flick of the wrist. The time of exposure should be less than half a second, so as to prevent more than one look at the word. At first the words should be short and of different shapes, such as *pill, here, pony,* and *cart.* As skill in quick recognition is gradually acquired, words of the same general configuration may be used in groups, such as *hall, bill, kill,* and *tell.* Longer and longer words can then be introduced, until the reader has developed to the point where he can recognize immediately words like *opposite* and *superiority.* Similar short-exposure practice should also be given in the reading of short phrases, such as "to me," "in the house," and "from the store."

According to Dolch, 50 per cent of the running words found in school reading material are repetitions of only 220 different words. He has published the list, which consists entirely of prepositions, conjunctions, adjectives, adverbs, and verbs (see 382). He reports that three or four weeks of practice on recognizing these basic words at sight produced remarkable improvement in reading, especially in speed and fluency. Improvement in comprehension also took place because the pupils no longer needed to waste energy on these common words and were able to concentrate better on getting the meaning. This list of basic sight words is very useful to remedial teachers.

When flashed exposures are used as a method for improving speed of word recognition, there is a possibility that the skill acquired in reading the cards may not carry over to the reading of the same words in connected material. This danger can be avoided by giving the pupil, after each flash card drill, connected reading to do which includes the words that have been practiced in isolation. When this is done there should be no difficulty in getting the desired transfer of training from the isolated drill to ordinary reading.

When slowness of word recognition is a real problem and the equipment is available, the use of a projection tachistoscope can be quite helpful.[5] Such an instrument consists of a lantern slide projector, to which a device like an oversize camera shutter is attached, which allows one to regulate the speed of exposure down to as little as 1/100th of a second. With it one can employ homemade slides or sets of slides which are commercially available.

Repetitions

The oral reading of many children is jerky and painful to listen to because of the way they continually repeat what they have already read. For instance, a child may read "The boy went for a

[5] The writer's preference is for the *Flash-Meter,* designed to be used with an overhead daylight projector, obtainable from the Keystone View Co., Meadville, Pa. Other similar devices are available: see p. 525.

walk with his spotted dog" in the following way: "The boy — the boy went for a — a walk — with his spo — spotted dog." Repetitions of this sort naturally cut down speed of reading, prevent fluency, and often interfere with comprehension. The treatment of repetitions depends on the particular cause that may be operating.

Some repetitions are due to slowness in word recognition. When the child comes to a word which he cannot recognize, he repeats the preceding words to give him more time to solve the unfamiliar one. These repetitions will drop out as greater skill in word recognition is achieved. Another possible cause of repetitions is the presence of faulty eye movements, so that the repetitions are simply the oral equivalents of regressive movements. Exercises of the sort that have been recommended for reversals of word order may be employed to good advantage when repetitions are due to regressive eye movements. A third cause of repetitions is failure to comprehend the reading material. The child loses the trend of thought of the sentence and goes back in order to pick up the thread of meaning again. As comprehension improves the need for repetitions of this sort will disappear. Finally, many children repeat because of nervousness or self-consciousness in oral reading. They need to have their confidence built up, and then their hesitations and repetitions will diminish. These children should be given opportunities to rehearse easy selections carefully and then to read the selections before children who are unfamiliar with the story. They also need large doses of encouragement and praise.

Refusal to Attempt Words

A common type of error in oral reading is refusal by the child to try to read a word. He may stop and wait to be prompted, may try to skip it without the omission's being noticed, or may simply say that he doesn't know that word. The majority of refusals are caused by inadequate word recognition techniques; they diminish in frequency as skill in word recognition improves. There are some children, however, who refuse to try words even when they have the equipment to work out the pronunciation of the word. This is nearly always due to the fact that the child has not yet built up confidence in his own ability. He has developed the habit of giving up quickly as the result of a long period of frustrated effort. He needs to be encouraged and gently prodded by remarks like, "I'm sure you can get that word if you try it." When this is insufficient, he may be given hints such as, "What would the word be if the first letter were *c* instead of *t*?" If it becomes evident that he cannot solve the word, he should be told what it is and allowed to continue. He should be praised for successful efforts, and should be reminded of previous successes if he shows an inclination to get discouraged. Refusals are problems of motivation rather than skill.

Phonic Devices and Word Games

There are a great many devices and games that can be used to add variety and interest to a program of training in word recognition. They serve very well to break the monotony which may otherwise cause a pupil's effort to slacken. A few of the popular ones that have been used will now be described.

1. *Lucky Wheel.* Two circles, one smaller than the other, are fastened together by a nail, brass pin, or buttonhook through their centers so that each can be rotated freely without disturbing the other. Initial consonants are printed around the outer circle and phonograms around the edge of the inner circle so that different words can be formed. By rotating the outer circle different initial consonants can be combined with the same phonogram, and by rotating the inner circle the same initial consonant can be combined with different phonograms. Many variations of this general idea have been devised. Such a wheel can be used as a basis for competitive games. Commercial materials of this type include the *Phono-Word Wheels* [6] (Sets A, B, 1, 2, and 3, covering initial consonants, consonant blends, prefixes and suffixes), and the *Webster Word Wheels* [7] (sixty-three wheels for use at grade four and above).
2. *Phonic Strips.* Three horizontal slits, close together and in line, are made across a 4x6 index card. Three other slits are made directly below them. A number of thin strips are prepared (by cutting up another index card) of a proper width so that they can be threaded through the slits in such a way as to expose only a small part of the strip. On one strip a number of initial consonants can be printed,

[6] Published by the Steck Co., Austin, Texas.
[7] Webster Publishing Co., St. Louis, Mo.

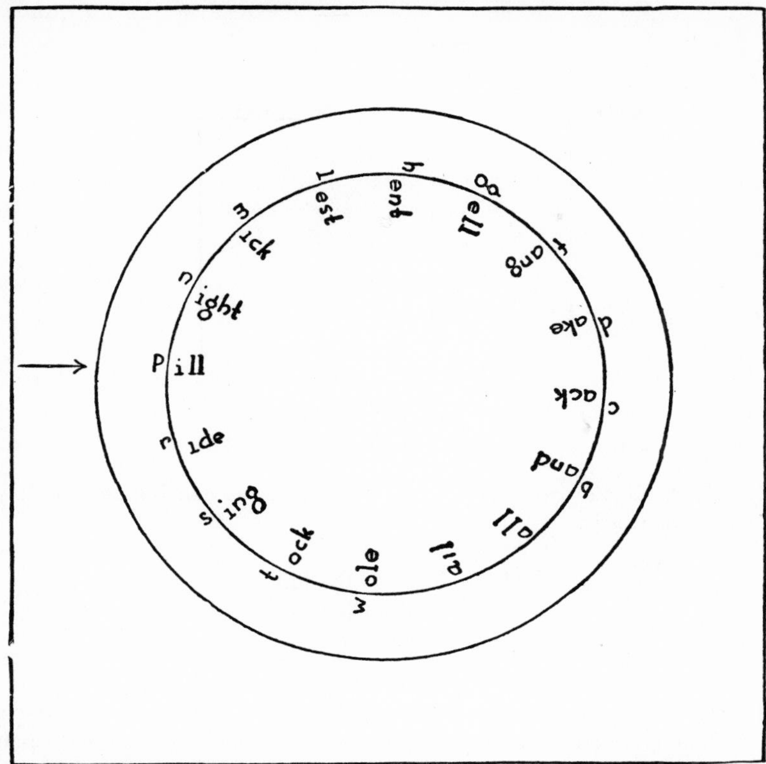

Fig. 40. "Lucky Wheel" for phonic practice; both outer and inner circles can be rotated.

one below the other, on a second strip middle vowels, on a third common word endings, and so on. By inserting the strips and moving them up and down a large number of different words can be formed. This device can be adapted for practice on beginnings, middles, or endings, and can be used with phonograms as well as single letters. The *Skill Builder* envelopes which accompany the *Building Reading Skills* workbooks (see p. 358) include several devices of this type.

3. *Rhymemaking.* Lines from several verses are printed on separate strips. The child is to pick out all the lines which end in the same sound and assemble them into a little poem. High poetic standards are not necessary. A sample verse:

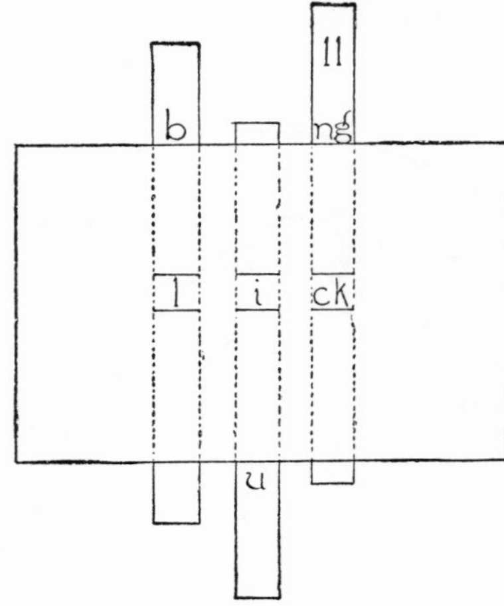

Fig. 41. A phonic card, showing how strip inserts can be used to form a variety of words.

The Indians on the hill,
  Led by Big Chief Bill,
Are standing very still,
  For they are out to kill.

4. *Darts.* A cheap dart and target set is used. Small cards with one phonogram on each are pasted to the target, and an initial consonant is pasted on each dart. If the child reads correctly the word formed when his dart hits a phonogram, he scores a point.
5. *Word-O.* Cards can be made modeled after Bingo or Lotto, with words instead of numbers, and the usual rules for such games can be used or modified. To teach words, the leader says the word as he holds up the card; the children look for the word on their cards and cover it if they find it; to review, the word is said but not shown. The first child who covers five words in a row or column and can identify them correctly wins.

   Commercial materials of this type include *Read-O* [8] and the *Group Word Teaching Game.*[9] Other adaptations, designed by Dolch to teach phonic principles, include the *Consonant Lotto Game* and the *Group Sounding Game.*[10]

[8] Augsburg Publishing Co., Morristown, Tenn.
[9] Garrard Press, Champaign, Ill.
[10] *Ibid.*

6. *Anagrams.* A cheap anagram set can be purchased, or letters can be printed on small squares of pasteboard. Word-building games of several kinds can be played. The *Embeco Word Builder* [11] is one of the few commercial sets that includes both capital and small letters, and is quite inexpensive.
7. *Spin the pointer.* Words are arranged around the outside of a circle, and the child tries to read the word at which the pointer stops. Failures and successes can be scored according to the rules of different games such as baseball and football. In baseball scoring a success is a hit and a failure is an out, and score is kept in terms of runs. By making slits into which word cards may be inserted, the same circle and pointer can be used indefinitely.
8. *Fishing.* One word, phrase, or sentence is printed on each of a number of cardboard cutouts in the shape of fish, to which paper clips are attached. The child picks up a fish by means of a horseshoe magnet on a string, and keeps it if he can read it correctly. Similar games can be devised involving pulling leaves off a tree, and so on.
9. *Racing.* A large race track is drawn and divided into boxes, in each of which a word is placed. Each child has a cutout auto of a different color. When a child's turn comes he spins a pointer which indicates a move of one, two, three, or four boxes. If he can read the word he advances his auto that many spaces; if not, he has to wait for his next turn.
10. *Word hospital.* Words that cause persistent difficulty are called "sick" words, and the child, as doctor, puts them to bed in a word hospital until he cures them (see Fig. 42).
11. *This to that.* Starting with one word, one of the letters in the word is changed each time, making a series of words, as: *his, him, ham, ram, ran, run.* The game can also be played with changing of two-letter combinations allowed, as: *sheep, sheet, shoot, shook, spook, spoke, broke.* Reading such a sequence is a welcome change from the monotony of word families, and provides an interesting form of review.[12]
12. It is possible to buy packs of playing card blanks, with decorative backs but no printing on the face side, from some playing card manufacturers. By printing the same word on four cards it is possible to make a "rummy" deck containing thirteen words, or to

[11] Milton Bradley Co., Springfield, Mass.

[12] Many other games and devices for teaching word recognition and word attack skills which can be made by teachers can be found in Russell, David H., and Karp, Etta E., *Reading Aids Through the Grades,* Revised Edition. New York: Bureau of Publications, Teachers College, Columbia University, 1951.

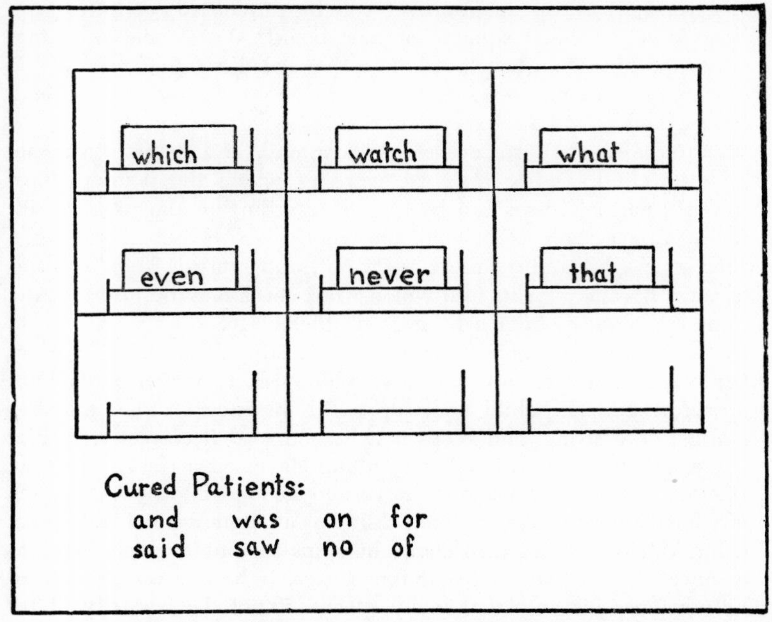

Fig. 42. A "hospital" for "sick" words. A word with which the child has persistent difficulty is printed on a small card and is put to bed (inserted in the slit corresponding to the mattress of the bed). When a sick word is cured, its name is entered at the bottom of the chart.

adapt the deck to the rules of other simple card games, such as casino. Oak tag cut into rectangles of appropriate size can also be used. Commercially available sets of cards which can be used to teach sight vocabulary or word attack skills include the following:

Basic Sight Vocabulary Cards,[13] by E. W. Dolch. The 220 commonest "service words" on individual cards. The same words on slightly larger cards are available as *Popper Words,* Set 1 and Set 2, each containing 110 words.

Picture Word Cards,[13] by Dolch. Cards with a picture and word on one side and the word only on the back, including 95 common nouns.

Take,[13] a Dolch card game involving matching the sounds of the beginnings, the middles, or the endings of words.

[13] Garrard Press, Champaign, Ill.

The Syllable Game,[13] by Dolch, designed to be used to teach syllabication in the middle and upper grades.

Go Fish,[14] an interesting card game well liked by remedial pupils, for reinforcing phonic learnings.

Vowel Dominoes,[14] played something like dominoes but involving the matching of sounds.

Grab,[15] available in three levels of difficulty, a card game involving word matching which can be played with several variations.

13. *Crossword Puzzles.* Commercial crossword puzzles of primary-grade difficulty are available.[16] For those who are advanced enough in their word recognition skills, *Scrabble* makes a fascinating word building game.

In addition to the game-type material just listed, the workbooks for developing word attack skills which were listed in the preceding chapter (see p. 358) provide material which is often quite helpful in corrective and remedial programs.

II. Teaching Word Recognition in Severe Disabilities

THE NONREADER and the severe case whose ability in word recognition is at or below second-grade level have as their main weakness the lack of a method of observing and studying words that helps them to remember and recognize the words in their reading. What they need first of all is to learn a method of attack so that they will be able to develop a sight recognition vocabulary. Three major methods for teaching word recognition to the severe reading disability case have been worked out; the kinesthetic, the phonic, and the visual. These three main methods have been tried in pure forms and also in many combinations.

Perception, Imagery, and Recall

When a child is unable to remember words after painstaking teaching efforts, the teacher is apt to wonder what is wrong with the child's memory. Sometimes the problem is one of difficulty in recall, particularly in cases where anxiety is strong and emotional

[14] Remedial Education Center, Washington, D.C.

[15] Obtainable from Dorothea Alcock, 324 E. College St., Covina, Calif.

[16] Primary Educational Service, Chicago, Ill.

blocking is severe. But often the main problem is not one of poor memory, but rather of failure to develop a mental image of the word which can be recalled at a later time. If there is no initial registration of the word, there will be nothing to remember.

The first step must necessarily be reasonably good perception of the word. Testing with brief exposures discloses that many severe reading disability cases perceive a word at first glance in very incomplete and hazy fashion, and additional looks at the word do little to amplify and improve this first impression. If perception has been unsatisfactory, the mental image of the word which the child forms cannot be any better.

It is also possible for initial perception to be fairly good, but upon closing his eyes and trying to "see" the word mentally the child has little or no visual image. Difficulty in forming mental images may be present not only for word forms but also for places or things.

The methods which have generally succeeded with severe cases all involve the development of clearer perception of words, and the provision of additional cues which lend vividness to the memory image so that it can be retained in memory. This is done either by tying in sensory and perceptual cues from other senses, as in the kinesthetic and phonic methods, or by systematic efforts to improve visual perception and imagery, as in the predominantly visual techniques.

The Kinesthetic Method

In 1921, Grace M. Fernald and Helen B. Keller described a method for teaching nonreaders which emphasizes tracing and writing as basic procedures. The following description of the method is based on the account given in Fernald's book.[17]

In the early stages, no printed material is used. At first the child is asked to tell the teacher a few words he would like to learn. These are taught one by one. As soon as he has learned a few words, he is encouraged to compose a little story, and is taught any words in the story that

[17] Fernald, Grace M., *Remedial Techniques in Basic School Subjects,* esp. pp. 33–35. New York: McGraw-Hill Book Co., Inc., 1943.

he does not already know. The compositions are at first dictated to the teacher and later written by the child. After the story has been read in written form, it is typed out so that he can read it the next day in type. The child's own compositions are the only materials used until a fairly large sight vocabulary has been learned.

The method of teaching words changes as the child's ability to learn words improves. Four stages are distinguished.

Stage 1. *Tracing.* The word is written for the child on a strip of paper about 4 inches by 10 inches, in large cursive writing (manuscript printing can also be used). The child traces the word with his finger in contact with the paper, saying each part of the word as he traces it. This is repeated until he can write the word from memory. He writes it on scrap paper and then in his story. Later the story is typed and read in typed form. Each new word that is learned is placed by the child in an alphabetical file. The following points of technique are stressed: (1) Finger contact is important; tracing in the air or with a pencil is less useful. (2) The child should never copy a word, but always writes from memory. (3) The word should always be written as a unit. (4) The child must say each part of the word either to himself or out loud as he traces it and writes it. (5) Whatever he writes must be typed for him and read by him before too long an interval; this provides transfer from the written to the printed form.

Stage 2. *Writing without Tracing.* After a while (days in some cases, weeks in others) the child does not need to trace most new words. He looks at the word in script, says it to himself several times, and writes it from memory. Library index cards with the words in both script and print form are substituted for the large word strips and are filed alphabetically. Essentially this is the same procedure as the visual-motor method described on page 320.

Stage 3. *Recognition in Print.* It becomes unnecessary to write each new word on a card. The child looks at the word in print, is told what it says, pronounces it once or twice, and writes it from memory. Reading in books is usually started about the time that this stage is reached.

Stage 4. *Word Analysis.* The child begins to identify new words by noting their resemblance to words he already knows, and it is no longer necessary to teach him each new word. Although phonic sounding of word parts is not allowed, skill in word analysis is gradually developed.

Total nonreaders are started at Stage 1. Children with partial disabilities are often started at Stage 2. No special techniques are used to overcome such difficulties as reversals or omissions; these are said to drop out without special attention, since the tracing-writing process enforces a consistent left-to-right direction and requires correct reproduction of the entire word.

Unique features in Fernald's method are the great emphasis on tracing and writing, the teaching of difficult as well as easy words from the very beginning, the use of the child's own compositions as the only reading material in the early stages, and the beginning of book reading on a fairly difficult level.

Kinesthetic reinforcement is recommended as a supplementary procedure both by those who place major reliance on visual word-study methods and by those who rely primarily on a systematic phonic method.

The kinesthetic method has produced very successful results with many severe disability cases, as Fernald's case histories show. It has several desirable features: (1) It enforces careful and systematic observation and study of words. (2) It makes necessary a consistent left-to-right direction in reading. (3) It provides adequate repetition. (4) Errors are immediately noted and corrected. (5) Progress can be noted by the child at practically every lesson. (6) The sensory impressions from tracing, writing, and saying the words reinforce the visual impressions and seem to be of definite value to children whose visual memory is very poor.

There are, however, several objections to the use of the kinesthetic method as outlined by Fernald. (1) The teacher has to direct and check every step in the child's work and teach him every new word until he has progressed far along the road to good reading. During the early stages, the child is unable to do any independent reading. The method is well suited to use in a special clinic school such as the one supervised by Fernald, in which the children were with the remedial teacher for a full school day five days a week, but is not so well adapted to a remedial setup in which the child has only a small number of remedial periods each week. (2) The vast majority of nonreaders can learn to recognize words by methods which are faster than the rather cumbersome tracing-writing procedure. The visual-motor method of word study (Fernald's Stage 2) is, however, very often helpful. (3) The writer sees no advantage in avoiding the use of easy books in the early stages of remedial work. He believes in starting book reading as early as possible, even if preprimers must be used, provided that the child's cooperation can be obtained.

Methods Based on Sounding and Blending

Systematic methods based on sounding out letters and blending the sounds together to make words are strongly advocated for severe reading disability cases by several authorities. Detailed descriptions of such phonetic programs have been given by Monroe,[18] Stanger, and Donohue,[19] and Gillingham and Stillman.[20]

The systems of sounding-blending recommended for nonreaders by these writers use the letter-by-letter method of blending. They start by teaching the child to sound and recognize individual letters. The next procedure is to teach the child how to blend sounds together so as to get recognizable words, starting usually with two- or three-letter words (*am, at, cat*). A good description of how to introduce blending has been given by Stanger and Donohue.[21]

> The letters *m a t* are put before the child. He is asked the sound of the first letter, then the sound of the second, and then of the third. Then he is told to make the sound of the first letter, and to hold onto it till he joins it to the sound of the second letter. It sometimes aids this blending process if the first letter can actually be moved close to the second letter, and then those two moved up to the third letter. This process of holding on to each sound till it joins the next sound is repeated, each time a little faster until *mat* comes as a whole word. In the very early stages of this work, the wise teacher will not let the beginner become too discouraged or impatient. If he has given the individual sounds correctly, she may help him in the final blending into an actual word.

In the systems employing blending as a basic method, new letter sounds are taught one at a time or in small groups. As new letters are learned, practice is given in blending and recognizing words composed of the letters already known. Soon short sentences and

[18] Monroe, Marion, *Children Who Cannot Read,* Ch. 5.

[19] Stanger, Margaret A., and Donohue, Ellen K., *Prediction and Prevention of Reading Difficulties.* New York: Oxford University Press, 1937.

[20] Gillingham, Anna, and Stillman, Bessie, *Remedial Training for Children with Specific Difficulty in Reading, Spelling and Penmanship.* New York. Sackett & Williams Lithographing Corp., 1940.

[21] *Op. cit.,* p. 129. Quoted by permission of the publishers.

stories composed of known words can be introduced. By the time a child has learned the consonant sounds, the long and short vowel sounds, and a few of the most common two-letter phonograms, reading in books of first-grade level can be started. After that the amount of time spent on phonetic drill is reduced, flash card exercises are used to promote quick recognition, and stress is placed on silent reading for comprehension. Three-, four-, and five-letter phonograms such as *ing, ight,* and *ought* may be taught, but most new words are studied as wholes and sounded out only when they cannot be read as wholes. Nonphonetic words, which comprise about 15 per cent of English words, must naturally be taught as wholes.

The writers who advocate blending as a basic method of teaching retarded readers make use of writing or tracing and writing as a supplementary method, used to teach nonphonetic words and words which the pupil has difficulty in blending.

If on the basis of diagnostic testing and sample lesson tryouts it seems likely that a child may make more rapid progress with a systematic phonic approach than with a predominantly visual or kinesthetic approach, there are many different phonic systems that may be used with success. The considerations which apply when phonics is used for remedial work are no different from those which apply in developmental instruction. At this point, therefore, it is desirable to review pages 330–338. Ear training is vitally important. Rigid adherence to any one method of sounding will inevitably produce difficulties due to the irregularity of the phonic structure of the language. As much as possible, practice should be given in applying phonic skills in meaningful context, rather than concentrating on drill with isolated words. As soon as it is feasible, words which originally have to be sounded out should be practiced for immediate sight recognition.

Gates has criticized the phonetic approach on the following grounds: (1) It is a "definite, rigid, hard-drill program." (2) It forfeits interest in the initial stages because real reading is not attempted. (3) It delays the reading of meaningful material much longer than the visual method does. (4) It is apt to produce slow, labored reading, with excessive amounts of lip movement.[22] These criticisms can be answered in the following ways: (1) Interest and motivation are created by evidence of successful progress. (2) When the child is introduced to genuine reading he has acquired a basis which insures successful accomplishment. (3) Fluency and comprehension can be built up when a thorough basis in word recognition has been established. (4) The method works, as Gates has said, in some cases where the visual approach does not succeed.

For the majority of reading disability cases, phonic instruction is more effective when used as a supplement to other procedures than when it is made the major method of attack in learning words. There are some children, however, whose previously disappointing progress becomes very rapid when they are changed to a systematic phonic method. In this issue, as in others, what is inadvisable for most children may be just the right thing for a few.

Methods Stressing Visual Analysis and Visualizing

In addition to the kinesthetic and phonetic approaches that have just been described, there is a third basic method which emphasizes visual analysis and visualizing. Such a procedure has been described and advocated by Gates. Words are taught as wholes, to be recognized at first on the basis of general shape or configuration. Pictures and illustrations are used freely as ways of introducing and giving clues to words. Workbook exercises are used to present new words and to give practice in word recognition and comprehension. The pupil is encouraged to close his eyes and visualize words, first part by part in left-to-right order, and then as a whole. Later he is asked to pronounce the word softly part by part while writing it. Phonic work and writing are used as supplementary devices when pupils seem not to be progressing satisfactorily without them. Familiarity with word elements is developed through finding similarities and differences in words that have already been learned. Gates has described the method as follows:

[22] Gates, A. I., *The Improvement of Reading*, Revised Edition, p. 448. New York: The Macmillan Co., 1935.

Words are introduced gradually and reused extensively. At first, the pupils recognize the words on the basis of general configuration and the more obvious component features. Gradually, assisted and directed by the teacher, the children learn to observe more details and more subtle features, to perceive them more quickly and accurately, to work out the recognition of unfamiliar words, and to acquire familiarity with new words in terms of these visual elements.

In this method, visual study is predominant. The writing (or kinesthetic factor) emphasized by the Fernald-Keller program, and the sounding (or phonetic factor) basal to the Monroe program are almost, or entirely, eliminated.

This program produces excellent results with certain disability cases. It is a rather adaptable method, in that perception can be based upon different features or words (such as large units or small units) as fits the aptitude of the individual, and refinement can be carried out to different degrees. It is direct and rapid, and harmonizes well with preception of whole words in full-fledged reading. In certain rare cases, however, it has shown limitations. In these cases, the introduction of writing in some form, or some direct phonetic instruction, or both for a preliminary orientation proved to be advantageous. In these cases, the visual study proved to be more useful after experiences with the slower and more detailed work with words. After once "catching hold" of the game by the other analytic studies, the visual study of phonetic attack upon larger units proved to be highly profitable.[23]

Essentially this program is similar to that advocated for teaching normal beginners by the authors of most basal readers. It differs mainly in that the pupil's learning is more carefully supervised and more attention is devoted to making sure that new words are introduced gradually and really learned than is the case in most classroom teaching. It is a program which assumes that the child has the capacity to learn as normal readers do but has been handicapped by some such factors as immaturity when first exposed to reading instruction, inefficient teaching, or something else which does not affect the child's present learning ability.

Stone's set of four workbooks entitled *Eye and Ear Fun* is designed to be used in a program of teaching word recognition such as that advocated by Gates. Practice is provided in discriminating between words which have first been learned as wholes. Word-

[23] Gates, A. I., *op. cit.*, p. 450. Quoted by permission of the publishers.

building games are included, and a variety of devices are given for enforcing careful comparison of words which are often confused.

A Combination Method

In Chapter IX it was pointed out that the majority of cases of reading disability do not have special types of mental defects, but result from such causes as lack of reading readiness when first exposed to reading instruction, uncorrected sensory defects, discouragement and emotional disturbance, and poor teaching. If that is so, the remedial work with those cases should not have to be radically different from the general methods used with primary-grade children. The writer's experience has shown that this conclusion is correct.

The majority of severe cases of reading disability (nonreaders or those with less than second-grade reading ability) show inattention to details in visual perception, have very poor phonic aptitude, and are slow and clumsy in handling pencil or chalk. The writer's practice is to start such children off at the beginning of the easiest preprimer in a modern set of readers and the accompanying workbook. The workbook provides abundant practice in matching the few words in the preprimer vocabulary with pictures, and between the repetition in the workbook and that in the preprimer, the child learns the words by being prompted every time he stumbles or forgets. As he progresses through additional preprimers and then through primers, the number of repetitions needed to learn new words gradually diminishes.

Some of the children need to be carefully pretaught the new words that they will meet in the next few pages of connected reading, in a more controlled way than the use of a workbook provides. For these children, each new word is printed on a card. It is studied by a look-and-say visual method, or by the visual-motor method (see p. 320), whichever seems to suit the child better. After a few words have been taught, the cards are shuffled and reviewed. Then the child reads the connected material in which the new words appear, and reviews his new word cards again. The cards are reviewed at subsequent lessons.

Rather than depend exclusively or primarily upon visual word study, as Gates recommends, the writer introduces phonics early and systematically. However, the majority of these children require a good deal of phonic readiness work before they can begin to apply phonics in word recognition. By the time the child has completed reading one or two primers and is ready for first-reader material, he has usually become sound conscious and pays attention to initial consonants, and sometimes to final consonants. Ear training is continued throughout the phonics program. More systematic teaching of phonics accompanies the use of first and second readers, following the procedures outlined in Table IX (see p. 351) but with adaptations for individual differences. Some children catch on to blending and can be given a systematic covering of vowel sounds, with the letter-by-letter sounding technique. Others never become proficient at blending and are taught vowel phonics through the use of a large number of word families or by initial consonant-vowel combinations. Case II in Chapter XIX describes in somewhat greater detail the procedure used with the typical serious reading disability case who lacks aptitude for phonics.

On the other hand, there are some children who seem, right from the start, to have poor visual perception but excellent phonic aptitude. Such a child is described in Case III, on pages 557–565. With such children it seems sensible to follow a procedure similar to Monroe's, with emphasis on the teaching of letter sounds and blending. Nonphonetic words have to be learned by these children also, and many of them need the visual-motor method because of their lack of success with a pure visual method. With some of these children, the hardest part of the remedial job is in persuading them to give up the practice of spelling the words letter by letter, in favor of a sounding procedure.

Few of the children seen by this writer have shown any need for tracing of the sort emphasized by Fernald. The visual-motor method of word study has, however, been very helpful to many, and supplementary practice in writing words from dictation on paper and at the blackboard is used considerably.

When resistance to the use of first- and second-grade readers is strong it is advisable to give up the use of books entirely for the time being, using instead a combination of experience stories and teacher-devised material. In such cases much time can be spent in the early stages playing games with word and sound cards, such as *Picture Word Cards, Go Fish,* and *Grab* (see p. 382). If a typewriter is available, the opportunity to use it is welcomed by most of these children. Fairly soon the child will be ready for first-grade books, such as the easiest of the *Cowboy Sam* [24] series or the Walt Disney story books.[25]

The Choice of Method

It is not always possible to tell, in advance of actual tutoring, what procedure will work best with a child. Sometimes deficiencies of visual perception, auditory perception, or motor control are so obvious that their bearing on the choice of methods is clear. With many children, it is helpful to try brief sample lessons with each of several word-recognition procedures (see pp. 213–218). In some cases, one finds the best procedure only by trying one method after another.

The remedial teacher must be resourceful. If, after a fair attempt to utilize one method, the pupil has not made adequate progress, the teacher must be willing to try something else. Adaptability to the pupil's needs is far more important than devotion to a particular plan of procedure. For example, Russell's teacher found that he was practically a nonreader and decided to use a systematic phonetic-blending method with him. He found out that the boy had had quite a bit of phonetic work in his first year and disliked it heartily. Russell said, "It's too hard, I can't do it." Thereupon the teacher switched to a whole-word method and Russell began to make progress.

Specific abilities and handicaps of pupils must be kept in mind. If a child has a handicap such as defective hearing, there are two plans open. One is to minimize his handicap by using a method in which his handicap will not interfere. On this basis the pupil with poor hearing would be taught by visualizing and writing; the pupil

[24] Beckley-Cardy Co.
[25] D. C. Heath & Co.

with poor vision or visual perception by phonic blending and writing; the pupil with poor muscular control by blending and visualization. The other plan is to attempt to build up his deficient ability. The child with poor hearing would be given training in hearing and discriminating sounds; the child with poor vision would be given training to sharpen visual perception of word and letter forms; the child with poor motor control would be given various exercises to improve his coordination, and much stress on writing. The present writer is inclined to favor starting with the idea of minimizing the handicap, and attempting to build up weak abilities later, after the child has made a good start. This would seem to be preferable from the standpoint of motivation, as it is more likely to insure successful progress from the very beginning of the remedial program.

A systematic experiment to determine the relative merits of different methods with retarded readers, confined to those with IQ's in the dull and borderline range, came out with the result that the visual method was most satisfactory, the phonic and alphabetic were least satisfactory, and the kinesthetic and mixed methods were in between.[26] This writer's experience has generally been favorable to a combined method, as described above. Individual differences are important and no one method works best with every retarded reader.

It seems likely that any remedial program in word recognition that provides adequate motivation, insures careful observation of words and word parts, and enforces consistent left-to-right habits in reading will succeed. The specific details of the method are less important than the fact that the major objectives are attained in one way or another.

Suggested Additional Reading

Durrell, Donald D. *The Improvement of Basic Reading Abilities*, Ch. 7.

Fernald, Grace M. *Remedial Techniques in Basic School Subjects*, pp. 21–82. New York: McGraw-Hill Book Co., Inc., 1943.

Gates, Arthur I. *The Improvement of Reading*, Third Edition, Ch. 16.

[26] Burt, Sir Cyril, and Lewis R. B., "Teaching Backward Readers," *British Journal of Educational Psychology*, Vol. 16, 1946, pp. 116–132.

KOTTMEYER, WILLIAM. *Handbook of Remedial Reading,* Ch. 7. St. Louis: Webster Publishing Co., 1948.

MONROE, MARION. *Children Who Cannot Read,* Ch. 5. Chicago: University of Chicago Press, 1932.

MONROE, MARION, and BERTIE BACKUS. *Remedial Reading,* Ch. 3. Boston: Houghton Mifflin Co., 1937.

RUSSELL, DAVID H., and ETTA E. KARP. *Reading Aids Through the Grades,* Revised Edition. New York: Bureau of Publications, Teachers College, Columbia University, 1951.

STANGER, MARGARET A., and ELLEN K. DONOHUE. *Prediction and Prevention of Reading Difficulties,* Chs. 9, 10, 11. New York: Oxford University Press, 1937.

· XV ·

Developing Understanding in Reading, I

THE HEART OF THE READING TASK is obtaining appropriate meanings from the printed page, and word recognition, which has occupied the stage for the preceding three chapters, is valuable only as it makes comprehension possible. This chapter and Chapter XVI are concerned with the problems of helping children to read with understanding.

Comprehension of what one reads is closely related, in the nature of the task, to comprehension of what one hears. Before one can understand, he must have sufficient mastery of the language to meet ordinary conversational needs. If the material is of a technical or specialized character, a certain amount of specialized information and vocabulary may be necessary. The possession of a level of mental ability adequate to follow the reasoning presented is needed for both listening and reading comprehension. Active attention is necessary in both if the train of thought is to be followed.

Reading, however, imposes additional tasks which are absent when one listens. For one thing, the words must be recognized if their meaning is to be appreciated. A second difference is that, in reading, one must organize the material into meaningful phrases and thought units, while in listening this is to a large extent done for the listener by the phrasing and expression of the speaker. A third point of difference is that in listening, the rate of comprehension is set by the rate of speech of the speaker, while in reading one has to learn to govern one's rate of reading so as to go fast enough to catch the flow of ideas, but not so fast as to miss too many of the details. Reading is similar to listening in many ways, but involves the need for additional skills.

In this chapter attention will be devoted to gaining meaning from words and from thought units of phrase, clause, and sentence size. Chapter XVI will take up specific comprehension skills, the essential study skills, and the nature of remedial work in comprehension.

I. Vocabulary Development

In our highly verbal culture an accurate understanding of the meanings of words is a necessary prerequisite for reading with meaning. Vocabulary is so closely related to comprehension and reasoning that a good vocabulary test can serve effectively as a measure of general intelligence, and most good intelligence tests contain many vocabulary items. A minimum essential for comprehension in reading is an understanding of the words used by the author. The development of a reading vocabulary which is both extensive and accurate is a necessary phase of good comprehension.

Types of Vocabulary

The first type of vocabulary knowledge that a person acquires is a hearing vocabulary. Most babies show that they can respond correctly to spoken words before they are able to use those words in their own speech. Hearing vocabulary develops earlier than speaking vocabulary, and throughout life the number of words to which a person can react appropriately when he hears them remains larger than the number which he can employ correctly in his own speech or writing. When children start to read, they begin to acquire a sight vocabulary. Gradually they begin to learn the meanings of words which occur in their reading but have not been in their previous vocabularies; they begin to acquire new meaningful vocabulary in reading. They also learn, through composition and spelling, to use a large number of words in their writing; these words, which are nearly always fewer in number than the speaking, hearing, or reading vocabularies, can be called writing vocabulary. A child's total meaningful vocabulary is the sum of all the words which he can understand or use correctly, whether in listening, speaking, reading, or writing.

In the writing of materials for beginners in reading, great care is taken to use only words whose meanings are already familiar to the children, or can be easily explained to them. The task of learning to recognize the words is hard enough without the added burden of having to learn new meanings at the same time. Because of this, the child's reading vocabulary is at first composed entirely of words which should already be part of his meaningful vocabulary. As the child progresses in reading, new words and ideas are introduced.

Size of Meaningful Vocabulary

Until recently, the majority of studies of the size of children's vocabularies seemed to indicate that the average child entered the first grade with a knowledge of the meanings of about 2,500 words, and increased his vocabulary at a rate of about 1,000 words a year in the primary grades, 2,000 words a year in the middle elementary grades, and 3,000 words a year in grades seven to nine, so that his vocabulary would be about 8,000 words in the sixth grade, and about 16,000 words in the ninth grade.[1] Wide individual differences were known to be present at every age. These older studies were based on samplings taken from word lists like the Thorndike *Teacher's Word Book,* or from small dictionaries, or upon counts of words used by children in their speaking and writing.

According to some recent data, the older estimates are much too low. Seashore constructed a vocabulary test based on a careful sampling of the Funk and Wagnalls *New Standard Dictionary,* an

[1] Excellent summaries of the older studies of vocabulary growth can be found in the following two sources:

Seegers, J. C., "Vocabulary Problems in the Elementary School," *Elementary English Review,* Vol. 16, 1939, pp. 157–166, 199, 234, 320, and Vol. 17, 1940, pp. 28–43. Also published as a pamphlet by the National Council of Teachers of English, Chicago.

Fries, C. C., and Traver, A. A., *English Word Lists,* Ch. VI. Washington, D.C.: American Council on Education, 1940.

unabridged dictionary which contains about 370,000 words, plus derivatives and compound words. Using this test, he estimated the basic vocabulary of the average college undergraduate as about 58,000 words; if derivatives, rare words, and compound words were included, the average rose to about 155,000 words.[2] Hartmann, using a sample of words from another unabridged dictionary, came to the conclusions that Alabama undergraduates could recognize meanings of about 215,000 words, and graduate students in education, about 250,000.[3] Smith, using Seashore's test with children in grades one through twelve, found a fairly steady increase in basic vocabulary from an average of nearly 17,000 words in the first grade to 32,000 in the sixth grade and 47,000 in the twelfth grade. Total vocabularies rose from 23,700 in the first grade to 52,000 in the sixth and 80,000 in the twelfth grade. Tremendous individual differences were found at each age and grade level.[4] According to Seashore, the older studies resulted in marked underestimations of vocabulary size because they were based on samplings of restricted word lists or abridged dictionaries and therefore did not give an individual a chance to show the full range of his word knowledge.

It is probable that some systematic error in these newer vocabulary studies has made the results come out so high. Possibly the method of sampling used favored common words with long dictionary entries over the less common words with briefer entries. Even allowing for such an error, we can conclude that most children learn thousands of words more than they can be systematically taught.

Causes of Deficiences in Meaningful Vocabulary

When a child has a small meaningful vocabulary, the first possible cause to investigate is intelligence. Low general intelligence shows

[2] Seashore, Robert H., "The Importance of Vocabulary in Learning Language Skills," *Elementary English,* Vol. 25, 1948, pp. 137–152; also Seegers, J. C., and Seashore, R. H., "How Large Are Children's Vocabularies?" *Elementary English,* Vol. 26, 1949, pp. 181–194.

[3] Hartmann, George W., "Further Evidence on the Unexpected Large Size of Recognition Vocabulary among College Students," *Journal of Educational Psychology,* Vol. 37, 1946, pp. 436–439.

[4] Smith, M. K., "Measurement of the Size of General English Vocabulary Through the Elementary Grades and High School," *Genetic Psychology Monographs,* Vol. 24, 1941, pp. 313–345.

itself clearly in retarded language development and difficulty in understanding and acquiring the meanings of words. The most important single test in the *Stanford-Binet Intelligence Scale* is one designed to measure the richness and accuracy of speaking vocabulary. One of the outstanding characteristics of the feeble-minded is their inability to understand words of a general or abstract nature.

Lack of intellectual stimulation and practice in the use of language are also important causes of vocabulary weakness. Words have meaning to a child only when they are related to things he has experienced or knows about. A child who has had a very restricted life is ignorant of many things that are commonplace to the average child, and so has not the basis for understanding words which refer to those things. Children whose parents are very ignorant or who speak a foreign language in the home are handicapped in their language development because they do not receive enough practice in hearing and speaking good English. Speech defects and defective hearing also interfere with the acquisition of a rich vocabulary because they cut off many conversational opportunities.

A child who likes to read enriches his vocabulary continually with words and ideas that he gains from his reading. When a child has made a poor start in reading he usually dislikes to read and thus gives up one of the best opportunities to expand his vocabulary. A vicious cycle is set up in which poor reading restricts the opportunity to learn new words, and failure to build up vocabulary prevents improvement in reading.

The factors that have just been described as hindrances to the development of meaningful vocabulary are the same ones that were described in Chapter II in relation to the language aspects of reading readiness. Causes which handicap a child in making a proper start in reading continue to interfere with his later progress if they are not corrected. The same general objectives that are involved in developing readiness for reading are also important for later training in the acquisition of vocabulary.

When, in reading, a child comes across a word and says that he does not know it, there are three possible explanations: (1) He may be able to pronounce it but has no understanding of what it signifies; (2) he may know the meaning of the word if presented orally but be unable to recognize it; and (3) he may be both unable to pronounce it and ignorant of its meaning. If a child has difficulties of the first type, he needs to have his meaningful vocabulary built up. If his difficulties are of the second type, he needs training in word recognition. If he is weak in both word recognition and meaningful vocabulary, both kinds of training need to be given simultaneously.

Providing a Background of Experience

The first essential in a program of vocabulary development is to provide children with a background of meaningful experience. Vivid first-hand sensory experience is the best basis for the development of accurate concepts. For this reason trips and excursions, when intelligently planned, are excellent for broadening children's horizons. The main difficulty with them is that in most schools they occur too infrequently to make a real dent in the problem. Also, when a trip is made the teacher often feels that he has done well if he gets the children back safely. The opportunities for developing meaningful concepts and vocabulary are too frequently neglected. When firsthand experience is not available, visual teaching materials, such as moving pictures, lantern slides, pictures, and charts, are the best substitutes. Storytelling and oral reading by the teacher are also valuable ways of imparting experience, especially in the lower grades. Practice in the use of language is highly important. Natural opportunities for intelligent listening and speaking arise in discussions, reports, informal conversation, and dramatics.

Developing Vocabulary through Wide Reading

The point of view has been advanced that a child should learn most of his new vocabulary simply by reading widely in interesting material. When reading matter is easy enough, a pupil can get a general idea of the meaning of a word from its setting or context, even if the word is completely new to him. If the word is an important one, he will come across it often enough in different settings to learn its meaning more exactly. If it is a word that occurs rarely, or is not a key word, it does not matter very much whether he develops a really accurate conception of it or not.

Some striking evidence in favor of this point of view was presented by Thorndike.[5] He made a word count of four and a half million words taken from books recommended for elementary school children. Of the 20,000 words in his *Teacher's Word List,* only 2,500 occurred frequently. Besides these, 18,000 words not in the list were found in the word count, of which 37 per cent occurred only once

THE THREE STRANGERS

This individual was one of a type radically different from the first. There was more of the commonplace in his manner, and a certain jovial cosmopolitanism sat upon his features. He was several years older than the first arrival, his hair being slightly frosted, his eyebrows bristly, and his whiskers cut back from his cheeks. His face was rather full and flabby, and yet it was not altogether a face without power. . . . He flung back his long drab greatcoat, revealing that beneath it he wore a suit of cinder-gray shade throughout, large heavy seals, of some metal or other that would take a polish, dangling from his fob as his only personal ornament. Shaking the water drops from his low-crowned glazed hat, he said, "I must ask for a few minutes' shelter, comrades, or I shall be wetted to my skin before I get to Casterbridge." [1]

Intelligent Guessing: What do you think each of these words means? Check your guesses with your dictionary.

1. radically ____________________
2. jovial ____________________
3. cosmopolitanism ____________________
4. revealing ____________________
5. ornament ____________________
6. glazed ____________________

Fig. 43. Part of a workbook exercise designed to develop skill in guessing meaning from context and checking by means of the dictionary; the material is at about ninth-grade level. From Hardy, Thomas, *Wessex Tales* (1888), quoted in Leavell, Ullin W., and Bailey, Matilda, *The Mastery of Reading,* Book 3, p. 14. New York: American Book Co., 1951. Reproduced by permission of the publisher, and reduced in size.

and only 39 per cent occurred more than four times. He concluded that "of the 60,000 or more different words that would be found in books recommended for reading by pupils in grade eight or below, the majority would occur only rarely, probably not oftener than once in three million words, or fifty books of the average size for juveniles." Because of the impossibility of teaching all or most of the

[5] Thorndike, E. L., "The Vocabulary of Books for Children in Grades 3 to 8," *Teachers College Record,* Vol. 38, 1936–37, I, pp. 196–205; II, pp. 316–323; III, pp. 416–429.

words that a child will meet in his reading, Thorndike recommended providing pupils with a wide variety of interesting books that are easy enough so that the new words and ideas can be learned from the context, as the best solution to the problem of vocabulary building.

It is probable that children in general would learn words more easily if writers would make definite provisions to help them to do so. Several ways in which the meaning of a word can be presented in context have been described.[6] Among the most helpful are the following:

1. The new word is set off by italics, quotation marks, or boldface type, to call attention to it.
2. A brief explanation or definition of the word is given in parentheses or in a footnote.
3. A clause or phrase which explains the meaning of the word is inserted in the sentence.
4. A synonym or substitute phrase is used to indicate the meaning (e.g., "a typhoon or terrific storm").
5. Similes and metaphors can be used.
6. The meaning of the word can be shown in a pictorial illustration.
7. A direct explanation of the word can be presented in a full sentence.
8. The sentence can be so written so that there is only one meaning that the new word could possibly have.

The greater use of these eight procedures by writers would make it easier for children to absorb new vocabulary directly from their reading.

For the child who easily guesses at meanings from context and reads widely, an extensive vocabulary is pleasantly acquired in this way. But those who most need vocabulary enrichment – the dull child, the verbally insensitive child, the slow reader, the child who does not enjoy reading – are not so likely to be reached in this way.

The poorer the child's reading ability, the harder it is to find easy, interesting books to fit his needs. The word-by-word reader has difficulty in using the context, and finds reading a slow process at best.

[6] Artley, A. S., "Teaching Word Meaning Through Context," *Elementary English Review*, Vol. 20, 1943, pp. 68–74.

Austin, Mary C., "Context Clues Aid Word Recognition," *The Reading Teacher*, Vol. 6, May, 1953, pp. 18–24.

Normal readers usually benefit from direct vocabulary instruction, especially with regard to the special vocabularies of content fields; [7] poor readers need such instruction even more.

What Word Meanings Should Be Taught?

There are too many different words in reading matter written for children to allow the direct teaching of the meanings of even the majority. How to select the important words that are worth teaching carefully is a real problem.

Teachers who are successful in providing reading material of appropriate difficulty for their pupils avoid much of this problem. When the reading material is easy enough, most of the new words can be taught directly without consuming too much time in word study.

When a choice has to be made of which words to teach, the first consideration is to select those words whose meanings must be understood if the selection is to be comprehended. Some words are essential to the meaning of a passage, others can be skipped without interfering too much with comprehension. With experience, a teacher can become skillful at picking out the key words in a selection.

Children are often confused more by a familiar word used in an unfamiliar sense than by a word which is totally new to them. A child who knows the word *strike* as meaning "to hit" may need help in understanding the use of the word in such expressions as *to strike it lucky, to go on strike, to strike a camp,* and so on. The learning of new meanings for old words is an important phase of vocabulary development.

There are a great many words which children should know eventually, but which may or may not be needed at a particular grade level. It would be helpful if there were a specific grade-by-grade list of words which should be definitely taught. Although many attempts have been made to establish such a list, the task is essentially impos-

[7] Gray, W. S., and Holmes, E., *The Development of Meaning Vocabularies in Reading,* Publications of the Laboratory Schools, No. 6. Chicago: Department of Education, University of Chicago, 1938.

sible, since any such list is based on the books of the past and will always lag behind the latest trends in interest and content. World War II, for instance, caused children and adults to become familiar with a great many military, technical, and geographic terms that normally would fall outside of any word list yet compiled. Nevertheless, there is a common core which makes up perhaps as much as 90 per cent of the running words in ordinary reading matter, and which can be identified by means of consulting available word lists. Some of the more useful word lists to those interested in reading vocabulary, as distinguished from writing vocabulary, are the following:

Thorndike, E. L., and Lorge, I., *The Teachers Word Book of 30,000 Words*. New York: Bureau of Publications, Teachers College, Columbia University, 1944. This is the latest revision of the Thorndike list, which started with the most common 10,000 words and was later expanded to 20,000 and 30,000. The list is based on a count of 10,000,000 words, partly from adult reading and partly from children's books. A symbol after each word indicates the thousand in which it belongs, and the words in the first 5,000 are marked to indicate first half or second half of the thousand. This has been the most widely used of all word lists.

Buckingham, B. R., and Dolch, E. W., *A Combined Word List*. Boston: Ginn and Co., 1936. An alphabetical list of over 19,000 words. The grade placement of each word is given as determined by a "free association" study by the authors. For each word, the Thorndike rating and the grade placements as indicated by eight other word lists are also given. This is a very useful list, because it shows the rating of each word on ten different lists. The lack of agreement concerning the grade placement of many words is clearly evident.

Durrell, D. D., and Sullivan, H. B., "Vocabulary Instruction in the Intermediate Grades," *Elementary English Review*, Vol. 15, 1938, pp. 146–148, 158, 179–184. Also printed in Durrell, *Improvement of Basic Reading Abilities*, pp. 355–391. Separate vocabulary lists for grades four, five, and six, including only words found in at least seven books for the grade, and excluding all words found in the Gates list for the primary grades.

The primary-grade word lists which have been described in Chapter XII, on page 332, are also very useful. All words which are common enough to find a place in primary-grade word lists should be known by children in the upper grades.

The Vocabulary Burden in Textbooks

Many studies have shown that entirely too many textbooks are loaded with unnecessary rare and technical words. This has been shown over and over again in studies of textbooks used in the teaching of science, the social studies, and arithmetic. Fairly typical are the results of a study of five arithmetic textbooks intended for use in the third grade.[8] There were marked differences in the general vocabulary used: one book had 50 per cent more repetition of words than another book. In the five books there was a total of 296 words which had a quantitative or arithmetical meaning. Of these words, 44 appeared in only one book and 19 in only two books. Twenty-four per cent of the technical words were used only once each in the books in which they appeared, and 55 per cent were used less than six times each. In addition, a large number of proper names were used which were difficult for many third-grade children to read.

As a result of studies like the one just summarized, a good start has been made in the publishing of textbooks in which careful attention has been given to the avoidance of an unnecessary vocabulary burden. There still is room for much improvement in this direction. The selection of textbooks which avoid the use of complicated verbiage and explain new terms clearly when they are introduced is one important way of reducing the vocabulary problem to teachable proportions.

The vocabulary problem is more acute in the textbooks of the content subjects than it is in general reading material. Many of the books used as texts in the elementary and secondary schools are written by specialists who have little understanding of the reading limitations of the children who are expected to use them. An invaluable source of assistance to the teacher who wants to know what words are most essential in subject-matter fields is the following:

Cole, Luella, *Handbook of Technical Vocabulary.* Bloomington Ill.: Public School Publishing Co., 1940. Includes subject-matter vocabularies

[8] O'Rourke, E. V., and Mead, C. D., "Vocabulary Difficulties of Five Textbooks in Third-Grade Arithmetic," *Elementary School Journal,* Vol. 41, 1941, pp. 683–691.

for arithmetic, secondary school mathematics, history, geography, English, and general science. Based on careful analyses of representative textbooks in each field of study.

Each of the content subjects has a vocabulary of its own that must be learned. One cannot expect a pupil to understand without assistance technical terms such as *dividend, factor,* and *decimal* in arithmetic, *longitude* and *latitude* in geography, and similar technical terms in other subjects. Whenever an important new concept is introduced there is need for a detailed explanation. Cole's *Handbook* is helpful in indicating which terms are likely to be worth teaching carefully.

It is not safe to allow pupils to pick out the words that they need to study. Even at the college level, it has been found that "the pupils most in need of vocabulary enlargement are too often the students least likely to realize their need or to appraise their limitations correctly." [9] This is even more true at lower scholastic levels.

Methods of Teaching New Words

Opinions concerning the best methods of introducing new words were studied by Addy, who secured questionnaire results from teachers and supervisors in 250 demonstration schools attached to teachers' colleges.[10] The methods which were considered most effective were: studying the context, noting the use of the word in the sentence in which it appears (also context), relating the word to former experiences, introducing words through the aid of activities, using concrete objects, and using visual aids. Other methods which were frequently mentioned but not considered most effective were: securing the definition from a dictionary, studying etymology (word origins), studying synonyms and antonyms, studying prefixes and suffixes, study of word combinations and compound words, and discussions of the most effective word to interpret a specific meaning. For fixing the meaning of words, twenty-eight different methods were listed. Those which received the highest number of votes were

[9] Bear, R., and Odbert, H., "Insight of Older Pupils into Their Knowledge of Word Meanings," *School Review,* Vol. 49, 1941, pp. 754–760.

[10] Addy, M. L., "Development of a Meaning Vocabulary in the Intermediate Grades," *Elementary English Review,* Vol. 18, 1941, pp. 22–26, 30.

regular conversation using new words, and practice in the selection of the most effective word to present a given meaning. Each of the many procedures had some defenders. Opinion was evenly divided concerning the merits of regular daily word study as compared to informal, incidental teaching of vocabulary.

The comparison of different teaching procedures in classroom situations is always a difficult task, and as yet there is not sufficient evidence to show which methods of vocabulary instruction work best at the different grade levels and with pupils of different degrees of ability. A study by Jenkins is illustrative of the sort of procedure that needs to be repeated at various grade levels.[11] Five English classes at the seventh grade were equated for ability on an intelligence test and a silent reading test. All classes were given the same general program in English. In one class (the control class) no special attention was paid to vocabulary development. Each of the other classes was given a different type of vocabulary study: (1) use of a reading workbook containing many varied type of vocabulary exercises; (2) individual word study, using index cards and much dictionary work, with students working in pairs; (3) emphasis on study of synonyms, antonyms, and special word lists; (4) intensive study of prefixes, suffixes, and roots. Best all-round results were obtained from the second and third of these procedures. The third procedure was helpful for all students; the second was more helpful to the inferior than to the superior students, and the fourth helped the superior more than the inferior students. It is probable that a combination method, employing the best features of each of these four procedures, would work better than any of the four used exclusively.

Explanation and Discussion

The conventional method of teaching new words is about as follows: The teacher looks through the selection in advance and picks out a few words that may need explanation. Before the children

[11] Jenkins, M., "Vocabulary Development: A Reading Experiment in Seventh Grade English," *Peabody Journal of Education*, Vol. 19, 1942, pp. 347–350.

read the selection, the teacher writes the new words on the board, explaining the meaning of each, using it in one or more sentences, and showing appropriate illustrative material if any is available. The children are asked to suggest other sentences in which the word can be used. The words are taken up in turn, and then the selection is read.

One difficulty with this procedure is the danger of relying on superficial verbalizations. Meanings that are clear to the teacher may be quite hazy to the child. Many of the classical boners are due to superficial and inadequate grasp of word meanings. It is not sufficient to tell a child that *frantic* means *wild*, or that *athletic* means *strong*; he may try to pick *frantic flowers*, or pour *athletic vinegar* into a salad dressing.

The other main difficulty with this procedure is the danger of spending too much time on word study. This can be avoided if the principles set forth in the preceding paragraphs are followed.

Some teachers prefer to have a group of pupils read the selection first, and then ask them at the end what new words caused them trouble. These words can then be explained in the usual way. Two advantages are claimed for this procedure: that the number of words pupils will ask about is nearly always less than the number that the teacher would have selected for preliminary teaching, and that the teaching arises from a need felt by the pupils, and therefore is more apt to be well motivated and to produce effective learning. This procedure can work well with children who are good readers; poor readers fail to ask about many of the words they do not know.

The Use of the Dictionary

As soon as possible, children should be taught to help themselves to acquire new meanings independently by making use of glossaries and dictionaries. Picture dictionaries can be used as early as the first grade, and are helpful additions to the library table through the primary grades and in upper-grade remedial work. Good picture dictionaries for use by children are:

The Golden Dictionary, by Ellen Wales Walpole. New York: Simon and Schuster, 1941. Beautifully illustrated in color.

A Picture Dictionary for Children, by S. A. Courtis and G. Watters New York: Grosset & Dunlap, 1941.

My First Dictionary, by Laura Oftedal and Nina Jacob. New York: Grosset & Dunlap, 1948.

The use of a simple glossary can be introduced as early as the third grade. From the fourth grade up, regular dictionaries can be introduced. The main drawback about stressing the use of dictionaries in the past was the poor type of dictionary that formerly was available for school use. School dictionaries published within the past ten years have to a very large extent overcome the former difficulties. Clear type, simple vocabulary in definitions and explanations, illustrative sentences, simplified guides to pronunciation, and abundant illustrations make them attractive for child use.

Most present-day teachers learned to use a dictionary by trial and error. Many have never learned how to find what they want quickly and easily, and so refer to a dictionary only as a last resort. A dictionary is a complex work, and in order to get children to use it willingly, it is advisable to prepare a planned sequence of lessons to teach elementary dictionary skills. The following outline lists the major dictionary skills that can be made the objective of planned lessons in the fourth, fifth, and sixth grades.[12]

1. Location of words in alphabetical order
   a. Learning the sequence of the alphabet
   b. Practice in determining which letter comes before and which letter comes after a given letter
   c. Arrangement of a list of words in alphabetical order according to first letter
   d. Arrangement of words having same first letter in alphabetical order according to second, third, and fourth letters
   e. Practice in opening the dictionary at a point near the word
   f. Practice in the use of a thumb index
   g. Learning how to use the guide words at the top of a page

[12] This list is a revision of the list suggested in:
Kelly, V. H., "The Use of the Dictionary in the Elementary Grades," *Elementary English Review*, Vol. 13, 1936, pp. 17–24.

2. Finding out the pronunciation of words
   a. Practice in reading words by syllables
   b. Interpretation and use of the accent mark
   c. Understanding of phonetic respelling
   d. Understanding and use of diacritical marks
   e. Location and use of the guide to pronunciation

Dictionary Lesson

Arrange the words below in alphabetical order according to the first two letters by numbering the words in each column. See the first column. "Berries" and "built" begin with "b". When the first letters are the same, look at the second letter. The letter "e" comes before the letter "u", so "berries" comes before "built".

Why does the word "citizen" come before "clubs"?

clubs	moving	trouble
drew	jamboree	rivers
each	map	unknown
berries 1	known	shelter
citizen	joined	used
deserts	learn	stockade
built 2	kind	town
explore	life	roads

Fig. 44. Example of an exercise in alphabetizing. From *Exploring Today,* Diagnostic Reading Workbook, Grade 6, p. 19. Reproduced by permission of The American Education Press, Inc.

3. Finding out the meaning of words
   a. Ability to interpret typical dictionary definitions
   b. Ability to select from several meanings listed in the dictionary the one which fits the present context
   c. Ability to find synonyms for a word
   d. Ability to relate derived forms of a word to the basic form

e. Ability to distinguish current good usage from obsolete or slang usage

Some reading workbooks intended for use in the middle grades contain a variety of useful exercises for the development of skill in the use of the dictionary. Helpful suggestions about ways to teach dictionary skills can be obtained from publishers of school dictionaries, such as Scott, Foresman & Co., the G. and C. Merriam Co., and John C. Winston Co.

Individualized Word Study

It is one thing to teach pupils how to use dictionaries and quite another thing to make sure that they will actually make use of them. Pupils must be stimulated to take advantage of the opportunities for self-help that dictionaries offer. Vocabulary notebooks are effective in encouraging the use of dictionaries. When such notebooks are used a pupil is expected to enter in his notebook new words that he meets in his reading, together with a brief description or explanation of each, and one or two sentences illustrating its use. Very important new words should be looked up immediately. Others can be allowed to accumulate until the pupil has fifteen or twenty new words, and then these can be looked up at one time. This procedure reduces the irritation many pupils feel if they have to interrupt their reading frequently to consult a dictionary.

The use of index cards of the usual 3 x 5 inch size is preferred to the use of notebooks by many teachers. The word is written on one side, and the pronunciation, definition, and one or more illustrations of the use of the word can be put on the back. An inexpensive filing box and set of alphabet guide cards can be used to give excellent practice in filing and locating in alphabetical order. Children can easily test themselves on their own cards, or they can work in pairs, each testing the other.[13]

Motivation is a big problem in keeping up an interest in vocabulary study. Teachers should not hesitate to talk about the importance of words as the bricks from which ideas are built, and should find

[13] Detailed directions for this type of procedure are given in: Cole, Luella, *The Improvement of Reading*, Chs. 8–10. New York: Rinehart, 1936.

varied ways of impressing upon their pupils the importance of using the right word to fit each idea. In order to prevent an initial enthusiasm for word study from waning, the teacher should check on the progress of each pupil and make it clear that the learning of new vocabulary is an important aspect of the work in English. Sometimes enthusiasm can be whipped up by staging a contest; for example, the class can appoint themselves "word detectives," and prizes can be awarded for the largest number of "missing" words located during a week or month.

Study of Verbal Relationships

There are many kinds of exercises and games that can be used to give training in word meanings through practice in various kinds of

Word Mastery Exercise 8

Time, 5 minutes. Number tried.......................... Number correct.......................

Draw lines under the right words. One is done to show you how.

Example: **Find some things that fly.**

<u>bird</u> third word <u>kite</u> sight night

A *bird* and a *kite* fly, so lines are drawn under them.

1. **Find some things a cow has.**

   corns horns thorns tail hail fail

2. **Find two pieces of jewelry.**

   king bring ring pin thin din

3. **Find two fruits.**

   fig pig dig peach reach each

Fig. 45. Part of a workbook exercise on vocabulary development that combines reasoning about relationships with the necessity for accuracy in word discrimination. From Bedwell, Robert L., and Hutchinson, Mary, *My Own Reading Exercises,* Book Two, p. 28. Auburn, Alabama: Prather Publishing Co. Reproduced by permission of the publisher, and reduced in size.

relationships between words. They can be adapted for either oral or silent work. In the latter case it is necessary to prepare mimeographed sheets or to write the questions on the board and use answer sheets. Many useful vocabulary exercises can be found in published workbooks. Some samples of different kinds of word-meaning exercises now follow:

Writing Words in Lists

Set I

Read these words. They are about games, food, and books.

1. pages	5. butter	9. bats	14. grapes	18. print
2. paper	6. milk	10. meat	15. chapter	19. skip
3. sugar	7. ball	11. pictures	16. cover	20. ice cream
4. bread	8. contents	12. jump	17. cards	21. marbles
		13. score		

Under "Games" write all the words about *games*.
Under "Food" write all the words about *food*.
Under "Books" write all the words about *books*.

Games	**Food**	**Books**
______	______	______
______	______	______
______	______	______
______	______	______
______	______	______
______	______	______
______	______	______

Number correct______

Fig. 46. One of many kinds of vocabulary exercises to be found in reading workbooks for the middle elementary grades. From Brueckner, L. J., and Lewis, W. D., *Diagnostic Tests and Remedial Exercises in Reading*, p. 41. Philadelphia: John C. Winston Co., 1935. Reproduced by permission of the publisher, and reduced in size.

Synonyms

1. What word means the same as: good? attractiveness? uncivil?
2. Underline the word that means the same as *quiet*: noisy, pretty, still, steady.
3. A tactful remark is: (1) rude (2) courteous (3) deceitful (4) intact.

4. List all the words you can think of that mean about the same as *happy*.

Opposites

1. What word means the opposite of: big? warlike? pretentious?
2. Underline the word that means the opposite of curved: twisted, bumpy, round, straight.
3. A *compulsory* act is not: (a) optional (b) contagious (c) necessary (d) repulsive.
4. Animated—lethargic. Same Opposite (Underline one.)

Classification

1. What are the parts of: an automobile? a plant? a city government?
2. A *wing* is a part of: (a) an animal (b) a bird (c) a fish (d) a plant.
3. Make one list of the fruits and another list of the vegetables in the words: orange, potato, pineapple, spinach, lettuce, pear, pea, grape, bean, lemon, squash, cucumber, strawberry, peach.
4. Make a list of all the kinds of clothing you can think of (or jobs, colors, animals, vehicles, etc.).

Analogies

1. Foot is to hand as shoe is to ________.
2. Good is to bad as light is to: bright, naughty, dark, happy.
3. Governor: state: : mayor: (1) city (2) town (3) country (4) president

The major purpose of the kinds of exercises just illustrated is to clarify the meanings of words through bringing out important relationships between ideas. As the child comes to grasp these relationships his understanding of the words becomes more accurate, and he is therefore able to use and interpret them more effectively. When in going over the answers to exercises like these it is found that some of the words are unfamiliar, the teacher can take the opportunity to teach the meaning of the words and also to add them to the child's reading vocabulary. Vocabulary tests can also be employed deliberately to afford opportunities for introducing and teaching new words.

Study of Prefixes, Suffixes, and Roots

A large number of English words start with prefixes. These little word parts have fairly constant meanings, and a person who knows the meanings of the more common prefixes can frequently make a fairly close guess as to the meaning of a new word, particularly when it is met in a meaningful context. Stauffer found that 24 per cent of the first 20,000 words in the Thorndike list have prefixes.[14] While the total number of prefixes is large, many of them are used but seldom, and fifteen prefixes account for 82 per cent of all the words in which prefixes appear. These fifteen prefixes can easily be taught in the fifth and sixth grades. They are as follows:

ab (from)	ex (out)
ad (to)	in (into)
be (by)	in (not)
com (with)	pre (before)
de (from)	pro (in front of)
dis (apart)	re (back)
en (in)	sub (under)
	un (not)

The rarer prefixes are also worth knowing, but probably should be left for individual study, or left for incidental consideration in connection with the learning of particular words that contain them.

The problem of the teaching of the meanings of suffixes is somewhat more complicated. This problem has been dealt with in detail by Thorndike, who pointed out that most suffixes in English have several different meanings, and that teaching the most common meaning may create confusion. The many questions concerning the teaching of suffixes are too complex to go into here. The reader who is interested should refer to Thorndike's monograph.[15]

A knowledge of the meanings of some of the more common Latin roots which are found in many English words is unquestionably helpful in attacking unknown words at a mature level. Roots like *port*, meaning to carry, *fac* or *fic*, meaning to make, and a few others can be easily learned by mature pupils. It is probable that nearly all of the help in learning new English words that is claimed as one of

[14] Stauffer, R. G., "A Study of Prefixes in the Thorndike List to establish a list of Prefixes That Should Be Taught in the Elementary School," *Journal of Educational Research,* Vol. 35, 1942, pp. 453–458.

[15] Thorndike, Edward L., *The Teaching of English Suffixes.* New York: Bureau of Publications, Teachers College, Columbia University, 1941.

D. Prefixes and Their Meanings

A **prefix** is a syllable that is placed in front of a root word to change its meaning. The prefix **re** means "again, or back." The prefix **un** means "not." Underline the prefix and write the meaning of each word below.

1. rebuild ....
2. unfriendly ....
3. repaint ....
4. unhappy ....
5. repay ....
6. redraw ....
7. untrue ....
8. renew ....
9. unnatural ....
10. unlike ....
11. recall ....
12. unlock ....

E. Words with Prefixes

Use the right word in each sentence below. The words that you add must have the prefixes **re** or **un**.

1. The boy was .... because he lost his cap.
2. You must .... the story that you read yesterday.
3. I can never .... you for all that you have done for me.
4. I am .... to pay for the vase that was broken.
5. We will have to .... the door to get inside.
6. The facts about the accident are ....
7. If you are ...., you may lose the game.

Fig. 47. A workbook exercise on prefixes that combines structural analysis with vocabulary development. From Leavell, Ullin W., and Davis, Betty E., *New Journeys in Reading,* The Reading Essentials Series, p. 20. Austin, Texas: The Steck Co., 1953. Reproduced by permission of the publisher, and reduced in size.

the benefits accruing from the teaching of Latin can be just as well secured from a few hours spent in consideration of the commonest Latin roots and prefixes. From one of the roots it is possible to build up a family of words, helping in the clarification of the meanings of those words, the root that is common to all of them, and the different shades of meaning created by their different prefixes and suffixes. Such a family might be *porter, import, export, deport, report, reporter, transport, portable,* and so on.

It takes a fairly high level of mental ability to understand a generalized meaning and to apply it correctly in particular situations, so as to be able to utilize a knowledge of word roots, prefixes, and suffixes effectively in attacking the meaning of unknown words. Such a level is probably not reached by the average student below the ninth- or tenth-grade level. In the elementary grades, only the brightest pupils are likely to be able to profit from such instruction.

Learning Fine Shades of Meaning

There are fads in the use of words, as in clothing styles. One year, everything commendable is "divine"; a year or two later, everything is "super," "sharp," or "crazy." Many children fall victim to the insidious habit of using a small number of stock adjectives and adverbs and fail to develop a command of a vocabulary that can express fine shades of meaning. In the upper grades, it pays to devote some attention to the comparison of words which express somewhat similar meanings. If a boy describes a party as a "lousy" time, instead of scolding him for the use of an inelegant word, it is more profitable to ask him to try to describe more exactly the way in which the party was "lousy." Was it boring, dull, dreary, disappointing? Were the refreshments insufficient, unappetizing? Discussions of this sort form one of the very best ways of awakening children to the desirability of stating their meanings with precision, rather than relying upon a few stock words whose overgeneralized meanings are worked to death. At the secondary school level, it is worth while to take time to acquaint students with the organization of a good thesaurus, such as Roget's *Thesaurus in Dictionary Form.*

REVIEW 2

A *Fill in the blanks in each paragraph with suitable words from the list below it. (The following changes will sometimes be necessary: "a" to "an," a singular to a plural, verb tense from present to past.)*

(a)

Overcome by .... exhaustion, we were lulled to sleep by the .... roar of the waters. When we awoke, the noise was even louder; we .... that the flood was getting worse. Hurriedly we climbed a high rock to .... the scene below. Then I began to.............. myself for my .... in dismissing the guide. The swollen river tumbled over the rocks with such force that its banks were .... in a misty spray.

conclude	*folly*	*shrouded*	*survey*
continuous	*reproach*		*utter*

Fig. 48. Part of a workbook exercise designed to give practice in using in context some words recently studied. From Hardwick, H. C., *Words Are Important,* Junior Book of Vocabulary Improvement, p. 20. New York: C. S. Hammond & Co., 1955; Agincourt, Ontario: The Book Society of Canada, 1955; published under the title, *The Right Word,* Huddersfield, England: Schofield and Sons, Ltd., 1956.

Learning to Recognize Implied Meanings

Much of the delicacy of expression in spoken and written language comes from the suggestion of ideas by indirect means. Figurative language may lend grace and charm to linguistic expression. It also frequently obscures the intended meaning.

To some extent ability to interpret ideas when they are presented through analogies, similes, metaphors, euphemisms, and circumlocutions grows from meeting such forms of expression again and again in settings which make their meaning clear. During wartime the public learned to read with understanding the indirect and euphemistic language used in military communiqués. For example, when one side announced that their troops had "reorganized their lines," it was clear that they were admitting a retreat. It does not take a young man long to realize that the plea of a headache, used to break a date, is usually a polite evasion. Few people are deceived by the "great regret" with which a public official's resignation is received by his superior.

Sensitivity to implied meanings also requires a fairly high level of verbal intelligence. The person who easily recognizes analogies and readily notes similarities and differences in concepts is likely to enjoy discovering the implied meanings in what he reads. The person who lacks facility in understanding verbal relationships is likely to grasp only the obvious stated meanings.

This page has three parts. In each part a word is used in two groups of sentences to show four different meanings. Write in the blank before each sentence in Group II the number of the sentence in Group I in which the word is used with the same meaning.

I

1. **All work and no *play* is not a good thing for anybody.**
2. **Molly will have a part in the school *play*.**
3. **I have always wanted to learn to *play* the piano.**
4. **Children should be taught that it is dangerous to *play* with matches.**

II

4..Never let a little child *play* with sharp scissors.
..1..*Play* is one of the best kinds of exercise.
2..We decided to make a *play* out of one of the stories in our reader.
.3..He could *play* the violin beautifully when he was five years old.

Fig. 49. Part of a workbook exercise to develop sensitivity to different meanings of common words. From Gray, William S., Horsman, Gwen, and Monroe, Marion, *Basic Reading Skills for High-School Use,* Teacher's Edition, p. 42. Copyright, 1948, by Scott, Foresman and Company, and reproduced with their permission.

Probably the best way to develop a real understanding of figurative or indirect language is through practice in paraphrasing. The attempt to restate another's thoughts in clear, unambiguous language of one's own is a crucial test of whether the thought has really been understood.

Materials for Vocabulary Development

Many vocabulary-building activities are provided in workbooks that are correlated with basal readers, and also in independent workbooks that cover a variety of comprehension skills (see pp. 454–456). Materials intended to be used for vocabulary development only are available from junior high school level up.

Hardwick, H. C., *Words Are Important.* New York: C. S. Hammond & Co. A series of several thin workbooks, junior high school and up, teaching some of the less common words of the Thorndike-Lorge *Teachers Word Book* in lessons of about 20 words each.

Hart, Archibald, and Lejeune, F., *The Growing Vocabulary.* New York: E. P. Dutton & Co. Contains an interesting and varied set of exercises for teaching secondary school words.

Hart, Archibald, *Twelve Ways to Build a Vocabulary.* New York: E. P. Dutton & Co. Varied practice exercises, for high school and college use; interesting style.

Miller, Ward S., *Word Wealth* and *Word Wealth Junior.* New York: Henry Holt & Co. Selected words of secondary school level, arranged in weekly units of about 25 new words each.

Christ, Henry I., *Winning Words.* Boston: D. C. Heath & Co. Secondary school level.

Greene, Amsel, *Word Clues.* Evanston: Row, Peterson & Co. A high school level book emphasizing Latin and Greek roots, prefixes, and suffixes; manual available.

Funk, Wilfred, and Lewis, Norman, *Thirty Days to a More Powerful Vocabulary.* New York: Wilfred Funk, Inc. Intended for adult self-instruction; lively style. Also available in a pocket-book edition.

Gilmartin, John, *Word Power.* New York: Prentice-Hall Book Co. A book designed for adult self-study including tests and answer keys, covering pronunciation, word origins and meanings.

Semantics

A comparatively recent development in the study of language and thought is the field of semantics, which means the study of the meanings of words. The semanticists believe that confusion with regard to word meanings is the source of much inaccuracy and false logic in both scientific and popular reasoning. Thus in the false syllogism: "No cat has eight lives; any cat has one more life than no cat; therefore any cat has nine lives," the confusion comes from using "no cat" in two different senses and substituting one for the other. By careful analytical study of exact meanings the semanticists expect to bring about a marked improvement in clarity of thought.[16]

What bearing the study of semantics will have on the teaching of reading is not yet entirely clear. It is obvious that if the semanticists have their way, much more time and attention will be spent on the clarification of word meanings and on the study of the way in which the meanings of words change in different contexts. Extremely careful study of the meaning of a writer would probably be stressed, with exact comprehension emphasized at the sacrifice of speed in reading.[17]

II. Reading in Thought Units

MODERN TEACHING of reading encourages children to read words in meaningful groups from the beginning. In first-grade material each line of print usually presents a sentence, or complete unit of thought. When sentences become too long to go on one line the authors are careful always to break the sentence at a division between phrases, and the fact that the two lines form a sentence is shown by indentation. This kind of typographical arrangement encourages the children to expect a line of words to convey a unified meaning. Even at

[16] For an understandable explanation of general semantics the reader may turn to one of the books written by Irving J. Lee, S. I. Hayakawa, Hugh R. Walpole, or Stuart Chase.

[17] The application of semantic principles in secondary school teaching is discussed in: Zahner, Louis C., chairman, *Language in General Education,* A Report of the Committee on the Function of English in General Education, The Progressive Education Association. New York: Appleton-Century-Crofts, 1940.

Types of vocabulary exercises based on semantic principles are described in: Tyler, C., "Semantics and Language," *English Journal,* Vol. 29, 1940, II, pp. 21–22.

Walpole, Hugh R., "Interpretive Exercises for the Middle Grades," in *Reading and Pupil Development,* pp. 70–77. Supplementary Education Monographs, No. 51. Chicago: University of Chicago Press, 1940.

the preprimer level, however, the sentence is not a complete, self-sufficient unit; from the beginning, each sentence is part of a sequence that tells a little story. The word has meaning as part of a phrase; the phrase, as part of a sentence; the sentence, as part of a paragraph; the paragraph, as part of a story. Gradually the children learn to grasp the meanings of larger and larger units.

Development of Phrase Reading

Oral reading provides a natural setting for the development of ability to read phrases as meaningful units. The alert teacher notices whether the child habitually groups his words, or tends to read in word-by-word fashion. It is important to distinguish whether hesitations between words are caused by slowness in recognizing the words or by the habit of paying attention to only one word at a time. If a child departs from reading in a connected, meaningful way only when difficulties with particular words slow him down, the problem is primarily a word-recognition difficulty rather than a phrasing problem. By encouraging children to read as if they were telling the story, the teacher encourages the child to read with natural expression.

Many primary teachers prefer to present new words, not in isolation, but in phrases or sentences. For practice in word recognition they use phrase cards instead of word cards. Such phrase cards can be used in various ways: as flash cards for quick recognition, in following-directions games, in assembling sentences on a wall chart, in answering questions by selecting the proper phrase card, and so on. They should be aware, however, that most primary-grade children cannot really perceive a phrase as a unit, and therefore depend on the first word and perhaps some distinctive feature of the card when phrase cards are used.

Comprehension questions can be used to direct attention to phrases. Oral questioning during a group reading lesson can emphasize phrase answers. For example, the following sentence occurs in a reader: "They got four windows and a door at the lumberyard." The teacher could ask, "Where did they get what they needed?" The correct answer necessarily requires reading "at the lumberyard" as a meaningful unit. Comprehension questions in written form, based on silent reading, can also require answers in phrase form. For example, on the same sentence, written answers could be requested to such questions as:

The boys got what they needed ______.
Underline the best answer:
The boys got what they needed
at the store. in the woods.
at the lumberyard. from their father.

The child whose progress in reading is normal does not need much special practice in reading phrases. Reading words in meaningful groups develops as part of the total pattern of reading skills, without having to be singled out for special attention.

Remedial Work in Phrase Reading

The child who reads word by word has difficulty in getting the meaning of a larger unit of thought such as a phrase, clause, sentence, or paragraph. He is unable to see the forest because of the trees. Because he is not anticipating meanings, he fails to utilize context clues and so makes unnecessary errors in word recognition. After he has read the words, he often has to go back and reread for meaning, and even then may find it difficult to understand the material.

There are two main ways in which the habit of word-by-word reading develops. Word-by-word reading is frequently a secondary result of slowness and inaccuracy in word recognition. The child has to concentrate most of his attention on recognizing or figuring out the words and has little attention left for the meaning. After the word-recognition difficulty has been overcome, word-by-word reading frequently persists as a habit.

Word-by-word reading can also develop as a result of much practice in oral reading of the mechanical reading-in-turn type, when there is little or no discussion of the meaning. If the teacher does not seem to be concerned with the meaning, many children are satisfied to disregard it. Sometimes they read orally with some expression and apparent attention to the thought, but questioning discloses that they have not been attending to the meaning and have made no effort to remember what they were reading. Such mechanical, thoughtless reading is often called "word calling." Children whose reading is of this sort frequently draw a distinction between "just reading" and reading in order to be able to remember and answer questions. It is important to note that a child who reads with percep-

Reading Phrases at a Glance

Draw a line under all the groups of words that answer each question. Try to read each phrase at a glance. Be ready to read your answers aloud.

1. Where is the bird?

on a branch	in a ship
on the ground	above the tree
on a book	above the ground
in a cage	above the flowers
in a tree	

2. Where is the ball?

under the fence	beside the book
under the bushes	on the grass
under the house	on the ground
beside the bushes	on the water
beside the flower	

Fig. 50. Part of a workbook exercise intended to provide practice in reading phrases quickly and accurately. From Brueckner, L. J., and Lewis, W. D., *Diagnostic Tests and Remedial Exercises in Reading,* p. 55. Philadelphia: John C. Winston Co., 1935. Reproduced by permission of the publisher, and reduced in size.

tible pauses between each two words may actually be understanding the material very well, while other children who sound as if they are reading fluently get little or nothing of the meaning.

Many different procedures can be helpful in overcoming word-by-word reading and faulty phrasing. Among the most helpful are the following:

1. In order to allow the child to concentrate on the phrasing and meaning, reading matter which is used for practice in phrasing should present few or no difficulties in word recognition and word meaning.

When you watch / a ball game, / you like / a front seat. / You even try / to help / the team / by cheering them. / You think along / with the players / in every play. / In this way / you actually / take part / in the game. Then you feel / that you helped / win it. / You can do / the same thing / when you read. / Come close / to the scene / of the story / and feel that / you are seeing / the incidents happen. / Think about / what you are / reading / or be one / of the characters. / You will then find / enjoyment / in reading, / and your ability / to read / will grow / and grow.

Fig. 51. Part of a workbook exercise intended to develop efficient phrase reading and to diminish frequency of regressions. From Leavell, Ullin W., and Davis, Betty E., *New Adventures in Reading,* The Reading Essentials Series, p. 118. Austin, Texas: The Steck Co., 1953. Reproduced by permission of the publisher.

2. It is helpful to provide a good model for the pupils to imitate. The teacher can read a sentence orally with somewhat exaggerated phrasing, and then have the children imitate her reading of the sentence. Reading of alternate sentences by teacher and pupils is also helpful. Some children gain considerable benefit from reading in unison with the teacher.
3. Practice can be given in reading printed material in which the phrases have been marked off by the teacher. A vertical line can be made in pencil between each two phrases, or each prase can be underlined. The following sentence is shown with the phrases marked off in three different ways:

   The boy|is going|to the store|for some milk.

   The boy is going to the store for some milk.

   The boy is going to the store for some milk.

4. When special material is typed, mimeographed, or printed by hand, perhaps the best way to set off phrases is to leave additional space between them. For example:

   The boy   is going   to the store   for some milk.
5. After the pupil has developed some skill in the use of marked reading material, he can be given an unmarked selection to mark off the phrases. His ability to group words properly can be quickly evaluated and faulty grouping can be corrected.

6. Practice can be given in the recognition of phrases as units during brief exposures. This can be done in a variety of ways.
   a. Phrases can be printed or typed on flash cards for practice in quick recognition. For use with a group, large cards with clear, black printing can be made. For individual practice, index cards of 3x5 inch or 4x6 inch size can be used. A cover card is lifted up and then replaced, using a flick of the wrist, as rapidly as possible; it is not possible to flash a card by hand too quickly for a reader to recognize a short, simple phrase.

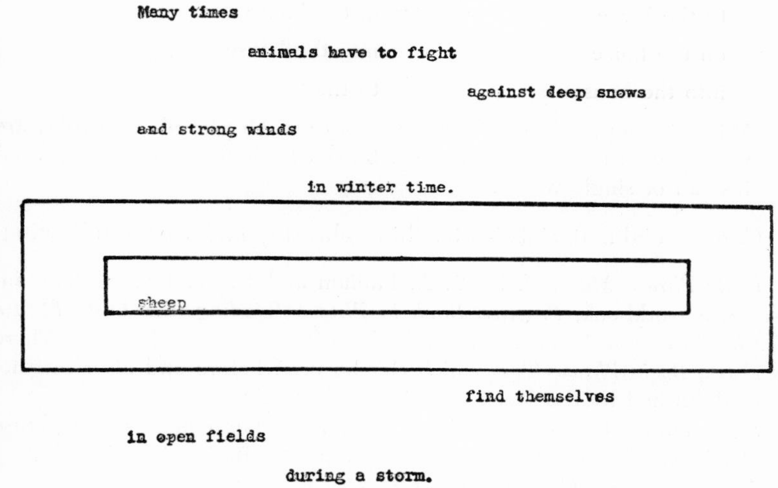

Many times

animals have to fight

against deep snows

and strong winds

in winter time.

sheep

find themselves

in open fields

during a storm.

Fig. 52. Practice material for reading in phrases. The strip of stiff paper is moved steadily down the page so that one phrase at a time appears in the opening.

   b. Phrase cards can be prepared and presented in a simple homemade tachistoscope (see p. 208) or in Durrell's cardboard tachistoscope (see p. 205).
   c. A projection tachistoscope such as the *Flash-Meter* can be used for very brief exposures of phrases as well as individual words (see p. 525). Some phrase slides for this purpose are available from the Keystone View Co.
   d. Material can be typed with one phrase on a line, as in Figure 52. A piece of stiff paper or cardboard with an opening the length of a full line is moved at a steady rate down the page, exposing one

phrase at a time. Some remedial teachers prefer to keep the opening stationary and pull the page up. In the latter case, it is usually necessary to paste several pages together so as to form a continuous strip.

7. Practice can be given in matching phrases. The same phrases are printed or typed in two vertical lists, side by side but in different order. The task is to draw a line from each phrase in the right-hand column, as quickly as possible. For example:

in the house	on the horse
to the horse	in the house
on the horse	into the house
into the house	to the horse

8. With a group, a form of phrase Bingo can be played. The rules are the same as for Word-O (see p. 380) except that phrases are used instead of single words.

Commercial materials for teaching phrasing include the following:

Basic Phrase Material, by R. A. Pulliam and U. W. Leavell. This includes a workbook, *Practice Book in Phrase Reading,* the *Basic Phrase Flash Cards,* Set 1 and Set 2, and *Phrase-O Game,* Set 1 and 2. There is also a *Basic Phrase Test* which can be used before and after instruction. Published by the Steck Co., Austin, Texas.[18]

Sight Phrase Cards, by E. W. Dolch. Each box contains 140 phrase cards, in which the words are taken from the Basic Sight Vocabulary and Picture Word Cards. Garrard Press, Champaign, Ill.

Tachistoslides, by Helen B. Knipp. A series of eighty prepared slides for use with a projection tachistoscope, using phrases and sentences of gradually increasing difficulty and length. The contents of these slides are given in: Knipp, Helen B., *Basic Vocabulary, Phrases, and Sentences for Early Reading Instruction.* Meadville, Pa.: Keystone View Co., 1952.

To compile a set of phrase practice exercises extensive enough for what one would need at intermediate grade levels it is necessary to take from each of several workbooks the few pages of relevant material, and add to the collection some teacher-constructed phrase material.

[18] See also: Pulliam, R. A., and Watson, Kathryn. "A Basic Phrase List for Use in Reading Instruction," *Elementary School Journal,* Vol. 46, 1946, pp. 513–518.

Whatever special types of practice may be used, it is important to make the child attempt to utilize his new skills in phrasing in his everyday reading. Unless the results of special drills are carried over into general reading, the time spent on them is wasted.

A word of caution is needed concerning the feasibility of getting slow, word-by-word readers to perceive phrases of two or three words in one quick glance. A college student who is well above average in reading ability will perceive a line of ten words in about four or five quick looks or fixations. An average high school student will require about six or seven fixations. To be able to average two words to each fixation is to be a very good reader. Obviously when a child is still somewhat slow and hesitant in recognizing single words, he should not be told to try immediately to see long phrases in one quick glance. The ability to set up goals which are within the child's reach in the near future is one of the marks of the expert teacher. If too high a goal is set at the beginning, discouragement will probably result.

Teaching the Use of Punctuation Marks

Some children become confused in reading connected material because they do not make use of the clues provided by punctuation. They have not learned to recognize a capital letter as a sign of the beginning of a sentence, a period or question mark as the end of a sentence, or a comma as a "partial stop" separating parts of a sentence. Children of somewhat higher reading ability may need assistance in the interpretations of semicolons, colons, and dashes. Simple explanation and supervised practice in noticing punctuation marks will usually overcome difficulties of this sort. If errors persist, coloring the first letter of a sentence in green, commas in yellow and periods in red is an effective way to emphasize the punctuation.

As a follow-up after the teaching of punctuation one can employ unpunctuated material. The pupil is given a selection that has been prepared with all punctuation omitted, and is asked to insert the necessary symbols. If he has difficulty, he should be asked to read the passage orally. He may need to repeat considerably before he is able to decide where the punctuation marks belong. If he makes errors, they should be corrected and the reasons for the correct insertions should be explained.

Improving Ability to Read Sentences

As a child improves his word recognition, enlarges his vocabulary, learns to read in phrases, and develops an appreciation of punctuation, his ability to read sentences improves. Little else is usually required other than to give him practice in reading sentences and answering questions on them designed to test his comprehension.

When it is evident that weaknesses in reading sentences are prominent features of a pupil's comprehension, practice should be given in reading sentences, with a specific question asked about each sentence. The essential ideas of most sentences can be tested by questions asking *who, what, where, when, how,* or *why*. Some sample types of sentences and questions are as follows:

1. A horse can run fast.
   What can a horse do? ______
2. Honest men can be trusted not to steal. True False
3. Do most automobiles have more than four wheels? Yes No
4. We were awakened by one of the servants who seemed alarmed.
   How did the servant feel? ______
   afraid happy angry disappointed
5. Although they had to endure many hardships, the soldiers at Valley Forge remained confident that they would win the war because of their faith in their leader.

   Check one: __ The soldiers were afraid that they would lose.
   __ The soldiers trusted their general to bring victory.
   __ The soldiers had an easy time resting at Valley Forge.

Difficulty in understanding sentences is related to the complexity of sentence structure. Simple sentences are usually understood without difficulty, provided that the pupil knows the vocabulary. Compound sentences with clauses joined by *and* or *but* are also generally easy. Complex sentences which contain subordinate clauses tend to be more confusing. When a pupil has difficulty in unraveling complicated sentences, guidance in sentence analysis is needed. Asking the pupil who the sentence is about, what did he do, to what did he do it, and so on, and showing him the answers when he cannot find them, is a servicable procedure. The use of formal grammatical terms such as "prepositional clause" may confuse the pupil more than it helps.

The understanding of dependent or subordinate clauses depends to a considerable extent on familiarity with the meanings of the words that are used to introduce them. For effective reading above the lower grades it is necessary to understand the shades of meaning indicated by the commonly used connectives. For reading of any degree of complexity, acquaintance with the following list is essential:

Who, which, what, that, from, whom, to which
How, like, so as, so that, in order to
Because, since, as
Until, as soon as, before, while, as, after, following
If, unless, provided that, whether, should
As well as, all but, hardly, except, without, although
However, moreover, therefore, nevertheless

One of the main reasons why these words may cause trouble is the fact that many pupils are not accustomed to speech and conversation which makes use of them to any extent. Practice in the construction of sentences employing these connectives is one good way to clarify their meanings so that they can be understood when they are met in reading. Paraphrasing or expressing the same idea in different words is another valuable form of exercise for this purpose.

This chapter has been concerned with the comprehension of words, phrases, and sentences. Understanding of these units of meaning is a basic necessity if the reader is to make sense out of longer selections. However, a mastery of the parts does not necessarily bring with it mastery of the whole; it is possible to read each word, phrase, and sentence correctly and yet not gain a comprehensive grasp of a connected selection. When the unit of reading matter is longer than a single sentence, as it usually is, higher-level comprehension skills are involved. These will be considered in the next chapter.

Suggested Additional Reading

BETTS, EMMETT A. *Foundations of Reading Instruction,* pp. 655–688.

COLE, LUELLA. *The Improvement of Reading,* Chs. 8, 9, 10. New York: Farrar & Rinehart, Inc., 1938.

RUSSELL, DAVID H. *Children Learn to Read,* Ch. 9.

TINKER, MILES A. *Teaching Elementary Reading,* Ch. 9.

YOAKAM, GERALD A. *Basal Reading Instruction,* Ch. 10.

· XVI ·

Developing Understanding in Reading, II

IN ORDER TO DEVELOP higher level skills in reading it is necessary to have a foundation in basic skills; if a child cannot recognize words, or is ignorant of word meanings, or cannot determine the natural meaningful groups into which words fall, it is useless to attempt to develop the more complex comprehension skills. Genuine reading situations, however, call for much more than the ability to read words, phrases, and sentences. They involve many different kinds of higher-level skills, which vary according to the reader's purpose and the requirements set by the reading material. The efficient reader is able to read in many different ways, adapting his mind set appropriately to the needs of each new reading situation.

In the first part of this chapter suggestions are given about how to develop the most important types of comprehension skills. In the second part, remedial problems in comprehension are discussed.

I. Developing Special Comprehension Skills

IN THE LIST of reading objectives given on pages 12–14, skill in comprehension was treated under ten headings. Two of these, vocabulary development and ability to grasp the meaning of phrase and sentence units, were discussed in the preceding chapter. The other eight will be considered below. Although the statistical experts are not in complete agreement about the components of comprehension,[1] in practical teaching situations the need to provide practice in reading with varied purposes and varied mind-sets is clearly evident.

Ability to Find Answers to Specific Questions

There are many reading situations in which the reader has a specific question in mind and reads to find an answer to that question. Sometimes the question is one which requires careful reading and analytical reasoning; for example, reading to find out why oxygen is essential for combustion to take place. In such reading the question provides point, purpose, and a way for the reader to determine if his reading was satisfactory: Does he have an answer? Children who have not had practice in reading to find answers to definite questions are likely to have difficulty in selecting the relevant from the irrelevant; even superior readers in the middle grades have difficulty in distinguishing between paragraphs that are helpful in providing information on a specific question, and paragraphs that are somewhat related but provide no information on that question.[2] At times, therefore, questions should precede reading, and the reading should be for the purpose of answering those particular questions. Written or oral answers, followed by discussion, provide a means for judging success and correcting errors.

Skimming to Find Answers to Specific Questions. One of the most important types of comprehension skills is the ability to skim rapidly over reading material. Two kinds of skimming can be distinguished. One kind involves rapid reading to find the answer to a very specific question, such as a name, a date, a telephone number, and so on.

[1] Davis, Frederick B., "The Factorial Composition of Two Tests of Comprehension in Reading," *Journal of Educational Psychology,* Vol. 37, 1946, pp. 481–486; Thurstone, L. L., "Note on a Reanalysis of Davis' Reading Tests," *Psychometrika,* Vol. 11, 1946, pp. 185–188; Davis, Frederick B., "A Brief Comment on Thurstone's Note on a Reanalysis of Davis' Reading Tests," *Psychometrika,* Vol. 11, 1946, pp. 249–255.

[2] Gans, Roma, *A Study of Critical Reading Comprehension in the Intermediate Grades.* Contributions to Education, No. 811. New York: Bureau of Publications, Teachers College, Columbia University, 1940.

Practice in learning how to skim for a specific item of information can be best provided through use of the kinds of material that are normally skimmed in functional reading. Some of the kinds of questions to which answers are found by skimming are as follows:

On what date did a certain event take place?
What is the Mason-Dixon Line?
Who was the American commander at the Battle of Saratoga?
What is the largest wheat-producing state?
What are the leading industries in Boston?
What is an Indian tent called?
What is Mr. John X. Smith's telephone number?
At what theater is a particular moving picture playing?

To give practice in skimming of this type, the teacher can prepare in advance a list of questions based on the reading matter to be used. The questions should be presented to the pupils before they read the selection, and they should be encouraged to find the answers as quickly as possible, and write them. After the pupils have finished, there can be discussion of the answers, with oral reading of the sentences which contain the answers, or the written answers can be collected and scored as a test. Material of many different sorts can be used. There is no reason why schools should not make greater use of such reading materials as daily newspapers for practice in skimming. Textbooks in the various content subjects can also be used to good effect.

The expert at skimming for specific information has developed a distinctive skill which is quite different from other types of reading. As he runs his eyes rapidly over the material, he does not absorb the meaning, but merely notices that what he is looking for is not there. When he comes to the desired item, it seems to stand out as if in boldface type. Some people are able to develop almost incredible speed in this sort of skimming.

Reading for Main Ideas

Skimming to Get a Total Impression. The other kind of skimming involves very superficial, rapid reading to get a general overall impression. Some of the situations in which this type of skimming is useful are as follows:

1. Looking over a chapter in a textbook, prior to serious study, in order to get an idea of the general scope of the chapter.
2. Sampling a few pages of a novel or other type of work to form an opinion as to whether it is worth reading.
3. Going quickly through an article on a controversial issue to find out the author's point of view, without bothering to note his specific arguments.
4. Looking through reading material to judge if it is likely to contain the kind of information one is seeking.
5. Examining reading material to decide if it is comprehensible or too difficult.

In this type of skimming, the reader must have a specific purpose. The teacher may suggest such reading activities as the following:

"John, look this book over and let me know if you think you would enjoy reading it." "Phyllis, look over these three books and decide which one will help you most in your selection of an Indian legend that the class could make into a play." "Harold, look through the section on mining in this book to see if it is too hard for you to read." As with other reading skills, improved efficiency in this type of reading comes gradually with motivated practice.

Reading for the Central Thought. One of the most valuable of comprehension skills is the ability to find the main idea or central thought in what one reads. To be able to select the most important thought from a mass of words calls for an ability to distinguish between essentials and nonessentials, between the most important idea and subordinate details or illustrations. It is a form of reasoning which involves comparison and selection. It is not strange, therefore, that children of below-average intelligence often have more trouble with this type of comprehension than they do in reading and understanding details.

Several different kinds of practice can be given to develop this type of comprehension.

1. In story reading, comprehension of the significance of an incident can frequently be tested by asking what feeling or emotion was felt by the main character during or after the incident.

2. Another form of question appropriate for story material is a request for a one-sentence summary of the incident.
3. In informational material, one can ask the pupils to select the main idea in each paragraph. The questions can take the form of multiple-choice items, in which the most adequate statement of the main idea is to be selected from other statements, or can call for oral or written answers in sentence form.
4. After skill has been attained in finding the central thought in single paragraphs, similar practice questions can be used, based on a short selection of a few paragraphs.
5. An excellent way of helping children to develop skill in finding and expressing main ideas is to have them practice writing headlines for selections, as though they were preparing the selections for a newspaper.
6. Another variation is to provide practice in making up a title for a selection, or in choosing the most satisfactory of several proposed titles. This can be done for both single paragraphs and longer selections.
7. Many authors provide headings, subheadings, marginal notes, introductory statements, final summaries, or other ways of emphasizing what they consider to be the most important ideas. Discussion of the use of these aids is helpful to the pupils, who otherwise might fail to use them.
8. Learning to find key sentences is helpful. In the upper grades and secondary school, children can be taught to look for a topic sentence which states the most important or most inclusive idea in the paragraph. Usually this is the first sentence, sometimes the last sentence.
9. Similarly, readers should learn to pay special attention to introductory and concluding paragraphs.

Reading to Follow a Sequence of Events

An essential part of the understanding of narrative material, whether fictional or historical, is the ability to note the order or sequence of events, to grasp the cause-effect relationships involved, and to anticipate the rest of the story. Practice in this type of comprehension can be given in many ways, of which the following are examples:

1. The most effective and most natural procedure is to ask for a retelling of the story. Omissions of significant events, changes in the order of events, and misunderstandings can easily be noted and corrected through discussion and rereading.

2. As a group or class exercise following silent reading, the major events described in the selection can be listed in scrambled order on the board or in mimeographed form, and the pupils can be asked to number them in the order in which they happened, or to rewrite the list in correct order.
3. The habit of thinking ahead while reading, and trying to anticipate the story, can be developed by presenting brief unfinished stories and asking the pupils to make up a suitable ending for each, or to select the most plausible of several suggested endings. In a longer story, the teacher can stop at a critical point and ask the pupils what they think will happen next.

Reading to Note and Recall Details

There are many reading situations in which it is just as important to note and remember significant details as it is to understand the main ideas. This is especially true in the type of functional reading called *study*, in which the purpose is to assimilate as thoroughly as possible the material presented by the author. Some pupils who are expert, rapid readers in fiction and who get the main thoughts easily in factual material seem to have little or no interest in details, do not notice them as they read, and cannot remember them later. Balanced training in reading should include practice in reading for details.

It is probable that in American education too much attention has been paid to details as such, standing alone and unrelated to the situations in which they have significance. This tendency is sometimes encouraged by teachers who make up tests consisting mainly of questions on minor points. A general fondness and esteem for the ability to recall isolated, unrelated bits of information is glorified in many of the radio and television quiz programs which have large audiences. There are too many questions that ask who, what, where, and when, and too few questions that call for meaning, significance, or analysis of relationships.

Ideally, children should be taught to see details in their relation to the major ideas which they support. Details have many functions in expository material: They provide concrete illustrations which make a generalization more meaningful; they provide evidence in support of a conclusion; or they show ways in which an idea can be applied. What is needed is not so much a disparagement of detail as encouragement of the ability to relate the detail to the major ideas.

Some of the kinds of practice in noting and recalling details in reading are as follows:

1. In informal discussion after oral or silent reading, the main thought should first be discussed. Then attention can be called to the details by such questions as:
   What are the ways in which this is shown?
   What evidence of the truth of this statement is presented?
   What applications of this idea are given?
   What are the places where this holds true?
2. An incomplete outline of a selection can be presented, with the main ideas filled in and blank spaces left for the details. After reading, the pupils complete the outline. See Figure 55.
3. Straightforward questions about details also have their uses. Questions can be put in multiple-choice, completion, or short answer form. The multiple-choice type is quicker to mark, but the other forms encourage a more attentive attitude while reading because they require recall rather than simple recognition.

Grasping the Author's Plan

Good writing is organized writing, in which the author starts with something he wants to say, thinks out the order, sequence, relative importance, and interrelatedness of the specific ideas he intends to convey, and plans his exposition accordingly. In fiction there are characters to be introduced, a setting to be described, and a line of action which, if well planned, leads up to a climax. In informational or factual writing there is usually an introduction, a body, and a conclusion or summary. There are differences between exposition and argument; between writing intended to inform and writing intended to persuade. The particular pattern a writer uses can vary greatly, but in well-written material the pattern should be discernible.

In books written for children, many types of clues are provided which can be used to discover the author's plan. A chapter may start with an overview and end with summary and questions for application. In between there are headings, subheadings, material in

UNIT 7

By the end of the American Revolution our country had been settled as far west as the Appalachian Mountains. The first people who crossed the mountains were explorers, like Daniel Boone. They had heard stories of the rich land in the interior, and they followed Indian trails to reach it.

After these explorers came traders, who wanted to trade with the Indians. Many of these traders traveled by canoes, following the courses of rivers to their beginnings in the mountains. When they reached the sources of these rivers, they took their goods out of the canoes and loaded them on pack horses for the rest of the journey The pack horses moved in caravans which sometimes traveled two thousand miles. The traders exchanged their goods with the Indians for furs.

Following the explorers and traders came pioneer settlers who decided to leave their small farms on the frontier and move still farther west. Often the father of the family went first. He would build a log cabin and cut down the trees on a few acres of land. While he was doing this, his family would arrange to sell the old home and the crops. With the money thus secured, they would set out on the long journey to join him. You might think that these people would want to stay in one place after they had had the hard labor of cutting down the trees and clearing their farms, but they did not. Some moved almost every year, one family moved nine times in ten years.

After these pioneer settlers came farmers, who meant to settle down and stay They bought the half-cleared farms. By the year 1800 three little towns had been begun west of the mountains, but the population in all three towns did not then number a thousand people.

---

acres An acre of land is equal to a square about 208 feet long on each side.
beginnings, starting places
caravans, large groups traveling together for safety
clearing, open space in a forest for a farm, made by cutting down the trees
decided, made up their minds.
explorers, persons who are the first to travel in new places and who bring or send back information about those places.
frontier, the line between the part of the country where people had just built new homes for the first time and the other part where no white men had built permanent homes.
interior, the part of a country away from the seacoast.
settlers, persons who move into a new country to make their homes there.
sources, starting places or beginnings.
traders, persons or merchants who exchange one thing for something else.

General Directions for Unit 7

Write your answers in the spaces provided. Under **GETTING WORD MEANINGS,** you will write words as answers; under **GETTING THE FACTS,** you will write A, D, or N as answers; under the other headings, you will write numbers as answers.

GETTING WORD MEANINGS. In the space at the right, write the underlined word which means:

1 paths, channels; routes, direction taken by 1
2 meet and unite with 2
3 occupied; colonized 3
4 gave for something else 4
5 expected, intended 5
6. products grown on farms for use as food 6
7 make plans; prepare 7
8 the first [persons], preparing the way for others 8
9 gotten, gained; obtained, acquired 9

20

Fig. 53. A workbook exercise intended to provide practice in vocabulary development and several types of comprehension skills. From Guiler, W. S., and Coleman, J. H., *Reading for Meaning*, Book 7, pp. 20, 21.

10. sources; origins; headwaters 10

11. traveling merchants 11

12. chose; reached a decision; resolved. 12

CHOOSING THE BEST TITLE. The best title for this selection is . . . .

1. The Life of a Pioneer Family
2. Kinds of People Who Moved West
3. How the Early Pioneers Traveled
4. Crossing the Appalachian Mountains

GETTING THE MAIN IDEA. The main idea in this selection is that . . . .

1. Different kinds of people went west in a definite order.
2. Some people went west in order to trade with the Indians.
3. The early traders frequently had to make very long journeys.
4. The families of pioneer settlers had to undergo many hardships.

GETTING THE FACTS. For your answer write A (agrees), D (disagrees), or N (not included).

1. Daniel Boone was an explorer. 1
2. The explorers were very kind to the Indians. 2
3. The traders did all their traveling by canoe. 3
4. The pioneer settlers moved west in covered wagons. 4
5. The pioneer settlers generally stayed in one place. 5
6. The traders often exchanged food with the Indians for fur. 6
7. By 1800 only two towns had been built west of the mountains. 7
8. A great many of the pioneer settlers were killed by the Indians. 8

MAKING AN OUTLINE. Make a partial outline of the selection by writing the numbers of six of the following items in the proper spaces.

1. Canoes
2. Farmers
3. Traders
4. Explorers
5. Flatboats
6. Railroads
7. Steamboats
8. Pack horses
9. Covered wagons
10. Pioneer settlers

I. What the traders used to carry their goods
   A. ....
   B. ....

II. *Order in which the people listed in the left-hand column moved west*
   A. .... C. ....
   B. .... D. ....

DRAWING CONCLUSIONS. It seems fair to conclude from this selection that .... and ....

1. The American Revolution occurred before the year 1800.
2. The pioneer settlers moved more often than the farmers.
3. The traders bought many farms from the pioneer settlers.
4. The pioneer settlers went west much earlier than the traders.

Pupil's Score ....

GRADE	5	6	7	8	9	10	11	12
SCORE	17	20	23	25	26	28	29	30

21

Philadelphia: J. B. Lippincott Co., 1955. Reproduced by permission of the publisher, and reduced in size.

bold type, marginal notes, and so on, which help the reader to determine what a particular section is about. Although the utility of these devices seems so obvious and the purpose so clear, many children need specific guidance in how to use these aids.

Following Printed Directions

One of the most important uses for reading in everyday life is to find out how to do things. In former times, children learned mainly by watching and imitating their elders. In modern life people must rely more and more on printed directions and manuals of procedure. The housewife with her cookbook, the auto mechanic with his printed specifications for different makes and models, the surgeon reading an account of a new type of operation, the worker filling out a social security application – all need to be able to read carefully and accurately, and to follow a series of directions precisely and in correct order. During World War II, the armed forces were able to train millions of men to become hundreds of different kinds of specialists largely because the men could teach themselves by following directions in printed manuals.

Practice in reading and following directions is best provided in relation to activities which children wish to carry out or skills which they want to learn. In many subjects, textbooks contain directions which can be used for reading practice. This is particularly true in arithmetic and science. Directions for handwork activities can also be used to good effect. If the task is one easily corrected or repeated, the children can attempt to carry it out without preliminary discussion, and the teacher can judge by the results whether the directions were properly read. If the task is a long one or involves expensive materials, it is desirable first to discuss the directions and clarify any misconceptions through rereading and further discussion.

Many different sources of material can be used. Boys like to work on directions from the *Boy Scouts Handbook*, magazines like *Popular Mechanics*, books such as *How To Make Toys*, directions for performing scientific experiments, and so on. Girls can be interested in cooking recipes, directions for sewing, knitting, making marionettes, and the like. When additional practice in following directions seems to be needed, workbook exercises can be employed.

Development of Critical Reading Ability

Nearly all reading tests now in use attempt to measure the success of the reading in understanding what the author has to say. Comparatively few have tried to find out how well the reader can evaluate what he reads.

An important type of critical reading involves comparison of two or more sources of information. Children are usually amazed when for the first time they find two authorities contradicting each other. An experience like that can serve as a preliminary to discussion of such questions as the reputation and prestige of each author, his impartiality or bias, the comparative recency of the two sources, and so on. Reading experiences of this sort develop naturally when children do wide reading to find data on a problem. The teacher should be alert to make use of such occasions as stepping stones toward a more mature attitude on the credibility of reading matter. In the study of current events, comparison of the treatment of an event by two newspapers of opposing points of view can form an effective point of departure.

A second type of critical reading involves considering new ideas or information in the light of one's previous knowledge and beliefs. The thoughtful reader asks himself: Is it reasonable? Is it possible? He does not, of course, automatically reject the unfamiliar idea or challenging conclusion, like the legendary farmer whose comment on the giraffe he saw in the circus was, "There ain't no sich animal." But he becomes doubly alert when he finds disagreements with what he has previously accepted as true.

One of the most important aspects of critical reading is the ability to detect and resist the influences of undesirable propaganda. In recent years, the molding of public opinion has become tremendously important in political and social affairs. While the term propaganda has sometimes been defined to include all activities which are intended to influence people in a given direction, concern has been centered mainly on the kinds that attempt to persuade people to believe or act in a biased fashion. "What we want people to be proof against is their being led by some form of misrepresentation or through some false claim to follow a course of action different from that they would follow if they were more fully informed." [3]

Effective methods of arming people against propaganda have not yet been developed. The Institute for Propaganda Analysis did praiseworthy pioneer work in studying propaganda techniques and in trying out methods for teaching children and adults to recognize them. Certainly every well-informed adult should be able to recognize and discount such common propaganda techniques as name-calling, use of glittering generalities, card-stacking, the use of testimonials, the "plain-folks" device, identification with an individual or institution of great prestige, and the band-wagon effect.[4] Experimental studies have shown, however, that even those who have learned through direct teaching to recognize propaganda techniques are little if any more immune to the persuasive effects of clever propaganda than those who have not had such teaching.[5]

Children who spend years in school and at home learning to accept the authority of parents, teachers, and books in unquestioning fashion grow up to be receptive, easy victims of propaganda. Independent, critical thinking cannot be taught in a special course. It must be learned as a way of action in innumerable situations, starting in early childhood. Children whose education is centered around the investigation of vital problems, who learn to investigate, to experiment, and to reason for themselves should grow up to be more able than the typical adult of today to resist propaganda influences.

The fact that education against propaganda has been ineffectual is shown clearly by the success of a book on reading which has made

[3] *Discussion Leaders' Guide.* New York: Institute for Propaganda Analysis, 1938.

[4] *Guide to the Analysis of Propaganda.* New York: Institute for Propaganda Analysis, 1937.

[5] Pressey, Sidney L., and Robinson, Francis P., *Psychology and the New Education,* Revised Edition, p. 248. New York: Harper & Brothers, 1944.

clever use of all of the recognized propaganda techniques. Lamkin's article is an excellent example of how to expose the difference between writing which involves slanting and distortion for propaganda purposes, and reasonably objective writing.[6]

Remembering What One Has Read

Many people, children and adults alike, complain that they understand what they read when they read it, but cannot remember it later. This is a serious complaint and one which deserves careful consideration.

There are, of course, large individual differences both in speed of assimilation and in permanence of retention. Some people have naturally better memories than others. However, the correct application of known and generally accepted principles of learning would enable most of these complainers to remember what they read far better than they do at present.

The principles listed below are not original, but can be found in almost every textbook of educational psychology.

1. Material is easy to remember in proportion as it is meaningful. It is very difficult to recall ideas that have been only partially understood.
2. Material that is well organized in the reader's mind is easier to remember than material which is unorganized. The efficient reader tries to grasp the author's plan and to understand the relationships between ideas and the relations between the major ideas and the facts or details which give them definite meaning.
3. Many people are aided in remembering what they read by outlining, summarizing, or taking notes as they read. Others obtain similar benefits from underlining significant points or writing comments in the margin.
4. An active intention to remember is an aid to recall. When one is determined to remember, one's attention seems better concentrated and one tends to read more effectively.
5. Recall should be selective. One cannot hope to remember everything that one reads. The points that one really wants to remember should be singled out for special attention.
6. A single reading is rarely enough. Most people have to do some

[6] Lamkin, F. Duane, "An Analysis of Propaganda Techniques Used in *Why Johnny Can't Read*—Flesch," *The Reading Teacher,* Vol. 9, December, 1955, pp. 107–117.

reviewing and rereading if they want to remember for any length of time.

7. After reading, one should try to recall the points worth remembering and recite them to oneself. If there is time, it is desirable to check one's recall by rereading and then recite again. At least half of the time spent (after the first reading) in trying to fix the material in memory should be spent in active recitation. Omission of this procedure is one of the most frequent errors of those who complain about their poor memories.
8. What we learn but never review or use is gradually forgotten. What we really want to remember must be refreshed by review from time to time.

Poor memory for what one has read, then, results from unselective, passive reading in the first place, followed by an overoptimistic failure to review and recite to oneself the points one wishes to remember. Both of these major faults are correctible.

Some teachers encourage reading without the intent to recall by the kinds of reading practice they give and the kinds of questions they ask. In most workbook exercises, the child is free to look back into the material if he cannot remember the answer. Unless some practice is given in answering questions with the book closed or the page covered, the child may become excessively dependent upon rereading. He may also learn to read the questions first and then read for the answers, a desirable procedure in many situations, but not suitable when one is trying to stimulate the ability to recall. Excessive reliance upon multiple-choice or true-false questions may also be harmful to recall, since such questions require only recognition of the correct answer and pupils may become quite skillful at recognizing what they cannot remember. It is therefore important to ask recall questions, and to provide at least some practice in reading with the intent to reproduce the gist of the material.

II. The Development of Study Skills

In order to put to good use the different types of reading comprehension that have been discussed in the preceding section, the efficient reader must also develop other abilities which are more properly called study skills. It is not the purpose of this section to take up in detail the host of specific techniques that are known to the experienced teacher of a special subject, which are more properly to be found in books on special methods. Instead this section will concentrate upon three study problems which are of quite general importance: locating information, reading graphic and tabular material, and outlining and summarizing.[7]

Learning to Locate Information

The most widely used tool in finding information is the index, a great timesaver to those who know how to use it. At about the sixth-grade level, definite lessons in the use of an index should be provided. Teachers in higher grades can profitably devote time to the development of this study skill, if their pupils show the need of it.

In an introductory lesson on the use of an index, one should start with a problem to which an answer is desired; preferably one that can be found in an available textbook. Pupils can be asked to suggest headings under which the information might be classified. For instance, information on the number of cattle raised in Colorado during the year 1938 might be sought in a geography book under several headings: Cattle, production; Colorado, cattle raising in; Production, of cattle; Meat, sources of; Livestock; and so on. After the most probable heading has been chosen in discussion, the group looks for that heading in the index. The other headings suggested can also be checked. When page references have been found, the group turns to the page indicated and skims to find the specific information desired. Skill in locating items in an alphabetical order should already have been developed through dictionary work. After the general procedure has been learned, the teacher can make up a series of questions to be answered by use of the index, similar to those shown in Figure 54.

When the technique of using a book index has been fairly well mastered, the pupils should be encouraged to try their ability on the

[7] Harris, Albert J., "A Program for the Development of Study Skills in the Middle and Upper Grades," pp. 62–71, Proceedings of the *Conference on Reading*, University of Pittsburgh, 1951.

Directions. The answers to the questions in Column 2 are found in the index below. First read the question and then find the desired answer by looking under the proper topic in the index. Then locate your answer among the possible answers given with the question and fill in the answer space in the margin which is numbered the same.

Study the samples carefully before you try to answer the questions.

Look at Sample A. In the index under "Oregon" you will find the word "lumber" and the page reference, 173. 173 is second among the answers given with the question; so the second answer space has been filled in.

Look at Sample B. See if you can find the page reference in the index. The correct answer space is marked.

Answer the remaining exercises the same way.

Index

Africa: 19–27; deserts, 216; houses of central, 182; irrigation in northern, 138; map, 55; mountains, 232; Negroes in, 179–181; topography, 181–282.

Astronomy: 22–24; defined, 23; American astronomers, 24; Lowell Observatory, 76.

Botany: defined, 35; study of, 36–38.

California: deserts, 209; grapefruit, 135; irrigation, 135–136; olives, 139; oranges, 132, 134; peaches, 139; petroleum, 263; rainfall, 135; salmon, 204–205; sand dunes, 210; temperatures, 135; truck farming, 122.

Samples.

A. What page discusses lumbering in Oregon?
1 **138** 2 **173** 3 **92** 4 **98** 5 **185** . . A

B. What page gives information about fisheries in Germany?
1 **156** 2 **235** 3 **83** 4 **205** 5 **82** . . B

1. On what page is information given about irrigating land in northern Africa?
1 **19** 2 **55** 3 **138** 4 **179** 5 **216**. 1

5. Under what word in this index is a reference given to the growth of oranges in California?
1 **California** 2 **grapefruit** 3 **oranges**
4 **ranching** 5 **Texas**. 5

6. On what page can a definition of astronomy be found? 1 **20** 2 **21** 3 **22** 4 **23** 5 **24** 6

Fig. 54. Part of a test designed to measure proficiency in the use of an index. Teachers can use similar questions to give practice in the use of the index in subject-matter textbooks, encyclopaedias, etc. From the *Iowa Silent Reading Test: New Edition: Elementary: Form BM*. Reproduced by permission of World Book Co.

indexes of encyclopedias, almanacs, or atlases. The use of the card index in a library should also be taught. The skills required for locating entries to encyclopedias and bibliographic sources like the *Readers' Guide to Periodical Literature* are similar in the main to those involved in using a book index. A suitable teaching sequence should include: (1) knowledge of the kinds of information that can be found in the different types of reference works; (2) practice in thinking up several relevant headings or entries under which the information might be found; (3) in works of several volumes, how to choose the correct volume; and (4) the interpretation of abbreviations commonly employed.

The use of the table of contents of a book should also be taught. Many people, when they want to find an item in an book, turn to the table of contents, locate the chapter and section in which the desired information is likely to be found, and then skim rapidly until they locate the desired point. However, for those who really know how to employ a book index, that is the faster and more efficient procedure.

Reading Maps, Graphs, Charts, and Tables

It is often possible for an author to present a large amount of material concisely in visual form by means of a map, a graph, a chart, or a table. Teaching children how to interpret these efficient aids to understanding is the responsibility of the teacher in each subject field in which they are used. Entirely too many students today have the habit of skipping past anything of this sort with the briefest glance. Teachers-in-training at the college sophomore and junior level are frequently unable to interpret the visual reading matter in their education textbooks. It is worth the time it takes to develop in each subject an understanding of these types of nonverbal reading materials.

Graphical representations of various types are being increasingly used, and more definite provisions are being made for teaching the interpretation of common types of graphical representation. For example, a recent series of arithmetic texts devotes twenty-six pages at the seventh-grade level to the explanation of different types of graphs and charts. Map-reading has always been an important phase of geographical study. As new types of graphical reading matter become more widely used, teachers should provide practice in their interpretation.

Outlining and Summarizing

No skill is more essential to the student of today than the ability to write an effective summary of what he reads. When all of one's study is from a single textbook, written notes are not absolutely essential. But when one's study involves consulting a variety of sources, most of which are in a library and cannot easily be taken out again when one wants to review, a satisfactory summary is indispensable.

In addition to its value for review, note-taking performs a useful function in enforcing selective, thoughtful reading. In taking good notes one must try to select the major from the minor points, decide what is worth recording, consider the relation of one idea to another, and rephrase the author's idea into a condensed but accurate restatement in one's own words. Passive, thoughtless reading is impossible when one is taking good notes.

In modern elementary schools, summarizing is a natural activity from the first grade on. Each experience story used in beginning reading is a little summary. In the planning of units or projects, the results of class discussions are summarized and organized in terms of main headings, and the questions or topics to be investigated are listed under their appropriate headings. As committee or individual reports are made, their important points are inserted in the unit outline. When they reach the higher grades, these children have a background of familiarity with the concept of an organized summary which makes it a comparatively simple task to teach them to apply the idea in their reading.

In teaching a group of children to outline, one should use material of a factual or textbook nature which is well organized and has a definite structure that is easy to detect. Material from scientific or social studies textbooks is generally most suitable. There should, of course, be some preliminary discussion of the importance of being able to outline what one reads. The teacher can point out that an outline shows the relative importance of each idea or fact, its relation to the other facts and ideas, and its place in the whole selection; that it is, in effect, the skeleton or framework of ideas which the writer has dressed up by expressing it in well-written sentences and paragraphs. The skilled reader easily finds the framework, while appreciating the decoration; the unskillful reader fails to discover the pattern of the author's thinking, which is expressed by the outline of what he has written.

Once motivation has been established, the task of the teacher is to present a series of graded practice exercises in outlining, in which the pupils are given a great deal of help at first and proceed gradually to do more and more of the outline by themselves. For the first two or three practices, the teacher should place on the blackboard a complete outline of the selection. After the pupils read the selection, the outline is discussed. In this meaningful setting it is easy to explain the system of progressive indentation and the sequence of Roman numeral, capital letter, Arabic numeral, small letter, and so on. When the group has learned the plan of a formal outline, the second stage is to give them an outline in which the complete skeleton is shown, but only a few of the headings are filled in. After reading, each pupil completes the outline, and discussion follows. Figure 55 shows the kind of help given at this stage. In a third stage, the structure of the outline is given but no headings are filled in by the teacher. In stage four, only the number of main headings is given, and in the final stage the pupils write a complete outline without assistance.

In a teaching sequence of this sort, learning how to condense a sentence into a few words can be achieved naturally though discussion of the most satisfactory way to state a given point in the outline. Different statements can be compared as to clarity and conciseness, and the best ones selected. The writing of acceptable incomplete sentences, the leaving out of unnecessary words, and the writing of what is sometimes called "telegram style" can be taught naturally in this way.

It is desirable to teach the use of the formal outline before taking

HOW CLOTH IS MADE

I. The history of weaving

    A. Hand looms

        1.____________________

        2.____________________

        3.____________________

    B. Development of power looms

        1.____________________

        2.____________________

II. How cloth is made today

    A. A modern textile mill

        1.____________________

        2.____________________

    B. Modern fabrics

        1.____________________

        2.____________________

Fig. 55. Example of the kind of partially completed outline used in the second stage of teaching outlining.

up the use of informal reading notes. The essential difference between good reading notes and a formal outline is the absence of the number-and-letter scheme. Learning to make a formal outline, is, then, desirable as a preliminary. Once one has learned to think in outline terms, the trappings can be discarded without losing the ability to reduce what one reads to its essential structure. The writing of a précis, or paragraph-type summary, lacks the organizational structure which is so important, and therefore seems to this writer to be a less valuable technique than outlining, although desirable in summarizing certain types of narrative material.

In going over samples of reading notes taken by hundreds of college students, the writer has noted that two faulty patterns seem to account for most of the poor specimens. Some students get into their notes only the major headings, ignoring all or most of the details; for reviewing, such notes are of comparatively little value. Other students take voluminous notes, almost paraphrasing the author, and sometimes quoting at length; they write too much, waste words, and fail to see the structure because they get lost in the details. It seems probable that the notes taken reflect the method of reading. Those in the first group just hit the high spots. They are after the main ideas, and because they often do not bother to read carefully the explanatory and descriptive material which explains and enriches these ideas, their understanding is often superficial and inadequate. The other type of student does not try to grasp the logical pattern or outline of the author's thoughts, and therefore often misses important relationships, fails to distinguish a principle from its illustration, and comes out with an undifferentiated, unorganized mass of information that is not in shape for use. The correction of these faults is not entirely a matter of revising the method of writing notes; it has to start back with the faulty reading habits that are reflected in the poor notes.

III. Materials for Developing Comprehension

In addition to the workbooks which are correlated with specific basal readers, there are many workbooks which provide useful practice material of different types for the fostering and sharpening of comprehension skills. Some of them require the answers to be written in, so that a new copy must be supplied to each pupil. Others are arranged for repeated use, with the answers to questions written by the pupil on separate paper. The teacher who wants to become acquainted with workbooks and what they have to offer should order one copy of each workbook that seems possibly suited to his needs, and inspect the contents carefully to get a clear idea of what it has to offer. Even if he decides not to use it, he may get suggestions from it concerning types of practice exercises that he can devise for use in his class.

An increasing number of independent workbooks is available for use in the elementary school.

Bedwell, R. L., and Hutchinson, M., *My Own Reading Exercises.* Auburn, Alabama: Prather Publishing Co. Books 2, 3, 4, 5, and 6, for those grades. Each workbook contains a variety of useful exercises under the headings of vocabulary and comprehension, with some speed-practice selections.

Brueckner, L. J., and Lewis, W. D., *Diagnostic and Remedial Exercises in Reading.* Philadelphia: The John C. Winston Co. A workbook suitable for use with retarded readers able to read fourth-grade material. Contains several pretests which can be used for diagnostic purposes, and good practice exercises of many types: word recognition, vocabulary, phrasing, central thought, details, and rate.

Wagner, Guy L., *et al., Readers Digest Reading Skill Builders.* New York: Readers Digest Educational Service, Inc. Two workbooks at each grade from three to six inclusive. Similar to the adult magazine in appearance and contain selections from it that have been simplified and shortened, with vocabulary and comprehension questions. Adult format and content make these acceptable to retarded readers of any age.

Leavell, Ullin W., and Davis, Betty E., *Reading Essentials Series.* Austin, Texas: The Steck Co. *New Avenues of Reading* (grade four), *New Journeys in Reading* (grade five), *New Adventures in Reading* (grade six). Include a variety of exercises on word analysis and phonics, dictionary use, phrase reading, and several types of comprehension skills. The varied selections are carefully graded in difficulty and words at or above grade level are explained. Teachers' editions available.

Gates, Arthur I., and Peardon, C. C., *Practice Exercise in Reading.* New York: Bureau of Publications, Teachers College, Columbia University. This is a series of sixteen workbooks. There are four levels of difficulty: III, IV, V, and VI, corresponding roughly in difficulty to those grade levels. At each level, there are four booklets: Type A, Reading for General Significance; Type B, Reading to Predict Outcomes; Type C, Reading to Follow Directions; and Type D, Reading for Details. Each booklet contains only one type of exercise, designed to develop the skill indicated by its title. These booklets parallel the *Gates Silent Reading Tests* for grades three to eight. Manuals containing answer keys are available.

Stone, C. R., and Grover, C. C., *Practice Readers.* St. Louis: Webster

Last summer I visited a lifesaving station. It is so named because the men stationed there are ready to save the lives of those who are in danger on the sea. When a ship is wrecked near the coast in a storm, these guards go out to save the crew and passengers. They use a large motorboat, which is kept in one of the buildings. The boat is pushed out to the water on a low wheeled truck. The front wheels are taken away by the guards and the back ones drop away by themselves. Then the lifesavers jump into the boat and are off to help those in danger Every day they practice launching the boat quickly This helps them speed to the rescue when someone needs their help.

1. When the boat is launched, the guards take away the (a) back wheels (b) rear wheels (c) truck (d) front wheels
2. Last summer I visited a (a) lighthouse (b) boathouse (c) training station (d) lifesaving station
3. The boat the guards use is a (a) motorboat (b) large ship (c) fishing boat (d) rowboat
4. The boat is pushed out to the (a) sand (b) beach (c) water (d) rocks
5. The boat is kept (a) in one of the buildings (b) in part of the house (c) on the ground (d) on the water
6. What drop away? (a) runners (b) back wheels (c) front wheels (d) slidings
7. The guards practice every (a) month (b) year (c) day (d) hour
8. The lifesavers jump into the (a) water (b) seaweed (c) boat (d) sand
9. The guards save the (a) ship in danger (b) food in the boat (c) fish in the sea (d) lives of the people
10. A lifesaver's work involves (a) treachery (b) complacency (c) responsibility (d) honesty

No. right	0	1	2	3	4	5	6	7	8	9	10
G score	**1.0**	**1.4**	**1.9**	**2.4**	**3.0**	**3.5**	**4.0**	**4.6**	**5.2**	**5.8**	**6.5**

Fig. 56. An exercise to increase rate of comprehension. A time limit of 3 minutes is allowed for reading and answering questions. From McCall, William A., and Crabbs, Lelah M., *Standard Test Lessons in Reading,* Book C, p. 24. New York: Bureau of Publications, Teachers College, Columbia University. Reproduced by permission of the publishers.

Publishing Co. Books I, II, III, and IV. Book I is about fourth-grade level in difficulty. Each exercise consists of a one-page selection followed by a page of questions of six different kinds, including main ideas, details, implied ideas, and vocabulary. Answer keys, answer sheets, and manual available.

McCall, W. A., and Crabbs, L. M., *Standard Test Lessons in Reading*, Revised. New York: Bureau of Publications, Teachers College, Columbia University. Books A, B, C, D, and E, about third- to seventh-grade difficulty. Each booklet contains 78 one-page exercises, consisting of a short selection followed by multiple-choice questions, to be administered with a three-minute time limit. Rough grade norms are supplied which are useful as a basis for progress charts. A manual of directions including answer keys and special answer sheets are available. Widely used in remedial and corrective programs.

Johnson, Eleanor M., *Reading Skilltexts*. Columbus: Charles E. Merrill Co. *Nibs* (grade one), *Nicky* (grade two), *Uncle Funny Bunny* (grade three), *Uncle Ben* (grade four), *Tom Trott* (grade five), *Pat, the Pilot* (grade six). Short factual selections, each followed by questions on main idea, getting facts, drawing inferences, vocabulary, and word analysis. Answer keys available.

Johnson, E. M., ed., *Diagnostic Reading Workbooks*. Columbus, Ohio: Charles E. Merrill Co. A series of workbooks from first grade through sixth grade. Titles are as follows: *Nip, The Bear* (grade one), *Red Deer, The Indian Boy* (grade two), *Scottie and His Friends* (grade three), *Adventure Trails* (grade four), *Exploring Today* (grade five), *Looking Ahead* (grade six). Each exercise consists of a selection followed by several different kinds of questions: main ideas, details, implications, following directions, word recognition, word meaning, etc.; the nature of the questions changes with the grade. Answer keys are available.

Nelson, Anna C., *Four and Twenty Famous Tales*. Chicago: Hall & McCreary. Fables and tales with comprehension checks, about third-grade difficulty.

Mertz, H. A., *Forty Famous Stories*. Chicago: Hall & McCreary. Brief versions of old tales at about fourth-grade difficulty, followed by comprehension questions. Content excellent, format mediocre.

Mertz, H. A., *Washington to Lindbergh*. Chicago: Hall & McCreary. Brief stories about outstanding Americans, with comprehension questions; about fifth-grade difficulty.

At the junior high school level many of the workbooks listed above will be suitable for corrective or remedial work. In addition there are some designed specifically for junior high school use.

Leavell, Ullin W., and Bailey, Matilda, *The Mastery of Reading*. New York: American Book Co. Books 1, 2, and 3, for grades 7, 8, and 9. Each of eleven chapters concentrates on one major objective, such as speed, vocabulary, locating reference material, problem solving, and so on. Usable with pupils whose reading is about two years below grade level.

Wilkinson, H. S., and Brown, B. D., *Improving Your Reading*. New York: Noble & Noble, Publishers, Inc. A hard-cover book of 361 pages containing pretests, sections on word recognition, phonics, oral reading, phrasing, eye movements, vocabulary, comprehension, recall, locating information, and final tests. This book is a reservoir of useful practice material for retarded readers of fourth-grade level or higher.

Hovious, Carol, *Flying the Printways*. New York: D. C. Heath & Co. A hard-cover book in which each chapter stresses a different reading skill. Tests of comprehension and rate are included. Teachers manual and key available. Widely used in junior high corrective programs.

Knight, Pearle E., and Traxler, Arthur E., *Develop Your Realing*. Boston: Little, Brown & Co. A hard-cover reader for junior high school stressing a variety of comprehension skills.

Gainsburg, J. C., and Spector, S. I., *Better Reading*. New York: Globe Book Co. A hard-cover book providing exercises in a variety of comprehension skills, popular in junior high corrective programs.

Guiler, W. S., and Coleman, J. H., *Reading for Meaning*. Philadelphia: J. B. Lippincott Co. Books 6–12, one for each grade. Each exercise contains vocabulary in context and several types of comprehension questions.

At senior high school level the available materials include both paper-bound workbooks and hard-cover books. Among the most popular are the following:

Gray, William S., Horsman, Gwen, and Monroe, Marion, *Basic Reading Skills for High-School Use*. Chicago: Scott, Foresman. Intended for ninth-grade use with somewhat retarded readers, it includes a review of phonic and word analysis skills and a variety of comprehension exercises.

Simpson, Elizabeth A., *SRA Better Reading Books*. Chicago: Science Research Associates. Book 1 is of fifth- and sixth-grade difficulty; Book 2, for seventh and eighth grades; Book 3, ninth and tenth grades. Timed reading selections followed by comprehension questions.

Murphy, George, and Miller, Helen Rand, *Reading for Fun; Reading for Experience*. New York: Henry Holt & Co. Contain varied practice materials on vocabulary and comprehension.

Witty, Paul A., *How to Become a Better Reader*. Chicago: Science Research Associates. Discusses effective reading and provides practice material for rate, different types of comprehension, and vocabulary.

Salisbury, Rachel, *Better Work Habits.* Chicago: Scott, Foresman & Co. Unsurpassed materials to develop outlining, note-taking and organization.

Knight, Pearle E. and Traxler, Arthur E., *Read and Comprehend.* Boston: D. C. Heath & Co. A variety of comprehension skills are emphasized in different chapters.

Johnson, Eleanor M., *Modern Reading.* Columbus: Charles E. Merrill Co. A series of three workbooks, carrying the style of the *Reading Skill-texts* into the secondary school levels.

IV. Overcoming Deficiencies in Comprehension

As with other faults in reading, poor comprehension can result from a variety of causes, and the nature of the remedial work to be employed depends on a diagnostic analysis. Sometimes inability to comprehend well is a secondary result of a more basic difficulty, such as low intelligence, poor word recognition, or a deficient vocabulary, which has to be the starting point of planning. In other cases imperfect comprehension seems to be a primary difficulty and should be attacked directly. In the following discussion, each of a number of factors that sometimes interfere with comprehension will be discussed, and the nature of the remedial work needed will be indicated. Where several factors are present, a number of different types of remedial activities may need to be carried on at the same time.

Intellectual Limitations

The significance of intelligence as an indication of the level of difficulty at which a child can reasonably be expected to understand reading material has been discussed in previous chapters (see pp. 222–228, 299–302). Verbal intelligence is highly correlated with scores on reading tests like the *Stanford,* which perhaps should be called tests of reasoning in reading. The dull child tends to understand only the directly stated, literal meanings of what he reads; implications, subtleties, and abstractions are particularly hard for him to grasp. When working with the mentally limited it is necessary to adjust not only the difficulty of the material to their abilities, but also the types of questions one asks.

Word Recognition Difficulties

Poor comprehension is sometimes the direct result of the fact that the child cannot read the words. In these cases, specific work on developing a sight vocabulary, overcoming confusions between words, and teaching a method of independent attack on words results directly in improved comprehension.

One cannot rely too heavily on test scores for an analysis of the relation between word recognition and comprehension. For example, a dull fourteen-year-old boy made the following grade scores on reading tests:

Stanford Primary Reading Test, Form D	*Grade Equivalent*
Paragraph Meaning	2.4
Word Meaning	3.0
Gray Oral Reading Paragraphs	1.9
Gates Word Pronunciation Test	3.1

One might be tempted to assume, because his vocabulary and word recognition scores were higher than his paragraph comprehension and connected oral reading, that the immediate remedial problem is primarily one of comprehension with the word problem less important. Actually, this boy's recognition of words was a painfully slow phonetic attack. For instance, he solved the word *peach* by saying under his breath *ch, each, peach.* On the word recognition tests, of which one is untimed and the other has a generous time limit, this slowness did not prevent him from working out a considerable number of correct answers. In connected reading, however, he had to stop so often to puzzle over words that he lost the flow of language and thought in any but the simplest reading matter. Only by listening to him read orally could one find out what was the major difficulty in his reading. In the early stages of remedial work with this boy, major emphasis had to be placed on clearing up his word recognition difficulties before he could be considered ready for stress on comprehension.

Vocabulary Deficiencies

With some poor readers, a major reason for poor comprehension is a meager and hazy knowledge of the meanings of words. If this is due to a foreign-language handicap or a culturally unstimulating environment, it is to a large extent improvable. There is, however, a fairly close relationship between general verbal intelligence and vocabulary knowledge; those who are retarded in verbal intelligence are insensitive to finer shadings and differentiations of meaning, and have great difficulty in understanding words of abstract or generalized meanings. When a meager meaningful vocabulary seems to be a major stumbling block to better reading comprehension, work to increase vocabulary is advisable, along the lines described in Chapter XV. One should, however, expect improvement in size of general vocabulary to be comparatively slow and should recognize that a child's mental ability sets limits to his ability to understand words which connote difficult ideas.

Poor Language Background

In the discussion of reading readiness in Chapter II, the importance of the language patterns which the child hears at home and in his neighborhood was discussed as it related to beginning reading. As the child progresses into the more difficult reading of the upper grades and secondary school, familiarity with the language patterns used by well-educated people becomes even more important. Some children, like the bookish little heroine of *A Tree Grows in Brooklyn,* overcome the language deficiencies of an uncultured environment by engaging in extensive reading and becoming steeped in the language patterns used by writers. These are the exceptions; the typical child growing up in such an environment spends little time with books, and as he gets older has difficulty with advanced reading material because the language patterns become so different from those used in his everyday life. The school cannot overcome this problem altogether, but can lessen it by providing many opportunities and incentives for practice in speaking well and hearing good English spoken.

Poor Comprehension Resulting from Inappropriate Rate

Comprehension may suffer when the rate of reading is either too fast or too slow. Some inaccurate readers need to be temporarily slowed down until they reach a satisfactory standard of accuracy; when that result has been attained, they can gradually speed up again while maintaining the newly achieved precision. Some very slow readers do poorly in comprehension because their many repetitions and hesitations break up the continuity of thought. The relation between rate and comprehension, and the procedures that are effective in coordinating them, are treated in detail in Chapter XVIII. For practice materials, timed reading exercises with thorough comprehension checks are usually desirable. The McCall, Crabbs *Standard Test Lessons in Reading* and the *SRA Better Reading Books* are materials frequently used with this type of problem.

Poor Concentration

Unquestionably, inability to concentrate one's attention on the meaning of what one is reading is a very important reason for poor comprehension. But lack of ability to concentrate is itself a result of causes, a name for the fact that the individual is unable to adjust to the requirements of the reading situation. Inability to concentrate is not in itself an explanation. Before one can take practical measures, one should try to find out what the reasons are that make it difficult for the person to concentrate, and then try to eliminate them. The causes will usually be found in the answers to one or more of the following questions:

1. Does the person suffer from eyestrain? Eyestrain resulting from farsightedness, astigmatism, poor eye-muscle balance, and so on, is a frequent and often unsuspected cause of concentration difficulties. Examination by an eye specialist is a desirable routine procedure. People who wear glasses may need a changed prescription.
2. Is he physically below par? There are many physical conditions which lower vitality and impair the ability to exert effort. Among poor readers, one should pay special attention to undernourishment, insufficient sleep, and thyroid dysfunction as possible causes of difficulty.
3. Is he generally overworked Accumulating fatigue resulting from an

effort to carry too heavy a load may bring on a decline in ability to concentrate.

4. Is the material he is trying to read much too difficult for him? The children who can maintain good effort and concentration when working on very difficult material usually do not become remedial problems.
5. Is he interested in what he is trying to read? A marked improvement in concentration sometimes occurs when more interesting material is provided.
6. Does he read in suitable physical conditions? For efficient reading, one should sit upright or bending slightly forward in a straight-backed chair, with good, glareless lighting, in surroundings free from distracting sights and sounds. While some people can read very well in unfavorable surroundings, the poor reader should give himself the benefit of good working conditions.
7. Do other thoughts keep running through his mind? One's attention can be focused well on only one thing at a time. To read well, one must be able to exclude other thoughts for the time being. When questioning discloses that the reader's mind runs off on other things when he is supposed to be reading, one has to try to determine whether this is a superficial habit which can be broken, or a symptom of a deep-lying emotional difficulty which needs expert treatment.

Some children who are musically inclined find tunes "running through their heads" while they read. Once they become convinced that this inner musical accompaniment interferes with their reading efficiency, they can usually by a voluntary effort at least reduce its interfering effect.

A regrettably large number of students deliberately invite trouble by attempting to do their reading and studying with the radio or television set going.

The tendency to slide away into daydreams when reading is an insidious one and is not easy to overcome. Easy, interesting reading matter helps. A very specific goal – so many pages to be finished within a time limit – also helps. The child who is interested in improving his concentration sometimes benefits by making a tally mark every time he finds his thoughts wandering, and recording on a progress chart the declining number of tallies.

In some cases, there seems to be a real obsessive trend. The child is bothered by ideas that are persistent and unwelcome, which seem to have a strong existence of their own and seem to resist all efforts to banish them from his mind. These thoughts may involve ideas of fear, shame or guilt, morbid speculations about sex, family relationships, death, horror scenes from movies, and so on. The treatment of a condition like this is best left to a psychiatrist.

In helping a child to develop better concentration, it is sometimes desirable to start with very small units. Two or three minutes of intensive silent reading is followed by discussion of the meaning of the material, and then a brief period of relaxation, before another practice exercise is tried. For work of this type, exercises such as are found in the *Practice Readers* and *Standard Test Lessons in Reading* can be used to very good advantage. When proficiency is attained in handling brief assignments of this type, longer selections can be gradually introduced.

Difficulties in Specific Types of Comprehension

In the first section of this chapter, several different kinds of comprehension skills were described, and the procedures that are useful for developing these skills in normal developmental reading lessons were discussed. If a teacher finds that a whole class is weaker in one or two of these skills than in the others, he will naturally try to provide corrective practice to develop the weaker skills. The same principle applies if the weakness is found in only a few pupils, or in a single pupil. With differentiated teaching methods it should, for example, be possible to give one group extra practice in reading for details and another group extra practice in getting a balanced comprehension program.

In general, remedial work for a specific comprehension skill can be of the same types as are used to develop that skill in normal readers. The use of published practice material in workbook form often reduces the teacher's burden, and allows the assignment of special types of reading practice that otherwise would be impracticable if the teacher had to rely entirely on practice material of his own construction. A file of comprehension exercises, classified by type as selecting main idea, reading for details, following directions, and the like, allows individualized teaching of comprehension skills and the assignment of extra practice in any kind of comprehension skill in which a pupil may be weak. Such a file can also include exercises made up by the teacher to supply types of practice that are not provided adequately in available workbooks.

Many of the shortcomings in comprehension that are discovered in the upper grades are caused, not by any particular difficulty in learning, but by the absence of any previous instruction to develop the missing skills. What is frequently called remedial work in comprehension turns out, in these cases, to be nothing but delayed first teaching.

In these two chapters the problems of developing understanding in reading have been surveyed. Much attention was given to vocabulary development, since word meanings are the raw materials of communication through print. Skill in gaining meaning from phrases and sentences usually develops in the context of a good developmental program, but may require corrective or remedial attention when the child becomes a word-by-word reader or has difficulty in following the thought pattern in complex sentences. Specific practice is needed in several different kinds of thoughtful reading, and systematic planning should be devoted to the sequential teaching of basic study skills. In the analysis of comprehension disabilities one has to analyze the reasons for defective understanding, and the remedial procedures must be selected accordingly.

Suggested Additional Reading

BOND, GUY L., and EVA BOND WAGNER. *Teaching the Child to Read*, Revised Edition, Chs. 13–15.

BROOM, M. E., *et al.*, *Effective Reading Instruction*, Second Edition, Ch. 8.

DURRELL, DONALD D. *Improvement of Basic Reading Abilities*, Chs. 7, 10.

MCKEE, PAUL. *The Teaching of Reading in the Elementary School*, Chs. 12–16.

RUSSELL, DAVID H. *Children Learn to Read,* Ch. 11.

TRAXLER, ARTHUR E. *The Improvement of Study Habits and Skills*, Revised Edition. Educational Records Bulletin, No. 41. New York: Educational Records Bureau, 21 Audubon Ave., New York 32, 1954.

YOAKAM, GERALD A. *Basal Reading Instruction,* Ch. 12.

· XVII ·

Fostering Reading Interests and Tastes

NEARLY EVERY STUDY of adult reading interests and tastes shows a tremendous consumption of fiction of inferior quality, a generally low level of popular taste, and a comparatively small number of people who read serious works of good quality. There are millions of adults in America whose voluntary reading is confined to newspapers, cheap magazines, and books (if they read books at all) of the murder mystery, Western adventure, and trashy love-story varieties. About half of the adult population rarely if ever read a book. About 70 per cent of the total reading of books is done by one-fifth of the population; only 30 per cent by the other four-fifths.[1] The long-time trends are somewhat more encouraging, since there is clear evidence that more good books, as well as more inferior ones, are being read today than ever before; but the room for improvement is tremendous.

Today's children are tomorrow's adults, and the reading habits, interests, and tastes formed during childhood determine to a great extent the adult reading patterns of the future. Building a lasting interest in reading, and developing an appetite for what is worth reading, are two objectives that have tremendous long-range signifi-

[1] Link, Henry C., and Hopf, Harry, *People and Books: A Study of Reading And Book-Buying Habits.* New York: Book Industry Committee, Book Manufacturers' Institute, 1946.

cance. Of what value is it to develop skillful readers, if the skill is used to little purpose in adult years? A good reading program must create the desire to read and help the individual to find pleasurable recreation in reading. It should also foster the desire to read for personal development, to learn more about the world, and to gain increasing understanding of people and society.

I. The Reading Interests of Children

Children who are beginning to read enjoy short, fanciful stories involving talking animals, fairies, and other mythical creatures. They also like realistic stories about children, with elements of surprise and humor. Interest in the fanciful usually increases until the age of eight or nine, and then gradually declines. During the primary grades sex differences in reading interests are not very marked. By the age of nine or ten, however, definite sex differences are apparent. Boys become absorbed in adventure and mystery tales. They also read fictionalized history and biography, and many of them read extensively on mechanics, science, invention, and material related to hobbies. Girls enjoy sentimental stories of home and school life, and usually develop an interest in romantic fiction between the ages of eleven and fourteen. They share the boys' liking for mystery and adventure, but usually do not care for reading related to science and invention. The boys, on the other hand, tend to ignore the human interest stories which are feminine favorites, and in general avoid anything that seems definitely feminine. Most children enjoy the "comics," both in newspapers and in the "comic book" form. There are frequently marked differences between what children want to read and what teachers and librarians recommend; many of the books which have been selected by adult committees as the best children's book of the year have been neglected on library shelves.[2]

[2] For summaries of the research on reading interests, see:
Terman, Lewis M., and Lima, Margaret, *Children's Reading*. New York: D. Appleton-Century-Crofts, 1937.
Rankin, Marie, *Children's Interests in Library Books of Fiction*. Contributions to Education, No. 906. New York: Bureau of Publications, Teachers College, Columbia University, 1944.

Voluntary reading usually increases in amount until the age of twelve or thirteen. In some schools there is a marked decline in voluntary reading which coincides in time with both increasing homework and the teaching of literature. In other schools, teachers are successful in maintaining the amount of voluntary reading and in helping adolescents toward mature tastes.

The reading interests of children do not correspond very closely to their felt needs for information. In a study involving 6,313 children, 4,531 parents, 212 teachers, and 169 librarians, it was found that children frequently turned to sources of information other than reading when they needed information, and regarded reading primarily as a recreational activity. Among the different fields of interest science was highest, and mystery, adventure, and stories about horses, dogs, and children also ranked high.[3]

In a study of data collected from 50,000 pupils in grades seven to twelve by 625 teachers, Norvell[4] found the special factors which aroused boys' interests to be: adventure (outdoor adventure, war, scouting), outdoor games, school life, mystery (including detective stories), obvious humor, animals, patriotism, and male characters. Unfavorable factors for boys were: love, other sentiments, home and family life, didacticism, religion, the reflective, extended description, "nature," form or technique as a dominant factor, and female characters. The special factors favorable to reading interest for girls were: adventure without grimmness, humor, animals, patriotism, love, other sentiments, home and family life, male and female characters. Unfavorable for girls were: grim adventure, extended description, didacticism, form or technique as a dominant factor, and "nature." Boys tended to give favorable ratings to novels, plays, short stories, and biographies of men; girls also rated these favorably and added biographies of women. Girls generally gave essays

---

Dunlop, Doris C., "Children's Leisure-Reading Interest," *Studies in Reading*, Vol. 2, pp. 81–105. Publications of the Scottish Council for Research in Education, XXXIV. London: University of London Press, 1950.

[3] Rudman, Herbert C., "The Informational Needs and Reading Interests of Children in Grades IV through VIII," *Elementary School Journal*, Vol. 55, 1955, pp. 502–512.

[4] Norvell, George W., *The Reading Interests of Young People*. Boston: D. C. Heath & Co., 1950.

and poems higher ratings than boys did. The reading materials commonly used in literature classes were liked better by girls than by boys by a more than two to one ratio.

On the whole, bright children read much more than the average child, have a wider range of reading interests, and are usually a year or two ahead of the average child in interest maturity. The mentally slow child reads less and generally has preferences which are slightly immature for his age, but more mature than those of younger children of his mental level.[5] At the secondary school level, however, little relationship was found between IQ level and liking for specific selections.[6]

Probably the most important single finding about reading interests, however, is the tremendous range of individual differences both in amount of voluntary reading and in the specific interests that are expressed. Even in a group of children who are similar in intelligence, age, and cultural background, the range of individual preferences is tremendous. While a knowledge of the general trends is helpful to a teacher in allowing him to anticipate the interests of his pupils, it does not relieve him of the responsibility of trying to discover the particular interests of each pupil.

Factors Influencing Reading Preferences

Quite a few years ago, Goodykoontz summarized the available evidence concerning illustrations in children's books as follows: (1) Children like books that have at least one quarter of the total page space devoted to pictures. (2) They prefer large pictures. (3) They prefer strong colors to black-and-white or to delicate pastel colors. (4) They like bold central groups, with few but striking details. (5) They prefer realistic to conventionalized pictures.

[5] Lazar, May, *Reading Interests, Activities, and Opportunities of Bright, Average, and Dull Children,* Contributions to Education, No. 707. New York: Bureau of Publications, Teachers College, Columbia University, 1937.

Thorndike, Robert L., *Children's Reading Interests.* New York: Bureau of Publications, Teachers College, Columbia University, 1941.

Lewis, W. D., and McGehee, W., "A Comparison of the Interests of Mentally Superior and Retarded Children," *School and Society,* Vol. 52, 1940, pp. 597–600.

[6] Norvell, George W., *op. cit.,* p. 5.

(6) They prefer pictures which show action or humor and tell a story. (7) Young children like a broader range of subject matter than they usually receive. (8) Young children do not care especially for pictures of child activities. (9) Older children like pictures related to in-school and informational activities.[7]

Since that summary was made, marked changes have taken place in the illustrations used in readers. Colorful covers have become general. Boxed-in small pictures have given way to pictures without definite margins, which sometimes spread across two pages. Line drawings with flat, primary colors have been supplanted by more lifelike pictures employing shading and a wide range of attractive tints. Illustrations occupy a greater proportion of the total page space and are more carefully integrated with the story. Fourth-grade children prefer illustrations that have a definite center of interest, are colored, and depict action.[8] Children prefer realistic pictures in color, but will choose a realistic black-and-white picture over a less realistic colored one.[9]

Accessibility and availability have a marked influence on children's choices.[10] The use of a public library by children is directly related to the distance of the library from the child's home and school. Increasing recognition of the importance of accessibility has been one of the major factors in the building up of library collections within schools. Each classroom in a well-equipped school today has a library collection of its own. Many elementary schools, as well as most secondary schools, have a central library collection, and the number of positions for librarians in schools has increased. Traveling libraries have been created to provide better library service to rural schools. In cities and towns, loan systems have become common by which a teacher can borrow a large assortment

[7] Goodykoontz, B., "The Relation of Pictures to Reading Comprehension," *Elementary English Review*, Vol. 13, 1936, pp. 125–128.

[8] Whipple, Gertrude, "Appraisal of the Interest Appeal of Illustrations," *Elementary School Journal*, Vol. 53, 1953, pp. 262–269.

[9] Rudisill, Mabel, "Children's Preferences for Color versus Other Qualities in Illustrations," *Elementary School Journal*, Vol. 52, 1952, pp. 444–451.

[10] Russell, D. H., "Reading Preferences of Younger Adolescents in Saskatchewan," *English Journal*, Vol. 30, 1941, pp. 131–136.

of books from a public library, and replace it with different books from time to time.

Children's preferences are influenced markedly by the attitudes of their teachers. In one study it was found that the book for which the teacher showed most enthusiasm was generally the one that the class came to like best.[11] Children's preferences are also influenced by the opinions of their friends, and to a lesser degree by the opinions of members of the family.

The Television Menace

A great many teachers believe, with some justice, that the main reason why their pupils do little or no reading at home is television. According to 1955 data, the average number of hours per week spent in watching television was, for different groups: elementary school pupils, 23.7; high school students, 14.3; parents, 21.2; and teachers, 12.5.[12] It may be reasonably concluded that three hours a day, which is a rough average for the elementary school, is excessive. The lure of TV was succinctly expressed by one youngster: "'It gives you stories like a book, pictures like movies, voices like radio, and adventure like a comic. Television has action while you stay in one spot.'"[13] As Witty and Shayon both point out, television is filling otherwise unmet needs in a somewhat satisfactory fashion. Regulating the amount of time spent in watching, while highly desirable if it can be carried out by the parents, does not solve the problem. A comprehensive approach would require improving community recreational facilities, working with parents to develop more active and creative forms of recreation in the home, helping children to develop and apply criteria for evaluating and selecting TV programs, and using television experiences as a background for motivating and enriching reading.

[11] Wightman, H. J., "A Study of Reading Appreciation," *American School Board Journal,* Vol. 50, 1915, p. 42.

[12] Witty, Paul A., "Children and TV: A Sixth Report," *Elementary English,* Vol. 32, 1955, pp. 469–476.

[13] Shayon, Robert L., *Television and Our Children,* p. 29. New York: Longmans, Green & Co., 1951.

Before the advent of television, the failure of many children to read at home was blamed on radio, the movies, and comic books. The comics will be discussed below. Both movies and radio now take up less of children's time than they did before TV, and much less is heard about their deleterious effects. Incidentally, research seems to indicate that listening to radio music while studying or taking a silent reading test does not interfere with efficient functioning, while listening to a variety program does interfere.[14] The fact is that if a child doesn't like to read he will find other things to do with his spare time, and if he loves to read he will find time for reading no matter what competing attractions there are. If a child finds reading to be easy, interesting, and accessible, we will not need to blame the mass media for capturing and holding his attention.

The Comics Problem

Many teachers are concerned over the great interest shown by children in the so-called "comic books," most of which contain adventure tales or portray the exploits of a superhuman character, while few make any attempt at humor. Practices range from that of the teacher who tears up each comic book that he finds in his classroom to that of the teacher who helps his pupils to set up a cooperative lending library of comic books. The interest in this problem is shown by the fact that already more than forty professional articles have been published about it.

Several studies have shown that reading comic books and the comic strips in newspapers is one of the most common leisure-time activities of children in grades four through six. Witty found that boys read more of them than girls do, and that a typical boy in these grades reads four comic books regularly, four others quite often, and another six occasionally; the average girl reads one or two regularly, two or three often, and another seven or eight occa-

[14] Mitchell, Adelle H., "The Effect of Radio Programs on Silent Reading Achievement of 91 Sixth Grade Students," *Journal of Educational Research*, Vol. 42, 1949, pp. 460–470.

sionally.[15] At least one child psychiatrist has said that the effect of reading the more violent comics is often more beneficial than harmful, because it gives the children some vicarious expression for their aggressive and hostile impulses.[16] Similarly a noted sociologist has challenged the notion that because delinquents read comic books, comic books cause delinquency.[17]

The amount of distorted spelling and poor English is not as great as most teachers believe; Hill found that only 5.4 per cent of the words in sixteen popular comic strips were distorted and doubted that there is any harm to children's vocabulary or spelling.[18] The reading difficulty of the printed matter in comics seems to be generally of fifth- or sixth-grade level.[19] On the whole, the research available does not seem to justify an alarmist point of view. Some improvement in the quality and moral implications of the most popular comics has accompanied the appointment of professional educators as advisors to some of the publishers of comic books.

It is futile, even if it were possible, to try to prevent children from reading the comics. Instead, one should attempt to help them to discriminate between the better and poorer types, and to use their comic book reading as a springboard toward the reading of stories and books that will satisfy the same interests at a higher level. The inclusion of freedom to criticize and compare comic books during a book-club meeting provides a basis for developing a group opinion which almost inevitably will frown on the worst specimens. The better ones, such as *True Comics* and *Classic Comics*, can be safely allowed a place in the classroom library. In the upper grades, a skillful teacher can lead the more voracious readers of comics into

[15] Witty, P., "Reading the Comics—A Comparative Study," *Journal of Experimental Education*, Vol. 10, 1941, pp. 105–109.

[16] Bender, Lauretta, and Lowrie, R. S., "The Effect of Comic Books on the Ideology of Children," *American Journal of Orthopsychiatry*, Vol. 11, 1941, p. 540.

[17] Thrasher, Frederick M., "The Comics and Delinquency: Cause or Scapegoat," *Journal of Educational Sociology*, Vol. 23, 1949, pp. 195–205.

[18] Hill, G. E., "Word Distortion in Comic Strips," *Elementary School Journal*, Vol. 43, 1943, pp. 520–525.

[19] Thorndike, R. L., "Words and the Comics," *Journal of Experimental Education*, Vol. 10, 1941, pp. 110–113.

reading books of the *Tom Swift* and *Tarzan* varieties and later to Jules Verne, H. Rider Haggard, and H. G. Wells. Anything to which children respond as enthusiastically as they do to comic books must have educational values that can be developed. The comic books of today may be pointing the way to the textbooks of the future.

Interest and Difficulty

Few people, whether children or adults, can really enjoy reading a book that taxes their skill. One of the reasons why so many children place reading low down on the list of their leisure-time activities is that, for the most part, the books which they have been given to read have been too difficult to allow easy and enjoyable reading.

Many a teacher finds that he has been given books to use as texts and readers which seem to be much too difficult for his pupils. When that happens the teacher must do the best he can with inadequate materials. Such a situation is all too prevalent in public schools, and is probably one of the reasons why normal development of reading skills is not more commonly achieved. The need for adequate reading materials is even more important for a remedial teacher. To handicap him with improperly chosen materials is to saddle him with a burden that he can carry only by the unnecessary expenditure of a great deal of effort.

In general, retarded readers should be given reading material which is not more difficult than the grade level at which they can read successfully. At the beginning of remedial treatment it is often desirable to give them materials which are at their independent reading level rather than at their instructional reading level. This insures successful reading from the beginning of the remedial work, and thus tends to stimulate effort. It also gives opportunity for fluent reading and for paying attention to thought getting — something which is overshadowed when much attention has to be devoted to the mastery of new vocabulary.

An inspection of the primary-grade books in seven currently popular series of basal readers shows very marked differences in vocabulary. The total number of new words introduced in the first grade varies from 235 to 375, with a median of 336; in second grade, from 296 to 663, with a median of 431; in third grade, from 480 to 956, with a median of 792; and in total for the three grades, from 1105 to 1955, with a median of 1575. If one fourth reader assumes a previous knowledge of 1900 words and another of only 1100 words, how similar can they be in difficulty? Differences in other factors which influence difficulty, such as sentence length, use of compound and complex sentences, paragraph structure, length and complexity of selections, and familiarity or strangeness of concepts, are also striking, but sometimes a book which is difficult according to one criterion is easy according to another.

Despite the pressure from teachers for simpler instructional materials, textbooks in the content fields continue to be difficult reading matter for the majority of children in the grades for which they are intended. Even when the vocabulary is not excessively difficult, the tendency to try to cram in as many facts as possible creates a "concept density" which makes for difficult reading.[20]

Estimating the Difficulty of Reading Material

Several different methods are employed in estimating the difficulty of the vocabularies of books. Most of them involve hours of laborious work for each book, and so are feasible only for a research worker who is able to devote the necessary time and effort. Fortunately there are many studies in print in which one can look up the difficulty of specific books. References to them will be found in the next section.

A classroom teacher who has had experience in several grades can usually form a rough estimate of the difficulty of a book by reading it through and studying a few of the pages carefully. In evaluating basal readers he will find the page-by-page lists of new words given in many recently published books to be helpful. The teacher should, however, check his personal impression by consult-

[20] Serra, Mary C., "The Concept Burden of Instructional Materials," *Elementary School Journal,* Vol. 53, 1953, pp. 508–512.

Mallinson, George G., Sturm, Harold E., and Mallinson, Lois M., "The Reading Difficulty of Textbooks in Junior High School Science," *School Review,* Vol. 58, 1950, pp. 536–540.

ing published studies of the difficulty of books whenever such lists are available.

In choosing a book for an individual child the teacher can estimate its difficulty by having the child read a few sample selections from the book and tell her which words he does not know. A book intended to provide practice in fluent reading of easy material should not have an average of more than two or three words in a hundred running words that are unknown to the child. Work-type materials may be satisfactory if not more than five out of one hundred running words are unfamiliar.

Research workers usually start their analysis of the vocabulary of a book by making a list of all the words used in it and the number of times each word is used. The word count can then be analyzed in a variety of ways. Commonly two or more of the following types of information are obtained:

1. The total number of words in the book. This is simply a measure of the length of the book.
2. The total number of different words used. The larger the number of different words, the more difficult the book tends to be.
3. The degree of repetition employed. The average repetition per word is obtained by dividing the total number of words by the number of different words. The higher the average repetition, the easier the book is.
4. The per cent of the words in a book that are used only a small number of times. The lower this per cent is, the easier the book.
5. The proportion of the words in a book that have been used in books previously read. This kind of information is extremely valuable for a teacher who wants to select a list of books to be read in sequence.
6. The proportion of the vocabulary of a book that is included in standard lists of common words. In general, the higher this proportion is, the more useful the book will be as a preparation for later reading.
7. The per cent of words of more than one syllable, or the number of syllables per hundred words.

Several formulas have been worked out by means of which the difficulty of a book or selection can be rated and given a numerical score, usually in terms of grade level. At primary-grade levels the most practical formulas are those devised by Spache[21] and

[21] Spache, George, "A New Readability Formula for Primary-Grade Reading Materials," *Elementary School Journal,* Vol. 53, 1953, pp. 410–413.

Wheeler.[22] Of the formulas appropriate for middle and upper grades, the Dale-Chall Formula is in highest favor, with several other usable formulas available.[23] The revised Flesch formulas have been widely employed in the rating of adult reading materials.[24]

II. Methods of Determining Reading Interests

Many elaborate techniques have been used in research studies on reading interests. Circulation data for newspapers and magazines have been compiled, the popularity of books has been studied by counting the number of times each was withdrawn from a library, and elaborate questionnaires have been used. Most of these methods are too complicated and time-consuming for use by the classroom teacher. Simpler methods are needed for general use.

One of the simplest and most effective ways of finding out a child's interests is to watch his daily behavior for indications of interests that could be followed up in reading. In schools in which children are encouraged to be spontaneous, they display their interests in many ways: in conversation, in play, in drawing, and in other activities that encourage self-expression. Donald's interest in aviation shows in his drawings and in the many airplane models that he builds. Lillian's interest in playing nurse can lead to reading a biography of Clara Barton. Tommy's devoted care of the class's rabbits suggests the reading of books of animal stories. The alert teacher can find many leads concerning possible reading interests by observing his children.

A second useful procedure is to arrange for a "hobby club" period,

[22] Wheeler, Lester R., and Smith, Edwin H., "A Practical Readability Formula for the Classroom Teacher in the Primary Grades," *Elementary English,* Vol. 31, 1954, pp. 397–399.

[23] Dale, Edgar, and Chall, Jeanne S., "A Formula for Predicting Readability," *Educational Research Bulletin,* Ohio State University, Vol. 27, 1948, pp. 11–20, 28, 37–54.

Russell, David H., and Fea, Henry R., "Validity of Six Formulas as Measures of Juvenile Fiction," *Elementary School Journal,* Vol. 52, 1951, pp. 136–144; this article is a good starting point for one who wishes to explore these formulas, and provides additional references.

[24] Flesch, Rudolph, "A New Readability Yardstick," *Journal of Applied Psychology,* Vol. 32, 1948, pp. 221–233.

or a period in which each child has a chance to tell about the things he likes to do in his spare time. This not only informs the teacher about the leisure-time activities enjoyed by the pupils, but also helps to popularize certain interests. An enthusiastic report about stamp collecting, a home aquarium, or some other hobby may start several other children on the same activity. Groups with similar hobbies can be established, and special reading matter supplied for each group.

A third useful procedure is to arrange for a quiet interview with each child. During the interview the teacher can encourage the child to talk about his likes and dislikes in games, movies, radio programs, the books he has read, what he wants to be when he grows up, and so on. Naturally the teacher must be liked and trusted by the children if he wants them to confide in him. The preparation of a mimeographed record form helps to keep such interviews fairly uniform in terms of the questions asked, and provides a convenient way of recording information. With large classes, it is often impractical to attempt to interview all of the pupils.

Finally, one can use questionnaires. Two kinds of questionnaires are shown. The check list in Figure 57 is useful for getting a comprehensive idea of the recreational interests of children. It can be used, as a group test, in grades three through nine. With poor readers, it may be necessary to read the items to the class. Earlier editions of this check list were used in several child study projects by the staff of the City College Educational Clinic and proved quite helpful. The questionnaire shown in Figure 58 was developed for use in secondary school remedial reading programs, but can be used as low as the fourth grade. It provides a detailed picture of reading interests, and also discloses interesting sidelights on emotional maturity.

An Example of Questionnaire Results

The interest and Activity Poll questionnaire shown in Figure 58 was used in three high school remedial reading classes. The boys in those classes were mainly of Negro or Latin-American descent; most of them were fifteen years old, had IQ's between 70 and 90, and were

THE CITY COLLEGE EDUCATIONAL CLINIC
RECREATIONAL ACTIVITIES CHECK LIST
By H.H.Abelson and A.J.Harris

Name.................................... Boy or Girl............ Age...........

School..................... Class........................... Date............

Directions: This is a list of things that some boys and girls like to do. Read each one. If you never do that thing, make a line through it. If you like to do it, make a check (✓) on the dotted line. If you like to do it very much, make two checks on the dotted line.

....

.... 1.Playing tag
.... 2.Cops and robbers
.... 3.Ring-o-levio
.... 4.Follow the leader
.... 5.Hide and seek

.... 6.Playing potsy
.... 7.Hop Scotch
.... 8.Jumping Rope
.... 9.Going on swings
....10.Roller skating

....11.Stickball
....12.Baseball
....13.Basketball
....14.Football
....15.Handball

....16.Swimming
....17.Going for walks
....18.Riding a bicycle
....19.Flying a kite
....20.Walking in the woods

....21.Going to a museum of art
....22.Going to a concert
....23.Listening to the radio
....24.Going to the movies
....25.Watching an athletic game

....26.Pitching pennies
....27.Just loafing
....28.Making bonfires
....29.Shooting dice
....30.Teasing

....31.Taking things apart
....32.Playing with electrical toys
....33.Building model planes or ships
....34.Experimenting with chemicals
....35.Making things with tools

....36.Modelling with clay
....37.Drawing and painting pictures
....38.Singing
....39.Playing a musical instrument
....40.Woodcarving or leathercraft

....41.Knitting or crocheting
....42.Sewing clothes
....43.Cooking or baking
....44.Making fudge or candy
....45.Stringing beads

....46.Playing card games
....47.Playing checkers
....48.Playing Monopoly
....49.Playing guessing games
....50.Playing Lotto or Bingo

....51.Playing with dolls
....52.Playing school
....53.Playing house
....54.Playing doctor or nurse
....55.Playing actor or actress

....56.Reading comic books
....57.Reading story books
....58.Reading fairy tales
....59.Reading sports stories
....60.Reading scientific stories

....61.Going to the library
....62.Writing letters
....63.Studying
....64.Keeping a diary
....65.Writing poems or stories

....66.Making a scrap-book
....67.Collecting stamps or coins
....68.Collecting shells or butterflies
....69.Keeping things neat
....70.Going to a museum of natural history

....71.Visiting relatives
....72.Visiting a friend
....73.Going to a party
....74.Just talking
....75.Being with a club or gang

....76.Social dancing
....77.Having a date
....78.Driving a car
....79.Playing postoffice
....80.Being with a group of boys & girls

....81.Being the leader of a group
....82.Arguing with someone
....83.Discussing politics
....84.Having a fight
....85.Being in a debate

Write in any other things you like to do
....
....
....
....

Fig. 57. A check list that can be used to study the recreational activities of elementary-school children. It can be administered to a class at a time. In the second, third, and fourth grades, it is advisable to read each item to the class. This check list may be reproduced in mimeographed form by teachers.

reading at fifth- or sixth-grade level. The findings have been summarized elsewhere [25] and are reproduced in part as follows:

A new questionnaire was constructed. It contains many questions which have been used before, with some new ones added. One of the new procedures, which seemed to be effective, was to provide a list of imaginary book titles and ask the subject to indicate which he would like to read and which he would dislike. The examiner read each question out loud, waited until all had answered it and helped with spelling when necessary, and then went on to the next item. In this way even the poorest readers were able to complete the questionnaire.

The results provide interesting information concerning the group. In certain individual cases the questionnaire was revealing and helpful. While there are always opportunities for misrepresentation in answering a questionnaire, it is believed that these boys took this questionnaire seriously and answered with a high degree of honesty and candor. An occasional response may have been facetious, and some falsification in reporting the amount and types of reading done is probable.

Leisture Time. Sports were the favorite leisure-time activities, being mentioned 48 times. Movies were second. Handwork such as building model planes was third. Reading books, social activities involving girls, traveling, visiting, listening to the radio, playing pool, playing cards, playing musical instruments, collecting stamps, eating, and "combing my hair" were also mentioned.

Reading. Thirteen of the boys said that they do not read comic books. For the other 32 boys, the median number of comic books read each week is 3, with 11 boys reporting 5 or more. The boys named 32 different titles, with *Batman, Superman, Captain Marvel,* and *True Comics* the most popular.

The magazines most frequently mentioned were *Life* and *Look,* both picture magazines. Altogether 17 magazines were mentioned, including *Esquire, Saturday Evening Post, Collier's, Reader's Digest, Popular Science, Time, Sports Stories, True Story, True Confessions.* The things liked best in magazines were pictures, stories, and war news; advertisements were liked least.

Seventeen boys reported that they had read no books just for fun during the preceding three months. The other 28 boys reported a median of 3 books read, with 6 boys reporting having read 5 or more. There was a

[25] Harris, Albert J., and Sternberg, W., "An Analysis of the Characteristics of Pupils in Three Remedial Reading Classes at the High School Level," *High Points,* Vol. 26, No. 7, September, 1944, pp. 43–59.

very wide range of titles, including *For Whom The Bell Tolls, Lover's Stroll, Moby Dick, Robin Hood, Lassie Come Home,* and *Guadalcanal Diary.* The truthfulness of answers in this section of the questionnaire seems to be decidedly open to question.

When the group was given a list of 42 fictitious titles and asked to indicate their likes and dislikes, marked individual differences appeared. The number indicating liking for a title ranged from 3 to 33, showing that discrimination was present. When the titles were classified under seven headings, the rank order of liking, from most to least, was: War Stories, Murder and Crime, Sport, Adventure and Exploration, How to Make Things, Science, and Love. When they were asked to check directly the kinds of stories they like to read, the group displayed somewhat less discrimination. The rank order of preference was in substantial agreement by both methods, with a correlation of .57. The use of specific titles, however, gave a more concrete and definite picture of actual preferences than the use of more general categories and seemed to be the better technique.

Counting first and second choices together, by far the most popular newspaper is the *Daily News,* with the *Times, Mirror, Journal-American* and *P.M.* following in that order. Attention is paid mainly to sports news, comic strips, and war news, in that order. ***No attention is paid to political news, commentators, or editorials.***

Movies and Radio. Eleven boys go to the movies more than twice a week, 20 go twice a week, 9 go once a week, and 5 go less often than once a week. Three quarters of the group like adventure, war and murder mystery pictures; more than half like musicals, comedies, Westerns and cartoons; less than one third indicate a liking for sad stories, love stories, or travel pictures. Of 67 different favorite pictures listed, pictures about the war formed an overwhelming majority, involving 54 choices.

Time spent listening to the radio ranges from 0 to 48 (!) hours a week; the median number of hours is 15. Comedy and mystery programs are the favorites with popular music in third place, and news, quiz programs, and plays far behind. Only 3 boys listed juvenile programs of the *Lone Ranger* type. Favorites were *Bob Hope* for comedy, *Mr. District Attorney* for mystery, and *Make Believe Ballroom,* for music. [Note: This survey was made before the advent of television.]

Sense of Reality. Interesting results were obtained from two questions designed to supply indications concerning wishes and desires. When asked what they would do with $1000, and given space for three answers, 18 boys said they would give all or part to their parents or mothers (none mentioned father). Thirty mentioned paying debts, buying War Bonds,

THE CITY COLLEGE EDUCATIONAL CLINIC

INTEREST AND ACTIVITY POLL

DEVISED BY ALBERT J. HARRIS

Name .... Class .... Date ....

The purpose of these questions is to find out what kinds of things boys of your age like and what kinds of things they dislike.

1. Who is your favorite movie star? ....
2. Who is your favorite radio star?..............................
3. Who is the greatest man in the world today?..............................
4. What things do you like to do most in your spare time?..............................
   (1) ....
   (2) ....
   (3) ....
5. (a) About how many comic books do you read a week?..............................
   (b) What comic books do you like best?
   (1) ....
   (2) ....
   (3) ....
6. What famous man would you most want to be like?..............................
7. What magazines do you sometimes read?
   (1) .... How often? ....
   (2) .... How often? ....
   (3) .... How often? ....
   (a) What do you like most in the magazines?..............................
   ....
   (b) What do you like least in the magazines?..............................
   ....
8. How many books have you read just because you wanted to in the past 3 months? .... What were their names? How did you like them?
   (1) .... Like? ....
   (2) .... Like? ....
9. If you had one thousand dollars ($1,000), what would you do with it?
   (1) ....
   (2) ....
   (3) ....
10. (a) About how many hours a week do you spend listening to the radio?
    ....
    (b) What are your favorite radio programs? List the one you like best, first.
    (1) .... (4) ....
    (2) .... (5) ....
    (3) .... (6) ....
11. What three changes would you make, if you could?
    (1) ....
    (2) ....
    (3) ....

Fig. 58. Questionnaire for determining reading interests. This form may be reproduced without special permission.

12. (a) What newspaper do you read most often?..........................
(b) What other paper do you read sometimes?..........................
(c) Make a 1 in front of the part of the newspaper that you usually read first. Now make a 2 in front of the part that you read second. Now make an X in front of any other part that you sometimes read.

....sports news	....war news
....comic strips	....fashion news
....editorials	....crime news
....store advertisements	....financial news
....movies and theatres	....radio programs
....political news	....headlines
....columnists	....news pictures

13. (a) About how often do you go to the movies?..........................
(b) Make an L in front of the kinds of movies that you like.

....adventure pictures	....comedies
....love stories	....sad pictures
....musical pictures	....murder mysteries
....war pictures	....Western pictures
....travel pictures	....cartoon pictures

(c) Name the three pictures that you have liked most in the past two years.
(1) ....
(2) ....
(3) ....

14. Here are the names of some books that you might like to read. If you think that you would like to read the book, make an L in front of it. If you do not know if you would like it or not, make a question mark (?). If you are fairly sure that you would not like to read the book, make a D.

.... 1. Wonders of the Electric Eye	....24. How to Repair Furniture
.... 2. Famous Football Games	....25. A Bomber Pilot's Story
.... 3. 1,001 Things You Can Make	....26. Ford of the F.B.I.
.... 4. War in the Desert	....27. Romance on the Range
.... 5. The Vanishing Corpse	....28. Big Game Hunting
.... 6. She Married the Boss	....29. Wild Animals and Their Habits
.... 7. Secret of Lost Gold Mine	....30. Life of Joe DiMaggio
.... 8. Modern Miracles of Medicine	....31. Inside an Airplane Factory
.... 9. Dick Jones, Fullback	....32. Great Battles of History
....10. How to Draw and Paint	....33. The Spider's Revenge
....11. Flying Against Japan	....34. Boy Meets Girl
....12. Murder at the Movies	....35. The Texas Rangers
....13. The Stolen Kiss	....36. Heroes of Science
....14. Famous Voyages	....37. Hold That Line!
....15. The Earth & The Stars	....38. How Engines Work
....16. Winning Plays in Basketball	....39. Heroes of Guadalcanal
....17. How to Take Good Pictures	....40. Famous Bank Robberies
....18. How to Defeat Germany	....41. The Dream Princess
....19. Famous Ghost Stories	....42. Mountain Climbing Adventures
....20. Dancing Sweethearts	
....21. Exploring African Jungles	
....22. The Story of Steel	
....23. The Home Run King	

15. What kind of stories do you like? Make an L in front of each kind of story that you like. Place a D in front of each kind that you do not like.

....science	....sport	....spy	....romance
....love	....crime	....travel	....adventure
....how to make things	....war	....history	....cowboy
....nature	....flying	....murder	....fighting

saving the money, or investing it. Forty-five would buy things: 15 want clothes, 10 want a house, 8 want a car. Three would set themselves up in business, only two mentioned giving some to charity, and one would get married!

When asked what three changes they would make if they could, 22 mentioned changes in school; 7 wanted to leave school or have less schoolwork, and 15 wanted to make assorted changes in curriculum, teachers, and subjects. Eleven mentioned a desire for peace and the end of the war. Nine showed a desire to abolish inequalities and discrimination. Fifteen would like to better themselves; they variously wanted fame, money, professional status, a job; one wanted to learn how to play baseball. Six expressed wishes of an altruistic sort. One boy said he had everything he wanted.

Summary. The questionnaire disclosed marked individual differences in the responses to every question. Differences in maturity were striking, as well as those involving specific likes and dislikes. Nothing was unanimously liked or disliked by the whole group. Many of them were keenly aware of economic inferiority or racial discrimination. The war was a topic of great interest as reflected in their reading and movie choices. Mystery and adventure were very popular. A strong liking for humor was evident in the radio and movie preferences. Interest in love and sentimentality was admitted by a minority of the group.

III. Creating and Enriching Reading Interests

One of the most crucial tasks in a reading program is the transformation of children whose attitude toward reading has been one of indifference or active dislike into avid readers. As long as progress depends entirely on what the children read under the eyes of the teacher, it is likely to remain slow. Spectacular gains in reading ability often result when the children begin to read a book or two a week, aside from class lessons. The most carefully planned lessons may bring disappointing results unless the teacher is able to ignite a tiny spark of interest and then nurture it carefully into a clear flame of enthusiasm for reading.

Creating Interest in Reading

The basic principles of successful work in developing reading interests have been admirably summarized as consisting of "a lure and a ladder."[26] The lure may be any of a variety of ways of enticing children to begin pleasurable reading. The ladder involves providing suitable reading matter which will intensify the child's interest in reading and in which he can gradually progress to reading material of superior quality.

The first essential is to provide physical surroundings in the classroom that will create an atmosphere favorable to reading. There should be a "reading corner" in every classroom. The furnishings for a reading corner do not have to be elaborate. A table or two, a few chairs, and book shelves are the essentials. Interest can be stimulated if, at the beginning of the term, the children build or paint the bookcases (sometimes improvised from orange crates), make and hang curtains, place colorful jackets on the books, and so on.

A good class library should contain at least fifty books. They should range in difficulty from some easy enough for the poorest readers in the class to others which will interest the most advanced readers. There should, of course, be a special collection of books of varied difficulty relating to the activity unit which is currently engaging the attention of the class. In addition, there should be fairy tales and legends, animal stories, adventure tales, stories with foreign settings, humor and nonsense, nature study and science, and at least some poetry. Current and back issues of the good children's magazines should find a place also.

A simple classification scheme makes it easier for the children to select books. The books can be arranged under a few simple headings — "make-believe," "real-life stories," "animals," "people and places," and so on. Some teachers use colored tabs, a different color for each reading group in the class, to help the children to find the books of appropriate difficulty for them. Of course, the daily class schedule must provide some free time for browsing and for independent silent reading if the reading corner is to function properly.

A teacher who makes it a regular practice to read fascinating stories to his class usually has no trouble arousing interest in reading.

[26] "Developing the Reading Interests of Children," A Report of a Committee of the Uppper Grades Study Council, Cincinnati, *Elementary English Review*, Vol. 20, 1943, pp. 279–286.

Children of any age through high school love to listen to a lively tale. A good book or story which the teacher has read to the class will find many readers when it is placed in the library collection. Children often show great interest in stories which are too difficult for them to read independently. After hearing the story, however, they can often read it with pleasure, since they have become acquainted with the author's style and have learned the meanings of the unfamiliar concepts and vocabulary that would otherwise be stumbling blocks.

Audience reading can be used to very good effect to foster independent reading. The nature of audience reading has been described on page 94. The desire to find and prepare a suitable selection to read to the class is a powerful incentive for many children, and creates a natural motive for reading with a critical and evaluative attitude. Through the short selections that are presented in an audience reading period, the listeners are exposed to samples from many different sources, and may have their interests awakened in books and stories that they might otherwise have overlooked.

Many teachers have made excellent use of a book club. Membership is open to the entire class. The usual requirements include possessing a library card and being ready to report on one book. The club elects officers, ordinarily a president and secretary, with sometimes a treasurer. Meetings may be held weekly, on Friday afternoons. At each meeting a few members are given the privilege of reporting on books they have read, telling whether or not they recommend the book, and, if they like, reading to the club some especially delightful portion. Greatly increased interest in book reading and marked improvement in critical ability and taste are the normal results of a well-run book club.

Some book clubs decide to have dues, which may be as little as a cent a week. The funds are used by a purchasing committee to buy materials for the class library collection. The judgment shown by a pupil committee in selecting materials to buy with club funds is often amazingly good, and the experience the children gain in visiting bookstores and inspecting books for possible purchase is invaluable. The handling of the funds also provides a real situation for the use of functional arithmetic. At the end of the year the purchases can be distributed to the members of the club, or left behind for the next class.

The Child Who Dislikes Reading

The procedures which have just been described are usually successful in creating a classroom atmosphere favorable to recreational reading and work well with the majority of children. With children who have a confirmed dislike for reading, special procedures may be necessary.

The first step in introducing such a child to pleasurable, voluntary reading is to locate a book that is easy, brief, and will attract and hold his interest. For this purpose it is desirable to try a book that has many pictures, few lines to a page, and comparatively few pages. The thinner the book, the better. Naturally, content should be chosen in relation to what is known about the child's interests. In the writer's experience, humorous books usually make an excellent start. Few children who can read them can resist the fun in *Mr. Popper's Penguins, The 500 Hats for Bartholomew Cubbins, Lentil,* and others. Many such books are included in the book list in Appendix B. After a successful first taste, the child is likely to want several more books of the same general type before venturing into a different type of content.

In introducing such a book, it is desirable to show the book, turn a few pages to show the illustrations, and then read enough of the story aloud to arouse a desire to know the rest of it. Then the child can be asked if he would like to continue reading by himself. It may be desirable to suggest that he read ahead five or ten pages. If by the next lesson he has read more than the suggested amount, the teacher knows that the procedure has been successful. From then on, the problem is mainly one of keeping the child supplied with a succession of suitable books.

Sometimes older children are reluctant to take books home because they are afraid that other children will notice the "baby books" and make fun of them. Supplying a large manila envelope in which books can be carried minimizes this difficulty.

After the child has made a good start in voluntary reading, he should be introduced to the public library (or to the school library, if there is one). If possible, the teacher should accompany him on his first visit, help him through the formalities of getting a library card, and show him where to look for books and how to take them out. For quite a while, he may need the assistance of a specific list of four or five suggested books to take with him; otherwise the long rows of books may be bewildering, and if his first few attempts at selecting his own books turn out poorly, he may become discouraged.

One should try to select reading material in accordance with a child's known interests until the habit of voluntary reading is well established. Some children want nothing but fairy tales, others disdain anything that is not true; narrow interests confined to animals, or airplanes, or blood-and-thunder should be respected as far as is possible.

A good children's librarian can be of invaluable help to both teacher and child in suggesting suitable books. A teacher of reading should, however, regard a continually enlarging acquaintance with children's books as an essential part of his own professional equipment. Aids to the location of reading matter of various kinds are discussed in the last part of this chapter.

Although primary motivation in voluntary reading comes from enjoyment of the reading itself, progress charts help here, as in other phases of reading improvement. A type of individual progress chart that appeals to all ages is shown in Figure 59 consisting of a bookcase, with books filled in as they are completed. Coloring the books with crayons adds to the attractiveness of such a chart. A popular kind of class record for voluntary reading is shown in Figure 60.

Expanding and Improving Reading Interests

While it is vitally important to help children to find reading matter that is closely related to their present interests, teachers should also try to broaden children's reading horizons. Children's interests are not fixed; they change as children get older, and are susceptible to many environmental influences, not the least of which is the influence of the teacher. There are many good ways in which children's

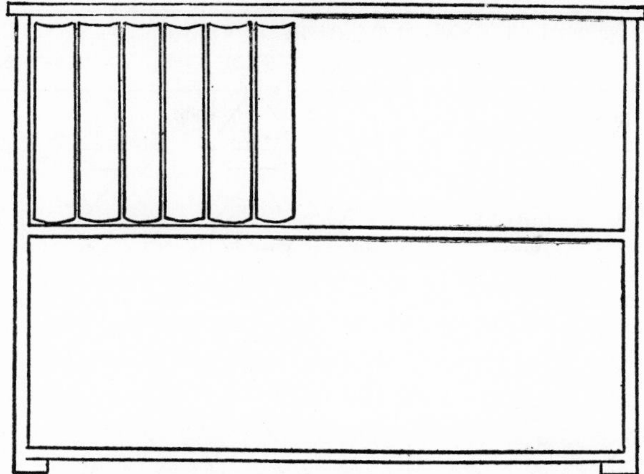

Fig. 59. A bookcase chart for recording independent reading. As the child finishes a book, he draws another book in his bookcase. If the bookcase is made about 6 x 9 in., the books will be large enough to allow printing the author and title on each, and the date completed. Coloring the books in crayon adds to the attractiveness of the chart.

reading interests can be improved and enriched. The worst way is to attempt compulsion through required assignments and detailed book reports.

An ingenious teacher can find many ways of suggesting new fields of reading and awakening interest in new books. One teacher has reported excellent results from interesting displays of the colorful jackets of books that were added to the class library.[27] Another teacher found that her pupils were reading nothing but fiction. To stimulate interest in nonfiction, she asked them to write on slips of paper the topics or questions about which they would like to find information. A card index of topics was set up, with book references listed for each topic. A marked increase in the reading of informational material was the result.[28]

An interesting approach, tried successfully by a seventh-grade

[27] Colburn, Evangeline, "A Device for Stimulating Reading Interests," *Elementary School Journal,* Vol. 44, 1944, pp. 539–541.

[28] Putnam, R. A., "Cultivating a Taste for Non-Fiction," *Elementary English Review,* Vol. 18, 1941, pp. 228–229.

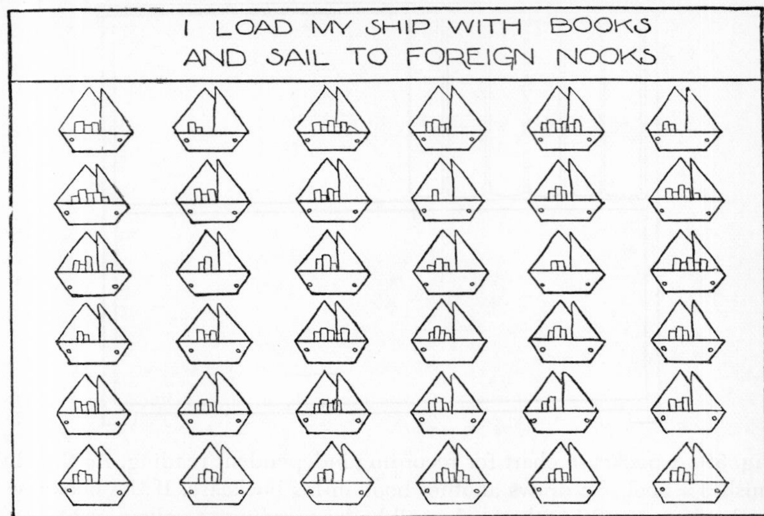

Fig. 60. Wall chart for recording supplementary book reading. Background is heavy colored pasteboard. Ships are cut out of colored construction paper, folded to form a pocket, and are held in place by brass fasteners. When a pupil has finished a book and has made a satisfactory report, the teacher prints the name of the book on a colored slip of paper and places it in the child's ship. Ships can be turned inside out and used with another class.

teacher, is worth relating. She gave her class, near the beginning of the term, a little talk on "Your Reading Diet." In it she started by reviewing the need of a proper diet of food for proper physical nutrition and growth. Then she drew an analogy to reading. Mystery stories were likened to dessert, and comic books to candy between meals. "What would happen to your digestion if you ate nothing but desserts and candy?" After some discussion, the class, which found the idea novel and stimulating, drew up a plan for a balanced eight-course reading meal: fruit cup, poetry; soup, current events; fish course ("brain food"), science and nature study; meat, biography and history; vegetables, special practice exercises in reading; dessert, fiction; milk, sports and hobbies; afterdinner mints, comics. Each child drew up a menu and filled in the titles of his reading as the term progressed. He could take as many helpings as he wished of the courses he liked best, provided that he ate at least one dish of every kind.

Convincing evidence has been presented by LaBrant [29] and others that a well-managed program of free reading leads naturally to the broadening and maturing of taste in reading. Children do not develop discrimination by being allowed contact only with superior reading matter; on the contrary, it is often found that the brightest children and most voracious readers read much that is of a trashy nature, as well as much that is good. Taste develops through comparison and contrast, not from ignorance.

An intelligent interest in current events should be one of the outcomes of education. Research studies have shown that elementary school children look first at the comic strips in newspapers. One study [30] found that boys in the intermediate and upper grades ranked sections of the newspaper in the following order: comics, sports, news, and photographic section. Girls ranked news below the comics but above sports and the photographic section. Only one-fourth of the children in the upper grades showed an interest in the news, and these usually limited their reading to a scanning of headlines and a hurried reading of the more appealing or spectacular items.

Some schools develop interest in news events gradually, through the regular reading and discussion of one of the weekly papers that are prepared for school use. Such papers as *My Weekly Reader,*[31] *Every Week,*[31] *Current Events,*[31] and *Junior Scholastic* [32] make it possible to introduce reading about current happenings as early as the first grade, and to continue it with reading matter appropriate to each grade through the elementary and secondary school years.

Another procedure that can be used at the upper levels is to devote some of the social studies time to current events periods, in

[29] LaBrant, Lou L., and Heller, Frieda M., *An Evaluation of Free Reading in Grades Seven to Twelve, Inclusive.* Ohio State University Studies, Graduate School Series, Contributions in Education, No. 4. Columbus, Ohio: Ohio State University Press, 1939.

[30] Witty, Paul, and Kopel, David, *Reading and the Educative Process,* p. 36. Boston: Ginn & Co., 1939.

[31] Published by American Education Press, Columbus, Ohio.

[32] Published by Scholastic Corporation, 220 E. 42 St., New York, N.Y.

which each child is expected to present a brief oral report about some interesting development in the news of the preceding week. This combines motivated independent reading in newspapers and news magazines, critical comparison of possible selections, practice in organizing a summary, and effective oral English work.

Poetry has become somewhat neglected in reading programs in recent years. The amount of space devoted to poetry in readers has decreased markedly, and the tendency to substitute wide individualized reading for uniform class study of specific selections has lessened the amount of attention devoted to poetry in the upper grades. There are many ways in which the modern teacher can awaken and develop an appreciation of poetry. One of the most important is the reading of well-chosen poems to the class by the teacher. A teacher who loves poetry and can read it well can make poems come alive for children. A second useful procedure is choral reading and speaking. Poems which the children enjoy can be prepared for group presentation. Choral reading is a comparatively new development, and one which is ideally suited to the development of an appreciation of poetry. At a simple level, the whole class can read the poem in unison. As the children become more expert, delightful contrast effects can be achieved through a balancing of solo parts and choral effects.[33] A third way in which interest in poetry can be developed is through encouraging children to prepare poems for presentation in audience reading periods.

IV. Locating Reading Materials

There is such a wealth of reading matter for children today that the task of selection is by no means easy. The purpose of this section is to acquaint the reader with sources in which he can look up recommended books and materials to meet all sorts of reading needs.

[33] Suggestions about choral reading can be found in:

Abney, Louise, and Rowe, Grace, *Choral Speaking Arrangements for the Lower Grades.* Boston: The Expression Co., 1937.

Robinson, Marion P., and Thurston, Rozetta L., *Poetry Arranged for the Speaking Choir.* Boston: The Expression Co., 1936.

Sister Mary Dorothy, R.S.M., *Choral Recitation in the Grades.* Washington, D.C.: Educator's Washington Dispatch, 1950.

Book Lists for Elementary School Children

The references described below are useful primarily for selecting books for children whose progress in reading is generally satisfactory, or for locating books to read to children. While age or grade designations are given in most of these references, they are usually quite broad — three year intervals — so that they are not very helpful in judging the reading ability required.

Children's Catalogue, Eighth Edition, Revised, compiled by Ruth Giles and Dorothy E. Cook. New York: H. W. Wilson Co., 1951. This volume of over 900 pages includes entries on 3400 titles, with reviews and a comprehensive system of cross-indexing by author, title, subject matter and grade levels. About 800 books are starred. Annual supplements keep this up to date until the Ninth Edition, due in 1956.

A Basic Book Collection for the Elementary Grades, Fifth Edition, compiled by a Joint Committee of the A.L.A., N.E.A., A.C.E.I., and N.C.T.E., Miriam Braley Snow, chairman. Chicago: American Library Association, 1951. A list of 1045 titles, classified according to the Dewey Decimal System and briefly annotated, with approximate grade levels and author and title index.

A Bibliography of Books for Children, compiled by Vera Peterson, Bulletin No. 37, 1954 Edition. Washington, D.C.: Association for Childhood Education International. About 1250 books, classified, annotated, and with broad age levels; limited to books costing more than $1.25; revised every two years. A companion list, *Children's Books for One Dollar and Twenty-five Cents or Less,* is also available.

Adventuring with Books, a Reading List for Elementary Schools, by the Elementary Reading List Committee, Mary Margaret Clark, chairman. Chicago: National Council of Teachers of English, 1950. Includes about 1,000 titles classified and annotated, with approximate grade levels and author and title indexes. Books related to personal development and human relationships are specially marked.

Combined Book Exhibit: Learning to Live in 1955, Basic Relationships to Life, selected by Christine B. Gilbert and Jean Betzner. New York: Combined Book Exhibit, 950 University Ave., 1955. Recent books from 47 cooperating publishers, classified, with emphasis on personal adjustment to life; annotated, with approximate age levels, author, title and subject index. Revised annually.

Subject Index to Books for Primary Grades, compiled by Eloise Rue. Chicago: American Library Association, 1943. Provides specific page references to 300 primary readers, 130 pamphlets, and 250 other books, on a wide variety of topics of interest to elementary school children. *A First Supplement,* published in 1946, added 225 titles.

Subject Index to Books for Intermediate Grades, Second Edition, compiled by Eloise Rue. Chicago: American Library Association, 1950. Over 1,800 titles analyzed under a very detailed alphabetical list of topics of interest to elementary and junior high school pupils; under each topic, relevant books are listed by author, title, specific pages, and approximate grade level.

Children's Books Too Good to Miss, by May Hill Arbuthnot and others. Cleveland: The Press of Western Reserve University, 1953. About 200 all-time favorites, arranged by age groups, with a one-paragraph review of each and several illustrations.

Growing Up with Books, compiled by the staff of *Junior Libraries.* New York: The Bowker Co., 1955. A tiny, very inexpensive (5¢ in large quantities) selected list of 250 titles, revised annually; excellent for use with parent groups.

In addition to these general basic references, there are many special lists dealing with historical fiction, poetry, plays, character education, extra large print, free and inexpensive materials, and so on; to attempt a comprehensive listing here would be impractical, since such a list is already available.[34]

Keeping up with the new books for children is a time-consuming task which can be eased through the use of the several reviewing services that are available; the person who wishes to do this should become familiar with the *Horn Book, Junior Libraries,* the *Booklist* of the American Library Association, the Sunday book review sections of the *New York Times* and New York *Herald-Tribune,* and the *Bulletin* of the Children's Book Service, University of Chicago Library.

Book Lists for the Secondary School

There are several book lists of high quality available for use in finding books of interest to junior and senior high school pupils.

Standard Catalogue for High School Libraries, Sixth Edition, compiled by Dorothy Herbert West. New York: H. W. Wilson Co., 1952. A selected catalog of 3610 books. The first part is arranged alphabetically

[34] Spache, George, *Resources in Teaching Reading,* pp. 66–71. Gainesville, Florida: Reading Laboratory, University of Florida, 1955.

and includes author and title references. The second part uses the Dewey Decimal classification and includes brief reviews. Especially recommended books are starred. Annual supplements provided until the next edition. A special Catholic Supplement is also available.

Books for You, a List for Leisure Reading for Use by Students in Senior High Schools, with 1954 Supplement, by the Committee on Senior High School Booklist, Mark Neville, Chairman. Chicago: National Council of Teachers of English, 1951. A classified and annotated list of about 1500 titles, with author index and title index.

Patterns in Reading, an annotated Book List for Young People, by Jean Carolyn Roos. Chicago: American Library Association, 1954. Intended for use by adolescents, this uses a classification of over 100 interest fields and gives brief annotations, with author and title index.

Basic Book Collection for Junior High Schools, edited by Elsa R. Berners and Mabel Sacra. Chicago: American Library Association, 1950. A relatively brief list, similar to the elementary and senior high school lists in organization.

Basic Book Collection for High Schools, Fifth Edition, compiled by a Joint Committee of the A.L.A., N.C.T.E., and N.E.A., Dorothea Dawson, chairman. Chicago: American Library Association, 1950. About 1700 titles, classified and annotated, with author and subject index.

Reading for Living, an Index to Reading Materials for Use in Human Relations Programs in Secondary Schools, by John J. DeBoer, Paul B. Hale, and Esther Landin, Illinois Curriculum Program, Bulletin No. 18, Circular Series A., No. 51. Springfield, Ill.: Office of Superintendent of Public Instruction, 1953. This book list is organized under such major headings as family and home relationships, financial problems, physical and health handicaps, and so on, with many subheadings; with one-paragraph annotations, author index and title index.

Booklets, Pamphlets, Newspapers, and Magazines

Some very good reading material is available in the form of paper-bound booklets and pamphlets. Since most of these are quite inexpensive, they make it possible to assemble reading matter on a wide variety of topics at little cost. Many of them are profusely illustrated and attractively made up. The following list is suggestive of the kinds of booklet materials that are useful:

Picture Scripts. Eau Claire, Wisconsin: E. M. Hale and Co. A series of very attractive booklets, grade levels one to four, on a wide variety of topics.

Follett Picture-Stories. Chicago: Follett Publishing Co. Thirty-five booklets dealing with natural science and social science topics, profusely illustrated; third- to fifth-grade difficulty.

Modern Wonder Books. Columbus, Ohio: American Education Press. A series of booklets, grades one to six, including fairy tales, social studies, and science topics.

Happy Hour Books. New York: The Macmillan Co. Each booklet deals with an occupation interesting to boys, such as policeman, fireman, engineer, airplane pilot, and so on. Fourth- or fifth-grade in difficulty.

Unitexts. Evanston, Ill.: Row, Peterson & Co. A well-written, beautifully illustrated series of booklets, on scientific and social studies topics, for intermediate and upper grades.

The possibilities in the little books obtainable at the toy counters of variety stores should not be overlooked. Many of these books are nicely illustrated and contain very simple reading material. Some excellent stories about animals, toys, trains, and so on, can be found, and useful books of riddles and books with printed directions for seatwork and construction activities can also be obtained.

Since the reading of newspapers and magazines bulks so large in adult reading, children should be given an opportunity to develop an acquaintance with these kinds of reading matter in school. Weekly newspapers are used in many schools to enrich the reading program and at the same time introduce current events into the social studies program. Daily papers can be used to some extent in the upper grades and secondary school. They can be used to give specific training in reading and interpreting weather forecasts, advertisements, and other sections, as well as the news portions. Magazines should have a place in the library collection. Many boys with narrow reading interests enjoy poring over such magazines as *Popular Science* and *Popular Mechanics.* Magazines of the digest type contain many interesting articles suitable for remedial use as well as for normal readers at the secondary school level. Picture magazines are always popular. The magazines published especially for children deserve more attention from the schools than they have been receiving.

Materials for Retarded Readers

It is often hard to select appropriate reading material for older children who are retarded in reading. Most of the books that deal with topics that interest these children are too advanced for them. Many of the books that are easy enough seem babyish to them because they are intended for younger children. This problem is of serious concern to the teacher of remedial reading.

If a child's retardation in reading is not very great, the chances are that he will accept readers intended for normal children one or two grades below him without much protest. This is especially likely if the book is not openly called a "second reader" or "fifth reader," but has an individual title like a storybook. If there is a discrepancy of several grades between the age of a child and his reading level, it is quite difficult to find suitable material. For this reason it is often desirable or even necessary to write special material for retarded readers. Suggestions for writing such material will be given later.

For children whose reading is above the primary level, the use of basal readers is not really necessary. Storybooks, informational books, workbooks, magazines, and newspapers can be employed to give variety and richness to a remedial program. The carefully graded vocabularies of recent primary-grade sets of readers, however, make them very desirable materials for the remedial instruction of children whose reading ability is below the fourth grade. They need an abundance of easy material for practice in word recognition, fluency, and comprehension, and it is difficult or impossible to supply enough specially prepared material for them. If such a child balks at reading a primer or first or second reader, his cooperation can usually be gained by a proper approach. He can be told that the book may be somewhat uninteresting for him because it is intended for younger children, but that he needs practice on easy reading and that this practice will make it possible to read and enjoy more suitable books. Another procedure that can be employed is to give the child opportunities to read stories to younger children.

Each teacher who works with slow readers gradually learns which books they will accept and enjoy, and which fail to appeal to them. The reports of experienced workers in remedial reading can be consulted in a number of published studies. A comprehensive listing is contained in:

Hill, Margaret Keyser, *A Bibliography of Reading Lists for Retarded Readers,* Revised, College of Education Series, No. 37, Extension Bulletin, State University of Iowa, Iowa City: State University of Iowa, 1953.

The following references, published since 1950, are especially helpful:

Spache, George, *Good Books for Poor Readers.* Gainesville, Florida: Reading Laboratory, University of Florida, 1954. An annotated list of about 1000 books, including adapted classics, trade books, remedial games, and so on, arranged by topic with author and title index. Difficulty levels are given, many based on use of Spache and Dale-Chall formulas; also estimated interest levels.

Annotated Bibliography of Selected Books with High Interest and Low Vocabulary Level. Curriculum Bulletin No. 22-IC-Ns. Indianapolis: Division of Curriculum and Supervision, Indianapolis Public Schools, 1644 Roosevelt Ave., 1954. Section I lists over 300 books under topical headings. Section II lists certain series of special interest for poor readers. Author index and title index.

Durrell, Donald D., and Sullivan, Helen Blair, *High Interest—Low Vocabulary Booklist.* Boston: Educational Clinic, School of Education, Boston University, 1952. Section I contains books published 1950–1952; Section II contains books published prior to 1950. In each section books are arranged by estimated vocabulary difficulty, and approximate interest levels are suggested. Some internal inconsistency is present.

Strang, Ruth, Gilbert, Christine B., and Scoggin, Margaret C., *Gateways to Readable Books,* Second Edition. New York: H. W. Wilson Co., 1952. Intended especially for use with adolescents of limited reading ability. A classified and annotated list, with ratings of difficulty; most entries are from fifth- to seventh-grade level; with author index, title index, and listing by difficulty level.

Fare for the Reluctant Reader, compiled for the Capital Area School Development Association by Bernice C. Bush, Anita E. Dunn and Mabel E. Jackson. Albany: New York State College for Teachers, 1951. A list of books, magazines, and audio-visual aids for the slow learner in grades seven to ten, arranged in thirteen topical chapters, with emphasis on books for grades nine and ten.

Hobson, Cloy S., and Haugh, Oscar M., *Materials for the Retarded Reader.* Topeka, Kan.: State Department of Public Instruction, 1954. Books in series form intended for use with poor readers.

The list of books in Appendix B has been drawn up specifically to aid corrective and remedial teachers in the location of titles that are suitable in both interest and difficulty. Many other book lists were consulted during its assembly, but the writer takes responsibility both for the selection and for the ratings of difficulty. So far as possible, the grade levels represent the independent reading level of the book; the instructional level would frequently be a grade lower. The listing is by grade level and all of the books included are judged to be interesting to children at least two years older than the difficulty level.

Books Written Especially for Retarded Readers

The availability of books written especially for use with older children whose reading ability is very limited makes remedial reading much easier now than it was twenty years ago. For those reading at or below second-grade level, the easiest books in the *Cowboy Sam* series (Beckley-Cardy) and the *Walt Disney Story Books* (D. C. Heath) are generally more palatable than primary-grade readers, while employing a reasonably well controlled vocabulary. The *American Adventure Series* (Wheeler Publishing Co.), popular over a wide range of ages, starts with *Friday the Arapaho Indian* at second-grade level. Dolch's *Pleasure Reading Series* and *Basic Vocabulary Series* (Garrard Press) are enjoyed by many poor readers at second- to third-grade level. *Desert Treasure* and *The Adventures of Canolles* by Hefferman (Harr-Wagner) represent original stories written at fourth-grade level for junior high school; *The Box-Car Children, Surprise Island,* and *Hidden Silver* (Scott, Foresman) are of third-grade difficulty. The *Childhood of Famous Americans* series (Bobbs-Merrill) contains fifty titles, mostly written at fourth-grade level, designed to interest a junior high school audience.

There are also very many simplified and shortened versions of famous books that are frequently used at secondary school level. Some of these are well done, others are quite poor. They range in difficulty all the way from third-grade level to eighth-grade level, so the fact that a book is a simplified version gives no indication of its actual difficulty. Stevenson's *Treasure Island,* for example, is available in four different simplified versions ranging from fourth- to eighth-grade level in difficulty. In the writer's experience, the most valuable of these are the collections of short stories, such as Kottmeyer's adaptations of *Tales from Sherlock Holmes* and *The Gold Bug and Other Stories* (Webster) and Moderow's *Six Great Stories* (Scott, Foresman). A listing of nearly two hundred books of this type, with difficulty levels estimated, has been given by Spache.[35] Many of these adapted classics are included in Appendix B.

Materials Written by Teachers and Pupils

It is often necessary, as has been pointed out before, to use stories especially to appeal to a particular child. The first step is naturally to find out what the child's interests are. It is easy to get the child's cooperation in such an undertaking, and he is usually very proud to dictate a story to the teacher and later read it in his own words. In addition to their interest value, such stories have an important advantage in that all the words used are from the child's own speaking vocabulary and therefore easy for him to understand; training in word recognition is therefore not hampered by comprehension difficulties. Stories written by one child are often enjoyed by other children. Scrapbooks of stories written by the children themselves have great interest as supplementary reading in remedial classes. The stories should be typewritten or printed.

A remedial teacher may also find it advisable because of a scarcity of suitable books to rely largely on material prepared by himself. Sometimes stories and selections from advanced books can be rewritten so as to be readable by retarded pupils. The value of stories and articles rewritten in this way has been demonstrated by research.[36] Unless a teacher has considerable originality, he will ordinarily be more successful in adapting the writings of others than in attempting to write completely original material.

In planning story-type or informational material for retarded readers it is a good idea to make each unit short enough so that it can be finished within one remedial period. A brief introductory statement may be used to give the pupil suggestions about the way

[35] Spache, George, *Good Books for Poor Readers,* pp. 37–49.

[36] Postel, H. H., "The Effect of Adapting Reading Materials to Seriously Retarded Readers," *Elementary School Journal,* Vol. 37, 1937, pp. 536–540.

in which the selection should be read. At the end of the selection specific questions should be included which may be answered in writing or may serve as a basis for oral discussion.

Materials written for remedial pupils should be written in a simple and straightforward style, and at a level of complexity within the grasp of the pupil. Compound and complex sentences may be used in moderation, provided that they do not contain many inversions of normal word order or other involved constructions. During the writing one should naturally try to use an easy word in place of a more difficult synonym whenever possible. After the material has been written, its vocabulary may be checked against one or more of the standard word lists to make sure that it does not contain an unreasonable number of unusual or difficult words. The best test of the suitability of the story, however, is the ease with which the pupil can read it.

The following two paragraphs illustrate how reading material can be simplified without any loss of essential meaning. The first paragraph contains more than a dozen constructions which are, according to Thorndike,[37] difficult for poor readers. They are printed in italics. The second paragraph is simple in sentence structure as compared with the first, and employs a much easier vocabulary. As usually happens, some of the life and color disappears when the material is simplified, but it is better for material to be less colorful than to be incomprehensible.

Michael O'Connell was a man's man. *Given to* smoking a briar, he disdained cigarettes *as being* effeminate. He would have been frequently the opposite of sober, *but that* liquor had no effect on him. *Having grown up* in a pugnacious atmosphere, one *had only to* mention a fight *for him to be* ready with both fists; and *strong as he was,* he rarely came out second best in a scuffle. He was a typical north woods bully, *save that* he never employed profanity. This was *the more* conspicuous *inasmuch as* wild oaths were generously interlarded in the conversation of his associates. One *cannot but* admire his fortitude *in declining* to participate in such an obnoxious custom.

Michael O'Connell was a man's man. He always smoked a briar pipe and thought that cigarettes were a woman's smoke. He drank quite often

[37] Thorndike, E. L., "Improving the Ability to Read," *Teachers College Record,* Vol. 36, 1934, pp. 123–144 and 229–241.

but never became drunk. He was always ready for a fight, as he had grown up among people who enjoyed a battle, and was so strong that he rarely lost. He was a typical north woods bully except that he never cursed. This was easily noticed because his friends used bad language most of the time. He was a brave man to refuse to join in such a bad habit.

Since writing special materials is very time-consuming, remedial reading teachers should make every effort to utilize the materials that are available in printed form. While there is a scarcity of materials written especially for retarded readers, fairly satisfactory materials are available for most remedial needs if the teacher knows where to look.

This chapter has stressed the importance of finding "the right book for the right child" as a way of increasing children's interest in reading for pleasure and providing a basis for the gradual maturing and refining of taste and critical standards. The child who reads extensively will make his own comparisons and will, in the long run, prefer sound writing and get to dislike trash. Even if he doesn't, an omnivorous reading diet is far superior to none at all. In the face of the competition from mass media, such as television, it takes both superior materials and clever salesmanship by teachers to develop the reading habit; without this habit, much of reading instruction is wasted.

Suggested Additional Reading

Adams, Fay, Lillian Gray, and Dora Reese. *Teaching Children to Read,* Chs. 14, 15.

Betzner, Jean. *Exploring Literature with Children in the Elementary School,* Practical Suggestions for Teaching, No. 7. New York: Bureau of Publications, Teachers College, Columbia University, 1943.

Bond, Guy L., and Eva Bond Wagner. *Teaching the Child to Read,* Revised Edition, Ch. 16.

McKee, Paul. *The Teaching of Reading in the Elementary School,* Ch. 17.

Russell, David H. *Children Learn to Read,* Chs. 12, 13.

Strang, Ruth, Constance M. McCullough, and Arthur E. Traxler. *Problems in the Improvement of Reading,* Second Edition, Ch. 16.

Witty, Paul A. *Reading in Modern Education,* Chs. 2, 5. Boston: D. C. Health & Co., 1949.

· XVIII ·

Improving Rate of Reading

IN TODAY'S LIVING there is so much to read that the ability to read quickly has become an important asset. The typical reader of a century ago, whose library may have consisted of the Bible, an almanac, and two or three treasured books read over and over again, had no need for speed. A literate adult in today's hectic world goes through more reading material in a week than his great-grandfather probably covered in a year. The college student who has to take six hours for what his instructor considers a three-hour assignment, the business executive who wishes he could get through his reports and mail in two hours instead of three or four, the physician who can't keep up with his professional journals – these are typical of the people who have made "speed reading" courses popular.

The average reader wastes a great deal of useful time in unnecessarily slow reading. There is abundant evidence that the typical high school or college student can increase his rate of reading by 25 to 50 per cent without any decline in accuracy of comprehension. The very slow reader can sometimes achieve an increase of 50 to 100 per cent in rate in a comparatively short time. If we assume, rather conservatively, that a typical pupil in the upper grades or secondary school spends two hours a day in reading, including recreational and study-type reading, an increase of 25 per cent in rate would release about three hours of his time each week for additional reading or for other activities. Over a year, the saving would amount to about 150 hours. An increase in rate may, in subjects requiring extensive reading, mean the difference between a C and an A grade; in the student's total program, it may mean the difference between being just able to meet study requirements, and having time for leisure.

I. Rate and Comprehension

THERE ARE two widely held contrasting beliefs about the relationship of rate to comprehension, both of which are wrong. Many people, both children and adults, believe that fast readers tend to be inaccurate, while slow readers make up for their plodding by getting more out of their reading. There is no evidence at all to substantiate this opinion. The contrasting belief is that fast reading is necessarily good reading, and slow reading is poor reading. While on the whole there is some tendency for fast readers as a group to comprehend better than slow readers as a group, there are so many exceptions to this rule that, as it is sometimes stated without any qualifications, it is almost as wrong as the other belief.

The degree of relationship between rate and comprehension varies with the age of the readers, the kinds of material used, and the methods used in measuring the two factors. In the primary grades one would expect to find a fairly high relationship, because slow reading at that level is usually caused by difficulty in word recognition which impairs comprehension also. At higher levels, the many research studies show great variations in results. Most of the correlations are positive but low, averaging around .30. There is some evidence that the correlation is high when the reading matter is very difficult (probably because poor comprehension makes rereading necessary) while there is little or no relationship when the reading matter is easy.[1] There is some evidence that in the upper levels of intelligence fast readers tend to be more efficient than slow readers,

[1] Tinker, Miles A., "Speed Versus Comprehension in Reading as Affected by Level of Difficulty," *Journal of Educational Psychology,* Vol. 30, 1939, pp. 81–94; Shores, Harlan J., and Husbands, Kenneth L., "Are Fast Readers the Best Readers?" *Elementary English,* Vol. 27, 1950, pp. 52–57.

while at the average and lower intelligence levels the slower readers tend to be more efficient, especially on difficult material.[2]

There is no one rate of reading that is appropriate in all situations; rather, the efficient reader varies his rate according to his purposes and the requirements of the material. Yoakam has distinguished four major rates of reading, and has indicated some of the kinds of reading situations in which they are appropriate:

READING RATES APPROPRIATE FOR DIFFERENT PURPOSES [3]

1. Skimming rate
   Work-type reading: to find a reference; to locate new material; to answer a specific question; to get the general idea of a selection.
   Recreational reading: to go through a book or magazine to get a general idea of the contents; to review a familiar story.
2. Rapid reading
   Work-type: to review familiar material; to get the main idea or central thought; to get information for temporary use.
   Recreational: to read narrative material primarily for the plot; to read informational material for pleasure or relaxation; to reread familiar material.
3. Normal rate
   Work-type: to find answers to specific questions; to note details; to solve a problem; to grasp relation of details to main ideas; to read material of average difficulty.
   Recreational: to appreciate beauty of literary style; to keep up with current events; to read with the intention of later retelling the story.
4. Careful rate
   Work-type: to master content including details; to evaluate material; to get details in sequence, as in following directions; to outline, summarize, or paraphrase; to analyze author's presentation; to solve a problem.
   Recreational: to read material with unusual vocabulary or style; to read poetry; to read with the intent of memorizing; to judge literary values.

The choice of an inappropriate rate of reading is sometimes an important factor in comprehension difficulties. Some children are

[2] Carlson, Thorsten R., "The Relationship between Speed and Accuracy of Comprehension," *Journal of Educational Research,* Vol. 42, 1949, pp. 500–512.

[3] Adapted from Yoakam, Gerald A., *Basal Reading Instruction,* p. 219. New York: McGraw-Hill Book Co., 1955.

given a reading diet which consists almost entirely of light, easy fiction, and become rapid, fluent readers. Later on, when they are expected to read materials which require careful study, they try to employ the same reading habits that are effective in their recreational reading. Then their tendency to read rapidly and superficially produces sad results. Other children are drilled carefully for accuracy from the very beginning. They find it easy to note details in their reading, but may experience difficulty in discovering the central thought of a selection or in following a sequence of events.

In regard to speed and comprehension, an individual may show one of three patterns: he may be retarded in both rate and comprehension; he may have a satisfactory rate but poor comprehension; or he may have satisfactory comprehension but be exessively slow.

When a pupil is poor in both speed and comprehension, the major efforts of the remedial teacher should be expended on the improvement of comprehension. Speed should not be emphasized at all until there is an adequate basis for reading with understanding. Many of the factors which interfere with comprehension also retard speed. As a pupil develops more effective word recognition habits, acquires a more extensive vocabulary, and learns to read in thought units, his speed will increase even though no attention is specifically devoted to it. This principle of stressing comprehension rather than speed when both are weak should be adhered to in all cases except those in which it is felt that excessively low speed is a major factor in preventing better comprehension.

Pupils who read at a rapid rate but whose understanding is poor likewise need training which emphasizes comprehension. Many of this group are context readers, whose difficulty is due in part to inadequate word recognition techniques. When that is true, emphasis should be devoted first of all to the improvement of word recognition. In other cases, the trouble may simply be due to an attempt to employ a rapid or skimming rate on material which requires careful reading. The first step in overcoming this difficulty is to explain to the child that he is underestimating the difficulty of the material and is not reading carefully enough. The second and major step is to check for comprehension everything that he reads. Many different kinds of reading matter and varied types of comprehension checks should be employed.

It is not advisable to place much stress on slowing down the rate of reading, since it is desirable to retain as much speed as is consistent with adequate comprehension. As the pupil learns through experience the degree of accuracy that is necessary in different kinds of reading, he will develop ability to adjust his rate to the requirements of his task.

When comprehension is satisfactory but rate is below normal, the remedial teacher can concentrate his energies directly on the problem of increasing speed. This is the easiest of all remedial problems, and one in which considerable improvement can be expected in most cases.

What Is a Normal Rate of Reading?

One of the most frequent questions that is asked of the teacher of reading is, "How fast should I be able to read?" It should be obvious from the preceding discussion that there can be no one answer to this question; the reader's rate should vary according to the kind of material he is reading and the thoroughness with which he wants to read it. Because of this, one can suggest a typical or normal rate for a specific kind of material, but should not encourage the mistaken belief that all kinds of material should be read at one standard rate. Norms or averages are good only for the kind of reading matter that was used in obtaining them. For this reason, the typical reading rates found by different investigators show marked differences. To take one example, the median rate of reading corresponding to a grade score of 9.0 on the *Iowa Silent Reading Test, Elementary,* Form AM, is 267 words per minute. On the *Iowa Silent Reading Test, Advanced,* Form AM, the median rate corresponding to a grade score of 12.9 is only 251 words per minute. The difference is probably due to the fact that the selections used in the Advanced test are more difficult than those used in the Elementary test.

Further light on this question is cast by the rates shown in Table X. This table shows the median rate of reading for each grade from two to nine, and grade twelve, as given in the norms of several

Table X. Median Rates of Reading for Different Grades as Determined by Several Standardized Reading Tests

	Grade								
	II	*III*	*IV*	*V*	*VI*	*VII*	*VIII*	*IX*	*XII*
Highest test	118	138	170	195	230	246	267	260	295
Median test	86	116	155	177	206	215	237	252	251
Lowest test	35	75	120	145	171	176	188	199	216

Note: The number of tests included in the above table is 7 for grades two and three, 8 for grades four, five, six, and seven, 6 for grades eight and nine, and 3 for grade ten.

standardized silent reading tests. There is a steady upward trend from grade two to grade nine, with the medians of the tests showing rates going from 86 words per minute in grade two to 252 words per minute in grade nine. However, the variation at each grade level is quite large. It should be noted that the top figure at each grade is not the rate of the fastest reader, but the median rate determined by the test which has the highest median. Similarly the lowest rates shown are not the rates of the slowest readers, but the median rate reported for one of the tests. The fact that the median for grade twelve is no higher than that for grade nine is in part due to the greater difficulty of the tests used at the high school level. However, one may take the rate of 250 words per minute as a rough estimate of the normal rate of reading for high school students and adults. Anyone at those levels who reads comparatively easy material at a rate much slower than 250 words per minute may be considered a slow reader.

Norms for rate of reading tend to be misleading, because results vary so much according to the nature of the material used and the type of comprehension checks employed.[4] As yet no one has at-

[4] *A Study of Various Methods of Appraising Rate of Reading,* Educational Research Series, No. 22. Toronto: Department of Educational Research, Ontario College of Education, University of Toronto, 1950.

Carlson, Thorsten R., "Effect of Certain Test Factors in Measurement of Speed of Reading," *Journal of Educational Research,* Vol. 44, 1951, pp. 543–549.

tempted to set up rate norms for the four different kinds of rates described above.

An efficient reader should vary his rate of reading over a wide range. In reading light fiction or easy nonfiction, a rapid rate is highly advantageous. A superior adult reader should be able to go through material of this sort at a rate of at least 400 words per minute; rates as high as 1400 words per minute have been reported, although such readers are extremely rare. A person's normal reading rate, for somewhat more careful reading, may be only two thirds as fast as his most rapid reading. In very careful reading, it may be sometimes desirable to slow down to less than one third of one's rapid rate.

Individual differences in rate of reading are great, and it is futile to hope to bring all slow readers up to the average. If one succeeded in bringing them up to the present average, one would find that the new average is higher than the old one, and there would still have to be as many below average as there are above average. Furthermore, when practice for improving speed of reading is given, those who are originally fast readers usually gain as much or more than the slower readers.

For example, in the spring of 1945 the writer conducted a little experiment in improving rate of reading with about fifty college students in educational psychology. The fastest reader improved from 450 to 700 words per minute; the slowest, from 175 to 250 words per minute. Each gain was important and valuable to the student who made it, although the difference between the two students was greater at the end of the experiment than at the beginning.

To some extent, rate of reading is related to rate of thinking. It does no good to try to read faster than one can assimilate ideas. Of two readers whose rate is 175 words per minute, one may be able to improve tremendously, while the other may already be close to his maximum rate of effective thinking.

One can test a person's rate on a standardized rate of reading test and let him compare his rate with the averages for different groups. However, the correct answer to the question, "How fast should I read?" is nearly always, "Considerably faster than you read at present." Instead of advising all to try to reach the average, and to be satisfied when they do, each reader should be encouraged to try to get close to his own maximum possible efficiency in reading. Few people, if any, ever reach this potential maximum.

II. Eye Movements

IN 1878 A FRENCH PHYSICIAN named Javal published the first account of systematic observations of the movements of the eyes during reading. His work stimulated others to work on similar problems, and by 1908, when Huey published the first important book on the psychology of reading,[5] a considerable store of information had been gathered. The early investigators were handicapped by clumsy, awkward, and sometimes painful apparatus, such as fitting a hollow plaster cup over the eyeball and attaching it by a string to a revolving drum. After Dodge invented a camera for photographing eye movements many important studies were made, notably by Dr. Buswell at Chicago.[6] A portable eye-movement camera called the *Ophthalm-O-Graph,* available for many years, is now out of production, but used machines can probably be obtained.[7]

When a person reads, his eyes do not move steadily along the line of print, but progress in a series of alternating pauses and quick jerky movements called *saccadic* movements. The pauses, which are called *fixations,* last only a fraction of a second each. The eyes see in reading only during the fixations. When one comes to the end of the line there is a smooth continuous movement back to the beginning of the next line. This is called a *return sweep.*

The efficient reader does not look at each letter separately as he reads, but usually sees one or two words at each fixation. The amount a reader can see at one fixation is called his *recognition span.* The more he can see at one fixation the fewer fixations are made. Some-

[5] Huey, Edmund B., *The Psychology and Pedagogy of Reading.* New York: The Macmillan Co., 1908.

[6] Buswell, Guy T., *Fundamental Reading Habits: A Study of Their Development,* Supplementary Education Monographs, No. 21. Chicago: Department of Education, University of Chicago, 1922.

[7] Manufactured by The American Optical Co., Southbridge, Mass.

times the eyes move backward to get a second look at something that was not clearly seen. Such a backward movement is called a *regression.* Good reading is characterized by a wide recognition span, a small number of fixations per line, and a small number of regressions.

The way eye movements are represented on a photograph is illustrated in Figure 61. The camera contains a roll of moving picture

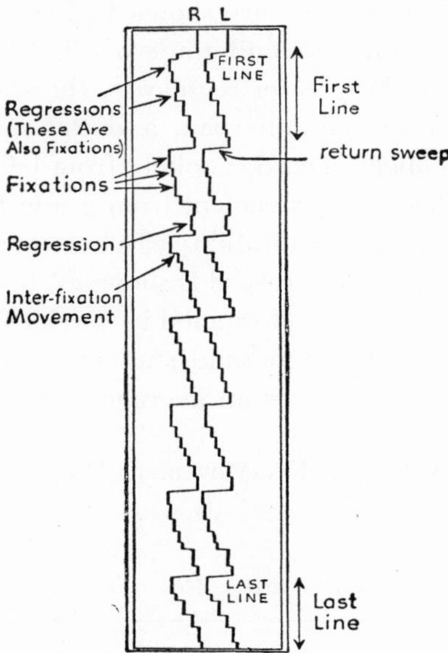

Fig. 61. Diagram showing how eye-movement characteristics are represented in a photograph. Reproduced by courtesy of the American Optical Co.

film which unrolls at a steady speed. A thin beam of light shines on each eyeball and is reflected onto the film. When the eye moves sideways between fixations, the turning of the eyeball shifts the beam of light so as to record an almost horizontal line on the film, and when the eye is motionless during a fixation, the unrolling of the film causes a vertical line to be made. The movements of both eyes are photographed simultaneously on the film, and their parallel movements give a sort of descending staircase effect. The duration of each fixation is shown by the length of the vertical line and the amount of print taken in during a fixation is indicated by the length of the horizontal line representing the movement between fixations. A regression is shown by a short horizontal movement to the left, and a return sweep from the end of one line to the beginning of the next line is shown by a long horizontal movement to the left.

Eye-movement photographs showing the progress in reading skill from the first grade to college are shown in Figure 62. Comparing the college reader with the second-grade pupil, it is easy to note the much greater speed, the greater regularity, the shorter duration of fixations, the wider recognition span, and the smaller number of regressions in the college record. Looking from left to right, we get an impression of steady improvement from grade to grade in all of these respects. Many reading disability cases are unable to do as well as the first-grade pupil whose record is shown.

Average performances, as determined by Taylor from photographs of the reading of over two thousand students, are shown in Table XI. The first-grade child makes an average of two and a half fixa-

Table XI. Eye-Movement Norms

Grade	*High 1st*	*2nd*	*3rd*	*4th*	*5th*	*6th*	*7th*	*High School*	*College*
Fixations per 100 words	250	200	175	140	125	120	115	93	80
Regressions per 100 words	60	50	40	30	25	23	21	17	10
Words read per minute	55	90	115	168	190	200	210	295	325

Adapted from Taylor, A. E., *Controlled Reading,* p. 126, 1937. By permission of the University of Chicago Press.

tions a word while the college student averages more than a word to each fixation. Regressions decrease from an average of two in every three words to one in ten words. Speed of reading increases from

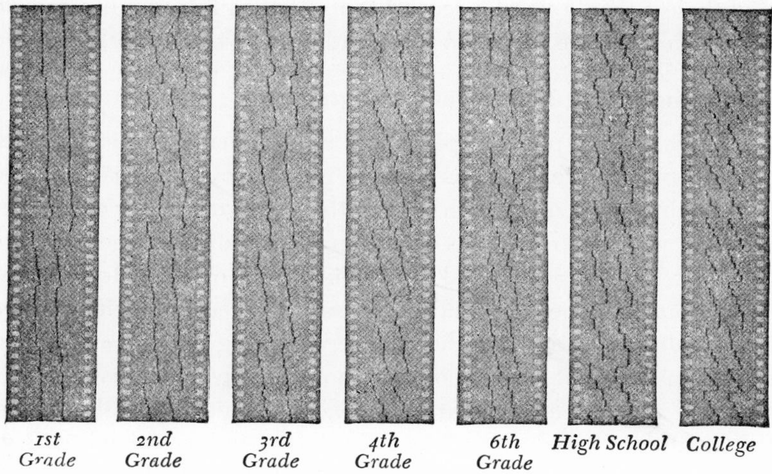

Fig. 62. Samples of eye-movement photographs. From Taylor, E. A., *Controlled Reading,* p. 128. Chicago: University of Chicago Press, 1937. Reproduced by permission of the publisher. Illustration supplied by the American Optical Co.

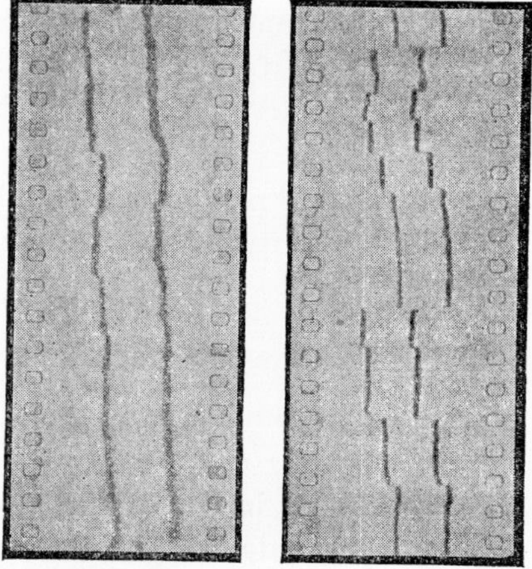

Fig. 63. Photographs of Mervin's eye movements in reading. Left, taken June 17, shows practically a letter-by-letter inspection, with the separate words indistinguishable. Right, taken June 25, shows clearly the improvement in perceiving words as units, although the fixation time on some words is very long.

slightly less than a word a second to more than five words a second. These averages are based on easy reading.

The Value of Eye-Movement Photographs

Eye-movement photographs show clearly many significant facts about a person's reading. As already pointed out, one can find out from such a photograph such data as the average number of fixations per line, words per fixations, duration of fixations, frequency of regressions, rate of reading, skill in going from one line to the next, and so on. In some cases the photographs detect difficulties in eye coordination, shown when the lines representing the two eyes do not remain parallel. It is evident that an eye-movement camera is a desirable piece of equipment for a reading clinic, especially for one that deals with reading problems at the secondary school, college, and adult levels.

The results of many research studies have shown that when selections of sufficient length are used, eye-movement photography with the *Ophthalm-O-Graph* gives reliable and valid measures of reading performance.[8] However, the expense of the apparatus and the necessity of having a trained technician to run the machine, develop the photographs, and interpret the results, makes the eye-movement camera a luxury which is impractical for most school and clinical situations. Its use will probably continue to be restricted to research laboratories and well-endowed reading clinics. Fortunately, eye movements can be studied in a reasonably satisfactory way without elaborate equipment.

Informal Measurement of Eye Movements

There are two procedures in common use for observing eye movements. One of them is the *mirror* method. The child is seated at a table on which he rests the book in reading position. The examiner sits slightly behind and to one side of him, also facing the table. A

[8] Anderson, Irving H., and Morse, William C., "The Place of Instrumentation in the Reading Program: I. Evaluation of the Ophthalm-O-Graph," *Journal of Experimental Education,* Vol. 14, 1946, pp. 256–262.

Tinker, Miles A., "The Study of Eye Movements in Reading," *Psychological Bulletin,* Vol. 43, 1946, pp. 93–120.

rectangular mirror, of the sort that can be purchased cheaply at variety stores, is placed on the table fairly close to the book and held by the examiner at such an angle that by looking at it he can observe the child's eyes.

The other method is called the *Miles Peep-Hole Method.*[9] An appropriate reading selection is mounted on a sheet of pasteboard. A small opening about one quarter of an inch square is made near the middle of the page between two lines. The examiner holds the sheet against his face so that he can look through the opening, and the child faces him and reads the selection. If the examiner is taller than the child, he should be seated and the child should stand, to make it unnecessary for the child to look up while reading.

The mirror method is the more flexible of these two, as any reading material can be used without special preparation. The peep-hole method, on the other hand, gives a somewhat clearer vision of the eye movements. These methods are not as objective and accurate as photography, but are good enough to provide most of the information that is sought.

In a third procedure, which this writer prefers, the reader holds a book on a level with his eyes as he reads, while the observer sits across the table and watches his eyes across the top of the book. This procedure can be used only for the top half of each page, as the reader's eyes are obscured by his eyelashes when he nears the bottom of the page.

It is advisable to practice on a few normal readers before attempting to observe the eye movements of a reading disability case. One should not attempt to watch more than one phase of eye movements at a time. The first three lines or so should be used to get settled. Then count the number of fixations in each of the next ten lines. The recognition span may be roughly estimated by dividing the average number of words per line by the average number of fixations per line. Next count the regressions in the following ten lines. Do not count the top or bottom lines of a page, or lines which begin or end

[9] Miles, W. R., and Segel, D., "Clinical Observation of Eye Movements in the Rating of Reading Ability," *Journal of Educational Psychology,* Vol. 20, 1929, pp. 520–529.

a paragraph. If there are so many fixations and regressions that they cannot be counted the tester should not be disappointed, as that fact in itself is highly significant. Norms for eye movements will be found in Table XI.

A third set of about ten lines of reading should be used to watch for any other significant facts. Some children have difficulty in making a return sweep at the end of a line, and so drop down to the end of the next line and follow it back to the beginning before starting to read it. This is obviously a wasteful procedure and interferes greatly with speed. Many children have difficulty in finding the beginning of a line and make extra fixations there. Other peculiarities may be found occasionally, such as a tendency to move the head rather than the eyes.

The Significance of Eye Movements

Photography or informal observation of eye movements discloses *what* the eyes do while the person reads; it does not provide an explanation of *why* they move as they do. Reading, like walking, is controlled by the brain. One cannot walk without legs, but the speed and direction of a person's walking are controlled by his central nervous system. In reading, similarly, the eyes are the servants of the brain. Regressive movements, for example, may be the result of many different causes. Among very poor readers, the most common cause of regressions is failure to recognize a word, necessitating additional inspection of the word. Some other causes of regressions are: failure to recognize the basic meaning of a word; failure to select the correct meaning of a word in its present context; inappropriate phrasing, spoiling the meaning and making rereading necessary; overlooking punctuation marks, confusing the meaning; inadequate perception resulting from an eye movement which overreaches the reader's span of perception; and external distraction which interrupts the reader's train of thought. Discovering that there are many regressions in a person's reading does not in itself explain the difficulty or indicate the specific nature of the remedial work needed.

In most cases, poor eye movements are not the cause of poor reading; they are symptoms of the fact that the reader is reading poorly.[10] The good reader is not aware of what his eyes do when he reads any more than he is aware of what his stomach does when he is digesting a tasty meal. If he tries deliberately to control his eyes while he reads, his concentration on the meaning suffers and his reading efficiency deteriorates. If a reader's comprehension and rate are satisfactory, his eye movements can be safely ignored. If his eye movements are poor, the remedial work should usually stress the basic elements of good comprehension – accurate word recognition, knowledge of word meanings, phrasing, good concentration, and so on. There are some who need training to overcome specific bad eye-movement habits, but they are definitely in the minority.

III. Elimination of Faulty Habits

EXPERIENCED TEACHERS of almost every skill know how important it is for the learner to perform smoothly and correctly before trying for speed. The music teacher knows how ruinous it is to allow a child to speed up too quickly. The swimming coach keeps his pupils swimming slowly up and down, ironing out the flaws in their technique, until he is satisfied with their form; only then does he let them begin to speed up. The golf professional cautions his pupils against trying to hit the ball hard. What he wants is a smooth, easy swing, which sends the ball a satisfactory distance without disrupting coordination. In these and in other complex skills, the basis of a highly expert performance is not the expenditure of a great deal of effort, but rather the attainment of a smooth, graceful, easy, relaxed, well-coordinated performance.

Reading is no exception to the principle that the attempt to develop speed should be postponed until good form has been achieved. Before trying to speed up the reading of a child or adult, one should try to establish fluent reading first. There are many faulty habits

[10] For more detailed presentation of this point of view, see the following:

Anderson, I. H., "An Evaluation of Some Recent Research in the Psychology of Reading," *Harvard Educational Review,* Vol. 7, 1937, pp. 330–339.

Tinker, M. A., "Motor Efficiency of the Eye as a Factor in Reading," *Journal of Educational Psychology,* Vol. 29, 1938, pp. 167–174.

Sisson, E. D., "The Causes of Slow Reading: An Analysis," *Journal of Educational Psychology,* Vol. 30, 1939, pp. 206–214.

which interfere with fluency in reading. These should be eliminated, or at least reduced in severity, before any pressure is exerted for greater speed in reading.

Excessive Word Analysis

Occasionally one finds a child whose reading is extremely slow because he inspects each word syllable by syllable or even letter by letter. Such cases were much more common in the days when phonics was overemphasized. Today they are less frequent but still do occur.

A good example of this condition is Mervin. When first seen, Mervin was twelve years old, had an IQ of 82, and was able to read at third-grade level but with first-grade speed. Sections of two photographic records of his reading are shown in Figure 63. These photographs were taken one week apart. In the earlier record, it is practically impossible to distinguish one fixation from another. His eyes went across the line letter by letter, or, at the most, two letters at a time. His rate of reading in this record was 53 words per minute. Between the two records he received six lessons, in which major attention was devoted to practice in the rapid recognition of words as wholes, and to phrasing. The second record shows a very marked change. He was now seeing words as words, not by single letters. His rate of 150 words per minute was still slow, but was an improvement of nearly 200 per cent in rate. The fixations were of excessively long duration, and there were several other faults in the total record of which only a part is shown here. But the major obstacle to his becoming a better reader had been overcome in just six lessons.

Slowness in Word Recognition

When it is found that words are perceived as units but that the child's reaction time is slow, speed of recognition can be gradually increased by direct practice in recognizing words which are exposed for only a brief duration. The use of flash cards has been discussed on page 318, and a simple easy-to-make hand tachistoscope is illustrated in Figure 19, page 208. The use of tachistoscopic exposure for speeding up perception and increasing the span of recognition is discussed below on page 525.

Word-by-word Reading

The harmful effect of reading each word as a separate unit has already been discussed, in relation to its interference with good comprehension. Obviously, reading in which there is a pause between each two words is unnecessarily slow reading. The cure for this habit is practice in phrasing, as described on pages 423–429.

Lip Movements and Subvocal Reading

One of the most common habits that retard speed in reading is the tendency to mumble or make lip movements during silent reading. Nearly all children learn to read through oral reading, which integrates the new printed language with previously acquired comprehension and speaking skills. Until the third grade, most children read just as fast orally as silently. By the fourth grade, however, the majority read somewhat faster silently. Since few people can talk intelligibly much faster than 200 words per minute, the persistence of the habit of forming each word with the lips and tongue prevents the growth of adequate speed in reading. True silent reading must be something other than inaudible oral reading.

It is not advisable to discourage lip movements in children whose reading is below third-grade level. At the third-grade level, children can be asked to try to read the way grown-ups do, without any movement of the lips. In most cases, reminding the child that he is not supposed to move his lips is all that is necessary. When the habit persists in spite of efforts to overcome it, one can prevent lip movements by having the child hold the tip of a pencil between his teeth.

At the high school and college levels one rarely finds real lip movement. Instead, the remnants of oral reading persist in slight movements of the tongue, throat, and vocal cords. The reader hears himself pronounce each word as he reads silently. Such reading is called *subvocal* reading. It is an important cause of slow reading at the upper levels.

One way of detecting subvocal reading is to place one's fingers gently on the reader's neck, just above and on both sides of the larynx. If he is a real subvocal reader, slight pulsing movements of the throat and tongue movements can usually be felt as he reads silently. Another procedure is to ask him to chew gum or candy while reading. If he complains that this spoils his concentration, one can be fairly sure that it has interfered with subvocal movements.

The attainment of true silent reading involves a gradual process of the type described as *cue reduction.*[11] This is the process by which a smaller and smaller part of a total stimulus situation becomes adequate to bring about a response that was originally made only to the total situation. Similarly, an original response involving action of the entire body may gradually be reduced until its significance is conveyed by a slight movement of one part of the body; the lifting of one eyebrow, for example, may convey the meaning of a paragraph of comment. In reading, both types of cue reduction take place. While the beginner must inspect each word carefully and often has to look at the separate letters, the expert recognizes most words in an almost instantaneous glance, and frequently sees a phrase as a unit. On the response side, the beginner has to read aloud to obtain meaning. Gradually he reduces the response to mumbling, to silent lip movement, to subvocal reading with tiny movements that cannot easily be detected, to a "hearing" of the words (in other words, having an auditory image without any detectable motor accompaniment), and finally, in a comparatively few exceptionally fast readers, to an instantaneous flash of meaning that seems to have no special motor or sensory accompaniment.

The first step in getting readers to progress beyond the subvocal stage is to make them aware of the problem and to explain the direction in which they should try to change. A purer type of silent reading gradually emerges as they engage in a series of speed drills, as described in the next section.

Finger Pointing and Head Movement

Two habits about which teachers are often too much concerned are pointing with the finger and moving the head while reading. Pointing with the finger is a crutch which some children need. It is an aid to children who tend to lose the place and to those with reversal tendencies, and it may help to develop progressive reading for

[11] Woodworth, Robert S., *Psychology,* Revised Edition, pp. 103–104. New York: Henry Holt & Co., 1929.

those who make too many regressions. Teachers are on the whole too anxious to have this habit stopped, and sometimes make a child stop pointing when he still has need of it. Pointing by itself does not interfere with rate of reading or comprehension, but it is often an accompaniment of excessive word analysis and word-by-word reading. As those faults are overcome, the pointing is usually discontinued by the child without the need of any pressure from the teacher. A card held under the line of print as a marker serves as a good intermediate step in doing away with pointing.

Moving the head from side to side is another habit which is not necessary for most individuals, but also not really harmful. The writer recently noticed in one of his college classes a boy whose head wagged from side to side like a pendulum as he read. On investigation, he proved to be the fastest reader in the class. He had not been aware of the habit, and when it was called to his attention he was able to stop it without any difficulty. There is no advantage in moving the head, except possibly for children who have mild difficulties in binocular coordination. Most head-waggers can give up the habit very quickly without ill effects.

Difficulty with the Return Sweep

Some children have difficulty in making a return sweep from the end of one line to the beginning of the next line. This is shown in the observation of eye movements by the fact that one or two extra fixations are made at the beginning of each line. There are a few children who, after reading a line, look back along the line and then drop vertically to the beginning of the next line. This habit results in taking nearly twice as long to read the line as is necessary. When difficulty in making the return sweep is discovered, one should look for evidence of eye-muscle difficulty or slow fusion, which at reading distance sometimes is a result of uncorrected farsightedness.

To develop greater skill in making the return sweep, which should be a single quick diagonal movement, one can use widely spaced lines, with diagonal lines connecting the end of each line with the beginning of the next line. The child is instructed to try to look along the diagonal when going from line to line. There is very little prepared material of this sort available (an example is shown in Fig. 64) and usually it is necessary to make up special material on the typewriter, starting with triple spacing and reducing to double spacing as the child improves. Often only a few days of practice are needed.

Paragraphs to Read

Read the paragraphs below. Be sure to read to end of each line and then to move your eyes along the dotted line to the beginning of the next line.

A little black and white dog lived in a barn. All he had to do was to keep mice out of the barn. One day he said, "I am going to stay away. I shall find something better than mice."

Soon a rabbit hopped by. The little

Fig. 64. Sample from an exercise to develop return sweep. From Brueckner, L. J., and Lewis W. D., *Diagnostic Tests and Remedial Exercises in Reading.* Philadelphia: John C. Winston Co., 1935. Reproduced by permission of the publisher, and reduced in size.

Regressions

The type of remedial work needed to reduce the frequency of regressive movements depends on the causes, which have been listed on page 516. Regressions are the eye-movement equivalents of repetitions in oral reading. When they are due to deficiencies or inaccuracies in word recognition or word meaning, attempting to train the eye movements will obviously be of little or no value. Any reader, no matter how skillful, will make a large number of regressions when reading material which is heavily loaded with unfamiliar words, peculiar or highly involved sentence structure, or very difficult ideas. However, if a tendency to excessive regressions persists as a lingering bad habit in a reader whose word recognition and comprehension are at a high level, specific exercises to overcome the regressions may be advisable.

A type of practice which is sometimes helpful in the reduction of unnecessary regressions is the use of *cross-line exercises.* In the beginning one uses a page prepared on the typewriter as shown in Figure 65. Exercises of this type are sometimes called saccadic exercises. The instructions are to go across the top line, taking one look at each letter, then follow the diagonal to the second line, and so on down the page. At the beginning of each remedial practice period the reader goes over this page three to five times, gradually speeding

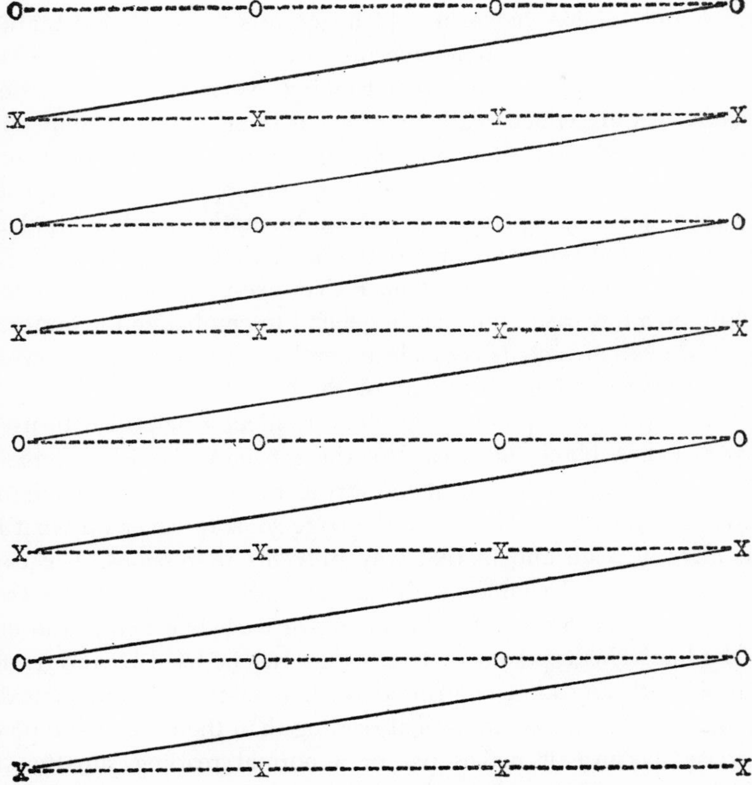

Fig. 65. A page of cross-line exercise, prepared on the typewriter.

up. After the reader has become skillful in using this page, a second page is introduced in which single words replace the meaningless letters. A third stage uses widely spaced phrases, three or four to a line.

One should not expect too great benefits from cross-line exercises. They serve mainly to convince the reader that he can go smoothly across lines without looking back. A direct transfer of the steady, evenly spaced movements, built up in this type of exercise, to connected, meaningful reading is not usually achieved.

The purpose of cross-line exercises is to develop a steady, regular sequence of eye movements. There is a substantial body of research and opinion, however, which supports the view that training eye movements is an ineffective procedure. Tinker concluded that there is a lack of evidence that training eye movements develops effective habits which really improve reading ability.[12] Somewhat later he modified his view only slightly, stating that "an occasional person may be benefited in reading by training the eyes to greater accuracy in sweeping from one fixation to another, such as the back sweep from the end of one line to the beginning of the other." [13] The present writer agrees with Tinker that eye-movement training is helpful in a few cases, but that in general to emphasize the improvement of eye movements is to place emphasis wrongly on the symptoms of poor reading rather than on the basic factors.

A second type of practice which is frequently helpful is to use a cover card. A blank index card of the 4x6 inch size is convenient. The reader starts the card at the top of the page. As he reads, he moves the card gradually down the page so as to cover up what he has already read, and in that way prevents regressions. The card should be slanted slightly with the left corner a little lower than the right, so as to cover the beginning of each line before the end of the line. This type of practice, which can be used by the reader himself with any kind of printed reading matter, should logically have a greater transfer to normal reading than the cross-line type of exercise, because it makes use of a normal reading situation to which only a slight addition has been made.

The elimination of regressions is also one of the purposes of the

[12] Tinker, M. A., "The Role of Eye-Movements in Diagnostic and Remedial Reading," *School and Society*, Vol. 39, 1934, pp. 147–148.

[13] Tinker, M. A., "Motor Efficiency of the Eye as a Factor in Reading," *Journal of Educational Psychology*, Vol. 29, 1938, pp. 167–174.

Tinker, M. A., "The Study of Eye Movements in Reading," *Psychological Bulletin*, Vol. 43, 1946, pp. 93–120.

several kinds of controlled reading practice which are described in the next section.

IV. Increasing Rate by Direct Practice

ONCE THE SLOW READER has reached satisfactory levels in word recognition and comprehension and has begun to eliminate specific interfering habits of the types described in the preceding section, he is ready for practice aimed directly at speeding up his reading. There are four main types of practice for increasing rate of reading: tachistoscopic training, controlled reading, timed reading, and extensive reading without specific emphasis on speed.

The Use of the Tachistoscope

A tachistoscope is a device which allows the presentation of visual material for brief intervals of time. It can range in complexity from a simple handmade cardboard device (see Fig. 19) to a complex laboratory instrument controlling the exposure time with great accuracy. In most of the recent work projection tachistoscopes have been used, consisting of a lantern-slide projector with a device like an enlarged camera shutter which can be set for exposures from a second or more to 1/100th of a second.

Commercially available tachistoscopes include the following:

AVR Eye-Span Trainer, Model 10. A hand-operated vinyl plastic tachistoscope, with prepared slides for practice with digits, words, and phrases. Audio-Visual Research, Chicago 5.

SVE Tach-adapter. A simple tachistoscope for use with slide or filmstrip projectors, with one speed, 1/25th second. Society for Visual Education, Chicago 14.

AVR Flash-Tachment, a hand-operated plastic attachment for 2x2 slide or filmstrip projectors, with approximate speeds from 1/25th to 1/100th second. Audio-Visual Research.

Flash-Meter. A large shutter, of metal and glass construction, with variable control of illumination and speeds ranging from "time" to 1/100th second; used with a Keystone Daylight Overhead Projector, the combination is a *Keystone Tachistoscope.* Masks permit exposure of any amount of material from a single word to an entire 3x4-inch slide. Usable with specially prepared or homemade slides. Keystone View Co., Meadville, Pa.

SVE Speed-i-o-Scope, a metal and glass tachistoscopic shutter very much like the *Flash-Meter,* usable with a variety of slide and filmstrip projectors; exposures from "time" to 1/100th second, and control of intensity of illumination. A less expensive model with only two speeds is also available. Society for Visual Education.

Timex, a tachistoscope shutter used with a projector, requiring the use of special filmstrips which can be projected at rates as fast as 1/150th second. Filmstrips with digits, words, and phrases are supplied. Expensive. Educational Developmental Laboratories, 15 Washington Place, New York City.

Perceptoscope, a very versatile projector for both tachistoscopic and controlled reading projection, using a unique system involving two filmstrips, one of which substitutes for a mask or shutter. Quite expensive. Perceptual Development Laboratories, St. Louis 5.

Although much pioneer experimental work had gone before,[14] present practice in the use of the tachistoscope stems mainly from the work of Renshaw. During World War II Renshaw developed a highly successful tachistoscopic method for training airplane spotters for the Navy. He also developed a system of training designed to speed up perception and increase the span of recognition, in which major attention was given to the use of series of digits. Average gains in rate of reading for groups were not highly impressive, although some spectacular individual gains were made.[15]

MacLatchy tried an experimental program in the first and second grades of several Ohio schools, in which visual training with a tachistoscope was the major feature. She concluded that this training helped the pupils in fluency and comprehension, and also helped in arithmetic.[16]

Cleland compared the relative effectiveness of four methods of tachistoscopic training with college students: digits only, words and phrases only, half of each period spent with digits and half with

[14] Dearborn, Walter F., "The Use of the Tachistoscope in Diagnostic and Remedial Reading," *Psychological Monographs,* Vol. 47, 1936, No. 2.

[15] Renshaw, Samuel, "The Visual Perception and Reproduction of Forms by Tachistoscopic Methods," *Journal of Psychology,* Vol. 20, 1945, pp. 217–233.

[16] MacLatchy, Josephine, "Bexley Reading Study," *Educational Research Bulletin,* Ohio State University, Vol. 25, 1946, pp. 141–168.

words and phrases, and fifteen sessions with digits followed by fifteen sessions with words and phrases. He concluded that tachistoscopic training at this level does increase rate of reading without loss of comprehension, and that the use of both digits and verbal material in each session was the most effective of the four methods.[17]

On the other hand, Manolakes found no significant differences in number of fixations, duration of fixations, span of recognition, or reduction of regressive movements in a group of Marine Corps officers as compared to an equivalent group given a nontachistoscopic reading improvement program; the nontachistoscopic group gained more in rate of reading.[18]

For readers who wish to learn more about the details, a clear step-by-step exposition of tachistoscopic procedures for reading improvement has been given by Barnette.[19]

As yet the amount of well-controlled experimentation is insufficient for drawing any firm conclusions on the real value of tachistoscopic training.

Controlled Reading

The *Metron-O-Scope*, a device which used reading material printed on specially prepared continuous rolls and had a three-shutter arrangement by which one third of a line at a time could be exposed, allowed the presentation of reading material at a rate which was selected by the instructor, and which could be increased at each practice session. It came in two sizes, one for individual and one for group use, but is now mainly of historical interest.

Motion picture films which presented one phrase at a time brilliantly lit against a fainter background of the rest of the page were the second venture in the creation of reading material that would control the phrasing and the rate of reading during practice. The original Harvard films, planned by Dearborn, were replaced by the

[17] Cleland, Donald L., "An Experimental Study of Tachistoscopic Training as It Relates to Speed and Comprehension in Reading," unpublished PH.D. Dissertation. Pittsburgh: University of Pittsburgh, 1950.

[18] Manolakes, George, "The Effects of Tachistoscopic Training in an Adult Reading Program," *Journal of Applied Psychology*, Vol. 36, 1952, pp. 410–412.

[19] Barnette, Gaspar C., *Learning Through Seeing with Tachistoscopic Teaching Techniques*. Dubuque, Iowa: William C. Brown Co., 1951.

Harvard University Reading Films, Second Series (Harvard University Press), a series of sixteen films suitable for college level work, with the speed of projection increasing from less than 300 words per minute to about 500 words per minute. These have been successfully used in many college and adult reading programs. The *Iowa High School Training Films* (Iowa State University) is a quite similar series of fourteen films with somewhat simpler material appropriate for high school use.

The *Controlled Reader* is a film-strip projector equipped with a variable speed automatic drive. Special film strips are provided which present connected reading material. A moving slot travels across from left to right, uncovered words and covering them again. The effect is much like that of a controlled reading film. Educational Developmental Laboratories, 15 Washington Place, New York.

The *Perceptoscope* (see p. 526) achieves the same effects as a controlled reading film by the simultaneous use of two filmstrips, one of which projects a page on the screen while the other gives extra brightness to one phrase at a time. In a situation in which extensive use of controlled reading is employed, the comparatively low cost of the films may justify the high initial cost of this projector.

These methods try to compel the reader to move his eyes in a set pattern and to fixate each word or phrase for a predetermined time interval. They make it impossible for the reader to slow down when he meets with difficulty or to reread. For that reason they are regarded with some suspicion by those who, like this writer, regard eye movements as symptoms rather than as causes of poor reading. As Dearborn pointed out, the machinery is intriguing, effective motivation is provided for most pupils to try to speed up their reading, and comprehension questions follow the reading so that attention to meaning cannot be neglected.[20]

Reading Pacers. A method for controlling reading rate without

[20] Dearborn, W. F., Anderson, I. H., and Brewster, J. R., "A New Method for Teaching Phrasing and for Increasing the Size of Reading Fixations," *Psychological Record,* Vol. 1, 1937, pp. 459–475: "Controlled Reading by Means of a Motion Picture Technique," *Psychological Record,* Vol. 2, 1938, pp. 219–222; Dearborn, W. F., and Wilking, S. V., "Improving the Reading of College Freshmen," *School Review,* Vol. 44, 1941, pp. 668–678.

imposing a set pattern of phrasing or a uniform rate of speed was worked out by Buswell, and involves the simple principle of a shutter which gradually covers a page from top to bottom at a speed which can be regulated.[21] Several devices using the Buswell principle and designed for individual practice are now available.

AVR Reading Rateometer. Uses a horizontal plastic bar as a shutter which descends over the page at a rate controlled by an electric motor; wide range of speeds; built-in rate calculator; comparatively inexpensive. Audio-Visual Research.

Keystone Reading Pacer. Uses a thin metal rod instead of a shutter so as to make looking back possible; electric motor provides wide range of speeds. Keystone View Co.

TDC Reading Rate Controller. Uses an opaque shutter which can descend over the page at a very wide range of speeds; electrical motor. Three Dimension Co., Chicago 41.

SRA Reading Accelerator. Uses an opaque plastic shutter which moves down over the page at a rate controlled by an electric motor; a portable nonelectric model also available. Science Research Associates.

Shadowscope Reading Pacer. Employs a horizontal beam of light reflected by a turning mirror so as to move steadily down the page; the intensity of the illumination can be reduced at will until the beam is barely perceptible, thereby producing an almost natural reading situation; speed controlled, as in the other machines, by an electric motor. Lafayette Instrument Co., Lafayette, Indiana.

These machines are widely used in high school, college, and adult reading programs. They provide individualized practice in which the learner can set his own rate at each practice session, and when the practice is followed by adequate questioning on comprehension, provide what seems to be a well-motivated procedure for guiding the learner toward gradually increased rate without loss in understanding.

The problem with these, as with all somewhat artificial methods of practice, is that the amount of carryover to natural reading situations is sometimes disappointingly small. How much of the favorable effect is the result of controlling the rate and how much is motiva-

[21] Buswell, Guy T., *Remedial Reading at the College and Adult Levels,* Supplementary Education Monographs, No. 50. Chicago: University of Chicago, 1939.

tion which could be secured by other nonmechanical procedures is impossible to estimate at present.

Increasing Rate through Motivated Reading

In contrast to the point of view which favors controlled reading is one which puts major emphasis on increased motivation in natural reading situations. The major causes of slow reading are considered to be lack of enough practice in reading easy, interesting material, and lack of motivation to improve speed.

From this point of view, a program for increasing rate of reading should have three major components. The first consists of overcoming specific interfering habits, as described in Section III of this chapter. The second involves motivating the reader to do a large amount of easy reading. This provides the abundant practice needed to develop fluency. The absence of vocabulary and comprehension difficulties in such material allows the reader to read easily, without the need to hesitate and reread that is created by difficult reading matter. If the subject matter is sufficiently interesting, the desire to find out what comes next provides natural motivation to read quickly, while the absence of pressure to read at a rate set by someone else eliminates strain and tension. Methods for developing greater interest in voluntary reading have been discussed in Chapter XVII.

The third phase of the program involves a series of timed silent reading exercises with comprehension checks. For these, one can use either published workbook selections, or general reading matter of a comparatively easy nature. The timed exercises strengthen motivation to keep the rate going up, provide a definite record of progress, and at the same time insure that comprehension does not suffer in the process.

There are several workbooks that can be used for timed reading in the upper grades and secondary school. The *Standard Test Lessons in Reading* by McCall and Crabbs [22] have been used successfully in many programs. Each page consists of a brief selection, followed by several multiple-choice questions. Three minutes are

[22] See p. 456 and Fig. 56.

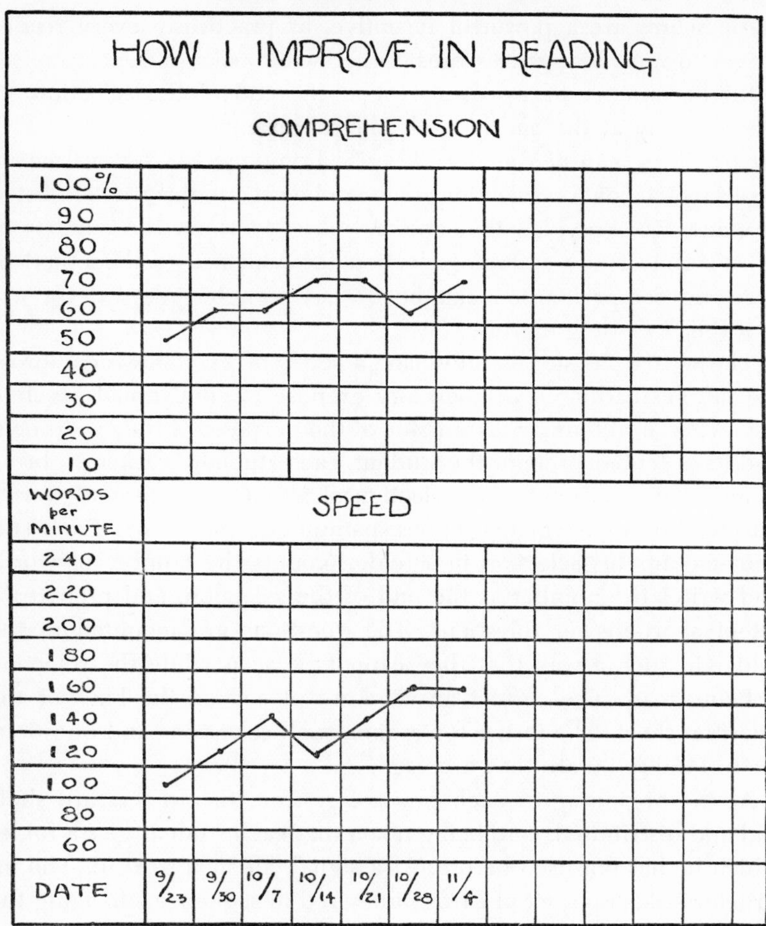

Fig. 66. Individual progress chart suitable for more mature pupils, for recording results on periodic informal tests.

allowed for reading the selection and answering the questions. If the reader goes too slowly, he cannot answer enough of the questions; if he reads carelessly or too rapidly, he gets too many answers wrong. In successive exercises he learns to read so as to increase his scores. Approximate grade scores are given for each exercise. These grade scores are a powerful incentive, as practically every reader strives to raise his grade scores. Other workbooks present exercises with the number of words shown at the end of the selection, or cumulatively at the end of each line; an example is shown in Figure 67. These can be timed as described on page 164. Several workbooks which contain selections that can be used in this way are listed on page 456. Provided that one is willing to count the number of words, almost any suitable selection for which a good method of checking comprehension can be devised can be adapted for use as a timed reading exercise.

The writer has successfully used a series of practices for improving rate of reading as a laboratory exercise in educational psychology. After a preliminary discussion of the purposes of the experiment and its potential value to the student, each student is asked to bring in an interesting nonfiction selection of about one thousand words, selected from current magazines, pamphlets, and so on. Each student mounts his selection in a folder, counts the number of words and writes the number at the end of the selection, and prepares a set of short-answer questions. The questions are mounted in the folder in such a way that they cannot be seen while the selection is being read. The correct answers are placed on the back of the question sheet. The instructor examines all selections and questions for suitability before they are used.

At the beginning of each practice session, the folders are shuffled and distributed, care being taken that each student gets a folder which he has not used before. At a signal, all start to read. The instructor holds up a set of cards numbered in sequence, changing the number each fifteen seconds. As each student finishes reading he jots down the number being displayed. He then answers the questions, and marks his answers by means of the key. Then he computes his rate in terms of words per minute.[23] Finally he enters his

[23] When the number is changed each 15 seconds, the rate is easily obtained by multiplying the number of words in the selection by 4, and dividing by the number exposed when the student looked up. The rate obtained is only approximate, because the time is correct only to the nearest quarter minute, but is close enough for practice purposes when the selections are long enough to take several minutes to read. If greater accuracy is desired, one can expose a new number every 10 seconds, and multiply by 6 before dividing.

Picking up Potatoes (214 words)

Read this story carefully. Then draw a line **under** the word below the question that is the **best** answer. Be ready to read the sentences in the story that show **that your answers are** correct.

Mr. Hart's potatoes were ready 5
to be dug late in June. Pete drove 13
two mules which pulled the potato 19
digger. This machine stuck its iron 25
fingers down under the potato vines. 31
It lifted out a clump of dirt and po- 39
tatoes. Then it sifted out the dirt 46
and laid all the potatoes in a row 54
on the ground. Fred and Jack 60
picked up the potatoes. Pete's two 66
small boys helped, and so did two 73
strange men who came to help with 80
the job. Before the first day's work 87
was over, Jack found that picking up 94
potatoes was the hardest work he 100
had ever done. Stooping over hour 106
after hour made his back ache. 112
The sun seemed to burn hotter 118
than he had ever before felt it. Mr. 126
Hart had a whole carload of po- 132
tatoes to sell. Jack was very sure 139
that if there had been many more 146
he would have left that farm. 152

Mr. Hart told Fred and Jack that 159
when he was a boy he had to dig the 169
potatoes with a hoe. That was just 176
as hard work as picking them up. Even 184
then they often cut the potatoes with 191
the hoe. The boys said they were 198
thankful that they did not have to 205
dig the potatoes as well as pick them 213
up. 214

1. When did Mr. Hart dig his potatoes?
   May June July August
2. What did he use to dig them?
   hoe plow machine hands
3. How many people picked up the potatoes?
   two four six eight
4. What kind of work was it?
   easy fun hard pleasant
5. How many potatoes did Mr. Hart sell?
   bushel quart wagon carload
6. What did Mr. Hart use to dig potatoes when he was a boy?
   hoe plow machine hands
7. How did the boys say they felt about the new way of digging potatoes?
   sorry angry happy thankful

Number correct__________

Fig. 67. An exercise which provides practice in timed reading, noting details, and motivated oral reading. Exercises of this general type are valuable and are used frequently in remedial programs in the upper grades and secondary school. From Brueckner, L. J., and Lewis, W. D., *Diagnostic Tests and Remedial Exercises in Reading*. Philadelphia: John C. Winston Co., 1935. Reproduced by permission of the publisher, and reduced in size.

rate and comprehension scores on a progress chart similar to that shown in Figure 66. Such practices usually take between ten and fifteen minutes.[24]

Repetition of this experiment with several classes has shown that substantial improvement is the rule. In Figure 68 the median results from one class of twenty-nine students are shown. The median improvement was 96 words per minute, an improvement of 39 per cent over the beginning rate of 247 words per minute. Accuracy scores varied somewhat, but ended up about as high as they were at the beginning. In the second and fifteenth practice sessions, approximately equivalent textbook selections were used. The total time spent was about three and a half hours, divided among the sixteen practice sessions. The rate of improvement obtained, considering the time spent, compares favorably with the results of any of the methods of controlled reading. Similar results have been obtained with several other classes.

No individual diagnosis was done in this class. Instead a volunteer committee looked up the causes of slow reading and reported their findings to the class. While many reported that they were helped by suggestions about the desirability of reading in phrases, and so on, this procedure did not meet the needs of all. Two students showed practically no improvement; for them, and for some whose gains were comparatively small, a better outcome might have been attained if the causes of their slowness had been investigated and special types of exercises had been provided as needed.

A similar procedure can be employed for practice in timed reading at any grade level from the sixth grade up. In the elementary school, the teacher would probably have to take the major responsibility for the selection and preparation of the selections to be used, but the rest of the procedure could be employed without change.

As compared with controlled reading in groups, this procedure has two major advantages: normal reading matter is used, and each stu-

[24] This procedure is an adaptation of a method first worked out by Goldstein and Justman. See: Goldstein, H., and Justman, J., "A Classroom Approach to the Improvement of Reading Rate of College Students," *Journal of Educational Psychology*, Vol. 33, 1942, pp. 506–516.

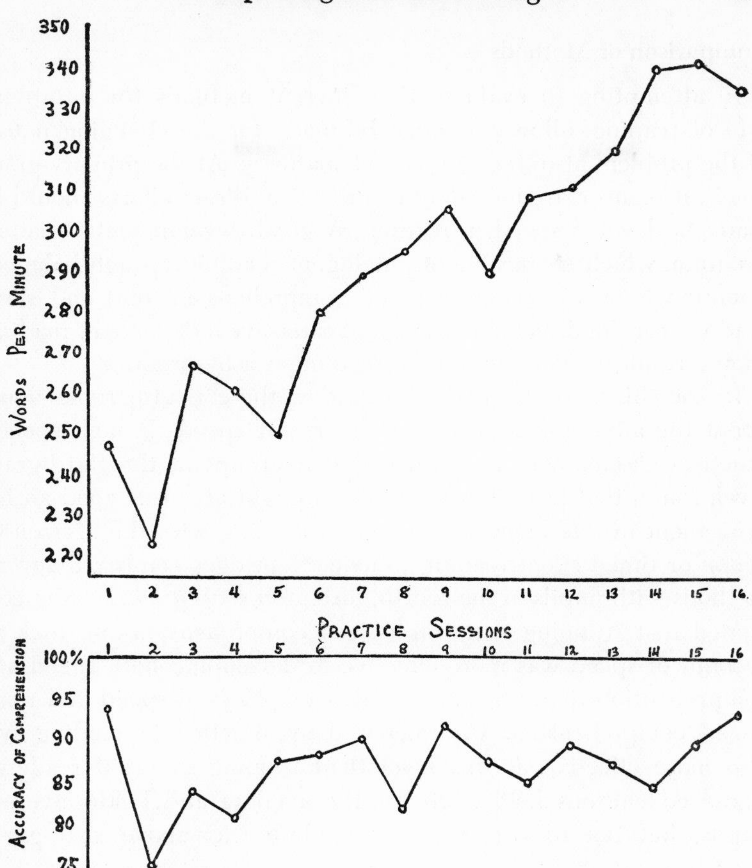

Fig. 68. Median rate and accuracy scores of 29 students in educational psychology who took part in 16 practice sessions for increasing rate of reading.

dent, although reading in a group, governs his own rate of reading and competes with his own past performances. It is really individual practice in a group situation. The material, having been selected by the students, is more likely to be appropriate in difficulty and interest appeal than material selected by the instructor might be.

Comparison of Methods

In attempting to evaluate the different methods for improving rate of reading, allowance must be made for the changing nature of the problem at different levels of maturity. At the primary-grade levels, it seems extremely doubtful that any direct efforts should be made to develop speed in reading. A good developmental reading program, which creates fluent, intelligent reading through balanced attention to word recognition and comprehension, oral and silent reading, careful directed reading and extensive independent reading, should result in adequate rate of reading as a by-product.

In the third, fourth, and fifth grades, there is also some doubt about the advisability of aiming at greater speed through specific practice. Cason, working with matched groups at the third-grade level, found that free library reading brought about as good an improvement in rate as either controlled reading with the *Metron-O-Scope* or timed silent reading practice.[25] Bridges compared several methods with pupils in the fourth, fifth, and sixth grades.[26] She concluded that "training that emphasized comprehension and took no account of speed was more effective in developing both speed and comprehension than was training that emphasized speed and minimized comprehension. Undirected daily practice in reading was also more effective at this level than training in rapid reading." These conclusions held good for the average and below average pupils, but not for those whose reading was above sixth-grade level.

At the college level, Westover compared the effectiveness of using the same practice material in the *Metron-O-Scope* as compared to a mimeographed version.[27] Both methods produced improvement, and there was no significant difference between the controlled and non-

[25] Cason, Eloise B., *Mechanical Methods for Increasing the Speed of Reading*, Contributions to Education, No. 878. New York: Bureau of Publications, Teachers College, Columbia University, 1943.

[26] Bridges, L. H., "Speed *versus* Comprehension in Elementary Reading," *Journal of Educational Psychology*, Vol. 32, 1941, pp. 314–320.

[27] Westover, Frederick L., *Controlled Eye Movements versus Practice Exercises in Reading*, Contributions to Education, No. 917. New York: Bureau of Publications, Teachers College, Columbia University, 1946.

controlled reading. Glock compared three methods, two of which used different controlled reading techniques while the third was motivated time comprehension practice without machinery.[28] Both reading rate and eye-movement patterns improved in all three methods.

At present, there is no reason to consider controlled reading superior to the procedure described above as motivated, timed reading. Traxler, in a comprehensive review of the literature on controlled reading, came to the conclusion that "the results of research studies that have been conducted so far do not provide clear-cut evidence either favorable or unfavorable to controlled reading." [29] In other words, the methods which do not require any special type of apparatus seem at present to give as good results as those which require elaborate equipment. The studies which have appeared since that summary would appear to support Traxler's conclusions. When the equipment is available, the writer's preference would be for a procedure which includes some tachistoscope practice and some controlled reading, but puts major emphasis on well-motivated practice sessions stressing both rate and comprehension.

Training for improved speed of reading should, in the light of present evidence, come in as a definite part of a development reading program at and above the sixth grade. Individual pupils may, of course, need remedial help at lower grade levels because of extremely slow reading; but for the majority, rate can be expected to develop as a by-product of a good reading program until the sixth grade. From then on, specific provisions for speeding up reading seem desirable, through high school and at least the first year of college. Unfortunately, in many school systems no attention is given to the teaching of reading above the sixth grade. The fact that so many high school and college students read at a rate which is at or below sixth-grade norms is probably due in part to the failure of the

[28] Glock, Marvin D., "The Effect upon Eye-Movements and Reading Rate at the College Level of Three Methods of Training," *Journal of Educational Psychology,* Vol. 40, 1949, pp. 93–106.

[29] Traxler, A. E., "Value of Controlled Reading: Summary of Opinion and Research," *Journal of Experimental Education,* Vol. 11, 1943, pp. 280–292.

schools to provide continued guidance in the acquisition of higher-level reading skills.

Suggested Additional Reading

Gates, Arthur I. *The Improvement of Reading,* Third Edition, Ch. 14.
Yoakam, Gerald A. *Basal Reading Instruction,* Chs. 11, 12.

· XIX ·

Case Studies of Reading Disability

WHEN THE DIFFERENT ASPECTS of diagnosis and remedial treatment are taken up separately, as they have been in the preceding several chapters, it is impossible to get an idea of how everything fits together in actual work with children. The present chapter attempts to bring the various threads together by presenting a few selected case studies in a fair amount of detail. The original records on any of these cases fill a thick folder, so that a great deal of condensation has been necessary, but an effort has been made to include all essential points and to give the flavor of uniqueness that was characteristic of each of these children.

The four cases which are presented below have been selected to show a wide variation in intelligence, cultural background, specific causal handicaps, and remedial procedures. While an attempt has been made to select different kinds of cases, no small group of case studies can do more than to suggest the variety of problems and personalities to be met. These four cases represent differences in age, sex, intelligence, social and cultural background, and patterns of causal factors. From the remedial side they show individual and small group work, differing approaches in teaching word recognition, varying emphases on vocabulary, comprehension, and rate, and unequal success in overcoming personality as well as reading problems. The diagnostic studies were either made by or checked by the writer, and the remedial teaching was carried on under his supervision.

Case I

Diagnostic Study

Alice was referred for private diagnosis and remedial teaching because of persisting lack of progress in reading. During the summer following a poor year in second grade her father had tried unsuccessfully to teach her, and the complete failure of these efforts convinced the parents that expert help was needed. When she was first seen she was starting the third grade and was 8 years 8 months old. The diagnostic study was made by a school psychologist.

General Impressions. Alice was a small, pale, blond girl with whom it was difficult to establish a relationship at first. She was wary and apprehensive, and at the mention of a reading test hid under the table. She openly expressed a marked dislike of reading, of school, and of learning situations in general. Eventually she complied enough to complete the diagnostic testing.

Physical Factors. Alice had been a premature baby and had always been small for her age. A successful operation for the correction of strabismus had been performed in June, at the end of the second grade. Medical study had disclosed no physical basis for her poor urinary control, which involved bedwetting and occasional wetting of pants in school. Although originally left-handed, she had started to write with the right hand in school while continuing to use the left hand for such activities as throwing and cutting; on lateral dominance tests she showed mixed hand dominance, right-eye dominance, mixed foot dominance, and some directional confusion. The mother was not aware of any pressure for this change having been exerted by any adult.

Abilities. Alice had superior general intelligence with an IQ of 121 according to the *Pintner-Cunningham*, given in school at the beginning of the first grade, and had scored a B rating (good) on the *Metropolitan Readiness Test* at that time. Clinical impressions were that Alice was a very bright little girl, functioning poorly because of emotional blocking. There was no evidence of any special intellectual defects.

Reading. The results of standardized reading tests were as follows:

Gilmore Oral Reading Test [1]
Accuracy R.G. 1.7
Comprehension R.G. 3.5
Gates Advanced Primary Reading Tests
Type 1, Word Recognition, R.G. 2.0
Type 2, Paragraph Reading, R.G. 1.7

Although silent and oral tests indicated reading ability at high first-grade level, informal book samples showed her instructional level to be primer, with many indications of frustration at first-reader level. She read very slowly and hesitantly in word by word fashion. Her sight vocabulary was limited and she did not make any attempt to figure out new words. She knew the sounds of all consonants except *g* and *q*, but none of the vowels; blending ability was good. Typical word recognition errors were *ball* for *boy, and* for *is, at* for *in,* and *has* for *is,* and she did not attempt such words as *man, does,* and *his.* There were a few reversals such as *was* for *saw.*

Other Schoolwork. Alice was up to grade level in arithmetic computation but refused to try any problems that required reading. She was able to do practically no spelling, and she joined in very few group activities.

Family History. Alice's father was a prosperous business man who was domineering, demanding, and authoritarian in his relationships with his wife and children. Her mother was a pretty, charming, and artistically talented woman who was also quite immature, egocentric, and indecisive. Alice's one sister, two years younger, seemed to be favored by both parents, and Alice hated her intensely. From the beginning of school Alice's father had exerted pressure on her for accomplishment she could not achieve, and as a result Alice had developed a strong dislike for both school and her father.

School History. Alice had gone to a private nursery school for two and a half years and then entered kindergarten at the age of 5 years, 8 months, in a public school in a wealthy suburban community. In

[1] The names of the forms used have been omitted. Throughout this chapter, when a test which has equivalent forms was administered to a child on more than one occasion, a different form was used each time.

kindergarten she wet her pants occasionally, continually tugged at a lock of her hair, hit other children and tried to win friends by bragging, and was tense and aggressive; the one favorable comment was that she listened attentively to stories. In first grade her progress was slower than most of the children but not entirely unsatisfactory; she was reading a primer and scored 1.8 on a standardized test at the end of the year; it was noticed that she became very easily discouraged. Her second-grade teacher found her work to be very inconsistent, and she seemed to make no headway in reading or spelling. At the beginning of the third grade the teacher found that when Alice was asked to read, she refused and put her feet up on the desk; she chewed her pencil, did very little, and refused to join group activities in the classroom or on the playground.

Emotional Adjustment. Much of the picture of her emotional adjustment has necessarily been covered above. Alice was clearly an unhappy, tense little girl. She had several nervous habits including nailbiting, hair-pulling, and enuresis. She was quite open in her expression of dislike for school and her sister, and spoke freely about how easy it was to "get Mother's goat." She seemed quite perceptive of the way others felt about her and aware of her feelings toward them. She obviously had deep feelings of inferiority and felt that people didn't like her because of her own shortcomings. She felt rejected and unloved by anyone. It seemed probable that she carried into her relations with other children her feelings about being outshone by her sister, and for this reason was hostile to other children and had great difficulty in either accepting or offering friendship. Similarly she was emotionally unable to accept the necessity of sharing the attention of her teacher with the other children in her class.

Toward the end of the first grade, Alice's evident unhappiness and frequent fights, quarrels, and tantrums at home had caused her parents to start psychiatric treatment for her. Treatment continued into the second grade, but was discontinued after eight months because of Alice's marked resistance. It was considered that Alice had improved somewhat in her feelings toward her father, but that the other problems had been left essentially unchanged.

Diagnostic Summary. Alice, a child growing up in a wealthy home, sent to good schools from the age of three on, developed a reading disability despite the superior intelligence and good readiness shown by tests at the beginning of the first grade. There was no clear evidence of a neurological immaturity or irritability, always a possibility in the premature. Her strabismus had probably intensified her inferiority feelings but probably had not interfered with clarity of one-eyed vision; since the operation her vision was apparently satisfactory. The directional confusion associated with her voluntary conversion to right-handedness probably had been more marked at the ages of six and seven than it was by the time of this diagnostic study, and probably was a contributing handicap. The emotional problems seemed of greatest importance, and involved feelings of rejection, intense sibling rivalry, projection of hostility upon classmates, and marked hostility to reading and other learning situations.

Recommendations. Despite Alice's hostility to reading, the failure of the combination of psychiatric treatment and good group instruction in school to induce reading improvement, followed by the father's unsuccessful efforts, made it desirable to try private remedial reading instruction. It was hoped that an experienced remedial teacher who could give exclusive attention to Alice and could provide warmth, acceptance, and the security of a stable, orderly procedure might prove effective. Because of Alice's hostility and defiance of people whom she perceived as being pliable or weak like her mother, the remedial lessons would have to be firmly structured at first. At the same time the tutor would have to make the learning situation as pleasant as possible, keep everything at a very easy, nonfrustrating level for some time, and avoid those activities such as silent reading toward which Alice seemed most resistant. Periodic discussions with Alice's mother and classroom teacher were planned so as to coordinate efforts.

Remedial Program

Alice was scheduled for three lessons a week, after school, with an experienced remedial reading tutor. The crucial first lesson was started with an inspection of the room, including discussion of souvenirs of trips the tutor had taken. The tutor remarked that many children came to her because they had trouble in reading and that they found the lessons to be fun. She then read a fairy story to Alice. They then went over to the bookcase to get an idea of the kind of stories Alice might like. Alice pointed to a preprimer which she had at home and said, "It's cinchy." Following this lead, the tutor suggested that they read a few pages in it together. The tutor expressed pleasure that Alice could read that well, and the lesson ended on an optimistic note. Alice told her mother that she had enjoyed the lesson and was looking forward to the next one. After this successful start there was never anything but eagerness for the lessons, and Alice insisted on coming even when she had a bad cold.

Materials. At the second lesson the tutor suggested that they try out a couple of books to see which would be best to use. Alice then read one hundred-word selections in another preprimer and an easy primer, making about the same number of errors in both. The tutor suggested that they should start the primer, and this was completed in about six weeks. It was followed by an easy first reader, another first reader, and Disney's *Here They Are.*

Alice felt safe with a book once she got used to it, and hated to give it up to start a new one. By February she was ready for second-grade material, and she covered most of the stories in two second readers and Dolch's *Why Stories.* She started an easy third reader in May. In school her teacher had placed her in a small group with three other children, and the group used readers about equal in difficulty to those being used by Alice's tutor. In January the tutor managed to get her enough interested in a story they started so that Alice asked to take it home to finish. After finishing several stories in this way, she began more systematic reading at home with *Cowboy Sam and Freddy* in March, and followed this with two more *Cowboy Sam* books.

Word Recognition. From the beginning Alice had no difficulty learning words by a visual method, although at times when she was upset, she blocked rather badly and seemed to forget much of what had been thoroughly learned. She enjoyed using the *Picture-Word Cards,* which she learned five at a time. New words in readers were pretaught before meeting them in connected reading, were printed on cards, and were reviewed each time until securely known. Because of Alice's evident good aptitude for phonics and need for independence in word attack, much attention was given to instruction in word attack skills. Parts of several phonics workbooks were employed. Since she already knew the sound of nearly all consonants, the short vowels were stresed, using *Happy Times with Sounds*, Book 2; these were fairly well mastered by the end of November. A scrapbook for vowels and word families was started, with pictures cut from old magazines. Then long vowels and the silent *e* were taught, and in February she moved on to the use of the *Jet Plane* workbook (third-grade level). Many informal games were played with anagrams and Word-O. Near the end of the year she did some of the exercises in *Phonics We Use*, Book D, and the Hegge, Kirk *Remedial Reading Drills*.

Language and Vocabulary. Alice had such an extensive vocabulary and was so quick to grasp meanings that little had to be done in this area.

Oral Reading. For the first several months, all reading was oral. Alice seemed to need the close attention of the tutor, and felt alone if she had to read silently. She read slowly, word by word, pointing with the index finger of her left hand. Pointing was not discouraged for a long time because it was considered an aid in eliminating the residues of her directional confusion. At times oral reading was very good, and at times very inaccurate. Sometimes the tutor read alternately with her or in unison with her to encourage and develop phrasing, fluency, and expression.

Silent Reading. Silent reading was introduced very gradually during the fourth month of tutoring. During the oral reading the tutor would ask something like, "What do you think will happen next?" Then they both would read ahead silently for two or three sentences to find out. Alice needed the feeling of security of having the tutor's full interest and support and for much of the year could not tolerate more than a small amount of silent reading. She began to do some independent silent reading at home, as related above.

Spelling. Around midyear Alice asked for some help in spelling.

The tutor used an easy second-grade spelling workbook, with which Alice was working individually in school, to teach her a systematic method of studying spelling words and to increase her confidence in her ability to do spelling. This occupied a few minutes of each lesson for about a month.

Comprehension. During the year the reading of each story was accompanied or followed by discussion. The tutor was impressed and sometimes amazed by the acuteness of Alice's comments. Her comprehension was far ahead of her word recognition skills for most of the year.

Creative Writing. During the spring the tutor introduced the idea of spending part of some lessons in writing original stories, and Alice responded to this with enthusiasm. Each story was typed for her, and she made a little booklet of them. Her stories were full of shootings, stabbings, and so on, and it seemed reasonable that this gave her some release for the hostile feelings that were troubling her. The stories were accepted and praised without any suggestions for improvement, and any impulses the tutor may have had to suggest interpretations were firmly suppressed.

Motivation. Perhaps the most important motivating factor for Alice was the fact that she had her remedial teacher all to herself, and the absence of jealousy made it possible for her to respond to the tutor's friendliness. One of the problems was that of overcoming her belief that the other children were so far ahead of her that she couldn't possibly catch up. Generalized praise was not effective; she had to be shown exactly what she had accomplished before she could believe it. Progress charts of many kinds were used: thermometers, corrals (a new post for each new word) when she was reading cowboy stories, a flower garden with a new blossom for each unit mastered, and the like. Reassurance, encouragement, and praise were employed very generously, but had to be based on some specific achievement. Alice's basic pessimism began to change. She said at one point, "I knew it was in me—it's coming out."

In November she had a setback when a little club of girls refused to admit her, the leader saying "No horrible child can be in." This reinforced her feeling that nobody could like her. She began wetting again and her reading slumped temporarily. By December she had recovered from this disappointment and was progressing nicely again. She no longer clung to the familiar and was willing to try a new book even if she thought it would be hard.

During the spring, as mentioned above, Alice began to do a little reading at home. This did not happen accidentally, but was carefully set up by the tutor to make it look and feel like a voluntary decision of Alice's. Home reading was never pushed, and at times when she did not want to do any, no pressure was exerted. Instead, the tutor would start an especially interesting story and leave it unfinished; sometimes Alice would take it home to finish, and sometimes not.

Results

By the end of February, retesting on the *Gates Advanced Primary* showed grade scores of 3.0 in Word Recognition and 3.2 in Paragraph Meaning, at a time when her instructional level was low second grade. Testing late in May gave the following results:

Gilmore Oral Reading Test
- Accuracy R.G. 3.4
- Comprehension R.G. 3.9
- Rate 72 words per minute, Slow

Metropolitan Achievement Tests, Primary II
- Reading 4.1
- Word Meaning 3.6
- Spelling 3.3

According to the tutor's evaluation in June, Alice had made very satisfactory gains. She was reading quite well in third-grade material. She had developed some confidence in her reading ability and was willing to try new and different kinds of reading material. She had made excellent progress in phonics and could sound out many unfamiliar words. Her oral reading was still slow and her phrasing was at times poor. Although not far below the national norms for her grade placement, she was still about three years below her mental level and about two years below the median for her classmates, most of whom were very superior readers.

The classroom teacher had had several conferences with the tutor and had done a great deal to help. For Alice's sake she had kept her group of the four poorest readers on material a little easier than three of them could handle, trusting extensive individual reading to make up the difference, and had tried in many ways to help Alice's social adjustment. Toward the end of the year she reported that Alice was taking part in group activities, was much more cooperative, and accepted suggestions more graciously than at the beginning of the year. She was still untidy in work habits and somewhat unorganized in her thinking and in taking care of details. Alice was still the poorest in the class in reading and spelling and the teacher recommended continuation of remedial help.

Remedial Reading: Second Year

During the first couple of lessons in September Alice said she had spent the summer at a camp and had not enjoyed it, and it was evident that much forgetting had taken place. The tutor went back to second-grade materials for a couple of weeks, and reviewed the phonic learnings of the previous year. She then introduced a third-grade book with many fairy stories which Alice enjoyed, spent part of the period on spelling, and began some silent reading exercises in workbooks of second- and third-grade level. Timed rate and comprehension exercises were started in *My Own Reading Exercises*, Book 2; in seven practice sessions her rate went from 141 words per minute to 198, with comprehension remaining close to 100 per cent. She continued with *Four and Twenty Famous Stories* (third-grade level) in which her rate went up to 237 words per minute by the end of November, and early in December began *Forty Famous Stories* (fourth-grade level), in which she started at about 180 words per minute. Good phrasing was emphasized in both oral and silent reading and several types of phrasing exercises were employed, including the use of a hand tachistoscope. In oral reading the tutor pretended to be an audience and encouraged looking up from the book and improved expression. Phonic exercises were selected as needed from several workbooks, and occupied much less time than in the first year.

After a short time on third-grade reader stories Alice moved on into an easy fourth reader. The tutor began to bring in many attractive library books. Early in November *Donald's Penguins* captured Alice's interest and she said she couldn't wait to get home to continue reading it. Other fanciful animal tales followed, and by the end of December she had read twenty books at home. Most of these were thin books of about third-grade level, but late in December a big step forward was taken when she completed *Eddie and Gardenia,* a mature-looking book of about fourth-grade difficulty. In school the teacher now had Alice's group reading in a fourth reader. Alice had shown a sudden spurt in spelling and began to get 100's quite often in the regular class spelling tests.

By December it was evident to the tutor that Alice's reading was already a little above the national norms for middle of fourth grade, and she raised the question with Alice of whether it would be necessary to continue remedial lessons much longer. Alice felt that she did not want to stop until she was up to the average for her class (which was now around sixth-grade level); she could not feel satisfied until she was at least able to keep up with the middle group. At this point it was evident that the main remaining problem was to keep her motivation up and to wean her away from her dependence upon the tutor, as she had no instructional needs that could not be met in school. It was decided to continue for another two months and then gradually cut down the frequency of the lessons, emphasizing meanwhile Alice's ability to continue to make gains through her own efforts, with the goal of terminating at the close of the school year. The teacher cooperated by promoting Alice to the middle group.

In a final evaluation, it was evident that Alice had made a great deal of progress in social adjustment as well as in achievement. At home, however, there was far less improvement, and it seemed advisable to suggest to the parents that they should get some professional guidance for themselves on how to improve the parent-child and sister-sister relationships.

Case II

Diagnostic Study

Elena was referred by the social work agency which was responsible for her, because she was doing failing work in school. She was first seen in September, when she was nine and a half years old and in the high second grade.[2]

General Impressions. Elena seemed to be an amiable youngster with an outgoing, friendly manner. She cooperated wholeheartedly and showed enthusiasm and delight with each new experience during the testing program. She worked calmly and persistently even with tasks that were too hard for her. Her rate of work was slow. Often she had difficulty in understanding directions. She showed limited understanding of English, spoke ungrammatically and with poor enunciation, and had difficulty in expressing her ideas. Spanish was spoken exclusively in her foster home, and Elena spoke very little English until she entered school.

Physical Examination. Elena was found to be well built and well nourished. At one time she had given a positive tuberculin test reaction. Her hearing was normal. She had nearsighted vision which was not completely corrected by her present glasses, and showed some fusion difficulty on the *Keystone Visual Survey*. She had unfilled dental cavities and fallen arches. She had consistent right-sided lateral dominance. Other medical findings were negative.

Abilities. Elena's intelligence was in the slightly inferior range. On the *Revised Stanford-Binet Intelligence Scale*, Form L, her MA was 8 years 0 months and her IQ was 84. This may have been an underestimate of her mentality because of her limited vocabulary and range of information, which seemed to be the result of a Spanish-speaking background. On the *Cornell-Coxe Performance Ability Scale*, a series of nonverbal tests, her IQ was 95, showing low average ability. Her drawings were above average in quality.

[2] This case and the two which follow it are from the files of the City College Educational Clinic, where the writer was supervisor of the Remedial Reading Service from 1940 to 1949.

Reading. The results of standardized reading tests were as follows:

Gray Standardized Oral Reading Paragraphs	Zero Score
Gates Primary Reading Tests	
Type 1, Word Recognition	R.G. 1.2
Type 3, Reading Directions	R.G. 1.6
Gates Word Pronunciation Test	R.G. 1.8

Her scores on reading tests indicated that she was practically a nonreader, scoring at beginning first-grade level on two of the tests. On the first paragraph of the *Gray Oral Paragraphs* she made sixteen errors.

An analysis of her errors showed that she had no systematic method for attacking words. She had a very limited sight vocabulary. She attempted to identify words according to their general configuration, such as *Mary* or *man* for *may,* or she tried to recall words from previous experiences, as when she read *jump* for *came* and *round* for *ball.* She knew the names of all the lower-case letters except for confusing *b* with *d, p* with *q,* and *p* with *g.* She was able to give the sounds of only a few consonants and was totally unfamiliar with vowel sounds.

Tests of sounding and blending indicated poor auditory discrimination, very inferior blending ability, and incorrect auditory associations. She lacked awareness of the relation between sounds and their visual symbols. She did very poorly on a sample phonics lesson, but was able to learn words very easily both with a straight visual method of study and with a visual-motor method.

Other Schoolwork. On a spelling test, she scored at low first-grade level. Many of her attempts at spelling bore not the slightest resemblance to the word intended, again showing a lack of phonic awareness. On the *Metropolitan Primary Arithmetic Test* her computational ability was 2.7, normal for grade placement.

Family History. Elena's parents were from Puerto Rico. Her mother died when she was one year old, and her father died of progressive paralysis when she was seven. She had grown up in a foster home in which Spanish was spoken exclusively. Her foster mother spoke a very broken English. The social agency reported that the boarding parents had been fond of her and had given her a good deal of attention, and that Elena was an affectionate child. The foster mother described Elena as a slow, easygoing child who was not nervous. She said that Elena had many friends but that she had "no brain." She said that Elena would not be allowed to go to the movies for six months if she did not do well in school. Elena gave the impression of being attached to her foster parents but of fearing stern discipline. She reported being punished with a strap when she did not know her lessons and being slapped when her face was dirty. She said that she was held responsible for the neat appearance of two other foster children in the home, aged three and four, and was slapped when they were not clean. She said that she helped with the dishes and housecleaning and washed her own underwear and that of the other children.

School History. Elena entered the first grade at the age of 5 years 9 months, after a term in kindergarten. She was in a slow first-grade class for one year, and then spent two years in the second grade. Her behavior in school was good and she seldom caused any trouble. However, she was inattentive in class and made little effort to concentrate on her work. She spent most of her time in class drawing pictures. She received good marks in penmanship, health education, music, nature study, sewing, and art, but was a nonreader and did very poorly in composition and spelling. Elena's attitude toward school was that "there are lots of nice things in school, arithmetic is easy, but reading and spelling are hard."

Emotional Adjustment. Elena said that she rarely went to the movies, and did not care to go much, because they gave her bad dreams. She liked to listen to musical programs on the radio, but was afraid of the scary programs. She reported having terrifying dreams and many fears. Her wishes were simple and concrete, involving skates, a big doll, and a doll carriage. She said that she enjoyed the supervised play activities on a nearby playground. She had one close friend, and seemed fond of the other children in her foster home. She seemed to be a warm, affectionate child, greatly lacking in a sense of security. The *Rorschach* test showed emotional disturbance, marked anxiety, and concern over security. She seemed to be somewhat inhibited. There was evidence of uneven mental functioning, some confusion in her concepts, and a tendency to arrive at hasty but erroneous conclusions.

Diagnostic Summary. Elena's reading disability seemed to arise from several contributing causes. (1) Most important was her lack of knowledge of English and very limited background of experience when she entered school. (2) She had entered the first grade when less than six years old, and was probably intellectually and socially immature, as well as lacking in cultural background. (3) Her poor auditory discrimination prevented her from utilizing phonic techniques as a method of word analysis. This lack of auditory perception seemed also related to her Spanish-language background. (4) Her vision was poor. She had obtained glasses after she had been in school for over two years, and did not achieve perfect vision even with the glasses. (5) Her general health was poor, with a condition of arrested tuberculosis. (6) Her emotional disturbance, involving many fears and preoccupation with the problem of security in regard to a permanent home, probably had interfered with her ability to focus her attention on school work.

Recommendations. It was decided to have Elena excused from school two afternoons a week in order to attend the Remedial Reading Service. A tentative program for the remedial instruction was laid out, the nature of which will become apparent from the description of the remedial work below. Medical recommendations included periodic checks of her eyes and lungs, dental care, and orthopedic treatment for her flat feet. The social agency was asked to try to modify the foster mother's attitudes in the direction of giving Elena less responsibility for the younger children and more time for play and relaxation; also to be less critical of her and to be gentler in correcting her. The school was asked to give Elena reasurance about her ability to succeed, to praise and encourage any genuine effort she might show, and to build on her superior performance in art and sewing as a means of providing her with earned approval.

Remedial Work

Elena was given individual instruction by a tutor, a college senior studying elementary school methods, who met with her twice a week for one hour lessons. One tutor worked with her in the fall and another tutor in the spring. She received a total of thirty-nine lessons between November and June, with interruptions caused by vacations, colds, and the uncooperative attitude of her foster mother. From the very beginning she was highly interested, anxious to learn, and avid for attention and approval. The remedial procedure was as follows:

Materials. During the year Elena read a preprimer and its accompanying workbook, a primer and its workbook, two other primers, a first reader and workbook, another first reader, a second reader and workbook, and nine other books of second-grade level, mainly readers. She also used *Eye and Ear Fun,* Book 1, during the second half of the year.

Word Recognition. At the outset a visual approach was used, because of Elena's total lack of phonic aptitude and her language handicap. She was started at a preprimer level. Words which she failed to recognize were printed on flash cards, studied by trying to get a picture of the word in her mind as she pronounced it, and reviewed until they were mastered. She increased her sight vocabulary rapidly by this method. Words with which she had special difficulty were written by her on a "magic slate" or on the blackboard. At this point she showed no awareness of the connection between sound elements in words and their visual symbols. Stress was placed on correct enunciation and pronunciation and on developing auditory discrimination. Her speech was indistinct, she left off plurals and endings, and confused the sounds of *d* and *g*, and *m* and *n*. Attention was called to similarities and differencies in word forms and sounds through workbook exercises, and through picking out from a pack of picture-word cards those which began with the same letter or ended with the same letter. Elena seemed to catch on to the idea of phonics rather suddenly when she was reading at the first-reader level. She then began to build word families, to attack new words by noting their similarity to words already learned. Sounds with which she had difficulty were associated with vivid meanings. The *wh* sound was taught through the word *whistle,* which she loved to do. Her most persistent difficulty was an *m-n* confusion. She was taught that *mmm* means delicious; I want *more; m* is more than *n.* Toward the end of the year she became able to divide long words into smaller, familiar units and to figure out words of several syllables; she was able to sound many words whose meanings were totally unknown to her.

Language and Vocabulary. Because of her imperfect mastery of English and very restricted experience, much attention was given to explanation of unfamiliar words and ideas. She was encouraged to speak freely of her life and thoughts, in full, clear sentences. Her fund of information was so incomplete that she was unable to understand some of the simplest concepts in first-grade readers. Illustrations in the books were fully discussed and a picture dictionary was frequently consulted. Her tutor, who became very fond of her, took her to the zoo and the circus. Elena's usage of English was faulty and ungrammatical. She thought that certain distinctions, such as between *was* and *were,* were entirely arbitrary. The tutor tried to get her to understand the distinctions between singular and plural, past and present, and so on, which she tended to ignore in her speech. Toward the end of the year some time was spent on synonyms, antonyms, and homonyms, studying such word pairs as *joy* and *join, threw* and *through,* and *curb* and *curve.*

Oral Reading. At the beginning, all reading was done orally. Most lessons included preteaching of new vocabulary, oral reading for fifteen or twenty minutes, a brief period for rest and conversation, silent work in the correlated workbook, correction and discussion of the workbook pages, practice in auditory discrimination and later in phonics, and a review of the new words. She read with good expression and intense absorption in the story from the start.

Silent Reading. At the fourth lesson, Elena asked to be allowed to take her book home. From then on she did a great deal of silent reading at home. She would bring back a list of the new words she had met, and would select the more enjoyable pages to read orally to the tutor. At no time was there any problem in motivating independent reading, except when the tutor gave her a book that was too difficult for her.

Comprehension. Comprehension was checked by means of exercises in the correlated workbooks and discussion of the stories read at home. Elena's errors in comprehension were not due to careless reading, but nearly always were the result of vocabulary deficiencies and lack of background information.

Speed. No attempt was made to encourage fast reading. Elena always read as fast as she could because she was anxious to find out the end of the story.

Motivation. The main form of motivation was a close feeling of affection that developed between Elena and her tutor. The tutor's approval was sufficient to keep her at a high level of interest in reading. A progress chart for number of pages read at home probably contributed to her desire to read independently but did not seem to be an important factor. Elena came for her lessons as early as she could and stayed until she was sent home. She often asked to be allowed to stay after her lesson and draw pictures or do some more reading. She was very proud of herself when her pictures were posted on a bulletin board, along with those of some of the other children.

Results

The results of standardized reading tests were as follows:

	Sept.	Jan.	May
Gray Standardized Oral Reading Paragraphs	0	2.1	3.1
Gates Word Pronunciation Test	1.8	2.3	2.8
Gates Primary Reading Tests			
Word Recognition	1.2	2.4	3.0
Reading Directions	1.6	2.5	2.8
Stanford Primary Reading Test			
Paragraph Meaning			3.4
Word Meaning			2.7
Total Score			3.1

At the time of final testing, she was reading fluently in the more difficult second readers and seemed ready for third-grade reading.

She had developed a high level of phonic skill and was able to blend words rapidly and successfully. From being essentially a nonreader she had become able to cope with the reading and spelling in school. Her reading ability was now only seven months below her mental age level.

At a final interview in June, Elena reported that her foster mother never got angry at her any more. This probably was the result of the efforts of the social worker at the agency, who kept in close touch with the remedial work and attempted to carry out the recommendations concerning Elena's treatment at home. Elena said that she was not bothered by scary dreams any more. "I'm a big girl now and I'm not afraid." She felt that the housework was easy for her. "The mop used to be bigger than me. Now I'm bigger than the mop. It's not too heavy any more." These feelings seemed to indicate a marked gain in self-confidence and self-reliance.

The school had also done its part. Elena had been fortunate in having a sympathetic and understanding teacher. She had given Elena many opportunities to read stories to the class. The teacher helped her with the difficult words in advance and provided ample time for preparation to avoid any embarrassment. The teacher had praised her improvement in reading and had moved her from the low group to the middle group in reading. Elena had also received praise for good work in drawing and music. Elena reported great improvement in spelling and geography, but was having some trouble with arithmetic. She said that she enjoyed school very much.

Case III

Diagnostic Study

Jimmy was referred for reading diagnosis by a mental hygiene clinic which had been working with him and his family for two years. When they had first seen him, he showed above average intelligence but was a nonreader. He had subsequently been in a remedial reading group in school for two terms but had made unsatisfactory progress. When first seen at the clinic he was 9 years 4 months old and was in the high third grade.

General Impressions. Jimmy was an attractive, snub-nosed boy with bright red hair. The first time he visited the clinic, he became nauseous and vomited before he arrived, an indication of emotional upset. After the purpose of the visit was explained to him, however, he quieted down and relaxed. In taking tests he understood directions well and worked quickly and with good attention. During oral reading tests he seemed quite nervous but the rest of the time he seemed at ease. He was talkative and emotionally responsive. His speech was poor; his voice was flat and nasal; he made many errors in usage; and his pronunciation was quite indistinct, with a marked lisp, and difficulty in pronouncing *l, r, j, g, sh, ch,* and other sounds.

Physical Examination. Jimmy was found to be tall for his age and a little below normal in weight. Vision was normal according to Snellen and Keystone tests. An audiometer test disclosed a hearing loss of 22 decibels (18 per cent) in each ear. His frenum (the membrane between the tongue and the floor of the mouth) was short, restricting his freedom of tongue movement and making him "tongue-tied." This had been treated surgically on three previous occasions. He showed consistent right-hand and right-eye dominance. The physician noted signs of emotional instability. Other medical findings were normal.

Jimmy had a long history of illness. Shortly after birth he underwent genital surgery and clipping of the frenum. At three months he had a severe case of pneumonia. Very bad tonsils and adenoids were removed at fourteen months. Before he was three he had mumps and chicken pox. At four and a half, a piece of furniture was dropped on his foot, breaking some bones and requiring many visits to a hospital clinic during the following year and a half. Throughout childhood he had been subject to frequent colds and digestive upsets.

Abilities. Jimmy's intelligence was well above average, with an IQ of 117 on the *Revised Stanford-Binet* and an IQ of 108 on a series of performance tests. He showed good comprehension and planning ability, superior auditory memory, and average visual perception and visual memory. No special intellectual defects were found.

Reading. Results of standardized reading tests were as follows:

Metropolitan Primary II Reading Test	
Paragraph Reading	2.2
Vocabulary	2.1
Gates Oral Reading Test	1.9
Gates Word Pronunciation Test	2.0

Although his test scores indicated reading ability of beginning second-grade level, they seemed to have benefited from much lucky guessing. When he was tried on oral reading in a series of graded readers, he made a great many errors even in the primer. His reading was slow, halting, inaccurate, and expressionless. Most of his errors were mispronunciations or nonrecognitions, with some omissions and repetitions.

He seemed to try to sound out unfamiliar words phonetically. However, his knowledge of phonics was very meager. He confused *m* and *n, n* and *v, b* and *d, p* and *q, k* and *f,* and *y* and *w.* He tended to pronounce all vowels as *uh.* The only two-letter combinations he could pronounce were *ee* and *oo.* As a result of his lack of knowledge of letter sounds and phonograms, his phonic efforts were almost always unsuccessful. Jimmy said that he had been taught, both in the classroom and in remedial work, by a completely visual method, and had figured out by himself the few sounds that he knew. He seemed to be anxious to learn how to read. In a sample phonics lesson he had difficulty with some of the letter sounds but showed excellent blending abiilty.

Other School Subjects. His spelling was at high first-grade level. He tried to use a phonic approach, as shown in such attempts as *yous* for *use, lev* for *leave,* and *bot* for *bought.* Letter confusions were shown in errors like *sona* for *summer, dekor* for *before,* and *moit* for *night.* On the *Metropolitan Primary II Arithmetic Fundamentals Tests,* he scored at high fourth-grade level, above his grade placement.

School History. Because of illness, Jimmy had entered kindergarten in May and attended for only eleven days. He did not like it because he felt that the other children knew more than he did. In the first grade, which he entered when exactly six, he wanted to play and did not pay attention or show any interest in reading. For several terms he did not want to go to school. His mother kept him home quite often when he said that he did not feel well. He repeated the first grade and then was promoted regularly. His conduct marks were B for the first year and then consistently C. In the third grade he was placed in a special remedial reading group in school, but showed little effort and made unsatisfactory progress. He said that he did not like the teacher and would not work for her.

Family History. Jimmy's parents had quarreled for years, and separated when he was three years old. His mother was a nervous, sickly woman, dependent upon relief and hard pressed to provide sufficient food and clothing. Jimmy felt bad about not having a regular father, and sometimes got into street fights when teased about it. His father visited the family occasionally, but paid little attention to Jimmy. Jimmy was the youngest of four children and did not get along well with his siblings, who regarded him as a pest. His mother criticized him and threatened to give him away, and at the same time had let him get his way since infancy by means of crying, nagging, sulking, and temper tantrums.

Emotional Adjustment. Jimmy's mother had sought the aid of the mental hygiene clinic two years before, because she was having difficulties with all of her children. The psychiatrist had concluded that Jimmy's behavior difficulties "seem to be related to certain neurotic developments arising out of the disturbed experiences in the family. It is apparent that he is troubled with feelings of rejection by his mother. . . . In his wish to maintain the attention of the mother he has allowed himself to be infantilized and overprotected by his mother." At that time he showed many fears, had a facial tic or twitch, and bit his nails. Jimmy, his mother, and an older brother had been receiving treatment at that clinic for two years and apparently all three had benefited. Jimmy was still, however, a highly sensitive, emotional boy with a chip-on-the-shoulder attitude, and was still a problem at home. The mental hygiene clinic felt that while his general adjustment had improved, his continuing reading disability had made him feel insecure and inadequate and had contributed to his restlessness, inattentiveness, and aggressiveness.

Diagnostic Summary. The three factors that seemed causally related to his reading disability were emotional instability, defective hearing, and poor speech. His emotional disturbance was thought to be the most important cause, resulting in inability or unwillingness to concentrate and pay attention in school. It, in turn, seemed possibly due in part to the series of illnesses, operations, and accidents in early childhood, but was probably related mainly to his broken home situation and his mother's inability to provide affection, security, or discipline. It seemed possible that he might have been transferring to his teachers (all women) some of the resentment he felt toward his mother. His poor speech seemed to be the result of his poor hearing and restricted tongue movement. His defects in speech and hearing probably explained why he had so much more difficulty with reading and spelling than with arithmetic.

Recommendations. Arrangements were made for Jimmy to attend the Remedial Reading Service twice a week. The mental hygiene clinic was to continue work with his mother and to try to secure more financial aid for the family. Medical recommendations were made concerning his hearing and the correction of his tongue-tie condition. The school was advised to discontinue remedial work in reading and to try to provide opportunities for him to gain approval through oral contributions and his good number work.

Remedial Work

Jimmy received twenty-seven lessons between December and June, a period of five months, during which there was a six-week interruption because of illness. He was given three lessons by the writer, five by one male graduate student, and nineteen by another male graduate student. He was intentionally assigned to men because of the assumption that he would accept instruction from them better than from women. The nature of the remedial work was as follows:

Materials. Jimmy read a preprimer, two primers, two first readers, two second readers, a third reader, several booklets of first- and second-grade levels, and selected exercises from the workbooks, *Eye and Ear Fun,* Book I, *Red Deer,* and *Scottie and*

His Friends. The major part of the book reading was done between lessons.

Word Recognition. Since Jimmy seemed to have good phonic aptitude, major attention was devoted to building up a systematic phonic attack. The letter sounds which he did not know were taught, and he was taken systematically through the first few exercises of the Hegge-Kirk *Remedial Reading Drills,* which emphasize letter-by-letter sounding and blending. Attention to hearing and pronouncing the words correctly was stressed, since he did not differentiate in his own pronunciation between such words as *man* and *men, cut* and *cot,* and so on. It took only a few lessons to teach the sounding of one-syllable words with short *a, o, i, u,* and *e* as middle vowels. Then a shift was made to incidental phonics, analyzing new words met during connected reading and building word families from them. By the end of the tutoring he was able to sound out almost any phonetically regular word of two or three syllables.

From the start, also, each new word in the readers was printed on a card and was learned by visual study, with visual-motor study used for the harder words. The word cards were kept in two envelopes, one marked "Do Know" and one marked "Don't Know." When, on a review, he recognized a word immediately, a check was made on the card. When a card had three checks, it was moved into the "Do Know" envelope. By the time he reached third-grade level in reading, this procedure was no longer necessary and was discontinued.

Language and Vocabulary. Because of Jimmy's indistinct speech and subnormal hearing, the tutor spoke with exaggerated distinctness and encouraged Jimmy to do likewise. Jimmy was willing to do so as long as he did not have to promise to talk that way with his friends. He had a wide range of word meanings and could successfully guess most new meanings from context, so not much attention had to be paid to concept development.

Oral Reading. Most connected reading during the lessons was done orally. At times the tutor read alternately with him, to encourage better phrasing and expression. At times he was asked to reread passages, for the same reason. Oral reading was emphasized so as to keep a very close check on his progress in word mastery and to locate the new words that he needed to learn.

Silent Reading. Since Jimmy was started on beginning first-grade material, he was able to read independently with ease and reasonable accuracy almost from the beginning. He willingly took his books home and, with his thermometer-type progress chart for pages read serving as a powerful incentive, sometimes read ahead as much as ninety pages between lessons. Because of the large amount of silent reading done at home, little time was devoted to silent reading during the lessons, except for the workbook exercises introduced in the latter part of the tutoring period.

Comprehension. Jimmy had a mental age of eleven years and was reading material of primary-grade level, so he rarely experienced any comprehension difficulties except when he misread the words. Comprehension exercises in workbooks were introduced when he reached second-grade level in his reading.

Speed. No attention was paid to speed until near the end of the tutoring. Then he was encouraged to give up pointing with his finger, was given some special practice in phrase reading, and was encouraged to try to read faster. When tutoring was stopped he was reading accurately but somewhat slowly. If tutoring had been continued, the development of greater speed would have become a major objective.

Spelling. At the sixth lesson, Jimmy asked for help in spelling. The tutor reported: "I agreed, and he then produced his speller, which he had brought with him. I tested him on twenty words from his grade list of which he got only three correct. I picked out six of the words (*matter, fruit, picture, lesson, our,* and *friend*) and taught them. Jimmy was told that most of these words are not spelled the way they sound. He said it wasn't fair, and I agreed with him. Each word was printed on a card, and Jimmy was instructed to look at the card, say the word, and then shut his eyes and try to see it. After he thought he could remember how the word looked, he was asked to print it from memory. Each word was reviewed until it was printed and written from memory several times without error. All of the words were learned except *fruit,* which was quite difficult for him." This was, of course, the visual-motor method. Jimmy was encouraged to use the same method of study in the spelling periods in school. No further help was given in spelling as such. An entry in the tutor's diary for March 25 reads: "Jimmy remarked that he received 100 per cent in a spelling test yesterday, and the boy from whom he usually copies got only 80 per cent. This pleased Jimmy no end."

Motivation. Both tutors were experienced in working with boys, and could talk with Jimmy in his own language and share his interest in sports. He got along very well with both of them from the beginning. His competitive spirit was high and his progress charts, on which were recorded the number of sounds learned, the number of words in the "Do Know" envelope, and the number of pages read, meant a great deal to him. He kept very careful track of his scores and would argue vehemently if he thought that the tutor had failed to give him a full score. From the beginning the tutors tried to show respect for his intelligence and gave him generous praise. This was easy, because he was a bright boy and made rapid progress.

An attempt was made, also, to change his mother's critical and disparaging attitude. For example, in March his mother remarked, in Jimmy's presence, that he read well in the clinic and at home, but did not do so well in school. She was told that he was doing splendidly, and was asked in private conversation to try not to express concern or discouragement about his schoolwork. In April, she complained that Jimmy was not doing any reading at home. Jimmy answered that he did his reading in spare time in school. The tutor said that he had confidence in Jimmy's desire to improve in his reading and that the progress he was making showed that he was doing his reading somewhere. "The troubled look on Jimmy's face turned into a smile and a look of triumph spread over his face as he turned to his mother, as if to say, 'So there!' "

Results

Retests in May with the *Metropolitan Primary II Achievement Tests* resulted in scores of 3.7 in Paragraph Reading, 3.4 in Vocabulary, and 3.1 in Spelling. On the *Gates Silent Reading Test,* Type D, given in school, he scored 4.0. He had started reading in a preprimer and was reading nicely in third-grade material when the tutoring ended. The gain, as measured by standardized tests, was almost two years in reading and over a year in spelling. He had acquired an efficient method of attack on new words and was confident of his ability to continue to improve in reading. His report card at the end of the term showed marked improvement in conduct and personality ratings as well as in work.

Jimmy's work in school was followed up for two years, during which his average mark was B plus. He was re-examined on two occasions.

Table XII. Changes in Jimmy's IQ and Reading before and after Remedial Reading

Stanford-Binet Form	*Occasion*	*IQ*	*Reading Grade Level*
L	Two years before remedial tutoring	113	Nonreader
M	Just before start of tutoring	117	High 1st
L	Just after remedial tutoring	132	High 3rd
M	One year later	125	Low 5th
L	One and a half years later	118	Low 6th

The results shown in Table XI indicated that Jimmy's ability to function on an intelligence test was stimulated during the period he received remedial help, the change of fifteen points being considerably more than a normal practice effect. Much of the gain was still present a year later, but at the last testing his IQ was back to where it was just before tutoring. During the first year after the remedial help he had continued to gain in reading at a good rate, but after that his rate of improvement in reading had slowed down. To what extent this was due to stopping remedial help too soon, or to the continued effect of living in an unhappy family, could not be certainly determined; it was felt that both were probably true in part.

Case IV

Diagnostic Study

When he was in the sixth grade, Bruce had been referred for psychological examination as a possible feeble-minded child because of very poor schoolwork. However, he was found to have average intelligence, so a diagnostic examination was arranged to study his severe disability in reading and spelling. He was 13 years 6 months old and in the low seventh grade in junior high school. Except for one month of private tutoring during the sixth grade, he had never had any remedial attention.

General Impressions. Bruce was a tall, very thin, nice-looking boy. He seemed very shy, indifferent, and inhibited. He never looked directly at the examiner but kept his eyes averted. He was totally lacking in spontaneity and self-confidence. He worked on tests with good effort and attention, but in a very unenthusiastic way. He usually gave one-word answers, said, "I don't know," or shrugged his shoulders. His voice was weak and expressionless.

Abilities. He showed average general intelligence, with an IQ of 97 on the *Revised Stanford-Binet.* His nonverbal abilities were slightly lower, with an IQ of 86 on a series of performance tests. No special intellectual deficiencies were noted.

Physical Examination. Bruce was found to be 6 inches above average height and 14 pounds below normal weight. His vision was normal according to Snellen and Keystone tests. Hearing, measured with an audiometer, was normal. On a series of laterality tests he showed right-hand and left-eye dominance. He had several dental cavities. No other defects were found. The physician noted that he was very apprehensive and nervous during the medical examination.

Reading. The results of several reading tests were as follows:

	Grade Score
Gray Standardized Oral Reading Paragraphs	3.0
Durrell Oral Reading, Rate	2.0
Stanford Primary Reading Test, Form D	
Paragraph Meaning	3.2
Word Meaning	2.7
Gates Word Pronunciation Test	3.4

These results indicated that he was at low third-grade level in word recognition and comprehension of silent reading, but was a very slow reader, rating at beginning second-grade level in speed of reading. His oral reading was labored, halting, and inaccurate. He hesitated and repeated frequently, and made many errors in word recognition, which he recognized and corrected only when they spoiled the meaning. He read word-by-word in a monotone. In silent reading he read very slowly and with lip movements.

Tests of phonic knowledge showed that he was unfamiliar with all of the short vowel sounds and with some consonant sounds. A marked confusion between *m* and *n* was evident. He tried to attack new words by spelling them and by guessing from the general configuration or the beginning of the word. Some errors were *him* for *her, window* for *wander, hare* for *hear, passing* for *passenger.* In sample lessons he did well with both a phonic approach and a visual-motor method of word study.

Other Schoolwork. His spelling was at second-grade level, and involved confusions, phonic inaccuracies, and disregard of word endings similar to the errors in his reading. His arithmetic was up to grade level. His other school subjects, except shopwork, were held down by his poor reading and spelling. In regard to history, he said, "What's the use? I know the answers, but I'll be marked wrong because I can't spell."

School History. Bruce had attended a parochial school for several years and was then transferred to a public school. Little specific information could be obtained from him or his family about his early school experiences. His mother was inclined to blame the parochial school for neglecting him. He said that in the sixth grade the teacher did not call upon him to recite because she did not expect him to know the answers, so he gave up trying to study. He liked junior high school better, particularly the shopwork and geography.

Family History. Bruce was the youngest of six children. His father had died when he was very young and his mother had worked for many years. He had three married sisters, two of whom had gone to college, a brother in the army, and a sickly seventeen-year-old brother who was described as a bookworm. At home Bruce was considered a good boy, but lazy. He would listen to the radio from five o'clock till bedtime. Two sisters had tried unsuccessfully to help him with his reading and spelling. The family was puzzled about his backwardness in school because at home he acted intelligently, had a good memory, showed a keen interest in current events, and had a good understanding of what was going on around him.

Emotional Adjustment. Bruce said that he had formerly had several friends, but was very lonesome since he had moved to a new neighborhood. His sister said that he was very self-conscious about his poor reading, and had successfully kept his friends from being aware of his difficulty by pretending to read when they did. He had avoided joining the Boy Scouts because he was afraid his inability to read and spell would have been shown up. His sister said that during the past year his attitude of indifference had become more noticeable and that often she had to repeat statements before getting any reaction from him. His main forms of recreation were the radio, the movies, and raising pigeons on the roof of his apartment house. His main wishes were for money, "brains," and friends. When asked if he liked to read, he replied, "Never. What do you want to read for?"

The *Rorschach* test indicated average intellectual ability but a narrow range of interests. There were indications that he was inhibited and fearful of making emotional responses, that he was evasive and noncommittal, and that when he felt anxious about a situation he was unable to face it squarely. However, he seemed to have a strong desire for better adjustment and to have a capacity for establishing friendly relationships in a situation in which he could feel at ease.

Diagnostic Summary. Bruce was found to be a boy of average general intelligence, with a severe disability in reading and spelling. His work in these skills was five to six years below his mental level. There were no indications of any special mental or physical defects that might explain his difficulties, with the exception of mixed lateral dominance. Since his reading and spelling were both free of reversal tendencies, the mixed dominance did not seem to be an important factor. The most likely explanation seemed to relate to unfortunate early school experiences, about which no specific information could be obtained. The fact that he had been allowed to continue in school for six years before any study was made of his backwardness seemed to show neglect on the part of his schools. His emotional attitudes of indifference and aloofness seemed to be more probably a result than a cause of his failure.

Recommendations. Arrangements were made with Bruce's school to excuse him three afternoons a week to attend a Remedial Reading Service. The specific recommendations concerning remedial work will be indicated in the description of the remedial work below. Suggestions were made to the school that he should be marked as far as possible on the basis of oral work, and that attempts should be made to draw him out in class discussions and to praise any contributions he might make. Medical recommendations included dental treatment and referral to a medical clinic for advice about enriched diet and tonics to improve his nutrition.

Remedial Work

Bruce was placed in a group of five boys, ranging in age from nine to fourteen, all of whom were reading at second- or third-grade level. The group met three afternoons a week from November through January and from March through May. For two months during the spring, Bruce was able to attend only once a week because of conflict with his school program. He was very regular in attendance and came to a total of forty-two sessions. The group was taught by three students who had had no previous remedial experience. The tutors took turns in leading group activities and giving individual help. Part of each session was devoted to group activities and part to individual work with a tutor. The remedial work may be summarized as follows:

Material. During the year, Bruce read three third-grade readers, two fourth readers, two fifth readers, part of a sixth reader, a few storybooks such as *The Story of Dr. Dolittle,* and several booklets of fourth- and fifth-grade level. Most of this reading was done at home, with a few pages read orally at each lesson. Selected exercises from several different workbooks were employed. Some time was also spent on reading in his history and geography textbooks.

Word Recognition. To develop a systematic method of word study, a phonic method was used, combined with practice in auditory and visual discrimination, using exercises in Hegge, Kirk, and Kirk, *Remedial Reading Drills,* and Durrell and Sullivan *Building Word Power.* Nonphonetic words were taught by a visual method. These were printed by hand on individual flash cards, were reviewed systematically until they were mastered, and were then presented in a hand tachistoscope for quick recognition. Bruce had developed fairly good phonic skill by the middle of the year, and attention was then shifted to syllabication and the use of the guide to pronunciation in a dictionary.

Vocabulary. The meanings of new words met in reading were discussed, and help was given in the use of a dictionary, both in locating words and in interpreting definitions. Vocabulary exercises of several types were employed, in the Brueckner and Lewis and Bedwell and Hutchins workbooks. Technical terms in history and geography were studied, taken from his textbooks and from Cole's *Handbook of Technical Vocabulary.*

Oral Reading. About ten minutes of each lesson were spent in oral reading, with the aims of developing phrasing and expression, and of checking on the adequacy of his word mastery. At times he read in unison with the tutor.

Phrasing. In addition to emphasis on phrasing in oral reading, phrase-reading exercises were used in workbooks, phrases were exposed in a tachistoscope for quick recognition, and phrase-matching games were played by the group.

Comprehension. Bruce was questioned orally on material read at home. Silent reading comprehension exercises of many different types were employed. These were taken from the *Practice Readers* by Stone and Grover, the *Practice Exercises in Reading* by Gates and Peardon, *Diagnostic Tests and Remedial Exercises in Reading* by Brueckner and Lewis, *My Own Reading Exercises* by Bedwell and

Hutchins, *Adventure Trails, Exploring Today,* and the *Standard Text Lessons in Reading* by McCall and Crabbs.

Speed. Besides the work in improving word recognition and developing phrasing, timed reading exercises were given. At each lesson, the group did two exercises in the *Standard Test Lessons* and entered their scores on progress charts. Informal rate tests were given from time to time. Bruce, however, made slower progress in this aspect of reading than in the others, and was still a slow reader at the end of the year.

Motivation. In planning the work with Bruce, major consideration was given to his emotional difficulties. A strong effort was made to make him feel at home, to help him develop friendly relations with the other boys and with the tutors, to develop a sense of achievement and build up his self-confidence, and to create a positive interest in reading. Progress charts were kept for several types of improvement. The boys were encouraged to compare their scores with their own previous scores rather than to compare scores with one another.

Results

Scores on the reading tests which were used for retesting were as follows:

Stanford Reading Test	*Oct.*	*Jan.*	*May*
Paragraph Meaning	3.2	3.7	5.3
Word Meaning	2.7	3.6	5.5
Total Score	2.9	3.6	5.4
Gray Standardized Oral Reading			
Check Tests, Set II	121 sec.	85 sec.	89 sec.
	18 errors	7 errors	1 error

(Norms for the second grade are 112 seconds, 6 errors; for the fourth grade, 62 seconds and 2 errors).

In addition to the tests which were systematically repeated, several other tests were used at various times for diagnostic purposes, including the *Gray Oral Paragraphs,* the Durrell *Analysis of Reading Difficulty,* the *Sangren-Woody Reading Test,* and parts of the *Gates Diagnostic Reading Tests.*

Analysis of the results showed a gain of about two and a half years in vocabulary, comprehension, and accuracy of oral reading. There was great improvement in his word recognition skills, his tendency to hesitate and reread had diminished markedly, and in general he showed much greater confidence in coping with all kinds of reading situations. His persistence in figuring out long and difficult words was noteworthy. However, his oral reading was still expressionless and his rate of reading was still very slow, at about low third-grade level. Although he was able toward the end to read sixth-grade material with satisfactory accuracy and comprehension, his scores on the standardized tests were held down by his inability to complete enough of the questions within the time limits.

Even more significant than the gains in reading were the changes in Bruce's emotional adjustment. These can be presented most vividly by extracts from the diary reports written by the tutors. They are presented in chronological order, and include comments from all three tutors.

My first impression of Bruce was unfavorable. He appeared to be extremely backward in his work and shrugged off every attempt to help him, as if he did not care about anything that was being done.

The first few times that I saw him he seemed to be completely indifferent to the work and also to the tutors and other boys.

Bruce acted so indifferent at the first phonic lessons that not only did he not look at me when he spoke, but sat in his chair in such a way as to practically have his back towards me. He did not speak to the other boys, and if they said something to him, he would just mutter a reply. He gradually sat around in his chair and one day he was almost enthusiastic. It happened this way. We decided not to use pencils on our magic slates and Bruce brought his pen holder and used the blunt side. I told him I thought it was a very good idea and next time brought pen holders for the other boys to use. Two of the other boys commented on Bruce's good idea. Bruce just shrugged his shoulders, but the very next day he showed more activity and joined our game for review sounds and played with us, not at us.

Bruce seems to be gradually finding his place in the group but he still indicates that he feels quite aloof from the whole thing. He attempts, with his facial expressions and shrugs of his shoulders and mumbling, to indicate that he really doesn't care. However, he is extremely disappointed when he doesn't win the Word-O game or when his work shows errors. He is extremely sensitive and becomes almost sulky if the others notice his errors.

After being absent yesterday, Bruce came in exceptionally cheerful. When we said we had missed him, he flushed and smiled. It was the first time I have seen him smile.

Seemed much more at ease in the group, occasionally laughing. Has become quite friendly with Frank.

Much more at ease. Makes comments freely. Smiles and talks with the other boys.

Today Bruce came up and told me that he had read three books, and gave me their names. It was the first time that he did not shrug his shoulders disparagingly when I asked him if he liked them.

At a final interview in June Bruce reported that he was passing all subjects except science, of which he had missed too many afternoon periods. He liked the shopwork best, and was planning to go to a vocational high school. For the summer, he was planning to stay at home, get a job, and spend time with his friends. He did not want to go to a farm because he would be too lonesome there. His attitude was open and friendly, and he seemed to be quite a different boy from the youngster of nine months before. In regard to reading, he thought he would be able to get along by himself and would not need any more special help.

Comments and Conclusions

THE FOUR CASES which make up the bulk of this chapter were selected to show how varied are the personalities, abilities, backgrounds, and special handicaps of children who develop severe reading disabilities. No two children are exactly similar in their instructional needs, and the remedial procedures used in these cases, successful as they were, should not be taken as models that can be employed without change with other children. Although each case has taken several pages to present, it has not been possible to do more than suggest the day-to-day fluctuations and the many unforeseen emergencies which the remedial teacher must be ready to meet as they arise. It is hoped, nevertheless, that these case summaries may give unity, vividness, and reality to the principles and procedures which have been described in previous chapters, and may help to point out different ways of getting started, of using time during remedial lessons, of adjusting and modifying the program as the child makes progress, and of maintaining relationships with parents and schools.

The range of intelligence in these cases was from dull to very superior, and in socio-economic status from that of a language-handicapped, culturally deprived orphan to a child of very well-to-do parents. Visual, hearing, nutritional, and other health problems were represented. Directional confusion was present in one case. Previous schooling ranged from excellent to poor, and one child (Jimmy) had reacted negatively to a previous remedial teacher. Two of the children had had previous psychotherapy which was only partially successful. Emotional problems varied: two were aggressive and hostile, one was friendly but fearful, one was apparently indifferent and aloof; all were unhappy.

The first three cases exemplify different methods of getting started with children who are almost nonreaders. Elena required a primarily visual method until she developed phonic readiness; Jimmy had responded poorly to a primarily visual approach and did very well with intensive letter phonics; Alice was able to profit from a program combining visual and phonic learnings from the start. Of these three, Elena might have made a good adjustment in a remedial group, but Jimmy and Alice seemed to need the close personal relationship which individual remedial teaching can provide. For Bruce, placement in a remedial group worked out well socially as well as educationally.

The remedial teacher whose heart is in his work usually comes to regard each child's problems as a battleground on which he is fighting for the child's chances for future success and happiness. There are few experiences which can equal the warm glow of satisfaction that such a teacher feels when a child is transformed from a frustrated and defeated individual into a person who has mastered a severe handicap and can look forward to the meeting of other difficulties with confidence and expectation of success. After once tasting the sweetness of such a victory, the teacher should be committed for the rest of his career to the principle of teaching children as individuals, respecting their individuality, studying their differences in aptitudes and learning ability, and adapting instructional practices to their needs. Into the hands of such teachers, parents can safely entrust the education of their children.

Suggested Additional Reading

BAKER, HARRY J. *Educational Disability and Case Studies in Remedial Teaching*. Bloomington, Ill.: Public School Publishing Co., 1929.

DURRELL, DONALD D. *Improvement of Basic Reading Abilities,* Ch. 15.

FERNALD, GRACE M. *Remedial Techniques in Basic School Subjects,* pp. 273–318.

GATES, ARTHUR I. *The Improvement of Reading,* Third Edition, Ch. 17.

STONE, CLARENCE R. *Progress in Primary Reading,* Ch. 12.

STRANG, RUTH, CONSTANCE M. MCCULLOUGH, and ARTHUR E. TRAXLER. *Problems in the Improvement of Reading,* Second Edition, Ch. 20.

APPENDIX A

An Alphabetical List of Tests [1]

In the following list, pertinent information is given about the tests that have been mentioned in the body of this book. All tests, regardless of type, have been arranged in a single alphabetical listing for easy reference. When the number of forms is not indicated, the test has only one form. The prices of manuals and other accessories are listed when they must be purchased separately. Information is based on the catalogs available at the time this appendix was compiled; changes in tests, forms, and prices may be expected as time passes. Current catalogs can be obtained from the publishers, whose abbreviated names are given as the last item in each entry; full names and addresses of the publishers are to be found in Appendix C.

Before ordering a test in quantity, it is advisable to make a tentative selection of several tests that might be suitable and write to the publishers for specimen sets. From an inspection of the test blanks, tryout on a few children, and careful reading of the manuals one can usually make an appropriate choice.

A O School Vision Screening Test

A revised, portable version of the *Massachusetts Vision Test*. Designed for quick screening to find pupils who need more complete visual examination. Includes tests of far-point acuity, farsightedness, vertical phoria, lateral phoria at near and far points. Complete material, in carrying case, $165.00. AMERICAN OPTICAL.

American Council on Education, Psychological Examination for High School Students

Grades 9–12. A group test of mental ability, yielding Linguistic, Quantitative, and Total scores. Working time, 55 min. Forms 1946, 1947, 1948, 1953. Test booklets, $2.75 per 25; answer sheets, $1.00 per 25; scoring stencils, $.25 per set; specimen set, $.50. ETS

American Council on Education, Psychological Examination for College Freshmen

A group test of scholastic aptitude for college work. Yields Linguistic, Quantitative, and Total scores. Working time, 60 min. Forms 1947, 1948, 1949, 1952, 1954. Test booklets $2.95 per 25; answer sheets, $1.00 per 25; scoring stencils, $.25 per set; specimen set, $.50. ETS

[1] In this listing, the names of publisher are abbreviated. Full names and addresses of publishers are given in Appendix C.

American School Reading Readiness Test, Revised

Kindergarten–beginning grade 1. Group administration. Working time, about 30 min. Separate norms for those who have and have not attended kindergarten. Test booklets, $2.25 per 25; specimen set, $.35. PUBLIC.

American School Achievement Tests, Revised, Form D

Primary Battery I, for grade 1. Includes reading and arithmetic. Test booklets, $1.85 per 25; specimen set, $.35.
Primary Battery II, for grade 2 and 3. Includes reading, vocabulary, arithmetic, and spelling. Test booklets, $2.25 per 25; specimen set, $.35.
Intermediate Reading, for grades 4–6. Paragraph meaning and vocabulary. $2.00 per 25; specimen set, $.35.
Advanced Reading, for grades 7–9. Paragraph meaning and vocabulary. $2.00 per 25; specimen set, $.35.
Reading Test for Senior High Schools and College Freshmen. Vocabulary, reading rate, and comprehension. Test booklets, $2.35 per 25; specimen set, $.50. PUBLIC.

Arthur Point Scale of Performance Tests

Age 4 to adult. A nonlanguage performance scale for measuring intelligence, to be used only by psychologists trained in mental testing. Working time, about 60 min. Form I, revised form II. Complete set, Form I, $90.00; Form II, $64.00; components available separately. STOELTING.

Bender Visual Motor Gestalt Test

An individually administered test involving the copying of nine specially devised designs. For use only by psychologists with special training. Design cards and directions for administering, $1.10; manual, $3.60. PSYCHOLOGICAL.

Brown-Carlsen Listening Comprehension Test

Grades 9–13. A test of ability to comprehend spoken language, administered orally to groups. Includes immediate recall, following directions, recognizing transitions, recognizing word meanings, and lecture comprehension. Working time, about 50 min. Forms Am, Bm. Answer sheets, $1.60 per 35; scoring keys, $.20; manual, $.30; expectancy chart, $.02; specimen set, $.50. WORLD.

Buckingham Extension of the Ayres Spelling Scale

Grades 2–9. A list of 1,000 common words, arranged in levels of difficulty; useful in remedial spelling as well as in testing. Per copy, $.30 with class record sheet. PUBLIC.

California Reading Tests

Primary, grades 1–3; *Elementary,* grades 4–6; *Intermediate,* grades 7–9; *Advanced,* grades 9–14. Each test has two main parts, vocabulary and comprehension, with several subtests in each part. Working time, 20 min. to 50 min., with provision for flexible time limits. These tests are revisions of the former *Progressive Reading Tests,* and are also published as the reading part of the *California Achievement Tests.* Two types of separate answer sheets are available for the Elementary, Intermediate, and Advanced tests. Forms AA, BB, CC; Form DD for all except Advanced. Test booklets, $.07 per copy; Scoreze answer sheets, $.07 per copy; IBM answer sheets, $.04 per copy; manual, $.25; scoring key, $.05, $.20, or $.60; specimen set, any level, $.50. CALIFORNIA.

California Short-Form Test of Mental Maturity

Preprimary, kindergarten, or beginning grade 1; *Primary,* grades 1–3; *Elementary,* grades 4–8; *Intermediate,* grades 7–10; *Advanced,* grade 9–superior adult. Yields mental ages and IQ's for language (reading) and nonlanguage (no reading) sections and for total test. A selection of subtests from the *California Tests of Mental Maturity.* Working time, about 20 to 52 min., but longer time may be allowed. Revised 1950, Primary 1953. Test booklets, $.08 per copy; Scoreze answer sheets, $.07 per copy; IBM answer sheets, $.04 per copy; manuals, $.25; scoring keys, $.05, $.20, $.40; specimen set, any level, $.50. CALIFORNIA.

California Tests of Mental Maturity

Preprimary Series, kindergarten–grade 1; *Primary,* grades 1–3; *Elementary,* grades 4–8; *Intermediate,* grades 7–10; *Advanced,* grade 9–adult. An analytical group intelligence test. Language and nonverbal items are used for testing memory, attention, orientation in spatial relationships, reasoning, and vocabulary. Provides separate MA's and IQ's for language, nonlanguage, and total scores. Working time, about 90 min.; exact timing not required. Language and nonlanguage sections can also be purchased in separate booklets. Separate answer sheets are optional. Test booklets, $.14 per copy; Scoreze answer sheets, $.07 per copy; IBM answer sheets, $.04 per copy; scoring stencils, $.05, $.40, $.60; manual, any level, $.25; specimen set, any level, $.50. CALIFORNIA.

California Test of Personality

Primary, kindergarten–grade 3; elementary, grades 4–8; intermediate, grades 7–10; secondary, grade 9–college. An analytical group personality questionnaire providing scores on self-adjustment and social adjustment. Working time, about 50 min. Forms AA, BB, each level (1953 revision). Test booklets, $.08 each; $2.80 per 35; Scoreze answer sheets, $.07; IBM answer sheets, $.04; specimen set, any level, $.50. CALIFORNIA.

Chapman-Cook Speed of Reading Test

Grades 4–8. A brief test of rate of silent reading. Working time, 2½ min. Forms A, B. Test booklets, $1.10 per 25; specimen set, $.30. EDUCATIONAL.

Chicago Non-Verbal Examination

Age 7–adult. A nonverbal group intelligence test that does not require any reading, and can be given in pantomime to those who do not understand spoken English. Time, about 55 min. Test booklets, $3.50 per 25; manual and scoring keys, $1.20; specimen set, $1.25. PSYCHOLOGICAL.

Chicago Reading Tests

Test A, grades 1 and 2. Word recognition and comprehension. Working time, about 30 min. Forms 1, 2. Test booklets, $3.50 per 50.
Test B, grades 2–4. Comprehension of words, sentences, and paragraphs, and rate of reading. Time, 42 min. Forms 1, 2. Test booklets, $4.00 per 50.
Test C, grades 4–6. Comprehension of words, sentences, paragraphs, maps, graphs, and rate. Time, 45 min. Forms 1, 2. Test booklets, $4.50 per 50.
Test D, grades 6–8. Similar to *Test C* but more difficult. Time, 45 min. Forms

1, 2, 3; also m-1, m-2, m-3 for use with separate answer sheets. Test booklets, $4.50 per 50; answer sheets, $.90 per 25. Complete specimen set, 4 tests, $1.00. HALE.

Children's Apperception Test

Ages 4–10. An individually administered projective test involving making up stories about ten pictures showing animals in social situations; for use only by psychologists with special training. Set of pictures, with manual, $6.25; record blanks, $6.30 per 30; supplement, with manual, $6.30; complete set, $17.00. PSYCHOLOGICAL.

Cooperative English Tests, Test C: Reading Comprehension

Test C1, for grades 7–12; *Test C2* for superior 11th and 12th grade and college students. Yields scores for speed of comprehension, level of comprehension, and vocabulary. Working time, 40 minutes. Forms R, T, Y, Z. Test booklets, $2.95 per 25; answer sheets, $.90 per 25; scoring stencil, $.15; specimen set, $.50, either level. ETS

Cooperative School and College Ability Tests

School Ability Tests, for grades 10–12 and superior 9; *College Ability Tests,* for college freshmen and sophomores, and superior grade 12. Group tests of mental ability designed to measure capacity for academic success. Each test has four parts, yielding a verbal score, a quantitative score, and a total score. Working time, 70 min. Level 1 (college), Forms 1A, 1B, 1C, 1D; Level 2, Forms 2A, 2B. Level 3, for grades 8–10, and Levels 4 and 5, for middle and upper grades, to be published. Level 1 or Level 2, test booklets, $3.25 per 25; answer sheets, $1.25 per 25; scoring keys, $.35 per set; specimen set, $1.50; Examiner's Manual, $1.00. ETS

Cooperative Vocabulary Test

For grades 7–12. A 210-item test, arranged in 7 equivalent scales of 30 words each. Can be used with flexible time limit, although normal working time is 30 min. Forms Q, Z. Test booklets, $2.50 per 25; answer sheets, $1.00 per 25; scoring stencil, $.30; specimen set, $.50. ETS

Coordinated Scales of Attainment

Primary Division. Separate batteries for grades 1, 2, and 3, each containing tests of reading, spelling, and arithmetic. Test booklets, any battery, $1.95 per 25; specimen set, $.30.

Grades 4–8. A separate test for each grade, providing a level of comprehension score; untimed. Also published as the *Nelson-Lohmann Reading Test.* Test booklets, $1.25 per 25, any grade; answer sheet (optional), $.60 per 25; scoring key, $.10; specimen set, five grades, $.50. EDUCATIONAL.

Cornell-Coxe Performance Ability Scale

Ages 6–15. An individual nonverbal performance scale for measuring intelligence. To be used only by psychologists trained in testing. Time, about 50 min. Complete test materials, including package of record blanks, $36.50; manual, $2.80; record blanks, $1.90 per 35. PSYCHOLOGICAL.

Critical Angle Board Test

An individually administered test for detection of tendencies toward directional confusion, involving simultaneous drawing with left and right hands on vertical surfaces at a variety of angles. Not available commercially. See reference, page 260.

Davis-Eells Test of General Intelligence or Problem-Solving Ability (Davis-Eells Games)

Primary Test, grades 1, 2; *Elementary Test,* grades 3–6. A group test of problem-solving ability which involves no reading. Working time, 60 to 100 min. in two or three sessions. Primary test blanks, \$3.80 per 35; Elementary, \$4.25 per 35; manual, \$.80; specimen set, either level, \$.35. WORLD.

Detroit Advanced First-Grade Intelligence Test

High first grade or beginning grade 2. A group test requiring no reading. Working time, 30–35 min. Test booklets, \$2.55 per 35; specimen set, \$.35. WORLD.

Detroit Beginning First-Grade Intelligence Test (Revised)

Beginning grade 1. A group test containing 10 short subtests, requiring no reading. Working time, 30–35 min. Test booklets, \$2.55 per 35; specimen set, \$.35. WORLD.

Detroit Primary Intelligence Test

Grades 2, 3. A group intelligence test requiring no reading. Time, about 35 min. Test booklets, \$2.05 per 25; specimen set, \$.40. PUBLIC.

Detroit Reading Tests

Test I, grade 2; *Test II,* grade 3; *Test III,* grades 4–6; *Test IV,* grades 7–9. Quick survey tests of silent reading for preliminary classification of pupils. Working time, *Test I,* 8 min.; *Test II,* 7 min.; *Test III,* 6 min.; *Test IV,* 5 min. Forms A, B, each test. Test booklets, \$1.65 per 35. WORLD.

Detroit Tests of Learning Aptitude

Ages 4–adult. An individual intelligence scale consisting of 19 subtests each with separate mental age norms, allowing a flexible choice of tests for diagnostic purposes. Record booklets, \$3.35 per 25; book of pictorial material, \$1.90; examiner's handbook, \$3.85; complete sample packet, \$6.50. PUBLIC.

Detroit Word Recognition Test

Grades 1–3. Test involves matching words and phrases with pictures. Working time, 4–6 min. Forms A, B, C, D. Test booklets, \$1.65 per 35; specimen set, \$.35. WORLD.

Developmental Reading Tests

Readiness test, beginning first grade. Test booklets, \$3.00 per 35.
Primer. Basic vocabulary test, \$1.50 per 35; general comprehension test, \$1.50 per 35.
Lower primary. Basic vocabulary test, \$1.50 per 35; general comprehension test, \$2.50 per 35. Forms A, B, C.
Upper Primary. Basic vocabulary test, \$1.50 per 35; general comprehension test, \$2.50 per 35. Forms A, B, C.
Intermediate, for grades 4–6. Basic vocabulary test, forms A, B, C, D, \$1.50 per 35; general comprehension test, forms A, B, C, D, \$3.00 per 35; basic study skills, forms A, B, C, D, \$3.00. LYONS.

Diagnostic Reading Tests

Higher level, grade 7–13. Includes a Survey Test with 8 forms, A to H, and a Diagnostic Battery with 8 separate booklets: vocabulary, silent comprehension, auditory comprehension, general rate, rate in social studies, rate in science, oral word attack, and silent word attack; forms A, B, of each part. Specimen set, all parts, $3.15; too many separate items to reproduce prices here. Norms, $.50; Interpretive manual, $2.00.
Lower Level, grades 4–6. Booklet I, comprehension and word attack; Booklet II, vocabulary, and rate; Section IV, word attack, oral, for individual administration. Forms A, B, each booklet. Test booklets, $.20 or $.18 each; directions, $.25; answer sheets, $.02; scoring stencil, $.15, $.30. COMMITTEE.

Dolch Basic Sight Word Test

The 220 words of the Dolch Basic Word List arranged on one sheet of paper for testing. $1.75 per 100. GARRARD.

Durrell Analysis of Reading Difficulty: New Edition

A battery of diagnostic tests for intensive analysis of reading problems. Includes a wirebound set of Reading Paragraphs, a cardboard Tachistoscope with a series of word lists, and an individual record blank. Provides tests of oral and silent reading, listening comprehension, word analysis, phonics, faulty pronunciation, and writing and spelling. Working time, 30–60 min. Record booklets, $3.35 per 35; Reading Paragraphs, $1.30 per copy; Tachistoscope and cards, $1.10; blank cards, $1.20 per 30; manual, $.45; complete examiner's kit, $3.25. WORLD.

Durrell-Sullivan Reading Capacity and Achievement Tests

Primary, grades 2.5–4.5; *Intermediate,* grades 3–6. The *Capacity* test is a nonreading group test of ability to understand spoken language as a measure of potential reading ability; the *Achievement* test is a test of reading comprehension with two parts, paragraph meaning and vocabulary. The *Primary* booklet includes both; the intermediate tests are published separately. Working time, *Primary,* about 45 min.; *Intermediate Capacity,* about 40 min.; *Intermediate Achievement,* about 35 min. Optional tests, 15–20 min. *Primary,* test booklets, $3.95 per 35; *Intermediate Capacity,* $2.55 per 35; *Intermediate Achievement,* $3.05 per 35; manual, $.25; specimen set, any test, $.50. WORLD.

Eames Eye Test: Revised Edition

A series of tests for screening out pupils whose eyes need professional examination. Consists of a manual, a lens, visual acuity card, near-vision card, two stereographic cards, card for testing stereoscope, astigmatic chart, record cards, and manual. All grades. Working time, about 10 min. Examiner's Kit, $6.40; record cards, $1.00 per 35. WORLD.

Gates Reading Diagnosis Tests, Revised

Tests for individual diagnosis of retarded readers from nonreader up through grade 5 level. Includes paragraphs for oral reading; phrase perception test; word lists for testing word recognition, word analysis skills, and spelling; tests of syllabication, reversible words, recognition of syllables, phonograms, and letter names and sounds; blending letter sounds. Forms 1, 2. Working time, about 60 min. Specimen set, complete, $1.60; record blanks, $.25 each; manual, $.60; pupil's reading material, $.65 each form; cards, $.10 a set. BUREAU.

Gates Reading Readiness Tests

Kindergarten–beginning grade 1. The first four parts can be given on a group basis; Test 5 must be given individually. Percentile norms for each part. Test booklets, $1.90 per 25; specimen set, $.35. BUREAU.

Gates Reading Survey

Grades 3–10. Provides separate measures of vocabulary, level of comprehension, rate of reading, and accuracy of comprehension. Working time, 60–90 min. Test booklets, $2.30 per 25; specimen set, $.35. BUREAU.

Gates Silent Reading Tests, Revised

Primary, grades 1 and 2. Three types, in separate booklets: Type 1, word recognition; Type 2, sentence reading; Type 3, paragraph reading. Working time, 15–20 min. each. Forms 1, 2, 3, each type. Test booklets, $3.30 per 100; $.04 each; specimen set, $.35.
Advanced Primary, grades 2 and 3. Type 1, word recognition, and Type 2, paragraph reading, in separate booklets. Time, 15–25 min. Forms 1, 2, 3. Test booklets, $3.30 per 100; $.04 each; specimen set, $.35.
Basic Reading Tests, grades 3–8. Four types, each in a separate booklet: Type A, general significance; Type B, predict outcomes; Type C, follow directions; Type D, reading details. Working time, 6–10 min. Forms 1, 2, 3, 4, each type. Test booklets, $3.30 per 100, $.04 each; specimen set, $.35. BUREAU.

Gilmore Oral Reading Test

Grades 1–8. An individual test of oral reading. Ten reading paragraphs of increasing difficulty, printed on heavy cardboard with spiral binding, and a record form for recording and analyzing errors and time, and checking comprehension. Forms A, B. Working time, 10–20 min. Reading paragraphs, $1.60; record blank, either form, $1.85 per 35; specimen set, $.50. WORLD.

Gray Standardized Oral Reading Check Tests

Grades 1–8. A series of brief oral reading tests. *Set I,* for grades 1 and 2; *Set II,* for grades 2–4; *Set III,* grades 4–6; *Set IV,* grades 6–8. Each set contains five tests of equivalent length and difficulty. Time, any test, 1–3 min. per pupil. Test sheets, $2.60 per 100, package containing 20 copies of each of five forms of one set; specimen set, one level, $.25; complete specimen set, $.70. PUBLIC.

Gray Standardized Oral Reading Paragraphs Test

Grades 1–8. An individual oral reading test consisting of a series of 12 paragraphs arranged in order of increasing difficulty. Score based on a combination of accuracy and rate. Time, 5–10 min. per pupil. Test booklets, $1.40 per 25; specimen set, $.25. PUBLIC.

Haggerty Reading Examination

Sigma 1, grades 1–3; *Sigma 3,* grades 6–12. A survey test of silent reading, covering vocabulary, sentence reading, and paragraph reading. Working time, *Sigma 1,* 20 min.; *Sigma 3,* 28 min. Test booklets, *Sigma 1,* $2.35 per 25; *Sigma 3,* $3.10 per 35. WORLD.

Harris Tests of Lateral Dominance

Ages 6 and up. A set of brief, easy-to-administer tests of hand, eye, and foot dominance. Working time, 10–15 min.; directions for abbreviated testing also included. Record blanks, $3.15 per 50; manual, $.65; A-B-C Vision Test, $2.00; specimen set, $.75. PSYCHOLOGICAL.

Henmon-Nelson Tests of Mental Ability

Elementary, grades 3–8; *High School,* grades 7–12; and *College* levels. Group intelligence tests presenting questions requiring reading; a carbon paper marking device provides easy scoring. Working time, 30 min. Forms A, B; Form C at the two lower levels. Test booklets, $1.85 per 25; specimen set, $.40. HOUGHTON.

Iowa Every-Pupil Test of Basic Skills

Elementary, grades 3–5; *Advanced,* grades 6–8. Test A, Silent Reading Comprehension, includes paragraph comprehension and vocabulary. Time, about 70 min. Test B, Work-Study Skills, includes map reading, use of references, and reading of graphs, charts, and tables. Series also includes language and arithmetic tests. Forms L, M, N, O. Test booklets, $2.00 per 25, any one test; manual, $.45; booklet of norms, $.25; complete materials for 25 pupils, $6.00; specimen set, $.40. HOUGHTON.

Iowa Silent Reading Tests: New Edition

Elementary Test, grades 4–8; *Advanced Test,* high school and college. Analytical silent reading tests including rate, comprehension, word meaning, and several skills in locating information. Working time, *Elementary,* 49 min., *Advanced,* 45 min. Forms Am, Bm, Cm, Dm, each level. *Elementary,* $3.05 per 35; *Advanced,* $4.10 per 35; machine-scored answer sheets (not required), $1.90 per 35; specimen set, either level, $.35. WORLD.

Iowa Spelling Scales

A list of 3000 words, arranged in spelling scales for grades 2–8. Now out of print. PUBLIC.

Kelley-Greene Reading Comprehension Test

Grades 9–12 and college freshmen. A survey silent reading test involving paragraph comprehension, finding answers to questions, and retention of information read; estimate of rate also obtainable. Working time, about 65 min. Forms Am, Bm. Test booklets, $4.75 per 35; answer sheets, $1.40 per 35; specimen set, $.35. WORLD.

Keystone Tests of Binocular Skill

An adaptation of the *Gray Standardized Oral Reading Check Tests* for use with the Keystone Telebinocular or other stereoscope. Equivalent oral reading selections are read with each eye separately, and with binocular vision. Complete set, including manual and record forms, $18.50. KEYSTONE.

Keystone Visual-Survey Service for Schools

Grade 1 and up. Includes a Telebinocular (stereoscopic instrument), visual-survey unit of 12 stereographs, color perception stereographs, nonlanguage charts, manual of instruction, record forms, parent notification forms, and carrying case. Working time, 10–15 min. Complete set, $248.00; Telebinocular, $187.00; visual-survey stereographs, $36.00; record forms, $.65 per pad of 50; parent notification forms, $.15 per pad of 50. KEYSTONE.

Keystone Visual-Survey Short Tests

Grade 1 and up. A series of 3 stereoscopic slides providing 11 brief tests of usable vision, fusion, depth perception, hyperphoria, and depth perception; to be used as a brief screening test to determine if more detailed testing is needed. For use in the Keystone Telebinocular. Slides, with manual and record forms, $21.00. KEYSTONE.

Kohs Block Design Test

Age 5–adult. An individually administered performance test, involving the reproduction of colored designs by placing colored blocks together. For use only by psychologists with special training. Set, including cubes, cards, record blanks, and manual, $7.00; record blanks, $1.50 per 25. STOELTING.

Kuhlmann-Anderson Intelligence Test, 6th Edition

Nine levels, one for each grade level, kindergarten–grade 6; one for grades 7–8, one for grades 9–12. A group test of general intelligence. Each level contains 10 subtests; content below Test E (5th grade) is largely nonreading. Total testing time, about 45 min. Test booklets, $2.65 per 25; Master Manual, $2.50; specimen set, $1.00. PERSONNEL.

Kuhlmann-Finch Intelligence Tests

Grade 1–high school. Tests I–VI for grades 1–6, junior high school test, and senior high school test. Group intelligence tests, completely nonverbal in first two booklets, and including largely nonverbal material in upper levels. Test booklets, $2.40 per 25; manual, $1.10; answer sheets (optional from grade 5 up), $1.00 per 25; answer key, for hand or machine scoring, $.25; specimen set, $1.50. EDUCATIONAL.

Leavell Analytical Oral Reading Test

Grade 1–high school. An oral reading test for individual administration in which paragraphs of increasing difficulty form a continuous story, with a record booklet for recording errors and answers to comprehension questions. Test booklets, reading section, $1.00 per 25; record section, $1.25 per 25; specimen set, $.30. EDUCATIONAL.

Leavell Language-Development Service

No age limits. The Hand-Eye Coordinator consists of a slanted surface on which are mounted stereoscopic lenses and a clip for holding stereoscopic slides, which are traced or copied. Complete set, including practice pads of line drawings, words, phrases, and digits, test sheets, and a manual, $28.50. KEYSTONE.

Lee-Clark Reading Readiness Test

Kindergarten–grade 1. Contains four tests of visual discrimination and recognition of similarities and differences in letter symbols. Working time, about 20 min. Separate norms for kindergarten and first grade. $2.80 per 35; specimen set, $.25. CALIFORNIA.

Lincoln Diagnostic Spelling Tests

Intermediate, grades 5–8; *Advanced,* grades 8–12. Designed to disclose causes or areas of difficulty; pronunciation, enunciation, and use of rules. Working time, 50 min. Forms A, B. Test booklets, $2.25 per 25; specimen set, $.50 complete. PUBLIC.

McGuffey Diagnostic Reading Tests

Intermediate, grades 4–6; *junior,* grades 7–9; *senior,* grades 10–12. Includes measures of syllabication, sound recognition, vocabulary, appreciation, rate of reading, and understanding; designed for group administration. Working time, 2 class periods. Test booklets, intermediate, $2.75 per 25; junior, $2.90 per 25; senior, $2.90 per 25; specimen set, any division, $.60. EDUCATIONAL.

Massachusetts Vision Tests

Grade 1 and up. Includes tests of far-point acuity, farsightedness, and eye-muscle balance at near and far points. Portable model. Complete equipment, $165.00. AMERICAN OPTICAL.

Metropolitan Achievement Tests

Primary I Battery. End of grade 1. Word and phrase recognition, word meaning, number knowledge, in one booklet. Time, about 60 min. Forms R, S, T. Test booklets, $2.70 per 35; specimen set, $.50.
Primary II Battery. Grade 2, beginning of grade 3. Reading comprehension, vocabulary, arithmetic fundamentals and problems, and spelling, in one booklet. Time for reading tests, about 35 min. Forms R, S, T. Test booklets, $3.30 per 35; specimen set, $.50.
Elementary Reading Test. Grades 3 and 4. Paragraph comprehension and vocabulary. Time, 45 min. Forms R, S, T. Test booklets, $2.70 per 35; specimen set, $.35.
Intermediate Reading Test. Grades 5 and 6. Paragraph comprehension and vocabulary. Time, 45 min. Forms R, S, T. Test booklets, $2.30 per 35; specimen set, $.35.
Advanced Reading Test. Grades 7, 8, first half of 9. Paragraph comprehension and vocabulary. Time, 45 min. Forms R, S, T. $2.30 per 35; specimen set, $.35. WORLD.

Metropolitan Readiness Tests

Beginning grade 1 or end of kindergarten. Yields a reading readiness score, a number readiness score, and a total readiness score. Working time, about 60 min., in two or three sessions. Forms R, S. Test booklets, $3.70 per 35; specimen set, $.35. WORLD.

Michigan Vocabulary Profile Test

High school, college, and adult. Measures vocabulary in eight different areas: human relations, commerce, government, physical sciences, biological sciences, mathematics, fine arts, and sports. Working time, about 50 min. Forms Am, Bm. Test booklets, $3.50 per 35; answer sheets, $1.40 per 35; machine keys, $.40; specimen set, $.35. WORLD.

Monroe Diagnostic Reading Examination

Poor readers of any age. A battery of diagnostic tests for individual administration. Includes 12 small charts comprising the *Iota* and *Word Discrimination* tests, supplementary tests, a record form, and a manual. Complete set, $10.00; record blanks, $3.75 for 25. STOELTING.

Monroe Reading Aptitude Tests

First-grade entrants, and nonreaders age 6–9, for measuring readiness for reading instruction. Includes visual, auditory, and motor control; speed and articulation in speech; and language development. Group tests, time, about 40 min.; individual tests, 10–15 min. per child. Test booklets, $2.65 per 25; test cards, $1.50; specimen set, $.50. HOUGHTON.

Monroe Revised Silent Reading Tests

Test I, grades 3–5. A very brief test of rate and comprehension. Working time, 5 min. Forms 1, 2, 3. $1.30 per 25; specimen set, $.25.
Test II, grades 6–8. A very brief test giving scores in rate and comprehension. Time, 5 min. Forms 1, 2, 3. Test booklets, $1.30 per 25; specimen set, $.25.
Test III, high school. A very brief test of rate and comprehension. Working time, 4 min. Forms 1, 2. Test booklets, $1.30 per 25; specimen set, $.25. PUBLIC.

Monroe-Sherman Group Diagnostic Reading Aptitude and Achievement Tests

Grade 3 and up. Group tests for use in reading diagnosis. Achievement tests include paragraph meaning, speed of reading, and word discrimination; also arithmetic and spelling. Aptitude tests include visual memory, auditory memory and discrimination, motor speed, and vocabulary. Complete set, including manual, norms, test cards, and record blanks, $1.97. NEVINS.

Morrison-McCall Spelling Scale

Grades 2–8. A booklet containing eight spelling lists of 50 words each, ranging from very easy to difficult. Copy, $.25. WORLD.

Mosaics Test

An individually administered projective test involving the creation of designs from plastic chips which are supplied in a variety of colors and shapes; for use only by psychologists with special training. Standard Mosaic set, including 456 chips, case, tray, and manual, $43.50; minor Mosaic set, including 228 chips, case, tray and manual, $27.00; record forms, $3.25 per 25; manual, $10.00 if ordered separately; filmstrip (optional), $7.35. PSYCHOLOGICAL.

Murphy-Durrell Diagnostic Reading Readiness Test

Early first grade. Measures auditory discrimination, visual discrimination and learning rate. Working time, Tests 1 and 2, about one hour; Test 2, about 20 min. of group instruction, and brief individual testing at three different times subsequently. Test booklets, $2.65 per 35; set of flash cards (required), $1.60; specimen set, $.35. WORLD.

Nelson-Denny Reading Test

High school and college. Vocabulary and paragraph comprehension. Working time, 30 min. Forms A, B. Test booklets with answer sheets, $3.35 per 25; answer booklets, $1.60 per 25; specimen set, $.50. HOUGHTON.

Nelson Silent Reading Test

Grades 3–8. Vocabulary and paragraph comprehension. Working time, 30 min.

Forms A, B. $3.35 per 25, including answer sheets; answer sheets, $1.60 per 25; specimen set, $.50. HOUGHTON.

Ortho-Rater

Master model, for rapid testing of large numbers of individuals; modified professional model for use in schools. Available with two sets of slides; a short set for very rapid screening, and a set of 12 tests for more comprehensive screening. Prices on application. BAUSCH & LOMB.

Otis Quick-Scoring Mental Ability Tests: New Edition

Alpha Short Form, grades 1–4. A group intelligence test requiring no reading. Same booklet is used for 45 items involving verbal directions, and 45 nonverbal items. Working time, 25 min. Test booklets, $2.30 per 35; specimen set, $.35.
Beta Test, grades 4–9. A group intelligence test assuming some skill in reading. Working time, 30 min. Forms Em, Fm. Test booklets, $2.30 per 35; answer sheets (optional), $1.00 per 35; specimen set, $.35.
Gamma Test, high school and college. A group intelligence test requiring reading ability. Working time, 30 min. Forms Em, Fm. Test booklets, $2.40 per 35; answer sheets (optional), $1.00 per 35; specimen set, $.35. WORLD.

Pintner General Ability Tests

Pintner-Cunningham Primary Test. Kindergarten–grade 2. A group intelligence test requiring no reading. Working time, 25 min. Forms A, B, C. Test booklets, $2.65 per 35; specimen set, $.35.
Pintner-Durost Elementary Test. Grades 2–4. *Scale 1, Picture Content,* has oral directions and requires no reading; *Scale 2, Reading Content,* has printed questions; the two scales are parallel in type of content otherwise. Working time, 45 min. each scale. Forms A, B. Test booklets, Scale 1, $3.60 per 35; Scale 2, $2.80 per 35; specimen set (combined), $.35.
Intermediate Test, Verbal Series. Grades 4–9. A group intelligence test with eight subtests, requiring reading ability. Working time, 45 min. Forms A, B. Test booklets, $3.05 per 35; answer sheets (optional), $1.40 per 35; machine keys, $.40; specimen set, $.35; manual, $.25.
Intermediate Test, Non-Language Series. Grades 4–9. A group intelligence test that requires no verbal skill or knowledge; can be administered with verbal or pantomime directions and requires no reading. Working time, 50 min. Forms K, L. Test booklets, $4.30 per 35; pantomime directions, $.25; specimen set, $.35.
Advanced Test, Verbal Series. Grade 9 and above. Similar to the intermediate verbal test but more difficult. Working time, 55 min. Forms A, B. Test booklets, $3.05 per 35; answer sheets (optional), $1.40 per 35; machine keys, $.40; specimen set, $.35; manual, $.25. WORLD.

Pintner-Paterson Performance Scale: Short Form

Ages 6–16. A nonlanguage performance scale for measuring intelligence, individually administered; for use only by psychologists with special training. Complete set, including apparatus, record blanks, and manual, $95.00; record forms, $2.00 per 25. STOELTING.

Rhode Island Intelligence Test, Revised (1955)

Ages 3–6. A group intelligence test using pictures, for which very high correlations with the Stanford-Binet are reported. Working time, 30 min. $2.00 per 25; specimen set, $.25. PUBLIC.

Rogers Test of Personality Adjustment

Ages 9–13; separate forms for boys and girls. A group personality test giving scores on personal inferiority, social maladjustment, family maladjustment, and daydreaming. No time limit; takes about 40 minutes. Test booklets, $2.75 per 25; specimen set, including both forms, $.75. PSYCHOLOGICAL.

Roswell-Chall Diagnostic Reading Test

A short series of tests for analyzing word recognition and word analysis skills. Untimed. Price on application. The authors, City College Educational Clinic, New York 31, N.Y.

Rorschach Technique

All ages above infancy. A projective test of personality, to be used only by trained psychologists. No time limit. Set of 10 plates, $10.40; individual record blanks, $2.70 per 35; location charts, $3.15 per 100; several books on interpretation available. PSYCHOLOGICAL.

Sangren-Woody Reading Test

Grades 4–8. A group silent reading test that provides separate measures for word meaning, rate, fact material, total meaning, central thought, following directions, and organization. Working time, 27 min. Forms A, B. Test booklets, $3.15 per 35; specimen set, $.35. WORLD.

Schrammel-Gray High School and College Reading Test

Grades 7–12 and college. Provides scores on rate of reading, comprehension, and comprehension-efficiency. Working time, 25 min. Forms A, B. Test booklets, $2.35 per 25; specimen set, $.40. PUBLIC.

Silent Reading Diagnostic Tests

Grade 3 and up. Booklet contains 11 tests for group administration, providing a detailed analysis of many phases of word attack and word recognition. Test booklets, $4.00 per 20. LYONS.

Spache Binocular Reading Test

Grade 1 and up. A test designed to measure the relative participation of each eye in a binocular reading situation; uses stereoscopic slides with different words omitted on each side. Contains three levels of difficulty. To be used in a stereoscope or Telebinocular. Complete set, including stereographs, manual, and record forms, $12.00. KEYSTONE.

Spitzer Study Skills Test

Grades 9–13. Measures five work-study skills: using dictionary, using the index, knowledge of sources of information; reading graphs, maps, and tables; and organization of facts in notetaking. Working time, about 3 class periods. Forms Am, Bm. Test booklets, $4.75 per 35; answer sheets, $1.40 per 35; specimen set, $.35. WORLD.

SRA Achievement Tests: Reading

Grades 2–4. Comprehension and vocabulary. Test booklets, $1.70 per 20; scoring stencil, $1.00; specimen set, $.50.

Grades 4–6. Comprehension and vocabulary. Test booklets, $3.55 per 20; IBM answer sheets, $3.85 per 100; scoring stencils, $.50, $1.00; specimen set, $1.35.
Grades 6–9. Comprehension and vocabulary. Test booklets, $3.55 per 20; IBM answer sheets, $3.85 per 100; scoring stencils, $.50.
Grades 6–9. Work-Study Skills. Test booklets, $3.55 per 20; IBM answer sheets, $3.85 per 100; scoring stencils, $.50, $1.00. SCIENCE.

SRA Reading Analysis

Achievement, Grade 3 and up. Designed as a group test useful in diagnosis of reading difficulties. Includes paragraph understanding, word discrimination, word recognition, and optional tests of spelling and arithmetic computation. Working time, 30–60 min. Forms A, B. About $3.00 per 20.
Aptitude, grade 3 and up. Designed to measure, on a group basis, some of the important psychological abilities required for successful reading. Includes visual discrimination and memory, auditory discrimination and memory, two motor tests, and vocabulary. Working time, about 60 min. Forms A, B. About $2.00 per 20. SCIENCE.

SRA Reading Record

Grades 8–13. Ten subtests: rate, general comprehension, paragraph meaning, directory reading, map-table-graph reading, advertisement reading, index usage, technical vocabulary, sentence meaning, general vocabulary. Working time, 40 min. Test booklets, $.49 each; self-scoring pin-punch answer pads, $2.05 per 20; profile sheets, $.50 per 20; specimen set, $.75. SCIENCE.

Stanford Achievement Tests

Primary Battery. Grades 1.9–3.5. Includes paragraph meaning, word meaning, spelling, arithmetic reasoning, and arithmetic computation. Working time for reading tests, 30 min. Forms J, K, L, M, N. Test booklets, $2.50 per 35; specimen set, $.35.
Elementary Reading Test. Grades 3.0–4.9. Paragraph meaning and word meaning. Working time, 35 min. Forms J, K, L. Test booklets, $2.00 per 35; specimen set, $.35.
Intermediate Reading Test. Grades 5, 6. Paragraph meaning and word meaning. Working time, 40 min. Forms J, K, L, M. Test booklets, $2.00 per 35; specimen set, $.35.
Advanced Reading Test. Grades 7–9. Paragraph meaning and word meaning. Working time, 40 min. Forms J, K, L, M. Test booklets, $2.00 per 35; specimen set, $.35. WORLD.

Stanford-Binet Scales, Revised

Ages 2–adult. An individual intelligence test of the Binet type; to be used only by psychologists trained in mental testing. Forms L, M. Record booklets, $4.15 per 25; manual, $5.20; condensed record forms, $2.00 per 25; printed card material, $3.40 per set; box material (for preschool levels), $22.25 including printed card material. HOUGHTON.

Terman-McNemar Test of Mental Ability

Grades 7–12 and college freshmen. A group test of intelligence requiring reading ability; stressing the verbal components of intelligence. Working time, 40 min. Forms C, D. Test booklets, $2.95 per 35; answer sheets (optional), $1.25 per 35; machine key, $.20; specimen set, $.35. WORLD.

Thematic Apperception Test

Elementary school to adult. A projective test of personality, to be used only by trained psychologists. Set of pictures with manual, $6.30. Psychological.

Traxler High School Reading Test for Grades 10, 11, and 12

Includes tests of rate of reading, story comprehension, and finding main ideas in paragraphs, using social science and science material. Working time, 30 min. Forms 1, 2. Test booklets, $2.50 per 25; manual, $.25; answer sheets (optional), $.05 per copy; specimen set, $.40. Public.

Traxler Silent Reading Test for Grades 7 to 10

Includes tests of rate of reading, comprehension, word meaning, and paragraph meaning. Working time, 50 min. Forms 1, 2, 3, 4. Test booklets, $2.50 per 25; answer sheets (optional), $.05 per copy; scoring stencil, $.25; specimen set, $.40. Public.

Van Wagenen Reading Readiness Test

First grade entrants. An individual test, covering information, ability to see relations, vocabulary, word discrimination, memory span for ideas, and speed of learning words. Not currently listed. Educational.

Wechsler Adult Intelligence Scale

Ages 16 and up. An individual intelligence scale, for use only by psychologists trained in mental testing; a revision of the *Wechsler-Bellevue*. Working time, about one hour. Record forms, $1.60 per 25; complete set, including box of test materials, manual, and 25 record forms, $21.00. Psychological.

Wechsler-Bellevue Intelligence Scale

Adolescents and adults. Form I has been superseded by the *Wechsler Adult Intelligence Scale*. Working time, about one hour. Forms I and II. Test materials, including 25 record forms, $17.50; manual "The Measurement of Adult Intelligence," $3.60; record forms, $1.60 per 25. Psychological.

Wechsler Intelligence Scale for Children

Ages 5–15. An individual intelligence scale, for use only by psychologists trained in mental testing. Gives verbal, performance, and total IQ's. Complete set, including manual and 25 record forms, $22.00; manual, $2.50; record forms, $2.00 per 25. Psychological.

Wide Range Achievement Test

Age 5–adult. An individual test of word recognition, spelling, and arithmetic computation. Time, 20–40 min. Test booklets, $3.00 per 50; specimen set, $.45. Psychological.

Williams Primary Reading Tests, Revised (1955)

Grade 1. Word recognition and paragraph comprehension. Working time, 25 min. Forms C, D. Test booklets, $1.25 per 25; specimen set, $.25.
Grades 2 and 3. Word recognition and paragraph comprehension. Working time, 25 min. Forms C, D. Test booklets; $1.25 per 25; specimen set, $.25; specimen set, both levels, $.40. Public.

APPENDIX B

A Graded List of Books for Remedial Reading

One of the major problems in selecting books for poor readers is the fact that the difficulty ratings provided in most of the children's booklists are not safe guides. In the lists which occupy the next few pages, books are assigned according to independent reading level. The grade placement for each book is this writer's personal opinion of the *minimum* level of reading ability necessary if a boy or girl is to enjoy reading the book independently, or with very little help. The books are arranged by grades, and alphabetically by author within each grade.

To be included, each book had to pass the test of having interest appeal to children at least two grades above the difficulty rating. Thus, all of the first-grade list are acceptable at least to third graders, all of the third grade list to fifth graders, etc. Three special symbols are used. An asterisk (*) indicates outstanding interest-appeal for poor readers. A "J" indicates that the book is accepted by many junior high school pupils; an "S" indicates acceptability to many senior high school pupils. Simplified and abridged versions are identified by the term "(adapt.)" after the author's name.

Most of the books in the present list have been published since 1946, and most of the books in the two previous versions of this list have been dropped because they are now so old that they are either out of print or probably soon will be. Of those that have been retained, the grade placement of some has been changed. Many of the older titles are available as Cadmus reprints. Full names and addresses of all publishers mentioned in abbreviated form below are given in Appendix C.

To select some books for a poor reader one should try to find books likely to appeal to his interests from those listed at his reading level. Assume, for instance, that one wants to select some titles for a twelve-year-old boy in seventh grade, who can read fourth-grade books with help and can read third-grade books easily. For this boy one should look through the third-grade list, paying special attention to those marked *J or J. Of course, his special likes and dislikes should be taken into consideration. An annotated booklist such as the *Children's Catalog* (see page 493) can be consulted for a brief review of the book's contents, if unfamiliar.

For older boys and girls with reading ability below third-grade level, the *Cowboy Sam* books and the Walt Disney books tend to be more palatable than most basal readers and story books written for primary-grade children; the individual titles of these two series are included in the lists below. Other series well represented by individual titles are the *American Adventure Series* (Wheeler), the *Childhood of Famous Americans* books (Bobbs-Merrill), the *All About* books and *Landmark* books (Random House), and the "First" books (Watts). Basal readers are not included in the lists below.

Suggestions for this list were obtained from many remedial teachers and from about a dozen of the more recently published lists of books for retarded readers. Particularly helpful were Spache's *Good Books for Poor Readers,* the Boston University *High Interest—Low Vocabulary Booklist,* Strang's *Gateways to Readable Books,* and several lists compiled by Mary Eakin of the Children's Book Service, University of Chicago Library. My wife has reviewed the difficulty ratings on many of the books in the light of her own use of them in remedial teaching. Final responsibility both for the selections and the difficulty ratings, however, is mine.

Grade I

Author		*Title*	*Publisher*
Barker		Little Sea Legs	Oxford
Battle		Jerry Goes Fishing	Beckley
Becker		Nine Hundred Buckets of Paint	Abingdon
Behn		All Kinds of Time	Harcourt
Boutwell		The Red Rooster	Aladdin
Brown		My World	Harper
Bulla		A Ranch for Danny	Crowell
Chandler	*J	Cowboy Sam; Cowboy Sam and Shorty; Cowboy Sam and Porky; Cowboy Sam and Freddy	Beckley
Dannecker		Happy, Hero and Judge	Abingdon
De Angeli		Just Like David	Doubleday
Disney	*J	Here They Are	Heath
Horn		We Live in a City	Ginn
Huber		Cinder the Cat	American
Huber		The Ranch Book	Macmillan
Huber		Skags, The Milk Horse	American
Huber		I Know a Story	Row
La Rue		Tiny Toosey's Birthday	Houghton
Lent	J	Straight Up	Macmillan
McCall		Bucky Button; The Buttons at the Zoo; The Buttons and the Pet Parade; The Buttons at the Farm	Beckley
Serl		In Rabbitville	American

Author	Title	Publisher
Stewart	Billy Buys a Dog	Reilly
Tresselt	Raindrop Splash	Lothrop
Unwin	Doughnuts for Lin	Aladdin

Grade II

Author		Title	Publisher
Anderson	*J	Friday, The Arapaho Indian	Wheeler
Anderson	*J	Squanto and the Pilgrims	Wheeler
Averill		Cat Club	Doubleday
Bacon	J	Turkey Tale	Oxford
Balet		Amos and the Moon	Oxford
Barr		Little Circus Dog	Whitman
Barr		Texas Pete, Little Cowboy	Whitman
Barr		Fireman Fred	Whitman
Beatty		Little Wild Horse	Houghton
Beim		Sasha and the Samovar	Harcourt
Beim		Twelve O'Clock Whistle	Morrow
Beim		Two is a Team	Harcourt
Bendick		All Around You	Whittlesey
Beskow		Pelle's New Suit	Harper
Bianco		Little Houses Far Away	Oxford
Bright		Georgie	Doubleday
Brock		Surprise Balloon	Knopf
Bromhall		Mary Ann's First Picture	Knopf
Brown		Little Fisherman	Scott
Brown		Merrylegs, The Rocking Pony	Scribner
Brown		Sleepy Little Lion	Harper
Buck		Country Boy	Abingdon
Burton		Exciting Adventures of Walco	McGraw
Burton		Katy and the Big Snow	Houghton
Caudill		Up and Down the River	Winston
Chalmers		Kitten's Tale	Viking
Chandler	*J	Cowboy Sam and the Rodeo; Cowboy Sam and the Fair	Beckley
Chapman		Child's Book of Sewing	Greenberg
Clark		Magic Money	Viking
Coats		The Story of Horace	Faber
Creekmore		Little Fu	Macmillan
Creekmore		Lokoski Learns to Hunt Seals	Macmillan
Dannecker		Fisherman Sims	Abingdon
D'Aulaire		Too Big	Doubleday
Davis		Timothy Turtle	Harcourt
Delafield		Mrs. Mallard's Ducklings	Lothrop
Deming	J	Indians in Winter Camp	Laidlaw
Deming	*J	Little Eagle	Laidlaw
Dennis		Burlap	Viking
Disney	*J	Donald Duck and His Nephews	Heath
Disney		Donald Duck's Toy Train	Simon
Dolbier		The Magic Bus	Wonder

Author		*Title*	*Publisher*
Duvoisin		Christmas Whale	Knopf
Eager		Red Head	Houghton
Fatio		Anna, the Horse	Aladdin
Fatio		The Christmas Forest	Aladdin
Flack		Boats on the River	Viking
Flack		Ask Mr. Bear	Macmillan
Flack		Tim Tadpole and the Great Bullfrog	Doubleday
Forbes		The Thirsty Lion	Crowell
Gannett		Elmer and the Dragon	Random
Gilbert		Mr. Plum and the Little Green Tree	Abingdon
Godden		The Mousewife	Viking
Hader		Chuck-A-Luck and His Reindeer	Houghton
Hader		Little Stone House	Macmillan
Hauman		Surprise for Timmy	Macmillan
Henry		Little Fellow	Winston
Heward		Billety Bob and the Big Brown Bear	McKay
Hoffman		Miss B's First Cookbook	Bobbs
Hogan		About Charlie	Dutton
Huber		It Happened One Day	Row
Huber		Rusty Wants a Dog	Macmillan
Huber	J	Skags, The Milk Horse	American
Hunt		Double Birthday Present	Lippincott
Hurd		Caboose	Lothrop
Ipcar		Animal Hide and Seek	Scott
Kinert		Little Helicopter	Macmillan
Kissin		Desert Animals	McKay
Kraus		A Hole Is To Dig	Harper
Kraus		The Backward Day	Harper
Krauss		I Can Fly	Simon
Lansing		The Pony that Ran Away	Crowell
Lathrop		Angel in the Woods	Macmillan
Lattimore		Bells for a Chinese Donkey	Morrow
Lenski		Cowboy Small	Oxford
Lenski		Little Airplane; Little Auto; Little Fire Engine; Little Farm; Little Train; Papa Small	Oxford
Lent	J	Straight Down	Macmillan
Lipkind		The Two Reds	Viking
Long		Faraway Holiday	Morrow
Love		April Showers	Crowell
Mathiesen		The Blue-Eyed Pussy	Doubleday
McGinley		Horse Who Live Upstairs	Lippincott
Meeks		Fireman Casey and Fireboat 999	Wilcox
Milhous		The Egg Tree	Scribner
Palazzo		Susie the Cat	Viking
Palmer	*J	Mickey Never Fails	Heath
Patton		The Little House on Stilts	Whitman
Patton		The Little River of Gold	Whitman
Paull		Pancakes for Breakfast	Doubleday

Author		Title	Publisher
Pease		The Book of Clothes; The Book of Food; The Book of Heat and Light; The Book of Houses	Nelson
Petersham		The Circus Baby	Macmillan
Petersham		The Rooster Crows	Macmillan
Politi		Juanita	Scribner
Politi		Little Leo	Scribner
Rey	*	Pretzel	Harper
Schneider		While Susie Sleeps	Scott
Schreiber		Bambino the Clown	Viking
Simont		Polly's Oats	Harper
Slobodkin		Seaweed Hat	Macmillan
Smith		Down the Road with Johnny	McGraw
Steiner		Sleepy Quilt	Doubleday
Stevens		Nippy	Webster
Snedden	*	Docas, Indian of Santa Clara	Heath
Snedden	*	Docas, the Indian Boy	Heath
Tippett		Tools for Andy	Abingdon
Tompkins		The Red Squirrel Twins	Lippincott
Tresselt		White Snow, Bright Snow	Lothrop
Webb		Song of the Seasons	Morrow
Wells		Beppo the Donkey	Doubleday
Wells		Coco the Goat	Doubleday
Wells		Zeke the Raccoon	Viking
Wiese		Fish in the Air	Viking
Wiese		Liang and Lo	Doubleday
Wiese		Wallie the Walrus	Coward
Williamson		Lion Cub	Doubleday
Withers		A Rocket in My Pocket	Holt
Wood		Great Sweeping Day	Longmans
Wooley		I Like Trains	Harper
Wooley		Schoolroom Zoo	Morrow
Zolotow		Park Book	Harper

Grade III

Author		Title	Publisher
Adrian		Firehouse Mystery	Houghton
Agle & Wilson		Three Boys and the Remarkable Cow	Scribner
Anderson & Regli	*J	Alec Majors	Wheeler
Anderson	*J	Pilot Jack Knight	Wheeler
Anderson	*	Billy and Blaze; Blaze and the Gypsies; Blaze and the Forest Fire; Blaze Finds the Trail; Blaze and Others	Macmillan
Anderson		A Pony for Linda	Macmillan
Anderson		Linda and the Indians	Macmillan
Anderson		Anderson's Fairy Tales	Appleton
Anderson		Stories I Like	Steck
Anderson		Sandra and the Right Prince	Oxford

Author		*Title*	*Publisher*
Andrews		Ten Boys Who Lived on the Road From Long Ago to Now	Ginn
Atkinson	J	How to Raise Your Puppy	Greenberg
Baer		Experiments Without Fire	Rinehart
Baldwin	J	Robinson Crusoe for Children	American
Bannerman		Story of Little Black Sambo	Grosset
Bannon		Billy and the Bear	Houghton
Barnum	J	Little Old Truck	Morrow
Barrow		Jamboree for Boys	Hart
Batchelor		A Cap for Mul Chand	Harcourt
Beals	*J	Chief Black Hawk	Wheeler
Beatty		Little Wild Horse	Houghton
Beauchamp		How Do We Know?	Scott
Beim		Alice's Family	Harcourt
Beim		Country Fireman	Morrow
Beim		Country Garage	Morrow
Beim		Eric on the Desert	Morrow
Beim		Danny and the Dog Doctor	Morrow
Beim		Kid Brother	Morrow
Beim		Smallest Boy in the Class	Morrow
Beim		Swimming Hole	Morrow
Beim		Andy and the School Bus	Morrow
Beim		Tim and the Tool Chest	Morrow
Bemelmans	J	Madeline	Simon
Bemelmans	J	Madeline's Rescue	Viking
Betts	*J	Squanto and the Pilgrims	Wheeler
Bianco		Good Friends	Viking
Bischoff		The Wonderful Poodle	Crowell
Bishop	*J	Five Chinese Brothers	Hale
Black	*	Dusty and His Friends	Holiday
Black		Maggie, A Mischievous Magpie	Holiday
Black		Summerfield Farm	Viking
Blough		Monkey With a Notion	Holt
Boutemps		You Can't Pet a Possum	Morrow
Brewster	*J	First Book of Baseball	Watts
Brewster	J	First Book of Cowboys	Watts
Brewster	J	First Book of Firemen	Watts
Brock		Three Ring Circus	Knopf
Brock		Till Potatoes Grow on Trees	Knopf
Bronson		Hooker's Holiday	Harcourt
Bronson		Coyotes; Turtles	Harcourt
Brooks		To and Again	Knopf
Brown		Crazy Quilt: the Story of a Piebald Pony	Scribner
Brown	*J	Little Pigs Picnic and others	Heath
Brown		Stone Soup	Scribner
Buck		In Woods and Fields; In Yards and Gardens	Abingdon
Bulla		Riding the Pony Express	Crowell
Bulla		The Secret Valley	Crowell

Author		*Title*	*Publisher*
Burton	*J	Mike Mulligan and His Steam Shovel	Houghton
Burton		The Little House	Houghton
Carlson	J	Make it Yourself	Abingdon
Carroll		School in the Sky	Macmillan
Caudill		Happy Little Family	Winston
Chandler	*J	Cowboy Sam and the Rustlers; Cowboy Sam and the Indians	Beckley
Chrystie	J	Riddle Me This	Oxford
Coatsworth		Boy with the Parrot	Macmillan
Coatsworth		First Adventure	Macmillan
Colby		Gabbit, the Magic Rabbit	Coward
Collin		Nils, The Island Boy	Viking
Crampton		The Pottlebys	American
Credle	J	Down, Down the Mountain	Nelson
Credle		Flop-Eared Hound	Oxford
Creekmore		Fujio	Macmillan
Crocker	J	Creative Carpentry	Houghton
Daugherty	*J	Andy and the Lion	Hale
D'Aulaire	J	George Washington	Doubleday
Davis		Picken's Great Adventure; Picken's Exciting Summer	Oxford
Davis		Roger and the Fox	Doubleday
Davis		The Wild Birthday Cake	Doubleday
Defoe (adapt.)	J	Robinson Crusoe	American
DeJong		Smoke Above the Lane	Harper
DeLeeuw		Blue Ribbons for Meg	Little
Deming		Indians in Winter Camp	Laidlaw
Denison		What Every Young Rabbit Should Know	Dodd
Disney	*J	Donald Duck and His Friends	Heath
Dobbs		Once Upon a Time	Random
Dolch	*J	"Why" Stories; Animal Stories; Folk Stories; Aesops Stories; Bible Stories; Fairy Stories; Famous Stories; Gospel Stories; Old World Stories	Garrard
DuBois		Squirrel Hotel	Viking
Dudley		Hank and the Kitten	Morrow
Duvoisin	J	Petunia	Knopf
Elting		First Book of Baseball	Watts
Emerson	*J	School Days in Disneyville	Heath
Engebretson	J	What Happened to George	Rand
Erickson		Cattail House	Children's
Erickson		Slip, Story of a Little Fox	Children's
Everson	J	Secret Cave	Dutton
Fatio		Anna the Horse	Aladdin
Faulkner	*J	Hidden Silver	Scott F.
Flack & Wiese		Story About Ping	Viking
Fletcher	J	Big Book of Cowboys	Grosset
Fletcher		Big Book of Indians	Grosset
Flexner	J	Puzzle Pond	Lippincott

Author		*Title*	*Publisher*
Finger		Tales from Silver Lands	Doubleday
Frisky		Captain Joe	Children's
Gag		Tales From Grimm	Coward
Gall & Crew		Here, There and Everywhere	Oxford
Gall & Crew		Ringtail	Oxford
Geisel	*J	And to Think That I Saw It on Mulberry Street	Vanguard
Geisel	*J	Horton Hatches the Egg	Random
Geisel		McElligot's Pool	Random
Graham		Timothy Turtle	Viking
Gramatky	*	Little Toot	Putnam
Gramatky	*	Loopy	Putnam
Grautoff		The Stubborn Donkey	Aladdin
Grey		Rolling Wheels	Little
Gulick		Dear Uncle Looy	Knopf
Hader		Big City	Macmillan
Hader		Billy Butter	Macmillan
Haywood		"B" is for Betsy	Harcourt
Haywood		Penny Goes to Camp	Morrow
Henderson		Cats for Kansas	Abingdon
Henderson	J	Why Cowboys Sing in Texas	Abingdon
Hoffman	*	Primitivo and His Dog	Dutton
Holt & Coggins	J	Lance and His First Horse	McGraw
Horowitz		Child's Treasury of Things To Do; Play-Alone Fun	Hart
Huber		After the Sun Sets	Row
Hurd	J	Toughy and His Trailer Truck	Lothrop
Jackson		Pantaloon	Simon
Jensen		The Flying Trunk	Scott
Johnson		Treat Shop	Merrill
Johnson		Joey and Patches	Morrow
Johnson	*J	Red Joker	Morrow
Johnson		Sir Lancelot and Scamp	Harcourt
Johnson		Snowshoe Paws	Morrow
Kiser		Sunshine For Merrily	Random
Kottmeyer, *ed.*	*J	Greek-Roman Myths; King Arthur and His Knights; Old Testament Stories; The Robin Hood Stories; The Trojan War	Webster
Krasilovsky		The Man Who Didn't Wash His Dishes	Doubleday
Kredel	J	Riddles Around the World	Pantheon
Lange		The Eskimo Store	Whitman
Laron		Bronco Charlie	Whittlesey
Lathrop		Skittle-Skattle Monkey	Macmillan
Lattimore		Davy of the Everglades	Morrow
Lawson		Edward, Happy and Joe	Knopf
Lawson	J	Watchwords of Liberty	Little
Leaf		Health Can Be Fun	Lippincott
Leaf		Manners Can be Fun	Stokes
Leaf		Noodle	Stokes

Author		*Title*	*Publisher*
Lewis		Puppets and Marionettes	Knopf
Lewis		Woodworking	Knopf
L'Hommedieu		Robbie the Brave Little Collie	Lippincott
Lindman		Snowboat	Whitman
Lorenzini (adapt.)		Pinocchio	Heath
Macmahon		Jack O'Moora and The King of Ireland's Son	Dutton
Mason		Happy-Jack	Macmillan
Mason		Herman, The Brave Pig	Macmillan
Mason	J	Hominy and His Blunt-nosed Arrow	Macmillan
Mason	J	Middle Sister	Macmillan
Mason		Timothy Has Ideas	Macmillan
McCloskey		One Morning in Maine	Viking
McClung		Ruby Throat; Spinx the Caterpillar	Morrow
McGinley		Blunderbus	Lippincott
Meeks		Fireman Casey and the Fireboat	Wilson
Moore	*	Old Rosie—The Horse Nobody Understood	Random
Morcomb	*	Red Feather	Lyons
Neurath		I'll Show You How It Happens	Chanticleer
Norling		Pogo's Farm Adventure; Pogo's House—Story of Lumber; Pogo's Lamb; Pogo's Letter; Pogo's Mining Trip; Pogo's Sea Trip; Pogo's Sky Ride; Pogo's Train Ride	Holt
Obermeyer	*J	The Six Robbens	Scott F.
Orton	*J	The Treasure in the Little Trunk	Lippincott
Palmer	*J	Mickey Never Fails	Heath
Park		Scratchy	Morrow
Parkin		The Red Carpet	Macmillan
Patton		Little Echo in the Hills	Whitman
Paull	J	A Horse to Ride	Doubleday
Pease		It Seems Like Magic	Rand
Pels		Easy Puppets	Crowell
Petersham		Mike	Cadmus
Petry		The Drugstore Cat	Crowell
Politi		Pedro the Angel of Olvera Street.	Scribner
Relyea		The Night the Storm Came	Aladdin
Renick		Nicky's Football Team	Scribner
Renick		Shining Shooter	Scribner
Rey	*J	Cecily G and the Nine Monkeys	Houghton
Rey	*	Curious George; Curious George Rides a Bike; Curious George Takes a Job	Houghton
Rey		Katy No-Pocket	Houghton
Rose (adapt.)	*J	Travels of Baron Munchausen	Longmans
Ross		Hungry Moon	Knopf
Ruly		Seatmates	Watts
Rushmore		Cowboy Joe of the Circus	Harcourt
Sawyer		The Little Red Horse	Viking
Schneider	J	Let's Find Out	Scott

Author		Title	Publisher
Schwalbach	J	Fun Time Crafts	Children's
Schwalje		Cezar and the Music Maker	Knopf
Scott		Judy's Baby	Harcourt
Scott		Little Wiener	Harcourt
Scott		Rip and Royal	Harcourt
Seuss, see Geisel			
Slobodkin		Magic Michael	Macmillan
Taber		The First Book of Cats	Watts
Tatham		First Book of Trains; First Flying Book	Watts
Thompson		Silver Pennies	Macmillan
Todd	J	Big Bag of Tricks	Hart
Todd	J	Tricks Every Boy Can Do	Hart
Tousey	J	Cowboy Tommy's Roundup	Hale
Tousey		Pony for the Boys	Houghton
Turner		When It Rained Cats and Dogs	Lippincott
Wagoner		Abigail Adams	Bobbs
Walters		The Snow Plow That Tried to Go South	Aladdin
Ward		The Biggest Bear	Houghton
Warner	*J	Boxcar Children	Scott F.
Warner	J	Surprise Island	Scott F.
Webb		Uncle Smith's Inventions	Holiday
Weir		Leif Ericson Explorer	Abingdon
Whipple		Airplanes at Work	Macmillan
White		The Story of Serapina	Viking
Will & Nicholas		Even Steven	Harcourt
Will & Nicholas		The Two Reds	Harcourt
Williamson	J	The First Book of Birds	Watts
Williamson	J	The First Book of Bugs	Watts
Wooley		David's Hundred Dollars	Morrow
Wooley		David's Railroad	Morrow
Wooley		Ginnie Joins In	Morrow
Wooley		Railroad Cowboy	Morrow
Wooley		Two Hundred Pennies	Morrow
Young		Prance A Carousel Horse	Crowell
Zarchy		Sewing	Knopf
Zim	*J	Elephants; Goldfish; Owls; Rabbits; Snakes	Morrow
Zoff		Riddles Around the World	Pantheon

Grade IV

Author		Title	Publisher
Agle	J	Three Boys and a Lighthouse	Scribner
Alcott	J	Little Men	Grosset
Alden		Why the Chimes Rang and Other Stories	Bobbs
Anderson		Anderson's Fairy Tales	Appleton

Author		Title	Publisher
Anderson	J	Black, Bay and Chestnut	Macmillan
Anderson	J	Fur Trappers of the Old West	Watts
Anderson	J	Wild Bill Hickock	Watts
Atwater	*J	Mr. Popper's Penguins	Little
Averill	J	Daniel Boone	Harper
Averill	J	Flash	Smith
Avision	J	Uncle Sam's Marines	Macmillan
Avision	J	Uncle Sam's Navy	Macmillan
Bailey	J	Miss Hickory	Viking
Baker		Necessary Nellie	McCann
Baldwin	J	Fifty Famous Stories Retold; Old Greek Stories; Stories of Don Quixote	American
Banning		Pet Pony	Knopf
Bannon		Billy and the Bear	Houghton
Bannon		Watchdog	Whitman
Barksdale		The Treasure Bag	Knopf
Barrie		Peter Pan and Wendy	Scribner
Beals	J	Rush for Gold	Wheeler
Bechdolt		Going Up	Abington
Beim		Beach Boy	Harcourt
Bennett	J	The Golden Encyclopedia	Simon
Bennett	J	Mick and Mack and Mary Jane	Doubleday
Beschof	J	Atoms at Work	Harcourt
Besterman		Quaint and Curious Quest of Johnny, the Shoe King's Son	Bobbs
Bethers	J	Perhaps I'll be a Sailor	Aladdin
Bialk	J	Taffy's Foal	Houghton
Bishop	J	Pancakes—Paris	Viking
Blackmore (adapt.)	*S	Lorna Doone	Scott F.
Blanek		The King and the Noble Blacksmith	Houghton
Blough	J	Tree on the Road to Turntown	Whittlesey
Bobenroth	J	Meriwether Lewis, Boy Explorer	Bobbs
Bonner	J	Couriers of the Sky	Knopf
Bonner		Something Always Happens	Knopf
Bontempts		Sam Patch, The High Wide and Handsome Jumper	Houghton
Bormann	J	Bridges	Macmillan
Bothwell		Little Boat Boy	Harcourt
Bothwell		Little Flute Player	Morrow
Bothwell		River Boy of Kashmir	Morrow
Bracken	J	Rodeo	Steck
Brindze	J	Gulf Stream; Story of Our Calendar; Story of the Totem Pole	Vanguard
Brock		Spooks, Spirits and Shadowy Shapes	Aladdin
Brock		The Topsy-Turvey Family	Knopf
Bronson	J	Cats; Coyotes; Turtles; Starlings	Harcourt
Bronson	J	Pinto's Journey	Messner
Bronte (adapt.)	*S	Wuthering Heights	Globe
Brooks	J	A Boy of the First Empire	Appleton

Author		Title	Publisher
Bulla	*J	Riding the Pony Express	Crowell
Bulla	*J	The Secret Valley	Crowell
Burton	J	Calico, the Wonder Horse	Houghton
Carmer	J	Hurricane Luck	Aladdin
Carmer	J	Wildcat Furs to China	Knopf
Cavannah		Our Country's Story	Rand
Chapman	J	Girl's Book of Sewing	Greenberg
Chase	J	Grandfather Tales	Houghton
Chase		Jack and the Three Sillies	Houghton
Clark		Looking for Something	Viking
Cleary		Henry Huggins	Morrow
Cleary		Ellen Tebbits	Morrow
Clymer	J	Trolley Car Family	McKay
Coatsworth	J	Plum Daffy's Adventure	Macmillan
Coblentz		Martin and Abraham Lincoln	Children's
Collection		Santas Footprints	Aladdin
Collins		Horace, the Hound that Howled	Dodd
Collodi		Pinocchio	Appleton
Coombs	J	Young Readers Baseball Series	Lantern
Coombs	J	Young Readers Football Series	Lantern
Cormack	J	First Book of Trees	Watts
Crampton		More Pottleby Adventures	Aladdin
Curtes	J	Winter on the Prairie	Crowell
Dalgliesh	J	The Bear on Hemlock Mountain	Scribner
Dalgliesh	J	Davenports Are At Dinner	Scribner
Dalgliesh	J	Davenports and Cherry Pie	Scribner
D'Aulaire	J	Abraham Lincoln	Doubleday
D'Aulaire	J	Benjamin Franklin	Doubleday
D'Aulaire	J	George Washington	Doubleday
D'Aulaire	J	Leif the Lucky	Doubleday
Day	J	Will Rogers, the Boy Roper	Houghton
DeAngeli	J	Jared's Island	Doubleday
Deleeuw		Nobody's Doll	Little
Dennis	J	Flip, Story of a Colt	Viking
Dennis		Holiday	Viking
Dickens (adapt.)	S	A Christmas Carol, and The Little Duke	Appleton
Dickens (adapt.)	S	A Tale of Two Cities	Webster
Dolbier		Magic Shop	Random
Doyle (adapt.)	*S	Cases of Sherlock Holmes	Webster
Dressel	*S	The Strange Paper Clue; The Man with the Pointed Beard; Find Formula X	Row
Driggs		Pitch Pine Tales	Aladdin
Dunham	J	What's In The Sky	Oxford
Duvosisin	J	They Put Out to Sea	Knopf
Eliot	J	Selected Stories from the Arabian Nights	Houghton
Elting		Patch	Doubleday
Elting	J	Trains at Work	Garden
Erikson		True Book of Animals of Small Pond	Children's

Author		Title	Publisher
Ets		Oley, The Sea Monster	Viking
Everson	J	The Secret Cave	Dutton
Eyre	J	Star in the Willows	Oxford
Fabres	J	Ann and Maryke	Winston
Faulkner	J	Melindy's Medal	Messner
Fenner		Giggle Box	Knopf
Fenner	J	Time to Laugh	Knopf
Fishel & Medica	J	Terry & Bunky Learn to Swim; Terry & Bunky Play Baseball; etc.	Putnam
Fisher		Over the Hills to Nugget	Aladdin
Fisher	J	Trapped by the Mountain Storm	Aladdin
Forbes	J	The Thirsty Lion	Crowell
Franklin	J	Shorty's Mule	Houghton
Friedman	J	Carol From the Country	Morrow
Friedman	J	Dot for Short	Morrow
Furness	J	Funny Riddles and Rhymes for Boys and Girls from 7–12	Hart
Gag		Tales from Grimm	Coward
Galt	J	Volcano	Scribner
Gannett	J	My Father's Dragon	Random
Geisel	*J	If I Ran the Zoo	Random
Geisel	*	Thidwick, the Big-Hearted Moose	Random
Geisel	*	The King's Stilts	Vanguard
Geisel	*J	The 500 Hats of Bartholomew Cubbins	Vanguard
Gerber		Gooseberry Jones	Putnam
Gibson	J	Arrow Fly Home	Longmans
Gilbert		Egbert and His Marvelous Adventures	Harper
Glendinning		Gertie, the Horse Who Thought and Thought	Whittlesey
Glick		Mickey, the Horse that Volunteered	McGraw
Goetz		The Hidden Burro	Morrow
Graham	J	Christopher Columbus, Discoverer	Abingdon
Grey	J	Elsa's Secret	Doubleday
Hanna, Kohn		Cross-Country	Scott
Harrison		Lonesome Bear	McGraw
Hatch		13 Danish Tales, Retold	Harcourt
Havighurst	J	High Prairie	Rinehart
Hawthorne		Wonder Book for Boys and Girls	Houghton
Haywood		Eddie and Gardenia; Eddie's Pay Dirt; Little Eddie	Morrow
Haywood		Penny and Peter	Harcourt
Heal	J	Golden Bowl	Lothrop
Hefferman	*J	Desert Treasure	Wagner
Hefferman	*J	The Adventure of Canolles	Wagner
Henry	J	Robert Fulton: Boy Craftsman	Bobbs
Henry	J	Sea Star	Rand
Hogeboom	J	Birds and How to Draw Them	Vanguard
Hogeboom	J	Christopher Columbus and his Brothers	Lothrop
Hogeboom	J	Horses and How to Draw Them	Vanguard
Holbury		Rowena Carey	Doubleday

Author	*Title*	*Publisher*
Holding	J Miss Kelly	Morrow
Holling	J Minn of the Mississippi	Houghton
Huber	It Must Be Magic	Row
Huntington	J Let's Go To The Brook	Doubleday
Huntington	J Let's Go to The Desert	Doubleday
James	J Cowboy in the Making	Scribner
James	J Young Cowboy	Scribner
Johnson	Magic Carpet	Merrill
Johnson	J Briar, A Collie	Morrow
Johnson	Cathy	Longmans
Justus, Tousey	Toby Has a Dog	Whitman
Kane	J Wild World Tales	Knopf
Karolyi	J A Summer To Remember	Whittlesey
Kipling (adapt.)	Captains Courageous	Scott F.
Kipling	Just So Stories	Doubleday
Lane	J River Dragon	Little
Larom	J Bronco Charlie	Whittlesey
Lattimore	J Little Pear, The Story of a Chinese Boy	Harcourt
Lattimore	Three Little Chinese Girls	Morrow
Lawrence	J Peach Tree Island	Harcourt
Lawrence	J Sand in Her Shoes	Harcourt
Lawson	J They Were Strong and Good	Viking
Leach	The Turnspit Dog	Aladdin
Leaf	Aesop's Fables	Heritage
Leaf	*J The Story of Ferdinand	Viking
Leeming	J Fun For Young Collectors	Lippincott
Lenski	J Boom Town Boy	Lippincott
Lenski	We Live in the South	Lippincott
Lent	J Flight 17	Macmillan
LeSueur	Little Brothers of the Wilderness	Knopf
LeSueur	Nancy Hanks of Wilderness Road	Knopf
Levine	J A Baby is Born	Simon
L'Hommedieu	Togo the Little Husky	Lippincott
Linderman	J Indian Why Stories	Hale
Lindman	Fire Eye	Whitman
Lindsay	J Johnny Appleseed	Macmillan
Lofting	J Story of Dr. Doolittle	Stokes
Lofting	Story of Mrs. Tubbs	Stokes
Long	J Oliver Hazard Perry	Bobbs
MacNeil	Between Earth and Sky	Oxford
Malcolmson	Yankee Doodle's Cousins	Houghton
Martin	J Golden Arrow	Tell
Martin	Lightning	Tell
Martin	Silver Stallion	Tell
Mason	Young Mr. Meeker and His Exciting Journey	Bobbs
McCloskey	*J Lentil	Viking
McCloskey	Make Way for Ducklings	Viking
McClung	Stripe: The Story of a Chipmunk	Morrow
McGinley	J All Around the Town	Lippincott

Author		*Title*	*Publisher*
McGinley		The Horse Who Had His Picture in the Paper	Lippincott
McGuire	J	Daniel Boone	Watts
McKinley	J	Harriet	Viking
McMeekin	J	The First Book of Horses	Watts
Meadowcroft	J	On Indian Trails With Daniel Boone	Crowell
Meigs	J	Swift Rivers	Little
Meyer	J	Picture Book of Astronomy	Lothrop
Meyer	J	Picture Book of Radio	Lothrop
Moderow (ed.)	*J	Six Great Stories	Scott F.
Munroe (adapt.)	J	The Flamingo Feather	Webster
Mukerji	J	Hari, the Jungle Lad	Dutton
Neurath	J	If You Could See Inside	Chanticler
Olds		Feather Mountain	Houghton
Oliver		Riding Days	Westminster
Orton		Eleven Mysteries	Lippincott
Orton	J	Mystery in the Old Cave	Lippincott
Orton	J	Mystery in the Pirate Oak	Lippincott
Parke		Scratchy	Morrow
Parks	J	Davy Crockett Young Rifleman	Bobbs
Parks	J	Little Long Rifle	Bobbs
Pauli		Lincoln's Little Correspondent	Doubleday
Philps	J	Toby on the Sheep Drive	Macrae
Pistorius	J	What Bird Is It?; What Butterfly is It?; What Wildflower Is it?	Wilcox
Poe (adapt.)	*S	Gold Bug and Other Stories	Webster
Powell	J	Junior Model Planes	Crowell
Pyle	J	Men of Iron	Webster
Reade (adapt.)	S	The Cloister & The Hearth	Longmans
Renick	J	A Touchdown for Doc	Scribner
Renick		Pete's Home Run	Scribner
Renick	J	Tommy Carries the Ball	Scribner
Retan		Santa's Footprints	Aladdin
Reynolds	J	The Wright Brothers	Random
Rifkin	J	When I Grow Up I'll Be A Flyer	Lothrop
Rigby	J	Moustachio	Harper
Rounds	J	Ol' Paul The Mighty Logger	Holiday
Rounds		Whitey and the Rustlers	Holiday
Rushmore		Cowboy Joe of the Circle	Harcourt
Ruskin (adapt.)		King of the Golden River	Appleton
Sandrus (ed.)	J	Eight Treasured Stories	Scott F.
Saroyan	S	My Name is Aram	Harcourt
Schneider	J	How Your Body Works	Scott
Schneider	J	Let's Look Inside Your House	Scott
Schneider	J	Now Try This	Scott
Schneider	J	You Among the Stars	Scott
Scott (adapt.)	S	Ivanhoe	Webster
Scott		Ripana Royal	Harcourt
Scott		Storytime Favorites	Random
Seuss (see Geisel)			

Author		*Title*	*Publisher*
Sewell (adapt.)	J	Black Beauty	Appleton
Seymour	J	Bird Girl—Sacagawea	Bobbs
Shannon	J	Dobry	Viking
Sharfman		A Beagle Named Bertram	Crowell
Shippen		Lightfoot	Viking
Singmaster	J	Sewing Susie	Houghton
Singmaster	J	Swords of Steel	Houghton
Slobodkin		Bixby and the Secret Message	Macmillan
Sperry	J	The Voyages of Christopher Columbus	Random
Spyri (adapt.)	J	Heidi	Appleton
Steele		The Golden Root	Aladdin
Stevenson		Abe Lincoln: Frontier Boy; Buffalo Bill: Boy of the Plains; Clara Barton, Girl Nurse; Kit Carson, Boy Trapper; Myles Standish, Adventurous Boy; Paul Revere, Boy of Old Boston; Pocahontas the Brave Girl	Bobbs
Stevenson (adapt.)	*J	Treasure Island	Scott F.
Stratton (adapt.)	J	When Washington Danced	Scott F.
Swayne	J	Great-Grandfather in the Honey Tree	Viking
Swift (adapt.)	*S	Gulliver's Travels	Steck
Taber	J	The First Book of Cats	Watts
Taber	J	The First Book of Dogs	Watts
Tatham	J	First Book of Automobiles	Watts
Tatham	J	First Book of Trucks	Watts
Thurber		The Great Quillow	Harcourt
Toles	J	Secret of Lonesome Valley	Wagener
Torry	J	Penny	Howell
Tousey	J	Cowboy Tommy	Doubleday
Tousey	*J	Davy Crockett	Whitman
Tousey	J	Jim Bridger, American Frontiersman	Whitman
Tousey	J	Kit Carson	Whitman
Tousey	J	Northwest Mounted Police	Rand
Tousey		Toby Has a Dog	Whitman
Travers	*J	Mary Poppins (and sequels)	Reynal
Turpin	J	Story of Virginia	Random
Untermeyer	J	Stars to Steer By	Harcourt
VanRiper	J	Lou Gehrig: Boy of the Sand Lots	Bobbs
Verne (adapt.)	S	Around the World in Eighty Days	Scott
Verne (adapt.)	S	Twenty Thousand Leagues Under The Sea	Scott
Wagoner	J	Julia Ward Howe: Girl of Old New York	Bobbs
Wagoner	J	Louisa Alcott: Girl of Old Boston	Bobbs
Wallace (adapt.)	S	Ben Hur	Webster
Watts	J	Dozens of Cousins	Whittlesey
Weil	J	John Quincy Adams, Boy Patriot	Bobbs
Widdemer	J	Harriet Beecher Stowe, Connecticut Girl	Bobbs

Author	*Title*	*Publisher*
Wilder	J Little House on the Prairie	Harper
Winston	J Famous Planes and Famous Flights	Platt
Wright	J Number Eleven Poplar Street	Abingdon
Wright	J Surprise at Sampey Place	Abingdon
Yates	J Amos Fortune: Free Man	Aladdin
Zaffo	J Big Book of Real Boats	Grosset
Zaffo	J Big Book of Real Building and Wrecking Machines	Grosset
Zaffo	J Big Book of Real Fire Engines	Grosset
Zaffo	J Big Book of Real Streamliners	Grosset
Zim	Elephants; Flowers; Frogs and Toads; Golden Hamsters; Goldfish; Great Whales; Homing Pigeons; Insects; Owls	Morrow

Grade V

Author	*Title*	*Publisher*
Adams	J The Pony Express	Random
Adams	J The Santa Fe Trail	Random
Adams	S Wonderful Year	Messner
Alcott	J Jo's Boys	Little
Alcott	J Little Women	Little
Altsheler	J Horsemen of the Plains	Grosset
Anderson	J Big Red	Macmillan
Anderson	J Fur Trappers of the Old West	Wheeler
Anderson	J High Courage	Macmillan
Anderson	*J Wild Bill Hickock	Wheeler
Andrews	J Cowdog	Morrow
Armar	J Waterless Mountain	Longmans
Averill	J King Philip, The Indian Chief	Harcourt
Bacon	J Mystery at East Hatchett	Viking
Baker	J Shasta of the Wolves	Dodd
Baker	J Stocky, Boy of West Texas	Winston
Bartman	J Yanks in Sicily	Whitman
Bass	J Thankful People	Caxton
Beals	*J Buffalo Bill	Wheeler
Beals	J Chief Black Hawk	Wheeler
Beals	*J Davy Crockett	Wheeler
Beals	J Kit Carson	Wheeler
Beeler	S Experiments in Optical Illusion	Crowell
Beeler, Branley	S Experiments With Electricity	Crowell
Beeler	S More Experiments in Science	Crowell
Benjamin	J Make Way For a Sailor	McKay
Bialk	J The Horse Called Pete	Houghton
Bialk	J Taffy's Foal	Houghton
Billings	J Diesel-Electric 4030	Viking
Black	J Big Book of Real Airplanes	Grosset
Blair	J Tall Tale America	Coward

Author		*Title*	*Publisher*
Blecker	J	Apache Indians: Raiders of the Southwest	Morrow
Blecker	J	The Crow Indians	Morrow
Blough	J	Monkey With a Notion	Holt
Blyton	J	Five Go Adventuring Again	Crowell
Bonner	J	Out to Win	Knopf
Bontemps	J	Fast Sooner Hound	Houghton
Bontemps	J	Slappy Hooper, the Wonderful Sign Painter	Houghton
Bowman	J	Pecos Bill	Whitman
Boylston	S	Sue Barton, Student Nurse	Little
Bridges	S	True Zoo Stories	Sloane
Brill	J	Copper Country Adventure	Whittlesey
Brindze	J	Boating is Fun	Dodd
Brink	*J	Caddie Woodlawn	Macmillan
Brink	J	Lad With a Whistle	Macmillan
Brink	J	Mademoiselle Misfortune	Macmillan
Britton	J	What Makes it Tick	Houghton
Bronte (adapt.)	S	Jane Eyre	Globe
Brown	J	Dick Whittington and His Cat	Scribner
Brown	J	John Paul Jones	Watts
Brown	J	Pony Farm	Scribner
Bryant	J	The Lost Kingdom	Messner
Buck	J	Jungle Animals	Random
Buff	J	The Apple And The Arrow	Houghton
Burbank	J	Narizona's Holiday	Longmans
Burnett	S	Secret Garden	Lippincott
Cameron	J	The Wonderful Flight to the Mushroom Planet	Little
Carmer	J	Too Many Cherries	Viking
Carmer	J	Windfall Fiddle	Knopf
Carveth	J	Jungle Boy	Longmans
Cavanah	S	Treasury of Dog Stories	Rand
Cervantes (adapt.)	S	Don Quixote	Dodd
Chase	J	Wicked John and the Devil	Houghton
Chrystie	J	First Book of Jokes and Funny Things	Watts
Clark	J	The Pennywinks	Bobbs
Clark	J	Pennywick Carnival	Bobbs
Clark	J	Poppy Seed Cakes	Doubleday
Clark	J	Thomas Alva Edison	Aladdin
Clemens (adapt.)	S	The Prince and the Pauper	Sanborn
Coatsworth	S	House of the Swan	Macmillan
Coatsworth	J	Thief Island	Macmillan
Coggins	*S	By Space Ship to the Moon	Random
Collier	J	The Story of Buffalo Bill	Grosset
Collin	J	Wind Island	Viking
Collins	J	Bush Holiday	Doubleday
Colum	J	Adventure of Odysseus and the Tale of Troy	Macmillan
Considine	J	The Panama Canal	Random

Author	*Title*	*Publisher*
Cooper (adapt.)	J Deerslayer	Sanborn
Cormack	J First Book of Trees	Watts
Cormack	J First Book of Stones	Watts
Cottler & Jaffe	S Heroes of Civilization	Little
Cromwell	J Six Good Friends	McGraw
Daringer	J Adopted Jane	Harcourt
Daugherty	J Daniel Boone	Viking
Davis	J Melody, Mutton, Bone & Sam	Doubleday
Davis	J Young Readers Sports Stories	Lantern
DeAngeli	J Bright April	Doubleday
Defoe (adapt.)	J Robinson Crusoe for Young People	Beckley
DeJong	J Picture Story of Holland	Harcourt
Dennis	J Palomino and other Horses	World
Dietz	J Jeff White, Young Woodsman	Little
Dillard	J Wishing Boy of New Netherland	Dutton
DiMaggio	*S Lucky to be a Yankee	Greenberg
Douglas	J Appleseed Farm	Abingdon
DuBois	J Peter Graves	Viking
Dumas (adapt.)	S The Black Tulip	Longmans
Dumas (adapt.)	S Count of Monte Cristo	Longmans
Dumas (adapt.)	S Three Musketeers	Sanborn
Dunlop	J Disappearing Island	Houghton
Dunlop	S Holly Hotel	Houghton
Dusoe	J Three Without Fear	Longmans
Eamer	J A Horse to Remember	Messner
Eaton	J That Lively Man, Ben Franklin	Morrow
Edmonds	S The Matchlock Gun	Dodd
Edmonds	J Tom Whipple	Dodd
Edmonds	J Two Logs Crossing	Dodd
Eliot (adapt.)	S Mill on the Floss	Globe
Enright	J Then There Were Five	Rinehart
Estes	J The Hundred Dresses	Harcourt
Estes	*J The Moffats; The Middle Moffat	Harcourt
Estes	J Rufus M	Harcourt
Evatt	J Mystery of the Old Merchant's House	Bobbs
Farmer	J Fish Hook Island Mystery	Doubleday
Fenner	J Cowboys, Cowboys, Cowboys	Watts
Fenner	J Fools, Funny Fellows	Knopf
Fennimore	J Bush Holiday	Doubleday
Fenton	J Us and the Duchess	Doubleday
Fenton	J Wild Folks at the Pond	Day
Ferguson	J A Horse of Her Own	Dodd
Fisher	*J Understood Betsy	Holt
Fluckiger	J Tuck	Coward
Forbes	J America's Paul Revere	Houghton
Foster	J Abraham Lincoln	Scribner
Foster	*J George Washington	Scribner
Franklin	J Tricky: Adventure of Red Fox	Houghton
Frost	J Let's Look at the Stars	Houghton
Fuller	J Manuel Goes to Sea	McGraw

Author	*Title*	*Publisher*
Furman	J Young Readers Dog Stories	Lantern
Garst	J Cowboy Boots	Abingdon
Garst	J Cowboys and Cattle Trails	Wheeler
Gatti	J Here Is Africa	Scribner
Gilbert	S Bird Dog Bargain	Holt
Gordon	S Romany Luck	Viking
Hall	S Buried Cities	Macmillan
Hall	J How the Pilgrims Came to Plymouth	Dutton
Hayes	J Skid	Houghton
Henry	J Album of Horses	Rand
Henry	J Always Reddy	McGraw
Henry	J Justin Morgan Had a Horse	Wilcox
Henry	J Misty of Chincoteague	Rand
Hogner	J Odd Pets	Crowell
Holberg	J At the Sign of the Golden Anchor	Doubleday
Holberg	J Restless Johnny: The Story of Johnny Appleseed	Crowell
Hough	S The Covered Wagon	Houghton
Huber	J They Were Brave and Bold	Row
Humphreys	J The Zoo Book	Holt
Hunt	J Story of the U.S. Marines	Random
Irving (adapt.)	J Rip Van Winkle: The Legend of Sleepy Hollow	Steck
Jagendorf	J Twenty-five Non-royalty Holiday Plays	Greenberg
Johnson, Jacobs	J Enchanted Isles	Merrill
Jones	J Spooks of the Valley	Houghton
Judson	J Green Ginger Jar	Houghton
Judson	J Lost Violin	Houghton
Judson	J Thomas Jefferson	Wilcox
Kieran	J Introduction to Birds	Garden
Kipling	*J All the Mowgli Stories	Doubleday
Kipling	J Jungle Book	Doubleday
Lane	S Let the Hurricane Roar	Longmans
Larom	J Mountain Pony	McGraw
Laverty	J Gold of Glanaree	Longmans
Lawson	J Ben and Me	Little
Lawson	J McWhinney's Jaunt	Little
Leaf	J Geography Can Be Fun	Lippincott
Leaf	J History Can Be Fun	Lippincott
Leeming	J Fun With Puzzles	Lippincott
Leeming	J More Fun With Puzzles	Lippincott
Leeming	J Tricks Any Boy Can Do	Appleton
Leighton	J Singing Cave	Houghton
Lenski	S Bayou Suzette	Lippincott
Lenski	J Judy's Journey	Lippincott
LeSueur	J Little Brother of Wilderness	Knopf
Lewellen	S You and Atomic Energy	Children's
Lewellen	S You and Space Travel	Children's
Lippincott	J Wilderness Champion	Lippincott
Lochlons	J Stretch Smith Makes A Basket	Crowell

Author		*Title*	*Publisher*
Lofting	J	Story of Dr. Doolittle	Lippincott
London	*S	Call of the Wild	Macmillan
Mason	J	Junior Book of Camping and Woodcraft	Barnes
Mason	J	Pony Called Lightning	Macmillan
Maw	S	Nikoline's Choice	Oxford
McCabe	J	I'll Take Cappy	Whittlesey
McCloskey	J	Centerburg Tales	Viking
McCloskey	*J	Homer Price	Viking
McGuire	J	Daniel Boone	Wheeler
McKean	J	Up Hill	Shady
McNeer	J	California Gold Rush	Random
Meader	J	Behind the Rangers; Cedar's Boy; Jonathan Goes West; Long Trains Roll; River of the Wolves; Skippy's Family	Harcourt
Meadowcroft	J	By Secret Railway	Crowell
Meadowcroft	J	Ship Boy With Columbus	Crowell
Meigs	J	The Covered Wagon	Macmillan
Meigs	J	Two Arrows	Macmillan
Melville (adapt.)	S	Moby Dick	Scott F.
Meyer	J	Picture Book of the Earth	Lothrop
Meyer	J	Picture Book of Molecules & Atoms	Lothrop
Meyer	J	Picture Book of the Weather	Lothrop
Molloy	J	Shooting Star Farm	Houghton
Morgan	J	First Chemistry Book for Boys and Girls	Scribner
Morrow	S	On To Oregon	Morrow
Morrow	S	Ship's Monkey	Morrow
Morton	J	Boy's Guide to Fishing	Greenberg
Nathan	J	Building of the First Transcontinental Railroad	Random
Neuberger	J	Lewis and Clark Expedition	Random
Nevin	J	Underground Escape	Westminster
Newell	J	Steppin and Family	Oxford
O'Neill	J	Picture Story of Hawaii	McKay
Orton	J	The Secret of the Rosewood Box	Lippincott
Parkhill	J	It's Fun to Make Things	Barnes
Parks	J	Bedford Forrest: Boy on Horseback	Bobbs
Parks	J	Dan Morgan: Boy of the Wilderness	Bobbs
Pease	S	Bound for Singapore	Doubleday
Pease	S	High Road to Adventure	Doubleday
Putnam	J	David Goes to Baffinland	Putnam
Putnam	J	David Goes to Greenland	Putnam
Pyle	J	Robin Hood	Globe
Pyle	J	Otto of the Silver Hand	Scribner
Queen	J	White Elephant Mystery	Little
Raftery	J	Snow Cloud	Morrow
Rankin	S	Daughter of the Mountains	Viking
Raymond	S	Linnet on the Threshold	Longmans
Reck	S	Automobiles from Start to Finish	Crowell

Author	Title	Publisher
Reed	J Sea for Sam	Harcourt
Reed	J The Stars for Sam	Harcourt
Renick	J Tommy Carries the Ball	Scribner
Retan	J Mystery of the Haunted Cliff	Aladdin
Reynolds	J Custer's Last Stand	Random
Rifkin	J When I Grow Up I'll Be a Farmer	Lothrop
Rifkin	J When I Grow Up I'll Be a Nurse	Lothrop
Rounds	J Rodeo, Bulls, Broncos and Buckaroos	Holiday
Rounds	J Stolen Pony	Holiday
Sackett	J Everglade Gold	Random
Salten	S Bambi	Grosset
Schneider	J Everyday Weather and How it Works	Whittlesey
Schneider	J Rocks, Rivers and the Changing Earth	Scott
Scott	J Mojave Joe	Knopf
Selsam	J Play With Plants	Morrow
Seredy	*J The Good Master	Viking
Seton	J Wild Animals I have Known	Scribner
Singmaster	J Swords of Steel	Houghton
Slobodkin	J Adventures of Arab	Macmillan
Slobodkin	J Space Ships Under the Apple Tree	Macmillan
Steele	J The Buffalo Knife	Harcourt
Stefansson	S My Life With the Eskimo	Macmillan
Stong	J Hirum the Hillbilly	Dodd
Strang, Roberts	*S Teen-Age Tales, Book 1, Book 2	Heath
Streatfield	J Movie Shoes; Skating Shoes; Theatre Shoes	Random
Swift (adapt.)	S Gulliver's Travels	Sanborn
Tarry, Ets	J My Dog Rinty	Viking
Thurber	J Great Quillow	Harcourt
Thurber	J Many Moons	Harcourt
Todd	J Tricks Every Boy Can Do	Hart
Tousey	J Bill Clark	Whitman
Townsend	J White Tailed Deer	Whittlesey
Travers	*J Mary Poppins	Harcourt
Travers	Mary Poppins Comes Back; Mary Poppins Opens the Door	Reynal
Trease	J The Secret Fiord	Harcourt
Tunis	S Keystone Kids; the Kid from Tomkinsville; World Series	Harcourt
Turner	J Let's Start a Stamp Collection	Lippincott
Twain (adapt.)	J Tom Sawyer	Scott F.
Twain (adapt.)	J Adventures of Huckleberry Finn	Globe
Undset	J Segurd and His Brave Companions	Knopf
VanderHaas	S Victorious Island	Harcourt
Waldeck	J White Panther	Viking
Warren	J Ride, Cowboy, Ride!	Harcourt
Warren	J The Golden Palomino	McKay
Watson	J Trooper, U.S. Army Dog	Houghton
Webster	S Daddy Long Legs	Appleton
Wheeler	J Stephen Foster and his Little Dog Tray	Dutton

Author		Title	Publisher
White	J	Charlotte's Web	Harper
White	S	Lion's Paw	Doubleday
Widdemer		The Wishing Star	Bobbs
Wilder		Little House in the Big Woods; Little House on the Prairie; On the Banks of Plum Creek	Harper
Wilson		Herbert; Herbert Again	Knopf
Wilson		Thad Owen	Abingdon
Wilson		This Boy Cody	Watts
Wulff		Let's Go Fishing	Lippincott
Zaffo		Big Book of Real Streamliners	Grosset
Zarchy		Let's Make a Lot of Things; Let's Make Something; Let's Make More Things	Knopf
Zim		Alligators and Crocodiles	Morrow
Zim		Rabbits	Morrow

Grade VI

Author		Title	Publisher
Alcott	*S	Little Women	Little
Alcott	S	An Old Fashioned Girl	Grosset
Alexander	J	Magic Show Book	Macmillan
Altsheler	J	Young Trailers	Appleton
Anderson	S	Tomorrow's Champion	Macmillan
Anderson	S	Touch of Greatness	Macmillan
Appel	J	Comanche	World
Arnold	S	Nose for News	Row
Atwater	S	Ski Patrol	Random
Atwater	S	Smoke Patrol	Random
Aviation Research Association, Inc.	S	How Planes Fly	Harper
Bachman	J	Great Inventors and Their Inventions	American
Baker	S	The First Woman Doctor	Messner
Banning	J	Submarine	Random
Barne	S	In the Same Boat	Dodd
Barton	S	Before Your Eyes	Row
Beals	J	The Rush for Gold	Wheeler
Bechdolt	S	Greg Sheridan, Reporter	Dutton
Bechdolt	S	On The Air	Dutton
Beim	S	Triumph Clear	Harcourt
Bell	S	Danger on Old Baldy	Morrow
Bell	S	Pirate of Toy Strait	Morrow
Bendick	J	First Book of Space Travel	Watts
Bendrick	S	Electronics for Boys and Girls	McGraw
Bethers	J	Perhaps I'll be a Railroad Man	Aladdin
Bethers	J	Perhaps I'll be a Sailor	Aladdin
Betz	S	Your Manners are Showing	Grosset

Author	*Title*	*Publisher*
Bianco	S Other People's Houses	Viking
Blakeslee	J Fighting Ships of the U.S.A.	
Blecker	J The Crow Indians	Morrow
Block	J Real Book About the Mounties	Garden
Bowen	S Fourth Down	Lothrop
Boykin	J This Way, Please	Macmillan
Boylston	*J Sue Barton, Student Nurse, and sequels	Little
Bridges	J Big Zoo	Viking
Brier	S Skycruiser	Random
Brill	J Copper Country Adventure	McGraw
Brill	J Madeline Takes Command	McGraw
Brink	J Magical Melons	
Brown, Betts	J John Paul Jones	Wheeler
Bugbee	S Peggy Covers the News	Dodd
Carter	S Into a Strange Lost World	Crowell
Cavanna	S Going on Sixteen	Westminster
Cavanna	S Two's Company	Westminster
Chalmers	S High Smoke	Viking
Chase	S Famous Paintings	Platt
Chase	S Sandhog	Row
Clemens	J Adventure of Tom Sawyer	Grosset
Coblentz	S Beggar's Penny	Longmans
Coe	S Road to Alaska	Messner
Coe	J Graven With Flint	Crowell
Comfort	S Treasure on the Johnny Smoker	Morrow
Conklin	J Guideposts of the Sea	Macmillan
Coolidge	S Greek Myths	Houghton
Coryell	J Scalp Hunters	Harcourt
Cottler	S Champions of Democracy	Little
Cottler	S Heroes of Science	Little
Cottler	S Map Makers	Little
Coyle	S Land of Hope	Row
Craig	S Danger is My Business	Garden
Curle	S Stamp Collecting	Knopf
Daly	S Smarter and Smoother	Dodd
Daringer	S Stepsister Sally	Harcourt
deKruif	*S Microbe Hunters	Harcourt
Deming	S Penny Marsh, Public Health Nurse	Dodd
Dickson	J Turn in the Road	Nelson
Dietz	J Jeff White, Young Woodsman	Little
Ditmars	S Animal Kingdom	Row
Drummond	J Monkey That Would Not Kill	Dodd
DuBois	J The Twenty One Balloons	Viking
DuJardin	S Practically Seventeen	Lippincott
DuSoe	J River of the Wolves	Longmans
Dusoe	J Sea Boots	Longmans
Eaton	S Gandhi: Fighter Without a Sword	Morrow
Eberle	J The Right Dog For Joe	Dodd
Edmonds	S Wilderness Clearing	Dodd
Eliot (adapt.)	S Silas Marner	Globe

Author	Title	Publisher
Elting	S First Book of Nurses	Watts
Emerson	S Father's Big Improvement	Lippincott
Enright	J The Saturdays	Rinehart
Erdman	S Fair is the Morning	Longmans
Everndem	J Knight of Florence	Random
Farley	*J Black Stallion, and sequels	Random
Farley	J Black Bay Colt	Random
Felsen	S Navy Diver	Dutton
Felton	J John Henry and His Hammer	Knopf
Fenner	J Horses, Horses, Horses	Watts
Fenner	J Yankee Doodle	Knopf
Fenton	J Us and the Duchess	Doubleday
Floherty	Behind the Silver Shield	Lippincott
Floherty	J 'Board the Airliner; Guardsmen of the Coast; Police; On the Air; Movie-makers; Fire Fighters	Doubleday
Floherty	J Watch Your Step	Lippincott
Franklin	J Monte	Houghton
Franklin	J Shorty's Mule	Houghton
Freeman	S Fun With Chemistry	Random
Garst	J Buffalo Bill; Custer, Fighter of the Plains; Kit Carson, Trail Blazer & Scout; Sitting Bull, Champion of His People	Messner
Garst	J Crazy Horse: Great Warrior of the Sioux	Houghton
Gilbert	S Arctic Venture	Holt
Gillis, Ketchum	S Our America	Little
Gilmore	J Model Planes for Beginners	Harper
Goetz	S Dragon and The Eagle	Vanguard
Goodwin	S Real Book About Space Travel	Garden
Graham	S Lou Gehrig	Putnam
Graham	J Story of Phyllis Wheatley	Messner
Griffin	S Here Come the Marines!	Howell
Haddock	S Blue Highway	Row
Halliburton	*S Royal Road to Romance	Bobbs
Harper	J Yankee Yarns	Dutton
Hart	S Big-Time Baseball	Hart
Henry	J King of the Wind	Rand
Heyliger	S Steve Merrill, Engineer	Appleton
Heyman	S Junior Quarterback	Morrow
Hill	S In Little America	Ginn
Hinkle	J Black Storm; Silver; Tawny; Shag, The Story of a Dog; Wild Fire And Other Stories	Morrow
Hogner	J Our American Horse	Nelson
Holt	J Wild Palomino	Longmans
Hubbard	J Vinnie Ream and Mr. Lincoln	Whittlesey
Huber, Salisbury	J These Are the Tales They Tell	Row
Hunt	J Better Known As Johnny Appleseed	Lippincott
Innes	Attack Alarm	Macmillan

Author	*Title*	*Publisher*
Jackson	S Call Me Charley	Harper
Jackson	S Rose Bowl Line Backer	Crowell
Jaeger	J Tracks and Trailcraft	Macmillan
James	J Lone Cowboy	Scribner
James	*J Smoky, the Cowhorse	Grosset
Judson	S The Green Ginger Jar	Houghton
Kantor	J Lee and Grant at Appomattox	Random
Keith	J Shotgun Show	Crowell
Keliher	S Picture Fact Books (a series describing occupations)	Harper
Kelley	S Egypt and the Holy Land	Black
Kjelgaard	J A Nose for Trouble	Holiday
Kjelgaard	J Explorations of Père Marquette	Random
Kneeland	J Smugglers Island	Houghton
Knight	S Secret of the Buried Tomb	Knopf
Knight	*S Lassie Come Home	Winston
Kyle	J The Provost's Jewel	Houghton
Lathrop	S Black River Captive	Random
Lathrop	S Northern Trail Adventure	Random
Law	J Fighting Planes of the World	Random
Lawson	J Smeller Martin	Viking
Lee	J Pioneers of Puerto Rico	Heath
Leeming	J More Fun with Magic	Lippincott
Lent	S Air Patrol; Aviation Cadet; Bombardier; Eight Hours to Solo	Macmillan
Lent	S This Is Your Announcer	Macmillan
Lindbergh	S North to the Orient	Harcourt
Lindbergh	S We	Putnam
Lippincott	J The Wahoo Bobcat	Lippincott
Lovelace	S General "Ike"	Crowell
Lownsberry	J Lighting the Torch; Boy Knight of Rheims	Longmans
MacGregor	J Miss Pickerell Goes to Mars	Whittlesey
Malcolmson, McCormick	J Mister Stormalong	Houghton
Malvern	S Ann Lawrence of Old New York	Messner
Martin	S Sea Room	Harper
Masefield	S Jim Davis	Nelson
Mason	J Animal Weapons	Morrow
McCracker	J Caribou Traveler	Lippincott
McCulloch	S Come, Jack	Houghton
McMeckin	J Kentucky Derby Winner	McKay
McSinigan	J Binnie Latches On	Dutton
Meader	S The Sea Snake	Harcourt
Miller, Dupont	S Bob Wakefield, Naval Aviator	Dodd
Mitchell	S Ships that Made U.S. History	McGraw
Montague	S Riders in Scarlet	Row
Montgomery	J Story Behind Great Inventions	McBride
Morgan	J A Pet Book for Boys & Girls	Scribner
Morgan	S Boy's Book of Engine Motors	Scribner

Author		Title	Publisher
Morgan	J	Messenger to the Pharoah	Longmans
Mulford	S	Bar–20 (Hopalong Cassidy)	Grosset
Munroe	J	Flamingo Feather	Harper
Murphy	J	Streamliner	Row
Nathans	J	Iron Horse	Knopf
Nordhoff	S	Pearl Lagoon; Derelict	Little
O'Brien	J	Return of Silver	Longmans
O'Brien	J	Silver Chief to the Rescue	Winston
O'Brien	*J	Silver Chief, Dog of the North	Winston
O'Brien	J	Valiant, Dog of the Timberline	Winston
Olds	S	Big Fire	Houghton
O'Neill	J	Picture Book of the Philippines	McKay
Pease	S	Black Tanker; Hurricane Weather; Jinx Ship; Secret Cargo; Shanghai Passage; Tattooed Man	Doubleday
Persing & Leary	S	Adventure Bound	Harcourt
Pratt	J	Monitor and The Merrimac	Random
Price	S	South Sea Adventure	John Day
Queen	J	Green Turtle Mystery	Lippincott
Queen	J	White Elephant Mystery	Little
Rankin	S	The Gentling of Jonathan	Viking
Ray	S	Story of Air Transport	Winston
Reed	S	The Earth for Sam	Harcourt
Rice	S	Mrs. Wiggs of the Cabbage Patch	Appleton
Rinehart	*S	The Circular Staircase	Grosset
Robertson	J	The Dog Next Door	Viking
Robertson	J	Ticktock and Jim	Winston
Rounds	J	Stolen Pony	Holiday
Rush	J	Duff, the Story of a Bear	Longmans
Sackett	J	Everglade Gold	Random
Salt	J	Automobiles	Putnam
Savery	S	Emeralds for the King	Longmans
Savage	J	Holiday in Alaska	Heath
Schneider	J	Everyday Machines and How They Work	Whittlesey
Scholz	S	Johnny King–Quarterback	Morrow
Shurtleff	J	AWOL, K-9 Commando	Bobbs
Shurtleff	J	Long Lash	Bobbs
Shurtleff	S	Two Against the North	Bobbs
Simon	J	The Royal Road	Dutton
Sperry	S	All Sails Set	Winston
Sperry	S	Call It Courage	Macmillan
Stapp	J	Escape on Skis	Morrow
Starbuck	J	The High Trail	World
Stevenson (adapt.)	J	Treasure Island	Longmans
Stevenson (adapt.)	J	The Black Arrow	Scribner
Strong	J	Wings over Wonder Island	Little
Sutton	J	Jemima, Daughter of Daniel Boone	Scribner
Swift	J	Little Blackrose	Harcourt
Terhune	S	Lad, A Dog	Dutton

Author	*Title*	*Publisher*
Theisen	S Heroic Deeds	Macmillan
Thurston	J Four Hundred Tricks You Can Do	Garden
Tousey	J Jerry and the Pony Express	Doubleday
Tunis	*S All American; Million-Miler	Harcourt
Urmston	J Plain Clothes Patricia	Doubleday
Van Loon	S Ancient Man	Liveright
Waldeck	J Jungle Journey	Viking
Walden	J Waverly	Morrow
Webberley	S The Secret of the Hawk	Ariel
Wellman	J The Haunts of Drowning Creek	Holiday
Whitney	J Mystery of the Gulls	Westminster
Wiggin	S Rebecca of Sunnybrook Farm	Houghton
Wire	S High Country	Westminster
Woody	S Starlight	Morrow
Worth	S They Loved to Laugh	Doubleday
Wyss	J Swiss Family Robinson	Macmillan
Yates	J A Boy and a Battery	Harper
Yates	J Amos Fortune, Free Man	Aladdin

APPENDIX C

List of Publishers and Their Addresses

The following list contains, in alphabetical order, the names and addresses of the books and tests mentioned in the two preceding appendices. Only one office is listed for each publisher. The abbreviation used in this volume is given first, then the full name and address.

Abingdon	Abingdon-Cokesbury Press, Nashville 2, Tenn.
Aladdin	Aladdin Books, 55 Fifth Ave., New York 3, N.Y.
American	American Book Co., 55 Fifth Ave., New York, 3, N.Y.
American Opt.	American Optical Co., Southbridge, Mass.
Appleton	Appleton-Century-Crofts, Inc., 35 W. 32 St., New York 1, N.Y.
Ariel	Farrar, Straus, 101 Fifth Ave., New York 3, N. Y.
AVR	Audio-Visual Research, 531 S. Plymouth Court, Chicago 5, Ill.
Barnes	A. S. Barnes & Co., 232 Madison Ave., New York 16, N.Y.
Bausch & Lomb	Bausch & Lomb Optical Co., 730 Fifth Ave., New York, N.Y.
Beckley	Beckley-Cardy Co., 1632 Indiana Ave., Chicago 16, Ill.
Black	Walter J. Black, Inc., Roslyn, N.Y.
Bobbs	Bobbs-Merrill Co., Inc., Indianapolis 7, Ind.
Bradley	Milton Bradley Co., Springfield, Mass.
Bureau	Bureau of Publications, Teachers College, Columbia University, New York 27, N.Y.
Cadmus	E. M. Hale & Co., Eau Claire, Wis.
California	California Test Bureau, 5916 Hollywood Blvd., Los Angeles 28, Calif.
Caxton	Caxton House, Inc., 9 Rockefeller Plaza, New York, N.Y.
Chanticleer	Chanticleer Press, Inc., 41 E. 50 St., New York 22, N.Y.
Children	Childrens Press, Jackson Blvd., Chicago 7, Ill.
Committee	Committee on Diagnostic Reading Tests, Inc., 419 W. 119 St., New York, N.Y.
Continental	Continental Press, Elizabethtown, Pa.
Coward	Coward-McCann, Inc., 210 Madison Ave., New York 16, N.Y.
Crowell	Thomas Y. Crowell Co., 432 4th Ave., New York, N.Y.
Dutton	E. P. Dutton & Co., Inc., 300 4th Ave., New York, N.Y.
Educational	Educational Test Bureau, 720 Washington Ave., S.E., Minneapolis, Minn.
Essay	Essay Press, P. O. Box 5, New York 24, N.Y.
ETS	Educational Test Service, Princeton, N.J.
Expression	Expression Co., Magnolia, Mass.
Faber	Faber & Faber, Ltd., 24 Russell Sq., London, W.C. 1
Follett	Follett Publishing Co., 1257 S. Wabash Ave., Chicago 5, Ill.
Garden	Garden City Books, 575 Madison Ave., New York 22, N.Y.
Garrard	Garrard Press, Champaign, Ill.
Ginn	Ginn & Co., Statler Building, Boston 17, Mass.
Globe	Globe Book Co., 175 Fifth Ave., New York 10, N.Y.

Greenberg	Greenberg, Publisher, 201 E. 57 St., New York 22, N.Y.
Grosset	Grosset & Dunlap, 1107 Broadway, New York 10, N.Y.
Hale	E. M. Hale & Co., Eau Claire, Wis.
Hall	Hall & McCreary Co., 434 S. Wabash Ave., Chicago 5, Ill.
Hammond	C. S. Hammond, Maplewood, N.J.
Harcourt	Harcourt, Brace & Co., 383 Madison Ave., New York 17, N.Y.
Harper	Harper and Brothers, 49 E. 33 St., New York 16, N.Y.
Hart	Hart Publishing Co., 114 E. 32 St., New York 16, N.Y.
Heath	D. C. Heath and Co., 285 Columbus Ave., Boston 16, Mass.
Heritage	Heritage Press, 595 Madison Ave., New York, N.Y.
Holiday	Holiday House, 8 W. 13 St., New York 11, N.Y.
Holt	Henry Holt and Co., Inc., 383 Madison Ave., New York 17, N.Y.
Houghton	Houghton-Mifflin Co., 2 Park St., Boston 7, Mass.
Keystone	Keystone View Co., Meadville, Pa.
Knopf	Alfred A. Knopf, Inc., 501 Madison Ave., New York 22, N.Y.
Laidlaw	Laidlaw Brothers, 328 S. Jefferson St., Chicago 6, Ill.
Lantern	Lantern Press, Inc., 257 4th Ave., New York, N.Y.
Lippincott	J. B. Lippincott Co., E. Washington Square, Philadelphia 5, Pa.
Little	Little, Brown and Co., 34 Beacon St., Boston 6, Mass.
Liveright	Liveright Publishing Corp., 386 4th Ave., New York 16, N.Y.
Longmans	Longmans, Greeen & Co., Inc., 55 Fifth Ave., New York 3, N.Y.
Lothrop	Lothrop, Lee & Shepard Co., 419 4th Ave., New York, N.Y.
Lyons	Lyons and Carnahan, 2500 Prairie Ave., Chicago 16, Ill.
Macmillan	The Macmillan Company, 60 Fifth Ave., New York 11, N.Y.
Macrae	Macrae Smith Company, 225 S. 15 St., Philadelphia 2, Pa.
McCann	James A. McCann Co., 188 W. 4th St., New York, N.Y.
McCormick	McCormick-Mathers Publishing Co., Wichita 1, Kan.
McGraw	McGraw-Hill Book Co., 330 W. 42 St., New York 36, N.Y.
McKay	David McKay Co., Inc., 55 Fifth Ave., New York 3, N.Y.
Messner	Julian Messner, Inc., 8 W. 40 St., New York 18, N.Y.
Merrill	Charles E. Merrill Books, Columbus 15, Ohio
Morrow	William Morrow and Co., 425 4th Ave., New York 16, N.Y.
Nelson	Thomas Nelson and Sons, 19 E. 47 St., New York 17, N.Y.
Nevins	C. H. Nevins Printing Co., Pittsburgh, Penna.
Noble	Noble and Noble Publishing Co., 67 Irving Place, New York, 3, N.Y.
Oxford	Oxford University Press, 114 Fifth Ave., New York 11, N.Y.
Pantheon	Pantheon Books, Inc., 333 6th Ave., New York, N.Y.
Personnel	Personnel Press, Princeton, N.J.
Platt	Platt & Munk, Inc., 200 Fifth Ave., New York 10, N.Y.
Psychological	Psychological Corp., 552 Fifth Ave., New York, N.Y.
Public	Public School Pub. Co., 509 N. East St., Bloomington, Ill.
Putnam	G. P. Putnam's Sons, 210 Madison Ave., New York 16, N.Y.
Rand	Rand, McNally, Skokie, Ill.
Random	Random House, 457 Madison Ave., New York 22, N.Y.
Readers	Readers Digest Educational Service, Inc., Pleasantville, N.Y.
Remedial	Remedial Education Center, 1321 W. Hampshire Ave., Washington 6, D.C.
Reilly	Peter Reilly Co., 133 N. 13 St., Philadelphia 7, Pa.

Reynal	Reynal & Co., 221 E. 49 St., New York, N.Y.
Rinehart	Rinehart and Company, 232 Madison Ave., New York 16, N.Y.
Ronald	Ronald Press Co., 15 E. 26 St., New York 10, N.Y.
Row	Row, Peterson and Co., Evanston, Ill.
Sanborn	Benjamin H. Sanborn and Co., 221 E. 20 St., Chicago 16, Ill.
Science	Science Research Associates, 57 Grand Ave., Chicago 10, Ill.
Scribner	Charles Scribner's Sons, 597 Fifth Ave., New York 17, N.Y.
Scott	William Scott, Inc., 8 W. 13 St., New York 11, N.Y.
Scott F.	Scott, Foresman and Co., 433 E. Erie St., Chicago, Ill.
Shady	Shady Hill Press, 7 Mercer Circle, Cambridge 38, Mass.
Simon	Simon and Shuster, Inc., 630 Fifth Ave., New York 20, N.Y.
Singer	L. W. Singer Co., Inc., Syracuse 2, N.Y.
Sloane	William Sloane Associates, 425 4th Ave., New York 16, N.Y.
Smith	Turner E. Smith, 441 W. Peachtree St., N.E., Atlanta, Ga.
Steck	Steck Company, Box 16, Austin 61, Texas
Stoelting	C. H. Stoelting Co., 424 N. Homan Ave., Chicago 24, Ill.
Stokes	Frederick A. Stokes Co., Inc., 521 Fifth Ave., New York, N.Y.
Tell	Tell-Well Press, Kansas City, Mo.
Vanguard	Vanguard Press, Inc., 424 Madison Ave., New York, N.Y.
Viking	Viking Press, 18 E. 48 St., New York 17, N.Y.
Wagner	Harr-Wagner Company, 609 Mission St., San Francisco 5, Calif.
Wahr	George Wahr, Ann Arbor, Mich.
Watts	Franklin Watts, Inc., 699 Madison Ave., New York 21, N.Y.
Westminster	Westminster Press, Witherspoon Bldg., Philadelphia 7, Pa.
Webster	Webster Publishing Co., 1808 Washington Ave., St. Louis 3, Mo.
Wheeler	Wheeler Publishing Co., 2831 S. Park Way, Chicago 16, Ill.
Whitman	Albert Whitman & Co., 560 W. Lake St., Chicago 6, Ill.
Whittlesey	Whittlesey House, 330 W. 42 St., New York 36, N.Y.
Wilcox	Wilcox & Follett Co., 1255 S. Wabash Ave., Chicago 5, Ill.
Wilson	H. W. Wilson Co., 950 University Ave., New York 52, N.Y.
Winston	John C. Winston Co., 1010 Arch St., Philadelphia 7, Pa.
Wonder	Wonder Books Inc., 1107 Broadway, New York, N.Y.
World	World Book Co., Yonkers-on-Hudson, N.Y.
World P	World Publishing Co., 2231 W. 110 St., Cleveland 2, Ohio

Index

Index